SPIRITUAL CONSCIOUSNESS

International Seminar
on
RELIGION OF SAINTS ('SANTS') - RADHASOAMI FAITH
Spiritual Consciousness Studies
SPIRCON 2010
NOVEMBER 12-14, 2010
Sesquicentennial Year of Radhasoami Faith, 2010-2011
Radhasoami Satsang Dayalbagh
DAYALBAGH EDUCATIONAL INSTITUTE
(Deemed University), Dayalbagh, Agra
SPIRCON2010
SPIRCON2010

Spiritual Consciousness

Edited by
P. SRIRAMAMURTI
PREM PRASHANT
ANAND MOHAN

Dayalbagh Educational Institute
(Deemed University), Agra, India

New Age Books
New Delhi (India)

SPIRITUAL CONSCIOUSNESS

Published by
NEW AGE BOOKS
A-44, Naraina Industrial Area, Phase-I
New Delhi-110 028 (INDIA)
E-mail: nab@newagebooksindia.com
Website: www.newagebooksindia.com

ISBN: 978-81-7822-443-5

First Edition: Delhi, 2013

Printed and published by
RP Jain for New Age Books
A-44, Naraina Industrial Area
Phase-1, New Delhi 110 028. India

Contents

FOREWORD

Prem Kumar
President, Dayalbagh Educational Institute &
President, Radhasoami Satsang Sabha, Dayalbagh, Agra, India

The subject of consciousness is now drawing wide attention. Although consciousness is something embedded in all our experiences, and is considered basic to all our knowing, no one seems to be knowing what exactly it is. The contemporary multi-disciplinary interest in the study of consciousness goes beyond philosophers, psychologists and neuroscientists to include physicists, information technologists and several others. Human beings, as conscious subjects, function at two levels. On the one hand their awareness is directed outward towards objects and events, fellow beings, their appearances and actions. On the other hand the awareness is sometimes focused inward in one's own thoughts and feelings and beings. The two knowledge domains necessarily raise relevant ontological questions regarding the primacy of the subjective and objective items of knowledge. The human experience is however, a confluence of the two. The objective component of the experience is subject to logic and rationality and application of scientific methods. The application of logic of objectivity in the realm of inner awareness has led to reductive exercises, designed to translate inner experiences into outward phenomena. There are broadly two approaches: the eastern and western, to the study of consciousness. The dominant trends that characterize eastern and western traditions, differ markedly in the emphasis they place on subjective and objective; on the presumed relations between the two and on appropriateness of methods to transform subjective items of experience into objective phenomena. In the western tradition, the emphasis has been primarily on the outward and the approach is rational and intellectual. Consequently the preferred method is scientific and the result is overwhelming concern with the physical reality. The central focus in the eastern tradition is on the inward. Reason is often seen as secondary to the inner experience. In the east, consciousness is regarded as an autonomous principle, grounded in spiritual foundations. In the west any such spiritual association is suspect. Objectivity of the phenomena is considered essential for it to be scientifically studied. Some behavioural psychologists have even declared that there can be no such thing as consciousness, while others have considered consciousness as an epiphenomena of matter. Some saw it as no more than neural events in the brain. Some consider consciousness as a process and the others as ability. Some looked at it as a state, while others regarded it as a function. Conscious experience in the human condition is clearly dependent on certain cortical processes which has led scientists to identify consciousness with brain functioning or as a study of brain. They, however, are not the same as the experience itself. A person may behave in many ways like a machine, yet one can function also as an autonomous being, exercising free will and self determination. Individuals have intentions, goals and objectives that may not be reduced to brain states. A person is believed to be different from a machine as some behaviours are not seen as being constrained by physical laws that control the brain functions, as exemplified by the evidence for para neural phenomena such as extra sensory perception and psycho-kinesis which seem to defy conventional physical laws and appear inexplicable in terms of known sensory-motor process. It may not be unreasonable to suppose that conscious experience, though dependent on neuro biological processes, may not be identical with or wholly determined by them. It is increasingly becoming apparent, that the theory which regards consciousness as an epiphenomena of matter or sees in it no more than neural events in the brain, is at best incomplete as it excludes from its consideration aspects of awareness that go beyond the categories of senses and understanding.

As mentioned, the emphasis in the east is on the psychological rather than only physical and preferred method is first person based introspection. In the west the focus is on the object of experience and preferred method is third person based observation and measurement. In the west, consciousness is generally equated with the mind or conceived as an aspect of the mind. In the eastern tradition, specially the Indian, basic distinction is made between consciousness and mind. Existence of pure consciousness is believed to be non intentional, whereas mental phenomena are regarded as essentially intentional. The two approaches can however be genuinely complementary for a fuller grasp of consciousness and its role in our being.

Sant Mat or the Religion of Saints is reflective of the best in the eastern tradition in this area. It is not rooted in any particular creed. It is a path which anybody can tread.

The teachings of Sant Mat are based on three essential beliefs:

(a) Belief in the existence of God or Supreme Being, the Original Source of energy which brought about the creation,

(b) Belief in the oneness of the essence of God and the spirit-entity in man, and

(c) Belief in the continuity of life after death.

To a follower of Sant Mat, God is not a matter of opinion. God exists as surely and certainly as his own spiritual self. He understands the oneness of the essence of an ocean and that of a drop of water. He has to move in the direction of his own spiritual self. He is convinced that the real self does not perish with the perishing of the physical body. It is immortal and will continue to exist and pursue the course Godwards even after the death of the present physical body.

According to the teachings of Sant Mat, human body is an epitome of the whole creation and an apparatus through which communion can be established with the various spheres and spiritual centres of the universe. It is believed that there are located in this body a number of force centres, technically known as *chakras*, with which are associated spiritual powers of a very high order and if these spiritual powers of the microcosm be properly developed and brought into action, it becomes possible for a devotee to establish communion with the spheres and spiritual centres of the macrocosm. The spiritual practices prescribed in Sant Mat raise the spirituality of a devotee to the required high pitch, and render it possible for him to tap his potential spiritual powers and bring them into action. The spiritual practices prescribed are *Sumiran*, *Dhyan* and *Bhajan* known by various names among the Persian Sufi saints and other religions prescribing meditational practices to devotee, so as to engage his attention in silent repetition of the Holy name at high force centres and in *Dhyan* focus at that centre and when the spiritual power dormant in that centre begins to show signs of awakening, he becomes fit for initiation in the *Bhajan* practices: contemplation of the spiritual sound which is the manifest form of the all-powerful current of spirituality emanating from the Supreme Fountain-head of all spirituality. The devotee can then proceed from stage to stage enjoying the rapturous thrills of various transcendental experiences, till one day he finds his spirit fully awake, freed from all contamination of mind and matter. One can also describe these movements of spirit from one force centre to a higher one as attaining different levels of consciousness and when it reaches the final destination, it acquires Supreme Consciousness – Supreme Intelligence, Bliss and Energy which are the attributes of the Supreme Being.

To quote Param Guru Sahabji Maharaj, the fifth Revered Leader of Radhasoami Faith, "Truth which we all love can never be comprehended with the physical instruments of science nor can Ultimate Reality, which we so much adore, be realized with the mental efforts of philosophy. These can be achieved only when the special spiritual faculty in human body is fully developed, when we shall be able to perceive Truth and realize Ultimate Reality in the same manner as we perceive and realize the Sun with our physical eyes. When this takes place we will be astonished and amused to find that Truth the goal of Science, Ultimate Reality, the goal of philosophy and God the goal of religion are the three names of same Supreme Essence."

The Seminar had drawn participants from different fields who are interested in the study of the phenomenon of Consciousness. These included scientists, neuro-physiologists, psychoanalysts, persons interested in eastern spiritual philosophy and religion, practitioners of spiritual meditation drawn from different backgrounds and followers of Sant Mat (Religion of Saints). The seminar was graced by Heads of Centres of Radhasoami Faith. The result is a rich harvest of ideas, thoughts and concepts and of facts, analyses and conclusions drawn from scientific experimentation and religious philosophies.

I hope the readers and researchers interested in the study of Consciousness would find the compilation useful and interesting and trust it will further advance the knowledge and understanding of this fundamental phenomenon of existence.

Dayalbagh
24th January 2013

PREFACE

The Religion of Saints sums up and extends the teachings of Saints and Fakirs of medieval and later times who have given the highest revelations culminating in *Radhasoami Faith*. Param Purush Puran Dhani Huzur Soamiji Maharaj revealed the *Radhasoami Name* and secret of *Radhasoami Dham* in 1861 on the Basant Panchami Day. The year 2010-11 marked the 150th year of the Foundation of the Radhasoami Faith. The Dayalbagh Educational Institute, founded in realization of the mandates of the Sant Satgurus of the *Radhasoami Faith* hosted an International Seminar on *"Religion of Saints ('Sants') – Radhasoami Faith: Spiritual Consciousness Studies"* (SPIRCON *2010)* from November 12-14, 2010.

The Dayalbagh Educational Institute declared as a 'Deemed to be University' in 1981 has implemented an innovative and comprehensive programme of education aiming "to bring about physical, intellectual, emotional and ethical integration of an individual with a view to evolving a complete man who possesses the basic values of humanism, secularism and democracy and who is capable of giving a fuller response to social and environmental challenges". As has been explained by Most Revered Prof. Prem Saran Satsangi, Chairman, Advisory Committee on Education, Dayalbagh Educational Institutions, education is imparted here at three levels. At the foundational level comprising the primary and middle school levels learning is by means of the well-known three "R's" namely, reading (w)riting and (a)rithmatic. Progressing to higher education and university education, scientific temper is inculcated and scientific methodology is adopted as a result of which education takes on the hue of another set of three "R's" characteristic of Science (duly blended with integration provided by systems approach) namely, Reductionism representing the analytical power of science, Repeatability of experimentation which is the strength of Science and Refutation of hypothesis by means of which Science has taken its spectacular strides in the modern world availing advancements in telecommunication technologies and Quantum-Nano-Computing. The third and highest level of education, however, is the level of Spiritual Education i.e. education pertaining to realms beyond the physical world called *Para Vidya* by Sages and Saints. It is ultra-transcendental knowledge of the *Nirmal Chetan Desh,* the Pure Spiritual Region revealed by the Param Sants and the essence of Satsang and *Sant Mat* or *Radhasoami Faith*.

According to Most Revered Prof. P.S. Satsangi, the order of the empirical world itself has an order, an underlying order of second degree, which rests on the Intuitive Consciousness that guides and prompts development of living systems, with apparently purposive and telic behaviour. Thus all human beings have some kind of programmed life given to them by the Supreme

Being. All of us at some time or the other experience a kind of conscious or sub-conscious precognition of it and as we get educated in Schools, Colleges and Universities and ultimately receive spiritual Education in Satsang that consciousness grows. We all have, in this way, a dynamically programmed life for the awakening and development of our consciousness. Science of Consciousness is in the process of its evolution. Modern scientists generally are concerned with empirical levels of consciousness that an ordinary man goes through.

Science and spirituality are getting reintegrated with their common interest in consciousness. The scholarly deliberations in two days at SPIRCON 2010 dedicated to the exploration of consciousness witnessed a grand convergence of scientists, spiritualists, philosophers, medical practitioners, and religious heads. There were a total of 16 Plenary Sessions, 9 Oral Paper presentation sessions and a Poster presentation session. Apart from these, the Inaugural Session, the Panel Discussion and the Valedictory Session drew much attention from the charged audience and the media persons. The Special Sessions were transmitted to 231 centres across the world including 201 centres all over India and 30 in other countries including USA, Canada, Middle East, Singapore, UK, Germany, Sri Lanka etc. which is one more way in which this Seminar is unique. More than thirty thousand people witnessed the sessions in various parts of the globe.

At the Inaugural Session, *Prof. P Sriramamurti* elucidated the link between religion and consciousness. He said that in religious traditions supremacy of spirit is taken axiomatically. Higher levels of spiritual consciousness are sought to guide our lives and it does not matter whether it is from the East or West, Hindu or Semitic. The *Inaugural Address* was given by *Revered Prof. Agam Prasad Mathur Sahab*, the present religious leader of Radhasoami sect, Peepal Mandi, Agra and Ex Vice – Chancellor, Agra University. Revered Prof Mathur Sahab fondly recounted his old associations with Dayalbagh and stressed the need to renew these associations. He recounted the basic tenets of *Radhasoami Faith* which for the first time described higher Spiritual Consciousness levels. He said that Spiritual Consciousness was explained by Param Guru Huzur Maharaj as "to acquire knowledge of the secrets and the order of Creation and the means of traversing the distance between his dwelling in the body (the pupil of the eye) and the abode of the Supreme Being, the Prime Source of everything; and to start on his journey with fervor and perseverance with the avowed object of one day reaching the presence of the most high and beloved Supreme Father". He enumerated several features that unite all the sects of *Radhasoami Faith* and said that all the sects have uniformly maintained these features. The '*Radhasoami*' greeting establishes brotherhood among all the Satsangis irrespective of their sect. He spoke about love and devotion to the current Guru being the cornerstone of salvation in Radhasoami Faith and exhorted people to go back to Param Purush Dhani Huzur Soamiji Maharaj and Huzur Maharaj.

"*Vision Talk*" delivered by *Most Revered Prof. Prem Saran Satsangi* (Chairman, Advisory Committee on Education, Dayalbagh Educational Institutions) provided a feast for body, mind and soul. The spiritual head of the

Radhasoami Faith, Dayalbagh, Most Revered Prof. Satsangi Sahab, provided a framework for scientific investigation into consciousness. He said that if scientists came out of the shell of prejudice and take recourse to intuition, they can make greater headway. "In fact, there are no great contradictions or chasms between scientific thought and the corresponding spiritual conceptualization. There is convergence of views to a large extent, he added." He further emphasized that Cosmology in Radhasoami Faith is also all inclusive with regard to various religions prevalent in the world. He proposed O-theory (Omni-quantum theory) as a complete theory that integrates all the currently known scientific theories and subsumes them by drawing a parallel between the 11 dimensions of String Theory and 11 *Lokas* that He listed with the highest *Loka* being *Radhasoami Dham* corresponding to the elusive 11th dimension of the string theory. He propounded the White Mountain Strategy, also alluded to indirectly by the Chief Guest, that will enable the adherents of Radhasoami Faith to scale the highest peaks of Spirituality which is a totally internal experience that does not interfere or cause trouble to anyone else.

Shri Prem Kumar, President Radhasoami Satsang Sabha and Dayalbagh Educational Institute, emphasized that the concepts and philosophy of Religion of Saints (Sant Mat) can give us a way for achieving peace in the strife torn world of today. He stressed that Fatherhood of God and Brotherhood of Man should be our ideal to establish Universal Peace.

Prof PN Tandon of National Brain Research Centre documented how recent years have witnessed a revival in interest in attempts to reconcile rational enquiry (science) and spiritual convictions (religion). He presented several recent attempts by renowned scientists who have taken bold steps to bridge this interrelationship. Research in systems concepts and systems understanding has expanded the range and depth of how we understand our world. The spiritual dimension of systems theory is being nurtured and developed at the DEI that is creating a spiritual model of man and the macrocosm. *Prof. Jack Ellis of York University, Toronto,* said the concept may hold the greatest potential for achieving a blending of Eastern understanding and Western knowledge. "The ultimate reality of systems theory is that there is only one system," he said. "Human beings are well equipped to think, reason, experience emotion, and most importantly, to grow spiritually."

Swami Jitatmananda ji, Vice-President, Ramakrishna Vivekananda Mission spoke about consciousness in modern science and Vedanta. Spiritual consciousness depends on the heightening of our heart, mind and consciousness and this can be attained by regular spiritual practices, he said: "There is a growing hunger to find divinity within. A 'Conscious Revolution' has come in science and people have already begun to look inward and outward for peace and contentment." While eastern masters regard consciousness as an independent source making subjective awareness possible, the West views consciousness as merely a quality of certain brain and mental states. However, all spiritual traditions assert that cortical processes alone cannot result in subjective awareness. It is the light of consciousness of spirit that shines on objects that make them subjectively realized. Mind is the medium and gateway between consciousness of spirit and the objective world. He expressed great happiness that the Dayalbagh Educational Institute was an exception and had taken the bold step of trying to integrate religious and scientific studies. He said that the DEI had organized this Seminar on Spiritual Consciousness and it was a step in the right direction. It would have to be replicated all over India for the betterment of our people.

Prof Subhash Kak, Oklahoma State University, USA provided an overview of Indian spirituality and its consideration of the problems of consciousness, freedom, sin, and meaning. It compared ideas of Indian spirituality with that of quantum physics, and showed that in both the universe is best viewed from the complementary perspectives of physical structure and observers. *Prof A. K. Mukhopadhyay, All India Institute of Medical Sciences, New Delhi* said that science, at present, works within the boundary of the universe that in turn is determined by the boundary of the cerebral cortex. He stressed on unconditional surrender to the Guru as a prerequisite to spiritual progress. He said that the flow of Grace from the Guru to the disciple is the highest form of psychotherapy and elucidated several interesting concepts combining deep medical and consciousness insights. *Prof. Daniel Gold of Cornell University* spoke about the approach of the Sant Mat or religion of saints to the study of consciousness. Gold said that central to Radhasoami philosophy is the belief that the soul is of the same essence as of God. Human beings can realize their soul and God while still in the body through meditation, which ultimately leads to awakening of spiritual consciousness. You can experience soul and God in your lifetime through meditation on the name, light and sound of God. Since God is spirit, one can know God by transcending body-consciousness. "Religion of the saints is very broad, and leaves out a lot of external rituals and traditions. The *Sant Mat* is inclusive with strong reformist attitudes," he said. He added, "Spiritual science of consciousness broadens the outlook of a person towards life and the whole of Creation." Other distinguished speakers including *Dr. Mark Graves, USA; Dr. Laxmidhar Behre, IIT Kanpur; Prof. Peter H. Toe, Canada; Prof. John. Grayzel, USA; Prof. Sangeeta Menon, NIAS, Bangalore; and Prof. B. Les Lancaster, UK* added delightful feast to the spiritual consciousness studies. There was a brilliant video presentation on "Consciousness and neuroscience" by *Prof. David C. Lane and Prof. Andrea Lane, USA.*

The absorbing Panel Discussion included stalwarts like *Prof. Daniel Gold, USA, Prof. P Sriramamurti, Seminar Chair, Prof. Mark Juergensmeyer, USA, Shri Prem Prashant, Vice-Preisdent, Radhasoami Satsang Sabha, Dayalbagh, Prof. Subhash Kak, US; Swami Jitatmananda ji, Vice-President, Ramakrishna Vivekanada Mission and Prof. Jack Ellis, Canada. Revered Kunwar Pal Sahab,* Spiritual Leader of Radhasoami Satsang, Dinode, who graced the occasion also participated in the discussion and said that there must be emphasis on '*Karni*', '*Guru Bhakti*' and following the Guru. The panelists also said that Spiritual Consciousness can be raised by devotedly following the teachings of the Saints, accepting the Guru as the Lord and freeing oneself from worldly desires. Right and regular practice of *Surat-Sabda-Yoga* can raise Spiritual Consciousness. Till the mind becomes enlightened it is necessary to sit at the feet of ones Guru.

The panel unanimously resolved that the study of Spiritual Consciousness must be promoted in all the Universities especially in DEI, and Experiential Science must be recognized as an accepted Science, and efforts must be made to bring Scientific Study of Religion in order to bridge the gap between the two. Efforts must also be made to organize an International Seminar on Spiritual Consciousness abroad in the next two years especially in USA. The panel also emphasized that in the Sant Mat greatest importance is laid on complete surrender at the feet of the Living Guru, in accepting Him as the Lord and performing selfless devotion and service.

The Valedictory Address was delivered by *Prof. Mark Juergensmeyer, USA* world renowned authority on Religious Studies in general and Radhasoami Faith in particular. His book entitled "*Radhasoami Reality*" is acknowledged as a classic on the subject. He is a scholar of repute with knowledge of several languages. He said that it was fascinating to see that the Faith that had started 150 years ago as a simple *Sadhu* camp had grown into a Global Religion. At the place where 90 years ago there were only sand dunes and pits, there exists a grand Colony where the Seminar is taking place. He said that this is an extraordinary development by any standards.

In a nutshell, the participants were in consensus that spiritual awakening alone could resolve individual and societal crises to establish a new world order of '*fatherhood of God and brotherhood of man*'. The thought provoking International seminar thus opened new vistas in awakening our conscious efforts towards better worldliness.

The presentations and deliberations at the seminar are now being brought out in a book form containing almost all the contemporary knowledge of *Sant Mat,* particularly the *Radhasoami Faith*. The editors hope that the readers will find this book of immense interest, both as a narrative of the first ever International seminar on *Radhasoami Faith* and secondly as a reference book of the contemporary views of international scholars on various aspects of the modern, natural religion, the *Radhasoami Faith*.

P. Sriramamurti
Prem Prashant
Anand Mohan
(Editors)

ACKNOWLEDGEMENTS

It is with immense pleasure that we acknowledge our deep gratitude to Most Revered Professor P.S. Satsangi, Chairman, Advisory Committee on Education, Radhasoami Satsang Sabha Dayalbagh, for the inspiration, initiative and constant Guidance in organizing the SPIRCON 2010 Seminar in the sesqui-centennial year of Radhasoami Satsang at Dayalbagh. We are grateful to all who have readily responded to the call and participated in the Seminar by way of giving Invited Talks, Paper Presentations, both Oral and Poster and above all extending their cooperation in the organization of the Seminar. Our special thanks are due to Most Revered Professor P.S. Satsangi for His Vision Talk which set the ball rolling and to Revered Professor Agam Prasad Mathur, former Vice Chancellor, Agra University and Head of Radhasoami Satsang, Peepal Mandi, for His Inaugural Address. We are grateful to our foreign delegates also who made it convenient to come all the way to present their papers and enrich the quality of proceedings. We gratefully thank Revered Kanwar Singh ji of Radhasoami Satsang, Dinod, Bhiwani and Revered Kehar Singh ji of Radhasoami Satsang, Taran Taran for gracing the occasion.

Our thanks to the staff and students of DEI who spared no effort in making the seminar a success and to the various Academic Committees for reviewing the Abstracts and papers and helping in so many ways to bring out this publication.

Fully aware of our limitations of knowledge, skill and resources, we humbly dedicate this volume at the Lotus Feet of Param Guru Huzur Dr. M.B. Lal Sahab, the founder Director and Architect of this great centre of education, the Dayalbagh Educational Institute (Deemed University), Dayalbagh, Agra, India.

Our heartfelt thanks to the President of DEI for his kind direction in steering this programme through. Our thanks are also due to the Alumni Association for their valuable support and financial help in organizing this Seminar.

P. Sriramamurti
Prem Prashant
Anand Mohan
(Editors)

I

EXCERPTS FROM

Discourses on Radhasoami Faith

BY

Param Guru Huzur Maharaj Sahab
[Pandit Brahm Sankar Misra]
Third Revered Sant Satguru of the
Radhasoami Faith, Dayalbagh

EXCERPTS FROM

Discourses on Radhasoami Faith

BY

Param Guru Huzur Maharaj Sahab
[Pandit Brahm Sankar Misra]
Third Revered Sant Satguru of the Radhasoami Faith, Dayalbagh

2-THE OBJECT OF RELIGION

2. A desire to acquire pleasure or to avoid pain appears to be the motive of all animate volition and acts. Involuntary actions and thoughts of animate existence also to some extent partake of this tendency, that is to say, there is co-operation, assimilation, or acceptance of the condition helpful or conducive to well-being, and there is resistance or receding in the case of a contrary condition. The terms, 'pleasure' and 'pain', have been used, here and elsewhere, in their most comprehensive sense, including all prospective and retrospective conditions, whether appertaining to self or connected with others.

3. It is clear that a motive, actuated by the impulse described above, can find a final resting place in such a state alone as is entirely free from pain and opposition of every description, and is one of supreme bliss. This is the object of religion in its extreme analytical aspect. A study of the laws of spirit-force, a clear and positive knowledge of the Supreme Creator and of the economy, genesis, and the object of creation, and of the true duty of the sentient entity in the universe, are other ends in view in a scientific study of religion.

17-THREE MAIN FACTORS OF HUMAN EXISTENCE

30. An analysis of the human body and its subjective functions discloses three main factors in the economy of human existence:-

1) The human frame and the appended senses, composed of solid, liquid, gaseous, calorific, and ethereal conditions of matter, along with the non-intelligent forces of nature, generated by the action of energy through the medium peculiar to each.

2) The mind associated with antahkarana (internal constitution) consisting of four functions, viz, (a) responses at the mental plane, which give rise to thought; (b) the spiritual or the attention-currents, by means of which thoughts are projected to their objectives and are associated with them; (c) intelligence, which is the source of comprehension and which is the lustre shed by the convergence of the spiritual current; and (d) the ego, which differentiates its comprehension from that of others.

3) The spirit-force, which gives vitality to the other two main factors and

without the help of which the other two factors would remain dormant and inoperative.

18-SIX GANGLIA IN HUMAN BODY

31. Besides the three main factors referred to in the preceding article, which represent three grand divisions, as it were, of the microcosm, six sub-divisions are further observable in the physical frame:-

1) The ganglion at the rectum- It performs the function of ejecting effete matter.

2) The ganglion at the organ of reproduction- Its main function is that of reproduction, that is to say, the formation of the seed which will eventually develop into the physical frame.

3) The nervous centre at the navel- It regulates digestion and furnishes physical material for the whole frame.

4) The ganglion known as the solar plexus which is situated at the lower end of the sternum- It regulates the economy of the entire human frame and is the region of feeling. Cases are not unknown where the collapse of the action of the heart and the cessation of the pulse did not effect the functions of this centre. The feelings and the sensory and the motor actions continued in such cases for some time, although the action of the heart had stopped. A shock to this centre resulting in a cessation of its functions would, however, lead to a complete collapse of the physical frame and of its subjective functions.

5) The ganglion at the throat- It regulates subtle respiration.

6) The ganglion situated midway between the two eyes, three-quarters to one inch inwards from the root of the nose- It is the seat of the spirit.

22-CORRESPONDENCE AND COMMUNION OF THE MICROCOSM WITH THE MACROCOSM

41. The correspondence and communion of the microcosm with the macrocosm takes place by means of apertures in the microcosm. The main factor of the communion is, however, the spirit or the sensory current permeating these apertures.

The law accordingly is that, for the perception of the macrocosm, the spirit-current must be associated at the proper apertures in the microcosm with substances and powers similar to those that exist in the macrocosm. Communion between the various spheres of creation and the nervous centres which correspond with them is established in accordance with the law specified above.

24-THE BRAIN AND ITS APERTURES

44. In the fissure between the two lobes of the brain there are twelve apertures, which provide the means for communion with the six sub-divisions of Brahmanda and with the six sub-divisions of the purely spiritual region. The apertures appertaining to Brahmanda are to be found in the grey matter, and those appertaining to the purely spiritual region, in the white matter. So far as the matter of the brain is concerned, whether it be grey or white, it is of very little importance. The innermost quarters within those apertures, by means of which

the microcosm is associated with Brahmanda and the purely spiritual region, are of supreme importance, and they are indispensable in our research. The following illustration, although it is rather of a rough character, will make our purport clearer. There is a slit in a wall of a dark room by means of which solar rays find access within. The opening itself is not composed of the materials of the wall, but it is in it. A person placed in this room would have to resort to the opening for holding communion with the rays and for getting out of the room, if he could become so subtle as to ride on the rays. Similarly, the innermost locations of the apertures of the brain, referred to, will have to be sought for holding communion with the higher spheres, and for eventually gaining access into the region of Brahmanda and those beyond them. The explanations given above are necessarily in the nature of ex cathedra statements, but they can be fully verified by the performance of the experimentations or devotional methods prescribed for the development of the brain centres.

27-SOUND, SIGHT, AND SPEECH-ESSENTIAL FACTORS OF EXISTENCE

49. The main media for getting the experience of the physical world and for expressing our experiences are the senses of sound, sight and speech. These, thus, constitute the initial means for the supply of the needs of the physical frame. Further, if these three functions were to become inoperative, the subjective powers would either disappear or they would undergo considerable deterioration, and life would be short.

50. The above remarks apply also to the senses and the subjective functions of the subtler and higher planes. But as they do not take an active part in the maintenance of the physical frame, their inoperative condition does not affect the physical existence. As these functions are not subjected to any regular training or exercise in the microcosm, they lie dormant, and the purpose for which they are provided in the human economy is not served. The methods of devotion and training, prescribed in the religious system we are explaining, represent three different forms of spiritual exercise for the development of each of the three functions in question respectively. The three forms of the exercise are:-

1) utterance of the spiritual name by the spirit-current,
2) contemplation of the spiritual form, and
3) attentively listening to the spiritual sound.

54-ADVENT OF RADHASOAMI DAYAL

86. When ground for true spiritual regeneration, was thus prepared for further development by the Saints and other adepts referred to, then the incarnation of the presiding deity of the highest spiritual region, viz, Radhasoami, took place. The tenets and teachings and the practical devotional methods of the religion of Saints, which had already been given out, were made manifest in their simplest forms, and the devotional practices rendered so easy of performance, that they can be attended to without difficulty and performed with success by human beings of both sexes and all ages, subject to the observance of certain simple

rules regulating the conduct of life and diet, etc.

87. The true genesis and object of creation, which had hitherto been an insoluble mystery and which had not been explained in detail by Saints even, were given out by most gracious Radhasoami in a complete form. The true spiritual articulation of the sound of the highest division, which had not been made known by Saints, was also disclosed by Him. To demonstrate the truth of all these revelations, arguments based on lines of pure inductive and deductive reasoning, and supported by illustrations taken from facts, which are within the access of ordinary observation, and by devotional or experimental experiences, were advanced in discourses of a most

extraordinary character, delivered during the holy service held under His august presidentship every day. The scientific presentation of the revelations made by Him, as unfolded in this book, is based on those discourses.

65-EXPLANATION OF THE SUPREME NAME 'RADHASOAMI'

102. The imitation in articulate sound of the first spiritual current, which is the beginning and the cause of all creation, is 'Radha', and the imitation of the wave or commotion that gave rise to this prime current is 'Soami'. The true holy name or the supreme mantra of the origin and source of all spirituality in creation is 'Radhasoami'; and when the true Supreme Being thus manifested Himself as Creator and evolved the creation, the wave and currents announced Him as Radhasoami in the vast region of spirituality first evolved. This true name is present everywhere in creation, and can be heard at the innermost plane where the spirit-current is acting. As each ray emanating from the sun carries with it the constitutional components of the sun, similarly, the prime action by focus and current, which are the constitutional components of creation in the beginning, is carried in the tiniest ray of spirit, and the sound, Radhasoami, could be heard in miniature if we could penetrate the surrounding layers and reach the innermost quarter occupied by the spirit-ray. The holy name, Radhasoami, has been announced above, as revealed by the incarnation of gracious Radhasoami, like other revealed mantras or holy names. It will, however, perhaps be more satisfactory to demonstrate to some extent, that the imitation in articulate speech of the sound of the spirit-current and of the spirit-focus is Radhasoami.

66-SEQUENCE OF SOUNDS, 'RADHA' AND 'SOAMI' EXPLAINED

103. Before proceeding with the explanation, it is desirable to remove a misconception that might present itself in connection with the explanation we have given above. As the commotion in the source of spirit must have preceded the first spiritual manifestation or first spirit-current, the question naturally arises why it should not be more correct to call the holy name 'Soami Radha', that is to say, in the sequence in which the action took place. The answer to this apparent anomaly is that the manifestation of the prime current took place by a process of attraction similar to that exercised by magnetism (vide Article 63). As the current always first flows outwards and then turns back towards the source, its action, so far as the creation is concerned, takes place first and subse-

quently the influence of the source affects it. In other words the source acts by means of currents. From the point of view of creation, therefore, the proper sequence is current first and focus subsequently, and the name Radhasoami is not therefore in an inverted sequence.

78-ETERNAL POLARIZATION IN THE SUPREME BEING

116. We have already stated in Article 11 and 13 that the spirit-force is the one which possesses prime energy, and that all the other forces of nature have been evolved by the association of this energy with media of different kinds. We have also said that the source of this prime spiritual energy, which is all-powerful, all-wise, and all-blissful, is the true Supreme Being Himself. The inference from what we have stated above, would accordingly be that there was an eternal polarization in the Supreme Being Himself.

79-THE TWO POLES

117. The region from which the spiritual force had been withdrawn, to some extent, was, in the technical language of the religion of Saints, the Feet of the Supreme Being and the other portion which was replete with spiritual energy was His Head. In scientific language, the two poles may be spoken of as the positive and negative poles of the spirit-force.

118. It is desirable to observe here that there was not a complete absence of spirituality from the negative pole. There was considerable residual spiritual energy in that pole, but there was, of course, a diminution in intensity. The impress of this eternal condition is to be found in the fact that the coarsest and densest matter is not completely devoid of energy.

119. The idea of the existence of eternal polarization of the kind we have been speaking of, may naturally appear to introduce an element of finitude in the infinite, as our ideas of polarization are always associated with finiteness of both poles. In comprehending the condition of the infinite, such associations should not, however, be pressed forward in all their details, and the difference in degree of the intensity of the spiritual force at the two poles alone should be kept in view. If we liken the negative and the positive poles respectively to a cloud floating in the sky and the sky itself, this would be the nearest approach, in visual presentation, to the polarization we have been speaking of. It is hardly necessary to say that this illustration at once dispels the idea of finitude which may have arisen in consequence of association of ideas, in as much as the cloud does not in any sense impose a limitation on the surrounding sky.

83-PRE-CREATIONAL CONDITION OF THE SUPREME BEING

124. It is clear from the explanation given above that before creation, the Supreme Being Himself alone existed, of course, in a state of spiritual polarization, as already stated. His condition was one of intense rapture within Himself, the entire mass of the infinite supreme spirituality constituting, as it were a single being. In this Supreme Being, there was no form, there was no colour, there was no demarcation. The intensest form of the bliss of love, the

most refulgent lustre, the all-knowing intelligence, the all-powerful energy- all these existing as one-constituted the essence of this August Supreme Being. The condition of the nether pole which was somewhat different, in consequence of a lesser degree of spirituality, from the all-full spirituality, viz, the Supreme Being referred to, was, of course, all known to the Supreme Being; but the lower pole itself did not actively participate in the all-conscious attribute peculiar to the complete spirituality surrounding it. It was in a trance-like condition of existence. There was a gradation in this pole, the portions adjoining the spirit-source being comparatively more spiritual than the portions close to, and at, the pole-centre. The spiritual deficiency, as already stated, had been produced in the region occupied by this pole by withdrawal of spirituality in the direction of the Supreme Being.

85-THE PRIME CURRENT PRECEDED BY COMMOTION IN THE SUPREME SOURCE

127. We have stated that this united action of the points represented the eternal subtle attraction, which for an inconceivable period had no appreciable effect in producing a further differentiation. In the fullness of time, however, accentuation of attraction began to make itself manifest. The spiritual depletion in the lower pole, which had already existed, began to be further polarized; in other words, spirituality in excess of that already withdrawn was further attracted towards the infinite ocean of the positive pole, viz, the Supreme Being, and the depleted portion, shorn further of its essence, receded farther from Him. This process which immediately preceded the creation continued to act for some time, and when the proper time arrived, the first great current of spirituality issued from that region of the supreme source which was nearest to the lower pole. The issue of this current was, of course, preceded by the commotion in that region, and it was a manifestation of the prime energy by means of a process of spiritualization similar to the process of magnetization (vide article 63), the object being that whatever was capable of constituting a region fit to form an extension, so to say, of the original spirit-source, should be located within the purview of the Supreme Being, and be so highly spiritualized that any deficiency in its spirituality, as compared to that of the supreme source itself, should not be subject to the conditions peculiar to the greatly accentuated depletion of spiritual energy in the nether pole of which we shall speak shortly.

86-THE SOUND AND SPIRIT CURRENTS

128. The uniting faculty of the spirit-force is the spiritual sound-current, and the centre-forming faculty of the same force constitutes the spirit-current. The two are dependent upon each other. The sound is the active form and the spirit is the focus form of the same force. The sound attracts and the spirit forms the reservoir. These distinguishing features of the two currents gave rise subsequently to the differentiation of sexes in animate existence.

87-THE PURELY SPIRITUAL REGION AND ITS SIX SUB-DIVISIONS

129. As the Supreme Being Himself was in a state of eternal polarization,

consisting of three distinct regions, viz., the infinite region of full spirituality, the region of the neutral zone, and the region of the lower pole, the sound and spirit currents, which emanated from Him at the time of creation and were, to some extent, like the two currents accompanying the process of animate respiration, also resolved themselves in the region, which was directly within the purview of the Supreme Being, into three divisions each. In the case of animate respiration, the oxygen which is taken in comes out with an admixture of one of the main constituents of the human frame, i.e. it comes out as carbonic acid gas. In the supreme being Himself, there is nothing else but pure spirituality of the highest degree, and therefore the out-coming breath (respiration) is steeped in this spirituality. The outward spirit-current is, therefore, as spiritual as the inward current of sound which is absorbed in Him. The three sub-divisions of the first set, i.e. those which came into existence as a result of the polarization of the sound-current, are known as Radhasoami, Agam (inaccessible), and Alakh (invisible); and the three sub-divisions of the other set, viz., those which came into existence as a result of the polarization of the spirit-current, are known as Anami, Sat Loka, and Bhanwargupha. As the spirit-current, which is one of attraction, extends outwards by a process of spiritualization, it has a somewhat lower location than the sound-current, which is one of pure, inward action. The second set of the three sub-divisions mentioned above accordingly occupies a lower position than that of the first set, and its spirituality, too, is of a somewhat lesser intensity. In the six sub-divisions we have mentioned, the two currents are not distinguishable and both act together, their joint action being similar to the conjoint, attractive and magnetizing functions of the magnetic force. The existence of these two currents, however, has given rise to the six sub-divisions referred to. Hitherto we have spoken only of the main sub-divisions of the spiritual regions evolved at the time of creation. We would now describe in some more detail the presiding deities and the denizens of these spheres.

91-MAHASUNNA-ITS SIX SUBTLE SUB-DIVISIONS

135. We have already mentioned that the spiritual regions constituted, as it were, an extension of the infinite region of the Supreme Being Himself. The six spheres, referred to, thus became a part and parcel of the supreme spiritual pole, and are, therefore, immune from all changes and dissolution. The creational process, explained above, which resulted in that part of the pre-creational neutral zone, which adjoined the supreme source, being converted into purely spiritual regions, caused a gap, as it were, below these regions. This vast gap is known in the religion of Saints as the region of Mahasunna. This constitutes the barrier between the spiritual regions and the regions of the Universal Mind or Brahma, which latter, as we shall presently explain, were evolved out of the lower part of the pre-creational neutral zone. As the gap, referred to, or Mahasunna, was constantly under the strain of the creational process employed in the evolution of the spiritual regions, it received a subtle impress of the purely spiritual regions, and subtle sub-divisions corresponding to the spiritual sub-divisions were formed in it. These subtle regions may be called sub-zones of the purely spiritual regions. The creational process of the subtle regions, referred to, was started by Soham Purusha, the presiding deity

of the lowest spiritual region, viz, Bhanwargupha.

93-EVOLUTION OF THE CONSTITUENTS AND SIX SUB-DIVISIONS OF BRAHMANDA

138. The issue of the currents of Kala Purusha and Adya from Sat Loka entirely removed from the sphere of Sat Loka that condition of lower spirituality which was not fit for association with purely spiritual regions, and at the same time supplied the necessary factors for the creation of Brahmanda. It may be observed here that the action of these two currents was outward, or contrary to the purely spiritual action, as their functions appertain to the region adjoining the region proper of the original nether pole. This region of Kala Purusha and Adya is known as Brahmanda, and its upper boundary is contiguous with the lowest part of the creation of Mahasunna, which lowest part is the sphere of Akshara Purusha (Imperishable Deity). This deity, being one of the subordinate deities of the sub-spiritual creation of Mahasunna, is like them almost immune from dissolution, and is accordingly called the Akshara Purusha. The currents of Kala Purusha and Adya formed the first focus in a somewhat commingled condition in conjunction with the seat occupied by Akshara Purusha. Here the two currents in question are respectively known as Purusha and Prakriti. As Akshara Purusha was an emanation of the purely spiritual region, he occupied with reference to Brahmanda the same position as that occupied by the individual human spirit with reference to the physical frame and the mind. His sphere is, therefore, known as the true Atma Pada (spirit-pole) of Brahmanda; and an adept who succeeds in effecting a union with Akshara Purusha, the great spirit of the nether pole, is most appropriately called a Mahatma (great spirit). The conjunction of Kala and Adya with Akshara Purusha, resulted in the supply of considerable vital energy to them and the work of creation of Brahmanda commenced forthwith. In accordance with the methods employed for the evolution of creation of the spiritual regions, currents issued forth from the Purusha, Prakriti, and the Akshara Purusha, and completed the work of creation of the spheres appertaining to them. These three currents are manifest in this sphere and are known as Tribeni. The focus or reservoir, which is directly below the seat of Akshara Purusha himself, is known as Mansarovara, and immersion in this reservoir of spirituality purified the adept, who reaches that stage, of all subtle impurities of Brahmanda that he may have imbibed during his upward journey through the region of the Kala Purusha, viz., Brahma or the Universal Mind. The point at which these three currents first converged is known as Trikuti, i.e. the place of three elevations or prominences. These three prominences are known as Meru, Sumeru, and Kailasa. Here the two currents which had come from Sat Loka manifested themselves as Brahma and Maya. As the original strata at this place were comparatively heavy or less spiritual, the creational shifting cast out a huge volume of cover-clouds composed of extremely fine constituents known as paramanus (molecules). These paramanus are infinitely finer than the ordinary molecules and ions we are familiar with and should not be confounded with them. The deficiency of spirituality in the region of Trikuti, as compared to the spirituality of the sphere above it, viz., Sunna or Dasamadwar, appeared in a much more pronounced form, and the visual effect produced by it was a highly refulgent, red hue, like that of the rising sun.

139. The three currents united in their course downwards from Trikuti, and two fresh main currents from Maya and Brahma also started downwards. The centre where these two currents took their third location is known as Sahasdal Kamal (the thousand-petalled lotus), and Maya and Brahma here assumed the form of Jyoti and Narayana (or Niranjana).

140. As the three currents referred to had started from a region of three prominences, the impress of the form of that region was imparted to the course carved out by them in their descent to Sahasdal Kamal. This path is known as Banknal (crooked tunnel). From the point from which the united three currents commenced their course downwards, the path goes up first and is then followed by a descent. These three currents are the subtlest latent forms of the three gunas (qualities) we shall speak of presently, one being highly charged with spirituality, the second with generative functions, and the third with the quality of destruction. At Trikuti these three currents and the currents of Maya and Brahma acting upon the molecules referred to produced five distinct (although very subtle and almost imperceptible) strata or layers in them. These are the subtlest forms of the five conditions of matter referred to in Article 12. The condition of matter produced by the Brahma-current was the Akasa tattva (ether); that produced by Maya was the Agni tattva (fire); and those evolved by the preservative, the generative, and the destructive qualities respectively were the Vayu (gas) the Jala (liquid), and the Prithvi (solid) tattvas (elements or conditions) respectively. The matter (or molecules), which had fallen downwards at the creational shifting applied at Trikuti, carried the impress of these five conditions downwards, and manifested itself at Sahasdal Kamal as the five distinct elements mentioned above. As these elements were much subtler than ions, and as they were highly charged with energy, they issued forth from Sahasdal Kamal as five distinct currents of radiance of different hues. The hue of ether or sky was of a dark bluish colour, that of fire, of red colour, and those of Vayu, Jala, and Prithvi, greenish, white and yellow colours respectively.

141. No sooner had the five tattavas emanated from Sahasdal Kamal, than they were subjected to further action. The three qualities and Jyoti and Niranjana, each acting on the five tattavas separately, produced twenty-five sub-constituents of the five tattavas, each possessing a distinctive property peculiar to it. These twenty-five constituents are known as the twenty-five prakritis or properties.

142. Concomitantly with the grouping of tattavas and prakritis in the manner indicated above, the creational process of constituting the sphere of Sahasdal Kamal was at work. Eight main currents were engaged in this creational work. These currents consisted respectively of the currents of Jyoti and Niranjana and of those of the three qualities split up into male and female currents each. It is because of these eight currents that the Sahasdal Kamal is also technically called the Ashtadal Kamal (eight-petalled lotus). Each of these eight currents first attracted and assimilated five distinct leaves, so to say, of the five tattvas.

Thereafter, each one of the individual leaves, so constituted, attracted and evolved twenty-five sub-leaves of the prakritis. These final leaves, thus arranged round the eight main currents, produced a ramification of one thousand petals, and the sphere is accordingly spoken of, with reference to them, as the lotus of one thousand petals.

143. After the formation of this lotus, the two currents of Jyoti and Niranjana took their final abode. They could not go down further, in consequence of the negative strata below Sahasdal Kamal being not suitable for their energy. The three qualities, which had hitherto remained concealed, as it were, within the sphere of Sahasdal Kamal, now issued forth as the three sons of Narayana, and became the deities of their respective spheres which are located one below the other. These deities are known as Vishnu, Brahma and Siva. Their spheres are in the order in which their names are mentioned. The evolution of these three spheres completed the set of the six sub-divisions of Brahmanda, which, as already stated (vide article 91), occupy the lower part of the pre-creational neutral zone. Hitherto, we have been speaking of the evolution of the constituents and of the six sub-divisions of Brahmanda. We now proceed to say something about the spirituality and the denizens of these regions.

96-THE TANMATRAS THE SUBTLEST PARTICLES OF MATTER

146. The matter or molecules which issued forth from Trikuti (vide article 93) was void of intelligence, although it was very subtle and pure and highly charged with energy. Simple covers out of such a material were, therefore, not sufficient for the perception of the outer world. At Trikuti, the five senses were created in their subtlest form, with the object of endowing the denizens of that place and those of the lower creation, with the necessary means of holding communication with, and acquiring a knowledge of, the surrounding creation. The subtlest and the minutest particles, technically known as tanmatras, were associated with each spirit, and they formed suitable media for receiving impressions from the five different kinds of matter already evolved there.

101-THE FIELD BELOW BRAHMANDA AND ORBITAL MOTIONS OF BRAHMANDA AND PIND

156. Below the spheres of Vishnu, Brahma, and Siva there is a vast field somewhat similar to Mahasunna. Although it is very much smaller than the latter, there is some minor creation in this field, and it serves as a boundary between the second and the third grand divisions of creation. At the lowest part of this boundary, the topmost sphere of the third division is situated with an upward opening into the regions of Brahmanda. This opening is known as the third til (the third or the subtle eye), and by means of it one can catch glimpses of the lower portion of Brahmanda. This opening is also the portal through which the spirit-entity passes from the third into the second grand division. The sphere, referred to above, bears a resemblance to the top sphere of Brahmanda, viz, Sunna. This is the moon-sphere of the third division of creation, and all spirituality is supplied to the lower spheres from this source. This sphere is above the sun, and is moving along with the latter around the lowest part of Brahmanda. Brahmanda, too, as a whole, is also subject to a similar orbital motion round the

purely spiritual region. This latter region or any portion of it, is not, however, subject to the motion of the kind referred to. As we shall explain later on, the two grand divisions of creation which are subject to orbital motion are alone subject to periodical dissolution also. In the purely spiritual region, there is no change or dissolution, and that region is accordingly eternal. The description we have given refers to that individual system of Brahmanda and of the third division of creation in which our solar system is located. In the Brahmanda as a whole, however, there are innumerable systems of the same type. The innumerable Universal Minds or Brahmas, with their consorts, the Adyas, as well as the innumerable spirit-centres of Brahmanda, were cast out like drops from a sea out of the spiritual current and the currents of Kala and Maya that descended down from the purely spiritual region into the vast expanse known as Mahasunna. Similarly, the innumerable solar systems we find in the plane of the third grand division of creation have been projected down by each of the individual systems of Brahmanda.

102-THE COMBINATION OF QUALITIES WITH PRAKRITIS FORMING EIGHTY-FOUR CURRENTS

157. The three Gunas (qualities) in their downward course became associated with the twenty-five prakritis mentioned in article 93, and also entered into combination with each other. Thus eighty-four compound currents, viz, seventy-five currents of matter and nine of the qualities referred to, descended into the third division of creation. These eighty-four subtle currents are known as the chaurasi laksh (the subtle eighty-four). The material constituents and the functions of all animate and inanimate creation in the third grand division have been evolved out of these eighty-four currents. The seventy-five material currents are in the nature of elements known to us, each endowed with separate properties in accordance with the nature of the various forces they were subjected to, and with reference to the tattvas from which their material element was derived.

104-THE SIX SUB-DIVISIONS OF PIND AND THEIR PRESIDING DEITIES

159. Besides the eighty-four currents referred to, current-emanations of Jyoti and Niranjan also descended into the third grand division of creation, viz, Pind. Their subtlest forms are associated with the presiding deity of the top sphere of this division, while the remaining two forms of each, which are comparatively speaking less subtle, are themselves the presiding deities at the next two lower spheres. Similarly, emanations from Vishnu, Brahma, and Siva have converged at the three lowest spheres of Pind respectively. The emanations from Jyoti and Narayana manifest themselves in the microcosm of a human entity as individual desire and mind respectively. The manifest forms of these two emanations in the human entity, where they exist as rays from the main currents, are to be found at the nervous centre which is located at the heart. There, the desire and the functions of the mind are at play. Their subtler forms are to be found in the nervous centres at the throat and at the seat of the spirit (vide article 18). Their functions are, however, not manifest and are perceived on development of the latent potentialities of the spirit. The three lower centres in the human entity are similarly imbued with the powers of Vishnu, Brahma

and Mahadeva respectively, and perform the functions of preservation, assimilation and procreation, and elimination of effete bodily matter respectively. The orbs of Pind region, which correspond to these six nervous centres, are respectively the Spirit or Moon-orb, the Sun, the Earth, Jupiter, Saturn, and Neptune. The other so-called planets are really minor orbs, and they render assistance to the main orbs to which they are nearest. These minor planets perform functions similar to those performed by certain sub-ganglia adjoining the main ganglia. Like the three lower ganglia in the human frame, which form a group, as it were, distinct from that of the three upper ganglia, the three lower orbs of Pind are to a considerable extent independent of the group of the three higher orbs. In accordance with the characteristics of its presiding deity, viz., the emanation of Vishnu, Jupiter is more or less independent of the Sun, the connecting link being the current of spirituality which descends down to the lowest sphere from the moon-orb. As the plane of this orb and the individual spirit or moon-orb are on the same level, this is spoken of as Chandra in astrological terminology and it is by means of this that the rasi or the characteristic of each human individuality is determined. This spiritual current is the source from which originally spirituality is supplied to all animate creation in the third grand division. This is also the orb from which another current known as jar chetan (vitality of inanimate objects) is supplied to the material constituents of Pind. The electricity which we find on our earth is a manifestation of the non-spiritual life-current we have been speaking of. In the holy scriptures of Saints it is mentioned as bijli (lightning). The subtle spheres of the five subtle currents of tattvas are below the moon-orb of Pind, and they are resplendent there in the hue peculiar to each. We quote below a couplet which contains the ideas we have stated above:-

पाँच रंग निरखे तत सारा।
चमक बीजली चंद्र निहारा।
फोड़ा तिल का द्वारा हो।।

The English version of the couplet would be as follows:-

The devotee saw the five elementary colours of the tattvas, beheld the flashes of lightning of the moon, and then forced open the third eye, viz, the portal of Brahmanda (vide article 101).

106-THE REGION OF HELL AND ITS DENIZENS

162. Below the lowest sphere of the third grand division of creation, exists the pole proper of the nether pre-creational region. There is no regular creation in it and it is a vast expanse of spiritual depletion, as it were. Whatever creation is there, is of a minor character, bearing some distant resemblance to sub-creations of Mahasunna and of the bottom portion of Brahmanda. This minor creation is known as the region of hell and is full of torments and woe. The denizens of hell are possessed of the vilest propensities and are ever tormenting those who have the misfortune of being cast into this place of correction and punishment.

107-GENERAL ECONOMY OF THE THREE GRAND DIVISIONS

164. So far as the regions of the first grand division are concerned, very little is required to be stated here. They are within the purview of the infinite Supreme Being and constitute His own region, as it were. At the time of creation, the spiritual regions were so spiritualized by the currents of spirit and sound that they do not stand in need of any further spiritualization. The residual pre-creational admixture of spirituality of lower order left during the first creational stage was eliminated at the commencement of the next creational step downwards, and the purely spiritual regions, as already stated before, are now perfect in every respect, needing no change or addition in consequence of lapse of time. Compared to the other two grand divisions, the expanse of the purely spiritual regions is immense. The case of the other two grand divisions of creation is different. Their spirituality is not so complete as to enable them to work independently, that is, without assistance. Accordingly, each part of Brahmanda with its innumerable Brahmas and Adyas has to be presented in turn before purely spiritual regions to receive the necessary help. This is the cause of the revolution of Brahmanda round the Sat Loka, the proper distance between Brahmanda and the purely spiritual regions being maintained during the course of the revolution in consequence of the contrary influence exercised by the nether regions below it. The nature of the relation of Brahmanda to the spiritual region, as described above, also obtains between the third grand division and Brahmanda. The third division is revolving round Brahmanda and deriving help therefrom as in the previous case. The tendency of Brahmanda and the third grand division is, however, all towards the extreme nether pole, as Brahmanda is situated in that portion of the pre-creational neutral zone (vide article-91) which adjoined the original nether pole. The continued action of the tendency, referred to, results in constant downflow of spirituality, which is eagerly absorbed by the nether regions which are so devoid of spirituality as sand is devoid of moisture. Those regions are, however, from their pre-creational constitution, unfit to retain for any considerable length of time spirituality of a higher degree than that originally allotted to them. The spirituality which has been collecting, so to say, from the continuous downflow, evaporates, as it were, and another current, upwards, is established. This upward current serves an extremely ameliorating purpose, specially in the third division of creation; for along with it, the denizens of the infernal regions and of the lower spheres of the third grand division, ascend to higher planes; but this current cannot go beyond the topmost spheres of the third division, and the highest point to which an entity may reach by this natural process of elevation is the moon-sphere. There the circle is completed by the two currents, and the downward course commences again. This circle is known as the *chakra* of chaurasi, and no one can get beyond it unless he is specially trained for access into higher regions. We have been speaking here generally of the regions of Brahmanda and Pind as a whole. We would now give further details of the conditions of individual solar and Brahma systems (i.e. of one Pind and one Brahmanda only) of the third and second grand divisions respectively.

108-MAHA PRALAYA AND PRALAYA

165.When an individual Brahma system (Brahmanda) has completed its vast cycle of revolution round the spiritual region, during which period it has been considerably exhausted by the assistance imparted to that part of the third grand division which is subordinate to it, it comes nearest to Sat Loka, that is to say, it is then in conjunction with the spiritual region; and the influence exercised upon it by that region is so great that the entire system of the Brahmanda and of its subordinate regions, is drawn up and reduced, more or less, to its pre-creational condition. This change is known as the maha pralaya (the great dissolution). The condition produced by this dissolution is maintained for such a period as is sufficient to impart to it the necessary spirituality for a reconstruction, and then the Brahmanda and the subordinate regions are again evolved in the manner of their original evolution. The dissolution of individual solar systems takes place on exactly similar lines, but the Brahmanda is not affected by their dissolution. The subsequent reconstruction of the solar systems is also similar to the reconstruction of Brahmanda. The dissolution of solar system is known as pralaya (dissolution).

111-THE CONSTITUTION OF MAN, A PERFECT MICROCOSM FIT FOR SPIRITUAL PROGRESS

168. The six ganglia, from the lowest at the rectum to that situated in the middle of the line joining the two pupils, are all kinetic in a human entity. The six planes of the third grand division are all, therefore, represented in a kinetic form in humanity. In accordance with the general law, which applies to all entities, the three upper ganglia of a human entity must necessarily be at work, as the location of man is on the lowest of the three upper spheres referred to, viz., on the earth. The momentum which the downward current from Brahmanda and that from the moon and sun orbs have acquired at the earth is very considerable. Its influence has, therefore, caused a development of the three lower ganglia (which correspond to the three lowest spheres of the third grand division) in a manner contrary to the general law that holds good in the case of Brahmanda and the purely spiritual regions. At the earth-level, therefore, both brute and human entities are endowed with the three lower ganglia in a highly developed form. In man, who is spiritually by far superior to all other animate entities on this earth, the three higher ganglia have not been denuded, to such an extent, of spirituality and energy, as a result of supplying energy to the three lowest nervous centres, as to render the former centres inoperative to any appreciable degree. The case of other entities is, however, different. Their spirituality being small, the downward drain has considerably affected the higher centres, and the subjective functions, specially the power of abstraction, have become considerably impaired. In many a case, their heart-centre is the seat of their spirit, and they can go on living even when their brain is removed. The downward rush of the current we have been speaking of is very powerful. Nobody can turn it in the opposite direction, unless the passions, which are all influenced by the current in question, are more or less subdued, and a constant watch kept over our actions to prevent an unnecessary and improper indulgence in them.

169. From what we have stated above, it is clear that man is the entity in whom six divisions of Brahmanda are reflected in a kinetic form. The apparatus for the reproduction of the divisions of Brahmanda in man is to be found in the brain (vide Article 23 and 24), and by means of the apertures provided therein which, in consequence of the reflex action taking place through them, contain in a potential state the powers found in Brahmanda, the spirit of man can, under proper training, get access into Brahmanda. As Brahmanda itself is a reflex image of the purely spiritual region, the currents which establish the reflex conditions of Brahmanda in the human microcosm, are associated with the reflex functions of the purely spiritual region. These functions are also, therefore, represented in the human brain, and apertures are provided therein for communication with and access into the purely spiritual region. Man, from his position in the universe and from the amount of spirituality he possesses, is thus endowed with a cosmos of his own, which is so constructed as to represent all the spheres of the entire creation from the highest spiritual source down to the creationless nether pole, and which possesses such apertures and potentialities as would enable the human entity to reach the highest mansion. In man, therefore, the true microcosm exits, and it is in consequence of this unique possession that he is considered to be superior to angels and to the denizens of Brahmanda. This is also the main reason for the incarnation of the true Supreme Being Radhasoami, of His beloved sons the Saints, of Brahma and of his prophets, etc. having taken place in human form. The denizens of Brahmanda too, when they become desirous of ascending into the spiritual regions, have therefore to assume human form which is possible on the earth-plane alone, as in this perfect microcosm alone the spiritual training, prescribed by Saints, can be performed. The spirits of Saints often visit the various spheres of Brahmanda with the object of revealing to the denizens thereof the existence and the bliss of the purely spiritual regions. As the denizens of Brahmanda are highly spiritual and pure, they find no difficulty in comprehending the revelations made to them, and they soon become imbued with a strong desire for reaching the purely spiritual regions. When this desire has sufficiently developed, then their advent into human form takes place. The bliss of Brahmanda is so great and enrapturing that it is the revelation about higher spiritual regions and their bliss alone which generates a desire of the kind we have spoken of.

124-THE GRACIOUS OBJECT OF CREATION

192. The Supreme Being is an infinite ocean of all absorbing rapture and love, of supreme intelligence from which nothing remains concealed, of supreme energy or spirit which supplies force and vitality to everything, and of supreme light whose lustre is indescribable. In this all-glorious condition, eternal and infinite, unaffected by anything, He exists. Association with such a source must necessarily produce the beneficial attributes of His essence. The pre-creational association with and subordination to the infinite source of the planes other than that of the infinite source were, therefore, pregnant with a supreme gracious object. When in the fullness of time the association was intensified, the lower strata burst forth into a glorious creation by the advent of a mighty

current of the essence of the Supreme Being. The region which was nearest to Him, and which in point of expanse was immensely greater than the rest of the creation itself became intelligent as a whole, and became attached for ever to the supreme source. The denizens of this region, too, whose numerical proportion compared to that of the denizens inhabiting other parts of creation, is inconceivably larger, woke up from a state of unconscious stupor into an immortal and immutable life of extreme rapture and bliss, susceptible in no way to the feeblest shadow of a condition of an opposite character. By far the largest portion of the pre-creational region below that of the supreme source became the recipient of a favour which is beyond description. It is hardly necessary to remark that the gracious object involved in organizing a creation of the region referred to is almost inconceivable, and the Supreme Being alone, Who is all-bliss, could conceive of such an object. In the evolution of other parts of creation, His object was not less generous. The pre-creational deficiency of spirituality prevented the other parts of creation from receiving in a full measure the benefit that had been showered by the Supreme Being, but the gracious object did not fail to effect its ends to the highest degree possible. The evils of the deficiency were mitigated and minimized, and such a place was assigned to those other parts in the economy of creation that eventually they always contributed to an enhancement of the bliss of existence. The evil we have referred to is almost nominal in the second grand division of creation, and when the time arrives for its manifestation, the great dissolution takes place, and the evil is not allowed to assert itself. In the second grand division of creation also, which constitutes the major portion of the fractional creation left behind after appropriation of the spiritual region by the Supreme Being, the object of creation was practically to confer almost ever-lasting bliss and happiness similar to some extent to that of the first grand division. The spirituality of the third grand division is of the lowest order, and evil tendencies, pains and torments are accordingly associated in a large measure with existence in this division. During the first three Yugas these, however, do not manifest themselves, and life with its joys is an immense boon compared to the pre-creational condition. In about the eighth part of the life of the third division, the denizens are under the direct influence of material and evil desires, and are afflicted with various sorts of troubles, anxieties, fear, etc. During that period, they have also to pay, in hell, the penalty of their evil acts. But these adverse conditions produce a shifting which results in the elimination of material covers, and at no distant date they become fit to receive the grace which accompanies the advent of adepts. If the time for the great dissolution has arrived, this grace comes direct from the gracious Supreme Creator of the purely spiritual regions, otherwise it descends from Brahmanda. In the former case, the denizens of the third division derive immense spiritual benefit, and a very large number of them is trained for admittance into the immortal regions of the first grand division. If, therefore, we consider the immensely large time allowed to all denizens for the enjoyment of existence, and the comparatively short period during which they are subject to pain merely as a corrective measure, the gracious object of creation in the lowest division becomes manifest in a very pronounced form, and the wisdom of the Supreme Being in all that He has ordained appeals forcibly. When the inherent powers of the spirit become developed to some extent, all occurrences and conditions, whether they be adverse or favourable to our well-being, show by unmistakable signs and in unmistakable ways the all-gracious object of the evolution of creation, and the devotee enraptured by a glimpse of that gracious object is translated into a condition which is one of ecstasy, love, and admiration of the Supreme Creator. If the effect is too strong, the faculties of expression are lost, and in that rapturous state he is in communion, as it were, with the Supreme Being. To know the object of creation by pure intuition, and not by the hazy methods of argumentation which hide the true view, is to know the gracious ordainment of the Supreme Creator. The school of spiritual training where such knowledge is acquired, is therefore a blessed institution and is specially under the supervision of the Supreme Being. Intellectual training and development, even of the highest possible degree, is not sufficient by itself for the purpose of comprehending in an experimental way the object of creation, and this should be kept in view when the object of creation is studied. Our knowledge is confined to the planes of three dimensions of this world. They are not, however, the only planes in this nature where action takes place and effect is produced. There are other innumerable planes which perform important functions in the economy of creation. They are, however, perceptible by intuition or the subtle senses of knowledge, and not by these physical senses. We do become, at times, cognizant of their action on the planes in our view, but such phenomena are so few and far between that a posteriori reason cannot build up an accurate conception on the basis of these occurrences of the other planes in question. It does not, therefore, appear to us to be unreasonable to observe that the subtle senses within us should be trained for the proper comprehension of the planes beyond the planes of three dimensions referred to, and that a reduction of everything to these three planes should not be insisted upon as a necessary condition of knowledge.

II

Vision Paper

Cosmology from the Twin Vantage Points of Radhasoami Faith and Systems Science

Revered Professor Prem Saran Satsangi
Chairman, Advisory Committee on Education,
Dayalbagh Educational Institutions, Agra, India

Vision Paper
Cosmology from the Twin Vantage Points of Radhasoami Faith and Systems Science

Revered Professor Prem Saran Satsangi
Chairman, Advisory Committee on Education,
Dayalbagh Educational Institutions, Agra, India

The original and the general structure of the system of Universe is revealed by the Merciful Saint[1] (Param Purush Puran Dhani Soamiji Maharaj, Shiv Dayal Singh Sahab) in His canonical scripture, *Sar Bachan Nazm (Poetry)* in its Chapter "Barahmasa" in the hymn for the twelfth month of "Jeth" in terms of 70 stanzas. The pre-creational state is described by stanzas 3 through 10 which translate as follows:

"Neither was there the Creator, nor Creature, nor Creation;
Neither was there Doer, nor Cause, nor Act, nor Impediment. (3)
Neither Seer, nor Seen, nor anything was visible;
Neither was there Unrevealed, nor Revealed, neither Position (Abode), nor Matter. (4)
Neither was there Qualifier, nor Quality, neither Beginning, nor End;
Neither was there Hidden, nor Exposed, neither Interior, nor Exterior. (5)
Neither was there Ram, nor Rahim (Merciful), neither Karim (Gracious) nor Keshav (Krishna);
Nothing was there, Nothing, Nothing was there then. (6)
Neither was there Smriti, nor Shastra, neither Gita, nor Bhagwat;
Neither was there Katha (Epic), nor Puran, neither Singer, nor Song. (7)
Neither was there Servant, nor Master, neither Devotee, nor Deity;
Neither was there Satnam (Refulgent Sat Chit Anand), nor the Nameless One. (8)
How often must I repeat, Nothing was there;
The Creation of the Four Worlds had not yet begun. (9)
What was there, I state now:
I (Supreme Being or Param Purush) was there in "Unmun" (Absolute self-absorption)
"Sun-Bisamadhi" (State of "Shunya Samadhi" i.e. Zero State of Deep Meditation). (10)

Post-creational evolution is given in Chart 1.

Radhasoami faith or Cosmology[2] is the Ultimate religious doctrine revealing the complete esoteric secret knowledge and therefore includes all the extant religions of the world.

Radhasoami faith[3] is the True faith, which gives information and the secret

---

[1] Param Purush Puran Dhani Soami Ji Maharaj (Shiv Dayal Singh Sahab). (2006). *Sar Bachan (Nazm)*. Dayalbagh, Agra: Radhasoami Satsang Sabha.

[2] Maharaj Sahab [Brahm Sankar Misra].(2004). *Discourses on Radhasoami Faith (with supplement)*. Dayalbagh, Agra: Radhasoami Satsang Sabha.

[3] Huzur Maharaj [Rai Bahadur Salig Ram]. *(1959). Prem Patra, Part III*. Discourse 22, pp. 315-321. Dayalbagh, Agra: Radhasoami Satsang Sabha.

of the True Being and explains the path and the method of proceeding to realize the same (i.e., the True Being). The True Being is One Who always remains the same and in Whom there is no change or alteration at any time. There are many grades of the "true being" in various religions. People call one who stays longer than another as "true being" and also believe so. However, the real True Being is One Who remains the same at all times in comparison to the entire creation and Who continued to exist even when there was no creation and Who would continue to exist as before even when there is no creation.

If any person proceeded in religion seeking for the True Being and found or saw a Region from which all creation lower to it appeared to have manifested or to have been created and also appeared to exist with its support and that seeker could not know the complete secret of that Region exactly as it really was, i.e., he could not reach its limits or find its extent, he accepted the Being there as the Creator of that creation and considered him to be the True Being or the True Region. Accordingly, there is Sun at the lowest level of hierarchy of the True Being followed by Brahma at the second higher level, Par-Brahma at the third higher level, Sat Nam Sat Purush at the fourth higher level, and finally the True Supreme Being (Merciful Radhasoami) of the Real and True Region at the topmost level.

In a new book, *Decoding Reality*: *The Universe as Quantum Information*[4], Vlatko Vedral takes us from Claude Shannon's definition of information – devised to improve the quality of telephone lines – to the growing recognition of its profound importance (comparable to the fundamental concept of mass-energy), its deep connections with entropy in the thermodynamics, and its reformulation for the quantum world. "Shannon's unit of information (bit) is defined in terms of a yes / no binary choice. But in the quantum world, yes / no gives way to 'both / and': when 'quantum' and 'information' are put together, a vast range of new understanding emerges; we find ourselves looking at the information content of blackholes, the potential of teleportation, how a deterministic universe might emerge from randomness, and fundamental questions about reality . . . The Universe, it would seem maketh itself."

Gottfried Wilhelm Leibniz, one of the inventors of Calculus, used the logic of Occam's razor, viz., the simplest explanation is usually best (held in highest esteem by scientists), in his proof of the existence of God. In view of Creation Ex Nihilo (Something from Nothing), he found it surprising that something rather than nothing exists in the Universe, given that nothing is by far the simpler state. The only reason he could find for something to exist at all is that an independent being (God) created that something. This for him was enough evidence to suggest an external influencer – the influencer being God, a supernatural being.

Quantum information requires a more generalized treatment than that proposed by Shannon. To quantify quantum information, instead of using the classical notion of entropy of a bit, one takes entropy of a qubit (first formulated by Ben Schumacher). In Quantum mechanical systems, the whole could be less than sum of its parts. Accordingly, the quantum entropy of two correlated

[4] Vlatko Vedral. (2010). Decoding Reality: The Universe as Quantum Information. New York: Oxford University Press.

quantum systems can now indeed be smaller than the entropy of each of them individually. The theory of quantum information is a superset of Shannon's information in that it reduces to Shannon information in certain cases.

From the point of view of information we can summarize two of the most important features of quantum theory; first, that qubits can exist in a variety of different states at the same time, and secondly, when one measures a qubit, it reduces to a classical result (a bit), i.e. one gets a definitive outcome.

Cosmology of Radhasoami Faith on one hand is consistent with all the extant religions in the world and on the other hand, it is also consistent with modern science as at the end of the first decade of the 21st century.

Accordingly, it is consistent with quantum theory (which has been called the most successful theory in the history of science for its sheer accuracy although it has strange implications) as well as Einstein's general theory of relativity (the modern theory of gravity, very different from the Newtonian theory of gravity, which visualizes that space and time form a dynamic geometric entity that curves in response to the energy that it contains, such that in extreme situations, the curvature may become singular giving rise to such important physical phenomena as black holes and big bang) and even the latest M-theory, the most general supersymmetric theory of gravity and the only candidate for a complete theory of the universe (which in order to predict finite quantities must have what is called supersymmetry between the forces of nature and the matter on which they act).

String theorists are now convinced that the five different string theories and supergravity are just different approximations to a more fundamental theory (called M-theory), each valid in different situations. No one seems to know what the enigmatic "M" stands for in M-theory. It may be "master", "miracle" or "mystery", or all three. "This M-theory is not a theory in the usual sense but a network of theories. It is bit like a map. To faithfully represent the entire Earth on a flat surface, one has to use a collection of maps, each of which covers a limited region. The maps overlap one another, and where they do, they show the same landscape" say Stephen Hawking and Leonard Mlodinow[5] in "The (Elusive) Theory of Everything" based on their new book, *The Grand Design*.[6]

One knows some of the properties of M-theory. First M-theory has eleven space-time dimensions. Also, M-theory can contain not just vibrating strings but also point particles, two dimensional membranes, three-dimensional blobs, and other objects called p-branes (where p runs from zero to nine). The fundamental laws of M-theory allow for different universes with different apparent laws – the laws of the four forces, and the parameters such as mass and charge that characterize the elementary particles – depending on how the internal space is curled. M-theory has solutions that allow for many different internal spaces, perhaps as many as 10^{500} = Googol[5], which means that it allows for 10^{500} different universes, each with its own laws. In *The Grand Design*[6], Hawking and Mlodinow argue that multiverse idea is not a notion invented to account for the miracle of fine-tuning of the universe for human life (the weak

[5] Hawking, Stephen and Leonard Mlodinow. (October 2010) "The (Elusive) Theory of Everything", *Scientific American India*. pp. 49-51.

[6] Hawking, Stephen and Leonard Mlodinow. (2010). *The Grand Design*. New York: Bantam Books.

anthropic principle) but it is a consequence of the no-boundary condition as well as many other theories of modern cosmology; and if it is true, then the strong anthropic principle (which says that perhaps our existence was a by-product of design or purpose) can be considered effectively equivalent to the weak one, putting the fine tunings of physical laws on the same footing as the environmental factors, for it means that our comsic habitat (now the entire observable physical universe) is only one of many, just as our solar system is one of many. In other words, the fine-tunings in the laws of nature can be explained by the existence of multiple universes which obviates the need for a benevolent creator (God).

Marcelo Gleiser[7], another renowned physicist, in his recent article "The Imperfect Universe: Can our knowledge of Nature ever be complete?" starts his essay with a statement: We are surrounded by the mysterious; but goes on to assert, "As we leave notions of mathematical perfection and final unification behind, what do we have left? A universe that thrives on the imperfect, on the manifestation of asymmetries from particles to galaxies, a universe that is no less fascinating for not hiding a 'mind of God'."

Why is it that in the two widely different contexts, these modern atheist-scientists appear so eager to deny the existence of God? The reason is not far to seek. Modern atheist-scientists have not been able to advance spiritually even to the first stage of reaching the top-most subdivision of the physical universe, viz., the Spiritual Orb, beyond the Sun, where an upward opening (Third Eye or Subtle Eye) or portal exists through which one can catch a glimpse of Brahmanda (the region of Universal Mind) to provide befitting answer to their doubts about the existence of God and His Grand Design.

The description of multiple universes as conceived by Radhasoami Faith is definitely authoritative[2] and represents Ultimate Reality. Scientific literature corroborates this description of multiple universes, but it is limited to the physical creation only. The dissolution of individual solar systems (Pinds or physical planes) would take place when these are drawn upto the sky above (Chidakash) and reduced more or less to pre-creational condition. On the other hand Great Dissolution takes place when the entire system of the Brahmanda and its subordinate regions, i.e. the Triloki itself would get dissolved. Of course, this is beyond the realm of science but Radhasoami Faith, for the sake of completeness, conceptualizes the Great Dissolution of the Triloki as well. When an individual Brahma system, i.e. Triloki has completed its vast cycle of revolution round the spiritual region, it comes nearest to Sat Lok, that is, to say it is in conjunction with the purely spiritual region. This triggers first the successive dissolution of individual Pinds (solar-systems) under the particular Triloki and later the great dissolution of the Triloki itself takes place. This is a great gracious act of amelioration and redemption. Even those spirits which are not redeemed get highly spiritualized and await sure redemption in the next cycle of evolution of Trilokis in the manner of their original evolution. Scientists Nicolai Kardashev and Michio Kaku[8] conjecture that man would

[7] Gleiser, Marcelo. (Spring 2010). "The Imperfect Universe: Can our knowledge of Nature ever be complete?" The New York Academy of Sciences Magazine, pp. 9-10.

[8] Kaku, Michio. (2008). *Physics of the Impossible*. New York: Doubleday.

advance to civilization of Type III with potential to utilize the enormous power of an entire galaxy colonizing billions of stars in it and exploiting also the power of the black hole in the centre of the galaxy. Accordingly, scientists surmise that the human civilization would be saved from dissolution by advancing to Type III civilization such that the whole civilization would leave the universe that is undergoing dissolution and go to another one. But the truth is that at that time the entire Pind and whole of Brahmand would contract to the size of Planck dimension (» 10^{-35} m) which is very small and the human body cannot withstand it. From a body of that contracted size one cannot recover human frame without going through the whole cycle of re-births or evolution. And there is also the cycle of "Chaurasi" (Eighty four subtle currents) to reckon with. One is not certain whether one would get a human body or some other body. There is no assurance of salvation before the Dissolution. They may have to take one or more births when the creation evolves again after the dissolution. To some extent, the scientists are right in imagining that they can save this civilization from destruction at the time of dissolution. We know that, when this life is over, the impressions are retained in Manakash or the space of the Mind, and therefore the progress that civilization has made is not entirely destroyed at the time of dissolution of this Pind or material region. When the next cycle of creation commences, the civilization can develop further from that stage. However, as the scientists do not believe in rebirth, the matter ends with the demise or dissolution of Pind. It is correct to the extent that when Pralaya (Dissolution) or Mahapralaya (Great Dissolution) takes place, all the spirit entities will be located in a Buffer Zone. When Pralaya, i.e. the dissolution of Pind takes place, the mind and Spirit would go to Chidakash and when Mahapralaya, the dissolution of Brahmand takes place, the mind too perishes. The spirits alone will be located in Mahasunna till the next cycle of creation takes place. If only the scientists were to concede certain basic facts and come to believe in rebirth and existence of God they may approach the Truth more closely in their investigations. For that matter, scientists keep trying and succeeding also in discovering the truth so far as material world is concerned. But they cannot reach beyond it because their investigations lack availability of adequate instruments and techniques. This is their limitation since they do not want to come out of their shell of prejudice. They think that spirituality is superstition and blind faith but, in fact, that is the correct belief system. They too would have to accept it sooner or later. I have pointed out earlier also that if the scientists take recourse to intuition they can make much greater headway. They would progress much farther than what they have achieved today. In fact, there are no great contradictions or chasms between the scientific thoughts and the corresponding spiritual conceptualization. Indeed, there is convergence of views to a large extent.

Now let us consider the conception of multiple universes in super string theory and Quantum Cosmology. They conceptualize this vast space as a Bath Tub, from which lots of bubbles – analogous to physical universes – keep popping in and out of existence. This shows this world is ephemeral, impermanent, prone to destruction. Their analogy is correct that this world is like the bubbles and is impermanent. However, having given this analogy, they do not wish to abide with it. They dream that they would make this world ever-lasting. But spirit alone is without decay or destruction, all other things are impermanent. Super string theory posits that the electron and the other subatomic particles are nothing but different vibrations of a string or other objects, p-branes (of dimension from 0 to 9), acting like a tiny rubber band or object. But the bizarre feature of Super string theory is that these strings can only vibrate in a specific dimension of space-time, viz., ten.

We are familiar with only the four standard space-time dimensions against the ten dimensions in the super string theory. This means that the other six dimensions must have collapsed, or curled-up, somehow. Another peculiarity is that there are five different versions of string theory. Surprisingly, scientists have found that, from the vantage point of the eleventh dimension, all five different string theories collapsed into one. In the eleventh dimension mathematical objects exist called the membrane (e.g. like the surface of a sphere)[8] or more generally p-branes. It perhaps means that the physical or material universe (Pind) itself was a p-brane, floating in an eleven dimensional space-time. This raises the possibility that our universe exists in a multiverse of other universes. Think of a vast collection of floating soap bubbles or p-branes. Each soap bubble represents an entire universe floating in a larger arena of eleven dimensional hyper-space. We might live on the skin or surface of just one of these bubble-universes. The super string theory (M-theory) was unique after all (with no contradictions), but only if we viewed it from the vantage point of the eleventh dimension. As the eleventh dimension curls up what is left of the p-brane is the ten-dimensional string. Since mathematically, there are five ways in which the p-brane can be sliced, this gives rise to five different string theories in ten dimensions. This visualization would appear to explain everything. In a way, you get the theory of everything. Thus it is the eleven dimensional string theory (M-theory) that is able to explain the physical material creation theoretically. The experimental proof is yet to be obtained. But people have great expectations from this super string theory (M-theory). However, even theoretically, the eleven dimensions of the super string theory explain only the third grand division of macrocosm, viz., the physical dimensional universe (or the Pind), still, leaving out of consideration the spiritual forces of the six subdivisions of Pind.

Any quantum force field in the physical universe is subject to duality between mind and matter (wave and particle) and therefore the principle of uncertainty implies that both position and momentum cannot be determined precisely. Similarly, any quantum force-field in the Region of Universal Mind is also subject to duality between spirit and mind and therefore can represent uncertainty. However, in the purely spiritual region, the quantum spiritual force-field is a special type which may be aptly described as Omni Quantum Spiritual Force Field whose distinguishing characteristic is that while it exhibits duality, it displays no accompanying uncertainty. Recall that there is considerable debate on "Dvait" (duality) and "Advait" (unity) in Vedas and Upanishads. "Advait" in the context of Brahman stresses that Atma and Parmatma are one and the same. On the other hand "Dvait" admits of duality of special kind in Radhasoami faith. It holds as an axiom that the Supreme Being (Merciful Radhasoami) is the unbounded and unfathomable Reservoir of spirit-forces of consciousness such that the spirits which become perfectly pure and merge with the Supreme Being (in the Purely Spiritual Region) exhibit duality at will. Accordingly, one would observe that in Radhasoami faith, although it belongs to 'Nirgun' tradition, there is still a lot of emphasis on Bhakti (devotion). Accordingly, even after merging in Radhasoami Dayal in Nirmal Chetan Desh (Radhasoami region), the spirit can separate out from Radhasoami Dayal (Reservoir or Source) at its free will and observe His Glory and worship Him (the deity) as a devotee. So there is no uncertainty in this duality and therefore, the concept of information acquisition, which is physical phenomenon, is irrelevant in the purely spiritual region. Notice that mind is an instrument or medium (somewhat like senses) through which the sentient entity, i.e. the spirit-entity, performs its subjective functions in the Region of the Physical Universe and the Region of Universal Mind (i.e. Brahmanda). Since there is no uncertainty nor any intervening medium of mind, true knowledge or intelligence (i.e. wisdom) is acquired or captured by the sentient entity (spirit-entity) in the Purely Spiritual Region, through intuition or consciousness. Thus true knowledge and primal force can indeed be sensed together such that omniscience and omnipotence are realized simultaneously, in the purely spiritual region. This is why it is preferable to use the nomenclature Omni-Quantum Spiritual Force-Field for the purely spiritual region in contradistinction to the ordinary Quantum Spiritual Force Field. There is a reference in the Diary of Param Guru Sahabji Maharaj of a "Haadi" or Maxim of Prophet Mohammad Sahab. On being enquired how he made communion with "Khuda" or "Allah", he replied that it was in two forms. One is through the sound of a bell and the other is through the intuitive prompts from a "Farishta" or Angel. That is how he acquired intuition or experiential knowledge. These descriptions fit the sub-division of Sahasdal Kamal where the divine bell sound is characteristically heard. But similar phenomena would also characterize enlightenment from higher regions of Trikuti, Sunna, Bhanwar Gufa, Sat Lok, Anami Lok, Alakh Lok, Agam Lok and ultimately Radhasoami Dham (abode) too. In each case, the mystic name and accompanying instrumental musical sound heard would be characteristic of the concerned spiritual abode accessed and the intuition gained would also arise from that particular spiritual sub-region.

M-theory family, as a network of theories, is the only candidate for a complete unified theory of the physical universe Einstein was hoping to find. Hawking and Mlodinow[5] conclude their essay in Scientific American (Oct. 2010) as follows, "It might be that to describe the universe, we have to employ different theories (in the M-theory family) in different situations. Each theory may have its own version of reality, but according to model dependent realism, that diversity is acceptable, and none of the versions can be said to be more real than any other. It is not the physicist's traditional expectation for a theory of nature, nor does it correspond to our everyday idea of reality, but it might be the way of the universe."

If one wishes to comprehend and bring into the fold of system modelling the other two grand divisions of creation, viz., Brahmanda (Region of Universal Mind) and Nirmal Chetan Desh (Purely Spiritual Region) one may have to propound Omni-Theory or O-Theory for Spiritual Systems as a hierarchical family of spiritual levels ranging from r = 1 to 11 representing 1. Spirit Orb of Physical Region; 2. Sahasdal Kamal 3. Trikuti 4. Sunna, of Brahmanda; 5. Maha-Sunna; and 6. Bhanwar Gupha, 7. Sat Lok, 8. Anami Lok, 9. Alakh Lok,

10. Agam Lok and 11. Radhasoami (Original Abode or Nij Dham with infinite degrees of freedom) of Purely Spiritual Region: so as to dovetail with the M-theory family of 11 dimensions for the Physical Universe.

The aforesaid O-theory family of models will be identified by their unique characteristic mystic names and divine musical instrumental sounds for each distinct level of spiritual hierarchy.

Furthermore, the O-theory family of models are founded on the fundamental axiom of spiritual consciousness and twin spiritual consciousness interaction and realization postulates as well as the fundamental axiom and postulates of Physical System Theory[9] with the corresponding Schematic and System Linear Graph for a rudimentary modelling framework for spiritual domains (as given in Appendix with its Figures A and B and Table 1).

It is known fairly accurately that the ordinary matter accounts for only 5%, of which only 1% is in the visible part of creation while the remaining is in the form of hot gas in between the stars and galaxies. Out of the remaining 95% of the matter-energy content of the universe, 23% is dark matter whilst the largest slice of nearly 72% is dark energy. Dark matter helps in forming structures and shape in the Universe and it is hoped that other creations in the long term future will come into existence as a result of it. The spiritual viewpoint also supports the belief that other creations will come into existence after dissolution and great dissolution. The dark energy of approximately 72% is in the nature of Antigravity force opposing the formation of new creation. However, should another phase of creation of Brahmandas and Pinds start with big bangs similar to the original ones, these would duly overcome the antigravity forces of dark energy. As already mentioned earlier, scientists conjecture that our galaxy might combine with other neighbouring galaxies as the outer universe expands at ever quickening pace leaving only our big galaxy visible with darkness surrounding us all around because all other galaxies would have run farther away from us. Locally, no object can travel at a speed higher than that of light, according to the theory of special relativity. However, in general relativity, space-time becomes a fabric, and this fabric can stretch faster than light. Accordingly, if the outer galaxies travel with a speed higher than that of light they would go out of sight of our galaxy and we would fail to get any signal from them. However, at present, we are fortunately so situated in space that we would get all the signals through COBE Satellite and W-MAP Satellite (and Planck Mission Satellite beginning 2009) even those at the time of Big Bang almost 13.7 billion years ago. However, scientists estimate that this fortuitous placement in space might change over the long term future such that in a few billions of years, we might be left as the lone illuminated galaxy in the visible space.

Marcelo Gleiser concludes his essay on "The Imperfect Universe" in the following words, "Current research indicates that simple life may not be so rare; but complex life, and, in particular, intelligent life, is a whole other story. The Search for Extra Terrestrial Intelligence programme, known as SETI, is 50 years old, but no radio signal from an alien civilization has been detected.

---

[9] Koenig, H.E., Y. Tokad and H.K. Kesavan. (1967). *Analysis of Discrete Physical Systems*. New York: McGraw-Hill.

Furthermore, the distances are vast, with current technology, it would take us over 110,000 years to arrive at the nearest star, Alpha Centauri. So even if there are other intelligent forms out there, we are, for all practical purposes, alone. This revelation should fill us with awe; we are how the universe thinks about itself. And for this reason, we have, the moral obligation to preserve life at all costs. Not bad for a species that has only a limited knowledge of reality."

Perhaps, these events might be indicative of impending dissolution of the physical universe. Their conjecture may well be right. The point of the matter is that there is no basic conflict whatsoever between the concept of creation held in Radhasoami faith and that propounded by scientists. There is full agreement between them except that the vision of scientists is limited to physical or material world only. Therefore, it is expected that a superior vision of the universe will result if we observe it from the vantage point of higher levels of consciousness. Accordingly, if we observe the material universe (Pind) from the higher level of creation, viz., the top-most Spiritual Orb beyond Sun in Pind Desh (Physical Universe) or Brahmanda, the reality would reveal itself more fully. Similarly, if we view the physical or material universe from the vantage point of the purely spiritual region the ultimate reality will be revealed. It is a similar phenomenon as referred to in the context of M-theory where from the vantage point of the eleventh dimension all five different string theories would collapse into one i.e., all the five theories would become a unified theory. This point is in keeping with the scientific view that if the observer rises to higher dimension than the observed phenomenon, then his investigation is likely to be closer to truth, i.e. free of any distortions. This conclusion is therefore supported from the scientific point of view also.

In conclusion, Cosmology in Radhasoami Faith is all inclusive with regard to various religions prevalent in the world. It has followed a Blue Ocean Strategy[10] in charting out an uncontested spiritual space of the fourth "Lok" i.e. the Grand Division of the Purely Spiritual Region which is Eternal beyond "Kshar" (perishable subdivision of 'Pind', 'And' and "Brahmanda", together known as Triloki (3 'Lokas'); 'Akshar' (imperishable presiding deity of 'Mansarovara' on the top of 'Brahmanda'); and 'Nihakshar' (without 'Akshar', viz., the vast expanse of Mahasunna as the barrier between Brahmanda and Nirmal Chetan Desh). Life, as practical religionists, of followers of Radhasoami faith, is life of better wordliness (neither worldiness nor unwordliness) which has evolved in response to four actions-framework of Blue Ocean Strategy[10], viz., eliminate rituals, orthodoxy, superstition etc., reduce unnecessary costs, wastage etc., raise standard and quality of Satsang, Seva, Abhyas etc. and create New Satsang Polity, New Devotional Method, New Surat-Shabda Abhyas etc. for Spiritual Value Innovation. Initiative has been taken by Radhasoami Satsang Sabha by adopting Murar Declaration – 13th June 2010 for forging Unity among different Radhasoami communities. Furthermore, a Conclave of Religious Leaders of various Radhasoami Communities is being organized on the occasion of SPIRCON 2010 on November 14, 2010 at Dayalbagh, Agra to promote fraternity, amity and heart-felt love and affection for each other

[10] Kim, W. Chan and Renee Mauborgne. (2005). *Blue Ocean Strategy*. Boston: Harvard Business School Press.

among Satsangis (followers of Radhasoami faith) across various Radhasoami Communities. As already stated earlier, the proposed O-theory of Spiritual Systems is fully consistent with the latest M-theory of Everything for Physical Universe.

While the Blue Ocean Strategy assigns uncontested space to all stake-holders in Science and Religion, making competition irrelevant, the "White Mountain Strategy", so to say, enables striving for achieving snow-white peaks and pinnacles of highest spiritual attainment for all adherents of Radhasoami Faith.

CHART 1 : POST-CREATIONAL EVOLUTION

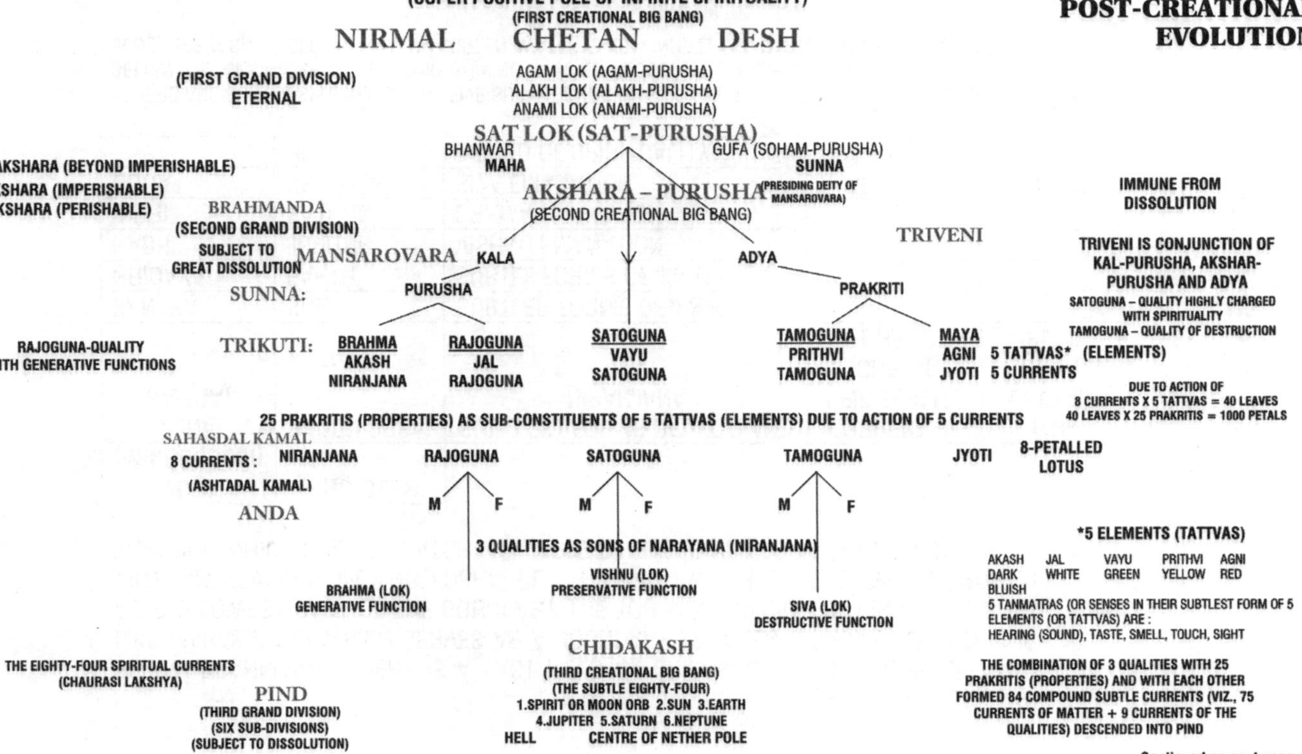

Continued on next page

BELOW BRAHMANDA THERE IS A VAST FIELD OF CHIDAKASH (WITH MINOR CREATION LIKE MAHASUNNA) WHICH SERVES AS A BOUNDARY BETWEEN BRAHMANDA AND PIND. AT THE LOWEST PART OF THE BOUNDARY THE TOP MOST REGION OF PIND IS SITUATED WITH AN UPWARD OPENING (TISRA TIL OR THIRD EYE OR SUBTLE EYE) OR PORTAL THROUGH WHICH ONE CAN CATCH A GLIMPSE OF THE LOWER PORTION OF BRAHMANDA

MAN (MICROCOSM)	PIND-DESH			
AJNA (NETRA)	MOON ORB*	SUBTLEST FORMS OF JYOTI AND NIRANJANA	CURRENT OF SPIRITUALITY (CHETAN DHAR)	JAR-CHETAN DHAR (BIJLI)
KANTHA	SUN	SUBTLER FORMS OF J & N		
HRIDAYA	EARTH	SUBTLE FORMS OF J & N		
NABHI	JUPITER	VISHNU EMANATION		
INDRI	SATURN	BRHMA EMANATION		
GUDA	NEPTUNE	SIVA EMANATION	ANIMATE	INANIMATE
	HELL	DEVOID OF SPIRITUALITY		

*THERE ARE SUBTLE SPHERES OF THE FIVE SUBTLE CURRENTS OF FIVE TATTVAS (THE FIVE PANCHBHUTAS) BELOW THE MOON-ORB OF THE PIND SHINING IN HUES PECULIAR TO EACH I.E. ETHER (AKASH) – DARK BLUE; FIRE (AGNI) – RED; AIR (VAYU) – GREEN; WATER (JAL) – WHITE; AND EARTH (PRITHVI) – YELLOW.

APPENDIX

O-Theory for Spiritual System Modelling in Cosmology
Physical System Theory Generalized for Spiritual System Modelling

The spiritual system theory framework presented in this section underlies the rudimentary systems modelling framework for spiritual domains of consciousness as shown in Figure A (with Post-Creational Evolution as summarized in Chart 1) and leads to the formulation of the corresponding abstract system linear graph model of Figure B. Notice that by identifying spiritual potential difference, an across variable, and spiritual force-current, a through variable, as the pair of fundamental complementary variables (Table 1) in conjunction with the system linear graph, the whole body of mathematical physical systems theory becomes available for developing models for spiritual domains. It must also be noticed that the system linear graph shown in Figure B is a simplified lumped parameter approximation while a graph-theoretic field-model would be more appropriate for rigorous representation[1]. Notice further that the simplified version gives complete solution for 52 each of spiritual potential difference variables and spiritual force-current variables without requiring solutions of any equation of the system model as implied by the branch equation count of zero. This pre-supposes that the precise states representing grades of closure (whether completely closed, closed to a large extent, closed to a medium extent, closed to a small extent or completely open) of the "intuitive" resonance operated switches in Figure A are known in advance such that the associated current sources (Nos. 36-52) are characterized deterministically in terms of specified spiritual current flows11.

[1] P.S. Satsangi, "Generalizing Physical Systems Through Applied Systems Research from "Real" Physical Systems through "Conceptual" Socio-Economic-Environmental Systems to "Complete" (Physical-Mental-Spiritual) Creational Systems", *International Journal of General Systems*, Vol. 35, No. 2, 2006, pp. 127-167.

Table 1 Examples of systems and complementary variables

System	X-across variable (effort variable)	Y-through variable (flow variable)
Electrical	Voltage	Current
Mechanical	Linear velocity (Rotational velocity)	Force (Torque)
Hydraulic/ Pneumatic	Pressure	Flow-rate
Transportation	Propensity or level-of-service or traffic density	Flow-rate
Economic	Unit price	Flow rate of goods and services
Ecosystem	Unit energy or Monetary cost	Material flow-rate
Information System	Treatment	Data flow rate
Quantum Information System	Quantum across variable directional vectors (Orthonormal unit basis vectors) "ket 0" and "ket 1"	Quantum through variable as quanta of information / computation flow-rates (qubits) with associated probability parameters (amplitudes) along directional vectors "ket 0" and "ket 1"
Spiritual	Spiritual Potential Difference	Spiritual Force-current (Inward:- Sound Current, Outward:- Spirit-Current)

Physical System Theory[9]

The discipline of Physical System Theory is based on the following Fundamental Axiom and Postulates.

Fundamental Axiom

A fundamental axiom is that a mathematical model of a component characterizes the behaviour of that component of the system as an entity and independently of how the component is interconnected with other components to form a system.

Postulates

(1) component postulate : mathematical description of each component by means of

(a) terminal graph: oriented line segment or segments where one orientation is used to represent both the across measurement and the through measurement reference, and

(b) terminal equation or equations; and

(2) mathematical description of how the components are combined to form the system as given by

(a) system graph postulate: system graph is a collection of component terminal graphs obtained by uniting the vertices of the terminal graphs in one-to-one correspondence with the union of the component terminals; and

(b) interconnection constraint postulates : fundamental cut-set and fundamental circuit equations. The aggregate of these mathematical equations is called 'system' equations. The theory of oriented linear graphs, developed as an abstract mathematical topic, is valuable in the analysis of systems as a means of achieving a simple systematic procedure for formulating the system equations.

For the sake of generalization of Physical Systems Theory to spiritual consciousness domains, it is necessary to supplement it with further formalization as follows:

Spiritual System Theory Framework

Fundamental Axiom of Spiritual Consciousness

The fundamental axiom of macrocosmic / microcosmic spiritual consciousness is that the origin of the macrocosm is an infinite spiritual energy source or reservoir known as the Supreme Creator or Being or Super Positive Pole accompanied by the omni-quantum spiritual force-field of consciousness ranging from the Super Positive Pole of full spirituality to the Nether or Negative Pole of depleted spirituality; and each constituent fundamental element of this omni-quantum spiritual force-field, known as the spirit-force of consciousness (monopole), is the one which possesses prime energy and that all other forces (mental or physical) of creation or nature have been evolved by the association of this spirit-force with media (mental or physical) of different kinds (Notice that the concept of "spirit-force" is no more intrinsically mysterious than "mass"). This gives rise to the quantum mind-force field which spans the Region of the Universal Mind and the Physical Universe, on one hand, while the quantum physical force fields – electromagnetic, weak nuclear, strong nuclear and gravitational span the third grand division, viz., the Physical Universe ("Pind") of the Macrocosm.

Microcosm-Macrocosm Consciousness Interaction Postulate

Man, a creation on planet Earth (the fourth subdivision from the bottom of the third grand division of macrocosm, represented by g_4 in Figure A) happens to be a perfect microcosm of the macrocosm in the sense that man possesses not only six ganglia (or "chakras") for interaction with the macrocosm by making communion with the corresponding six subdivisions of the macrocosmic division of the physical / material region but also six nerve-centres (or "Kamals") in the grey matter of the brain for accessing the corresponding six subdivisions of the macrocosmic division or region of Universal Mind as well as six other apertures (or "Padams") in the white matter of the brain for communicating with the corresponding six subdivisions of the macrocosmic division of Universal Spirit or purely spiritual regions.

(Notice that the degree of spiritual consciousness (or spiritual potential) of the macrocosm, pertaining to its three grand divisions ranging from the purely spiritual region (i.e. the macrocosmic division of the Universal Spirit) through the region (or macrocosmic division) of Universal Mind to the physical / material region (or macrocosmic division) together with their six subdivisions each, varies in descending order of magnitude.)

Universal Consciousness Realization Postulate

The religion of Saints prescribes a systemic methodology of the meditational practice of "*Surat*" (spirit force) – "*Shabda*" (spiritual sound currents) – "*Yoga*" (union) for uniting the spirit force of a human being with the "characteristic" spiritual sound currents[2], which emanate from the various spirit centres ($e_6 - e_1$; $f_6 - f_1$; $g_6 - g_1$ shown in Figure A) in different regions and sub-regions (i.e. grand divisions and sub-divisions) of the macrocosm for realizing corresponding levels of increasing degree of consciousness (or spiritual potential) from the lowest subdivision (g_1) of the macrocosmic division of physical / material region through the macrocosmic division of the Universal Mind to the highest subdivision of the Supreme Creator or Being (e_6) of the purely spiritual region.

The object in view is to realize the highest degree of macrocosmic consciousness (spiritual potential) corresponding to e_6 in Figure A, i.e. God (the goal of religion) or Ultimate Reality (the goal of philosophy) or Truth (the goal of Science) which are but three names of the same Supreme (Spiritual) Essence, as defined by the fundamental axiom of spiritual consciousness by means of awakening the 18 hidden subtle senses or centres within man as a microcosm implied by $g_1' - g_6'$, $f_1' - f_6'$; e_1'-e_6' in Figure A, and as referred to in the Universal Consciousness Realization Postulate invoking the meditational practice of "*Surat Shabda Yoga*" of unifying the spirit force of man with the "characteristic" sound-currents emanating from spirit-centres at various levels of consciousness (or spiritual potential). However, this requires rigorous training and practice under the guidance of an adept or mentor or 'Guru'.

[2] This is somewhat akin to the Cosmic Background Microwave Radiation emitted at the time of the Big Bang (marking the beginning of creation of physical universe) which is being detected even to this day by devices such as COBE (Cosmic Background Explorer) Satellite as the Microwave Relic of the Big Bang to study the state of the physical universe soon after its birth.

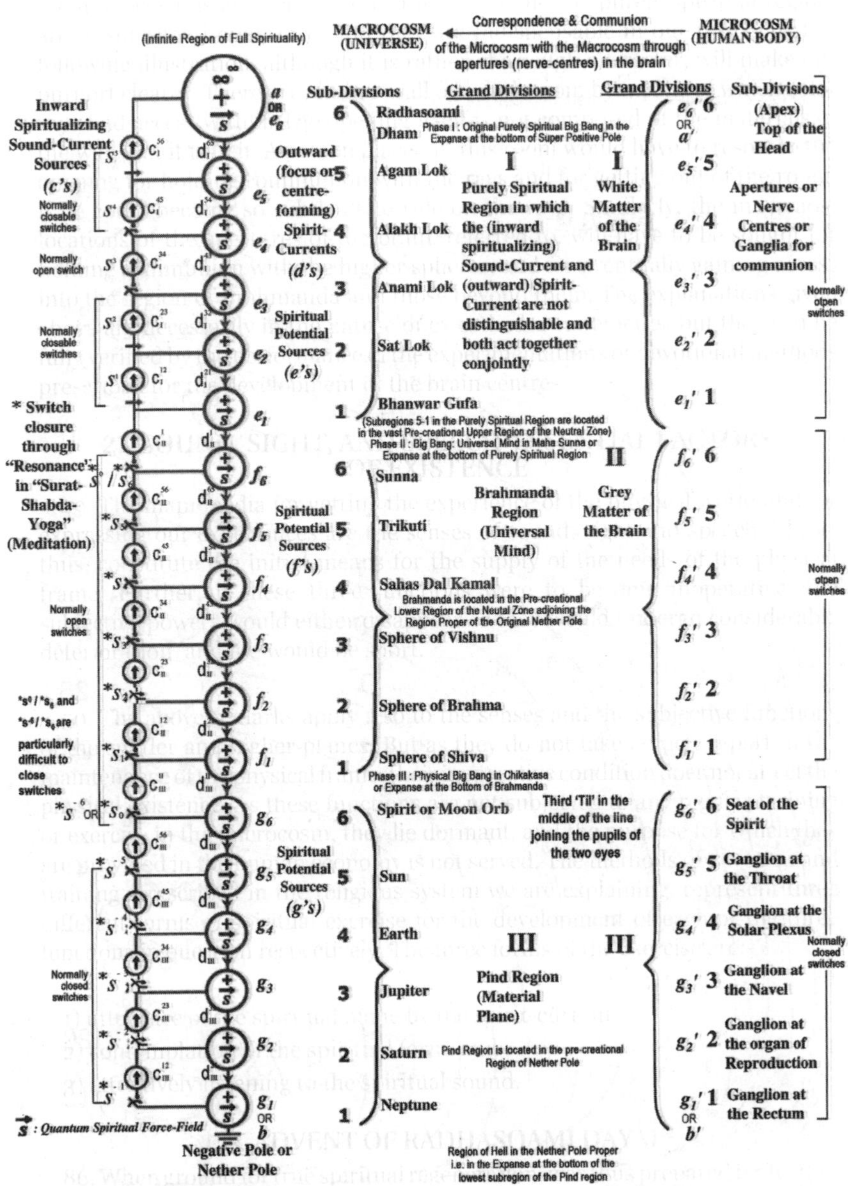

Figure A Schematic : A Rudimentary Modelling Framework for Spiritual Domains

(The entire creation is evolved out of the pre-creational Nether Pole)

The second sub-division sphere of a set of six sub-divisions of each grand-division of Macrocosm or Human-Microcosm is the one which is endowed with generative function :

e.g. e_2 (Sat Lok), f_2 (Sphere of Brahma); and g_2' (Man : Ganglion at the organ of reproduction)

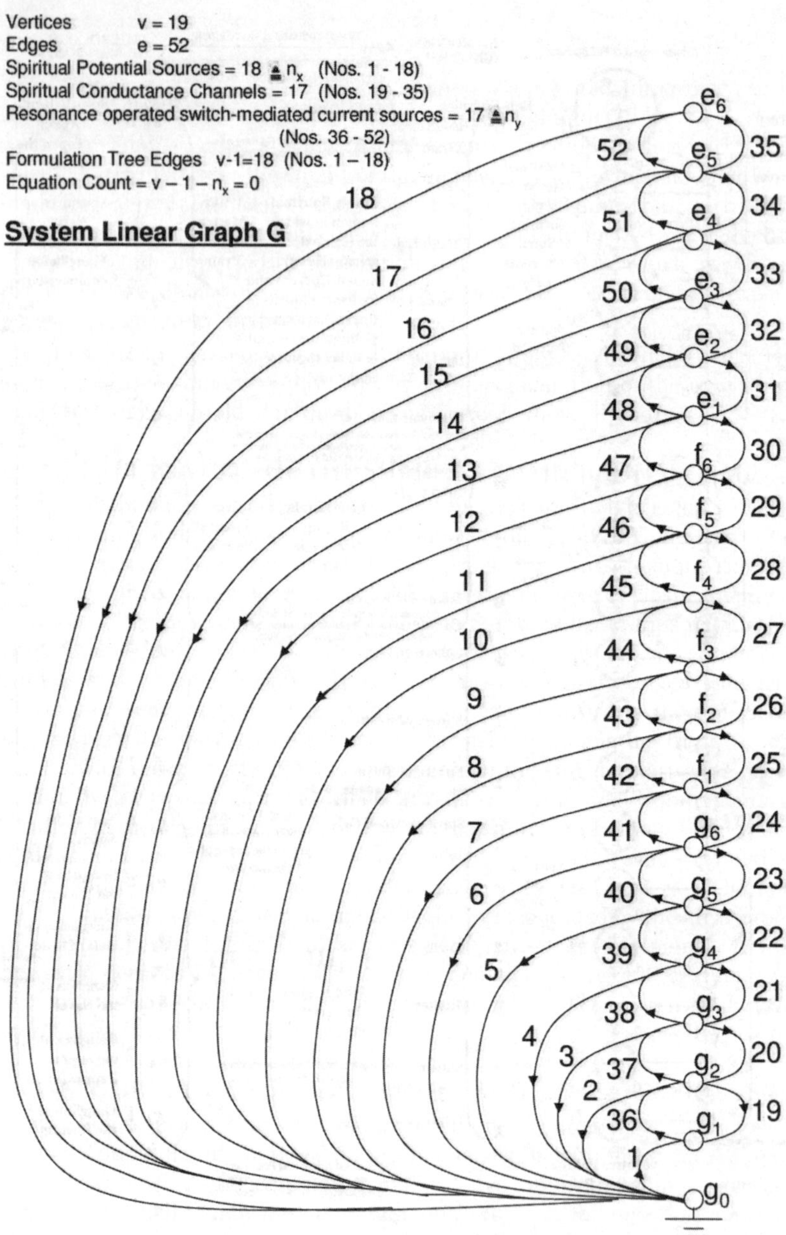

Figure B System Linear Graph Model G :

A Rudimentary Modelling Framework for Spiritual Domains

III

Spiritual Consciousness – An Explanation

Revered Professor Agam Prasad Mathur
Former Vice-Chancellor, Agra University, Agra, India

Thereafter, each one of the individual leaves, so constituted, attracted and evolved twenty-five sub-leaves of the prakritis. These final leaves, thus arranged round the eight main currents, produced a ramification of one thousand petals, and the sphere is accordingly spoken of, with reference to them, as the lotus of one thousand petals.

147. After the formation of this lotus, the two currents of Jyoti and Niranjana took their final abode. They could not go down further, in consequence of the negative strata below Sahasdal Kamal being not suitable for their energy. The three qualities, which had hitherto remained concealed, as it were, within the sphere of Sahasdal Kamal, now issued forth as the three sons of Narayana, and became the deities of their respective spheres which are located one below the other. These deities are known as Vishnu, Brahma and Siva. Their spheres are in the order in which their names are mentioned. The evolution of these three spheres completed the set of the six sub-divisions of Brahmanda, which, as already stated (vide article 91), occupy the lower part of the pre-creational neutral zone. Hitherto, we have been speaking of the evolution of the constituents and of the six sub-divisions of Brahmanda. We now proceed to say something about the spirituality and the denizens of these regions.

95. THE TANMATRAS THE SUBTLEST PARTICLES OF MATTER

148. The matter or molecules which issued forth from Trikuti (vide article 93) was void of intelligence, although it was very subtle and pure and highly charged with energy. Simple covers out of such a material were, therefore, not sufficient for the perception of the outer world. At Trikuti, the five senses were created in their subtlest form, with the object of endowing the denizens of that place and those of the lower creation, with the necessary means of holding communion with, and acquiring a knowledge of, the surroundings or about. The subtlest and [illegible] particles, technically known as tanmatras, were associated with each spirit, and they formed suitable media for receiving impressions from the five different kinds of matter already evolved there.

96. THE FIELD BELOW BRAHMANDA AND ORBITAL MOTIONS OF BRAHMANDA AND PIND

149. Below the spheres of Vishnu, Brahma, and Siva there is a vacuum zone very similar to Maha Sunna, although it is very much smaller. There is no [illegible] creation in this field, and it serves as a boundary between the second and the third grand divisions of creation. At the lowest point of this zone, the topmost sphere of the third division is situated with an opening towards the regions of Brahmanda. This opening is known as the third til (the third or the subtle eye), and by means of it one can catch glimpses of the lower portion of Brahmanda. This opening is also the portal through which the spirit-entity passes from the third into the second grand division. The sphere referred to above bears a resemblance to the top sphere of Brahmanda, i.e. Sunna. This is the main sphere of the third division of creation, and all spirituality is supplied to the lower spheres from this source. This sphere is above the sun and is moving along with the latter around the lowest part of Brahmanda. Brahmanda, too, as a whole, is also subject to a similar orbital motion round the

Spiritual Consciousness – An Explanation

Revered Professor Agam Prasad Mathur
Former Vice-Chancellor, Agra University, Agra, India

Spiritual consciousness is to explore the knowledge of the spirit and its origin or reservoir through intuitive realization. The proper course of attaining higher levels of spiritual consciousness for a sincere lover of the Supreme Being, according to Huzur Maharaj – the second Guru of Radhasoami Faith - is **"to acquire knowledge of the secrets and the order of creation and the means of traversing the distance between his dwelling in the body (the pupil of the eye) and the abode of the Supreme Being, the prime source of everything; and to start on his journey with fervour and perseverance with the avowed object of one day reaching the presence of the Most High and Beloved Supreme Father."**

Love and devotion are the basic driving forces to attain success in life, whether temporal or spiritual. As a scientist, unless driven by a passionate zeal to find the truth, finds it difficult to surmount the hurdles in his path, so does a spiritual seeker, devoid of love and devotion, fail to attain any tangible result in his spiritual pursuit. Love and devotion are therefore the cardinal values in any endeavour to succeed. The medieval Bhakti traditions ushered by saints laid great stress on love and devotion for *Guru* and the Supreme Being. Radhasoami Faith, which is the culmination of the *Sant* traditions, lays great emphasis on love and devotion for the *Guru* and the Supreme Being. Huzur Maharaj says that "a heart devoid of love or affection is as hard as stone and does not form a suitable receptacle for the light of Heavenly Grace and Mercy... The Supreme Being loves and takes special care of those who love Him with all their heart and soul and gradually draws them towards Himself - The Centre of Pure Light and Attraction."

Bhakti has been defined as "the worship of a personal deity in a spirit of love." *Bhakti* is adoration and devotion fixed upon the Lord after acquiring knowledge of the attributes of the adorable one. Thus, *Bhakti* is the emotional aspect of religion; its root lies in the feeling or affective side of human consciousness.

Sants such as Kabir Sahab, Guru Nanak, Dadu Dayal, Paltu Sahab, Jagjivan Sahab, and Tulsi Sahab inspired the humanity and led it from darkness to light through their mystic revelations and easy teachings. The message they delivered to the suffering humanity forms the backbone of *Santmat*. Nabhaji says, "Kabir refused to acknowledge the caste distinctions or to recognise the authority of the six schools of Hindu philosophy, nor did he set any store by the four divisions of life prescribed by *Brahmins* (ब्राह्मण). He held that religion without *Bhakti* was no religion at all and that asceticism, fasting and alms-giving had no value if unaccompanied by *Bhajan* that is devotional practice."

The mission of Kabir Sahab was to preach a religion of love which would unite all castes and creeds.

The traditions of Kabir Sahab were continued by Guru Nanak. The mission of Guru Nanak was the unification of the Hindus and the Musalmans so that the wound of society might heal up and the conflict of religions might end. Guru Nanak preached that there is one God in the world and no other and that Nanak, the son of God, speaks the Truth. For Guru Nanak, God is great, high, formless (*nirakar*) and flawless (*niranjan*) and when manifested is the *satguru*.

The main contribution of the religious movement started by Guru Nanak is a union of *Bhakti* and *Yoga*, as asceticism of the heart combined with the fulfillment of the worldly functions of body and mind, the recognition of a living *Guru* who reincarnates himself in the successor, the idea of *Satsang* and religious recitation with love and fervour.

The mysticism of the Sufi sect is apparent in the concept of Supreme Being who is regarded as the manifestation of Love and Light. He is all love and can be attained only through love. The devotee should take true shelter (*saran*) and keep full faith and devotion in His feet for the attainment of salvation. The Muslim mystic who sets out upon the path of union (*wasl*), of absorption (*fana*), always needs a spiritual guide, for they say that if a man has no teacher, his Imam is Satan. The whole machinery of Sufi Monism moves round the pivot of preceptor (*Pir or Sheikh*). The notable Sufi saints were Maulana Rumi, Shams Tabrez, Hafiz, Mujaddid Alif Sani and others.

With Tulsi Sahab, a new rational and logical thinking sprang up in *Sant* traditions. Tulsi Sahab tried in an absorbing manner to explain the *Sant* teachings rationally and logically. Thus a new tendency of harmonious blending of metaphysical concepts and scientific reasoning dawned in the nineteenth century. The message of Tulsi Sahab was one of unity and synthesis of the true *Sant* teachings.

The Radhasoami Faith moved a step forward. The leaders of this sect, as best as they could, tried to rationalize the abstruse metaphysical concepts, simplified the *Sant* teachings and laid great emphasis upon the need of the *Guru* of the time. They put forth in a vivid manner the intricacies of *Shabd*, the practice of *Surat-Shabd-Yoga* and clearly spelled out the secrets of cosmogony.

For the attainment of perfect salvation, Radhasoami Faith shuns all paraphernalia and external observances and rituals. It has emphasized upon the pure love in the holy feet of the Supreme Being and the *Guru*.

Meaning of the Holy Name 'Radhasoami'

It is the Name of the True Supreme Being.

In the Radhasoami Faith, the ultimate reality is Radhasoami. In Hinduism and its branches the ultimate reality is *Brahman* (czã) and Isvara. *Brahman* is considered to be the highest reality in *Vedanta*. The founders of Radhasoami Faith, however, came forward with a new concept. According to them, the *Brahman* of *Vedanta* is limited to the second grand division of the creation which they call 'spiritual-material region". They hold that the *Brahman* is not the true Supreme Being or the highest reality because he is not perfectly free from mind and matter. They assert that though spiritual components predominate in *Brahman*, there is *Maya* latent in the seed form and a Supreme Reality having the least admixture of *Maya* cannot be styled as the highest truth. They envisaged the highest and the first grand division of creation as the region of the true Supreme Being who is absolutely spiritual and totally free from mind and matter. Such a Supreme Being they have named as 'Radhasoami'. In view of the said difference between Radhasoami and Brahman, the meaning of the word is not Krishna or the Lord of Radha. A casual observer however gets confused and straightaway starts interpreting it for Krishna, as Farquhar did when he observed: "It is necessary also to realize that the real meaning of Radhasoami is Krishna as Lord of Radha (His cowherd mistress in the latest cycle of myth) that Soami is only a curious phonetic misspell of Swami."

A careful study of the beliefs and practices of the faith shows that symbolic worship is totally rejected in it. The founders have openly criticized the traditionalism and ritualism of Hinduism. As such their, Supreme Being cannot belong to that category. besides, the name of Lord Krishna occurs in the writings of the first *Guru* who designates Krishna as the incarnation of a lower region who can never grant salvation to the *jivas*.

It is the True Shabd and Dhunyatmak Name.

The founders assert that Radhasoami is a *dhunyatmak* name because it is the true *shabd*. *Shabd* is energy and sound both. When there was no creation, pure and absolute spiritual energy rested in an ellipsoid. Through divine will, creation started and the Supreme Being first manifested Himself as *shabd*. The creativity in the pure spiritual energy led to a commotion which was accompanied by a pure spiritual resonance or a holy sound. The founders of the faith assert that Radhasoami is the all-pervading sound force in creation and a devotee can listen to this resonance within himself during the spiritual practice.

Soami is Ocean and Radha its First Wave.

The founders of the faith have a few allegorical interpretations to put forward to explain the two components of the word – *Radha* and *Soami*. The second guru says that the Supreme Being may be compared to an ocean. A creative ocean cannot be perceived without commotion. The first wave of the endless ocean is *Radha*. The original current is not different from, but is identical with, the ocean itself and as it comes out so it is ever drawn towards it. The creative ocean, therefore, is *Soami* and the first original wave just identical to the ocean is *Radha*. The two together form the supreme ocean full of spiritual bliss and truth. Hence Radhasoami.

A Scientific Explanation.

Pt. Brahm Sankar Misra, in his writings, tried to explain the name on scientific grounds. According to him, the components of *Radha* and *Soami* represent in their letter form and in articulate speech the sound accompanying the spirit current and its focus. Comparing the action of the spirit force to that of a magnetic force he says: "The ions of Ether observed in a magnetic field are subject to two forces (given out by the two poles of magnet). At one pole, it is storage of energy and at the other it is its depletion. The ions are subjected to tremors. This is the first effect in the sphere of the attractive force. Similarly, prevailing attraction in spirit force can resolve into attraction currents which are made up of a series of attractive impulses. The letter sound *Radha* is accordingly the nearest approach in articulate speech of the subtle sound accompanying the action of the spiritual current. *Soami* is the prime source of the currents". Thus Radhasoami is the source of all creation.

It Denotes Two Spiritual Components: the Lover and the Beloved

Radhasoami Faith is the religion of pure and spiritual love. Love denotes two components, the beloved and the lover. The prime source of all love and spiritual energy is the beloved and is therefore known as *Soami*. The first wave of love and spiritual energy arising from its source and then being attracted towards it again is the lover and therefore is known as *Radha*. The Supreme Love is Radhasoami, identifying both the components and fusing them into one.

Radha is Adi-Surat and Soami is Adi-Shabd

As already explained, Radhasoami is the spiritual resonance reverberating incessantly in the highest region of creation where no mind and matter exist. The original resonance of *Adi-Shabd* (First sound) is *Soami*. *Radha* is the creative force which emanated from *Adi-Shabd*. In other words, *Soami* is the storehouse of the *shabd* and so it is called *Adi-Shabd*. *Radha*, being the first creative force, having its source in *Adi-Shabd*, and completely identical to it, is known as *Adi-Surat*. Radhasoami together signify the storehouse of *shabd* which is sound and energy both. In the human manifestation Soamiji Maharaj is *Soami* and Huzur Maharaj is *Radha*.

The special features of Radhasoami Faith can be summariszed as follows:

1. ***A New Concept of the Supreme Being and His Abode.*** The founders claim that the concept of the Supreme Being as enunciated by them had so far been unknown. They call Him as *Sat Purush* Radhasoami *Dayal*. The Brahman with both His aspects, *vachya* and *laksh*, is dependent upon the Supreme Being Radhasoami for His own existence and creation. The founders assert that the *Brahman* of Hinduism, *Allah* of Islam and *God* of Christianity are the Lords of the spiritual-material region or the second grand division of creation which is not free from mind and matter. *Brahman* is in fact *Kal* or the universal mind with purest form of matter latent as seed in Him. *Brahman* and His region cannot escape change, decay or dissolution. The founders envisage a new concept of the Supreme Being who is absolutely free from mind and matter and is the ocean of love, peace, intelligence, bliss, mercy, light and spirit. He is all-pure and all-spiritual and His abode known as *Radhasoami Dham* or *Dayal Desh* is also all-pure and free from any admixture. The spirit entities are the

particles of the true Surpeme Being and as such their original abode is *Dayal Desh*. A worshipper of *Brahman*, they hold, will not attain true salvation because freedom from mind and matter will not be attained even after the attainment of *Brahman*. Those who strive for total redemption from the cycle of birth, death and rebirth must, therefore, try the attainment of *Dayal Desh* - the region of *Radhasoami Dayal*.

2. ***The Theory of Spiritual Sound is Scientifically Explained.*** The founders assert that *Surat-Shabd-Yoga* is an improvement upon *sahaj yoga* of the medieval saints - *Shagal-i-awaz* of Sufis, *prananyam* and *hathyoga* of Hinduism. They base their spiritual practice upon the theory of sound. According to the founders, sound is the real guide of the spirit-entity. As in a dark and dense forest, they argue, one can find out the way to destination by catching the sound coming from a certain direction, so a practitioner of *Surat-Shabd-Yoga* listens intuitively to the spiritual sounds resounding in the different regions of creation. In the course of spiritual practice, the spirit-entity can catch the eternal sound-current which is refulgently resonant in the highest region. Then alone it can attain the highest ecstasy and bliss leading to true salvation. The founders give a scientific explanation of the theory of the spiritual sound-current. Describing the economy of creation in detail, they hold that the theory of 'spiritual sound' has been testified in many religions of the world.

3. ***A Practical Religion - Blending of Bhakti and Yoga.*** The founders of the faith have essentially made it a faith of actual practice and behaviour. The philosophical moorings and thought-processes are subsidiary elements in it. It is through practice alone that teachings would prove efficacious. The founders of the faith set the motto: "Practise and observe the results yourself". They introduced a mode of spiritual exercise - *Surat-Shabd-Yoga* – and claimed to have based it on scientific lines. The practitioner of this *yoga* would derive practical benefits in the world and feel no pain at the time of death. An *abhyasi* dies while living. He gets absorbed in the bliss and ecstasy of higher and spiritual life and attains the status of a *sthitpragya*. Hardly does he feel the joys and sorrows of the world. The founders assert that *Surat-Shabd-Yoga* is the easiest and best of all modes of *yoga* ever practised in the country in the past or present. It can be practised by all alike - men, women, old, young, rich and poor. A person leading a family life with all his temporal preoccupations can practise it as effectively as a recluse.

The faith also presents a harmonious blending of *yoga* and *bhakti*. The key to *Surat-Shabd-Yoga* lies with the *Guru* of the time. A practitioner must, therefore, practise *bhakti* of the *Guru* as a prerequisite to successful performance of *yoga*. When the practitioner serves the *Guru* with body, mind and soul and with all love and humility and dissolves his ego, he himself witnesses a transformation of his life within and without, and achieves remarkable progress in spiritual pursuit. The founders have, thus, delivered the message of love on practical grounds. They have affirmed that the path of love excels everything. True and selfless love is itself the *yoga*. *Surat-Shabd-Yoga* is the devotional mode of self-realization.

4. ***Emphasis on Love and Devotion.*** Reviving the *bhakti* traditions of Medieval India, the founders of Radhasoami Faith emphasize the devotional aspect of religion. According to them *bhakti* alone would bring salvation to the suffering humanity. One should engender true love for the formless Supreme Being and take shelter (*saran*) in his divine will (*mauj*). In a nut-shell, Radhasoami Faith is a gospel of love. Love towards the holy feet of Radhasoami Dayal, love towards the *Guru* of the time and love with all the human beings is its cardinal message. Love, therefore, is the keynote of the Radhasoami Faith.

5. ***Advocacy of Guru-Bhakti.*** The tradition of *Guru-bhakti* (devotion to the *Guru*) has been revived by the exponents of the Radhasoami Faith. The guru, they believe, is the manifested Supreme Being and as such it is *Guru-bhakti* through which one would attain redemption from the cycle of birth, death and rebirth. A total surrender of body, mind and soul at the feet of the *Guru* is a pre-requisite of *bhakti*.

   The relationship between the Supreme Being, the *Guru* and the *Jivas* has been well compared with ocean, its wave and a drop. The Supreme Being is the ocean of all bliss, light, life, sound and truth. The *Guru* is the wave which is always in union with the ocean and not different from it and the *Jiva* with the same attributes is a drop far away from the ocean. This contact between the drop and the wave is the true *Bhakti*. Therefore, emphasis has been laid upon establishing contact between the *Guru* and the disciples at all levels, that is, physical, mental and spiritual. This contact would be developed through the company of the *Guru*, both external and internal. The external company of the *Guru* is called the 'external *satsang*' and the internal company of the *Shabd* form of the *Guru* is called the 'internal *satsang*'.

   Such an ideal devotion had been practised by Huzur Maharaj towards his *Guru*. The source of eternal solace is, thus, the *Guru* of the time. The founders assert the necessity of choosing the right *Guru* and renouncing the false one. They have warned followers against the dangers of being led away by ignorance and compulsion at the time of selecting the *Guru*. They further assert that only when the essential form (*shabd-rupa*) of the *Guru* has been revealed to the follower through inner experience, he should adopt one as his *Guru*; otherwise the *Guru* should be treated as 'elder brother or a friend or a *sadhguru*".

6. ***The Four Essentials of Radhasoami Faith.*** There are four essentials on which this faith bases its tenets:

   I. Sant Satguru

   II. Sant Shabd or Satnam

   III. Satsang

   IV. Sat Anurag (sincere love for the Supreme Being and *Sant Satguru*)

   By the *Seva* and the *Satsang* of the *Guru* the spirit entity would slowly and slowly shake off the coverages and would be able to catch the sound currents and one day reach the Ultimate Abode. The whole process may take a period of four lives which may be shortened in the case of more ardent devotees.

7. ***The Doctrine of Grace and Mercy.*** The most significant feature of this faith is the doctrine of Grace and Mercy. The Supreme Being is full of grace and mercy, so is His human manifestation. Therefore, the natural attributes of *Sant Satguru* are grace and mercy. Huzur Maharaj has said, "Grant Merciful Radhasoami Thy Grace and Protection." The human beings are so infirm and helpless that they cannot perform the prescribed spiritual exercise. They will always need assistance of superior spiritual personage. Huzur Maharaj has showered the Supreme grace and mercy, particularly on the practitioners of the *Surat-Shabd-Yoga*, and generally on all such *Jivas* who seek shelter from the miseries and sufferings of this world, and dependence of the devotees on His kind patronage and protection shall always be required. In a nutshell, we can describe it as the Doctrine of Grace and Mercy.

8. ***It Provides a Midpath.*** The teachings of the Radhasoami Faith lay stress on a midpath. One should neither renounce the world, nor become over-absorbed in it. It is essentially a faith of detached participation in worldly activities. The founders of the faith assert that true love and devotion at the holy feet of *Radhasoami Dayal* will generate true detachment from the world. Thus as a *grihastha* (householder) one can fulfil worldly duties and still be a true *virakta* (unattached being). It is in fact a unique message to people engaged in materialistic pursuits.

9. ***Corporate Life.*** Striking a balance between spiritualism and materialism, attachment and detachment, God and the world, the Radhasoami Faith teaches the lesson of corporate life and better-worldliness. It emphatically professes that one should adopt honest means to earn one' livelihood. Religion is not only an ethereal pursuit, but a positive remedy to all socio-religious maladjustments. The followers believe that with the foundation of Radhasoami Faith in 1861, there came into being not only a faith but also a new way of life. They assert that followers of different religions who have always been enjoined upon to practise abstinence and austerity, have often slipped into a life of indolence for want of an impelling motive for better living. Therefore, there is an emphasis in the faith on honest living as a precondition to spiritual progress. The faith, thus, holds corporate living to be an essential concomitant of enlightened living. The socio-economic progress on religious lines is a novel contribution of the Dayal Bagh group.

The Radhasoami Faith has gained popularity in modern India as a simple cult of love and devotion. It has made an impact on people who are fed up with materialistic trends of the present age. It provides a solution to those who are eager to embrace a religion which is free from external ritualism but full of intuitive contemplation and devotionalism.

The faith is growing every day. However, the founders of the faith have clearly spoken against proselytization and have introduced it primarily for genuine seekers or *samskaris*. It has been able to attract seekers after truth as also those who are prudent, sensitive and able to see the efficacy of a true religion. People of lower strata of society, primarily villagers, who have joined the faith, have sought relief in the principle of spiritual equality. The faith also appears to interest those who believe in mystic revelation. Some Muslims belonging to *Sufi* and other liberal schools of Islam have joined it as they see a resemblance between their *shagal-i-awaz* and its *Surat-Shabd-Yoga*. Some Europeans and Americans are also drawn towards the faith as their own materialism has failed to offer them real happiness.

There are strong integrating elements in the norms of life and principles of moral conduct among the followers of Radhasoami Faith. Irrespective of their belonging to different leaders and different satsang centres, they greet each other with the holy name of *Radhasoami*. This salutation is not only unique among them but it also knits them in a common bond. Another affinity in various groups is the daily routine of *satsang* or holy service whose programme is largely the same. The special meetings of *satsang* are held on special occasions when followers assemble in large numbers to pay homage to their *Guru*. The special features of such congregations are also similar at the different centres.

The annual *Bhandara* of the past *Gurus* is observed with zeal and enthusiasm by almost all branches and groups. The basic spirit of the *Bhandara* is maintained by all leaders and no satsang centre has yet stopped it. The annual meet and community dinner present an ideal of the essential unity of the faith. The followers of Radhasoami Faith are not only strict vegetarians but they also observe total abstinence from liquor and intoxicants. No change is yet discernible in different centres with regard to the "do's" and "dont's".

The practice of a common devotional and spiritual exercise - *Surat-Shabd-Yoga* - is followed by all branches and groups. It signifies their basic unity. Leaders of almost all groups lay primary emphasis on the fundamental importance of *Shabd* and *Guru* of the time. All of them strictly believe that the secrets of *shabd* would be revealed through the aegis of *Satguru*. They grant initiation by explaining to the initiatee the fixed point of concentration and a definite posture for *yoga*. They provide almost identical information regarding the performance of inner practice. The followers of Radhasoami Faith have the common basic idea of self-help and the community is very active and enterprising in this regard. With self-help they march forward to mutual help.

The message of true and selfless love is so poignantly preached and practised in the faith that it could never be extinguished. The *Surat-Shabd-Yoga* would escape all decadence. Therefore, if one really wants solace, and attain spiritual consciousness, it is advised that he should completely surrender at the feet of Radhasoami Dayal, and my call is - **"Go back to Soamiji Maharaj and Huzur Maharaj in order to march forward on the path of salvation with the grace and mercy of the *Sant Satguru*."**

IV

Basic Aspects of Consciousness

Chapter 1

Mysterium Tremendum

DAVID CHRISTOPHER LANE
California State University, Long Beach, California, USA

ANDREA DIEM LANE
Mt. San Antonio College, California, USA

Abstract
The conflict between Science and Spirituality stems from a linguistic confusion over what the term "matter" means and what it ultimately implies. The authors explore why the conflict is trapped in a linguistic conundrum and discuss what the seeds are for a future Science of Consciousness – neurophysical and / or mystical.

Prologue

The conflict between science and spirituality primarily stems from a linguistic confusion over what the term "matter" means and what it ultimately implies. This first came into sharp focus for me when I was attending the annual graduation ceremonies at Mt. San Antonio College in June of 1990. I had only been hired the year before so I was relatively new to the proceedings. As I was getting ready to walk in with my philosophy cohorts, dressed as we were in our long robes and mortar boards, another young professor from another department came up to me in a visibly irritated mood. After we exchanged pleasantries, he pulled out an issue of Plato's Cave, the new journal that I founded along with some students a few months prior. He queried, "Why would you allow this blasphemous claptrap to be published?" Before I could respond, he proceeded to rip the small magazine to pieces in front of me and threw it on the floor and walked away in disgust.

A mathematician friend of mine witnessed the spectacle, and asked, "What was that all about?" I responded that I didn't exactly know, but I mentioned that it concerned a recent issue of Plato's Cave, which contained an interview with Patricia Churchland, an eminent professor of philosophy at UCSD who had more or less invented the new field of neurophilosophy where ancient questions are examined in light of the latest discoveries in physics and neuroscience. The title of piece was *The Neural Basis of Consciousness, a Glorious Piece of Meat, and the Dalai Lama.* One of my star students, Meredith Doran (who is now a professor of French literature at Penn State), had conducted the interview and I thought she had done a superb job in capturing the ins and outs of Professor Churchland's scientific view of how philosophy should be conducted in the future.

Right then, another professor chimed in and said, "Oh, Dave, that guy who just verbally assaulted you is a fundamentalist Christian and he thinks your publication contradicts the Bible and insults his religion." A few other colleagues also confirmed the same and it became clearer to me why he would be upset by

Churchland's advocacy of eliminative materialism.

Yet, as I pondered over this episode, I couldn't help but wonder why certain religious persuasions are so troubled by sciences' reduction of man to mere material, given that matter itself was and is as mysterious and as glorious as anything conjured up in our spiritual imaginations. Before we tackle what matter is and why an updated definition of what it portends can radically upend the persistent and pernicious dualism driving much of our religious resistance to science and its naturalistic underpinnings, I would like to indulge the reader in a thought experiment.

A Dialogue in Sach Khand

Clearly, the following is a metaphor pushed to its hyperbolic extreme, but I think it drives home an often overlooked point. Imagine finding yourself in a transcendental realm of bliss and that within this ultimate region you and your companions strike up a conversation soul to soul. You inquire, "What are we made of?" And, one of your blissful friends replies, "Light, of course. We are beings of light and that is our core constituent." How would you hypothetically "feel" if someone did indeed inform you that you were a body of pure unalloyed light?

However, let's descend back to terra firma, and ask a different question. Now when we are in the here and now and a philosopher or a friend tells us that we are just material and just the body, or, when the Nobel Prize winner, the late Francis Circk says that consciousness is just a bundle of neurons or when Patricia Churchland indicates we are just three pounds of meat, how do we feel about that? In sum, how do we feel when we are told that we are just this stuff, just this body, just the re-composition of this world?

One could, of course argue at this juncture that this very feeling is why dualism arose in the first place. We feel that we are more than our bodies and, as such, that there is something transcendent in us. This primordial distinction, which appears to have arisen in most Homo sapiens, has no doubt influenced much of our religious and philosophical outlook. But I think the real confusion is in our fundamentally distorted understanding of what matter actually is. We tend to think that matter and spirit are opposites and that focusing on one discounts the other and vice versa. Yet, the real problem may be linguistic and not existential. In other words, it may be the outdated definitions and mythological remnants inherent in those definitions that have caused us so much unnecessary confusion. In order to make this point crystal clear, we will need to take a tour of "matter" and find out why it is so much more than gray and flat.

What's the Matter

Although the origin of the word matter (derived from mater) is of relatively recent origin, it is intriguing to note that it appears to have been derived from the word mother, which in light of this article is revealing indeed.

One can start from any object to get a glimpse into what matter may be, so for our example let's use a book. On my desk right now I have a copy of the annotated edition of Charles Darwin's famous *On the Origin of Species* published by the Belknap Press of Harvard University Press, which contains a complete facsimile of Darwin's 1859 first edition. In examining the book, we not only discover a certain hardback binding, a nicely designed dust jacket, but 537 pages filled with small print. However, if we look at just one of the pages within this book, we soon realize that it is made of a fine quality paper, which undoubtedly was derived from some dead tree for the purpose of utilizing pulp.

But what is a tree? A simple definition from a dictionary might explain it thus, "a plant having a permanently woody main stem or trunk, ordinarily growing to a considerable height, and usually developing branches at some distance from the ground." Yet, if we probe further we discover that such a plant is made up of much smaller constituent parts such as millions of cells, which in themselves are made of even smaller bits called molecules which, in turn, are comprised of billions, nay trillions, of atoms. Indeed, every physical composition on planet earth is essentially the reconfiguration of atoms.

Now the question, 'what is an atom?', will give us a deeper insight into what matter actually is. The term atom was first coined by Democritus (influenced no doubt by his teacher Leucippus) who argued that things are made up of indivisible particles which cannot be cut further. By the turn of the 20th Century this view became modified when Max Planck and others realized that atoms contained smaller bits, such as a nucleus and an electron. And those in turn contained smaller units still, including photons, quarks, and so on. Richard Feynman, the famous physicist and architect behind quantum electrodynamics (QED) once quipped that if he had to reduce all of human knowledge into one intelligible sentence he would write, "Things are made of littler things that jiggle"

This is a profound understanding of material structure and not merely a humorous slogan as Feynman is getting right to the heart of the issue. Matter isn't just one thing. It is rather a scaffolding project of many layers, each of which reveals a different aspect of what matter can do under differing circumstances.

Reconfigure atoms in a certain way and you get the Taj Mahal, reconfigure another way and you get a football stadium, reconfigure it still more and you get Mt. Everest, and reconfigure those same units and you get millions of different species trying their best to adapt to a whole eco system which itself is a larger network of reconfigured atoms.

And even the nucleus itself is, contrary to what Leucippus and Democritus opined some 2,600 years ago, divisible. Depending on the element, atoms come in different weights (depending on the number of protons within the nucleus and the number of electrons manifesting outside its chambers). Yet, even when we get to the very core of matter, we find yet another layer and our understanding of what is actually going on turns indeterminate.

As Sir Arthur Eddington once stated concerning the strange underpinnings inherent in quantum theory: "Something unknown is doing what we don't know".

The latest theoretical conjectures concerning the basis of matter has more or less coalesced around the four fundamental forces in nature: 1) gravity; 2) Electromagnetism; 3) strong nuclear force; and 4) weak nuclear force. Einstein's General Theory of Relativity is a radical explanation of gravity, whereas quantum mechanics has provided a remarkably accurate theory regarding electromagnetism, with strong and weak nuclear forces being also understood within its fold. However, scientists are troubled that general relativity and quantum theory do not mesh together, since one is classical and determinate whereas the other is revolutionary and indeterminate and being at odds with one another they together do not provide us with either a grand unified theory (GUT) or a theory of everything (TOE).

Thus for decades there has been a quest for a more fundamental theory which can reconcile the world of quanta with the world of gravitons. The most viable candidate so far has been a reworking of string theory which has evolved into a nested series of mathematical models most popularly known as M-theory. Stephen Hawking explains in his latest book, The Grand Design: "M-theory is not a theory in the usual sense. It is a whole family of different theories. Ours is not the only universe. Instead M-theory predicts that a great many universes were created out of nothing."

But even here the notion of nothing is itself caught in an epistemological confusion, since the very word nothing is literally nonsensical in this context and, as such, is merely a placeholder for the breakdown of both our physics and our language.

Most problematic for physicists is the upsetting discovery that pure and unadulterated objectivity breaks down at the quanta level where Heisenberg's uncertainty principle serves as a sort of information cul du sac. Yes, you may know relatively the momentum of a single particle, but at the expense of not knowing its position and vice versa. The absolute certainty that was bubbling forth since Newton's day as the hallmark of science got obliterated when it was realized that Chance was at the heart of nature. This is why Einstein wrote to Max Born that he didn't study physics to find out that God plays dice.

But in light of M-theory and the multiverse hypothesis not only does God (and God here is, of course, merely a metaphorical way of saying ultimate Nature or Reality) play dice but she/he does so in the dark countless times. Thus the laws of physics in this universe could be quite different in a divergent universe and given that M-theory implies a vast multiplicity of universes, it is odds, and not necessarily design, which gives rise to the peculiar circumstances of our present astronomical reflections. As Niels Bohr, one of the early pioneers in quantum mechanics, warned, "Those who are not shocked when they first come across quantum mechanics cannot possibly have understood it."

Bohr became the champion of the single most popular philosophic interpretation of the new physics, which would later be known as the Copenhagen interpretation because of the location of his institute. In many ways, Bohr's reasoning is akin to what we find in Plato's allegory of the cave, as found in his Republic, but with one very telling caveat. In Plato's story we learn that prisoners shackled in the cave cannot actually see the light itself that is casting the varying shadows on the wall. And only later when unhinged can they progress from the rudimentary impressions to clearer shapes and outlines until the full luminosity of the light explains more fully how all these images were generated.

In the quantum mechanical world we are in a similar position, since we cannot actually know both the position and the momentum of any single electron, but only its probabilities and even then how we measure such an outcome predetermines its wave or particle manifestation. What the electron is "really" doing nobody knows.

Apparently nobody can know what a single bit of matter is ultimately doing, since even that definition of "bit" of matter is itself a construct, a theoretical map in order to make sense out of one aspect of what appears at such minute levels of matter. What we get when we penetrate the subatomic realm isn't, to quote Kant, the thing in itself, but only what appears visible to our intervening devices. And since we cannot intrude into that realm without some type of instrument (even a single photon cascading off an electron causes a disruption of the assumed virgin state), we don't unlock nature pure and pristine, but as nature reacts to our measuring devices. In other words, we cannot unlock nature as nature, or electron as electron, or matter as matter, since we are invariably altering what we are examining.

We might occasionally acknowledge this interference even at the macroscopic level (sociologists and psychologists are well versed in interpreter's biases in grappling with raw data), but at the quantum level it looms so large and is so evidential that its impact cannot at any instance be ignored. Heisenberg's principle of uncertainty isn't merely a temporary limit to man's knowledge, according to Bohr, but a fundamental statement about what that knowledge is.

It is for this reason that Plato's allegory is instructive, since we are not in the position of the narrator to look objectively upon the cave from the outside and the inside simultaneously. Rather, we are the prisoners in the cave and only from that position can we both induce and deduce what may or may not be ultimately real, but in so doing we are still at the Kantian level of phenomena. What quantum mechanics revealed was precisely this epistemological limit and how it plays out in trying to form a picture about reality. Reality we can never know, since that very concept is itself a fiction which implies that we can somehow act as an objective narrator to the entire cosmos, with a 360 degree purview and a level of certainty which implies that we are impartial witnesses to a play with a beginning, middle, and an end. No, we are literally like the prisoners in Plato's allegory of the cave, limited by our very existence in what can and cannot know. For Bohr this wasn't merely a philosophical extension of his Kierkegaardian leanings, but the very result of what quantum mechanics revealed about our ability to come to grips with nature and how it responds to our introspections. As Bohr put it, "It is wrong to think that the task of physics is to find out how Nature is. Physics concerns what we say about Nature." Or, as Bohr himself discovered, "For a parallel to the lesson of atomic theory regarding the limited applicability of such customary idealizations, we must in fact turn to other branches of science, such as psychology, or even to that kind of epistemological problems with which already thinkers like Buddha and Lao Tzu have been confronted, when trying to harmonize our position as spectators and actors in the great drama of existence Everything we call real is made of things that cannot be regarded as real." It is little wonder, therefore, that so many eminent scientists have had such ambivalent reactions and feelings to the implications of quantum mechanics.

Hence, when we look at the very essence of matter we discover that it has no such essence, at least not something that can be related to our common sense notions of the world. In fact, our very common sense breaks down when we examine the rudimentary basis of matter itself. Our evolution has bounded what we can and cannot know about the world around us. Because of this our brains are not well adapted to understand either the very large or the very small. We are quite literally middling creatures that have been shaped for eons of times to survive in eco-niches where our food and prey are accessible to our five apertures. What this means, of course, is that whenever we venture beyond our middle earth by extending our senses to the very large or very small, we have to acclimate ourselves anew.

The history of science is a record of how man achieved such acclimations and how, in turn, such new insights transformed his understanding of how the universe actually works. Whether it was Galileo's telescope (seeing a pock marked moon versus a polished lunar surface) or Copernicus mathematical equations (indicating a solar based orbital system versus an earth centered one), in each case sensory or mental breakthroughs led to revolutions in scientific thought. It may be no exaggeration to say that whenever man has altered his bodily or cranial limits he has extended his world, a world which is forever linked to the limitations of what his senses can and cannot reveal.

To say that neurology is ontology is merely to state the obvious. But what sometimes gets lost in such clichés is that man's brain state is never static and thus his world is never the same as well. Change the neural apparatus and one transforms the universe. Not necessarily because the brain creates such realities, but rather because the limitations of one's cranial capacities predetermines what is accessible or knowable about any given aspect of reality. Change those neural coordinates and thereby change one's intellectual map. All of this is necessary preface to understand why the human mind has an almost innate difficulty in understanding quantum theory- a theory which takes into account things so infinitesimally tiny that even our best analogies freeze our minds in a state of wonder. Ludwig Wittgenstein gives us a fruitful glimpse of just how contradictory quantum physics can be and why it demonstrates prima facie its almost inherent illogical nature. Writing several years before the discovery of Werner Heisenberg's Nobel Prize winning discovery of the uncertainty relations in the subatomic realm, Wittgenstein states in his famous Tractatus Logico-Philosophicus:

Today, of course, quantum physicists state the opposite of Wittgenstein's logical necessity about the behavior of matter and point out that indeed a particle can be in two places at the same time, even if that space and time is limited in its regional and temporal import.

What Wittgenstein captured (quite unwittingly since his Tractatus dates from the latter part of the First World War) was how a rational, logical mind would be upended by the implications of quantum theory. Moreover, he provides us with a framework for why it may be so difficult for many of us to actually "get" quantum theory. As Richard Feynman, the well-known architect behind Quantum Electrodynamics (QED) once quipped, "I think I can safely say that nobody understands quantum mechanics."

Therefore, a very strong argument can be made that the real problem with materialism (the idea everything that arises is nothing but permutations of matter) isn't that it is the exact opposite of spirit or that it somehow diminishes human consciousness, but rather that we do not properly appreciate what the world actually means and what it entails. To say something is "just" matter is akin to say something is "just" light (which matter, by the way, also contains).

Even when inter theoretic reductionisms hold true there is no "just" about it, since the very phenomena under inspection doesn't love its mystery by being contextually or algorithmically comprehended. If someone says that the Atlantic is merely H2o, the ocean and all its magnificence isn't lessened by such molecular equations. The trouble isn't with matter or our tendency to ground all properties to it, but rather that we are assuming that matter is one thing when it is completely the opposite of that.

Science will undoubtedly expand our previous limits and horizons, but we will inevitably be stuck with our own neural constraints from the very beginning. And herein lays the great human dilemma: the limits of our skull are the limits of our understanding. Yes, we may augment our brains with artificial devices in the future, but even here we will only confront a new limit time. If we don't know what a single thing ultimately is (even if we can know various things about a material item, we are circumscribed in our knowledge about comprehending all of its various dimensions and interconnections), do we even know where we are ultimately?

What this means is that even if we forego religion and spirituality and opt for a purely materialistic understanding of what surrounds us, we are still touching moment to moment a mystery that transcends our ability to grasp it. And, ironically, the dilemma isn't between matter and spirit, but the persistence of wholly inaccurate and misleading definitions of them. To echo the immortal words of Ludwig Wittgenstein, there isn't a philosophical problem inherent in this supposed dualism but a confused use of reifications embedded in our languages. Simply put, our use of the term matter is mostly a linguistic confusion and as such has blinded us from the radical mystery to which it consistently points us towards.

The implications here are enormous for spiritual disciplines which wish to be viewed as promoting a scientific outlook. Any meditational discipline that wishes to be seriously taken as a science must ground itself in the very thing it wishes to transcend. But as I wish to make crystal clear, nobody transcends matter as such. Instead what are transcended are bad definitions. To risk a reframed pun here, there is nothing the matter with matter as a grounding concept, if we first understand that the term itself is under constant evolutionary pressure in that what it entails changes with more and more study.

What this means is that meditational traditions would be much better served if they stopped resisting a purely materialistic explanation of their given inquiries. At first this may sound heretical or even contradictory (given what the spiritual enterprise presumes), but it is not if we realize that a purely material explanation for inner experiences is precisely what we should expect if we understand science and its definitional aims in a larger purview.

Science cannot diminish the spiritual quest if that quest is concerned with truth and not merely dogmatic assertions taken at face value. However, spiritual paths must be open to varying interpretations and must (and this is the kicker that most paths tend to resist) be open to falsification. In other words, for any endeavor to be justifiable regarded as "scientific" it must be willing to be corrected, to be changed, and to be wrong.

While much of spiritual literature advertises itself as scientific, we find that the very basis of almost all scientific endeavors, that of theory making, is dismissed since it interferes with certain strongly held religious beliefs. For example, when a particular guru instructs the neophyte to go within the laboratory of one's own body to verify the factualness of their respective theology, he doesn't mention that such subjective experiences should be open to varying interpretations of what they could possibly mean.

This version of science is more akin to an elaborate food recipe, where the would-be chef needs to follow a set of given instructions in order to know how to make a chocolate cake or a vegetarian pizza. Applied science is successful only after certain facts are well established and known. But at this juncture, any proposed spiritual science is still in its infancy, even if some traditions would like to suggest otherwise.

Such versions of science are similar to a computer program like basic or UNIX where if you follow just the right set of protocols you will invariably end up with a repeatable outcome. But this leaves out the most vitally important aspect of science, something which only few meditational teachers seemed to grasp, which is that science isn't a thing but rather a process of discovery and along that pathway there will be false starts, differences of opinion, falsifications, tentative hypotheses, and theories and even facts that are always subject to alteration or even wholesale elimination.

For instance, it may be one thing for a religious tradition to say, "There is no better method than that of the Sound Current, which is an ancient and natural science. It was designed by the Creator Himself, is within every one of us, yet whole nations and entire countries of the world are ignorant of it". But, it is quite another thing for them to claim that such a description is part and parcel of a genuine science. Notice that the preceding quote concerning Shabd yoga isn't alleging to be merely a scientific endeavor to be placed alongside biology or chemistry, but rather is emphatically stating (quite categorically one might add) to be more fundamental than even physics since it was created by God himself as a path back to him. While a devotee may believe this to be the case, it is fairly obvious to an outsider that this assertion is not a scientific claim as much as a dogmatic one in the guise of scientific dressing.

This is important to understand since a genuine scientific endeavor worthy of its name cannot ad hoc cherry pick which aspect of science they wish to utilize. In cases like this it as if science is employed as a form of advertising to reach interested seekers who may have been turned off by more exclusive forms of religious dogmatism. While it appeals to the rational authority of science, it does so by claiming that Shabd yoga is the highest of all sciences, apparently forgetting in the process that any scientific endeavor worth the appellation must be open to revaluation and correction. Nowhere do we find in most meditational literature a consistent theme of falsification, where past Gurus and their ideas are corrected, changed, or overthrown. What we do find, however, is a paradoxical selection of quasi scientific language which appears to be offering a potential experimental procedure to validate inner spiritual experiences.

Surprisingly, Shabd yoga or any meditational discipline that wishes to be viewed as a genuine science would be best served if, instead of first resorting to dogmatic axioms about its ultimate truth claims or appealing to unassailable authorities in its lineal past, it looked for ways to falsify itself. A good example of how to do this can be found in Charles Darwin's *On the Origin of Species*, where in just one sentence he explained how his whole theory of evolution by natural selection could be wrong. Wrote Darwin,

"If it could be demonstrated that any complex organ existed, which could not possibly have been formed by numerous, successive, slight modifications, my theory would absolutely break down."

Here Darwin points the pathway by which his whole theory could be turned upside down. Any spiritual endeavor desiring to be taken seriously as a science must do the same.

Seeds for a Future Science of Consciousness

As for whether science can indeed decide the physicality of consciousness I think the answer is affirmative, even despite science's methodological naturalism. Quite simply, if consciousness is indeed beyond physics or anything within its known laws, then no matter how hard we try to ground mind to its neural structures there will always be something missing in such reductions. And, interestingly, this gap will loom even larger because our physical science will be unable to adequately explain it. Thus, one could argue that such a physicalist approach will shine a much more illuminating light upon the problem by showing exactly where, when, and how awareness is not the result of physical properties. But if we forego this grounded scientific quest prematurely because of already accepted quadrant categorizations (the type that religions want to pose as already confirmed hierarchies) then we can and will succumb too easily and too readily and too naively to the Transcendental Temptation. Or, to invoke Ken Wilber's pithy parlance, you cannot make a pre-rational and trans-rational fallacy distinction (distinguishing that which is truly within the five senses from that which is not) unless you have a deep and rich and nuanced understanding of all that is indeed pre-rational. How else can one determine that which is truly trans-rational?

A science of consciousness, therefore, must start with the brain. Science, in other words, can indeed point to that which is not physical because of its ultra-focused aim. Science can upend itself quite easily. The fact that it hasn't yet is why we remain so confident in its methods and its discoveries. But if in the future it comes across something that cannot be reduced to the four forces of the universe, we will be forced to reconsider. But what has happened in the past and what is still happening today is that we want to invoke transcendent explanations too quickly in order to salvage a sense of the numinous, forgetting in the process that even if all things are indeed material bits the mystery of all this (and here comes the pun) isn't lessened by one bit.

What is matter anyways?—from organisms to cells to proteins to molecules to atoms to electrons to light? The most famous equation in modern physics is Einstein's $E=MC^2$ which if we pause for a second is as mysterious as anything written in our ancient religious scriptures and measurably more radical. My point is that the resistance we have to reductionists who say, we are "just matter" is because we tend to think of matter as flat. It is, of course, anything but. Thus may be the reason we opt for dualism or the idea that something must be "beyond" matter is because we haven't come to grips to the amazing plasticity and mystery inherent in matter itself.

In other words, we are using an extremely outdated and misleading definition of matter and in so doing losing sight of the wonderfulness of what physics and neuroscience is saying. We are not lessened because we are just matter, just as we wouldn't be lessened in Sach Khand if we were made of just "light." Frank Visser, author of Thought as passion, rightly captures our semantic confusion when he queries, "How on earth could cells and molecules lead to felt states? Forget about psi- psychology itself is as paranormal as you can get!"

At first glance it does seem to absolutely amazing how we could get from molecules to self-awareness. But, the same could be said about life itself. How can it be that a three letter sequence of DNA strung together in varying sequences can produce a giraffe, a shark, and a human being? Indeed, rearrange atoms and you can get a chalk board, a cruise ship, an orange, and the moon. But get it we do. Likewise, getting from a cell to a self-aware human being isn't a stretch if we understand how the complex arrangement of atoms can indeed produce things that we cannot possibly imagine to exist, but which played out over time do indeed exist.

Therefore, the problem that we have with the physicality of consciousness is the same resistance that our ancestors had with understanding probabilities and how very simple algorithmic sequences can produce truly astonishing complex varieties, the likes of which boggle our imagination. That we cannot imagine how matter produces consciousness tells us how limited our imaginations are when it comes to the wonders of physics. We shouldn't confuse our intuitive limitations with how the world works.

Physics is the most mystical endeavor known to humankind, if one truly comes to grip with the multi-dimensional aspects inherent in any particle that arises. If one takes thinks of hydrogen and oxygen in isolation, it would be inconceivable to imagine that their combination would bring forth water. But that is precisely what occurs and nothing "more" is needed. Therefore, the "inconceivability" of something shouldn't be used ad hoc as a precursor for invoking the divine. Patience, in other words, is a highly necessary virtue if we wish to avoid making pre/trans leaps. We have an almost built-in dualism within our awareness which gives us the convincing sense that our selves are not our bodies.

However, one could just as easily argue that if consciousness is akin to an electromagnetic wave then stopping production at its source would indeed cancel the television show. The brain, in this purview, is the production facility and because of its centrality to self-reflective awareness, it seems fairly obvious that if you destroy the central nervous system you have killed consciousness. Saying consciousness is physical doesn't detract from its majesty in the least, since as we have repeatedly mentioned matter itself is to use Rudolph Otto's religious terminology, mysterium tremendum and ganz andere. We have to turnaround our understanding of matter and also how we view ourselves in the process. Matter is multi-dimensional and if the reconfigurations of tiny atoms can give us nature's wide diversity (from a rose to an airplane to a sunset to a cup of java to repeated episodes of I Love Lucy), then a complex set of billions of neurons may also give rise to varying degrees of awareness.

Or, we could use reverse engineering to give us a clue about why awareness is directly connected to physics. The difference between a rock and a chimp isn't something transcendent, but rather due to the complexity of atoms and molecules clustered within the central nervous system of our simian friends. Look to the complexity of matter first and you will readily see why and how awareness arises in some material objects and not in others. Invoking Gods or spirits of Eros is literally nonsensical, particularly when the physics of neuroscience is still in its infancy. Before we succumb to the transcendental temptation, may be it would be prudent to show some patience and let our empirical science have a deeper stab at the problem first.

Then, I would suggest, the science of consciousness would be on much firmer footing and would make much greater strides in its mystical search. The radical key for any newly emerging science is its willingness for self-correction. To assume, as too many meditational disciplines do, that the map has already been charted and all that is necessary is to embark on the voyage, is to neglect science's most vital feature: the unexpected. If all that is to come is already expected and predicted (without variation or exception) then we are no longer engaging in a scientific endeavor but rather a tautology designed to merely confirm a certain religious ideology. While such a religious ideology may indeed turn out to be true, it shouldn't be conflated with what science endeavors to do and thus confusing the religious impulse with the scientific impulse is doomed to failure.

Perhaps this may explain why some scientists feel that the most promising way to tackle the subject of consciousness is by a process of eliminative materialism. Simply put, if the phenomena cannot be explained fully and comprehensively by mathematics, then one turns to physics, and if that too is incomplete, then to chemistry, then to biology, then to psychology, then to sociology, etc. The old joke is that if none of these academic disciplines can explain it then it is perfectly okay to say, "Well, God did it."

In other words, try to explain it simply first. This is why Occam's razor (Entia non sunt multiplicanda praeter necessitate. "Don't multiply entities beyond necessity") is such a powerful weapon in science and why ideas such as Hume's Maxim ("That no testimony is sufficient to establish a miracle, unless the testimony be of such a kind, that its falsehood would be more miraculous than the fact which it endeavors to establish.") and Laplace's Dictum ("The weight of evidence for an extraordinary claim must be proportioned to its strangeness.") serve as helpful guide posts. Edward O.Wilson has captured this same spirit in his book, Consilience, which suggested that a unification of the sciences and humanities should be predicated upon a deep and robust understanding of what Bertrand Russell called 'natural facts."

It is not that only simple things exist or that there may not be something beyond the rational mind, but only that to genuinely uncover these transcendent phenomena one must eliminate lower level categories first. When we scientifically advanced in astronomy, medicine, and physics we replaced the old and outdated concepts of our mythic past with new and more accurate terminology which reflected our new found understanding of our body and the universe at large. Thus, instead of talking about Thor, the Thunder God, we talked instead about electrical-magnetic currents. Thus, instead of talking about spirits as the cause of diseases, we talked about bacteria and viruses. Thus, instead of talking about tiny ghosts circulating throughout our anatomies pulling this or that muscle, we talked about a central nervous system. In sum, we "eliminated" the Gods or spirits in favor of more precise and accurate physiological explanations. Hence, the term: "eliminative" materialism.

As a materialistic explanation evolves over time, it will either eliminate or reduce hitherto inexplicable phenomena down from the celestial region to the empirical arena. And in so doing, help us to better understand why certain events transpire in our body, in our mind, in our society, and in our world. Eliminative materialism is reason writ large. The glitch, though, is that we have allowed eliminative materialism to change our thinking about almost everything except ourselves. When it comes to understanding our own motivations, we have (as Churchlands' point out) resorted more or less to "Folk Psychology," utilizing terms such as "desire," "motivation," "love," "anger," and "free will," to describe what we believe is happening within our own beings. The problem with that is such terminology arises not from a robust neuro-scientific understanding of our anatomies but rather arises from a centuries old mythic/religious comprehension of our very consciousness.

And that's the rub. Where we have moved away from such religious language in the fields of physics, astronomy, chemistry, and biology, in talking about ourselves we are still stuck in pre-rational modes of discourse. Where astronomy reflects the latest theories of the universe, where medicine reflects the latest theories of diseases, in talking about ourselves we tend to reflect ancient theories of human psychology. And in order to get a better understanding of human consciousness, neurophilosophy argues that we focus our attention on developing a more comprehensive analysis of the brain and how it "creates" self-reflective awareness.

In so doing, we can then come up with a more neurally accurate way of describing what is going on within our own psyches (pun intended). Thus, instead of using the term "soul" we might instead use phase-specific words to describe the current state of awareness which are more neurologically correlated. We have already done this slightly when it comes to headaches. Due to our increased attention to various pains and to the various drugs that are effective in treating them, we have become more aware of how to differentiate and thereby treat varying types of head pain- from Excedrin (very good for migraines because of the caffeine and aspirin combination) to Advil (very good for body and tooth aches).

Hence, the neurophilosophical way to understand one's "soul" is to ground such ideas in the neural complex. Now if consciousness cannot be explained sufficiently (Occam's Razor only works if it can indeed explain the given phenomena accurately) with just recourse to the brain, then that form of reductionism has actually helped, not hindered, the case for religionists or transpersonalists since it has exhausted the neuronal possibilities. What this implies, of course, is that any meditational discipline worth its salt should be completely unafraid of what a critical and materialist science would make of it, since such skeptical scrutiny could only enable us to better differentiate illusory factoids from the truth.

Even the most profound spiritual experiences may themselves be the result of brain process of which we remain unaware. This doesn't discount the beauty or bliss of such numinous journeys, since there are many things we enjoy that are indeed the result of physical machinations. For instance, my fondness for surfing (even with my lack of smell) has not disappeared because I know something about the physics of waves. The majestic beauty of a rose isn't lessened by our deeper grasp of its molecular parts. As Feynman once illustrated when he pointed out to his artist companion that a physicist's understanding of a flower doesn't detract from its beauty, but only adds to it since he can appreciate so many other levels that usually go undetected.

In light of how reductionism actually works when applied to real life situations, I am surprised that there are not more strong advocates of it coming from those most deeply interested in mysticism. Blaise Pascal once wrote that those with little faith will have little doubt and those with great faith with have great doubt. While I appreciate his religious syllogism, I don't think he extends it far enough. The logical consequence of his couplet should end with "and those with infinite faith will have infinite doubt." Because it is through doubt and skepticism where more, not less, evidence for the transcendent will arise since such critical scrutiny raises the bar for acceptable proof much higher than those who tend to believe on anecdotes alone.

Yet, any deep understanding of matter as multi-dimensional must take into consideration the first person experience of one's own consciousness. If we think we can eliminate qualia, or what David Chalmers called the "hard problem" in understanding self-awareness we are both deluded and mistaken, since it is our very awareness in which all questions of human affairs have arisen. In this regard, I think Indian mystical traditions, in particular, have offered us a radically new analogy by which to view consciousness.

Levels of Awareness

Imagine that the only state of consciousness that existed was, in fact, our dream world. Further imagine that in such a state an unusual person (we will call him Ramana) confronts you by claiming to have access to a hitherto unknown level of awareness which he calls the "waking" world. Ramana further argues that all experiences within the dream state are subsumed (indeed produced) by a waking brain which is inaccessible to dreamers. And therefore the attempt by the majority of dream materialists to reduce waking phenomena down to their dream stuff is completely wrong and misleading, since the truth of the situation is completely the opposite. The dream is happening because of the waking state brain (in another realm) not the apparent dream brain which looks to be generating awareness from itself and from its extended environment. Ramana's ultimate point is a very simple one. While it may seem to overwhelmingly clear that the dream brain causes the dream world, the fact is that a transcendent state of being is its real cause and origination.

What to make of such a claim? If one were grounded in "dream stuff" methodologies, one might ask for some convincing evidence of such a world (let's call this thinker Churchland). To which Ramana might reply that it was impossible to actually transport such waking stuff into the dream world, since the very moment one attempts to do so it instantly transforms into dream material. Churchland, ever the skeptic, might then rejoinder that Ramana's bold claim lacks proof and as such warrant no further attention. Or, she might argue that Ramana's waking excursions were just modifications of his own dream brain and that what he thought was higher and transcendent was neither, since his numinous experiences were the result of neural dream discharges within his own dream skull.

At this juncture, Ramana may argue that to see the proof of his claim one must be willing to do a most radical experiment. One must literally "die" to the dream state in order to properly access the waking state. When that happens, then Churchland will actually have the extraordinary evidence she demands. Of course, Churchland might balk at this suggestion since dream death seems a bit extreme to prove a point.

Churchland may persist and query Ramana again and say, "Why can't you produce something in our present state of awareness which would give us confidence that your claims are true?" In addition, is it not possible that you are wrong, Ramana, since your recollection of the waking state must be recalled in and through your present dream brain? How do you possibly know that the dream brain couldn't produce what you wrongly believe is higher?

Ramana may then point out that the certainty of any experiment rests upon an uninspected axiom: that the present form of awareness is somehow the best and final arbitrator of all other states of consciousness. Why this is so isn't an ontological fact and if other superluminal forms of awareness do exist then exploring them may help us contextualize our present dream state.

At this state then Ramana could encourage Churchland to take up the experiment by practicing a method that he himself used. Using one's own self-awareness asks what the source of such luminosity is. According to Ramana, that very inquiry will lead to a deep questioning of what one takes to be "real" and "permanent" and will eventually prompt one to emerge into the waking state, which itself is the larger context behind the dream world. In such an awakening, the erstwhile skeptic will immediately discover that dream stuff was not the real cause behind dreaming. Rather, it was a physical brain in a completely different state of awareness.

The gist of this argument is that saying everything was caused by the physical brain may appear to be perfectly sensible in this present waking state awareness, but may in truth be completely wrong if indeed there were higher states of awareness in which this and other states were subsumed.

More precisely, even if a purely materialist position absolutely convinced us that matter and only matter gave rise to our self-awareness, we could still be quite mistaken. The dream analogy or Fritz Staal's "Three ants in a room analogy" or Plato's allegory of the cave or Edwin Abbot's Flatland all address, to varying degrees, the idea of a multi-dimensionality to consciousness. The waking state does indeed seem certain until we fall asleep. Likewise, a lucid dream appears real until we wake up. If that is the case with two states, is it really that unreasonable to think of a third or a fourth state that would show the relativity of our present state?

I think the overriding reason that many of us find the previous analogy persuasive is because we intuit or know from our own experiences that when one is in a higher state of awareness it makes the waking state look like a dismal and shadowy dream. It seems as if neuroscience was merely the logical extension of Flatland thinking, of taking the dream brain too seriously, and snuffing out the possibility that deep meditation of self-inquiry could actually lead beyond the rational mind into realm thought impossible by physicalist thinking. Of course, a whole host of thinkers have postulated this as well, ranging from early Gnostics to modern day mathematicians and quantum physicists. But one of the great difficulties confronting such perennialist thinking is that arguing by analogy or by experiential inquiry doesn't easily translate as "evidence" or "proof" in the nuts and bolts world of everyday life.

Yes, there seems to be little question that amazing states of consciousness exist and that almost all humans can access such under certain conditions. Even the most skeptical of scientists will concede the plasticity of awareness. But such a phenomenological acceptance doesn't mean that we have agreed upon what these experiences actually mean or portend. The impasse between materialists and mystics isn't over whether UOE's (unified oneness experiences) or NDE's or OBE's or any other illuminated "E" Experiences exist, but how to best interpret and explain them. In other words, how do we decide or know that consciousness isn't reducible to the known laws of physics and neuroscience? We have already reduced water to its chemical make-up of H2o and nobody seems too concerned that we have more or less eliminated Neptune as a guiding explanatory principle. One could argue that science is one long (and quite successful) history of what occurs when humans discover a physical explanation for what was otherwise regarded as the province of God or metaphysics.

If this has been the case for explaining almost the entire known universe, from electromagnetism to gravity, why shouldn't science also be successful in explaining human awareness? And aren't mystics and spiritualists and religionists too prone to explain their numinous encounters with outdated modes of thinking? As I argued in the Politics of Mysticism:

"But, the argument goes, the devoted mystic will say that his or her experiences are authentic (because of the utter certainty of the encounter) and the experiences of others, especially if they belong to a rival group which splintered off after a succession dispute, are misguided, secondary, or illusory. So what we actually have in effect here in terms of truth claims is not essentially different than that of a fundamentalist. The mystic is right by virtue of his/her inner attainment and everybody else is wrong (no matter how politely we may gloss over it: karma or chance?) because he/she happened to get the right Guru and the right path (and by right we mean "highest").

But notice how the mystic is not calling into question or doubt his/her own truth claims. For example, one rarely finds a completely agnostic posture among disciplines about the relative status of his/her Guru. Why not? Because just like the fundamentalist he or she is not trained to severely doubt interior revelations of truth, primarily because they appear so real when they occur. It is one thing to state that my inner experiences have convinced me that I am on the right track: quite another to them make judgments on the veracity of other meditators' experiences.

To strike a sociological note here, it becomes fairly apparent that culture plays a significant role in the ultimate interpretations of inner experiences. What at first glance appears to be a simple, sweet path to enlightenment turns out to be on closer inspection a political contest over religious claims-claims, I should add, that have been transformed by the cultural landscape of when and where they take place. We may wish that mysticism was devoid of culture, or personal bias, or religious prejudice, but it is almost wholly entrenched in it.

Why? Because we never apprehend inner lights and sounds and beings divorced of their interpretative network. In other words, our socially conditioned minds are always flavoring, always transforming, always contextualizing whatever we perceive, whether those sights be inner or outer. And it is exactly when my experiences are personal and internal that I am most subject to error. We have yet to discern a normative corrective for mystical encounters. Sure we have templates to gauge inner experiences, their relative efficacy and so on, but since most individuals have no mastery of leaving their bodies we are subject to tremendous imprecision and tremendous speculation. Yet do we admit to this impasse? Do we acknowledge our immaturity in the spiritual arena?

And even if analogies cannot constitute evidence, they can at the very least prompt unexpected voyages which can on their return trips provide the tangible evidence that was missing at the outset—witness Charles Darwin and his five year journey on the H.M.s. Beagle or Captain Cook's encounters in Tahiti and beyond.

What kinds of evidence can a mystic proffer that would convince neuroscientists that their very paradigm may need to be transcended?

Perhaps the evidence we seek is by its nature transcendent and not amenable to empirical test claims? If so, then we are truly not in a Newtonian or Einsteinian world anymore and we should straight up admit it. That is, if mysticism is indeed a "transpersonal" science then it may just have to go alone and forget convincing us flatlanders otherwise. I say this because if consciousness is indeed multi-dimensional in an ontological sense then it won't be possible to reduce one state to another without concealing its most important features.

If this is indeed the case, as some mystics have argued, then we may be confronting the limits of what has been tantalizingly termed the Chandian Effect. It was so named because Faqir Chand was the first Sant Mat Guru to speak at length about the "unknowing" aspects of visionary manifestations. In this context, the Chandian Effect designates two major factors in transpersonal encounters: 1) the overwhelming experience of certainty (ganz andere/mysterium tremendum) which accompanies religious ecstasies; and

2) the subjective projection of sacred forms/figures/scenes by a meditator/devotee without the conscious knowledge of the object/person that is beheld as the centre of the experience. The Chandian Effect in the realm of mystical experiences is weakly analogous to Heisenberg's principle of uncertainty in subatomic physics. The more "certain" or "real" the mystical encounter seems, the less likely one is to believe that such is the product of subjective projection or transference. This invariably causes deep epistemological consternation, since what makes us certain that something is indeed real is the result of our own deeply felt subjectivity (even if dressed up in objectivist language).

This explains, albeit only partially, the great transformation that occurred to Ramana Maharshi of South India. Paul Brunton in his book *A Search in Secret India* retells it:

"He [Ramana] was sitting alone one day in his room when a sudden and inexplicable fear of death took hold of him. He became acutely aware he was going to die, although outwardly he was in good health. He stretched his body prone upon the floor, fixed his limbs in the rigidity of a corpse, and closed his eyes and mouth... 'Well, then,' said I to myself, 'this body is dead. It will be carried stiff to the burning ground and then reduced to ashes. But with the death of the body, am I dead? Is the body I? This body is now silent and stiff. But I continue to feel the full force of myself apart from its condition. 'These are the words with which the Maharishee [Maharshi] described the weird experience through which he passed... He seemed to fall into a profound conscious trance wherein he became merged into the very source of selfhood, the very essence of being. He understood quite clearly that the body was a thing apart and that the I remained untouched by death. The true self was very real, but it was so deep down in man's nature that hitherto he had ignored it."

As Ramana himself gracefully said:

"There is only one consciousness and this, when it identifies itself with the body, projects itself through the eyes and sees the surrounding objects. The individual is limited to the waking state; he is expected to see something different and expects the authority of his senses. He will not admit that he who sees the objects seen and the act of seeing are all manifestations of the same Consciousness-the 'I-I' [Real Self]. Meditation helps to overcome the illusion that the Self is something to see. Actually there is nothing to see. How do you recognize yourself now? Do you have to hold a mirror up in front of yourself to recognize yourself? The awareness is itself the 'I'. Realize it and that is the truth."

This mystical resonance is quite understandable since the experience brings forth its own definite and convincing certification, just as the waking state does after a good night's sleep. But herein arises a pertinent observation. Our conviction that something is real or certain doesn't mean that we cannot be mistaken. We most definitely can be.

If we can anatomically be mistaken when it comes to ordinary reality, which we can easily double check, then it seems we are confronted with much larger issues of literal confusion when it comes to alternative states of consciousness. Of course, Michael Shermer, founder of Skeptic Magazine, critiques the natural/supernatural divide from a different angle:

I don't think a union between science and religion is possible for a logical reason, but by this same logic I conclude that science cannot contradict religion. Here's why: A is A. Reality is real. To attempt to use nature to prove the supernatural is a violation of A is A. It is an attempt to make reality unreal. A cannot also be non-A. Nature cannot also be non-Nature. Naturalism cannot also be supernaturalism.

In a natural worldview, there is no non-natural or supernatural. There is only the natural and mysteries left to explain through natural means. Believers can have both religion and science as long as there is no attempt to make A non-A, to make reality unreal, to turn naturalism into supernaturalism. The only way to do this for theists is to posit that God is outside of time and space; that is, God is beyond nature-super nature, or supernatural-and therefore cannot be explained by natural causes. This places the God question outside the realm of science. Thus, there can be no conflict between science and religion, unless one attempts to bring God into our time and space, which is a violation of the principle of A is A.

If we substitute mysticism or transcendent consciousness for religion, Shermer's argument is that there is an indissoluble gap between science and spirituality. And any attempt to bridge the two is a violation of the simple principle that A is A. While I am not quite convinced by Shermer's verbal sleight of hand, I do think he is on to something that deserves closer inspection.

For instance, if consciousness is indeed brain based then neurology should be able to help us better understand how it arises from material structures. Mysticism or the pursuit of higher states of consciousness, therefore, will also be part and parcel of such neurological studies, and will not be beyond its jurisdiction. However, if consciousness (or some part of our awareness) is not physically produced then science will not be able to comprehensively explain it as such. This implies that science will eventually confront a border it cannot cross.

Chapter 2

Seeds of Transformation: Small Step towards a Unity of Humanity's Consciousness and Conscience

JOHN GRAYZEL
University of Maryland, USA

Abstract

This paper offers the consideration that human consciousness is an ongoing dramatic transformation from a consciousness that resides in the individual to a consciousness that resides in the species. This new level of consciousness is a necessary adaptation to the tremendous surge in the interdependency of humanity in terms of sheer numbers, of people and transactions and the speed at which they occur. Such intensity is overwhelming established human social, economic and political systems, as well as those of the natural world. Having overwhelmed natural systems, humankind must now fully assume the responsibility for the future of the earth itself. Consciousness of this phenomenon itself is the first step in a process that must end both with a new unity of consciousness on the part of all humanity and a new "unity of conscience" among all people.

By a unity of conscience is meant a shared understanding and commitment to a set of foundational principles that can serve as the accepted final justifications on which a new global civilization inclusive of all people can be built. The intended purpose of this paper is to make us not only more conscious and aware of this process and the choices before us, but especially as to some specific small steps we can take right now to become its dynamic agents. It is suggested that the decision on the part of each of us as to whether to engage as progenitors of this transformation, or remain only as inert elements being affected by it as it occurs, is a choice of free will presented to us. Our decision depends on the exercise of our spiritual nature and, in particular, on our capacity for love, which is the spiritual expression of the force of attraction that is behind all great transformations and as such potentially the most powerful force we can harness for the transformation of the human race.

Introduction

NASA has provided a timeline of universe that is shown in Figure 1.

It is divided into thirteen and a half stripes and these stripes represent thirteen and a half billion years that the present universe has existed. We can see how the universe has progressed along those thirteen lines from the Big Bang at the beginning to the present. Where we are now is so small that we can't locate ourselves on this scale. During this period, one starts with light, that goes into quantum explosion, that goes into darkness, that then goes into light, then it goes into gases, then consolidating the galaxies, then becomes

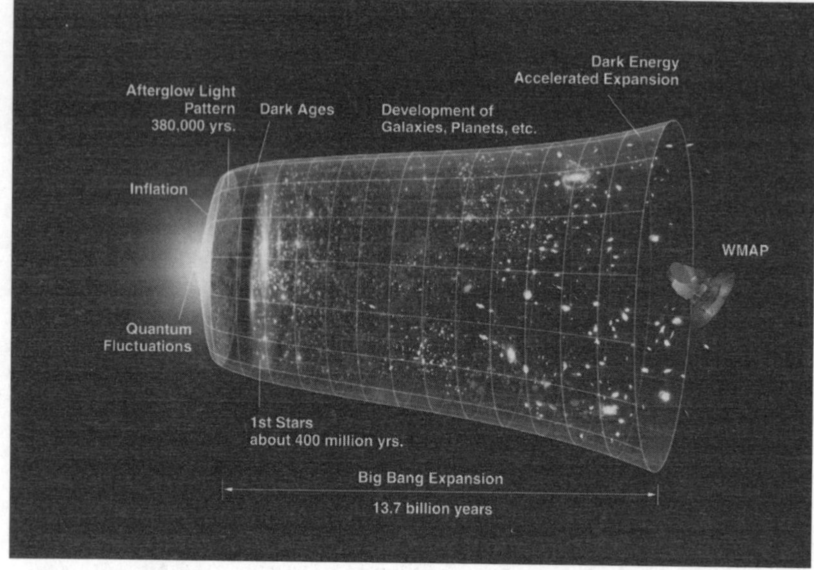

Figure 1

suns, then becomes planets, where the initial elements of hydrogen and helium and additional elements of periodic table come, where planets form, where life begins on planets. It's a progression which is very important to explain everything. Scientists also explain how things came to be and write laws in support of this explanation. But looking forward from where we are now from seven billion years ago nothing can be predicted; when was there only hydrogen and helium or the emergence of the periodic tables or that there was hydrogen and oxygen to make water till there was water or there were gases which turned to stars until there were stars. So there is confusion in our ability to explain and predict the laws of the past and in imagining future predictions where periodic transformations reconstitute in ways for which never before any knowledge existed. We only know that it does happen but don't how it happens.

What seems to happen is a small, for which some physicists give a fancy phrase like "crease in the cloth of time" and an era in space. In a pebble or a piece of sand in an oyster, nucleation occurs over a period of time and the piece of sand in an oyster becomes a pearl. So the little piece becomes a planet, it becomes a mass. It gathers gas until it becomes the sun and the sun becomes so hot that it begins to create a new dynamic energy that bursts forth as actual new elements. Likewise, Dayalbagh is a manifestation of a phenomenon in which nucleation occurs when we create a centre of attraction and over time, it brings forth other elements and finally through its dynamic interactions brings forth an actual transformation. This is essentially different from invention and discovery. We do invent things, we discover things, and we imagine things. But we really imagine discovering the recombination of what we know. We don't imagine things that really don't exist. There comes a time for transformation.

We are in a time of such transformation because what we are seeing precisely is a type of frenetic, dynamic consolidation of things. Also such things that seem to exist are now engaged in a process of both disintegration and integration. They are coming apart and they pair structures and they seem to be coming together in a very frenetic fashion in new structures. That's how towns grow. The small towns later became great cities. The entire world is slowly turning into a traffic jam. We use to have cars, roads and everything is coming together and everything is just going to solidify into a big traffic jam around the entire world.

It's unlikely to forecast what's going to happen in future and it is even not possible to predict that something will happen. And we can't sense it but we are right now in one of these periods of transformational frenzy. Why don't we recognize it? There are many reasons; like our minds are not prepared. We have special interests but to some extent this is also a matter of courage and courage to me is a spiritual quality. It really takes courage to think that there is going to be a major transformation. It's amazing that we don't want to contemplate it. I don't know how many of you who have gone to the USA have ever visited the Yellow Stone Park, which is the national park in California. That's famous because it's like a mystery land. You walk over it and these hot guiles or hot water fountains of different colors come up and it looks spectacular. And what most people don't understand though is that they think they are walking on ground and there are pools of hot water. They are actually walking on the top of an active volcano. There is an active volcano and that volcano has erupted approximately once in every 60 million years and erupted approximately 60 million years ago. And 200 million years ago when it erupted, it covered New York State on the other side of America with ten feet of ash. We always have to have the courage of contemplating and the ways we do it are our using metaphors. Because metaphors are our ability to take things we understand and reduce them to levels, but they are not analogies, they are just symbols.

We take something that has structure and that has qualities that we think we can attribute to something else though we know that something else may manifest those structures and qualities in a different fashion. And if we do that may be we begin to reduce the size that we can imagine and deal with some other problems we have. Now, in American English, it is very interesting, the metaphor of the seed very often is used as everything going through a seed. The city is seedy and therefore the metaphor is decay, everything is falling from the trees and everything seems to be decaying and just spreading itself on the ground in tiny little morsels or particles and it's a rejection and metaphor of death. The time has come to realize that we are disintegrating in certain elements that have held our societies together and we have to reject them. And what are those? There's competition everywhere. We now have to transform into a society where there is mutuality of existence, where each of us is a mutual reinforcement to the maximization of the other person's potential and not a competition against each other. We also have to realize that we are not living in a world of individuals and the greatest thing is that the seed is not a separate seed. It's one of thousands of seeds; its eventuality is to make a forest and a whole new ecology, a whole new environment. Similarly, we have to realize that the age of individualization has passed and we are disintegrating as individuals. What we also have to see is that in the age of matter where everything is materialistic, we have to understand that the materialistic is merely the packaging for the soul and the spirit. Most people actually see that we can no longer deal with the world as it is. Information comes too fast for our minds to process it. We diagnose children with syndromes, with attention specific syndromes. There is nothing wrong with their attentions, they just don't have time, the opportunity, and it's not their minds that are wrong, it's the circumstances. Nature can no longer heal herself. Nature engaged in the process of thousands of years of adaptation and in one day we can do to nature what in the past could have been done with one atomic bomb. What this has done to our system is that it has disintegrated it. So now a new system has to launch, one of re-integration. Now this is where the seed comes in. It is a powerful metaphor of reintegration because if you think of what a seed is, we realize that we have a gigantic tree which is a great metaphor of all spiritual religions. It condenses and consolidates into the seed all its potentials and it packages its seed and prepares it to be launched into a new journey, into a new environment. And it is in that new environment that the seed will again emerge but in ways that are different, that are adapted to that new environment even though it comes from a mother tree that came from another environment.

If we want to be seeds of that transformation, what do we have to do? Now whether we want to be seeds, I believe is a matter of our free will. And there is no other word for it other than the expression of our own spirituality. But what is it we have to do? First of all we have to be centres of attraction as the seed brings together all the elements of the tree; we have to begin to be centres of attraction. Not of rejection, not of differentiation. We have to act as agents of unity bringing together a fragrance just like how the little seed brings together all the elements of the tree from which it comes. We have to bring that together. And lastly we actually have to develop capacities so that those elements can then interact in a fashion of mutuality of assistance/existence so they work together. You know when we started as an organism, we started as a stem cell, we started as an undifferentiated cell and then we begin to differentiate, but don't differentiate in some chaotic manner. We should differentiate in way that harmonizes. The differences within us create a larger entity of consciousness. So those are the three initial things we have to do. We have to attract, we have to generate unity among the fragrance, and we have to establish our own capacities for actually working in mutuality.

Now how can we do that? What really has to be done? What is that great spiritual change? This happening is summarized below:

1. We need a new unity of consciousness. We have discussed all the amazing things about conscious levels that we can achieve as individuals. But the time I believe has come where we are entering a new consciousness as a species or even something beyond our species, just as each of us carries around more different organisms, then there are people working on the planet but we see and think of ourselves as one. We are in the processes of seeing an emergence of a new type of unity of conscience.

2. The second thing is the unity of conscience in diversity. It's not one thing; if you look along this time line every new transformation is more complex than the one before it. The earth is far more complex than the sun. The sun is far more complex than the gases. So as we go on the unity in diversity increases with the glory of new transformation.

3. And the third unity is unity in reflection. We need a unity where we really begin to exchange the mental and spiritual processes that we feel within ourselves and within each other. Not just share them but actually exchange and reflect them.

David Bohm working with the Krishnamurti foundation realized that we have to move from debate and discussion to dialogue because he saw in front of his own eyes two of his best friends Neils Bohr and Albert Einstein get to a point where they could not discuss anything, they wouldn't even talk to each other because they disagreed about theories of probability. So we have to go to dialogue and not just discussion.

The second thing we have to do is we have to get rid of the process of negotiation. The world is built on negotiation, from the market to diplomacy. We have to move through true processes of consultation where we forget my interests and your interests and we look at the problem that actually faces us. And we contribute to it whatever we can and whatever will come out is with a common understanding not one in which we distribute the benefits in a way that doesn't get anybody everything that they want and really doesn't solve the problem.

The third thing we really have to do is disengage ourselves from the reigning theories and disciplines we belong to that create boundaries in ideologies and that say "this is how I'm different from you"; these very factors will keep us from coming together. This can begin within our family. Today husbands, wives and children can really understand each other if they would be just create a capacity for dialogue. If we really want to learn how to consult with each other, we are going to have to work within our own institutions, our schools, our politics or economics, to break down the barriers that now actually are how we identify ourselves, economists don't really talk to the social scientists, they teach their own theories, their own paradigms, they put them together, they purposely create boundaries.

Lastly if we want to really bring ourselves together in action we are going to have to do it on matters of common purpose such as the climate change, the injustices in the world and peace. And the way we are going to have to begin is to realize that we are in a period of transformation. So anything that happened in the past doesn't matter. It may matter for history, it may matter for insight. But it doesn't matter who did the injustice. What matters is what we do today. Just make sure that the injustice does not continue. That's what matters today.

Last thing is, we have to understand that we can't do this as individuals. We're not just ships upon an ocean anymore. Just like the cells in our body, are an individual's, we are a part of the flotilla. And as a ship across an ocean needs a lighthouse to guide it or star to guide it. So we need that as a group. So we need to develop a unit of conscience. Not just consciousness. By conscience it is meant, a unity of core simple foundations that really are going to guide our unified efforts together, and recognize what they are. The only things that can make us do this are to realize the true power of love. Love is the only ultimate mode of action that can bring us together. The love of the mother who restlessly feeds a child, the child grows up and gives the mother trouble, and yet she loves the child and nurtures that child. That's the love we need to discover and reassert.

If we do that then only can we move forward. There is a quote on the power and the need for love by Pierre Teilhard de Chardin, a very famous catholic philosopher and a social scientist:

"The day will come when, after harnessing space, the winds, the tides, gravitation, we shall harness for God the energies of love. And, on that day, for the second time in the history of the world, man will have discovered fire."

Chapter 3

Brain, Self and Consciousness: Their Interrelations

SANGEETHA MENON
National Institute of Advanced Studies, Bangalore, India

Abstract

Brain is arguably the most important part of the human body studied to understand the working of sensation, emotion, and consciousness. The single unit of information and experience that connects sensation, emotion, and consciousness is agreed to be the "self". There are two major streams of discussion on the self. Self is debated as a cognitive concept that helps tie the missing ends between the physical and psychological functions; and, self is argued to be the locus of conscious experience. However different the arguments for these two positions are, it is agreed that human behaviors, attitudes and emotions are intricately tied to the neural structures on one side, and the indivisible experiential self on the other. Brain and self are the common threads that are used by neuropsychiatry, neuropharmacology, and philosophy to get some hold on one of the most intractable problems of humankind, namely, "consciousness."

Introduction

There are discussions primarily centered on three important ideas or concepts (Brain, self and consciousness) which we all are grappling with and perhaps the entire humanity is trying to figure out because it looks like these three central ideas define our existence in totality. Of course, the word consciousness has become very attractive and it has attracted everyone's mind, whichever discipline they follow and people are brought-in a kind of multidisciplinary approach to understanding this perhaps very enigmatic idea, we all know or we all may experience what consciousness is. But the moment we try to understand it, it stands at least a few centimeters away from us and perhaps that is what is making consciousness the most elusive idea that the more we try to understand it as a concept, as a person it leaves us behind. It's very important to understand or acknowledge the place of these three concepts, brain, self and consciousness as perhaps the three basic realities. The whole of human existence perhaps can be defined by these three and my attempt in this discussion is to present before you a couple of ideas which might interest you in seeing the inter-relations between these three concepts.

We all have a fair idea of what the brain is. It weighs three pounds and has about hundred billion neurons and each of these neurons have thousands of interconnections with other neurons and this basically makes the mechanisms behind all the experiences which we have. And apart from the very complex cortical areas and connections, the neurochemistry and electrical processes define the human experiences. A few speakers mentioned about another important function of the brain namely the neuroplasticity which makes the brain a very flexible organ. We talk about people in that way that oh he's a very flexible, open minded person in a sense that the brain is a very open minded organ. It welcomes ideas, forms new connections, ready to change, welcome new events in terms of forming new experiences. So when a part of the brain which governs a certain function gives way, another part of the brain comes in and forms a new connection. It's a continuously evolving and cooperative organ. Perhaps it is this very complex nature of the brain that gives rise to what is called as the binding problem which perhaps also defines the central enigma behind the concept of consciousness. Some two decades back which is called as the binding problem. The binding problem is basically the following. That how do the quantitative, discrete, physical neural processes and events give rise to experiences which is qualitative, unitary, subjective and very personal? It's very interesting to pause for a second and see the transition which is taking place here. How can a quantity become a quality? Or how can quantity generate quality. It's also interesting that in terms of conscious experience, it's no more the neural processes or events which become more interesting but subjective person, the experience behind every conscious experience, the person behind every conscious experience, the personal identity of that person, the emotional richness of the person, the qualities the person possesses.

So it's very interesting that from an intricate pattern of this discrete neural processing's a person emerges with a rich complexity in terms of very different kinds of qualities. This also gave rise to eternal question which of course by now is very famous, sorry for the repetition if some of you would be knowing it, this is called as "The Hard Problem and the Easy Problems" of David Chalmers, a mathematician turned philosopher. He said that how the quantitative discrete, the quantitative physical processes give rise to subjective qualitative subjective experience is a hard problem. Perhaps it cannot be explained. But then there are a set of other problems called the easy problems which perhaps can be answered. With the advancements in medical techniques, brain imaging techniques and so on because basically the easy problems will talk about the mechanisms behind the sensations and perceptions we have. But quite often what happens in fields like cognitive sciences and so on is to misquote a sensation or a perception or a process behind sensation and perception as that which constitutes consciousness. And in this kind of attempts a particular sensation is taken as a whole to explain the person in his or her entirety. Perhaps it is this attempt which has given rise to a set of questions for anyone who is interested in understanding consciousness. She be a philosopher, a medical scientist, a physicist, artist or a literature person, a poet, which is first is can we have a working definition of consciousness. Because one problem behind the understanding of the mystery behind consciousness is that we often get into a kind of homogeneity where everything can be explained as consciousness. It has become a word which includes everything and excludes nothing. It's very interesting as in terms of an inclusive term but also if we follow certain patterns of science and scientific methodology we have to perhaps apply a simple law of parsimony which is kind of using a fewer terms and explain consciousness. This is a valid method but at least it gives some clarity as to what perhaps each one of us mean by consciousness.

So, the first question in terms of understanding consciousness would be to have a working definition. What do we mean by consciousness, whichever discipline it is, perhaps we can list the terms which we use in understanding this very complex concept? The other is where is consciousness? It looks like, it's pretty clear for most of us, it's just a matter of touching it, it's somewhere near, but the moment we try to touch it, it leaves us and it makes itself; therefore more attractive.

Where is consciousness, this again is a question which interests many scholars working in this area and there are very interesting concepts in terms of neurobiology for example one very popular is to identify neural correlate of consciousness which is basically to address the functions of consciousness as situated in certain cortical areas. This of course has given rise to various problems at least in terms of understanding the neuroplastic nature of consciousness. So it looks like, even a simple function which we have in our day to day life is governed by not one central area of the brain but many areas of the brain and they have a cooperative behavior.

The third question is when does consciousness happen? Is there a point in the evolutionary scale of our origin that consciousness happens? Can we have a chart where we can say that from a rudimentary sense of awareness to more complex levels of cognition to further metacognitive levels such as introspection and reflection and so on? So when does consciousness happen? Can we chart a scale? This will be another important question we should address in order to see the inter-relationship between brain, self and consciousness.

The fourth question which is raised by neurophilosophers who are heavily influenced by evolutionary biologists that why do we need a concept of consciousness. This is not my question. It's a question of some of the critiques. It's an interesting question. But the question perhaps undermines the complex nature of subjective character of consciousness. Why do we need the concept of consciousness? Perhaps the semantic structure of the linguistics behind the language which we use, the structures which we form in everyday life can explain many things and perhaps we don't need a grand theory of consciousness. This is one important question many neurophilosophers are engaged in their answers, responses, critiques.

The most important question comes in the fifth place and, this question comes after the four questions - What is consciousness? Can we have a working definition? Where is consciousness? Can we give a place to that so that we know where exactly to find it? Whether it is the spirit or mind or some of the cortical areas? Can we have a somewhat rough idea when did it happen or where did or when did consciousness happen and the fourth is why do we need a concept of consciousness? What do we mean by a concept of consciousness? These four questions give a lead to perhaps the fifth important question about consciousness; who is asking about it? Who is asking about the problem of consciousness? Because often like many other scientific problems, we think consciousness is also an object which can be placed over the table and say look here, here it is. So there's this interesting expression in the brain in the back. The most important question which again makes the consciousness tantalizing subject is - who is asking about it. And that is why there is a need of a personal engagement in understanding consciousness. We may get approximate answers about the rest of the questions of what, where, why and when. But to get into the secret planes and the real taste of consciousness, it's important for any researcher to ask the fifth question, who is asking about it? Who is framing the general framework in order to understand the consciousness? And by asking that question the investigator places her or him as component of the problem of consciousness. That is why perhaps the end of the day the search for consciousness becomes something which is very intimate, something which is very personal and the questions are influenced by our own reflection and ability to redefine those questions.

It may be reiterated that the central problem in consciousness studies is a problem of personal identity. How do we understand the identity with which we carry and which we share, with our neighbors and others who come across and the rest of the universe. The question is about who is asking about consciousness or who is interested about the question of consciousness brings the most important concept in which underlies the problem of consciousness which is self. In fact it is very difficult to address the problem of consciousness without the concept of self and that times have gone when psychologists and perhaps others influenced by psychology of fright have stopped asking questions related to ego. There are no more questions related to ego when it comes to consciousness. And the medical literature has redefined these questions, today the questions are no more about ego. Today questions are about self and personal identity. How do we understand self? Perhaps that is the reason William James has become an important figure for us to go back and look at his ideas. His own definition of self is very interesting and has a sense of humor behind it. The concept of self also comes across to us between other ideas which are subtle in nature. It needs a lot of attention for us to understand. One is the experience or the content of any experience whether it is perception or whether it is hearing or whether it is seeing or tasting or touching or a complex sense of experience which involves all these or whether in terms of memories, in terms of love, compassion, jealousies and insecurities so on and so forth, there is a content for the experience. Which you can objectify, identify and perhaps to a great extent keep it on the table and sell it, here is my content of experience. But then there is something else which will not allow us to reduce. And we all are bothered about reductive methods. The more we try to reduce the self, the more we see that the subtle core of the experience, which will not admit us to reduce because the more we reduce, the more we see it. The more we try to reduce the experience in more magnanimity it comes. Any amount of reduction takes us to yet another phase of the experience.

These are the two ideas which are interesting philosophies, eastern and western from time immemorial. That we are able to understand what could be called as the content of experience and one who is studying the content of experience or watching the content of experience. There is a quote which is a very beautiful verse from "Drig Drsya Vivekam" Roopam drishyam locanam drik. It gives you series of seer, seen gradations that anything which you see there is a seer and it looks like that particular framework is persistent in all our experiences. And the only way perhaps to see the seer alone is to have perhaps more and more inclusive methods of not just understanding including many things in our experience. And this is also important for us to see the idea of experience in a larger framework. When we talk about experience in general we talk about experience in the waking stage; just the normal experiences which we all have. But what is the range of our experiences? The range of our experiences is not limited to this very formal gathering or the very formal space defined by this hall. We move from public to private spaces in our everyday life. And we have perhaps which is commonly excepted and regarded as public which is the day to day life experiences defined by basic emotions of love, jealousy, happiness, pleasure, pain, fear, anger and memories. In fact the role of the memories in defining experience is something which is very fascinating to investigate because the moment we narrate an experience the experience is not a pure experience. It gets influenced by the baggage of memory which is sitting all around us. The moment we try to understand an experience in that moment something else comes from the previous moment or the memory influences something else which is yet to come from the future. The role of memory in understanding human experience extremely important because though we tend to take the default experience as the present moment, even the present moment is very much influenced by the memories we all carry. They cover our own personal private memories. And of course added to it are the archetypal memories which you mentor, our own traditions talk about. The other set of experience is the odd experiences which could be called as the odd experiences. These are generally limited to psychological and neurological experiences of different kind.

The odd experiences and the inexplicable experiences which largely constituted by the experiences talked about by the neuropsychiatrists and neuropsychiatric literature which is very interesting to read about, which tells us that how the boundary of self is shifting. The third set of inexplicable experiences which are constituted by larger spaces and traditions of religion, aesthetic traditions, mystic and meditative experiences. So we have a set of day to day experiences which is kind of qualified by the public space, the odd experiences which is largely defined by the neuropsychiatric literature, and inexplicable experiences which all of us would have at some point in our life. So the concept of experience itself is so complex that we have to understand in a general framework, which alone could give us perhaps some idea of its relation with the brain and self in large. The basic framework one would keep in mind to understand the intricate nature of consciousness is to have some idea of the brain because it is not something which can give up or give way. And the second is experience because experience gives us the mystery of moving from something which is completely physical to something which is subjective. The third one is very central to all of us is the concept of Being. Because that indicates to us the core in each of our experience and gives us a first person intimacy in which lies the truth, beauty and goodness of idea of consciousness.

Chapter 4

Meditation, Ethics and Contemplation Science

JACQUES VIGNE
Paris, France and Haridwar, India

Abstract

The present theoretic-experimental paper on meditation, ethics and contemplative science is based on the last 30 years of my work in the field of psychiatry and as a Sadhaka of spirituality in India. Perhaps there is no great discrepancy between science and spirituality. An attempt has been made to explain, through practical areas of research in the meditative practices, the spiritual expressions of the Dalai Lama, other Saints of India and the philosophers of the west. In search of universal ethics, it has been attempted to explain three universal ethics - individualism, perfectionism and rationalism. An effort has also been made to explain that compassion and empathy is a solid basis for ethics although there maybe some critics questioning this. This paper also highlights how positive emotions can lead to good mental health.

Towards a Contemplative Science

In my experience of first being a student of mathematics and physics, then a medical student, and later a psychiatrist, followed by 25 years as a researcher and sadhaka in India, I never felt any major discrepancy between science and spirituality. Each was right in its own right. However, being originally from a Catholic milieu, I could see around me that finding a harmonization between the two fields could be a heavy trial and headache, for quite a few believers. I could as well observe that believers had endless questions about how to reconcile creation as presented in Biblical mythology and the hard data of modern sciences. Not only in this area, but also procreation and reproductive health, they painfully realized that the realm of God as defined by them beforehand was shrinking by the day. For instance, it was the role of God before to give children, now; there are all kinds of the scientific techniques in order not to have them or on the contrary, to activate the process of having them.

Especially in the field of neurosciences and psychology, subjectivity is much less taboo than before. It has been due to the collaboration of open-minded scientists, meditators as well as spiritual teachers. At first, there was the publication of collected research papers by the movement of Transcendental Meditation headed by the late Mahesh Yogi and from 1985 onwards, we have benefited from the dialogues between the Dalai Lama with scientists, under the aegis of the Mind and Life Institute. The Dalai Lama himself has been invited to preside over a conference in Washington where thousands of neuroscientists had gathered. It was a landmark conference in the dialogue between contemplative traditions and modern science. From this entire movement the notion of contemplative science emerges, where the term ' subjectivity' is not taboo anymore. Robert Walsh, physicist by training and then student of Tibetan Buddhism and able translator of the Dalai Lama, wrote a book in 2001 on the subject of removing this taboo of subjectivity. The Dalai Lama himself underlines that the best field of collaboration between spirituality and science is the domain of psychology. I don't claim this because I am a psychiatrist! On the contrary, I chose the domain of psychiatry 30 years ago because I was interested in consciousness as well as the practice of meditation and I definitely wanted to create a bridge between psychology and religions and spiritual teachings.

It is interesting to observe the Dalai Lama, during his dialogues with scientists; first and foremost he presents the four Noble Truths as a law of psychology: the central question is alleviating suffering. The spiritual chief of the Tibetans went beyond simple dialogues, he helped to find the subjects to be studied, like Tibetan Yogis, who were brought to western laboratories, and then they tried to evaluate, with modern measurement, the characteristics of different states of attention as described and practiced in the Tibetan tradition.

For meditators, the question of energy of the subtle body is at the forefront. In this sense, there are direct links with the notion of kundalinî in Yoga and the channels of acupuncture and reflex therapy. With this kind of meditative introspection, one clearly improves the direct knowledge of the link between body sensations and basic mental activity. All types of meditation develop this awareness, but it may be expressed more or less clearly and explicitly depending upon the traditions.

Actually, every branch of science has its preferred instruments - the telescope for astronomy, and the microscope for biology. If you invert them and take a microscope to look at the planets, you will go nowhere. In the same vein, the inner world of subjectivity has also its preferred instrument, meditation. First, the instrument should be calibrated and the researchers should learn how to use it. Here lies the main difference between the Western and traditional Eastern approach. Even great Western psychologists did not have the knowledge, and did not take the time to fine-tune any practice of concentration and meditation. That is why they had great difficulty to see or even conceive the subtle realities of the mind. They could not even reason over these parts of reality, because they merely could not see them without the so called microscope required for perception. Meditation is thus the best instrument for the exploration of consciousness, a genuine "cerebroscope".

Here, we come to the question of evidences: for the hard sciences - they lie in biochemistry and brain electricity or imagery. For meditators, they reside in the perception of the current of sensations (skt nâdîs, tib tsa), of the *chakras*, and the absorption in some archetypical visualizations. However, there have been already some bridges which have been established: I think the book of Hiroshi Motoyama: Theories of the *Chakras* - Bridge to Higher Consciousness. Brain imaging represents the recent revolution in neurosciences: at last, it was becoming possible to observe the brain and its process of thinking "live".

The relationship between spirituality and science has expanded and become a wide subject. We should mention for instance Ken Wilber, who has done substantial work in this area. He was first inspired by Shri Aurobindo and his ideal to embody spirituality in the world and combining it with new ideas of evolution. From that base, he worked a lot by himself, and now he has written quite a few books, in addition to what is found on the Internet.

From the Buddhist side also, a lot of publications appeared. The Dalai Lama, although now 75, continues conscientiously to participate in the meetings of the Mind and Life Institutes. He explains clearly that the aim of these meetings of Buddhism and science is not to convert people to this persuasion, but to serve humankind, so that people could become better persons. Meditation is a common heritage of humanity. Nobody can claim his copyright on it. Let it be used as widely as possible for the betterment of the mind. It is the need of the hour, and actually it is an eternal need. For this work, there are of course hurdles and obstacles to pass. However, the success will depend on our quality of vision. To quote Etty Hillesun, a young Belgian mystique who died in the Nazi concentration camps, but did not manifest hatred against anyone: "The great obstacle lies always in the representation, not in reality."

In Search of a Universal Ethics

Out of five people in the world at present, only one or two are religious. In France, only 22 per cent of people still believe in a personal God, and moreover, the survey from which I quote this data was conducted seven or eight years ago, this proportion has probably decreased by now. An important subject of discussion in France and Europe is the theory and practice of a lay spirituality - it means in this context, without any personal God and Church. Even French Christians are deeply and collectively shaken, and their last national convention a few months ago had as a title: "Do we still need God?" Here is a hot debate!

One can see three poles from which to find universal ethics:

- Individualism: Is defined as everything that promotes the development of the individual. This theory is clearly tempting, even alluring for modern Western minds, which value this kind of development.
- Perfectionism: the human being is called to perfection, he strives for it, and this very striving will render him fully ethical: That is the viewpoint of the religious and spiritual traditions.
- Rationalism: Logic is only enough to show us that human beings are equal, and so, human rights must be clearly defined so that they could be applied practically by way of politics and social work.

A famous French thinker, Edgar Morin, who passed away recently, had published, maybe 15 years ago, one of his last books called Ethics, where he does not speak at all of Christianity or of any personal God. Actually, modernity is fed up with the sectarian view of ethics in some form of religions. In these religious forms, everything which can help to disseminate the creed is considered good, and everything or everyone which impedes this development is considered bad, even satanic. The French Revolution has been a deep-felt reaction against this kind of half-ethics which boils down to no ethics at all. When speaking of monotheism, it is very interesting to note that its expansion has been based on iconoclasm, i.e., destroying the Gods of others religions and countries which were globally labeled 'idols'. Now, modernity takes this iconoclasm to its logical conclusion, and destroys the ultimate idol which is the concept of a unique and almighty God. It somewhat finishes the job. It could be seen as the return of a violent karma or a kind of boomerang effect, which is quite logical and understandable.

When we keep in mind this historical context, the approach of Buddhism and Jainism based not on belief, but on ethics directly, sound more modern, healthy and viable for the future of humanity.

In this sense, let me tell what I heard of a friend of mine, who is a doctor in France but from Iranian origin. A few months ago, she lost her father. He had been an intellectual and liberal, and had assumed the direction of an important educational Institute in Teheran before the Islamic revolution. When his last hour came, while his emotional wife was invoking the Prophet as she had been conditioned to do from childhood, he had the name of Zoroaster and Buddha on his lips. I see in that anecdote a symbol of our time. To speak of another Iranian intellectual, Daryush Shayegan, who is a professor of philosophy - who wrote a book entitled Light comes from the Occident. In it, he acknowledges that the Century of Lights, the European 18th-century had been indispensable to our modernity, but he concludes his last chapter by saying that for founding a universal ethics, Buddhism was the fittest candidate. This converges with the opinion of Vivekananda, who, even being an adept of Hinduism, acknowledged that "Buddhism was the only rational religion".

A contemporary French critic of religions and free thinker, Regis Debray, drew an interesting parallel between religion and technology: religions, according to him, like cultures, represent dividing factors, creating competitions, quarrels and eventually wars. Technologies, on the contrary, are unifying factors, because they can spread quickly the world over and work in the same way from one side to the other of the planet, whatever the beliefs of people may be. However, we could argue to the contrary that there is a common foundation in all religions, for instance the process of devotion, which works in about the same way in every tradition. The meditative techniques also may work in the same manner, all that is needed to recognize it is some translation of notions from one path to another.

Compassion and empathy, seems to give a solid basis for ethics, although there may be some critics and caveat – they might claim:

- Compassion may be just sentimental and elicited more by pity or a superiority complex than out of real empathy for the other.
- If compassion is connected with religion, then, it cannot be universal.
- Compassion is too personal; the need of the hour is a general principle which could be applied equally for the masses all over the world.

Whatever these critics may say, compassion could be a good basis for large-scale action. Call it empathy, altruism or whatever you want, but something of this kind must be there if you want humanity to develop well, and even if you want it to survive. The Golden Rule enunciated by the Jewish sage Hillel in the first century before the Common Era is as valid today as before: "Do not do to anyone else what you would not want to be done to you".

Individualism must also be questioned: it is also a kind of new religious belief to imagine that the individual has unlimited rights. It became fashionable a few years ago to celebrate the anniversary of the Declaration of the Human Rights, which took place at the beginning of the French Revolution. But most people forget that eight or nine years later, during the Directory, after the dark phase of Terror where 50.000 people were killed, the French had been sobered in their revolutionary zeal, and wrote a Declaration of Human Duties. Very few people have observed the anniversary of this Declaration... Could it be the effect of the banal ego, forever more prompt to assert its rights than to acknowledge its duty?

In this discussion about ethics, the Dalai Lama has an interesting argument, as a Buddhist, on a universal ethics based on God: "What about animals, especially social animals? (Like primates or dolphins) They have a limited form of altruism and it also seems they have a very good sense of responsibility to the common good, but without any religion!" When some animal species could have the beginnings of basic ethics without any God, why not the humanity as a whole?

The development of a spiritual psychology in the biblical religions has been overshadowed and thwarted by a bigoted idea of devotion. If someone was trying to understand the mind directly, as did the Buddhist and as is doing modern psychology, he was suspected not to have faith in the almighty action of God, and he was put aside, if not burned alive. This kind of bigoted obscurantism has been sadly effective to impede the development of an objective psychology for more than a millennium in the West.

Even modern psychotherapy has its own weaknesses, the instrument for introspection is not as fine tuned as it should be, and for instance the notion of concentration and of the spiritual teacher is very hazy for most of the psychotherapists. True, there is an increase in self-knowledge, they are definitely a lot of publications on psychology, be they popular or academic, but not much increase in self-control is observed. There is some related humor in this sense: Someone comes in a nightclub, goes to the bar and orders a beer. The waiter serves it, and the visitor takes up the glass, looks at it, turns it upside down and goes away without adding a word. Rather dismayed, the waiter calls him while he is walking out: "You are crazy; you'd better go to a psychiatrist!" One month later, the same visitor turns up again, and reenacts the exact same scenario. The waiter had of course recognized the strange fellow and asked him: "Did you not to go to the shrink, as I had told you?" The man replied: "Yes, actually I did!" The waiter said "So, I can see there were definitely no results!" to which the man replied "Yes, there were"! Before, I had this behavior, but I felt very guilty, now, I still have it, but I don't feel guilty anymore!"

A sound basis for ethics is what goes into one's own happiness and others' happiness, in parallel if one can say. There are now 8000 researchers working in the world on the psychology of happiness, it makes an important difference with the last generation where almost all the psychologists were focused on pathologies and depression. Matthieu Ricard was a French young scientist, doing his Ph.D in biology with François Jacob and later received a Nobel Prize. After this, he became a monk in the Tibetan tradition, and is now a well-known writer on Buddhism and the West, as well as the translator of the teachings of the Dalai Lama into French. In a meeting with him in Kathmandu, we conversed on different topics. He has written among other things, a famous book, Plaidoyer pour le bonheur, a title which could be rendered as A case for happiness. It has been translated into many languages. It draws its sources from Buddhism as well as from Western moral literature, modern psychology and daily life. In it, he quotes a clear example leading us to think about what happiness really is. He was with a friend of his in Hong Kong. One day, the latter told him that he wanted to earn one million dollars in 10 years, and then to stop, to do nothing and be happy. After 10 years, he met him again, he had not accumulated one million, but three, and Matthieu asked him whether he was happy. He answered: "No, I feel I have wasted 10 years of my life!" To quote from the same book, Matthieu Ricard reminds us of Shantideva, a Mahayana sage of the 8th century in India who wrote about the ideal of compression and equanimity. He says for instance in a logical way: "If there is a remedy, there is no reason for discontent, and if there is no remedy, neither there is any reason nor discontent..."

Positive Emotions as a Basis for Good Health and Universal Ethics

The main impression of psychologists who are open to a holistic view of the human being is that positive emotions are good for oneself and leads to long-term health, as well as the good health of others; so, they are thus able to provide us with a solid basis for universal ethics. Daniel Goleman, a well-known American specialist of emotions, has developed the idea of emotional intelligence. He is also interested in Buddhist meditation and he speaks of the of the body dharma and the right laws of the body. Bodhidharma was also the Indian monk who introduced Buddhism into China in the fifth century. These newly-discovered laws of the interactions of the mind and the body by different channels are now gathered in a new science, which took shape from the 80s, the psycho-neuro-immuno-endocrinology.

Let us start by giving a series of example on how emotions directly affect health. A study by William Redford of Duke University on 2000 workers is significant in this sense. They were evaluated for their feelings of hostility and were examined again after 25 years to see their general health and death rate. 20 per cent of the ones with a low level of hostility had died, while 30 per cent of the ones with a high level of hostility had died from different causes, including accidents. This means that a high-level of hostility increased the risk of death of 50 % after a quarter of a century. The same author has done the same kind of study with other groups, and sometimes, he has found an increase much larger, up to 500%.

If the subject has already had a heart attack and is subject to fits of anger, he is two or three time more prone to death after 10 years than the other group of people who had the same basic heart problem but no fits of anger.

There are lots of evidences that depression disturbs the recovery of serious diseases, like heart attacks, breast cancers, or hip fractures among the elderly. Friedman, of the University of California at Irvine, made a Meta study of a hundred studies on emotions and health. His conclusion is that negative emotions double the risk of serious diseases. Even the simple fact of repressing one's own emotions increases notably the risk of asthma, hypertension, colds, and relapses of breast cancer.

From the aspect of immunity, one observed a regular relation between the augmentation of a T-cell and the augmentation of the time of practice of meditation. T-cells are important links in the proper working of the immune system.

Pessimists are dismayed in the case of failure, while optimists are more flexible, they understand that everything changes, and they know how to wait for better periods of time. Besides, the feeling that we have control over our life helps us to be optimistic, and even to live longer. For instance, in an elderly home, if one again gives some control to a group of members, they halve their death rate after one year. In the same sense, social support helps a lot: it increases the number of cancer killer-cells in women with breast cancer by 30 per cent, it means the ability to fight the disease and the same social support decreases the death rate by 50 percent after 10 years.

An interesting study links solitude and stress: a monkey, alone in its cage, is submitted to flash lights and loud banging sounds, and so, it experiences a lot of stress. If there are two, the stress is divided by two, and if they are five monkeys in the cage, there are no signs of stress at all. This experiment should be taken with a grain of salt: there are many cases where people gather and party to escape and mask stress because they merely don't want to see impending danger. The result may be that they fail to organize their defenses, and finally, they are destroyed. So stress may have some utility.

In an important study, the sense of joy has been shown to be the single most important factor for survival from breast cancer. As for laughter and the watching of comic films, it increases the T-cells and diminishes the cortical, which is directly linked to stress. We can suppose that a meditator who is able to develop humor in a relationship with oneself and who can look to one's own mind as a comic film will benefit by a higher immnunity level. These kinds of studies could point out mechanisms on how meditation helps to reduce the incidence of cancer or the incidence of relapses after a first treatment.

To conclude, we can open the perspective and enlarge the debate: there is a major advantage in separating ethics and the concept of God: it helps people to feel responsible, and they don't need to be submissive to a powerful entity to live happy and healthy. Many in modern society will see that as the sign of maturity, and at least the Buddhists or Jains will not be shocked by this approach as it is what they have adopted from the beginning.

The immune system is now looked upon as a second brain, Lymphocytes are like traveling neurons, they are linked not by synapses, but by binding proteins which help to recognize each other. Nerves are effective because they are connected at the end to muscles, in the same way, the immune system is effective because at the end of the chain, there is a group of B-cells which can act directly by liberating antibodies which will smear the bacteria and finally destroy them. In the same way as the brain develops a feeling of identity, the immune system has very accurate individuality, hence the rejection of the transplants at times.

The time has come to clarify a simple question in psychotherapy: should one advice a subject to assert his ego, or to reduce it? We should distinguish according to the level of the person. Some people are very inhibited, for instance because of having been crushed by their parents during their childhood. For them, a certain dose of ego assertion would be good. They have a tamasic ego; going to the upper level in the form of the rajasic ego will be helpful for them.

But beyond that, there is the sattvic ego which becomes more and more tenuous and transparent, finally becoming only a very clean veil enveloping the central light of the Self.

To finish this discussion on emotions, let us tell a story to illustrate how our negative emotions are able to create their own reality: 'A man had a puncture in his car tire in an isolated place at sunset. He realized he had forgotten his screw jack. He saw an isolated house at some distance, and walked towards it. On the way, he was brooding over the situation in a negative manner: "Maybe the man there will be afraid to see me knocking at his door while darkness is falling and he may be an egotistical man wondering if I will never give him back his jack. Perhaps he will be angry with me because I disturbed him. Finally, he knocked at the door, and as soon as a gentleman opened, our anxious driver shouted to his face directly: "You, damned egoist, keep your jack; I will manage without it, and go to hell! He turned around and went back empty handed towards his car.

The Emotional Aspects of the Right and Left Hemispheres

To put it in a nutshell, there is a centre in the frontal left cortex which is connected to positive emotions. The symmetrical centre in the right is connected to anxiety. The specialization of hemispheres is a very old affair: paleontologists have found crab shells dating back several hundred millions of years. They accurately examined the marks on the claws of the crabs and could conclude that these crabs where 'right-handed' or, one should say, 'right-clawed'.

In meditation, it is traditionally advised to hear the nâda through the right ear, or to also concentrate on the right eye. Râmana Maharshi used to advice (in the practice of Yoga), the absorption of attention into the right side of the thorax, as a support to the meditation of the Self. Really, there is a direct connection between the right side of the trunk and the left hemisphere, hence the positive effect. As for the eye and the ear, anatomically, the cranial pairs of nerves do not cross the middle plan of the head, except for the optical nerves. However, it seems that the habit of the body image anyhow associates strongly the right side of the face and of the head to the right side of the body in general, and this association is strong enough to be able to 'overwrite' the influence of the cranial innervations.

There is an interesting neonatal reflex: when a newborn baby hears a sound on the side, not only does he turn his head on that side, but he has a contraction of the corresponding arm and leg on the same side of the body. Then, by hearing the sound of silence through the right ear, even an adult in deep meditation, will have probably the beginning of a reflex reaction in the shape of an awakening and stimulation of the right side of the body below the head.

To summarize the difference between right and left hemisphere, we could say that the right hemisphere represents the 'quick withdrawal', and the left is the 'detailed approach'. This approach is also linked to tenderness, and the coming close of a mother to her infant. This closeness brings a smile to the babies face with the stimulation of the periorbicular muscle below and on the side of the eyes (which produces what is sometimes called 'the crowfeet'). The smile made only with the corner of the lips is a social smile, which babies produce for strangers. The same difference between a social smile and a sincere one also exists among adults. This opposition between detailed approach and quick withdrawal is a convenient way to order emotional reactions in a unique spectrum. Thus, researchers can classify them in a continuous way. The other classification is not continuous but discrete and is based on the usual basic emotions, happiness, sadness, fear, surprise, disgust and anger.

We could mention an interesting experiment about the method of listening to sounds through the right side. The context seems not to be very spiritual, but we will make the link with meditation in the end. The study was about audition and emotions. Psychologists went to meet people in a noisy nightclub, and asked them for cigarettes. When they were on the side of the right hear of the subjects, not only could they hear the demand more easily, but had the tendency to respond to it positively more often. Could we not say that the nâda is the call, the demand of the Absolute, and that we have better luck trying to answer it positively?

As for the Tibetans, they don't really have a term for emotions; they speak of sensations, feelings, sentiments, and afflictions, klesha-s in Sanskrit. This includes some emotions like anger, but also ignorance, skepticism, and erroneous conceptions. Actually, they put a lot of cognitive factors into the group of afflictions. This is logical, because people are not bad in themselves, but they simply, out of ignorance, do not know how to deal with their inner world.

One way of meditating on emotions is to use antidotes: it is possible to have a quick succession of love or hatred, but it is not possible to have these two contradictory emotions at the same time. The French philosopher Alain, from the past century, said: "One movement excludes the other. If you extend a friendly hand, this excludes using a punch".

The Work of Pr Kabat-Zinn on Meditation in the Hospital

Pr Kabat-Zinn is the Head of the Department of Medicine in the University of Massachusetts Medical Centre. It is a large hospital with 400 beds and thousands of outdoor patients. He developed a method of meditation for patients which is now taught in 200 other hospitals in the States. Already in 1991, he presented his work to the Dalai Lama in Dharmashala during a meeting of the Mind and Life Institute. In fact, what he taught to people was a classical course of vipassana meditation, but he changed the appellation to replace it by the usual behaviorist vocabulary, with terms like mind body stress reaction and so on. He spread the course over eight weeks, so that it could be done on an outdoor basis, with two and a half hours every weekend, and one day of retreat after the first week - of eight hours in silence, with only the help of teachers. Moreover, the patients were asked to sit 45 minutes every day, and they were warned that it is stressful to stay such a long time without doing anything... Kabat-Zinn adds with a pinch of humor that it is almost anti-American to make this exacting demand on normal citizens! What is remarkable is that 86% of people who started the course went to the end of it. This is an excellent result in comparison with the usual medical treatments, where only 25 per cent of people actually complete the required cure. This is still more interesting, because the people were under-average Americans; it means they had serious diseases, which are frequently connected to disturbing emotions and gross errors in lifestyle. What is also interesting is that after four years, 45% of people continued to sit at least 15 minutes three times a week and globally follow the course prescriptions about the need of awareness in daily life. This was without any outer reinforcement or reminder.

About the medical results, it has been observed a 25% reduction of medical symptoms, and a 35% decrease of psychological complaints about anxiety, depression etc. More important, even in this short a course, there has been a real personality change: this has been examined by different tests, for instance a 7% increase in the capacity to cope with stress. According to the specialists of personality, a global augmentation of 7% on a full group is really significant.

As for the methods, Kabat-Zinn remained quite classical. He had himself followed a teaching of Vipassana in Burma. He prescribes also hatha-yoga for the body, and lying down for the meditative practice. The American professor apologized when he explained this to the Dalai Lama, but said that if he asked his American patients right away, to start the lotus pose, he would not have any client for the next session... They do a lot of breath observation, a little bit of choice less awareness meditation at the end of meditation, fully knowing that it is the most difficult meditation process because it is the most simple. In between, they mostly take the support of body scanning. The main problem is not being aware whether people are stressed or not, most of them are, but they do not know it. This body scanning is first a way to clearly identify that yes, there is a problem.

In this sense, there is an interesting test in experimental psychology: people who are known to be anxious were asked to look a complex image, with one part of it showing disturbing contents. At the same time, the movements of eyes were recorded, especially by monitoring the direction of acute vision. It has been observed that they did not even look at the disturbing area of the image, and when they were asked to comment on the picture, it seemed like they had not even seen that part. Actually, what probably happened is that they did actually see the disturbing part with their peripheral vision; it elicited some more anxiety in them which they were not able to cope with, and so they just shunned it. This mode of functioning is probably equally valid for the inner view of the body and sensations, the tendency being to shun disturbing areas of the body. Hence the usefulness of full body scanning, which remedies this kind of suppression, and also the importance of starting by observing the breath, in order to calm the mind, reduce anxiety and then be able to see more clearly what is going on inside the body and mind. Usually, especially in modern life, people have the habit of always being busy with something. The motto is "Keep on going". Going through the different parts of the body allows a gentle transition between outer busyness or activism on one hand, and inner quiescence on the other.

Body scanning should be made with a main instruction: "do not let the sensations spread in other parts of the body, remain focused on one part only where you accept any arising sensations". Usually, sensations in a part of the body have the tendency to spread, for instance if we have the beginning of anger, we will clench the fist, then increase the tension in the jaws, and then there will be tension in the belly and in the sole of the feet, and at last a small series of locations will be tense and the full emotion of anger will be there, well rooted in different parts of the body and it will be very difficult to get rid of. So, it is more effective to stop the process, if one may say, in the egg. It means to limit it at the level of local sensation. Indeed, the chain of sensations evolves into an emotion and finally binds, while, conversely, breaking the chain right away liberates it. Disturbing emotions are like a cobra which stands to bite. If you cut the snake into slices, it won't be able to stand or bite. Another image could be that of epilepsy. The fits and convulsions are due to an excess of synchronization either in parts of a hemisphere, or in all of it, or in both. In the later case, we have general epilepsy, with the loss of consciousness and usually a loss of motor capacity too, i.e., fall and convulsions. We could consider emotions as a kind of specialized epilepsy, which over synchronizes a series of parts of the body and obscures the clarity of mind. For instance, a fit of anger is really like an absence and a coming out of the normal and healthy mind for some time. In this sense, people may have difficulty to remember what they have said or done. On the contrary, by 'de-synchronizing' the sensations coming from each part of the body, we will effectively prevent these 'para-epileptic attacks', Of course, most of the time during normal days, we are not agitated by over consuming emotions, but still, we are somehow chronically poisoned by minor forms of them, for instance small irritations against nears and supposedly dears who always repeat the same mistakes and have not changed an inch for the past several years, etc.

What is a remarkable also in these meditation practices for serious patients is that even people who could not gain a sizeable reduction of pain were pursuing their sessions three years after. They explained that it enabled them to cope better with the unchanging pain. In general, when people are asked what did they find in this meditation training, they insist on increased awareness, and their realization of the fundamental truth: "I am not my thoughts, and hence not my suffering."

Actually, 'medicine' and 'meditation' come from the same Latin root, which means not only to cure and to care, but also to measure. Meditation indeed is that: moderation, measure in the appreciation of oneself and of the situations, re-establishing a just proportion between oneself and the others, and also between the different parts of oneself, like sensations, feelings, reason, instincts, ideals, etc.

Here is a good piece of advice about relaxation and meditation too: "Be so relaxed that even if you see tensions that you cannot relax for the time being, you accept it in a relaxed way..." Even people with medical problems, like cancer, said they could benefit from this meditation training. There were instructed in a very simple way: "Care for what is right with you, the doctor will care for what is wrong" The aim of the method was not to erase the problem completely, but learn how to accept it and accept globally things as they are. Finally, this new approach for modern medicine tends to underline a shift between curing and healing, between just taking a magic pill and caring for the whole of the body-mind-soul complex.

For Indian doctors and therapists, this model of Kabatt-Zinn should be a case for deep thinking, a challenge of sorts. These practices of meditation came from the Buddha, hence from Indian tradition. They are now taught in 200 American hospitals, but what about Indian health centers? Certainly, there are some attempts here and there, but there should be much more happening. If not, it will be like Indian herbs which are used since millennia in ayurvedic medicine, but which have suddenly been patented in America by a new dynamic company... Sleepy Indians will be left behind!

All these observations and research on the link between positive emotions and good health, hence longer life, help to better identify the link between medicine and meditation, in fact, it somehow comes back to Taoism, which was not as much metaphysical as Indian thought, and not obsessed by martyrdom for the glory of the one God as in the Bible and in the religions which derived from it. In Taoism, the aim is a good, happy and long spiritual life. They have developed holistic methods for that, including alchemy which was connected with medicine at that time, and also techniques of meditation. Perhaps there is something to learn from them.

Seeing the experimental proofs that positive emotions provide good health and long life is good news for the three quarters of humanity who are non-religious people looking for a solid basis to found their ethics. To go one step further and be a little provocative, we could add that it is good news also for people who are supposed to believe in a God but are not quite sure that he exists. In that case, they will at least have the solace that the endeavor they made to develop positive emotions will be good, even if they were ultimately mistaken about their metaphysical conceptions.

Many people, although apparently integrated in a social network, feel lonely inside and suffer from it. A western psychiatrist, Howard Cutler, wrote three books with the Dalai Lama, starting by The Art of Happiness. He asked him once whether sometimes he felt lonely. He was almost sure that he would answer 'yes', because he knew him for the past 30 years, and he had observed that he was very sincere about his own feelings. Surprisingly, the Dalai Lama replied: "Never!" He then explained that the feeling of solitude comes from the lack of active compression. Although he is very busy as head of State in exile and spiritual leader, he tries to connect with people, and even when the first trial is a failure, he still tries again by other ways and at other levels. Often people feel that it is the duty of others to make the first step, and not the reverse. If the other is also thinking in the same line, life reduces itself to a juxtaposition of small spheres of solitudes, and becomes actually rather grey and dull. To continue with the Dalai Lama, he says very clearly, that with his experience of life, he is now just 75, he realized that what was important in religious and spiritual life was not what people believe, but rather whether they were a good person doing good or not.

The Notion of Awareness and the Limitations of Neurosciences

An Asian Buddhist monk asked the scientist who was recording his brain waves: "Do you have a machine to measure awareness?" The researcher realized he did not, he was just recording some kind of global brain activity. Certainly, with the brain imaginary, one can be more precise and know quite a few details, but what about this synthesis which is awareness? Measuring awareness is still a distant dream. If there is no way of measuring it, how is it possible to build a science about it?

Actually, if you look inside the field of sciences itself, you observe a discrepancy between hard and soft sciences. What is considered as valid evidence in psychology and sociology will be just empty talk for physics and chemistry. Nonetheless, it would be hard to deny to soft sciences the very name of sciences.

If you delve deep into all these questions, you will realize that Western psychology needs itself a good psychotherapy, to cure its megalomania of sorts: that is its belief that it has discovered depths of psychology, and the unconscious mechanisms, while the meditative techniques in the East are dealing also with that for the last two or three millenniums. Moreover, Western psychology, except in it parts about neurology and experiments in laboratories, is not really a science. Psychotherapy remains an art, and so much the better.

The most knotty question that arises in the dialogue between spirituality and neurosciences is the question of reductionism. The general assumption of neurosciences is that consciousness is a succession of the brain. Of course, some great researchers like Sir John Eccle, a Nobel Laureate, are clearly against this. But if consciousness is independent of the brain, then how do you objectify it or how does one measure it, is the main issue? The Dalai Lama is of the opinion that this might be possible one day.

Another question is why modern science has being working mainly on cells and chemistry, and the yogis on the notion of centers and channels of energy? Here, I think that the answer is rather simple, out of mutual ignorance. Now that a dialogue with more mutual knowledge is possible, it is important to work together to have a fuller of view of the picture. In this sense, there is a branch of this field which is called kundalini research. One 450 page book has been released on this subject, edited by John White. It is quite complete on this field, balancing the traditional and modern approaches. We also spoke before of the book on *chakras* and channels by Hashimoto.

In fact, there should be no taboo in the choice of subjects of scientific investigation. One big taboo so far has been subjectivity in itself, it was an anathema for instance by behavioral psychologists, this dogmatic attitude is fortunately receding. Certainly, there are subjects which need to be handled with precaution. For instance, in the field of kundalini awakening, there are a lot of false experiences which are disturbed forms of sexual awakening, more related to hysteria or to borderline conditions. In the field of drugs, especially with the auto experimentation, we are obviously on dangerous grounds. Still, there were psychiatrists, like the French Moreau de Tours in the 19th century, who experimented with hashish to be able to describe very correctly its effects, and his observations are still valid. There is a French doctor too, Jacques Mabit, who is working on the effect of the Amerindian herb ayahusca. He has a center in Peru which has show good results; for difficult problems like detoxification of heroin or alcohol for instance.

Of course, we should take seriously the notion of initiates in secret traditions, some knowledge can be easily misused, and caution is necessary. Moreover, the guru will give his instructions according to the level of a particular disciple, they are usually not universal. On the other side, for instance, the Tibetans techniques of visualization were considered to be the exclusive secret of Himalayan yogis in their caves at the beginning of the 20th century, but they have found practical applications with techniques like Caycedo's sophrology in the French and Latin world, and mental imagery against cancer with Simonton in the States. We have seen the same process with Vipassana and the considerable work of Professor Kabat-Zinn. Of course, there are negative aspects in this evolution, for instance commercial tantrism both in modern India and in the West.

Another obstacle to the scientific study of spiritual phenomena can come from the meditators themselves when they are asked to collaborate. Matthieu Ricard told me for instance that Chinese Buddhist monks had difficulty in accepting the recording of their brain during meditation, because they were afraid like schoolchildren that the conclusion of the test could be that, after 20 or 30 years of endeavors, their meditation was bad and fruitless... But it is not like this, theses studies are made out of curiosity, it is the natural tendency of the human mind to go and see what is going on in a particular place, be it the brain.

At the beginning of my stay in India, I visited a few ashrams which had installed a laboratory for research on meditation. I had the global impression that the big shortcoming of their undertaking was a lack of review of literature. They just did with their limited equipment what has been done already a hundred times, especially in the West, 20 or 30 years ago. As we say in French, they 'dashed into a door already opened'. The basic principle of scientific research is to first do a good review of literature, to identify exactly those areas which need clarification or innovation, and then only to start the research. If not, the experiments will be only a kind of advertising aimed at showing to the naive believer that the technique of a given ashram has some physiological good effects. But in fact, all the methods of relaxation and concentration have some good effects.

Since we speak of awareness, we should ponder shortly on what is the sense of ego. From the neurological point of view, it seems there is a centre of the ego near the corpus callosus, it means the junction between the two hemispheres. This seems logical, since consciousness is born and nourished out of comparison, by pondering and balancing one side with the other. This is the role of the corpus callosus to enable this kind of work, to provide the neuronal wiring for this.

It is important also to reconcile between the Vedanta and Buddhism regarding the question of ego: when Buddhism says there is no atman, it corresponds to the ego, the individual atman of Vedanta. As for the universal atman, a school of Buddhism still deny it fully, while others accept the existence of a fundamental consciousness, or a 'storehouse of knowledge', âlaya vijñâna, like in the Yogâchâra school. Certainly, Buddhism likes to content itself with the idea of vijñâna, a temporary consciousness which works as a reaction to vedâna, ie sensations and feelings. Understanding the functioning of this temporary consciousness, we would say in computer sciences the RAM, the active working memory, is enough to get liberation. According to them, there is no need of an eternal consciousness, which is not only not provable, but also not needed.

Now that we are going to reach the last part of these reflections, it is important to reflect for a while on the question of concordism. This is a term of science of religions which describes the deep-seated tendency among believers, to make concordances, agreements, between the recent scientific discoveries and some parts, even only verses or words, of the sacred Scripture. This tendency should be taken with a grain of salt: for too often, there is a confusion of level, between the golden age of religion, which is the way to express in mythological form that it comes from pure consciousness and from the Self, and real history with an evolution from ignorance to more knowledge on the scientific level. One has to accept this paradox: a child of 10 or 12 at present knows more exactly about the physical world than any prophet or rishi of yore.

I lived in a Muslim country, Algeria, for 15 months teaching and practicing psychiatry. I had some contacts and exchanges of views with a Sufi brotherhood. Like the whole Muslim world, they had been very impressed by a book on the Koran and sciences which had been written by a French explorer, the Commandant Cousteau, who had converted to Islam. I did not read the book fully, but I heard a lot about it. The attempt was obviously naive: Cousteau was taking a single verse or sometimes even an isolated word of the Koran, and trying to show it was predicting some scientific discovery. This kind of simplistic interpretation is just not convincing, but it has been a big success in the Muslim world, because they are deeply anxious about the growing invasion and power of modernity in front of the tenets of their faith. This book was visibly a kind of attempt of reassurance, but it could convince only the ones who were ready to be convinced.

Actually, when an ideology wants to be totalitarian, it wants to interfere with sciences. This has been the case for Stalin, who was dictating to biologists, what conclusions they had to find to be in line with the party.

It is interesting to see that among modern Muslim fundamentalists and terrorists, we find people who have a high level of study, like a Ph.D in sciences. But when you look at their exact field of study, you see that it is usually some kind of technology, in material sciences, and almost never in psychology or psychiatry. I remember when I worked in Algeria as a psychiatrist, not one of my colleagues, be they psychiatrists or psychologists, were even remotely tempted by fundamentalism. Actually, they saw too clearly the manipulation of mind it involves, and the mix of paranoia and depression it expresses.

Let us nuance our critique of 'concordism'. One can say it is a naïve attempt as far as hard sciences are concerned, but it is relevant in the field of psychology, particularly if you are interested in archetypes. Those images that have given inspiration to millions have definitely something in them; they are able to stir a deep chord in the human heart. They can be taken over by modern psychology, by keeping in mind that if we want them to be really effective and active, they need to be concentrated upon for a long time and with full energy,

After speaking of concordism, we can say a word about creationism. The main problem is with the religions of the Book, like Christians and Muslims who are dogmatic over their view of creation. Certainly, the Catholic Church has taken some steps back since a few decades ago, but the basic problem remains almost the same. If the personal God is not able to intervene in creation, not even to fabricate one speck of dust, how on earth will he be able to change the heart of every human being, and to judge them at the end of the time? In the conception of Vedanta and Buddhism, one can say that the world has always existed, although it has evolved and undergone cycles. In this context, people will be more at ease with the scientific cosmology. And may be the silence of Buddha about this question, expressing that he doesn't know, is more honest, because during his time, one did not know anything scientific about the origins and beginning phases of the universe. Now, we have more hard facts and knowledge to think about matter in a proper way.

Another illusion of pseudoscience is to apply a kind of Darwinism to the evolution of religion. According to this conception, the more a religion is important in quantity, the better it should be, according to the law of Darwinian competition for life and supremacy. There is the spiritual argument of Swâmî Râmatîrtha: he explains, not without humor, that if the number of devotees should be the sign of the value of a religion, certainly, the religion of Satan will be the best of all: actually, he is the one who has the greater number of devotees, addicted as they are to the ideas of violence, lust, avidity, anger, etc Moreover, a simple reflection will show that epidemics may spread to a good part of humanity without being for the good of it.

The research on parapsychology is very important for the future: it will help to integrate into the field of science all those phenomena which appear in different traditions, but have been only related to different gods or even to a unique one. There are quite a few people working on this subject, we may mention, for instance, Marilyn Schlitz and the IONS, Institute of Noetic Sciences in California. They have definitely proved that thought has power. It was not so much a question of quantity of people having the same thought at the same time than the intensity of the feeling accompanying it. Somehow, it is like a rocket propelling a satellite into orbit. Marilyn Schlitz honestly says that with her team, they have found nothing connecting this power of thought to a personal superior entity, whatever his name.

There is a dynamic organization which organizes conferences on psychology and spirituality in India, the Yoga Psychological Association of India, (YPAI). I participated in their conference in Hardwar, it was in 2007 if I remember well.

A last reflection on awareness and sciences: until not so long ago, the departments of philosophy and psychology in the Indian universities were reunited. It was the same case some time ago in the West. Now this tendency has come back in an interesting way in Germany. A young philosopher, Richard-David Precht, studied the neurosciences and psychology in depth and made an understandable synthesis of all this in a book which has become a best seller in Germany and has now been translated in several languages. He has given a humoristic name to his work who am I, and if I am, how much? He understood that he was lost as a traditional philosopher, as well as the general public was, in front of the mass of disorganized information, so he worked hard to organize all this new material. Modern philosophy should not be only a repetition of the history of philosophy, but be able to explore and somewhat digest new fields of knowledge.

Returning to Contemplative Science

There are differences between a musician and a musicologist: the first one practices an art whereas the second speaks about it, analyzes it, etc. However, it is difficult to imagine a competent musicologist who would not have any practice in music, nor a taste for it. He would be simply 'out of sync' with his subject. This analogy holds good for psychology and neurosciences on one side, and meditation and the subjective practice of awareness on the other. Even with a simple knowledge of meditation, therapists can do a lot of good, as Pr Kabat-Zinn has demonstrated for the past 30 years. There are quite a few psychotherapists who have understood the importance of a daily practice of meditation for themselves. Let us wish that this tendency will grow both in quantity and in quality.

To conclude, it will be interesting to speak about Matthieu Ricard who was a top scientist and is now a monk in Tibetan Buddhism and about what objective reality is, and what could be a foundation for a spiritual search. "What is to be understood under the label: 'objective knowledge'? The nature of particles is unknowable independently of our systems of measurement. Likewise, a universe independent of every human concept is unknowable by the human mind. Who is attached to the reality of phenomena? The Mind again. In spiritual practice, what do we act on? On the mind! Should we succeed in unblocking the wrong perception of the solidity of the world, perception which leads to endless suffering, then we will reach objective knowledge. It will not be the one of natural physics, but of the mechanism of suffering and of the experimental verification of the results of this science of the spirit.

Why should we consider that experimental verification could apply only for physical phenomena? Based on this point of view, only the quantitative and physical sciences would deserve the name of exact sciences. In order to be exact, a science must start with a few hypotheses, proceed with rigor in the field of experiments, to eventually validate or contradict its hypotheses by the results of those experiments. There is no reason at all why the criteria should be limited to the physical, or so called objective field.

Nothing, except mind itself, will enable us to recognize the ultimate nature of mind. If introspection has failed as a scientific method in the context of Western psychology, it is because those who used it had not developed the adequate instruments to conduct their experiments. They did not have the least training nor the least knowledge of the contemplative domain and ignored the techniques allowing to calm the mind in order to observe its profound nature. It is just as someone who would use an instable voltmeter and conclude that it is impossible to study the tension of an electric current... Skepticism is understandable, but not the lack of interest, of desire to verify the validity of a different approach. The problem exists also in the other sense; I have known Tibetans who refused to believe that men could have gone to the moon!"

This field of contemplative science is a lesson in humility. Nobody knows the full picture, but if we accept to collaborate, many interesting discoveries will come out. Moreover, this work of unification is positive; the Bhagavâd-Gita would say sattvic, in a well-known verse (18, 20):

Sarvabhuteshû yenai'kam bhâvam avyayam îkshate
Avibhaktam vibhakteshu tah jñânam viddhi sâttvikam

"This knowledge by which the imperishable Being is seen in all existences, undivided in the divided, knows it as sattvic".

Chapter 5

Consciousness and Science: Mutual Understandings and Conflicts

RANDHIR TIWARY
Bharat Electronics Limited, Ghaziabad, India

Abstract

This paper discusses the complex nature of comprehending the concept of consciousness. Ordinary and altered states have been dealt with very briefly to explain conscious experience of the world in different conditions. Its physical and metaphysical dimensions, the information processing model in mind and development of self-consciousness as life progresses which gets firmly attached to outside world and experiences resultant vagaries as it is subject to mercy of this fast changing physical world in dimensions of space, time and matter. The paper also highlights the potential of returning of this self ego to a transcendental pure state of consciousness by withdrawal from this material world which is referred in Indian Philosophy as a state of "Sat-chit-ananda" i.e. the truth, unchanging eternal being, ever blissful which being our original state from where we descended to this physical world.

The same has long been the aim and purpose of religion as it frees one from cycle of birth and death. This paper then deals with the limitation of traditional methods of science to study consciousness and a new emerging outlook that new tools of quantum methods may throw better insight for understanding this topic. This has resulted in paradigm shift by science and convergence to the religious concept of consciousness that it is a fundamental entity and responsible as creator and sustainer of this vast ever expanding creation. It also includes the arguments of scientist who have dualist view on consciousness and physical causation. It also touches on the greatest gift of God to sentient who possess the faculty of intuition which is ever evolving and one day is progressing to explore the mysterious world of our being with more clarity surpassing the restrictions and bounds of logic of mind and traditional scientific discipline. There is growing enthusiasm that one day religion, philosophy and science will converge to the same Truth as our consciousness further evolves.

The Concept of Consciousness

For centuries people have tried to understand the abstract nature of consciousness and the effort is still on to unfurl its mystery. Empirical evidences and deterministic, logical approach falls short in fully understanding consciousness. It manifests in many dimensions and states but nevertheless many of it eludes our ordinary perception. Its meaning we know as long as no one asks us to define it. Consciousness lies at the root of all knowledge. It exists, but to identify it is like trying to locate the sun through dark clouds. It may be defined as a subjective awareness of some aspects of ongoing mental (psychical) processes. Near death experiences gives an indication that consciousness extends beyond physical being and may survive beyond death.

It has probably been the challenge of understanding consciousness more than any other field of science that has forced us to come to grips with the deficiency of Physics or science to explain everything. We have come far with our technology but are stumped when it comes to understanding our own consciousness. Understanding intangible affecters will open up new frontiers in science and provide us with even greater opportunities to improve the quality of our lives.

Ordinary States of Consciousness

When we view it as awareness of various cognitive processes: sleeping, dreaming, concentrating, and making decisions then Consciousness may be broadly categorized as:-

- o Waking Consciousness
- o Altered State of Consciousness
    - Daydreaming and fantasy
    - Sleep and its stages
    - Dreams
    - Drug altered consciousness
    - Hypnosis
    - Meditation and path to higher consciousness.

Waking Consciousness

It is the mental state that encompasses the thoughts, feeling, and perceptions that occur when we are awake and alert. It is usually action or plan-oriented. It is tuned in to the external environment. It is true that we are exposed to a vast variety of stimuli. We select to pay attention to what seems the most important at the moment.

Stream of Consciousness

Pieces of information are received from various sensory modes; sent to areas on the cerebral cortex. The processing is by nature very orderly but mostly we fail to appreciate it. The thalamus scans these areas. Each scan is a single image or "moment of consciousness" but experience is much beyond sequential images but a sum result of many complex processes which are all not always understood by science and the measuring resources available with scientist. One point of view is that consciousness is a small peak emerging from a reservoir of large mass of unconscious mental representations accumulated by evolutionary processes in the mind and stored in the cerebral cortex.

Many reject the idea that people are driven by mainly unconscious motives but operate mostly by their free will and volition.

Awareness of the World Around

Our sensory apparatuses are affected by external stimuli such as photons and air vibrations. They in turn send neural signals into our brains, and we are conscious of the external world.

As we move about in the external world our brain is constantly changing the internal map. What we know as the external world is, in actuality, a navigation room in our minds that is essential for computing our interactions within our environment. It is this navigation room that we experience as the external world. The characteristics of the subject that we are studying are the characteristics of the model. The model creates everything that we call appearance or experience. The mind doesn't deal in real things but it models and processes information. The only world that we know is an information process.

The information world that is our own experience is a parallel world to the real world, yet it is utterly different. It is a world of appearances without substance, whereas the real world is a world of substance without appearance.

What we consider consciousness to be is the aspects of our mind that are simultaneously experiential, in the focus of attention and "self" referencing. For often, when our attention is intense we forget our "selves" and only see what we have accomplished after it is done, even if the processes involved active reflection. We often find ourselves agitated or in a daydream while our attention is applied unconsciously. Consciousness, by the above definition, would be useless without that vast unconscious processing which applies our knowledge to understanding our sensorial images. What we call consciousness is a small slice of what it is to be ourselves.

Day dreaming and Fantasy

Day dreams are effortless shifts in attention away from the here-and-now into a private world of make-believe. They occur about every 90 minutes or so. Studies show they are variations on a central theme. Day dreams and dreamers may fall into categories:

- Positive
- Negative
- Scattered
- Purposeful

Sleep

Sleep – a natural state of rest which is by nature cyclic characterized by:

- A reduction in voluntary body movement
- Decreased awareness of the surroundings
- Sleep deprivation impairs cognitive skills to a great extent

"Going to sleep" implies losing awareness and failing to respond to a stimulus that would produce a response in the waking state.There are several stages of sleep:

o Stage 1 (brain produces high amplitude theta waves, which are very slow brain waves, lasts only a brief time (around 5-10 minutes).

o Stage 2 (bursts of rapid, rhythmic brain wave activity known as sleep spindles. Body temperature starts to decrease and heart rate begins to slow. Lasts for approximately 20 minutes).

o Stage 3 (deep, slow brain waves known as delta waves begin to emerge and is a transitional period between light sleep and a very deep sleep.).

o Stage 4 (is a deep sleep that lasts for approximately 30 minutes.)
o REM (known as rapid eye movement sleep. It is characterized by Eye movement, increased respiration rate, increased brain activity.

Dreams

Dreams are vivid, visual and auditory experiences that occur primarily during REM periods of sleep. The average person has 4 to 5 dreams a night. It accounts for 1 to 2 hours of total sleeping time. Dreams consist of a sequential story or series of stories. Both external and internal stimuli may modify an ongoing dream; they do not initiate dreams.

Drug-Altered Consciousness

Psychoactive drugs are substances that change people's moods, perceptions, mental functioning, and behavior Many of these drugs have been used for thousands of years. The most common are:

- Hallucinogens, LSD, Marijuana, Barbiturates and Opiates
- Depressants like Alcohol
- Stimulants: Caffeine, Nicotine, Amphetamines, and Cocaine

Motives for use have changed. Today they are used for recreation rather then religious or cultural purposes. They have become stronger and more addictive over the years

Hypnosis

Hypnosis is a trance like state in which a person responds readily to suggestions. In mid-18th century Europe, Anton Mesmer began putting people into trances to cure their illnesses. That is how the term Mesmerism came into vogue. Its effectiveness depends upon how suggestible people are. It can ease the pain of certain medical conditions

Meditation

Any method of concentration, reflection, or focusing of thoughts undertaken to suppress the activity of the sympathetic nervous system and to experience beyond ordinary sensory perception is meditation. There are

- Zen Meditation – It concentrates on respiration
- Sufism – It relies on dancing and prayer
- Transcendental Meditation – It encourages repetition of a mantra-sound that relaxes the practitioner
- Surat Shabd Yoga - It is a rekindling of the inner portals dormant normally within human beings which take one to a higher sense of consciousness through realization of self and then to various states of infinite reservoir of consciousness transcending space, time and matter.

In meditation, the person is fully aware that he has reached a stage beyond his apparatus of thoughts of mind and bodily senses, a state which is not easily describable but nevertheless real and highly blissful.

Consciousness: An Information-processing Model in the Material World

The explanation of consciousness conforms to a primarily easily observable belief that there is only a material world. Despite that, we have no true notion of what it means to be physical/material. We have no access to the world outside of our minds. Our mind is an information process that creates our 'selves', our sense of being an observer, a subject of experience and the world that we observe and experience. Information and information processing are intangibles that arise out of the specificity of dynamic relationships in the brain. Experience is the only characteristic of consciousness that is something. Because experience is something that doesn't have to be material. Experience is what-it-is-like to be in a particular state of something physical in our brain.

It is clear that experience is a characteristic of the physical brain but there is still much exciting territory to puzzle over in understanding the neural correlates of experience. We will not be able to appreciate what experience is if we don't advance beyond trying to experience it. There is no subject of experience. There is only a 'self' that has lived a life of illusion.

Experience is all that there is that is real in our world. It is the media on which the mind formulates consciousness. Conscious images are formed in experiential states. The forms are a Map that represents the external environment. Everything that we consider to be the world is only our own mind's analogy for the world. We experience the world because of this process and the world we experience is this process. It is an information process. We do not experience real things. Things only exist for us as the shapes of experiential states even if they are a tiger leaping at us or the arms of our lover. Consider the fact that this is the only world you have ever known. You haven't been able to compare it to the real world. That possibility simply doesn't exist because the world you know would not exist if it were not for intangible information processing being carried on a physical substrate within your skull.

Here is listed a sample of different types of experiences reported which gives some insight into how complex the process of consciousness is and the way it manifests into innumerable experiences which is often not based on external sensory stimuli and puzzles deterministic scientific analysis most.

FACTOR – HARMONY WITH THE UNIVERSE

- A feeling of total love for all living creatures
- A feeling of divinely inspired power that inspires others
- A feeling of unity with "everything"
- A feeling of "direct experience of the essence"
- A discovery of a new value/beauty of familiar matter or object
- Being sunk in pleasant, positive feelings of happiness, peace and joy
- An experience of a guidance of an "internal voice"
- A feeling of devotion to God

FACTOR – UNUSUAL REALITY

- A feeling of leaving one's body and being able to observe this
- A feeling of a contact with ineffable reality
- Darkness that fills the mind – being sunk in dark abyss
- Loss of sense of reality to which we are normally conditioned
- An experience which may be communicated only by metaphorical or paradoxical statements
- A feeling of loss of self-consciousness, while aware
- A feeling of spacelessness
- A feeling of disorder in time

FACTOR – MAGICAL INFLUENCE

- A feeling that external power influences my thinking
- A feeling that an external power controls my behavior
- An impression that another ego exists in my personality
- An impression of hearing of one's own thoughts
- A feeling of unusual abilities like telepathy, healing, precognition
- A feeling that observed events may have a hidden meaning
- A feeling of possession by a negative power
- A feeling of spiritual protector from the "other world"
- An experience of mysterious changes in surroundings

Consciousness is not a system in a vacuum by any means. It is more like the executive department of the nervous organization of the organism. The conscious mind is a dynamic system that is responsible for gratifying the needs of the inner milieu of the organism and navigating the organism as a mobile entity in the environment in which the organism must survive. It is not directly involved with controlling the functions of the inner milieu but the organism's internal conditions such as hunger, thirst, body temperature and fatigue are summarized and reported to it. It in turn is driven by these conditions to cause the entity of the organism to perform actions that will change or gratify those conditions. The mind primarily directs the activities of the whole organism. It does this through control of the musculoskeletal system.

Consciousness is a dynamic relationship driven by the need to gratify conditions that keep the body in equilibrium internally and within the environment. These needs are generated in the body and are summarized and reported to the mind where they are felt as drives and emotions and where they motivate one's intelligence to devise action plans to gratify them. The mind contains an image of the body that intelligence identifies as the organism, which it is to serve.

Development of Self-consciousness in Sentient

As we reflect upon our own consciousness, it seems that there must be an experiencer -- an individual self that is having these experiences, making all these decisions, and thinking all these thoughts. But what is this self? What is it really like? What does it consist of?

Questions such as these have intrigued and puzzled philosophers for centuries. Some, like the Scottish philosopher David Hume, spent much time searching within their experience for something that seemed to be the true self. But all they could find were various thoughts, sensations, images and feelings. However hard we look, we never seem to find the self itself.

Not finding an easily identifiable self at the core of our being, we look to other aspects of our lives for a sense of identity. We identify with our bodies, with how they look, how they are dressed, and how they are perceived by other people. We identify with what we do and what we have achieved; with our work, our social status, our academic qualifications, where we live and who we know. We derive a sense of who we are from what we think about our theories and beliefs, our personality and character.

There is, however, a severe drawback to such a sense of self. Being derived from what is happening in the world of experience, it is forever at the mercy of events. A person who draws a strong sense of identity from their work may, on hearing that their job is threatened, feel their sense of self is threatened. Someone else, who identifies with being fashionably dressed, may buy a new set of clothes every time the fashion changes, not because they need new clothes, but because their sense of self needs to be maintained. Or if we identify with our views and beliefs we may take a criticism of our ideas to be a criticism of our self.

Any threat to our sense of self, triggers fear. Fear is of great value if our physical self is being threatened. Then we need to have our heart beat hard, our blood pressure rise, and our muscles tense. Our survival may depend on it. But this response is totally inappropriate when all that is being threatened is our psychological self.

Having our bodies repeatedly put on full alert is a principal cause of stress. We can easily end up in a permanent state of tension, opening us up to all manner of physical illnesses. Our emotional life may suffer, leading to anxiety or depression. Our thinking and decision making can likewise deteriorate.

Fear also leads to worry. We worry about what others might be thinking of us. We worry about what we have done or not done, and about what might or might not happen to us. When we worry like this, our attention is caught up in the past or the future. It is not experiencing the present moment.

Perhaps the saddest irony of all is that this worry prevents us from finding that which we are really seeking. The goal of every person is, in the final analysis, a comfortable state of mind. Quite naturally, we want to avoid pain and suffering, and feel more at peace. But a mind that is busy worrying cannot be a mind that is at peace.

Other animals, not having language, do not think to themselves in words, and do not experience many of the worries that we do. In particular, they do not experience all the worries that come from having a vulnerable sense of self. They are probably at peace much more of the time. Human beings may have made a great leap forward in consciousness, but at our present stage of development we are no happier for it -- quite the opposite.

Higher consciousness of Sat Chit Ananda

Returning the mind and then self to this simple pre-linguistic state of consciousness is not easy. A lifetime of conditioning makes it hard to stop thinking and let go. This is why many spiritual teachings include practices of meditation designed to quieten the voice in the head, and bring us to a state of inner stillness. In Indian philosophy, this state is called Samadhi, "still mind". Furthermore, it is said that when the mind is still, then one knows the real self, and the nature of this self is, according to the ancient Vedic and Upanishad teachings, sat-chit-ananda.

It is Sat - "the truth, unchanging, eternal, being". It is always there, whatever our experience. It never changes. It is not a unique self; it has no personal qualities. It is the same for everyone. It is the one undeniable truth -- the fact that we are conscious. It is Chit -- "consciousness". It is not any particular form or mode of consciousness, but the faculty of consciousness. It is that which makes all experience possible. And it is Ananda -- "bliss". It is the peace that passes all understanding that lies beyond all thought. It is the state of grace to which we long to return; from which we fell when we began to fill our minds with words.

This is the self that we have been seeking all along. The reason we have had such difficulty finding it was that we have been looking in the wrong place. We have been looking for something that could be experienced -- a feeling, a sense, an idea. Yet the self cannot be an experience. It is, by definition, that which is experiencing. It is behind every experience, behind everything I see, think, and feel.

What the mystical traditions around the world seem to be saying is that the self, that sense of I-ness that we all feel, but which is so hard to pin down or define, is actually consciousness itself. The pure self is pure consciousness -- the faculty of awareness common to all sentient beings.

Moreover, when we come to know this to be our true essential nature, our search for identity ends. No longer is there any need to buy things we don't really need, say things we don't really mean, or engage in any other unnecessary and inappropriate activities in order to reinforce an artificially derived sense of self. Now we discover a deeper inner security, one that is independent of circumstances and events. Here is the peace we have long been seeking. It is right here inside us, at the heart of our being. But as with the self, we have been looking for it in the wrong place -- in the world around.

Science and Consciousness

As a field of endeavor, traditional science lays heavy emphasis on empirical measurement. The common dictum is, "If it can't be measured, it is not science". As present-day scientific instruments are incapable of directly measuring the soul, consciousness, and non-physical realms-at least for now-conclusive direct evidence for the soul cannot be said to exist. Mounting indirect evidence, however, is available through ingeniously designed experiments in quantum physics, parapsychology, and other scientific disciplines; the systematic study and analysis of the accounts of people who report transpersonal, transcendent experiences, and the formulation of mathematical equations that theoretically support the existence of multidimensional "hyperspace" beyond the physical universe.

Perhaps our expectations for science are too high. The province of science is best limited to theoretical understanding of consciousness and the soul, and not as a direct aid in helping us experience the soul. In the future, however, may be scientific instrumentation will play some role in furthering the soul's exploration.

There is a growing body of renegade scientists who in recent years have ventured into the domain of the spiritual in an attempt, both to interpret the seemingly inexplicable findings of their experiments and to validate their intuitions about the existence of a spiritual dimension of life. Many cases are rooted in an interpretation of the experimental data of quantum physics (the physics of elementary particles), with a myriad of findings and theories in fields from artificial intelligence to astronomy to Hindu, Islamic, Christianity and other religious mysticism with an attempt to show that the discoveries of modern science are in perfect accord with the deepest mystical truths.

They believe that the universe, in order to exist, require a conscious sentient being to be aware of it. Without an observer, he claims, it only exists as a possibility. In the world of science, many have done their own mathematics. Marshalling evidence from recent research in cognitive psychology, biology, parapsychology and quantum physics, and leaning heavily on the ancient mystical traditions of the world, scientists are building a case for a new paradigm that, ***"a view that consciousness, not matter, is the foundation of everything that is".***

The current worldview is that everything is made of matter, and everything can be reduced to the elementary particles of matter, the basic constituents—building blocks—of matter. The cause arises from the interactions of these basic building blocks or elementary particles; elementary particles make atoms, atoms make molecules, molecules make cells, and cells make brain. But all the way, the ultimate cause is always the interactions between the elementary particles. This is the belief—all cause moves from the elementary particles. This is what we call "upward causation." So as per this view, what human beings think of as their free will does not really exist. It is only an epiphenomenon or secondary phenomenon, secondary to the causal power of matter. And any causal power that we seem to be able to exert on matter is just an illusion. This is the current widely accepted paradigm by most traditional scientists.

Now, ***the opposite view is that everything starts with consciousness.*** That is, consciousness is the ground of all being. In this view, ***consciousness imposes "downward causation."*** In other words, our free will is real. When we act in the world we really are acting with causal power. This view does not deny that matter also has causal potency—it does not deny that there is causal power from elementary particles upward, so there is upward causation—but in addition it insists that there is also downward causation. It shows up in our creativity and acts of free will, or when we make moral decisions. In those occasions we are actually witnessing downward causation by consciousness.

The idea that consciousness is the ground of all being is the basis of all spiritual traditions. There is a philosophy called "idealism" which is opposed to the philosophy of "material realism". Idealism says consciousness is the only real thing but material realism holds that only matter is real. But in the West, that kind of idealism has usually meant something that is really dualism—that is, consciousness and matter are separate. Whereas in the East, Idealism is the mainstream philosophy. In Buddhism, or in Hinduism where it is called Vedanta, or in Taoism, this is the philosophy of everyone.

In scientific world, what had been happening was that for many years quantum physics had been giving indications that there are levels of reality other than the material level. How it started happening first was that quantum objects—objects in quantum physics—began to be looked upon as waves of possibility. Now, initially people thought, "Oh, they are just like regular waves." But very soon it was found out that, no, they are not waves in space and time. They cannot be called waves in space and time at all—they have properties, which do not jibe with those of ordinary waves. So they began to be recognized as waves in potential, waves of possibility, and the potential was recognized as transcendent, beyond matter somehow.

But the fact that there is transcendent potential was not very clear for a long time. Then Aspect's experiment verified that this is not just theory, there really is transcendent potential, and objects really do have connections outside of space and time. What happens in this experiment is that an atom emits two quanta of light, called photons, going opposite ways, and somehow these photons affect one another's behavior at a distance, without exchanging any signals through space instantaneously.

Einstein showed long ago that two objects can never affect each other instantly in space and time because everything must travel with a maximum speed limit, and that speed limit is the speed of light. So any influence must travel, if it travels through space, taking a finite time. This is called the idea of "locality." Every signal is supposed to be local in the sense that it must take a finite time to travel through space. And yet, Aspect's photons—the photons emitted by the atom in Aspect's experiment—influence one another, at a distance, without exchanging signals because they are doing it instantaneously—they are doing it faster than the speed of light. And therefore it follows that the influence could not have traveled through space. Instead the influence must belong to a domain of reality that we must recognize as the transcendent domain of reality.

Henry Stapp, who is a physicist at the University of California at Berkeley, says this quite explicitly in one of his papers written in 1977, that things outside of space and time affect things inside space and time. There's just no question on this that what happens in the realm of quantum physics when you are dealing with quantum objects. Now of course, the crux of the matter is, the surprising thing is, that we are always dealing with quantum objects because it turns out that quantum physics is the physics of every object. Whether it's submicroscopic or it's macroscopic, quantum physics is the only physics we've got. So although it's more apparent for photons, for electrons, for the submicroscopic objects, scientists' belief is that all reality, all manifest reality, all matter, is governed by the same laws. And if that is so, then this experiment is telling us that we should change our worldview because we, too, are quantum objects.

The early work, like *The Tao of Physics*, has been very important for the history of science. However, these early works, in spite of supporting the spiritual aspect of human beings, all basically held on to the material view of the world nevertheless. In other words, they did not challenge the material realists' view that everything is made up of matter. That view was never put to any challenge by any of these early books. In fact, many later books which are challenging it squarely and which are still based on a rigorous explication in scientific terms. In other words, the idea that consciousness is the ground of being, of course, has existed in psychology, as transpersonal psychology.

Within quantum physics, there is a view to recognize that all the paradoxes of quantum physics can be solved if we accept consciousness as the ground of being. The unique contribution has paradigm-shifting potential because now we can truly integrate science and spirituality. In other words, earlier works held on to a fundamentally materialist paradigm, the paradigm is not shifting, nor is there any real reconciliation between spirituality and science. If everything is ultimately material, all causal efficacy must come from matter. So consciousness is recognized, spirituality is recognized, but only as causal epiphenomena, or secondary phenomena. And an epiphenomenal consciousness is not very good. I mean, it's not doing anything. So, although earlier books acknowledge spirituality, the spirituality is ultimately coming from some sort of material interaction.

The kind of exuberant statement that mystics make could not be made on the basis of epiphenomenal consciousness. It can be made only when one recognizes the ground of being itself, when one cognizes directly that One is all. So long as science remains on the basis of the materialist worldview, however much you try to accommodate spiritual experiences in terms of parallels or in terms of chemicals in the brain or what have you, you are not really giving up the old paradigm. You are giving up the old paradigm and fully reconciling with spirituality only when you establish science on the basis of the fundamental spiritual notion that consciousness is the ground of all being.

The present science has shown not only quantum paradoxes but also has shown real incompetence in explaining paradoxical and anomalous phenomena, such as parapsychology, the paranormal—even creativity. And even traditional subjects, like perception or biological evolution, have much to explain that these materialist theories don't explain. However, if we do science on the basis of consciousness, on the primacy of consciousness, then we can see in this phenomenon creativity, real creativity of consciousness. In other words, we can truly see that consciousness is operating creatively even in biology, even in the evolution of species. And so we can now fill up these gaps that conventional biology cannot explain with ideas which are essentially spiritual ideas, such as consciousness as the creator of the world in quantum physics, as I said earlier, objects are not seen as definite things, as we are used to seeing them. Newton taught us that objects are definite things, they can be seen all the time, moving in definite trajectories. Quantum physics doesn't depict objects that way at all. In quantum physics, objects are seen as possibilities, possibility waves. So then the question arises, what converts possibility into actuality? Because, when we see, we only see actual events. That's starting with us. "Quantum measurement paradox." It is a paradox because who are we to have this conversation? In the materialist paradigm we don't have any causal efficacy. We are nothing but the brain, which is made up of atoms and elementary particles. So how can a brain which is made up of atoms and elementary particles convert a possibility wave that it is? It itself is made up of the possibility waves of atoms and elementary particles, so it cannot convert its own possibility wave into actuality. This is called a paradox. Now in the new view, consciousness is the ground of all being. So who converts possibility into actuality? Consciousness does, because consciousness does not obey quantum physics. Consciousness is not made of material. Consciousness is transcendent. One sees the paradigm-changing view right here—how consciousness can be said to create the material world? The material world of quantum physics is just possibility. It is consciousness, through the conversion of possibility into actuality, that creates what we see manifest. In other words, consciousness creates the manifest world.

The entire physical universe only existed in a realm of countless evolving possibilities until at one point, the possibility of a conscious, sentient being arose and that, at that point, instantaneously, the entire known universe came into being, including the fifteen billion years of history leading up to that point.

It turns out that the idea has been around in cosmology and astronomy under the guise of a principle called the "anthropic principle." that is, the idea has been growing among astronomers—cosmologists anyway—that the universe has a purpose. It is so fine-tuned, there are so many coincidences, that it seems very likely that the universe is doing something purposive, as if the universe is growing in such a way that a sentient being will arise at some point.

The question arises: for whom was the cosmos created? Was it for all sentient beings? And the universe is us. That's very clear. The universe is self-aware, but it is self-aware through us. We are the meaning of the universe. We are not the geographical center of the universe—Copernicus was right about that—but we are the meaning center of the universe. The transcendent dimension is developed extremely well in Indian philosophy, whereas the transcendent dimension in the West is hidden in the cave of a very few esoteric systems such as the Gnostics. To supplement the above, famous and great scientist Einstien says,

> *"I am convinced that He (God) does not play dice."*
>
> *"God is subtle but he is not malicious."*
>
> *"Science without religion is lame. Religion without science is blind."*
>
> *"My religion consists of a humble admiration of the illimitable superior spirit who reveals himself in the slight details we are able to perceive with our frail and feeble mind."*
>
> ---- Albert Einstein.

When Einstein died, researchers were interested in examining his brain to see whether there was something special about it that made him a genius. His brain is still in a jar at Princeton University. We're not going to find what makes one person smart and one person stupid by looking at their brains, unless, of course, there's an obvious physical impairment. So we're not going to find the source of intelligence and the soul in the material world. Every brain has a genius possibility but there is something beyond the brain, an observer which governs it and that is what spiritual scientists believe is a presence of special state of consciousness.

Dualist View on Consciousness

The dualist is perfectly within rights to maintain full confidence in reasons for thinking that consciousness could never be explained in physical terms alone. David Chalmers, a dualist gives a stunning conclusion that subjective consciousness continues to defy all objectivist explanations. If consciousness cannot be explained in physical terms alone, either it is itself fundamental, or else some sort of nonphysical, non-phenomenal property. Thus, a complete theory will have two components: physical laws, telling us about the behavior of physical systems from the infinitesimal to the cosmological, and what we might call psychophysical laws, telling us how some of those systems are associated with conscious experience. These two components will constitute a true theory of everything.

Let science take its course; see how our conceptual and empirical resources unfold over time. Dualists think that not all the facts are physical facts. They think that there are facts about phenomenal consciousness that cannot be explained in purely physical terms—facts about what it's like to see red, what it's like to feel the cold touch of ice etc..

Phenomenal properties emerge from their physical bases in some causal or quasi-causal fashion. That is how the property dualist both maintains a reasonable respect for the physical sciences, while simultaneously claiming that phenomenal properties are genuinely new additions to the world.

Once we accept that materialism is false, it becomes clear that, we have to look for a "Y-factor," something additional to the physical facts that will help explain consciousness. We find such a Y-factor in the postulation of irreducible psychophysical laws.

A physical theory gives a theory of physical processes, and a psychophysical theory tells us how those processes give rise to experience. We know that experience depends on physical processes, but we also know that this dependence cannot be derived from physical laws alone. The new basic principles postulated by a non-reductive theory give us the extra ingredient that we need to build an explanatory bridge, nothing in this approach contradicts anything in the physical theory; we simply need to add further bridging principles to explain how consciousness arises from physical processes. However a close examination reveals that the laws will not explain consciousness; they will at best predict it. Scientists can look around the world and draw up complex and sophisticated correlations between the physical and the phenomenal. They can do MRI scans and lesion studies and so forth, and concludes that some physical process P is always accompanied by experience E. But for a brute-law dualist, these are mere correlations. They will enable us to inductively predict that the next person who is in brain state P will probably also have experience E. But they will not at all tell us why or how?

God Consciousness and HIS Guidance through Intuition

Through the intuition, God's Intelligence guides the human species, just as He guides animals through instinct mostly. However, another great difference is that mankind has the capability of not only receiving intuitive guidance from his Creator, but the ability to come to truly know the Creator, to develop a genuine relationship with the Most Holy One. This developing spiritual intimacy leads to what the early mystics called Divine Union. But first you must go through the initiations of Illumination and Self-Realization.

While intuition is an innate faculty within you, and quite often functions when you least expect it, this process must be developed and fine-tuned in order to operate in a much fuller capacity. This is why you practice the Spiritual Disciplines, such as Concentration, Visualization, Meditation, Contemplation, and of course Prayer. These are tools for fine-tuning the intuitive function.

It is true that quite often you will have a hunch, or intuitive flash, or strong impression for no apparent reason, and it will turn out that you were absolutely right. There have been countless reports of premonition. There have been saints, avatars, gurus or simple religious devotees who could hear the voice of God. The prophets had the ability to prophesy. Others have definite abilities in clairvoyance and clairaudience. These are deeper aspects of Intuition, or what many call the Sixth Sense, which is a catch phrase for psychic abilities. Certain mystical schools refer to these abilities as avenues of experiencing Cosmic Consciousness, or the Consciousness of God. As the consciousness of an individual grows in deeper awareness, and expands toward the Mind of God, he begins entering God's Consciousness. Understand that this development takes place specifically while the soul is unfolding through the spiritual Initiations, because these are an intrinsic part of the whole development of Cosmic Consciousness.

The fact is that the finite mind of human beings is limited in this material world, especially as they depend only on five senses, and use these with not as much awareness as they should. However, our species has six senses actually, but uses the sixth one far less than the other five. Mankind's sixth sense is the manifestation of his intuition. It is this faculty of intuition which one must seriously learn to develop. This is the bridge, which leads you into God's Consciousness. Without developing and using it, you remain in the mundane state of self-consciousness, which means your spiritual journey will be much slower.

Developing the intuition leads to expanded awareness of things around you and within you. You will perceive things without logical reasoning, receive insights beyond the normal scope of the mind, and become spiritually sensitive to things the normal five senses do not penetrate. With practice and discipline, realities on a deeper level will open up to you increasingly, for your limited mind will be surrendering over to the Greater Mind of God, just as you will be giving up your will for God's Will to manifest in your life.

One of the most important tools for developing the intuition is meditation. It quiets the mind and opens the heart to the voice of God. As you practice the Spiritual Disciplines, especially concentration, these are primary tools in learning to meditate effectively. You become more spiritually sensitive to certain feelings or receiving impressions or insights that are from God in essence, which is true intuition.

There are other techniques for developing the intuitive faculty, other than meditation, simply mute your mind, get focused and centered within, and become receptive to inner impressions, and a repetitive mantra at a particular seat of human faculty brings realization of that needed intuitive experience.

Intuition is a valuable spiritual gift of grace given to us by God in His immense love for us that we may become one with our Divine Source. One should develop it and use it wisely.

View of Consciousness in Sant Mat

The following are the prevalent views of Consciousness in the Sant Mat.

1. The Supreme consciousness is formless, infinite and unlimited and its current in form of Shabda (holy word) issued from Him in the beginning of the creation and descended downward and at some stage assumed color, form and outline creating different regions each having a presiding deity and its own characteristic and covered by gross or subtle created substance called Maya which gets going by the presence of the same original conscious current.

2. The covers of Maya (gross and subtle body and mind) gets thicker and thicker as one descends to lower regions but sustains and further grows only in the presence of that formless same original spirit current which is not easily recognizable to the sentient being.

3. Those who recognize their existence due to the presence of the current try to free themselves from the clutches of Maya and ascend upwards. As per Sant Mat religion it is possible for the spirit to ascend from one region to another region until it reaches the region of the final and ultimate form. That form would then enable it to have the experience and knowledge of the formless region and make it reach there.

4. The only method is to catch hold of the spirit current (Shabda) through which he was created and ascend upwards and pass through all curtains. If he aligns himself through "Bhakti Marga" and "Surat Sabda Yoga" to a presiding diety who has out of mercy taken a form of this region but is always in communion with the Supreme formless consciousness (referred as "Sant Satguru"), his task of complete salvation from bounds of Maya becomes possible and he merges back with the supreme consciousness. Or else in past many ended in intermediate regions depending on the diety to whom they aligned and thought it to be their last destination and as a consequence could not completely get out of the clutches of time and Maya and again fell back to lower regions once their period of stay in the elevated region was over.

5. The most important revelation in clear terms by Sant Mat religion is the reassertion that the functioning of the entire creation is carried out through consciousness and is the supreme observer and master. The same exposition is found in the text of the world's two biggest religions- Christianity and Islam. It is declared: - "It was word and only word in the beginning. Everything has come out from word and is sustaining due to word and it is the will of the word that everything created gets annihilated back to word." The source of this word has been given different names viz God, Allah with attributes which are inexhaustible to be described in this limited world of ours but nevertheless means same in essence. In other words, all kind of knowledge, art and skill and all kinds of things, appliances, machines etc. which are found in the world are all the creation of this same conscious spirit found flowing maximum in human beings which is the most dominant creation of this physical world. The outward maintenance and organization of this world is being carried on by the same

consciousness which is same as the essence of the creator.

6. This is something which the science discipline has been refuting or partially accepting but is also realizing that accepting theoretically the presence of consciousness as a fundamental solves many of the paradoxes which are posed during unified field theory and quantum analysis. In coming times this will be an interesting area of research and progress is expected.

Summary and Conclusion

There are at present many major but conflicting schools of consciousness theory and research. Each of these schools has something irreplaceably important to offer.

1. Cognitive science tends to view consciousness as anchored in functional schemas of the brain/mind.

2. Introspectionism maintains that consciousness is best understood in terms of intentionality, anchored in first-person accounts.

3. Neuropsychology views consciousness as anchored in neural systems, neurotransmitters, and organic brain mechanisms.

4. Individual psychotherapy tends to view consciousness as primarily anchored in an individual organism's adaptive capacities.

5. Social psychology views consciousness as embedded in networks of cultural meaning.

6. Clinical psychiatry field increasingly tends to view consciousness in strictly neurophysiological and biological terms.

7. Developmental psychology views consciousness not as a single entity but as a developmentally unfolding process. This includes higher stages of cognitive, affective, somatic, moral, and spiritual development.

8. Psychosomatic medicine views consciousness as strongly and intrinsically inter-active with organic bodily processes.

9. Non-ordinary states of consciousness, from dreams to psychedelics, constitute a field of study that, its advocates believe, is crucial to a grasp of consciousness in general.

10. Eastern and contemplative traditions maintain that ordinary consciousness is but a narrow and restricted version of deeper or higher modes of awareness, and that specific injunctions (yoga, meditation) are necessary to evoke these higher and exceptional potentials. Moreover, they all maintain that the essentials of consciousness itself can only be grasped in these higher, post-formal, and non-dual states of consciousness.

11. What might be called the quantum consciousness approaches view consciousness as being intrinsically capable of interacting with, and altering, the physical world, generally through quantum interactions, both in the human body at the intracellular level (e.g. microtubules), and in the material world at large (psi). This approach also includes the many and various attempts to plug consciousness into the physical world according to various avant-garde physical theories (bootstrapping, hyperspace, strings).

12. Subtle energies research has postulated that there exist subtler types of bio-energies beyond the four recognized forces of physics (strong and weak

nuclear, electromagnetic, gravitational), and that these subtler energies play an intrinsic role in consciousness and its activity. Known in the traditions by such terms as prana, ki, and chi.

One thing seems to be that the reality of consciousness is multidimensional and has no boundaries. The various school of study view reality within their own restricted dimensions or disciplines and arrive at different interpretations of truth and presently all standpoints of view have to be taken in account so that one day an integral approach of consciousness develops when science, religion and philosophy converge to the same conclusion. It is the consciousness which will only let things happen; only it's a question of progress in religion, science and philosophy with time and how vividly consciousness evolves in us to unfurl its unadulterated, multidimensional truth.

References

Antony, Michael V. (2008). Are Our Concepts Conscious State and Conscious Creature Vague? *Erkenntnis*, 68(2), 239-263.

Chalmers David J. (1997). *The Problems of Consciousness*. Arizona, USA: Department of Philosophy, University of Arizona.

Claus, J. (2000). Omnipresent Consciousness and Free Will, Freedom of Choice - A Real Solution to the Problem. First published in *German Magazine, Nr. 10*. (Translated from German by Mary Rose).

Huzur Maharaj [Rai Bahadur Salig Ram Sahab] (2006). *Sar Updesh*. Agra, India: Radhasoami Satsang Sabha, Dayalbagh.

Ken, W. (1997). An Integral Theory of Consciousness. *Journal of Consciousness Studies*, 4 (1).

Pandit, M.P. (1986). *The Yoga of Knowledge Based on Sri Aurobindo's Synthesis of Yoga*. USA: Lotus Press.

Wolf, Fred Alan (1998). The Soul and Quantum Physics. Rosen, Eliot Jay (Ed.). In *Experiencing the Soul: Before Birth, During Life, After Death*. (pp. 245-252). Carlsbad, CA, USA: Hays House.

Chapter 6

A Fundamental Understanding of the Comprehensive Characteristic of Consciousness

VIMLARANI CHOPRA AND MITALI SHARAN
Houston, TX, USA and Los Angeles, CA, USA

Abstract

This paper explains the basic working of the conscious mind. Emphasis is laid on the word "conscious"; and not on the mechanical working of the brain. Consciousness is an individual's perception of his own internal mental state, a private universe of his own. The science of knowing the past, present and the future is a part of meditation known to disciples of various religions. As per various creational postulates when the ego was created it formed the mind, the body, and the senses of the gross world. All of this involved action or karma. The 'Creational Systems Theory' published by Revered Professor Satsangi Sahab, The eighth Sant Sat Guru of Radhasoami faith clearly explains the essence of the Supreme Spiritual Current manifested in the Sant Satguru for the redemption of Jivas who are the Microcosm of the Macrocosm after the annihilation of their karmas. A scientific exploration of all these states of consciousness by experimentation of Surat Shabda Yoga comprises the science of Ultra-transcendental Consciousness.

Introduction

Consciousness is variously defined as subjective experience, awareness, wakefulness, or the executive control system of the mind. The words "conscious" (adjective) and "consciousness" (noun) cover a wide variety of mental phenomena and are used with a diversity of meanings being applied both to whole organisms (creature consciousness) and to particular mental states and processes (state consciousness). The words "conscious" and "conscience" are used quite differently today, it is likely that the reformation emphasis on the latter as an inner source of truth played some role in the inward turn so characteristic of the modern reflective view of self. Consciousness is the subject of much research in philosophy of mind, psychology, neuroscience, cognitive science, and artificial intelligence. Issues of practical concern include how the presence of consciousness can be assessed in severely ill or comatose people and whether non-human consciousness exists and if so how it can be measured. Many questions are unanswered and science cannot explain as to at what point in fetal development consciousness begins; and if computers can achieve a conscious state (1). The subconscious mind is also mostly unknown to us, but that is where all our vibrations and impressions are stored. The subconscious mind has a storage capacity that includes everything from the creation of each soul up to the present moment and into the future. It retains all records of actions and karmas.

What is Consciousness?

Understanding consciousness involves a multiplicity of questions that have been posed and the sorts of answers they require. The relevant questions can be:

- The Descriptive Question: What is consciousness? What are its principal features? By what means can they be best discovered, described and modeled?
- The Explanatory Question: How does consciousness of the relevant sort come to exist? Is it a primitive aspect of reality, and if not how does (or could) consciousness in the relevant respect arise from or be caused by non-conscious entities or processes?
- The Functional Question: Why does consciousness of the relevant sort exist? Does it have a function, and if so what it is it? Does it act causally and if so with sorts of effects? Does it make a difference to the operation of systems in which it is present, and if so why and how?

Theories of Consciousness

These questions focus on describing the features of consciousness, explaining its underlying basis or cause, and explicating its role or value (2). Is consciousness a fundamental feature of reality in its own right, or does its existence depend upon other non-conscious items, be they physical, biological, neural or computational? Consciousness is especially resistant to explanation in physical terms because of the inherent differences between our subjective and objective modes of understanding. Many theories of consciousness have been proposed which vary in their theoretical aims —cognitive, neural or quantum mechanical to model consciousness as a natural feature of the physical world. The nature and basis of consciousness cannot be adequately understood within the framework of classical physics but must be sought within the alternative picture of physical reality provided by quantum mechanics (3).

Types of Consciousness

An animal, person or other cognitive system may be regarded as conscious in a number of different senses: sentience, wakefulness, self-consciousness, conscious states, transitive consciousness, etc. One can refer specifically to phenomenal consciousness, access consciousness, reflexive or meta-mental consciousness, and narrative consciousness among other varieties. Consciousness in medicine (e.g., anesthesiology) is assessed by observing a patient's alertness and responsiveness, and can be seen as a continuum of states ranging from alert, oriented to time and place, and communicative, through disorientation, then delirium, then loss of any meaningful communication, and ending with loss of movement in response to painful stimulation. Consciousness in psychology and philosophy has four characteristics: subjectivity, change, continuity and selectivity. The word "Conscious" is endowed with the power of knowing one's own thoughts and actions, and definition of "consciousness" is the perception of what passes in a man's own mind. Access consciousness is the experience whereby information in our minds is accessible for verbal report, reasoning, and the control of behavior is less mysterious than phenomenal consciousness. Phenomenal consciousness is simply know-how and often governs our behavior. Events that occur in the mind or brain that are not within phenomenal or access consciousnesses are known as subconscious events (4). Computer scientists working in the field of Artificial Intelligence have pursued the goal of creating digital computer programs that can simulate consciousness. Some of these quantum mechanics theories offer descriptions of phenomenal consciousness, as well as quantum mechanical interpretations of access consciousness (5).

Anatomically the human being is composed of two elements, body and mind, and that conscious experience resides in the human brain often, associated with human consciousness and the rational soul. Subconscious mind goes on storing each action-reaction whether it happens in dreaming or wakeful states. It is the greatest computer chip ever created with the capacity to record trillions of bits of data. At the point that a reaction from an action is set in motion, that particular karma emerges out of the subconscious mind with its own force and motion, dependent upon time and space. If the spirit force has gone beyond time and space, it is free of karma. The circular motion of karma is such that it will meet or converge whether we are conscious of it or not (6).

Functions of Consciousness

Consciousness can be considered as a supremely functional adaptation of living organism and suggests a variety of functions in which consciousness plays an important role, if not essential, roles: prioritization of alternatives, problem solving, decision making, brain processes recruiting, action control, error detection, planning, learning, adaptation, context creation, and access to information. Hence, consciousness can be considered as a part of an organism's survival kit, allowing planned rather than instinctual responses. Awareness of self allows a concern for one's own survival, which increases the drive to survive, although how far consciousness is involved in behavior is an actively debated issue (7).

Regarding the primary function of conscious processing, a recurring idea in recent theories is that phenomenal states somehow integrate neural activities and information-processing that would otherwise be independent. Obviously not all kinds of information are capable of being disseminated consciously (e.g., neural activity related to vegetative functions, reflexes, unconscious motor programs, low-level perceptual analyses, etc.). At this point it is important to mention that spirituality is directly related to inner consciousness of humans and directs all actions of all humans directed towards worldly and spiritual progress (8).

Transcendental Consciousness as per Radhasoami Faith

Prime Spiritual Energy possessed by the Supreme Being is all-powerful, all-intelligent and all-blissful. All the forces of nature have evolved by the association of this energy with different media in different planes. When the energy is withdrawn to the higher plane from a plane which is not its original plane of existence but is capable of manifesting there, it is called latent energy. The distinctive feature of matter is that it exercises a restrictive influence on the spirit force. The individual constituents of matter like atoms, ions or still subtle particles, exercise restraint over the spiritual force that is imbibed by them.

This creation is therefore capable of inversion and as a result everything in this creation gets transformed into subtler conditions surcharged with energy (9). The Supreme Being, all Gracious, brought this creation into existence, which burst forth when a mighty current of Infinite Spirituality made its advent into the different strata of the nether pole. His object was not in any way less generous in the evolution of the other parts of the creation dependent on their spirituality. The description of the process of creation and explanation of the reasons for superiority of the human frame (according to the Radhasoami Faith) presented above clearly are based on systematic study. Indian tradition stands for unity of consciousness and integration of knowledge. Prime Spirit force is Sat, Chit and Ananda – Truth, Consciousness and Bliss. The mission of the entire mankind is to know the Ultimate Knowledge and attain salvation, as per Radhasoami Faith. An integrated approach to knowledge of the Self, the Prime Spirit Force and worldly knowledge alone can give the right world view and save mankind. For this, the development of Consciousness Studies is the foundation (10).

Conclusion

Science and Religion will culminate in the emergence of a Science of Ultra-transcendental Consciousness which includes consciousness of all inner realms spoken of in all religions. There is unlikely to be any single theoretical perspective that suffices for explaining all the features of consciousness that we wish to understand. Perhaps no aspect of mind is more familiar or more puzzling than consciousness and our conscious experience of self and world. Human irrationality and selfishness without consciousness and spirituality have been great obstacles in the realization of the ideal of Human Unity and salvation of Universe.

References

Amadei, G., Bianchi, I, and Sander, L.W. (2008). *Living Systems, Evolving Consciousness, and the Emerging Person: A Selection of Papers from the Life Work of Louis Sander*. New York, USA: Analytic Press, Psychoanalytic Inquiry Book Series, 26.

Brennan, M. (2010). *Curating Consciousness: Mysticism and the Modern Museum*. Cambridge, Massachusetts, USA: MIT Press.

Combs, A. (2009). *Consciousness Explained Better: Towards an Integral Understanding of the Multifaceted Nature of Consciousness*. St. Paul, MN, USA: Paragon House.

Frohock, F. M. (2000). *Lives of the Psychics: The Shared Worlds of Science and Mysticism*. Chicago, USA: University of Chicago.

Kriegel, U. (2009). *Subjective Consciousness: A Self-Representational Theory*. Oxford, UK: Oxford University Press.

Mathur, V., and Kumari, K.M. (2009). Grades of Consciousness: A Systems Perspective. *Literary Paritantra (Systems)*, 1, 45-49.

Squires, E. J. (1990). *Conscious Mind in the Physical World*. Bristol, UK; New York, USA: A. Hilger.

Sriramamurti, P. (2007). Science and Spirituality: Towards a Science of Ultra-Transcendental Consciousness. *DEI Journal of Science and Engineering Research*, 14, 229-236.

Sriramamurti, P., and Patvardhan, C. (2007). Creational Process According to Radhasoami Faith. *DEI Journal of Science and Engineering Research*, 14, 261-273.

Tye, M. (2009). *Consciousness Revisited: Materialism Without Phenomenal Concepts*. Cambridge, MA, USA: MIT Press.

Chapter 7

Spiritual Consciousness: Different Phases of Life and its realization

A. VASDEV RAJU
SRF Ltd., Gurgaon, india

A. CHARAN KUMARI
Dayalbagh Educational Institute (Deemed University), Agra, India

Abstract

Spiritual Consciousness is a philosophical concept related to higher regions. Everyone can realize the effect of Spiritual Consciousness during their life time, but the degree of Consciousness varies from person to person based on the intensity of the link that one has established with the Source of Consciousness – Supreme Father Huzur Radhasoami Dayal. The jivas on the earth go through various phases across the spectrum of the life cycle and definitely realize the effect of Consciousness in different modes. In this paper, we identified the two broad phases of the human life. The first phase is childhood and student life. During this phase, the simple mandates to follow are Education (adhyayan), Community Service (seva) and Physical exercise (vyayam). The second phase is the adult life. In this period, the principles to be adopted are Satsang, Seva, Spiritual Practices (Abhyaas) and discharging duties. The only way to realize Spiritual Consciousness during different phases of oneslife cycle is to sincerely execute the mandates and principles suggested by the Supreme Father from time to time; to experience better worldliness through "Fatherhood of God and Brotherhood of man" and also for achieving the ultimate objective of life – redemption from the cycle of birth and death.

Introduction

Spiritual Consciousness is highly philosophical and is related to higher regions. Everyone can understand the concept of Simple Consciousness with a little effort. It is quite difficult for a lay man to understand the concept of Spiritual Consciousness. ***Chait + anyata (consciousness)*** means - the inner power of decision making between right and wrong / attaining a state of purity and bliss/ experiencing extreme happiness. Once a person starts introspection and realizes the effect of the state of the mind, then he can understand that his journey of realization of consciousness is in progress.

A person can only realize the effect of consciousness while the things are under control or out of control. But it is very difficult for him to assess the impact of consciousness as it depends on person's state of mind, act and distance from the source of Consciousness.

Based on the strong faith and realization of Consciousness during each and every step of our lives, an attempt has been made to identify the effect of Consciousness during the two broad phases of life.

Existence of Consciousness

It is a strong realization among most of us that Consciousness exists all over the place in the creation. But the degree of consciousness may be different. It is like the growth of a sapling into a big tree. All the saplings definitely grow day by day but the degree of growth is directly proportional to the factors like sunlight, water, nature of soil etc.

Degree of Consciousness

Degree of consciousness depends on various factors like association of inner self with the source of Consciousness, surrounding environments, clarity of thoughts/act etc. It is depicted in the diagram- Fig.1.

The diagram reveals that degree of consciousness has direct correlation with the reservoir of spirit force - Param Purush Puran Dhani Huzur Radhasoami Dayal, whose mission is to redeem the jivas from the cycle of birth and death (Jiva Uddhar). Therefore, for focused and timely attainment of the ultimate objective it is imperative to follow the mandates/directions given by the Supreme Father from time to time and to have better worldliness through "Fatherhood of God and Brotherhood of man".

The diagram also reveals that the Sun provides light(consciousness) to the entire earth and the Sun gets light from higher region(Bharmanda) and

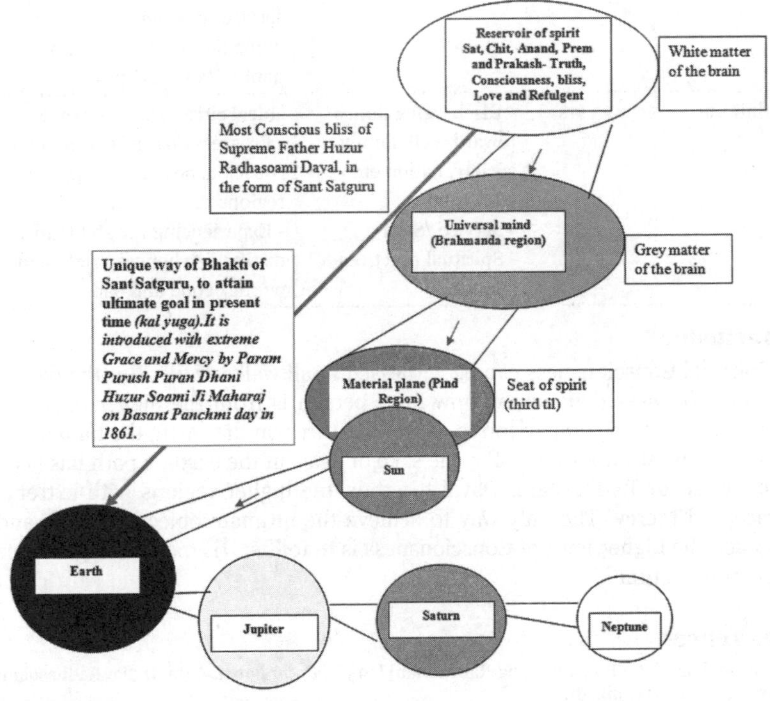

Fig.1

Note: The diagram is based on Prem Patra of Param Guru Huzur Maharaj (Second Revered Sant Satguru of Radhasoami Faith) and Rudimentary modeling framework for spiritual domains of Most Revered Gracious Huzur Prem Saran Satsangi Sahab.

Bharmanda gets consciousness from the white matter region(complete consciousness). Indeed consciousness on earth is very insignificant in comparison to different regions existing above.

Different Phases of Life and Consciousness

The pre-requisites for experiencing consciousness would be based on ones willingness to experience the same without using artificial, materialistic tools/ methods. The following table indicates the two broad phases in the life of a human being and the simple ways to achieve the Spiritual Consciousness.

Phase of life	Approx. age	Expected act/behavior	Experience of consciousness
Child hood and student life	Up to 22 yrs	-Education (Adhyayan) -Servicefor community (Seva) - physical exercise to keep a good physique (Vyayaam)	-attention towards studies - all round development of personality - building of innovative and creative mind - Character building -Devotion towards social service, spiritual activities like doing *Sumiran* of the holy name- Radhasoami.
Adult life	>= 23 yrs	- Discharging duties towards self, family, society, nation etc - Satsang - Service /Seva - Spiritual practices (Abhyaas)	-Ideal citizen/human being - Progress on self realization of consciousness/attaining higher regions - Experiencing the ability to distinguish between right and wrong/ good and bad

Conclusion

Spiritual Consciousness can be witnessed in all walks of life. But the degree of Consciousness depends on how far a person is from the higher region of Consciousness. In comparison to all the creatures on the earth, the human life has the highest importance. For the sake of jivas on the earth, a path has been laid by Huzur Radhasoami Dayal to attain the higher regions with extreme Grace and Mercy. The only way to achieve the ultimate objective of life and to reach the higher level of Consciousness is to follow His mandates/guidance from time to time.

References

Huzur Maharaj [Rai Bahadur Salig Ram Sahab] (1958). *Prem Patra*. Agra, India: Radhasoami Satsang Sabha, Dayalbagh.

Maharaj Sahab [Pt Brahm Sankar Misra Sahab] (2004). *Discourses on Radhasoami Faith*. Agra, India: Radhasoami Satsang Sabha, Dayalbagh.

Satsangi, P.S. [Revered Prof. Prem Saran Satsangi] (2003). Reality and Truth vis-à-vis Wisdom (via Aparavidya and Paravidya). International Conference of the Association of Asia-Pacific Operational Research Societies. Delhi, India.

Chapter 8

The Scientific Quest of Higher Consciousness: Supreme End of Spirituality

RICHA SATSANGI
Dayalbagh Educational Institute (Deemed University), Agra, India

Abstract

Consciousness is the seed of all creation and is a multifaceted puzzle. Consciousness is defined as basic awareness. Consciousness involves thoughts, sensations, perceptions, moods, emotions, dreams, and an awareness of self. It involves phenomenal experience, self-awareness, feelings, choices, control of actions, model of the world etc. Self consciousness is associated with the mind and higher consciousness experiences are beyond the realms of mind and can only be experienced by the spirit. The third eye (pineal gland) is a portal through which consciousness can be expanded through focused attention/ meditation. Consciousness at every step involves increase of knowledge, intelligence, bliss, power, perception and wisdom. In everyday consciousness, the attention current is outwardly disposed, through meditation it can be focused, thus becomes most powerful. Spiritual consciousness is beyond body experiences and is mystical. The human body is a perfect microcosm of macrocosm. Man is endowed with the special instrument of discrimination of judgment, of analysis and synthesis, which is unique. He has to develop this and utilize it to its best purpose. Through this instrument he can realize the Immanent Divinity. Consciousness can be increased by rendering kinetic portals present in the human brain.

Introduction

Reality can be understood in two ways as Science and Spirituality (religion). Scientists look at the world from the viewpoint of four quantities viz. Space, Time, Energy and Matter (STEM). Saints see this as arising from consciousness. In speculative convergence, Universal Spiritual Consciousness (USC) constitutes the foundational premise for understanding the unity between science and spirituality. In religion this (USC) has been given varying names and forms such as GOD, Supreme Being. In science, USC is a unified force field revealing itself through space, time, and consciousness (STC). Sharma (2005) has represented this geometry as space time consciousness. Consciousness is the origin of two collapsed variables of ST& EM. Unfolding of these variables leads to realizing the supreme consciousness (Fig1a). Upanishads, Vedas, Sant Mat and Sufi discourses are authentic and authoritative, which shine in pristine glory and where enough data is available for mastering this quest. By Surat Shabd Yoga the spirit can be Quantum teleported to regions of higher consciousness.

Modern day scientists know that consciousness is the omniscient, omnipresent, all pervasive substance behind existence, the source of every event, condition and circumstance experienced in life. In these scientific expositions the divine nature of a human being is forgotten; that he has higher order of spiritual potential. The brain is indeed a prerequisite for all conscious experiences but it is not a generator; rather it is a transmitter. Through cognitive studies it has been revealed that it is the Soul that manifests through the body and mind. Intelligence and cognition are the faculties of the soul and are its media of expression of consciousness. Through the mind, the soul performs the functions of the brain and activates the nervous system. Mind and soul can get dissociated from the arousal mechanism on their own or by drugs or hypnotism. Functions of selection and rejection as well as correction of data belong to the soul. Therefore, guidance of man to higher levels of consciousness and life can be achieved only through the awakening of spiritual faculties.

Quantum theory awareness is, facilitating to understand science behind smallest particles. Soul which is subtlest is aware, omnipotent, and omniscient. Like all energy fields, it also has a reservoir which is Universal consciousness (God) and soul particle which is entangled with it. Will, intention and interests are of mind and soul, which channelize the activity of the brain in the desired direction. The soul has self awareness and it can produce changes in the brain. Experiential and operational unity besides neurological unity, is due to the soul.

Scientific Outlook: Neurobiological Approach

The hypothalamus, thalamus and prefrontal lobes and other parts of brain are merely the mechanism for exteriorization or inhibition of emotions though the emotions belong to mind and soul. When these subtle planes are acted upon through nerve centers, communication with the macrocosmic spheres corresponding to them is established and the powers of the presiding deities of these spheres are imbibed. The brain from which the lower nerve centers have been created is similarly associated with very subtle planes. They do not belong to that part of creation, but to the higher regions of creation viz., to those of the universal mind and to those of the source of the pure spirit, the true Supreme Being. By developing the latent powers of these planes in the brain, communion can be established with Brahma and the true Supreme Creator. This function of the brain emphasizes the supreme importance of this organ in the economy of the microcosm.

In the fissure between the two lobes of the brain there are twelve apertures, which provide the means for communion with the six Subdivisions of Brahmanda and with the six sub-divisions of the purely spiritual region. The apertures (kamals) appertaining to Brahmanda are to be found in the grey matter, and those appertaining to the pure spiritual region (padams), in the white matter. Higher consciousness is thus experience of Supreme or Universal consciousness and can only be experienced by meditation. Brain Energy Supports the State of Consciousness (Shulman et al 2009). The most striking result is that the energy consumption supporting neuronal firing in the conscious- awake, baseline state is one to two orders of magnitude larger than the energy changes during stimulation (Fig 1b). The modern quest to understand the relationship between the subjective, conscious mind and the objective, material brain is focused on the empirically tractable problem of isolating the neuronal correlates of consciousness (NCC), the minimal set of neuronal events and structures jointly sufficient for any one specific conscious percept. The quality of consciousness depends on the quality of the mind; and the quality of the mind depends on the emotional and physical quality of the brain. All mind power comes from the brain that is developed to its highest potential.

Scientific Outlook: Quantum Mechanics Approach

Quantum effects show up most readily at the subatomic level, but empirical research into large-scale systems has also demonstrated that mind can influence matter. However, Planck's length, which is what obtained at the beginning of the physical universe, is 10-35 metre, i.e. almost four times exponentially as subtle as nanotechnology (i.e. nano). As we reach an even subtler entity, we reach the mind domain (zero mass, zero dimensions); if we get further subtler, we reach the spirit domain. So it can be visualized what kind of a sub-sub-sub-microscopic technology the Supreme Being invokes in bringing about the Universe (Macrocosm) into existence. Quantum teleportation is estimated to be still 50 years away; the spiritual quantum teleportation is already a reality which can be experienced by a meditationist through practice of "Surat Shabda Yoga".

Spiritual Approach: Conscious Energy Fields

Man is endowed with faculties of perceptions of higher order than those of the familiar knowledge, senses and mind. The subtle fields co-exist within the same space, and influence each other. Their distinctiveness lies in the fact that each has its own unique type of energy and rate of vibration. The aura is made up of at least seven bands or (subtle) bodies: the Etheric, the emotional, the mental, the astral and the causal, soul and spiritual. The *chakra* centers are affected by both light and sound, especially when used in conjunction with each other. The human body has seven *chakras* or energy levels. The *chakras* are dimensional portals within the subtle bodies which take in and process energy of a higher vibrational nature so that it may be properly assimilated and used to transform the physical body (Fig 1c). Each *chakra* has what is called a bija mantras "seed sound". These seed sounds are the symbolic representations of the energy pattern of each *chakra* and hold its essence.

Ra-dha-Soa-mi which is dhyunyatamak (ever resonating, ever gener-

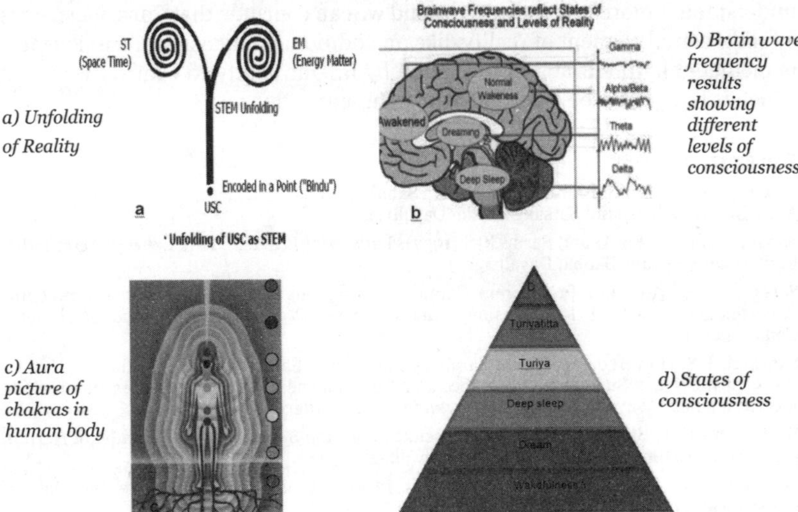

a) Unfolding of Reality

b) Brain wave frequency results showing different levels of consciousness.

c) Aura picture of chakras in human body

d) States of consciousness

Fig 1: Higher consciousness

ating in universe) sound (word) when used as a mool-mantra for all *chakra* consciousness, leads to immense effects and to higher conscious levels, even beyond Brahmanda or universal mind region. When the mind becomes concentrated, one pointed, inward, it peers into the latent part of unconsciousness and there it finds a glittering light. Aim of meditation is to go into the silence from where wisdom flows with all its majesty. It leads to intuitive knowledge, and then one perceives reality. Ultimately, the stage is reached where the *chakra* or centre with which God-perception is possible, becomes kinetic. The consciousness of mind is derived from the consciousness of the spirit and all the activities and the functions of mind are due to this reflected consciousness. Beyond the seventh *chakra* (shashara) it's a purely spiritual path and experiences (Fig 1d). Beyond Turiya state its purely spiritual consciousness (Atmapad). Consciousness is thus completely understood only by developing spiritual faculties and reaching the plane of higher consciousness by itself. All physical science tools and techniques cannot completely comprehend it. It is the supreme end of spirituality.

Conclusion

The human eye cannot delve into the minute or the magnitude. It cannot read the mystery of a virus or an atom or stellar universe. Therefore, scientists rely on the telescope or microscope. Similarly, sages are able to experience Divinity through the eye of knowledge, gained by following the dharma of moral conduct and spiritual discipline. It is hard to obtain the eye of wisdom; it requires purity of consciousness, moral awareness and spirituality. Therefore, it is only through the spiritual journey that one can experience higher consciousness, not via any scientific tools or techniques. Systems theory of Revered P.S. Satsangi (2007) explains one fundamental axiom and 3 creational postulates in a scientific way and is a solution, explanation, for the origin of consciousness and how it can be developed to its fullest attributes. The holistic approach of science will help in solving this quest. Like a true scientist we should experience this by ourselves and understand it more precisely. In the end we can conclude that Consciousness is a fundamental element of reality, like an additional dimension. Consciousness is mediated by the brain, not excreted by it. Our ability to connect with that which is larger may be a normal state of human beings.

References

Maharaj Sahab [Pandit Brahm Sankar Misra Sahab] (2004). *Discourses on Radhasoami Faith*. Agra, India: Radhasoami Satsang Sabha, Dayalbagh.

Sahabji Maharaj [Sir Anand Sarup Kt.] (1957). *Yathartha Prakash*, Part 1, 2 & 3. Agra, India: Radhasoami Satsang Sabha, Dayalbagh

Satsangi, P.S. [Revered Prof. Prem Saran Satsangi], and Sahni, V. (2007). A Systemic Experimental Study of Macrocosmic Consciousness. *Proceedings of National Systems Conference*, 1-7.

Satsangi, P.S. [Revered Prof. Prem Saran Satsangi], and Sahni, V. (2008). Study of Human Consciousness as a Surrogate of Macrocosmic Consciousness via Scientific Measurements of Electromagnetic Wave Radiations. *National Systems Conference*.

Sriramamurti, P. Science of Spiritual Consciousness - the Super Science. *Dayalbagh Herald*, Agra, India: Radhasoami Satsang Sabha, Dayalbagh.

Shulman, R.G, Hyder, F. and Rothman D.L. (2009). Brain Energy Supports the State of Consciousness. *Psyche, Vol 15, No 2*.

Chapter 9

Collective Consciousness

GAZAL MATHUR
Dayalbagh Educational Institute (Deemed University), Agra, India

Abstract
Humanity is now burdened by a boding sense of futility. The strife of modern day society is taking its toll on a physical, mental and spiritual level. The more we enmesh ourselves in materialism – the greater is our internal discontent. So does it stand to reason that we separate ourselves from this society that we perceive to be the root cause of our discontent - a hermitage of sorts – OR does the answer lie in its exact contrast? Will the act of 'coming together' redeem us and lead us to the path of true salvation? This paper deals with 'Collective Consciousness' – a concept with which we are just coming to terms with. Religion has always propagated collectivity but it is with the advent of a scientific postulate that science and religion seem to have come full circle. Quantum Entanglement delves into the possibility - that at the metaphysical level, we are but mere parts of a greater whole. Parapsychology experiments with the concept of a universal consciousness, almost as if we are all plugged into the same mainframe and merge on some esoteric level. Will Humanity finally become a unified whole and imbibe the true essence of "Fatherhood of God and Brotherhood of Man"?

Collective Conscious

"There lies strength in numbers". A phrase that most of us are well acquainted with, yet I feel, have not truly grasped its overwhelming purview.

In fact, in recent days - this phrase (for me) has been the source of an internal upheaval – one which embodies a sense of revelation, euphoria and also a burdening sense of responsibility.

We are not only answerable to ourselves but to humanity as a whole and our individual actions are directly correlated to the future of the universe. Quite a burden to bear! This especially comes as a somewhat rude awakening to a society which has been nurtured on the premise of "each man for himself"

But on the other hand "strength in numbers" creates a welcoming cocoon, a newfound brotherhood and a confidence that at the end of the day we are all like the colors of the spectrum contained in the color white – a unified whole!

Collectivity is a concept that has always been advocated by religion and has been an appeal to the masses to live, think and pray together but the benefactor in society's eyes has always been the individual himself i.e. the confirmation to social and religious tenets would create the perfect environment for an individual's eventual social and spiritual development. Where this still holds true, it is now with the advent of a new scientific supposition that a paradigm shift has been created. The belief that there may be no individual to begin with – just parts of a Singularity. So, it is with this paradigm shift that the true purport of 'collective consciousness' comes into play.

Emile Durkheim first used the term 'collective consciousnesses' to describe traditional/primitive societies and how religion played an important role in uniting members through the creation of a common consciousness. In societies of this type, the contents of an individual's consciousness are largely shared in common with all other members of their society, creating a mechanical solidarity through mutual likeness. But where Durkheim's reference was more to 'conscience' or the moral binding of a society rather than 'consciousness', it is our modern scientific community that has now taken a "quantum leap" in the understanding of what a collective consciousness really is. It delves into what the scientific basis of a collective consciousness is and whether it is possible for a group of people to establish one stable collective consciousness field.

We now know that atoms and molecules are composed of nothing but electromagnetic fields whose energy comes from a source that is not yet measurable by most conventional methods. As our understanding of this universal energy increases, we conclude that it is intelligent and that it can directly interact with our consciousness.

In modern Quantum Mechanics, most physicists now realize that the outcome of an experiment is dependent on the 'experimenter' or the 'observer'. So, the outcome of the experiment can dramatically change based on the perception of the observer. Thus creating a direct link between consciousness and our physical world!

Even in Parapsychology, tests conducted by PEAR (Princeton Engineering Anomalies Research) and Roger Nelson's Global Consciousness Project show conclusively that human consciousness can affect the outcome of seemingly random procedures such as, among others, in the case affecting computerized random number generators.

Biologist Rupert Sheldrake and others have conducted several experiments that show how 'psi' or extra sensory abilities are now not only the stuff of science fiction but conclusively demonstrate that people can sense the thoughts and intentions of others across space and time.

This research includes studies on a common experience called "the sense of being stared at." By separating two people in a laboratory setting, with the first person hooked up to equipment that monitors his or her nervous system and the second person staring at the first person at random intervals on a closed-circuit television, researchers have collected evidence for the existence of this phenomenon with statistical "odds against chance" of 3.8 million to one.

Sheldrake has also demonstrated in a number of studies that we can assist each other's learning across distances, without any external interaction or communication.

In one study, for instance, a group of individuals completed a newly created crossword puzzle, and their average completion times were recorded. The same puzzle was then broadcast to millions via Television, for the viewers at home to complete. Subsequently, a new group, which had not seen the puzzle at all, finished it significantly faster than the original group, suggesting that as a result of so many individuals having done the puzzle, knowledge of the puzzle was somehow etched into the field of collective consciousness, making it increasingly easier for others to solve.

So is mankind standing at the door of a new awakening? Has science and religion finally come full circle for they now seem to be speaking the same language where the collective mind, body and soul converge into a Unity or Oneness?

It stands to question here that if there is a collective consciousness – how do we strengthen this bond? Could the elemental emotion of love be the answer? It may be love for our fellow man or love for the Divine or Supreme Being.

Love, this romanticized human emotion, is the tendency for entities within the Unified field to increasingly vibrate to a point of Singularity and is capable of affecting us in a very real physiological manner.

It causes more motion in the nervous system and throughout the body – the pupils dilate, heart rate accelerates, skin conductivity changes, perspiration increases, breathing is accelerated and neurological processes flow more quickly, leading to greater inspiration.

Love manifests itself as a radiant motion and can permeate humanity in just the same manner as a ripple exhibits motion and permeates through a body of water.

This subsequently leads to the assumption that if your consciousness is creating ripples, then the greater the amount of love – the greater is the vibrational fusion with the energy of Creation.

The conclusion here is but a simple one – the most complex of problems usually have the simplest of cures. All the strife, angst and suffering in the world may be alleviated through the simple process of coming together. "*Herein lies the strength in numbers*"

References

Grace Davie, G. (2007). *The Sociology of Religion*. Sage Publications.

Wilber, K. (2001). *The Theory of Everything*. Dublin, Ireland: Gateway.

Chapter 10

Spiritual Consciousness: An Essential Kinetic Force

T.P. RAO AND T. SHEETAL PYARI
Dayalbagh Educational Institute (Deemed University), Agra, India

Abstract

The world is full of misconceptions and still too elusive to appear to be real, happy and permanent. The world is a place to compete as well as to become complete. If human beings only compete without 'completeness' then the end result would be ephemeral happiness. Completeness leads to knowledge of 'real', 'ultimate realty', 'perceived truth', 'truth' & 'ultimate truth' leading to the knowledge of life beyond this world of material plane with physical senses. This leads to everlasting happiness & better quality of life. Param Guru Huzur Sahabji Maharaj had said "Education, more education – education made perfect –is the only panacea for our country's ills and evils." Education leads to understanding being made better to distinguish right from wrong. The perfect education with concepts of broad based value education leading to high moral values in an individual leads a person towards consciousness who further becomes fit to gain spiritual consciousness.

Introduction

No matter to which society/group/association they belong, human beings have always been in a cyclical race for proving themselves better or superior to their fellows. This race has led to many problems in the social fabric of the human setup, although these may be brushed aside as offshoots of competition or, at times, as excuses for those who fear to compete. It is often said "We may fail in our attempt, but let us not fail to attempt". While this statement is, in itself, positive and encouraging to growth and gainful momentum in any society, when viewed in isolation the final results may not be conducive to the society for whom the human being ultimately works.

Compete vs Complete

The world is a place to compete and, also, to become complete. If human beings just compete without trying to become complete, then the end result is bound to be lopsided with only short-term understanding and happiness.

What is meant by the word 'complete'? It is the asking of basic, fundamental questions about the purpose of existence in this world; to try and understand the difference between the 'real' and 'ultimate real', as against the 'perceived truth', 'truth' and the 'ultimate truth' of life; and life and knowledge beyond this world of material plane/senses.

Further, it can be said that whereas when humans compete, they produce some positive and some negative results in society (as listed below), it is the quest to complete that would result in an everlasting state of happiness, and a better quality of life for present and future generations of society.

Positive effects of competition:

- Growth
- Prosperity
- Happiness
- Development
- Peace
- Efficiency
- Rules/regulations
- Power
- Knowledge
- Education
- Intelligence

Negative effects of competition

- Lopsided growth
- Groups of haves and have-nots
- Disgruntlement
- Corruption
- Inefficiency
- Degradation of moral value system
- Absolute power centers
- Social disorder
- Economic power zones
- Violence/wars leading to destruction
- Exploitation of economically weak

The question that now very simply arises is: what method should be adopted for the development of human life that can balance material requirements and their quest on one side, with real consciousness leading to spiritual consciousness and permanent happiness, on the other? It is the search for ultimate happiness and imperishable pleasure, as against transitory and ephemeral happiness, that would bring real happiness, prosperity and permanent growth.

Consciousness

Consciousness can be expressed, in simple terms, as being in a wakeful form of life where we see, understand, express and analyze with the use of an intelligence of mind that has been trained and tuned by education and learning through the physical senses.

Let us see this from a layman's point of view. The mind of a person gets a message through the eyes and analyses it, interpreting and extracting information from it against the backdrop of his education and standing. This individual is a social animal, who lives in a group which has further and smaller sub-groups, such as his family etc.

Now, in normal circumstances, every individual is biased towards the smaller sub-group and, only later starts calculations within his mind for the betterment of the larger group to which he belongs. This calculation is based on the requirements of the individual from society (or any particular part or individual of it). Based on the need of the particular individual at that particular point of time, a decision is taken to act in a particular manner.

In order to decipher the meaning and analyze the outcome of the information or the decision, the individual explains to himself that he has acted on the information that was received by him to "the best of my ability". Further justification is put forward by his mind, that society at large and its benefits/needs have been kept in mind before any final decision was taken or initiated, based on the information that was churned/pruned in the background, and on the knowledge/educational abilities that he acquired during his life.

It can very well be ascertained that this whole process is transient and individualistic. It is also very short-lived and impermanent.

There must be some method, then, to make an individual capable enough perform acts in life that are wide-based, deep-rooted and of a permanent nature.

Education and Consciousness

Param Guru Huzur Sahabji Maharaj said "Education, more education – education made perfect –is the only panacea for our country's ills and evils."

Education leads to better understanding; it also helps a person distinguish

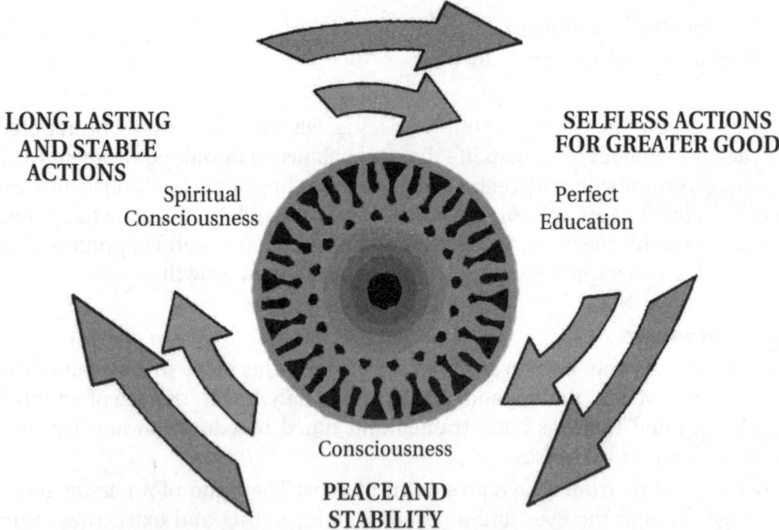

Fig: 1 Perfect education leads to spiritual consciousness; such elevated personalities work selflessly for society at large. Their work has long-lasting effects for peace & stability.

right from wrong. It creates the ability for consciousness with limited frame set-up, as it is perfect education as prescribed by Huzur Sahabji Maharaj that would ultimately lead to improvement in the state of consciousness with better clarity of thoughts.

Perfect education, which develops the following concepts of value education, leads to better consciousness which, in turn, makes one fit to gain spiritual consciousness:

- Broad-based, inter-disciplinary
- Integrated, value-based
- Education teaching dignity of labour
- Education teaching humility and truthfulness
- Inculcating high moral values
- Education for social work
- Education for simple living and high thinking
- Education aiming towards a well-rounded personality of the individual.

The base of consciousness is education, and hence, perfect education is a must for the development and containment of the mind, and to enhance the ability to evaluate right and wrong in terms of the larger canvas of human kind and away from small, individualistic views.

A great saint said-

"Think like a genius,
Work like a giant,
Live like a saint."

It is the ability to be a genius and still be a saint that leads to higher consciousness. Value-based education helps in developing an individual who is fit to live in society at large. This individual would bring about long-term and ever-lasting changes in the world around him, because he has the ability to think better, analyze better and, ultimately, sustain better. Thus, education is immensely important in the development of consciousness, which, in turn, leads to higher, spiritual consciousness and the quality of saintliness. It is only through the enlightenment of the spiritual faculties that a person can make his inner intelligence kinetic.

It is not necessary to renounce the world to open the inner eye. It can well be done by the complementary performance of worldly chores along with spiritual practices under the guidance of a perfect spiritual teacher or Guru. The Guru imparts this unique 'sadhana' to transport an individual from this 'pind desh' to the all-refulgent, glorious, eternal and permanently peaceful 'lok'.

Spiritual Consciousness-Ultimate Source of Peace for Mankind

It is the spirit of detachment from the world and its objects which is most important for a person's peace of mind. Once his mind is in control and does not have any attachment to materialistic objects of the world, then comes the sense of 'tyaga' which leads to actions which are not selfish in nature. Such a person performs actions with societal benefit in mind, as he is above attach-

SPIRITUAL CONSCIOUSNESS AND PEACE

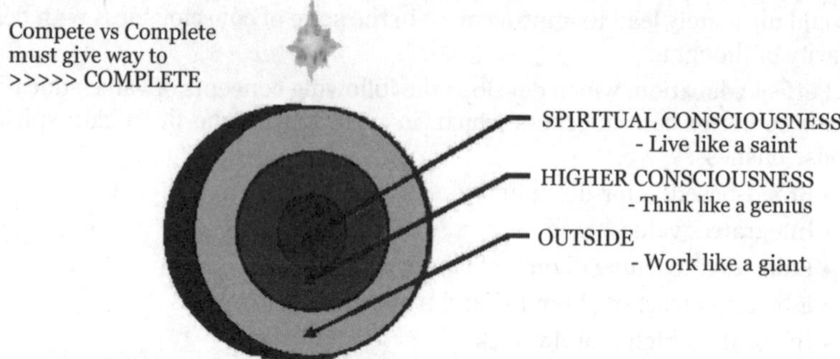

Balance in life is attained by making higher faculties kinetic with the help and grace of a GURU or a SPIRITUAL LEADER which leads to inner contentment which further leads to peace and stability. Such individual takes **selfless actions for society at large with lesser conflicts and increased cohesiveness.**

Fig: 2 Grace of the Guru helps in self contentment-one must do complete surrender

ments. Spiritual consciousness leads to the breaking of all bondages. This leads towards righteous actions of the 'karta'. It is the 'detached involvement' stage of life that, with the blessings of the Guru, helps the individual to reach a higher plane of consciousness–above the stage of consciousness–and guides him to perform only such actions that do not look at short-term gains. These actions reduce the negative effects of any development/ progress which competition brings about in the world.

Spiritual consciousness thus would have a sustained action plan leading to greater stability with peace and tranquility in the world.

As stated in the *Bhagwad Gita*

"He whose undertakings are all free from the will of desire, whose work is burnt up in fire of wisdom, him, the wise call a man of learning."

Once the mind is under control, is free from desire, rises above the material plane and starts thinking of the end of life and beginning after the end- the mind has peace –that is the ultimate need of man- kind.

Moral and ethical values teach us all the way of life which leads, in turn, to a better life.

Conclusion

Perfect education helps us to evaluate right and wrong and gives us the ability to search for the perfect Guru, under whose guidance and teachings we must take forward selfless actions that benefit society at large.

Consciousness through education helps in the attainment of higher and spiritual consciousness, which further leads to action without desire. Such actions are the source of permanent happiness and peace in the world.

The concept of 'better worldliness', as propounded by Param Guru Huzur Sahabji Maharaj, where mutual existence of all with respect being the right of all, is the ultimate mantra for peaceful coexistence of all mankind in every nation.

The flame of desire to search for the perfect Guru and then surrender to Him in unequivocal terms would lead to spiritual consciousness. This surrender to the Guru has to be unconditional and complete, with rationality taking a back seat. The thinking powers which the mind possess are of this plane, and hence not in consonance with higher transitory planes. We must learn to leave the 'pind desh' and transport ourselves to the higher plane which the Guru ordains for us at the appropriate time, with His help. But, such a time would come only when we control our minds and surrender to Him.

References

Bhagavad Gita.

Lal Sahab [Dr. Makund Behari Lal Sahab] (2007). *Bachans of Param Guru Huzur Dr M B Lal Sahab*. Agra, India: Radhasoami Satsang Sabha, Dayalbagh.

Lohrey A. (1997). *The Meaning of Consciousness*. Michigan, USA: University of Michigan Press.

Maharaj Sahab [Pandit Brahm Sankar Misra Sahab] (1988). *Discourses on Radhasoami Faith*. Agra, India: Radhasoami Satsang Sabha, Dayalbagh.

Sahabji Maharaj [Sir Anand Sarup Kt.] (1935). *Huzur Sahabji Maharaj's Speech*, The National Problem of India, Allahabad, India.

Sahabji Maharaj [Sir Anand Sarup Kt.] *Bachans of Huzur Sahabji Maharaj*. Agra, India: Radhasoami Satsang Sabha, Dayalbagh.

Saxena P. K., and Chaturvedi, D. K. (Eds.) (2005). *Theology, Science and Technology: Ethics and Moral Values*. New Delhi, India: Vikas Publishing House.

V

Consciousness in Sant Mat and Other Religions

Chapter 11

The Scientific Spirit in Sant Tradition, A Twentieth-Century Example

DANIEL GOLD
Cornell University, New York, USA

Abstract

This paper discusses the several spiritual traditions that were prevalent since the fifteenth century. Most of these traditions focused on the Lord / Guru to be worshipped and to engage oneself in spiritual practices as well. A comparative of the spiritual practices of the Sant Mat ,the Religion of Saints, and other spiritual yogic practices prevalent in Northern India are presented by the author through a narrative on the Life and yogic experiences of Malik Sahab. He had primarily adopted Sant Mat teachings but Malik Sahab also shared and exchanged the spiritual & yogic knowledge of the Gurus / Sants of the time following other traditions.

As emphasized in central papers by Professors P.S. Satsangi and P. Sriramamurti, the scientific spirit in religion foregrounds the importance of experience—ideally replicable experience—together with an impulse towards the coherent systematization of knowledge. In this way, the scientific spirit seeks to make comprehensive rational sense of the realities we actually perceive. Yet even as attention to experience and rational understanding remain crucial, there are often other, less system-oriented aspects of the scientific spirit that can come into play within religious life. These include: a spiritual curiosity that can lead to new experimentation; a refusal to explain away persistent inconsistencies as current understandings encounter new experience; and a realization that even as knowledge often increases through practical problem solving, the growth of knowledge also sometimes demands basic paradigmatic shifts in thinking. The Hindi Sant tradition—which was only very loosely organized, gave weight to the authority of individual gurus, and could get iconoclastic—had plenty of room for these latter aspects of the scientific spirit along with the former. Today I want to tell the story of a twentieth-century sant who did not hesitate to exercise them. I'll begin, however, by introducing the tradition itself.

The Hindi Sants flourished in North India from about the fifteenth century and continue in different forms today. They comprise one of the last of the traditions of devotional poets in vernacular languages that began in South India in about the sixth century CE. These traditions are all somewhat different from one another, and in the case of the Hindi Sants, two particularities stand out. First, the Sants were devoted to a Lord, who was without qualities, nir-guna in Sanskrit. Theirs was an aniconic, formless divinity. Although he could present himself through internal lights and sounds and a feeling of loving attraction, he was not normally seen in the image of a traditional deity such as Krishna or Shiva, as has been most often the case in Indian devotional traditions. Second, from the beginning, the Sants employed in their verse a particular language of yoga that strongly suggests that some of them, at least, did spiritual practices that entailed paying attention to sounds heard in the body.

Although the variants of Hindi sant tradition were diverse, the verses that its members commonly acknowledged shared some widespread characteristics. In addition to its use of a characteristic yogic language, Sant verse also very frequently extols the Guru, or Satguru, "the True Guru." Praising the Guru is, of course, common in many Indian traditions, but because the Sants recognize no traditional image of the Lord, the figure of the Guru can carry much weight both as a focus for devotion and as a basis for yogic authority. The Guru of Sant verse can thus become a locus of mystery. Depending on context, the Guru may be interpreted as a living person, a founder of a lineage, the transcendent Lord, or some combination of these at once. The Sants also sing conspicuously of śabda, which literally means word or sound. This term is also polyvalent, and can refer to the words of the Living Guru, the songs of a past Guru, the internal sounds that feature in important traditions of Sant practice, or to a primal sound power of which these are all manifestations.

The polysemy in the central terms of Sant verse lends it to both esoteric and more exoteric interpretations. As in many popular traditions, there have certainly been many devotees and probably some figures living as Sants who did little or no meditation practice and for whom the Sant verses had largely exoteric significances. Indeed, some movements invoking past Sants, such as the Raidasis, have been interpreted largely as movements of sociopolitical protest. But one likes to believe that for the great Sants of the past and some of their disciples the verses also had esoteric meanings, tied to practice, and this does seem to have been clearly the case in some eighteenth and nineteenth century lineages. The early Sants—especially the first and best-known Hindi Sant Kabir—were oral poets with a great many verses coming down in their names. It is very hard to know which of these verses can be traced to the historical figures or to be sure about their original esoteric meanings. In part because of this I will focus on figures from the later lineages, which have more stable textual sources, and on their continuing oral commentaries about practice.

The yogic language of the Sants seems to have derived from that of the Naths, a popular tradition of yoga that was current in Kabir's day. It includes common terms such as those for major yogic veins (idā, pingalā, sushumnā) together with less familiar Hindi terms that are now regularly used to indicate areas of concentration in the head. These include terms such as the spotless, or spotless light (Niranjan Jyoti), three-peaks (Trikuṭī), the void (Sunna), and the whirling cave (Bhaṃvar Guphā). The Naths were known as exponents of Haṭhayoga, which entails practices of the body such as pranayama and taps the latent psychic energy known as Kuṇḍalinī. It seems reasonable that early Sants, too, were conversant with the conventional yoga of the body, even if many didn't practice it much. Certainly, the eminent Hindi scholar Hazari Prasad Dwivedi, echoing many other Indian scholars, suggests this is the case. Interpreting Kabir in relation to older yoga and tantra, he notes: "Kabir of course never made clear reference to Kuṇḍalinī, but he was definitely fully aware of this principle" (Sahaj Sādhanā, p.36).

Older, tantric-style yogas, too, know a series of points in the head that are pierced by Kuṇḍalinī as it rises, often accompanied by sound, usually called Nād. In the Nath texts, the Hindi terms adapted by the Sants seem to refer to some of these points, which were probably experienced in a withdrawn yogic way. By the eighteenth century, however, the terms were clearly used in some Sant lineages to refer to experiences of loving devotional ecstasy. Later Sants, moreover, find authority for their usage in verses like these attributed to Kabir, where lights and visions are accompanied by sounds:

Kabir sees a bright shining lotus,
A spotless, risen sun.
Night's darkness disappears: he hears
The horn of unstruck sound.

Kabīr Granthāvalī 9:36

There heavens are thundering, nectar drips down,
Banana trees bloom, and the lotus shines bright:
Where just His few real slaves are found,
Kabir is bound in adoration.

9:35

Perhaps even in Kabir's day Sants had found a way to give new devotional depth to a more quietistic experience that they also knew.

At any rate, as later lineages began developing experiential theologies, the esoteric meaning of śabda becomes something more than internal sound, the "horn" and "thunder" just mentioned. It can also be experienced as a stream into which the devotee merges and which carries him or her along. These lines, part of a verse discourse addressed to the Gulalpanthi poet Bhīkhā, describes the soul leaving the body through śabda, which is first referred to as Anhad Nād, Hindi for the parallel Anāhata Nāda of the yogis. In the late Sant esoteric usage, the void (Sunna), where the disciple here encounters the śabda, normally refers to the region of the mid-forehead:

In the sky-void, Bhikha,
All things have a place.
Anhad Nād, Sabd, vital forces
Consciousness, I tell you.
That void lives in the body—
Manifest in all, in all unmanifest.
When someone comes in touch with it
He finds the Guru's śabda.
The body doesn't merge with it.
The soul does, though, and leaves the body,
Going off in śabda.

(Mahātmāoṃ kī Bānī, p.205).

Paltu Sahib of Ayodhya, an eighteenth-century Sant from the same lineage, offers a lighthearted song apparently describing his ecstatic condition. He came from a merchant caste and plays with his caste identity:

Who will keep my shop now, hey, who will keep the shop? (Refrain)
The goods are all at Trikuṭī, Suṣumnā's got a mattress on the floor;
My main store's at the tenth door, where sits endless Lord. (1)
idā, pingalā, my two scales—they hang from the soul's strings.
I'll grasp the crossbeam of true sound, and weigh out piles of pearls. (2)
The sun and moon will keep up watch on heaps of primal stuff
Climb to turiyā, set up shop—that's how I'll take charge. (3)
The master Satguru's interceded; I've met sweet-seller Rām.
He's sounded the drum at Palṭū's house, who keeps getting paid back a hundred-twenty-five percent (4).

(Palṭū Sāhib kī Bānī, vol. 3, song 81, p.28).

Yet even when favoring devotional rapture, literate Sants throughout the tradition were almost necessarily aware of the general Hindu yogic formulations and incorporated them in their verse. Still, even though mentioning them, they seemed not always to encounter them seriously. Maluk Das, for example, a seventeenth-century figure wrote many verses in a typical Sant style, lauding śabda and Guru, but he also composed concise descriptions of the six *chakras* (Maluk Das, p. 187) as well as of the eightfold exercises of Patanjali's classic eight-limbed yoga. His descriptions of the *chakras*, however, are most formulaic, and his treatment of the eight-limbs is a devotional rewriting of it. He ends, as does Patanjali, with nirvikalpa samadhi, the samādhi "without change":

Then you've stepped into samādhi [8]: no object there at all
Hari's there then face to face, the seer merges with the seen
This is turiyā, how you know Him, what there is to know
Its nirvikalpa, says Maluk Das, nirvāna's abode (82-83).

This is a joyful, face-to-face encounter with the Lord, but doesn't seem to be like anything ever hinted at by Patanjali. The Sant on whom I will focus in the rest of my talk, known to his devotees as Malik Sahib, also spoke of an experience of nirvikalpa, but it was probably an experience closer to Patanjali's, a more serious encounter that evoked a response quite different from Maluk Das' above.

Malik Sahib, whose given name was Mansingh Kushwah, was born in 1909 in the Chambal valley, not far to the south of Agra, and lived much of his life in the city of Gwalior. I met him in Gwalior more than forty years ago while serving as an American Peace Corps volunteer and formed a lasting bond with him. In talking about him, I will draw both on a published biography (Miśra, 1999) and on some of my own memories.

Like many Sants, Malik Sahib was a householder and worked for a living, with a career in the middle ranks of government service in Gwalior State and its successors in the Indian union. After taking early retirement in 1952, he built a large house on the outskirts of Gwalior city that doubled as an ashram, where he passed on in 1983. Although Malik Sahib never had much training in modern science, he was well versed in some Indian sciences and practiced techniques of experiential observation and comprehensive synthesis common in different ways to both traditions. He was also, throughout his life, something of a spiritual adventurer—always curious, keen to experiment, and ready to face new theoretical problems squarely as they arose.

As a young man studying at Sardar's school on Gwalior Fort, they say, Malik Sahib had been long puzzled by verses of Kabir. He consulted with his teachers, but didn't get any satisfying answers until he came into contact with Lala Shyamlal, known as Guru Data Dayala. This Guru traced a lineage to Soamiji Shiv Dayal Singh, the source of the Radhasoami lineage, through Soamiji's younger brother Pratap. The Radhasoamis, who began in the mid-19th century and have branched into several sublineages, are the current main self-conscious bearers of Sant tradition, cultivating the late esoteric strand that the early 19th-century Sant Tulsi Sahib called Sant Mat. Malik Sahib became an ardent disciple of Guru Data Dayala and brought others to him and Sant Mat; when his Guru passed on in 1940; Malik Sahib had experiences that he felt authorized him to offer initiation in the tradition himself (Miśra, 83-91). The managing committee at the Guru's ashram, however, had other ideas, although it in fact never managed to find a viable successor.

So Malik Sahib continued on his own, holding religious gatherings where sayings of the Sants were read and discussed and giving initiations. He thus made his own group of disciples in different towns as he moved around his home region in government service. At this point we see him as one of a number of initiating Gurus in the mid-twentieth century who traced a lineage to Soamiji, most doing so with sincerity whatever we think about their qualifications. Unlike many of these Gurus, however, Malik Sahib was institutionally unattached. From the perspectives of both history of science and history of religions, this fact is very important. For even as it limited his influence, it gave him full freedom to experiment. Malik Sahib would thus sometimes tell stories of his earlier years about meeting with one or another little known spiritual practitioner and attempting to verify whether the internal experience that person talked about was true. For his major spiritual experiment after he started to give initiations himself, however, he proceeded with circumspection.

Already in the 1940s, Malik Sahib had formed a cordial relationship with Swami Vishnu Tirth of Dewas, whom he met while the latter was visiting a disciple serving in his office. Vishnu Tirth traced a lineage to Swami Narayan Tirth of Madaripur, East Bengal—the source of a Shaiva śaktipāt lineage with several extant branches throughout India. Members of this lineage spoke of arousing Kuṇḍalinī energy to cultivate a type of spiritual consciousness that Malik Sahib recognized as qualitatively different than the type he knew through his śabda practice. Despite their different experiences, Malik Sahib and Swami Vishnu Tirth had mutual respect for each other as adepts, seemed to value each other's company, and visited each other regularly (Miśra 94-95).

In 1952 Malik Sahib became acquainted with the Swami's Guru, Yogendra Vijnani, still alive and a householder like Malik Sahib, and five years later had the occasion to host him in Gwalior. The two got to know each other better, and the visiting Guru suggested a yogic exchange ("Hamārā āpkā kucch lenā denā hai") [Miśra, p. 124]. He seemed to have something specific in mind. Malik Sahib humbly responded that he himself had nothing to offer ("Ham kyā de sakte hai? Hameṃ bas Lena hi Lena hai"), but he was clearly open to the idea. He knew about the power of śabda and had heard much about the power of Kuṇḍalinī. How were they related? He had enough experience of gurus in the lineage to think that their spiritual states were worthwhile. Why not see what they were?

Over a week the next year beginning at the spring festival of Holi, Malik Sahib stayed with Yogendra at Rishikesh and managed to assimilate the essence of his spiritual consciousness, but—as sometimes happens with experiments—he had not fully anticipated all the results. Not only did he himself experience Yogendra Vijnani's śakti, but his disciples previously initiated into Sant Mat began feeling its effects, too. This, however, seems to have been part of Yogendra's design. In a letter written a month after Malik Sahib left Rishikesh, Yogendra reminded him that he had suggested that something like this might happen when they were together in Gwalior (Miśra, p. 127). Yogendraji seems not to have fully understood the path of the saints, but saw in Malik Sahib a fit successor to his own lineage.

Although in retrospect, disciples think of the meeting of Malik Sahib and Yogendra Vijnani as a blessing, its immediate results could seem problematic. As presented to Malik Sahib, the Radhasoami and śaktipāt-tradition practices had been two distinct spiritual paths having their own theological bases and leading to different experiences. The Radhasoami practice emphasized listening to sounds heard in the head and cultivating love for the divine; this could lead to experiences of consciousness being drawn up rapturously by a sound current through a series of stations beginning at the point between the eyebrows. Making sense of these experiences intellectually is a theology that bears some resemblance to dualistic Western gnosticisms—with a demiurge seeking to keep souls enthralled in the world and a true Lord pulling them home to the highest heavens—but which in fact isn't so common in Hindu-oriented contexts (Shyam Lal, 1923). The śaktipāt practice, by contrast, was monistic, grounded in understandings about the essential unity of Shiva as ultimate consciousness and Shakti as divine power. It had devotional aspects to be sure, but it did not highlight the experiences of intense, blissful love that were featured in the Radhasoami tradition. Instead it was said to lead relatively quickly to clarity of consciousness through an awakening of the consciousness-force in the body, a force often referred to as Kuṇḍalinī śakti. The internal subtle-physical emphasis in the practice Malik Sahib now offered was no longer oriented predominantly toward the centers in the head; the well-known bodily *chakras* of later Hindu yogas also now came seriously into play.

For both disciples and guru, these two experientially and intellectually divergent traditions needed to be integrated. For the disciples, experiential integration was foremost. The disciples still experienced some of the ecstatic love associated with śabda, but now often in the six bodily *chakras* as these were purified by the Kuṇḍalinī śakti through familiar yogic processes of prāṇayāma and postures as well as through some less familiar means. As the disciples progressed and were able to bring their consciousness fully to the point between the eyebrows, they were more likely to successfully catch the audible śabda in the higher regions. What kept Malik Sahib's two practices together for the disciples was the centrality of the Guru's grace in both: it now provided a wider variety of experiences, but they were all recognized as coming from the same source. For the Guru, the experiential integration of the Sants' śabda and the yogis' Kuṇḍalinī seems to have been immediate, but he still needed to formulate their interrelationship rationally. This would entail a paradigmatic shift away from the Sant Mat teaching in which he had found intellectual groundings and into the broader Indian traditional sciences of the subtle body. Malik Sahib, however, had previous experience in moving between these two discourses.

Unlike Kabir and some of the earlier Sants, but like many later ones, Malik Sahib never fully renounced the established traditions. He lived as a Hindu householder, if giving priority to the inward interpretation of myth over the outward performance of ritual. While still a young man, he wrote interpretations of the esoteric meanings of mythic figures such as Krishna and Hanuman that derived from his experiences of inner worlds as a Sant Mat practitioner. Later he would, conversely, look at the Sant Mat yoga from the point of view of the larger Hindu tradition. The force of loving attraction featured in that śabda practice, he said, was the āhlādini śakti spoken of by the ancient sages, the power of delight. Malik Sahib was not alone in making this move. Hazari Prasad Dwivedi in one of his works on the Sants—I think it's the one titled simply Kabir—also considers the āhlādinī śakti when discussing the Sants, noting the term's appropriately suggestive derivation: its base form hlādin (from the Sanskrit root hlād) means pleasing or delighting, but with the slight change of the liquid r to l, we get hrādin (from Skt. hrād) which means roaring or sounding: āhlādinī śakti then connotes the power of delightful sound.

Malik Sahib's experience gave him a particular practical perception of how āhlādinī śakti works. He understood it to rise up the front of the body, starting from the svadiṣṭhāna cakra, in the genital area. Following a line of Sant teaching, he said it could be triggered by nām, "name" —a word or phrase repeated internally or externally and taken as the voiced co-efficient of the unstruck śabda. Eventually the nām merges with the breath (prāṇa) and reaches the point between the eyebrows. From there the loving journey of the Sant Mat yoga practitioner truly begins. The Kuṇḍalinī, he said as most do, travels up the spine, in the back of the body. He added that it then travels up over the head and down to the point between the eyes. From there yogis are also able to merge into the highest consciousness through unstruck sound, moving through the increasingly higher points of concentration sometimes shown in yogic diagrams. They are, however, likely to do so without the āhlādinī śakti, experiencing a quietistic, enstatic calm, not an ecstatic loving bliss. Those oriented towards yoga and devotion both experienced unstruck sound, but differently.

In psychically synthesizing the practices of gurus from two different traditions, Malik Sahib both complicated his inner world and enriched it. He was also literally able to see it as complete. Looking to the directions of the body spoken of in Hindu lore, he talked about the path of śabda/āhlādinī śakti as the eastern path. This was the path in front, which offered feelings of love and objects to vision: it was the path to the true Vishnu. The path of Kuṇḍalinī, up the back, was in the west, the direction of the setting sun. It was the path leading to Shiva as ultimate consciousness. The Eastern path was like a train ride: it took some time, but you got to see some marvelous sights along the way. The Western path was like an airplane flight, a potentially quicker way to the goal, but offering no sights. Depending on their temperaments, devotees could progress differently.

Malik Sahib thus had real experience of two different ways in which spiritual consciousness could develop in the subtle body, and tried to give each of them their due. But personally, he seemed to prefer the devotional train ride, enjoying the stops along the way. Even as most new disciples were engaged largely in the śaktipāt path, Malik Sahib would still have Sant verses from his own lineage and the broader tradition read during the regular evening service. He would engage with those verses deeply, as did some of the older disciples, and in his final years he seemed to increasingly enjoy them and the states they led him to. Although in his public discourses he would always try to be theoretically evenhanded in discussing his two lineages, I heard him say a number of times, when pressed, that the Sant Mat states were "higher." And once I remember him expressing a strong distaste for nirvikalpa samādhi, which he referred to as "death." He seemed to have experienced this end of classical yoga in a way more like a yogi than did Maluk Das in his devotional reworking of nirvikalpa read earlier, and he didn't particularly like it. Malik Sahib, I think, preferred the devotee's continuing ability to personally taste the sugar over the monist's total absorption into the sugar cube. In the end, after experimenting seriously in the inner worlds, he remained a devotee in the tradition of the Sants.

References

Baba Saheb Rambaran Das (2005, 1993). *Mahātmāom kī Bānī.* Bhurkura, Gazipur, 205, (The manuscript on which this book is based has recently been edited by Dr. Indradeva as *Rām Jahāz: Nirguna "Satanāmīi" Siddhapīth, Bhurakurā se Sambaddh Gyārah Santom kī Bāniyom kā Samkalan,* 1st ed, Naī Dillī, India: Namana Prakāsan).

Das, Malūk and Vamsi, Baladeva (2002). *Sant Malūk Granthāval.* Delhi, India: Parameśvarī Prakāśan.

Lal, Shyam [Guru Data Dayala] (1923). *Retransformation of Self.* Lashkar, Gwalior, India: G. S. Niwas.

Miśra, P. (1999). *Divya Caritāmrit*. 2nd ed. Gwalior, India: Adhyātm Sādhnā evam Śiksan Kendra, Adhyātm Niketan.

Pārasnāth Tivārī (1961). *Kabīr Granthāvalī*. Prayāg, India: Hindī Parisad.

Paltū Sāhib (1974). *Paltū Sāhib kī Bānī, part 3, Sant Bānī Pustakmālā*. Song 81. 28. Allahabad, India: Belvedere Press.

Chapter 12

The Path to Higher Consciousness in Kabbalah and Allied Traditions: An Approach from Neuroscience and Psychology

B. LES LANCASTER
University of Maryland, USA

Abstract

In broad terms the mystical tradition within Judaism is focused more on the attempt to understand the nature of God than it is on inner states and the nature of mind. Given that the primary source for knowing God derives from His act of revelation through which the Torah is given to humankind, the majority of mystical texts are hermeneutic in form. Judaism holds that God's essence and His ways may be known through study of scripture. One of the most respected of Jewish exegetes, Nachmanides (1195-1270), articulated the mystical approach to the Torah by asserting that its letters may be viewed as comprising the name of God; whilst the exoteric approach through which its letters are grouped into words conveying stories and laws, when understood esoterically the letters constitute nothing other than the name. And, for the Kabbalist, the name is no mere appellation but a glyph of the essential nature of that which is named. Thus knowledge of God is achieved through deciphering the Torah, and Judaism developed subtle and sophisticated approaches to the hermeneutic enterprise which are used to this end.

Introduction

Despite the seemingly outward orientation of the work of exegesis, at the mystical level the same exegetical activity takes on distinctly inner connotations. In the first place, Kabala holds that God and humans are isomorphic (Idel, 2005; Shokek, 2001) and consequently knowledge of God implicitly implies knowledge of self. Secondly, the hermeneutic process itself entails an experiential dynamic. The exegete enters into a state which is considerably more visionary than would normally be associated with mundane scholarly, interpretive work. "Hermeneutics is a practice of the recovery of vision," writes Boyarin (1990, p. 449). Explicating further, he writes that hermeneutic practice—the core of Judaism—enables "the unmediated vision of God's presence" to be recovered.

This distinctive form of hermeneutic practice is termed Midrash. Its centrality to the very heart of Judaism is symbolically conveyed by the Talmud's statement that the phrase darosh darash (Leviticus 10:16) comprises the central two words of the Torah (Ḳiddushin 30a). It can easily be seen that these words are forms of the Hebrew verbal root (meaning search or inquire) from which the word Midrash derives. The Torah is the essence of Judaism, and the hermeneutic process of Midrash is the essence of the Torah. Another allusion conveying the experiential dynamic of Midrash comes from a commentary on the biblical book of Ezekiel noted by Wolfson (1994). Ezekiel begins with the verse "...the heavens were opened, and I saw visions of God." Drawing on the important exegetical device of gematria (based on the fact that Hebrew letters have numerical value), the author of the commentary observes that the Hebrew word niftechu 'were opened' equates numerically to the Hebrew Midrash, implying that this hermeneutic practice opens the path to heaven and enables visions of God.

Boyarin (1990; see also Wolfson, 1994, p. 327; Wolski, 2010, pp. 2-3) cites the following Midrash as the key source for understanding the experiential dynamic of hermeneutic practice:

Ben-Azzai was sitting and interpreting [making midrash], and fire was all around him. They went and told Rabbi Akiva, "Rabbi, Ben- Azzai is sitting and interpreting, and fire is burning all around him." He went to him and said to him, "I heard that you were interpreting, and the fire burning all around you." He said, "Indeed." He said, "Perhaps you were engaged in the inner-rooms of the Chariot [theosophical speculation]." He said, "No. I was sitting and stringing the words of Torah [to each other], and the Torah to the Prophets and the Prophets to the Writings, and the words were as radiant / joyful as when they were given from Sinai, and they were as sweet as at their original giving. Were they not originally given in fire, as it is written, 'And the mountain was burning with fire' (Deut. 4:11)?" [Song of Songs Rabbah, p. 42]

There are many fascinating allusions in this Midrash. Suffice it to note here that the fire surrounding Ben-Azzai is to be understood metaphorically as portraying the profound inner state achieved through the exegetical imagination. The self-same experience of the divine as that vouchsafed to those present at the revelation on Mt. Sinai is available to him through his hermeneutic practice.

My interest in this article focuses on the kinds of inner state conveyed in kabbalistic literature and how we might understand them in contemporary psychological terms. It is axiomatic that the states can only be evaluated in relation to the practices through which they might be achieved. Accordingly, my analysis extends beyond descriptions of the states themselves into a consideration of the psychological basis of the practices promulgated in kabbalistic literature by means of which the mystic aspires to these higher states of consciousness.

In her study of the Zohar, the principal text of the Kabala, Hellner-Eshed (2009) identifies three main states of mystical consciousness: 'Rose' consciousness, 'Tree of Life' consciousness, and 'White light' consciousness. The naming of the first state as Rose consciousness derives from the Zohar's opening discourse on the "Rose of the valley" depicted in the biblical Song of Songs. Just as the whole edifice of the Zohar opens with this metaphor, so Rose consciousness is viewed by Hellner-Eshed as the initial mystical state through which the further states may be accessed. For the Zohar, the rose depicts the Shekhinah, the feminine face of the divine and divine presence in the world. Rose consciousness is accordingly the state through which one becomes aware of the divine presence. There is an intensification of the senses, through which one discerns an extra quality in the world. The world of the senses is no longer merely a collection of images; it becomes a rich tapestry through which the ultimate Hand is glimpsed.

The Tree-of-Life consciousness to which Rose consciousness opens is named after the central glyph of the Kabala. The Tree of Life depicts the entirety of creation from the ultimate source—the first stirrings to action in the recondite mind of God—to the final manifestation of the divine presence in the physical universe. For Hellner-Eshed, this state of consciousness is characterised by centeredness and an inner knowing of all things. It conveys at one and the same time both the centre of the Tree of Life and its totality. It is a state of presence and stable clarity, through which one may aspire to influence the mysterious dynamic of the Godhead.

White-light consciousness brings awareness of the oneness and unity at the heart of all being. It may be identified with the undifferentiated roots of thought, and depicts the alignment of the human mind with the "amorphous dimension that precedes order and language" (Hellner-Eshed, p. 349). Whereas Rose consciousness is depicted as having a feminine quality and Tree-of-Life consciousness as being masculine, White-light consciousness transcends any duality associated with gender.

Which of these states might be appropriately applied to Ben-Azzai's 'fire' in the above extract? It is noteworthy that two 'levels' are indicated in the Midrash: The presence of 'fire' suggests to Rabbi Akiva that Ben-Azzai was involved in the 'work of the chariot,' a term denoting visionary and mystical practice (and a topic forbidden to be taught to the kind of group around Ben-Azzai, as implied in the Midrash—which is why "they" brought it to Akiva's attention in the first place); Ben-Azzai's answer suggests that his 'fire' was burning on account of less esoteric practice, namely more normative hermeneutic work. Evidently, there could be two altered states to which the term 'fire' might be applied: one associated with intensive exoteric hermeneutic work, and the second entailing esoteric work. An insight into the more esoteric practice may be discerned in the writings of Abraham Abulafia (1230 – after 1291), who notes that the Hebrew Merkavah ('chariot') is etymologically related to the Hebrew word for 'combination,' harkavah. This allusion connects the 'work of the chariot' with complex techniques which involve permuting and combining Hebrew letters and the names of God. A further allusion is given whereby Ma'ase Merkavah, Hebrew word for 'work of the chariot' is shown to be identical numerically with Shem b'Shem, meaning 'Name with name' (i.e. combining one divine name with another name). One of Abulafia's pupils, Rabbi Gikatilla writes explicitly:

> Know that the letters of the Honourable name, whose secret is YHWH, are exchanged by combining them with the letters that follow the letters of the name. This is the secret of the Merkabah, and you must be aroused concerning the great matter contained therein (cited in Idel, 1989, p. 51).

I shall return to the esoteric practices described by Abulafia later. For the present I wish to propose that Ben-Azzai's 'fire,' which arises when exoteric hermeneutic work reaches a peak of intensity, should be identified with Rose consciousness. The state aroused by esoteric combinatorial practice is more appropriately related to Tree-of-Life consciousness. In making these proposals, I am aware that I am bridging between two strands of Kabbalah that many view as distinct—the sefirotic tradition (which examines the principles of emanation—the sefirot—and the Tree of life through which the sefirot unfolds) and the more ecstatic path involving combining letters and names. I doubt that these should be treated as wholly separate, especially as far as states of consciousness are concerned. Whilst the Zohar primarily explicates the Tree of Life and the sefirot, it is clear that a fascination with mystical states lies within its pages. I see no reason to doubt that the fraternity depicted in the Zohar experienced states akin, if not identical, to those associated with the ecstatic strand of Kabbalah.

I suggest that these two states, Rose consciousness and Tree-of-Life consciousness, are the most interesting from the point-of-view of psychology. The nature of White-light consciousness cannot effectively be described in terms that have currency within most schools of psychology. Rose consciousness, by comparison, seems to entail an intensification of those processes that characterise mundane consciousness, and the knowing beyond normal bounds associated with Tree-of-Life consciousness may be the result of the conscious mind gaining access to normally unconscious material. But what lies behind these statements? My interest here lies in operationalizing these notions: what are those processes that become intensified in Rose-consciousness, and how do they lead to the opening of unconscious thought which characterises Tree-of-Life consciousness?

In order to answer these questions, I shall first present a model of perception and memory that enables a detailed analysis of consciousness. The model is presented in Figure 1, and is more fully explicated in Lancaster (2004). I have elsewhere examined and refined the model's view of the stages of perception in relation to that given in the Abhidhamma of the Theravada school of Buddhism (Lancaster, 1997). Indeed, a key feature of the model concerns its attempt to integrate introspective insights such as those generated in Buddhist schools with data drawn from recent research in cognitive neuroscience.

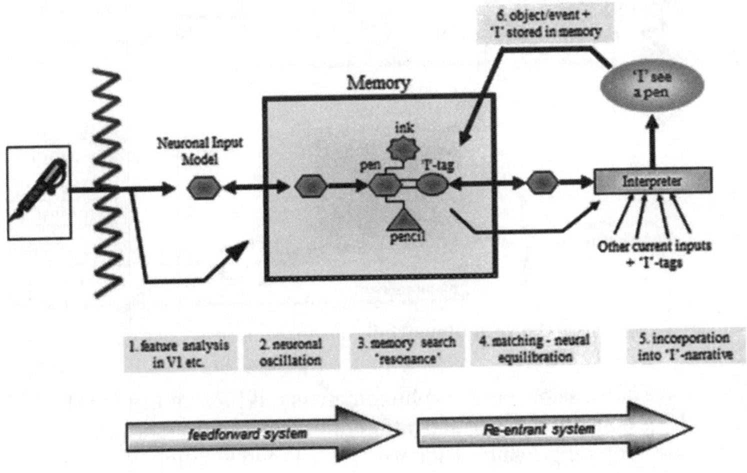

Figure1. A model of the stages in perception (after Lancaster, 2004).

In brief, the model conceptualises the functions of the feed forward and re-entrant neural pathways involved in processing of sensory input. The process of feature analysis generates a neuronal input model which activates structures in memory having features in common with the current input. In psychological terms, the activated structures are associations to the input model. It should be noted that this memory function is preconscious, occurring within the first milliseconds of the input arriving at the senses. The re-entrant system then becomes involved in an attempt to match the activated memory structure with the input model. If it matches then it is selected for inclusion in what I call the 'I'-narrative, and other activated associations become inhibited. The term 'I'-narrative is intended to convey the fact that on-going perception is effectively a narrative construction in which the central feature is the ego, or 'I'. It should be noted that 'I' is viewed not as a substantive pre-existing entity but rather as a kind of hypothesis constructed by the interpretative systems to give retrospective coherence to the on-going mental activity (see Lancaster, 2004 for detail).

As far as consciousness is concerned, it is only the output of the entire system that may be identified with normal, mundane consciousness. However, I identify different dimensions of consciousness, each of which is associated with a specific stage in the model, as illustrated in Figure 2.

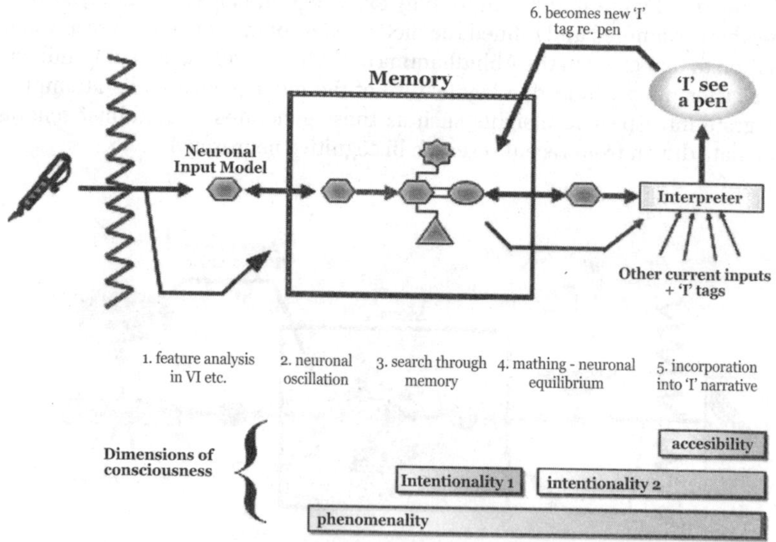

Figure 2. Dimensions of consciousness

The essence of consciousness, its phenomenality, is present from the time the input model is constituted. The activation of preconscious associations entails a form of intentionality which I identify with Freud's notion of the primary process. Accordingly I term it intentionality 1. Intentionality 2, by contrast, is the dimension relating to the match between input model and activated associations. It is reality-oriented, corresponding to Freud's secondary process. Finally, accessibility represents the output, the 'I'-narrative. This dimension is paramount in the form of consciousness that Block (1995) identifies as access consciousness. These dimensions are, as it were, cumulative in the sense that when I am conscious of some object (such as the pen in Figure 1), intentionality 2 is directly expressed in my field of experience, intentionality 1 carries the associations to the object but these remain inaccessible to the 'I'-narrative, and phenomenality pervades the whole experience. A crucial point to note is that recognising these differing dimensions of consciousness overcomes the problematic distinction between 'conscious' and 'unconscious' realms of mind. The associations activated by the input model, for example, are not strictly 'unconscious' but they are inaccessible to the 'I'-narrative.

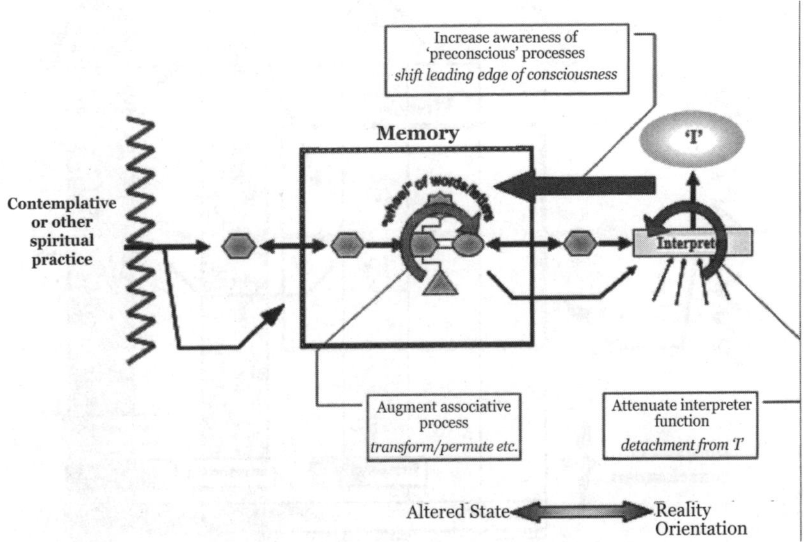

Figure 3. The effects of spiritual practice

Armed with the above model and my operationalization of the effects of spiritual practice, I can now return to the states of consciousness found in Jewish mysticism. An immediate set of parallels present itself since I have identified three dimensions of consciousness in addition to that of accessibility which dominates the normal I-focused state, and Hellner-Eshed (2009) argues that the Zohar portrays three mystical states of consciousness. Beyond the simple concordance of number here, the real issue is whether the putative correspondences encompass the features of experience that, on the one hand, would accompany the dimensions of consciousness I identify, and, on the other, characterise the Zohar's mystical states. In other words, my real interest concerns whether operationalization of the effects of spiritual practice as conceived in the model might meaningfully be applied to the mystical states identified by Hellner-Eshed.

I am proposing that each of the dimensions of consciousness will dominate a specific state of consciousness (Figure 4). In the normal state, accessibility is dominant. It is important to note that accessibility in the context of this model concerns the ability of the narrative 'I' to needs and desires. Thus, for example, in an everyday conversational mode, I might be conscious not only of the words spoken by others, but also of the ramifications of their words in relation to my own interests and of the various ways in which I might assert myself more strongly in order to achieve those goals I deem valuable. Such consciousness entails accessing all the information relevant to those concerns. The egocentric orientation of the accessing that is taking place in such contexts should be evident from reflection on one's own mundane experience.

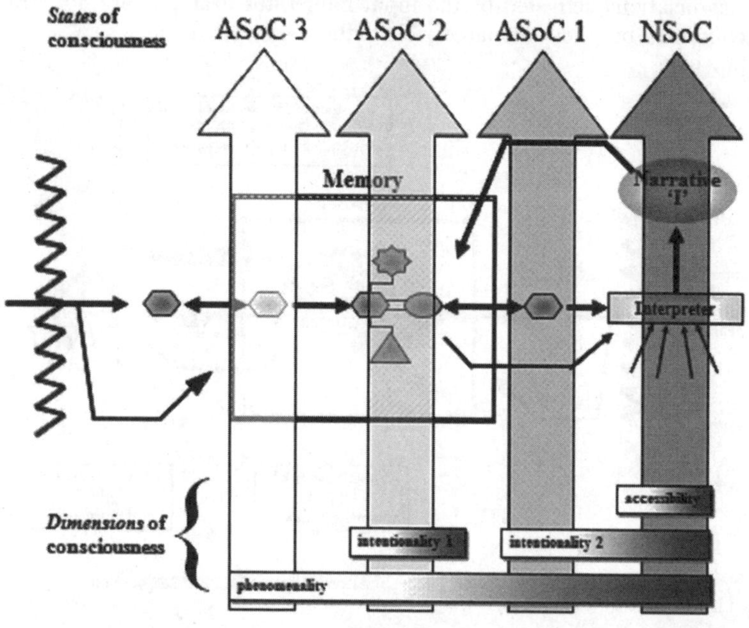

Figure 4. Dimensions of consciousness and corresponding altered states of consciousness.

There is a feature of the above figures which I have not yet explained that comes in at this point. I have proposed a 'tagging' system whereby information present in any given moment of consciousness becomes stored in conjunction with the 'I'-model that had been constructed at that time. In effect the 'I'-model becomes a tag attached to the memory. Accordingly, I refer to it as an 'I'-tag (see figures above). Whilst this posited 'I'-tag system can be instructive in relation to spiritual and mystical notions of the intractability of egocentric states; it was advanced in the first place (Lancaster, 1991, 1993) to account for extensive observations in cognitive neuroscience on the nature of implicit memory. In short, the evidence suggests that apparent disorders of memory may arise from inconsistencies in the 'I'-tagging system rather than failures of information storage per se. Details of this need not concern us here; I simply wish to stress the role of the 'I'-tag system in effecting the ability of a current construction of 'I' to access those schemata which can enhance consolidation of its own status.

If the role of the 'I'-narrative is attenuated, the centre of consciousness shifts to the left one step, moving from the normal state of consciousness (NSoC) to altered state of consciousness 1 (ASoC 1). As portrayed in Figure 4, ASoC 1 will be characterised by intentionality 2 in the absence of the narrative 'I,' meaning that the accessing of egocentric information (as in the above example of a conversational scenario) will be attenuated. An individual in ASoC 1 will be focused on the immediate object of attention without distraction by diverse associations or by thoughts deriving from the narrative 'I.' The state might best be captured by referring to it as a mindful state of consciousness.

A further leftward shift leads to ASoC 2, in which intentionality 1 becomes dominant. The state would be similar to ASoC 1 inasmuch as egocentric thinking attaching to the narrative 'I' is attenuated, but differs from the first altered state to the extent that associational activity dominates. ASoC 2 would accordingly be characterised by the same level of focus as in ASoC 1 but the individual would be focusing on diverse associations to the primary object of attention. To anticipate somewhat the argument below, the kind of ecstatic hermeneutic activity discussed earlier as characterising Jewish mystical approaches would exemplify ASoC 2.

Finally, ASoC 3 entails phenomenality in the absence of intentionality, which means content less state of consciousness. As mentioned earlier, there is little that can be said about such a state from the psychological point-of-view. The origin of phenomenality remains a mystery; there are no definitive studies of brain function, for example, that would enable us to assert unequivocally that phenomenality is uniquely a function of the brain. Phenomenality may be generated by neurones, but equally it may be a fundamental property of the universe and/or derive from a realm that is transcendent to physical reality. We simply do not know.

To what extent do these altered states correspond to the states described by Hellner-Eshed (2009) on the basis of her close analysis of the Zohar? Correlations of this kind can be notoriously problematic in that one set of parameters can be made to fit with another where there is weak specification of the parameters and potential bias on the part of the one making the 'fit.' I cannot exclude my bias (to the extent that I would obviously like to see my model supported by the evidence from analysis of Jewish mystical states), but I do claim that the operationalization of neural and cognitive events in the model and the level of insight Hellner-Eshed brings to her analysis lend a distinctive value in the correspondences suggested here.

The intensively hermeneutic orientation of most kabbalistic work might suggest that it is the augmentation of associative activity as depicted in Figure 3 that characterises the tradition. Indeed, the phrase "wheel" of words / letters which I placed around the figural representation of the associations to sensory input derives specifically from ideas promulgated within the kabbalistic tradition (see Lancaster, 2005). The 13th-century Sefer ha-Bahir encourages the mystic to probe into the concealed meanings of words by exploring what it terms the "wheel" of each word, clearly an allusion to the associations that 'revolve' around the word. In an earlier work, the Sefer Yetzirah, this wheel imagery is applied to the Hebrew letters. God is portrayed as realising the work of creation through permuting the letters:

He placed them in a wheel .... The wheel revolves forwards and backwards.... How? He permuted them, weighed them, and transformed them. Alef [the first letter] with them all and all of them with Alef; bet [second letter] with them all and all of them with bet ... (Sefer Yetsirah 2:4-5).

At the same time as depicting the linguistic technique by means of which God creates His world, the Sefer Yetzirah encourages the mystic to emulate the divine, giving rise to esoteric practices involving intensive ways of permuting and combining letters, as mentioned earlier in my discussion of Ben Azzai's state of consciousness symbolised by fire. To repeat my conclusion from the earlier discussion, associative practice lies at the root of the two altered states of consciousness captured by the terms 'Rose' and 'Tree-of-Life,' the former brought about by intensive, yet normative, hermeneutic activity and the latter engendered by anomian concentrative techniques involving esoteric working with divine names and letter permutation. Here is not the place to go into extensive detail, but it will be clear to anyone who reads Abulafia's works that a fluid associative faculty is central to these latter practices.

Connecting this with the model presented in the above figures, it seems evident that in the Jewish tradition the leftward shift representing a move into mystical states of consciousness is strongly driven by augmenting the associative process. I suggest that Rose consciousness equates to ASoC 1 in Figure 4. Hellner-Eshed (2009) specifies intensification of perception and emotion, and augmentation of associative processes as being amongst the key properties of Rose consciousness. These changes accord with what I would predict for ASoC 1 inasmuch as this state includes heightened focus on the perceptual objects—the matched schemata in the figure—with little distraction by the ruminations of the 'I'-narrative. Whilst my model does not deal with emotion, it is reasonable to assume that the attenuation of the 'I'-narrative would similarly increase focus on emotion.

The next correspondence to consider is that between ASoC 2 and Tree-of-Life consciousness. In asserting the appropriateness of this correspondence I have in mind the richer sense of knowing and sense of engagement in the dynamics of the Godhead as specified by Hellner-Eshed. ASoC 2 is a state bringing increased contact with the unconscious (Lancaster, 2004), akin, for example, to the state accessed through active imagination in Jung's scheme of the psyche and the process of individuation. Due to the limitations of a static representation, the figures cannot capture the extensive ramifications of the associative process. The associations depicted in the figures are simply trivial connections to a mundane stimulus at a single moment. In reality the associations should be understood as comprising panoply of ever-changing images, which are inaccessible from the NSoC. It is this process of accessing such normally unconscious imagery and, more especially, of making controlled contact with the effervescent process that continually activates complex associations, which, I suggest, brings the sense of a wider sphere of knowledge to the individual experiencing ASoC 2.

I think we can gain additional insights into ASoC 2 / Tree-of-Life consciousness by considering further the complex linguistic practices advocated by Abulafia. His goal is attainment of 'prophetic' consciousness, which Idel (1986, 1989) conceptualises as an expansion of the mind. Again, to put it in psychological terms, such expansion may be aligned with an opening to previously unconscious dynamics. I do not mean this to imply some rather limited Freudian-style notion of repressed content. Rather I have in mind a state in which complex associations can be explored—the mind opening to a wider field of cognition, as it were. I have explored elsewhere (Lancaster, 2000, 2004) the reasons why specifically linguistic esoteric practices may be especially potent and eventuate in this widening of cognitive functioning. In essence, language structures the cognitive connections which define our mundane sense of ego and world. The 'I'-tags are like knots, to use one of the terms Abulafia applied in this context, that bind us to a limited scale of being, and language is the rope—to extend the analogy—that connect the knots. Deconstruction of language—as brought about by the intensive techniques of breaking words into letters—might be conceived as deconstructing the ego and its world. The esoteric working with the divine names in this deconstructed state reties the knots to a higher level of being:

... Man is [tied] in the knots of world, year and soul [i.e., space, time and persona] in which he is tied in nature, and if he unties the knots from himself, he may cleave to He who is above them.

He must link and change a name with a name, and renew a matter, to tie the loosened and to loosen the tied, using known names, in their revolutions with the twelve signs and the seven stars, and with the three elements, until the one tying and loosening will strip off from the stringencies of the prohibited and permitted, and dress a new form for the prohibited and permitted (extracts from Abulafia's works, cited in Idel, 1988, pp. 135 and 136-137).

What is the "new form" to which the mystic aspires according to Abulafia? The goal of esoteric practice for Abulafia is a level of intellect which is divine in scale, namely the Active Intellect, and it is only when operating from here that the mystic can initiate new forms. In this extract the 'new form' would seem to involve insights affecting the normative practice of religion. Elsewhere there are suggestions of creating a "new universe" (Idel, 1989, p. 103), intimating the more magical nature of these practices. From the perspective of the model advanced here, the 'untying' of 'I'-tags frees the mind from its limited mode of operation. Experientially, this facilitates an expansion of self (Pappas & Friedman, 2007), understood not as ego inflation but as a widening of the field of awareness. Whether freeing the mind from egocentric functioning is all there is to the highest mystical states must remain an open question. Should we regard the Active Intellect as no more than an outmoded metaphor, or might there be levels of intellect ontologically distinct from the brain? These are questions that take us beyond the reach of models based in psychology. My notion of an indexing system that is central to the content of consciousness need not in itself limit our horizons; it may be that immersion in the world of divine names substitutes, as it were, a higher-order tagging system than that dominated by 'I'-tags, since the divine is an ocean of unlimited potentiality.

Ultimately, of course, neuro-cognitive explanations appear to impose reductive limits on the value of the kinds of higher states to which practices such as Abulafia's are directed. However, the question can reasonably be asked as to whether the brain state generates the mystical state of consciousness or is some kind of necessary receiving condition for the higher level of mind (cf. Fingelkurts & Fingelkurts, 2009). From the kabbalistic perspective all is built on correspondence: the lower reflects the higher and the higher may be known through understanding the lower (Lancaster, 2011, in press). Let me close, therefore, by emphasising that assigning links between features in my neuro-cognitively-based model and various mystical states of consciousness does not imply reductionism. The neuro-cognitive processes conceptualised as underpinning ASoC 2 may be all there is to this state or they may furnish us with a valuable key for understanding and 'tuning into' a more profound level of intellect than the normally active. It is doubtful that any contemporary term does justice to that profound fount of knowing and being which the mediaeval mystics had in mind by their term, Active Intellect. Perhaps what you cannot name, you cannot know. But that which may stand just beyond the reach of psychologically-grounded explanatory models should not be discounted when exploring the interface between psychology and mysticism.

References

Block, N. (1995). On a Confusion About a Function of Consciousness. *Behavioural and Brain Sciences*. 18. 227-287.

Boyarin, D. (1990). The Eye in the Torah: Ocular Desire in Midrashic Hermeneutic. *Critical Inquiry*. 16. 532-50.

Fingelkurts Al. A. and Fingelkurts An. A. (2009). Is Our Brain Hardwired to Produce God or is Our Brain Hardwired to Perceive God? A Systematic Review on the Role of the Brain in Mediating Religious Experience. *Cognitive Processing*. 10. 293-326.

Hellner-Eshed, M. (2009). *A River flows from Eden: The language of Mystical Experience in the Zohar*. Translated by Nathan Wolski. Stanford, CA, USA: Stanford University Press.

Idel, M. (1986). Infinities of Torah in Kabbalah. In G. H. Harman and S. Budick (eds.), *Midrash and Literature*. New Haven, USA: Yale University Press.

Idel, M. (1988). *The Mystical Experience in Abraham Abulafia*. Translated by J. Chipman. Albany, NY, USA: State University of New York Press.

Idel, M. (1989). *Language, Torah, and Hermeneutics in Abraham Abulafia*. Translated by M. Kallus. Albany, NY, USA: State University of New York Press.

Idel, M. (2005). *Enchanted Chains: Techniques and Rituals in Jewish Mysticism*. Los Angeles, USA: Cherub Press.

Lancaster, B. L. (1991). *Mind, Brain and Human Potential: the Quest for an Understanding of Self*. Shaftesbury, Dorset and Rockport, Massachusetts, USA: Element.
Updated e-edition available at
http://www.amazon.co.uk/Mind-Brain-Human-Potential-ebook/dp/B0064TJD4K.

Lancaster, B. L. (1993). Self or No-Self? Converging Perspectives from Neuro-psychology and Mysticism. *Zygon: Journal of Religion and Science*. 28. 509-528.

Lancaster, B. L. (1997). On the Stages of Perception: Towards a Synthesis of Cognitive Neuroscience and the Buddhist *Abhidhamma* tradition. *Journal of Consciousness Studies*. *4*. 122-142.

Lancaster, B. L. (2000). On the Relationship between Cognitive Models and Spiritual Maps: Evidence from Hebrew Language Mysticism. *Journal of Consciousness Studies*. *7*. 231-250.

Lancaster, B. L. (2004). *Approaches to Consciousness: The Marriage of Science and Mysticism*. Basingstoke, UK: Palgrave Macmillan.

Lancaster, B. L. (2005). *The Essence of Kabbalah*. Arcturus (UK) and Chartwell (USA).

Lancaster, B. L. (2011). The Hard Problem Revisited: from Cognitive Neuroscience to Kabbalah and Back Again. In H. Walach, S. Schmidt, and W.B. Jonas (eds.). *Neuroscience, Consciousness, and Spirituality*. Springer.

Lancaster, B. L. (In press). The Cognitive Neuroscience of Consciousness, Mysticism and Psi. International Journal of Transpersonal Studies.

Pappas, J. D. and Friedman, H. L. (2007). The Construct of Self-Expansiveness and the Validity of the Transpersonal Scale of the Self-Expansiveness Level Form. *The Humanistic Psychologist. 35:4*. 323-347.

Shokek, S. (2001). *Kabbalah and the Art of Being*. London, UK: Routledge.

Wolfson, E. R. (1994). *Through a Speculum That Shines: Vision and Imagination in Medieval Jewish Mysticism*. Princeton, NJ, USA: Princeton University Press.

Wolski, N. (2010). *A Journey into the Zohar: An Introduction to the Book of Radiance*. Albany, NY, USA: State University of New York Press.

Chapter 13

Transcendent Systems: A Community of Saints

MARK GRAVES
Santa Clara University, Santa Clara, California USA

Abstract

Systems scientists have organized human systems into four levels: physical, biological, psychological, and social-cultural. Two additional levels are meaningful for incorporating the findings of modern physics and the dialogue between science and religion: a lower, subatomic level that models quantum phenomena and a higher transcendent level that captures shared values and norms across religions and cultures. Drawing upon the American philosopher of religion Josiah Royce, transcendent systems would depend upon the shared interpretations of the communities out of which they emerge. Because of the importance of human exemplars (saints) in forming constructive transcendent systems, one can consider some communities' collective minds as extensions of the minds of the founding and sustaining exemplars. For example in Christianity, the church and its communities of saints would form the body and mind of Christ's spirit. By examining emergent processes across levels, one can use empirical methods to discern among transcendent systems and make a more informed selection among the cultural and religious frameworks that might lead to one's chosen values.

Human Systems

A *system* is a collection of interacting elements that form an integrated whole. The elements coordinate their interactions along functional divisions to yield functional capabilities for the system, i.e., the system does something and the elements accomplish that work. The system as a whole has an organization and the activity of its interrelated elements brings about local order, i.e., they both reduce local entropy. As a whole, the system has continuity of identity, and its behavior necessarily and sufficiently depends upon the independent activities of its elements, i.e., the system depends on its constellation of elements, all of its elements, and nothing but its elements. Those elements may themselves be systems with their own elements and subsystems. Because a system as a whole accomplishes something that none of its elements accomplishes alone, a system does not reduce to its elements nor their independent interactions.

Several researchers have distinguished what simplifies to four levels of inquiry for the scientific study of human systems. Ludwig von Bertalanffy (1975) organized scientific disciplines and systems into four levels in his General System Theory and suggests physical, biological, psychological/behav-

Acknowledgements. Some of this article depends upon material previously published in my *Mind, Brain, and the Elusive Soul: Human Systems of Cognitive Science and Religion* (Aldershot, Hants, England; Burlington, VT: Ashgate, 2008); "The Emergence of Transcendental Norms in Human Systems." (Zygon 44, no. 3, 2009); and *Insight to Heal: Co-Creating Beauty amidst Human Suffering* (Eugene, Oregon: Cascade Books, 2011).

ioral, and social scientific disciplines; his goal for General System Theory was to discover general rules about systems that crossed those four levels. AA Abrahamsen observes that scientific disciplines may be differentiated by specialization of focus and distinguishes four levels of focus: the physical world, living organisms, the behavior of living organisms, and human culture. (Bechtel and Abrahamsen, 1991)

Arthur Peacocke organizes his eight levels of part-whole hierarchies of nature into Abrahamsen's four levels of focus. (Peacocke, 1993) Claus Emmeche and his colleagues also propose four similar levels: physical, biological, psychic, and social though, they do not propose a strict hierarchy because the biological depends only on the physical while the psychological and sociological are interwoven and involve the emergence of self-consciousness and institutions. (Emmeche et al., 2000) (Emmeche et al., 1997)

For simplicity, one can model most human activity as occurring on physical, biological, psychological and cultural levels where the boundaries occur in biochemical, neurological, and linguistic systems, respectively. In addition, to capture the casual relationships that give rise to the physical laws and spirituality, one needs two additional levels.

Six Levels of Human Systems

The *subatomic* level separates the unknown (and perhaps ontologically indeterminate) foundations of modern physics from the well-understood atomic physics and chemistry in the physical level. When physical reductionists describe reducing the world to physics, they frequently claim reduction to the physics of atoms, efficient causation, and Newtonian mechanics. Although that physics provides a necessary foundation for chemical, biochemical, and biological processes, twentieth-century physics discovered quantum effects such as non-locality, Heisenberg uncertainty, and wave-particle duality, which nineteenth-century physics could not explain. The lower (subatomic) level consists of phenomena studied in quantum mechanics and quantum electrodynamics and perhaps theorized phenomena in string theory or quantum gravity. I call the level subatomic because its effects are most apparent on the scale smaller than atoms and quickly drop off at larger scales. The higher physical level consists of physics and chemistry above the level of the atom. An open scientific question is whether the subatomic phenomena can be explained by the mechanistic processes of the atomic level (in which case, one physical level with atomic and subatomic aspects would remain appropriate) or whether the mechanistic processes of the atomic level result (i.e., emerge) from the interactions of non-local, non-mechanistic relationships of, say, energy and space. As considerable evidence suggests the latter more likely than the former, I will treat subatomic phenomena as belonging to a separate level.

The *physical* level describes the mechanistic interactions between particles, atoms, and molecules. It includes the disciplines of physics and chemistry, especially mechanics and thermodynamics, and physical chemistry. The lower aspects of the level involve atoms and their constituents. Other disciplines in the physical level not required for the study of the person include geology, astronomy, and optics. Higher disciplines in the level relevant to human systems include organic chemistry and some aspects of biochemistry. Biochemistry acts as a bridge discipline between the disciplines in the physical level and biological level.

The *biological* level begins with biochemistry and includes molecular biology, cell biology, and biology of the entire organism, such as botany and zoology. Neuroscience studies the brain from a biological perspective and constitutes the highest discipline within the biological level in that it depends and builds upon the other required biological disciplines. In particular, the discipline of human cognitive neuroscience bridges the biological level with the higher psychological level.

The *psychological* level describes the behavioral and mental aspects of individual living organisms. In particular, organisms with brains appear to have interesting (psychological) properties correlated with the biological activity of the brain. Some scholars would attribute unique properties to humans based on the phenomena studied at this level, such as intelligence or abstract reasoning, but close examination by comparative psychologists suggest to some researchers that only gradients of properties shared by many animals distinguish humans. For example, some dolphins and higher primates show abilities comparable to human children in self-awareness, communication, and problem solving; even honey bees may have the ability to communicate and generalize; and microscopic worms can learn new behaviors. One of the early goals of artificial intelligence is to create those computational systems with intelligent behaviors (rather than biological systems). It appears that the associative networks of the brain are key to the adaptive behaviors and mental processes studied at this level. However, there appears to be one property developed only by humans—creation of arbitrary, abstract symbol systems, specifically languages.

The *cultural* level depends upon the interaction of two (or more) organisms with the ability to generate, communicate, and share arbitrary, abstract symbol systems, namely language. (Deacon 1997) From shared language, humans develop a variety of social products in literate societies, including written text, laws, institutions, governments, rituals, drama, art, poetry, and religions. Disciplines in the cultural level include linguistics, sociology, history, cultural anthropology, philosophy, law, mathematics, theology, and all the humanities. Groups of other animals may interact socially and develop properties that no individual organism has, such as systems of dominance relationships and group personalities; and these relational and group properties influence human culture, too. The higher disciplines in the level that study poetry, ritual, and theology, appear to use the shared symbols systems of language to refer to (signify) phenomena, experiences, or other constructs that language does not easily describe, which requires higher-level systems to model.

The contemporary philosopher of science and religion Philip Clayton in *Mind and Emergence* (2004) suggests an additional emergent level of spiritual or *transcendent* activity, which emerges from mental (and cultural) activity, and I describe using the Interpreter-Spirit of the pragmatic philosopher of religion Josiah Royce (2001 [1913]). This level begins with ethical principles, such as justice, and includes constructs noticed in inter-religious dialogue. Although cultural-level systems can describe the relationships of people within groups, it lacks the systemic power to describe value or purpose to relationships between those groups. Clayton's higher level of transcendence does not fit within the four levels of focus in human scientific inquiry. In addition to occurring outside the realm of natural science, the level also may include what Samuel Alexander calls the emergence of deity, and provides a scientific placeholder for Ian Barbour's limit or boundary questions, which facilitate dialogue between the discipline that raises the question and the discipline that explores it. (Barbour, 1997) Religious studies researchers, such as Steven Katz (1978), indicate that the various states of mystical religious experience appear to be the outcome of epistemological activity, which in turn depends upon culture, though psychologists and neuroscientists who study religious experience typically assume it culture-independent. They mistakenly ascribe universality to phenomena that emerges from culture yet transcends it. (For a discussion, see Bulkeley (2004).) From a systems perspective, one must denote the system to which various religious and mystical experiences relate, even if one cannot specify any intrinsic properties of that system. Some systems have emergent properties that transcend cultural systems, and this paper describes some emergent systems that form a higher, transcendent level.

The disciplines of the six levels investigate aspects of human existence frequently ascribed to a person's body, mind, and spirit with subatomic, physical, and biological systems typically modeling one's body; psychological and cultural systems typically modeling one's mind; and transcendent systems capable of modeling one's spirit.

Emergence

How do these levels relate?

Emergence captures the apparent novelty in the world where the whole appears greater than the sum of its parts. Emergence describes how simple objects interacting in simple ways can give rise to the complexity in the world, it addresses how these complexities appear as a coherent whole and combine with other emergent complexities, and it explains how those interacting complexities weave together to give rise to stability in the world rather than fragility.

Emergent properties may appear from interactions that one would not predict from the properties of the components. When hydrogen (a highly flammable gas) and oxygen (a gas necessary for fire) combine, they produce water—a liquid that puts out fire. When sodium (a silver¬-white metal that reacts strongly with water and other substances) combines with chlorine (a toxic green gas), they form sodium chloride or table salt—a common substance in ocean water necessary for life.

In emergence, all the prior properties and processes remain the same. Only something new is added. Emergence is a type of change where everything already existing endures, but something new comes to be—namely a new constraining relationship. When one adds a drop of water to a glass, water is added, but air at the top of the glass is removed (pushed out of the way by the falling drops). When surface tension emerges as a property of water, no properties of the air, the glass, or the water are removed.

In emergence, all the existing, actual properties and processes remain the same, but a future possibility is removed while another possibility becomes actualized. When hydrogen and oxygen combine, they eliminate the possibility of combining with different elements through covalent bonds. When sodium and chlorine combine, the properties of those atoms remain, but some of the possible effects of their separate reaction with other substances are removed. Emergence eliminates some possibilities by realizing others. As the hydrogen atoms share their electrons with the oxygen atom, the two atoms bond, and that bond of shared electrons has certain properties that neither atom had separately. The physical level emerges from subatomic interactions. These properties of the bond, such as a 120° angle between the two hydrogen atoms bonded to the oxygen atom in a water molecule, contribute to other emergent properties, such as the six-fold symmetry of a snowflake. One can describe such emergent phenomena as relationships between different components where something novel arises or emerges in the relationship between parts.

To examine emergence in human systems by analogy from physical systems, atoms can interact with each other to create emergent properties of temperature or surface tension by bouncing off each other or synchronizing orbiting electrons. Human individuals can interact with each other through conflict to create a violent or litigious society or through empathy to create a harmonious one. Likewise human societies can interact with each other in a closed system (such as on Earth) to create a violent, warlike planetary cultural system or a harmonious one.

In covalent bonds, e.g., a sodium and chlorine atom bonding to form table salt, the atoms share an electron and the electron participates in both atoms. A cultural system may lack a component, such as an individual idea or artifact, that another society provides resulting in a synthesized cultural system. Historical Christian examples include the integration of Platonic thought into Christianity by Augustine, and the integration of Aristotelian thought into Christianity by Thomas Aquinas. In biological systems, numerous atoms interact in a variety of ways. In some systems, a significant bond transforms the entire system. A phosphorylated protein, a conformational change to a protein structure, formation of a protein complex, passage of calcium ions into a neuron, each have a biological consequence that cannot be modeled from a purely physical perspective.

When an individual in a cultural system makes a decision to act nonviolently, that person can transform the cultural system in the same way that a significant covalent bond can change a biological system. Something occurred in the British soldiers when Gandhi's followers allowed themselves to be beaten under British law. In the American Civil Rights movement, an emergent property appeared when US citizens saw blacks beaten by agents of state or local governments. Two coherent, autonomous, self-maintaining cultural systems interact at a place of possible and partially expressed violence, yet both systems become surprisingly transformed in a way that one cannot model in either cultural system.

Another example of transcendent-level emergence occurs in dialogue between Christians and Buddhists (or Muslims) when each practitioner recognizes in the other's founder an insight to understanding the practitioner's own religion. In sustained dialogue respectful of plurality, one finds a new, cross-cultural (cross-religion) relationship that strengthens the coherence, integrity, and autonomy of each system.

The US military has studied what makes an effective unit and discovered that camaraderie and the ability to work as a team greatly impacts unit effectiveness. Other studies have examined suicide bombers who either surrendered or hesitated and were captured. (Caryl, 2005) Speculation suggests that terrorist cells become effective through similar mechanisms to other military units with a shared, often ideological vision. A frequent thread among suicide bombers who decided not to act is their reports of seeing a mother and young child. Although each society has strong, intracultural relationships to form autonomous systems, and the interaction between the cultural systems includes high conflict behaviors such as military and terrorist actions, something occurs when a terrorist sees a mother and young child in the opposing cultural system who the terrorist is about to kill. Something surprising, unpredictable, and highly efficacious, i.e., emergent, occurs that transcends the suicide bombing attempt. Perhaps the terrorist training demonized the opposition to an extent that a mother's love was excluded from the terrorist system's shared worldview. Although suicide bombing and military actions can occur between two cultural systems, something emergent happens when some suicide bombers see a mother and young child that breaks down the prior coherence, integrity, and self-maintenance of the system (Collier and Muller, 1998).

Spiritual Communities

How does spirituality emerge in transcendent-level systems?

I locate human spirituality within community and describe how those emergent spiritual tendencies transcend and can outlast any particular group of individuals. Communities manifest in many forms, and a readiness to relate can maintain and propagate values and ideals through shared interpretations of experience. Those shared interpretations can guide discernment, ethical decision-making, and interpretation of religious experience. That understanding of human social, cultural, and historical relationality can also illuminate other possibilities for discovering the spiritual within the natural world.

A group may compensate for the flaws and biases of an individual member. As long as the limitations and wounds of the individual do not amplify or react with each other, the tendencies of the individuals may combine into healthier social interaction that supports a variety of weakened human conditions. In some cases a significant overlap or interaction among wounded individuals may twist the tendencies of the group in a dysfunctional and eventually self-destructive direction, but in general, the human propensity for social relationships will stabilize and resist annihilation of the group and its collective tendencies.

However, human relationships that create spirituality have characteristics that distinguish them from other human and natural relationships. To continue using Christianity as an example, as that is the tradition with which I am most familiar, a Christian community is called to more than just a self-perpetuating existence that mitigates the imperfections of its members. Christianity is the way of the Cross, where one bears the wounds of others in love and embraces the impoverished, mourning, meek, hungry, persecuted and suffering other in service. A Christian community also reaches out beyond the narrow confines of self-validating shared interests and relates in service to the suffering of others. The commitments of a Christian (and other religious) communities require engagement with Nature's unfolding and continuing creation, especially in places of human suffering.

A group becomes a community through love and acceptance of difference, not the removal of difference. The diversity also increases the capacity of the community to respond creatively to unanticipated situations, and may increase group stability. A community needs enough commonality and structuring relationships to create order and prevent the community disintegrating into a disconnected collection of individuals. A community also needs enough diversity and variation to support dynamic relationships and avoid collapsing into a stagnating, homogeneous group that substitutes for a single idealized individual.

Philosophy of Community

What turns a collection of individuals who interact with a shared language into a community?

When a group of individuals share a commonplace or identity with high social cohesion, that group forms a community. The group will likely share many beliefs and goals and disagree on other ones, but as I use community, it has some common vision, value, or concern. The unity and diversity of how the individuals in community respond to the world in attempting to live out the common vision strengthens the group's cohesiveness and promotes coordinated actions. The breadth of insights across individuals becomes a strength of the community with the shared vision directing the community as a whole and the plurality of perspectives enabling the group to enact that vision in a variety of situations.

A community acts in many ways more like a whole person than just a collection of individuals and brings personal experience into a social collective. Although communities—like people—have wounds and limitations, a community generally has greater cohesion than other social structures because its rich interpersonal relationships coordinate and amplify the distributed decisions of its members. M. Scott Peck (1987) defines community in terms of deep respect and true listening for the needs of others in community. In classical cognitive terms, a community shares a heart, mind, and will that results in social cohesion rather than self-interest.

In the communities I describe, individuals commit to a principle, norm, cause, vision, or value, which they individually hold and collectively share and which transcends the survival of a particular social group. By committing to a shared cause or vision, the members of a community create the unity that holds the community intact rather than expect the community to meet the individual's interests while also maintaining its own existence. The communal cohesiveness emerges from the distributed commitment to a shared vision or value instead of existing as an independent social structure. Because the individuals work and communicate to enact, articulate, and interpret the shared vision rather than simply to maintain that social structure, the ideal community does not draw resources from the individual beyond what is needed for the common vision.

Although communities require a shared vision, that vision must be such to support a common spirituality. A vision tied to a particular person, social institution, or cultural trend will fail to support a sustained activity. Drawing upon the early twentieth-century, pragmatist philosopher of religion Josiah Royce (1995 [1908]), I suggest that visions, which include a commitment to the right of others to commit to alternative visions support a harmonious spirituality. The inclusion of alternative vision supports both the diversity of interpretations within a community and the harmonious interaction with other communities that have possibly conflicting views. Additionally, the commitment-to-the-right-to-commit excludes support of social structures that dominate individuals or that subvert their individual freedom to choose their own transcending vision or norm. In the ideal case, a community would emerge from the congruent decisions and interpretive activity of its members without their additional effort, but, in practice, the limitations, wounds, and failures of individuals and interpersonal relationships require additional work by the community as a whole.

Community of Interpretation

In Royce's *The Problem of Christianity* (2001 [1913]), he explores the relationship between individuals and community. He distinguishes among types of communities that consist of a collection of selves that share some particular cause, memory, expectation, or hope. For Royce, in the type of community he called "a community of memory," each member accepts as part of one's life and self the same past events that each fellow member accepts. Any group of people who individually remember or commemorate the same past events, such as the founding of a nation or the death of a particular person, forms a community of memory with reference to that event (or events). Similarly, a community of expectation (or hope) consists of individuals who accept as part of the member's individual life the same desired future events. A richer type of community combines the sharing of past and future with shared lives where the members advance collectively toward proximate goals using their individual gifts. A community depends upon the interpretation that each individual members gives to that individual's own self, past, and future.

Diversity is essential to making a group a community. The individual cannot melt or merge completely with the community, but must retain distinction for the community to exist as relationships between the distinct individuals. Otherwise the community would degenerate into a group with a single perception of the world—incapable of the differences needed to form diverse interpretations. A community requires unity in terms of pasts and hopes and requires diversity of its members.

When each person attempts to interpret a past event with a future hope while also interpreting each other's interpretation, Royce calls that ideal a "community of interpretation." That process occurs in true loyalty as each attempts to become loyal to loyalty by examining the behaviors of each other to determine one's own action in remaining loyal to one's cause and most of all to loyalty, and that commitment resists annihilation of the community and its shared interpretive process oriented toward its cause.

Atoning Love

For Royce, a community also includes atoning love where the community is willing to forgive any repentant member and has the creativity to posit an atoning act that makes the world better than if the member's betrayal had never occurred. Somewhat surprisingly, Royce holds the community responsible for forgiving a member that injures the community rather than require that individual to repair the harmful action. Because the community as a whole maintains its social cohesion, the community must restore that cohesion while interpreting the treasonous or wounding act as part of the shared life and history of the community. The community cannot undo the consequences of the harmful act without subverting the interpretive process or denying the right of the offending member to make mistakes in pursuing the shared vision. The offending member does have to repent and continue a commitment to the shared vision to accept the community's forgiveness as a part of the community. In addition to forgiveness, the community must find a creative response to the harmful act that makes the world better than if the treason never occurred. The community cannot undo the act to develop a response that makes the world exactly the same as if the treason had not occurred, and responses that make the world and community almost as good as before would eventually erode the community, so the community must atone in a way that turns the harmful act constructive. The repentant member of the community will likely participate in the atoning act, but the community as a whole must use its shared interpretive process to posit the act as part of the shared vision.

In healing a community, a creative act can restore the community's responsiveness to the world and its members to better than it was before the wound. The community incorporates the creative deliberation as an aspect of its shared interpretative process and the creative response to the wound as part of its history. Even without an intentional harmful act by one of its members, a community can still heal by transforming inadvertent or external wounds into responses that make the community better than it was before the wound. Like the surprisingly novel effects of covalent bonds in physical systems, a creative act by some members of a community can radically change the possibilities for a community.

In summary for Royce, each individual in a community interprets the shared memories, shared hopes, shared lives, and atoning love. In shared memory,

---

[1] Experiments on theory of mind often involve a false-belief task where a subject watches an experimenter hide an object, such as a ball, under one of two boxes as a second person observes. The second person leaves the room, and the experimenter switches the location of the ball. Where does the subject believe the second person will look when that person returns? Under the second box where the subject knows the ball rests or under the first box where the subject knows the second person saw it placed. Adult humans expect the second person will look under the first box, where that person believes the ball was placed, but human infants, very young children, and most (if not all) non-human primates indicate (through a variety of experimentally verified nonverbal cues) that they believe the second person will look where the ball now actually rests, not where the second person thinks the ball rests. Before a particular age, humans lack a theory of mind, and cannot separate their own beliefs about the world from the different beliefs another person might hold.

each member accepts as part of one's life and self the same past events that each fellow member accepts, such as remembering or commemorating the founding of a nation or the death of a particular person. Similarly, in shared hopes, individuals accept as part of the member's individual life the same desired future events as other members. In shared lives, members advance collectively toward proximate goals using their individual gifts. By atonement, Royce means the community is willing to forgive any repentant member and has the creativity to posit an atoning act that makes the world better than if the treason had never occurred. In a community of interpretation, the shared interpretive process leads to a collective interpreter that Royce calls Interpreter-Spirit.

Interpreter-Spirit

In the shared interpretive process, the community gains a collective interpretation of events that no single individual may hold. The community may reach a general consensus even though every individual lacks some detail or perspective. As a whole, the community can interpret events in a way that does not reduce to the interpretations of the individuals. That interpretation will continue to develop as additional members join and leave the community, and the prior communal interpretants will influence future interpretations. The community's interpretive process has causal power and shifts how individuals interpret events. Because the community's diverse perspectives and historical memory enrich the interpretive process beyond the capacity of any individual, the individual may adapt to the community's interpretation to better live out the individual's commitment to the shared vision.

Because the interpretive process may outlive the lives of individual members in a long-standing community and influences the actions and tendencies of others, one can fruitfully consider the "Interpreter of a community" as having agency. The interpreter of a community distributes its actions over the members of a community and orients itself toward the shared vision. It helps maintain social cohesion and responds when members stray from their commitment. Ideally, in an egalitarian community, the community in its entirety could share in all the communal decisions; though, in practice, the governance structure would need to orient itself toward discerning the decisions of the community's Interpreter.

The dynamic Interpreter has the role that Josiah Royce characterized as Spirit. The interpreter of a community emerges from the mental processes of individuals, and occurs in Royce's community of interpretation when each person interprets a past event with a future hope while interpreting another's mind to a third person. The interpretation provides a relational structure of the individual within community by relating the individual perceptions and the community-provided conceptual framework embedded in language. In other words, interpretation emerges from shared meaning, which, in a pragmatic understanding, results from the effects of the constraints placed on the community by the individual members. Any community would have a "spirit," i.e., interpreter, though some "spirits" would have more interesting emergent properties and relationships than others. This use of spirit resonates with an awareness of the "spirit" of a family, city, nation, church, organization, etc. For Christian theology, communities of interest include the family, local congregation, all Christians, and all humans. In particular, one can talk of the emergent Spirit of the Christian Community (or "Beloved Community" for Royce and Martin Luther King Jr.) and the emergent Spirit of Humanity.

Collective Minds and Embodied Spirituality

Contemporary social scientists and psychologists have identified a human capacity to have "theories" of another person's mind. A person's theory of mind gives that person the ability to reason about another person's beliefs and desires separately from one's own.[1] Royce's community of interpretation depends upon the capacity of humans to hold their interpretations of the world distinct from their knowledge about the interpretations of others. The ability for humans to form collective interpretations depends upon our capacity to hold and communicate multiple interpretations of the world.

Memory provides the conceptual knowledge that permits one to categorize experience, regardless of whether one categorizes that experience as natural, religious, or mystical. For a group of individuals, they may also share what the French philosopher and pioneering sociologist Maurice Halbwachs (1992 [1925]) called a "religious collective memory." In contemporary work, the cognitive sociologist Eviatar Zerubavel (1997) expands upon Halbwachs' work to identify thought communities—groups of people who perceive, remember, and think in a way that is distinctively different from the ways other groups do. However, the thought community, and its religious collective memory, still consists of human individuals with particular memories and experiences. It is through the individual minds that the shared community takes form. For Royce, a community is group with a will to interpret a shared founding event that interprets itself as the individuals interpret each other, and the ideal goal of the community becomes the shared interpretation of each other in the context of the founding event.

Neuroscience examines the brain of individuals, but some of those scientific insights can also inform one's understanding of collective memory. The percepts, categorization, and concepts used to store and organize individual memories derive from shared biological functions across the species, socially constructed language, and cultural norms. A person's distributed human memory persists as neural connections in the hippocampus that connect to other neural networks in the modal-specific processing and association areas. Although Western individualism suggests encapsulating the individual brain as isolated from other organisms, each person's hippocampus has greater similarity to a different person's hippocampus than it does to the first person's perception and other functional brain areas. Communication within an individual's aggregated brain often occurs more quickly than across brains, which require verbal and nonverbal communication, but that is not always the case, as in brain damage, psychological intervention, or Socratic instruction. In many, though obviously not all respects, one may view the neural associations formed in the hippocampus of an individual's distributed memory as connecting to shared social memories across "larger synaptic clefts" from one individual's motor cortex to another individual's sensory neurons. Rather than direct biological activation through neurotransmitters and ion flow, social interaction occurs through behavior and sensation, and in the case of language, cultural systems can emerge. Although antithetical to American individualism and a challenge to traditional philosophical constructs of self, other cultures would find that interrelatedness and solidarity as confirming there presumed cultural norms.

How does one embody one's participation in transcendent level systems?

At the cultural level, one shares interpretation within community of those oriented toward some spirit. At the psychological level, one makes decisions according to communal values. At the biological level, one's brain adapts to have appropriate neurological tendencies to support discerned decisions. At the physical and subatomic levels, one embodies values maintained by the transcendent system.

Cultural memory exists as real as individual memory and may persist for longer. Recognizing the biological basis of a collective thought, memory, and mind not only provides scientific foundation for a significant cultural concept, I argue viewing the individual brain as a part of the collective better indicates the actual distributed nature of an individual's thought and memory to those with European-American culture's incorrect presuppositions of Newtonian mechanics and Cartesian separation of mind from body. Cultural memory can include the interpretive constructs necessary for an Interpreter-Spirit and thus extend the memories of founding and sustaining religious exemplars. Those memories can influence the interpretive processes of individual and collective minds for a community.

References

Barbour, I. G. (1997). *Religion and Science: Historical and Contemporary Issues*. San Francisco, USA: Harper.

Bechtel, W., and Abrahamsen, A. (1991). *Connectionism and the Mind*. Oxford and Cambridge, Massachusetts, USA: Blackwell.

Bertalanffy, L. V. (1975). *Perspectives on General System Theory: Scientific-Philosophical Studies*. New York, USA: G. Braziller.

Bulkeley, K. (2004). *The Wondering Brain: Thinking about Religion with and Beyond Cognitive Neuroscience*. New York, USA: Routledge.

Caryl, C. (2005). *The New York Review of Books*, 15.

Clayton, P. (2004). *Mind and Emergence: From Quantum to Consciousness*. New York, USA and Oxford, UK: Oxford University Press.

Collier, J. D., and Muller, S. J. (1998). In *Emergence, Complexity, Hierarchy and Organization, Selected and Edited Papers from the ECHO III Conference, Acta Polytechnica Scandinavica, MA91* (Farre, G. and Oksala, T.) (Eds.). Espoo, Finland: Finish Academy of Technology.

Deacon, T. W. (1997). *The Symbolic Species: the Co-evolution of Language and the Brain*. New York, USA: W.W. Norton.

Deacon, T. W. (2003). In *Evolution and Learning: the Baldwin Effect Reconsidered*. Weber, B. H., and Depew, D. J. (Eds.) Cambridge, Massachusetts, USA: MIT Press.

Emmeche, C., Koppe, S., and Stjernfelt, F. (1997). *Journal for General Philosophy of Science*. 28. 83 -119.

Emmeche, C., Koppe, S., and Stjernfelt, F. (2000). In *Downward Causation: Minds, Bodies and Matter*. Andersen, P. B., Emmeche, C., Finnemann, N. O., and Christiansen, P. V. (Eds), Aarhus, Oakville, Connecticut, USA: Aarhus University Press.

Goodenough, U., and Deacon, T. W. (2003). *Zygon*, 38, 801-819.

Halbwachs M., and Coser, L.A. (1992 (1925). *On Collective Memory, The Heritage of Sociology*.

Chicago, USA: University of Chicago Press.

Katz, S. T. (1978). *Mysticism and Philosophical Analysis*. New York, USA: Oxford University Press.

Peacocke, A. R. (1993). *Theology for a Scientific Age: Being and Becoming--Natural, Divine, and Human*. Minneapolis, USA: Fortress Press.

Peck, M. S. (1987). *The Different Drum: Community-Making and Peace*. New York, USA: Simon and Schuster.

Royce, J. (1995, 1908). *The Philosophy of Loyalty*. Nashville, USA: Vanderbilt University Press.

Royce, J. (2001, 1913). *The Problem of Christianity*. Washington, D.C., USA: Catholic University of America Press.

Zerubavel, E. (1997). *Social Mindscapes: An Invitation to Cognitive Sociology*. Cambridge, Massachusetts, USA: Harvard University Press.

Chapter 14

Consciousness in Modern Science and Vedanta

SWAMI JITATMANANDA
Shri Ramakrishna Vivekananda Mission, India

Abstract

Science has already entered into the domain of religion and spirituality. New physics has moved "light years" away from 19th Century physics overthrowing strict causality. Consciousness creates the world outside and everything is pervaded by consciousness. According to Max Planck Consciousness is fundamental. Brain is a hologram. The fundamental unity and interconnectedness in the Universe can be comprehended by it. Mind or consciousness is non-physical, it is spiritual. There are four levels of consciousness; (1) Brain-Stem-Consciousness; (2) Limbic Stem Consciousness; (3) Cortical Consciousness; (4) Supra-Cortical Consciousness; where man can feel cosmic consciousness. The process of downward causation and 'emergent interactionism' should be understood. Science now accepts the power of Faith and 'subjective belief'. A consciousness revolution is in the offing. Thought is a force and meditation brings it in touch with infinity. Meditation of OM leads to the realization of Infinity. The extra-terrestrial God is seated inside human heart. In establishing God in man a 'Consciousness Revolution' has come in science. As predicted by Vivekananda, Vedanta Philosophy will be inundating the civilization of tomorrow. There will be spiritualization of our materialistic civilization. People have already begun to look upward and inward for peace and contentment.

Introduction

Science has already entered into the domain of religion and spirituality. According to Arthur Eddington, "...religion first became possible for a reasonable scientific man about the year 1927 ... If our expectation should prove well founded that 1927 has seen the final overthrow of strict causality by Heisenberg, Bohr, Born, and others, the year will certainly rank as one of the greatest epochs in the development of scientific philosophy". The new physics has moved "light years away: from 19th century Physics, says A.D. Reincourt. And the demolition of strict causality by Heisenberg's Uncertainty Principle has been consistently applied. (A.D. Reincourt: The Eye of Shiva: William Marrow, 1981, p. 23, 30, 196)

Since 1927 with Heisenberg's discovery of the Uncertainty Principle it was found that in quantum world of subatomic particles like electrons, the presence of the observer or the act of observation alters the final outcome of the experiments. It was realized for the first time that the 'experimenter' is also a "participator" in the quantum world. The mind or the consciousness of the experimenter in the quantum world became a part of quantum calculation. After Heisenberg's experiments nothing is purely objective anymore. The objective reality is inextricably connected with the experimenter's subjective consciousness. Michel Tablot in his book Mysticism and New Physics coined the word 'Omnijective', to define a reality in the Quantum World. Heisenberg was awarded Nobel Prize in physics for this historic discovery of uncertainty principle. [1]

Consciousness Creates the World Outside

If the reality outside is a combination of the object and subject, which is primary, subject or object? Nobel physicist Schrodinger's discovery of wave-equation showed that consciousness is the primary. The equation shows that the same particle can move both as a particle and a wave at the same time. It is a strange situation.

Schrodinger tried to explain this phenomenon for our macro world. Schrodinger's wave equation suggests that two or more things can happen at the same instant at the same spot through his now celebrated thought experiment known as Schrodinger's cat. From this came 'Many Worlds Interpretation' which is also known as Everette- Wheeler interpretation of Q.M. It tells, in short, that our consciousness creates the reality outside. There is no purely independent objective Reality outside. And here, for the first time, Consciousness, took the driver's seat in quantum physics which can project two or more universes at the same instant. This is known as 'parallel universe theory'. How is it possible? Nobel physicist Eugene Wigner suggests that our consciousness alters the world by altering us.

Now a question has been raised by physicists. What if two observers observe the same thing in two different ways? Then the external reality may appear as cat to one, and dog to another. This is popularly known as a paradox, called Wigner's friend. Wigner poses this problem, where Wigner and his friend look at the external reality in two different ways. What is the final solution? "The solution is deceptively simple", says physicist Amit Goswami in his book The Self Aware Universe, "Consciousness is one. The consciousness that chooses, that exerts free will, is the same in all of us. This is what biologist Roger Sperry pointed out more than a decade ago; "Brain as computer hardware needs mind to make meaning out of its programs. The same as it is with a TV set. It takes us, our minds, to make meaning out of the movement of electrons on the TV screen."

Vedanta says it is the same consciousness which creates the external Reality according to individual's will, desire and mental makeup. On a half-moonlit night stands a man-like pillar in half-light, half-shade. The thief looks at it and sees as Policeman. The lover looks at it and finds his beloved. Vedanta goes deeper, and says that it is consciousness which moves the mind. Drik Drishya Viveka, a 1000 years old Vedanta text, says, "The inner organ (mind) which is but a modification identifies itself with the reflection of consciousness, imagines various ideas in the dream. And the same inner organ or mind (identifying itself with the body) imagines objects external to itself in the waking state with respect to the sense-organs. ...The external reality is the object seen, the organ of vision the seer. Again this organ of vision becomes seen and the Self of consciousness is the seer. The Self within is the eternal witness which cannot be

[1] Major ideas and facts in this article have been collected from *Modern Physics and Vedanta and Holistic Science and Vedanta*, by Swami Jitatmanda. Both the books are published by Bhartiya Vidya Bhavan, Mumbai-7.

seen." Kena Upanishad says, "Consciousness, which makes the body function, is called Mind of mind, Life of life, Speech of speech, Sight of sight and Hearing of hearing. It is that by which the mind thinks but which mind cannot grasp. It is that by which the eyes see but which cannot be seen by eyes; that by which the ears hear, but which cannot be heard by the ears; that by which life breathes, but which cannot be breathed by life". It is called Brahman or cosmic Consciousness above this world of relativity which men normally adore. The Katha Upanishad brings the simile of chariot in order to explain the higher importance of Consciousness of Self. "Know the soul (the cosmic consciousness or Chit) inside the body as the master of the chariot, the intellect as the charioteer, and mind as the reins." (Katha Upanishad:1:3:3)

Almost in the style of a Vedanta philosopher Schrodinger shows how unreasonable it would be for a scientist to reject Heisenberg's indeterminacy which gives primacy to one's consciousness. After pointing out that no scientist can find satisfaction in 'declaring himself a pure mechanism', Schrodinger examines the two propositions; i) my body functions as a pure mechanism according to the laws of nature. ii) yet I know, by incontrovertible direct experience that I am directing its motion of which I see the effects, that may be fateful and all important, in which case I feel and take whole responsibility for them'. While in the waking state we seem to determine our acts, in sleep or unconscious state human body functions although no voluntary will is exerted for its functioning. ? Who runs the heart, liver etc. during sleep? Schrodinger's inference on these two questions is, "I think, that I (I in the widest meaning of the word that is to say, every conscious mind that has ever said or felt 'I') am the person, if any, who controls the 'motion of atoms' in the state of deep sleep according to the laws of nature'. Vedanta calls it 'Aham Brahmasmi': The individual consciousness becomes one with the universal consciousness in the Turiya state, which is even beyond the state of deep dreamless sleep or sushupti. (Erwin Schrodinger: mind and Matter, Cambridge University Press, 1967, p. 92) This Universal Consciousness is the Cosmic or the one-all-pervading consciousness from which all the other individual consciousness is derived.

Schrodinger, writing on the unity of consciousness in Quantum Physics, declared: In all the world there is no kind of framework within which we find consciousness in the plural. This is simply something we construct because of the temporal plurality of the individuals. But it is a false construction... The only solution to this conflict, in so far as many are available to us at all, lies in the ancient wisdom of the Upanishad". This ancient wisdom, according to Schrodinger is Atmen=Brahman, or 'I am the whole universe' (Erwin Schrodinger: My view of the World, London, Cambridge University Press, Chapter-4)

Today Consciousness and its function of cognizance have taken a key position in modern science. An "absolute silence of all our scientific imagination towards the fact of cognizance is most painful", said Schrodinger, and "it is because our science – Greek science is based on objectivities, whereby it has cut itself from an adequate understanding of the subject of cognizance of the mind. It is precisely the point where our present thinking does need to be amended, but by a bit of blood-transfusion from eastern thought."

If everything has consciousness, then is it going to be an infinite plurality of consciousness in different entities? Vedanta says consciousness is one. Consciousness is extra-physical and therefore infinite. Infinity cannot be two. Erwin Schrodinger echoes Vedanta and says, "The only possible alternative is simply to keep to the immediate experience that consciousness is a singular of which the plural is unknown; that there is only one thing and that what seems to be a plurality is merely a series of different aspects of this one thing, produced by a deception (the Indian MAYA)

On January 25, 1931, OBSERVER published an 'Interview with Max Planck' by J.W.N. Sullivan. In answer to the question, "Do you think that consciousness can be explained in terms of matter and its law?" Max Planck answered that he did not. "Consciousness", Max Planck continued, "I regard as fundamental. I regard matter as a derivative from consciousness. We cannot get behind consciousness. Everything that we talk about, everything that we regard as existing postulates consciousness." (C.E.M. Joad: Philosophical Aspect of Modern Science, Urwin Books: 1963, p.42).

Everything is Pervaded by Consciousness

The Isa Upanishad tells us that everything is enveloped in an all-pervading consciousness. The Upanishadic Rishis realized that this universe of both animate and inanimate objects, is permeated by one all-pervading consciousness or Brahman (Sarvam khalu idam Brahma- Chandogya Upanishad: 14:1). According to Spinoza every particle thing or being is a modification of the infinite substance, i.e. God. To Spinoza any inanimate object is also 'a thought of God'.

Today science is approaching this truth through its experiments. In 1957 Nobel physicist Richard Feynman, through a series of B.B.C. lectures interpreted the Probability-Wave theory of Max Born and showed that electrons working as 'probability waves' are waves, but waves which choose their own course of action. Feynman demonstrated through the double-slit experiment that electrons or photons, while moving like waves, betray a strange element of intelligence and choice when they choose to enter one of the two slits in the double-slit experiment on the screen. How does the particle (electron) find the right path?... all your instincts on cause and effect go haywire when you see that the particles decide to take the path that is going to give them minimum action. "Physicists found themselves dealing with energy" writes Gary Zukav, "that somehow possessed information". (Gary Zukov: The Dancing Wuli Masters: Flamingo Edition, London. 1984, p.90) Physicist Jack Sarfatti writes, "I suspect that the general relativity and quantum theory are simply two complementary aspects of a deeper theory that will involve a type of cosmic consciousness as the key concept".

Long ago 1899 Sir J.C. Bose began a comparative study of the non-living object like metals and the animals. Experimentally he found that metals became less sensitive if continuously used, but return to normal state after a period of rest. The discovery of the 'fatigue of metals' led Bose from the domain of physics to physiology. Subsequently, Bose found that plants also responded in the similar way like metals or muscles. In 1901, May 10, Bose demonstrated all his experiments in England, and concluded with words: "How can we draw a line of demarcation and say, here the physical ends, and there physiological begins? Such absolute barriers do not exit.... It was when I came upon the mute witness of these self made records, and perceived on them one phase of a pervading unity that bears within it all things, it was then that I understood for the first time a little of that message proclaimed by my ancestors on the banks of the Ganges thirty centuries ago. 'They who see but one, in all the changing manifoldness of this universe, unto them belongs Eternal truth – unto none else, unto none else.' (Peter Tompkins and Christopher Bird: The Secret life of Plants, Penguine Books, 1974, USA [chapter on J.C. Bose]).

Swami Vivekananda the greatest rational interpreter of modern times explains the holistic background of the living and the non-living; "Now, when we study metaphysics, we come to know the world is one, not that the spiritual, the material, the mental, and the world of energies are separate. It is all one, but seen from different planes of vision. ...Whatever is, is one. Let us say, it is a sort of tapering existence; the thickest part is here, it tapers and becomes finer and finer. The finest is what we call spirit; the grossest, the body. ...The end and aim of all science is to find the unity, the one out of which the manifold is being manufactured, that one existing as many". Spirit is non-physical, and therefore infinite. Consciousness is also infinite. There cannot be two infinites. The Spirit, the non-material Self, and the all pervading consciousness, according to Vedanta, is one and the same.

Brain is a Hologram

In 1920 Neurophysiologist Karl Lashley discovered that in spite of partial damage to the brain, a man could perform all the functions controlled by the brain's missing parts. Some sense organs might have been disrupted but memory of specific events was not disturbed. Stanford Neurologist Karl Pribram interpreted Lashley's findings by saying that the structures responsible for memory were distributed in much the same way that the images of a hologram are enfolded in all its parts. "Brain is a hologram," Pribram concluded. Each brain cell, in this case, reflects the whole brain in a miniscule way. Pribram went still further like a Vedanta mystic. "What if the real world isn't made up of objects of all? What if it's a hologram perceived by a Supreme Perceiver?" (The Holographic Paradigm: Ed. By Kenliber: 1982, Shambhala Publication, p.7)

In 1977, Karl Pribram, held out a holistic universe and a holistic world view as the core of future science: "This is science as it was originally conceived in the pursuit of understanding. The days of the bold-hearted technocrat appear to be numbered." Lord Krishna in the Gita says: "I have interpenetrated through the entire universe, like pearls strung on one string." Pribram admitted that this holographic concept of a Holistic universe was first given to the world by Eastern philosophy. He said: "Eastern philosophy has come into western thought as in the past...whether it will stick this time or we will have to go around once more will depend on you. The spirit of the infinite could become part of our culture and not a little far out".

Fundamental Unity and Interconnectedness in the Universe

Einstein refused to accept Heisenberg's uncertainty principle. There cannot be 'Einstein asserted any uncertainty in science. "God does not play dice: Einstein said" in 1933 Einstein propounded that there must be a 'Hidden variable' somewhere which is responsible for this uncertainty. However, until the time of Einstein's death, no such 'hidden variable' nullifying Heisenberg's uncertainty principle was found. In 1961 Nobel physicist Winger proposed that it is the 'consciousness of the scientist which is itself the hidden variable' that decides which outcome of an event actually occurs. A question of measurement arises only when human observation intervenes. Winger asserts that it is impossible to give a description of quantum mechanical processes 'without explicit reference to consciousness'. (M. Talbot: Mysticism and New Physics, p.34).

In order to disprove uncertainty principle Einstein proposed Einstein-Podolski-Rosen Paradox. It was experimentally verified in Bell's Theorem. In short, this theorem proposes that if uncertainty principle is valid then two paired particles at infinite distance cannot communicate instantaneously. A particle placed at a distance of eight lakh miles will take a few seconds as all communication can move as fast as the speed of light is 186000 miles per second. This is the fastest communication speed in the universe, according to Einstein, to communicate between two particles. But after the experiment on Bell's theorem by David Bohm of London, and Clauser and Freedam of USA, it was found, contrary to Einstein's theory, that the connection was almost instantaneous.

Scientists however doubted the experiment. In 1982, Alain Aspect, along with the colleagues Jean Dalibard and Jerald Rodger, added the refinements necessary to make the result unequivocal. The group used photons produced by atoms of mercury vapor excited into a higher energy state with a laser beam as their paired particles. Then, with the aid of switching mechanisms that could operate in the billionths of a second, fast enough to catch a photon after it had left its source, before it had traveled more than a few yards away. Aspect, Dalibard, and Rodger proceeded to measure the angles of polarization of stream of countless paired photons. They found that the 'correlation between photons scattered in opposite directions was far greater than would be expected. In fact it was almost instantaneous. How was this instantaneous communication possible? The co-relating particles must have traveled faster than the light speed or they had a super luminal Connection. But according to Einstein it is not possible. Vedanta says no such connection is necessary. It is a holistic universe. No communication is necessary in this fundamentally interconnected universe (M. Talbot: Beyond the Quantum, Bantam New Age Book, 1988, p.32)

It is a Holistic Universe

With the EPR effect, Einstein, without knowing it, opened the Pandora's Box, as Gary Zukav said, in modern physics. It postulates the existence of a fundamental interconnectedness between two similar particles separated by any distance in the whole universe. (Gary Zukov: The Dancing Wuli Masters, New York Willium Marrows, 1979, p.314)

Following a successful verification of Bell's Theorem, David Bohm offers the idea of the universe of 'unbroken wholeness', of an 'implicate order', on which 'the explicate order' survives. Physists Henry Stapp writes: "An elementary particle is not an independently existing analysable entity. It is in essence a set of relationship that reach outward to other things." (Fritzof Capra: The Turning Point, N.Y. Simon & Schuster, 1982, p.81).

Michel Talbot writes on experiments of Bell's theorem in his latest book Beyond the Quantum: "Perhaps the most intriguing aspect of Bohm's theorem is how it might apply to our understanding of the human mind." If every particle of matter interconnects with every other particle, the brain of an individual itself must be viewed as infinitely interconnected with all the brains in the rest of the universe. "Bohm believes that such a mind-boggling interconnectedness might even shed light on the phenomenon of consciousness itself," writes Talbot. (Michel Talbot: Beyond the Quantum, p.52-52, 55-56) if the universe is interconnected, as Bohm's theory suggests, then according to M.Talbot, every human brain-work interpenetrates every other human brain-work and establishes that there is one single cosmic brain or cosmic intelligence which in modern science is known as the Anthropic Principle.

Bell's Theorem has proved that the universe is a "stupendous multi-dimensioned hologram" where each part is "infinitely interconnected" with the rest of the universe. Following the conclusions of Bell's Theorem, David Bohm believes that such 'inter connectedness' proves the existence of a holistic universe. The experiments on Bell's theorem influenced modern thinkers. Arthur Koestler used the word 'holon' instead of electron or proton, because every particle is connected with every other particle of the universe. The movements of subatomic particles have been called 'holomovement'.

Mind or Consciousness is Non-physical: It is Spiritual

Still newer thinking about mind and Brain and its function began with new discoveries. British neurologist John Eccles won the Nobel Prize in 1963 for his pioneering research on the synapse in the Brain. Eccles discovered that the early burst of discharge in SMA was not due to stimulation by another cell in the SMA region or elsewhere in the brain. He concluded that "we have here an irrefutable demonstration that a mental act of intention initiates the burst of discharge of a never cell. The SMA (supplementary motor area) gets a non physical signal and starts according to the direction of his signal. The time difference between the non-physical signal and physical action is only 1/50th of a second. When there is a fire, we switch off the line, but between the decision and action there is this time difference. Eccles believes that "the non-physical mind" entered our physical brain during embryological development and thus, according to Eccles, it is conceivable that such non-physical mind lives even after the death of physical body and brain (Beyond the Quantum: Michel Tablot, Bantam New Age Book, 1988, p.93) Science consciousness or the Mind of mind, is non-physical it is spiritual. In fact Consciousness is always spiritual. It is transcendent above the material world.

Professor George Wald, Professor Emeritus at Harvard University, was awarded Nobel Prize for his research in biochemistry of vision. Wald asks a pertinent Question: "But I know that I see. It reacts to light; so does a photoelectrically activated garage door. Does the frog know that it is reacting to light, is it self-aware? Now the dilemma, there is nothing whatever that I can do as a scientist to answer that kind of question" In his own style Wald speaks of stark similarity between modern discoveries and ancient Indian finding: "Let me say that it is not only easier to say these things to physicists than to my fellow biologists but easier to say them in the West. For when I speak of mind pervading the universe, of mind as creative principle perhaps primary to matter, any Hindu will acquiesce. Will think, yes, of course, he is speaking of Brahman. The Judeo-Christian-Islamic god constructed and does so in cycles, time without end. And as the Upanishads tell us, each of us a share in Brahman, the Atman, the essential Self, ageless, imperishable. The universe, mind-stuff; and yes, each of us shares in it. (Dialogue with Seven Nobel Laureates: Bhakti-Vedanta Institute, Kolkata-700059, 2004, p.14).

George Wald spoke about the latest trends in brain-mind study: "Some years ago I talked about this with Wilder Penfield, the greater Canadian neurosurgeon... I asked him, 'Why do you think consciousness is in the brain?' He chuckled and said, 'Well, I will tell you one thing, it's not in the cerebral cortex." Prof. Wald then gave his own ideas on the mind-brain-consciousness relation: 'Though consciousness is the essential condition for all sciences, science cannot deal with it... Consciousness itself lies outside the parameters of space and time that would make it accessible to science. That relation carries an enormous consequence. Consciousness cannot be located. It has no location...' Wald quotes a number of outstanding physicists in support of this idea. Physicist Von Weizsacker (1971) gives a new and intelligible interpretation of quantum theory of what he calls his 'Identity Hypothesis': "Consciousness and matter are different aspects of the same reality." "Biologists" says Wald, "tend to be embarrassed by consciousness". [2]

Four Levels of Consciousness

Dr. A.K. Mukhopadhyay, AIIMS, New Delhi, discussed more clearly four kinds of consciousness. First, Brain-stem-consciousness is personified in the strictly mechanical movement of the body like the soldier's marching according to the direction given by the leader. The second is Limbic-system-consciousness which drives one to seek pleasure and avoid the unpleasant. Basic motivations of this level of consciousness are thirst, hunger, and sex. Those who are solely limbic-system conscious, are concerned only about their own pleasure. They can do anything for their own sensual gratification. People dominated by this consciousness are generally known as selfish.

Still higher level of consciousness is cortical consciousness which originates in the cerebral cortex... All creative imagination and aesthetic activities belong to this cortical consciousness. Under its dominance people emerge as geniuses or leaders in various fields of science, religion, politics or sociology. The leading idea of these geniuses in the various fields of human endeavour constitutes human values.

A pure 'cortical-consciousness' is without any motive. That is why artists feel that art is for art's sake. It is a joy in itself, and feels no need of satis-

[2] George Wald, paper on *Life and Mind in the Universe* NCERT Seminar, New Delhi: Feb. 1987.

fying the creator or anybody else. Today's medical scientist, according to Dr. Mukhopadhyaya, is finding the existence of **A Fourth Dimension – 'Supra-cortical Consciousness'**. That is the level of consciousness where man can feel the 'cosmic consciousnesses' through his own individual consciousness, either through meditation or various mystical experiences. [3]

Downward Causation: Mental Forces Act on Body

Nobel-scientist R.W. Sperry who has conducted extensive experiments on split-brain subjects, rejects reductionist explanation of mental phenomena which says all mental phenomena can be ultimately reduced to physical and chemical reactions. He argues instead for the existence of something like downward causation. It is technically known as 'emergent interactionism' of consciousness on matter. Sperry explicitly states that, "mental forces or properties exert a regulative control influence in brain physiology. How does the 'mental force' exert a downward causality on physical brain matter? Sperry explains, "Once penetrated from neural events, the higher order mental pattern and programs have their own subjective qualities and progress, operate and interact by their own causal laws and principles which are different from, and cannot be reduced to those of neurophysiology.

By 1970s, "this causal view of mind", writes Sperry, "had become the centre of a paradigm battle in behavioural science, with a possibility of further spreading into all sciences. From the standpoint of the brain's functional organization and cognitive processing, one can hardly overrate the commanding, central-control influence of the human belief system as a shaper of both individual and social behavior." Science is turning, according to Sperry, from "the micro material to the macro mental paradigm".

Science Accepts the Power of Faith and Subjective Belief

Roger W. Sperry thinks, "Subjective belief is no longer a mere impotent epiphenomenon of brain activity. It becomes a powerful impelling force in its own right. I no longer need to keep my religion and my science separate. This new outlook arose as the unforeseen, secondary result of long search for a better answer to the age-old mind-brain problem... As things stand, I no longer need to believe, as I belong upward through the "fundamental forces of physics" in a totally mindless and purposeless cosmos, indifferent to human concerns." (A Search for Belief to Live by Consistent with Science: Article by Roger W. Sperry quoted in Cosmic Beginning and Human Ends, Edited by Mathews and Vergese Open Court, Illinois, 1995, p.314-315).

Consciousness Revolution

Sperry also thinks that religiously deep-rooted beliefs or faiths are no longer illusions. They are sometimes overwhelmingly functional: "Subjective belief is no longer a mere impotent epiphenomenon of brain activity.

It becomes a powerful impelling force in its own right. I no longer need to keep my religion and my science separate. This new outlook arose as the unforeseen,

[3] NCERT seminar New Delhi, Feb, 1987, paper on *States of Consciousness, A Holistic View.*

secondary result of a long search for a better answer to the age-old mind brain problem. As things stand, I do longer need to believe, as a scientist, that I and my world are governed solely from below upward through the 'fundamental forces of physics' in a totally mindless and purposeless cosmos, indifferent to human concerns. In our new downward-control paradigm we are moved and surrounded in the modern world by higher, more-evolved vital, mental cultural and other social forces".

The related so called New Age movement of the past two decades, which has increasingly challenged Judeo-Christian and other traditions of Western Culture, I believe also has its foundation in the consciousness revolution." (Goswami: The Selfaware Universe: Bantam, New York, 1995, p. 271).

Thought is a Force

Science has discovered five kinds of forces in the universe-gravity, electricity, magnetism, strong nuclear force (which binds the atomic nucleus) and the weak interaction force (which allows subatomic particles to escape from the bondage). India discovered a sixth force-thought which is the most powerful of all the forces. Vivekananda says: "What is thought? Thought is a force, as is gravitation or repulsion ... Force is supplied to us through food, and out of that food, the body obtains the power of motion etc. Finer forces, it throws out as what we called thought... From the infinite store house of force in nature, the instrument called Chitta (mind-stuff) takes hold of some, absorbs it, and sends it out as thought." (Rajayoga) "The greatest force is derived from the power of thought. The finer the element, the more powerful it is. The silent power of thought influences people even at a distance because mind is one as well as many," says Swami Vivekananda.

Science Discovers How Meditation Brings us in Touch with Infinity

Recently a team of three American brain scientists led by Andrew Newberg, experimented on what happens in our brain during deep meditation. Their historic experiment had been graphically described in their brain-storming book. Why God Won't Go Away (Ballantine Books. N.Y. 2001, p. 1-14).

An adept in Buddhist mediation admitted that during the state of deep meditation he feels at the depth of his consciousness that he is inextricably connected with the whole of creation. How did this experience come to him repeatedly? He himself agreed to be examined in laboratory. This team of doctors tugs a twine on his brain to signal the gradual changes in the brain functioning as the meditation deepens and reaches the peak experience. They injected a tracer into his blood which gets locked with brain cells for hours. A Single Photon Emission Computed Tomography Camera (Known as SPECT), which is a high tech imaging tool, and which can detect the movement in the brain, was now connected with meditator's body. Increased blood flow in any part of the brain corresponds with heightened activity in that area.

The finished scan images unusual activities in the top rear section of the brain which is a highly specialized bundle of neurons. This is known as Posterior Superior Parietal lobe. This team termed this spot as OAA (Orientation Association Area). The primary function of OAA is to orient the individual in his space-time universe. It is in short, the organ by which one responds to the external world, for instance, takes own hands away from fire, redirect the steering when a frontal crash seems plausible, or take a stick when a cobra chases and so on.

When meditation began the eyes got closed. Immediate realities like the wall in front, got blocked. Still memories of past began to emerge in meditation. Before meditation, the scan showed furious neurological activity of person who was still responding to external reality. This furious neurological activity of the brain generally "appears on the scans in vibrant bursts of reds and yellows." As the meditation deepened this scan of bright yellow and red got slowly replaced by "cool green & blues", colours which indicate a sharp reduction in the activity levels inside the brain. In deep meditation OAA does not function. Brain scientist so long understood that the OAA (Orientation Association Area) never rests. Why was there a sudden cessation of activity of OAA during meditation?

OAA responds to external reality of our space-time universe which is a limited universe. Our universe is a small finite universe with a diameter, according to Einstein, of 1035 miles. In deep meditation the finite universe slowly disappears. What remains when the immediate reality of finite universe is blocked from our consciousness? To what remains is non-physical infinite beyond space-time, beyond all limits.

Newberg concluded: "As our study continued, and the data flowed in, Gene (another scientist) and I suspected that we'd uncovered solid evidence that the mystical they described as the absorption of the self into something larger-were not the result of emotional mistake or simple wishful thinking, but were associated instead with a series of observable neurological events, which, while unusual, are not outside the range of normal brain function. In other words, mystical experience is biologically, observably, and scientifically real."

"Every meditation is direct super consciousness. In perfect concentration the soul becomes actually free from the bonds of gross body and known itself as it is... He who has known God has become God. There is nothing impossible to such a free soul", says Swami Vivekananda. (Complete Works, Vol. 4p. 226).

Repetition and Meditation on OM Leads to the Realization of Infinity

In India the commonest practice for meditation begins with repetition of OM. OM is constituted of four dimensions- A.U.M and the great active silence, after M. The repetition of OM is a powerful spiritual practice. The Upanishads teach the students to repeat 'OM' or Om along with God's name. A few minutes' repetition of 'OM' brings a freshness, new energy, and deeper concentration.

The Chandogya Upanishad and Prasna Upanishad teach the young students the science of Om. The repetition of Om (AUM) makes us eminent in the world of common men (Bhuh), brings eminence in the world of knowledge, (Bhuva) and also brings eminence in the world of saints (Swah). It makes us powerful enough to resist obstructions and rise above them. "Repetition of OM and self-surrender to the lord will strength the mind, and bring fresh energy", Says Swami Vivekananda. The silence after AUM leads to infinite beyond words, sounds, time and space.

One who repeats OM gets a new superhuman body just as a serpent gets new skin after the winter (Yatha padodarah twacha vinirmchyate)- say the Prasna Upanisad (5.5). Repetition of OM with its four foundations; AUM and the unspoken great active silence after M-reveal the mystery of the infinite, the Effulgent Reality. (Chatusringa Avamita Gaura) – says Mahanarayana Upanisad (12:9).

Conclusion

Biologist Roger Sperry believes that the new culture of tomorrow "has its foundation in the consciousness revolution". The Extraterrestrial God, sitting in a heaven, has been seated inside human heart, the Infinite has been found to be inextricably with the finite. Science has established God in man. Sperry called this revolution as "Consciousness Revolution".4

New avenues were sought to explore mind. E.F. Schumacher wrote in his book A Guide for the Perplexed of new consciousness' which would help scientists 'to seek self-knowledge in the inner world of the scientist himself.

The most important characteristic of life is evolution. If thought can change the body by the process of downward causality, then higher thought backed by higher cosmic Consciousness can create cosmic personalities. The men without frontiers like Buddha, Christ, or Vivekananda. Sri Ramakrishna used to say that weaker insects evolve by constant thinking into another kind of more powerful insect. Stronger animals prey on the weaker ones. A tiger might have survived by killing a deer. But Jesus evolves into Christ by going to cross or Siddhartha Gautam becomes the Enlightened One, by death-defying sacrifice and spiritual struggle for the highest spiritual evolution or Buddhahood. "Human evolution is not biological but psychosocial", says post-Darwinian biologist Julian Huxley. Inner struggle or Internal burning which Indians call tapasya leads to higher human revolution. Schrodinger strangely advocates this view in his celebrated book What is Life (Cambridge, 1965). The essentially non-physical or spiritual Consciousness is influencing more and more the world of science.

The 'Consciousness Revolution' predicted by Roger Sperry and other scientists, is fulfilling Swami Vivekananda's prophecy that Vedanta philosophy will inundate the civilization tomorrow. It would bring the thought wave of "Immanent God" or Universal Consciousness or God hidden in every being. And this will be, as Vivekananda dreamt, the beginning of spiritualization of our materialistic civilization. The prophecy is coming true. America's best-selling author Dennis Wholly writes in the 1997s:

"We are in a spiritual revolution. This is going to be called God's decade. It is a decade of higher awareness... We are in the midst of a great spiritual revolution and people are looking upward and turning inward in their search for peace and contentment."

(Dennis Holly: *The Miracle of Change*: 1997, Pocket Book, New York, 1997, p.98-99)z

Chapter 15

कबीर पंथ और राधास्वामी मत में निहित दर्शन, साधना और आध्यात्मिक चेतना

स्वामी प्यारी कौड़ा
कला संकाय, डी.ई.आई. आगरा
साहबदास कौड़ा
विज्ञान संकाय, डी.ई.आई. आगरा

"क्या परम आनन्द की अवस्था मुमकिन है और अगर मुमकिन है तो सचमुच मौजूद भी है? और अगर मौजूद है तो किस प्रकार से यानी किस साधन व उपाय की मदद से उसकी प्राप्ति हो सकती है?" "चेतनशक्ति यानी जीवात्मा के नियम क्या हैं? सच्चा मालिक यानी सत्करतार किसको कहते हैं? रचना कैसे और किस निमित्त रूपवती हुई? जीव के लिए इस संसार में रहते हुए मुनासिब कर्त्तव्य क्या होने चाहिएँ?"[1] राधास्वामी मत के तृतीय आचार्य परम गुरु महाराज साहब द्वारा प्रस्तुत इन प्रश्नों के उत्तर पाने के लिए कबीरपंथ और राधास्वामी मत के दर्शन, साधना व आध्यात्मिक पद्धतियों में निहित समानताओं को जानना आवश्यक होगा, जिनमें इन प्रश्नों के वैज्ञानिक उत्तर अन्तर्निहित हैं।

परमतत्व – कबीरपंथ की ईश्वरवादी षाखाएँ समस्त दृश्य–जगत का सारभूत तत्व ब्रह्म को मानती हैं।[2] (कबीरपंथ परम तत्व को 'सत्यपुरुष ' नाम देता है।) समस्त सृश्टि का मूल तत्व सत्यपुरुष अनादि है। जो आदि, अन्तरहित और स्वप्रकाशित है।[3] निर्गुण ा, निराकार, अनन्त होने के कारण परम तत्व इन्द्रियों का विशय नहीं है।

"मन बुद्धि चित्त पहुँचे नहीं तहाँ, अवरण पुरुष विराजे जहाँ
अगम, अगाध, गाध के नाहीं, ज्यों के त्यों प्रभु आप रहा हीं।"[4]

राधास्वामी मत में भी सत्तपुरुष तीन लोक से ऊपर चौथे पद में बास करने वाला है। अलख व अगम लोक के भी पार राधास्वामी धाम है, जहाँ अनामी पुरुष विराजते हैं, और पूर्णमुक्ति उनके चरणों में पहुँच कर ही संभव है।

"सत्तपुरुष चौथे पद बासा। संतन का वहाँ सदा बिलासा।।
सो घर दरसाया गुरू पूरे। बीन बजे जहाँ अचरज तूरे।।"[5]

शब्दस्वरूपी – कबीरपंथी ब्रह्म को शब्द स्वरूपी मानते हैं। कबीरपंथ में शब्द स्वरू पी साहब को अनादि, अविनाशी, चेतन, विदेह, अखण्ड, सर्वव्यापी, अलिप्त, निःतत्व, निरवयव, अक्षर, निःअक्षर (वर्णातीत) और सगुण, निर्गुण, द्वैताद्वैत से न्यारा माना गया है।

"सार शब्द है मुक्ति दाता, कहं लग करे पुकारा।
चैतन्य सहित सबही में व्यापक, है पुनि सबसे न्यारा।।"6

राधास्वामी मत में भी सतपुरुष को शब्द स्वरूपी माना गया है। सुरत शब्द योग में सतगुरु ही शब्दस्वरूप में परिवर्तित होकर सुरत को अपने संग जोड़कर निजधाम ले जाते हैं।

"शब्द ने रची त्रिलोकी सारी। शब्द से माया फैली भारी ।।
शब्द ही घट–घट करे पुकारी। शब्द फिर अलख अगम से न्यारी।।"[7]

निःअक्षर – कबीरपंथी ग्रन्थों के अनुसार पदार्थ तीन हैं – क्षर, अक्षर और निःअक्षर। माया क्षर है, आत्मा अक्षर है और परमात्मा निःअक्षर। कबीरपंथ जिस परमतत्व को निःअक्षर कहता है, उसे सार शब्द नाम देता है ।

"निःअक्षर वह रूप अनूपा। सार शब्द निःतत्वस्वरूपा।"[8]

राधास्वामी मत में सतपुरुष को क्षर, अक्षर और निःअक्षर से परे माना गया है –

"क्षर, अक्षर, निःअक्षर पारा , बिनती करे जहाँ दास तुम्हारा।।"[9]

सत्यपुरुष की अभौतिक दिव्य देह की कल्पना भी कबीरपंथी महात्माओं ने की है। सत्यपुरुष की दिव्य देह का अंग प्रत्यंग अतुलित सौन्दर्य और प्रभा से युक्त है –

"अमर चीर सोहे अस अंगा। सूर्य मणि सो अधिक सुरंगा।।
दंत सुरंग शोभित अति भारी। मानों मणि बत्तीस बिचारी।।
भाल रूप का कहाँ बखानी। चन्द्र किरण मानो लपटानी।।"[10]

राधास्वामी मत में भी परम पुरुष पूरन धनी राधास्वामी दयाल के स्वरूप का वर्णन कबीरपंथ से मिलता जुलता है। हंस हंसनी उस अगम्य अगोचर रूप के दर्शन कर निहाल होते हैं जिसके एक एक रोम में करोड़ों सूर्यों की छबि समायी हुई है –

"करूँ आरती राधास्वामी, तन मन सुरत लगाय।
थाल सजा सत शब्द का, अलख ज्योति फहराय।।
सुन्न मँडल धुन साराँगी, किंगरी बजे अनूप।
कोटि भानु छबि रोम इक, ऐसा पुरुष स्वरूप।।"[11]

जीवात्मा – कबीरपंथ की अद्वैतवादी विचारधारा यह स्वीकार करती है कि स्वयं ब्रह्म ही देह धारण कर जीव कहलाता है।

''ब्रह्म देह धरि जीव कहावे, पांच स्वादरति सो दुःख पावै।''[12]

सभी अद्वैतवादी दर्शन आत्मा का अनादित्व स्वीकार करते हैं। कबीरपंथ भी जीव तत्व को अनादि मानता है।"राधास्वामी मत सिखलाता है कि कुलमालिक और सुरत का अंशअंशी भाव संबंध है, और जैसे पानी के एक बिन्दु और सिन्धु का एक ही जौहर है। ऐसे ही सुरत और कुल मालिक का भी एक ही चैतन्य जौहर है। रचना की क्रिया के आरम्भ होने से पूर्व सब सुरतें कुल मालिक में लीन थीं।"[13] कुलमालिक सागर हैं तो सुरत एक बूँद के समान है।

''सुरत बुंद सत सिंध तज , आई दसवें द्वार ।
वहाँ से उतरी पिंड में , बसी आई नौ द्वार ।।''[14]

माया – कबीरपंथ के अनुसार – सृश्टि रचना की इच्छा से सत्यपुरुष ने अपने विभिन्न अंशों से सहज, अंकूर, इच्छा, सोहं, अचिन्त, अक्षर, निरंजन आदि विभिन्न पुत्रों को उत्पन्न किया। निरंजन दुष्ट और अभिमानी था, अतः सत्यपुरुष ने उसे अपने राज्य (सत्यलोक) से निश्कासित कर दिया। निरंजन ने अपने लोक का निर्माण करने की इच्छा से तप करके सत्यपुरुष से पहले नक्षत्र, पर्वत, पृथ्वी आदि जड़ सामग्री प्राप्त की। पुनः जीवन शक्ति प्राप्त करने के लिए तप किया। सत्यपुरुष ने जीवन शक्ति देकर, अपनी इच्छा शक्ति से उत्पन्न एक अश्टांगी मोहिनी कन्या (आद्या) को भेजा। निरंजन ने इसे बलपूर्वक अपनी भोग्या बनाया। ब्रह्मा, विश्णु, महेष इन त्रिदेवों के जन्म के उपरान्त निरंजन अन्तर्द्धान हो गया। अब आद्या (माया) ही स्वयं को समस्त ब्रह्माण्ड और सृश्टि का उत्पत्तिकर्त्ता बताने लगी। निरंजन के रहस्य को उसने अपने पुत्रों से भी छिपाए रखा। संसार में अपनी और अपने तीनों पुत्रों की पूजा का प्रचार करने के लिए माया ने विभिन्न अवतारों, तीर्थों और चौरासी लाख योनियों की रचना करके जीवों को अपने जाल में उलझा लिया। जीव भी सत्यपुरुष को भूलकर आद्या और उसके पुत्रों को ही सर्वोपरि समझने लगे। निरंजन के समान उसकी अर्द्धांगिनी भी कबीरपंथ में तिरस्कृत ही है। कबीरपंथ में माया को सर्वत्र भ्रमात्मिका, बन्धनस्वरूपा, हेय और निम्नशक्ति के रूप में देखा गया है। कबीर कहते हैं –

"माया महाठगिनी हम जानी।
तिरगुन फाँस लिए कर बोले मधुरी मीठी बानी।"

राधास्वामी मत में भी निरंजन को काल कहा गया है, और उसकी संगिनी माया द्वारा जीवों को भरमा लेने का वर्णन मिलता है।

''माया काल बिछाया जाल, अपने स्वारथ करें बेहाल।
यह घर काल बसाया आन, तुमको लाया हमसे मांग।''[15]

जगत – निरन्तर उत्पत्ति स्थिति और लय इन तीन लक्षणों से सत्ता को दर्षन में 'जगत' संज्ञा दी जाती है। कबीरपंथी साधकों के समक्ष रहट की घरिया के समान

गतिमान संसार है, जिसमें उत्पत्ति लय का क्रम निरन्तर है –

"ऐसा यह संसार है जैसी रहट की घरिया।
एक रीति फिरि जाए, एक आवे फिरि भरिया।।"[16]

राधास्वामी मत में जगत की निरन्तर उत्पत्ति स्थिति व लय का वर्णन मिलता है। यथार्थ प्रकाश में सर साहब जी महाराज ने स्पष्ट लिखा है – "जब वर्तमान रचना का उद्देश्य पूरा हो जाएगा, अर्थात् निरमल चेतन देश में निवास पाने योग्य सुरतें परम गति को प्राप्त हो जाएंगी, तो महाप्रलय की क्रिया से समस्त पिण्ड और ब्रह्माण्ड सिमट जाएँगे, और फिर रचना का नया चक्र जारी होने पर महासुन्न के भण्डार से सुरतों का दूसरा समूह नए ब्रह्माण्डों और पिण्डों में उतरेगा, और नयी रचना का पसारा फैलेगा, और उसका उद्देश्य पूर्ण होते ही तीसरा समूह मैदान में आवेगा। इसी प्रकार अनन्त काल तक रचना और महाप्रलय की परम्परा जारी रहेगी।"[17]

भक्ति एवं सतगुरु का महत्त्व – कबीर परात्पर ब्रह्म के अनन्य उपासक थे। कबीरपंथ की छत्तीसगढ़ी शाखा के अनुसार मुक्ति के लिए भक्ति एक आवश्यक तत्त्व है। निष्काम नाम साधना और भक्तिभावना मनुष्य को आवागमन के बंधन से मुक्त करती है ।

"जब लग नाता जाति का, तब लग भक्ति न होय।
भक्ति करे कोई सूरमा, जाति वरण कुल खोय।"[18]

राधास्वामी मत तो गुरु की भक्ति का मत है। सतसंग की असली क्रिया गुरूभक्ति है। गुरु की महत्ती आवश्यकता पर बल देते हुए परम गुरु प्रेम सरन सतसंगी जी ने परम गुरु मेहता जी महाराज के भण्डारे पर फ़रमाया – "राधास्वामी मत गुरु का मत है।"[19] परम पुरुष पूरन धनी स्वामी जी महाराज द्वारा रचित सारबचन पोथी में गुरु की महत्ता पर निम्न शब्द प्रकाश डालता है –

"गुरु की कर हर दम पूजा। गुरु समान कोई देव न दूजा।
गुरु रूप धरा राधास्वामी। गुरु से बढ़ नहीं अनामी।।"[20]

परम गुरु साहब जी महाराज ने लिखा है – "सतगुरु की शान का इल्म किसी को नहीं है, और न पहचान ही हो सकती है। लेकिन जिसको वे खुद पहचान बख्शें, वह पहचान सकता है।"[21]

नाम – नाम साध्य भी है और साधन भी। कबीर पंथ में कहा गया है कि अद्‌भुत चैतन्य शक्ति से संपन्न नाम संजीवनी मूल है। जिसके कान में प्रवेश होते ही अवगुण छूटने लगते हैं, दुर्मति दूर हो जाती है, और हृदय में अलौकिक प्रीति का उदय होता है। संचित कर्म और करोड़ों जन्मों के पाप भी नाम से भस्म हो जाते हैं –

"कोटि जनम के पातक होई। नाम प्रताप जाएं सब धोई।।"

राधास्वामी मत में भी स्वामी जी महाराज ने अपनी पुस्तक 'सारबचन' के बचन नं. 2 में असली व निर्मल नाम राधास्वामी बताया । उन्होंने राधास्वामी नाम की महिमा के विशय में कहा है–

"राधास्वामी नाम , जो गावे सोई तरे ।
कल कलेश सब नाश, सुख पावे सब दुख हरे।।"[22]

सतसंग – सतसंग का अर्थ है सतस्वरूपी ईश्वर के भक्तों का संग। सतसंग बिना विवेक संभव नहीं है, और विवेक के बिना सद्जीवन का विकास संभव नहीं है, जो मुक्ति के लिए आवश्यक है। कबीर पंथ सतसंग के महत्त्व पर बल देता है –

"सत्यस्वरूपी ईश्वर कहिए। ताके भक्तन संगत गहिए।
तासु नाम सतसंग कहावे, सो संगत गहि जिव तरि जावे।।"[23]

राधास्वामी मत के द्वितीय आचार्य परम गुरु हुज़ूर महाराज ने सतसंग की महिमा का बखान करते हुए फ़रमाया है – "संत अथवा राधास्वामी मत में सतसंग नाम ऐसी सभा और संगत या जलसे का है, जहाँ कि सच्चे मालिक का निर्णय और उसकी महिमा और उससे मिलने के सच्चे रास्ते और जुगत का बयान होता होवे। परम पुरुष पूरन धनी स्वामीजी महाराज ने सतसंग के महत्त्व पर लिखा है –

"करो री कोई सतसंग आज बनाय।
नर देही तुम दुर्लभ पाई। अस औसर फिर मिले न आय।।"[24]

प्रेम – परम तत्व के प्रति रागात्मकता भक्तिमार्ग की विषेशता है। जिसकी तीव्रतम अनुभूति के लिए साधकों ने प्रायः घनिष्ठ मानवीय संबंधों का प्रतीक रूप में प्रयोग किया है। इसलिए पिता–पुत्र, माता–पुत्र, सखा–मित्र, सेवक–सेव्य, गुरु–शिष्य, पति–पत्नी आदि विविध संबंधों के माध्यम से प्रेम की अभिव्यक्ति भक्ति साहित्य में मिलती है। कबीरपंथी धरमदास जी पिता–पुत्र संबंध में प्रार्थना करते हुए कहते हैं –

"कोटिन ऐगुन बालक करई, मात पिता चित्त एक न धारी।
तुम गुरु मात पिता जीवन के, मैं अति दीन दुखारी
सदा भरोसे रहूँ तुम्हारे, तुम प्रतिपाल हमारी।"

दाम्पत्य प्रेम के रूप में कबीर सत्यपुरुष को दूल्हे के रूप में और स्वयं को दुल्हिन मानते हुए कहते हैं –

"दुलहिनी गावहु मंगलाचार।
हमारे घर आए राजा रामभरतार।।"

राधास्वामी मत में भी सुरत के सतगुरु से प्रेम के विभिन्न रागात्मक संबंधों का वर्णन

मिलता है।

''परम गुरु परम पितु परम प्रिय नाथ मम।
आदि पुरुष आदि हितु आनी जग तारिए।।''[25]

विरह – विरह प्रेम का शाश्वत जीवन है। आत्मबोध के कवि के अनुसार है।संत सतगुरु से परमपुरुष और उनके देश की बातें सुनकर पूर्व संबंध के कारण अनन्य प्रेम का उदय होता है, वह अपरोक्षसत्ता 'प्रियतम' बन जाती है, और साधक को अपनी विरहित अवस्था सालने लगती है।

"सतगुरु आवो हमारे देस निहारों बाट खड़ी।।
वाहि देस की बतियां रे, लावे संत सुजान।
भूल गई तन मन धन खारा, व्याकुल भया सरीर।
विरह पुकारे विरहनी, ढरकत नैनन नीर।।"[26]

राधास्वामी मत पर दृष्टिपात करें, तो हम पाते हैं कि विरह द्वारा मालिक को पाने में सुरत दीवानी होकर उनकी पुकार करती है। वह प्रिय की दूरी से विचलित होकर पुकार उठती है –

"मैं तो पड़ी री दूर निज घर से। मेरा दरशन को जिया तरसे।
छिन–छिन पिया की याद सतावे। जल नैनन सों बरसे।।"[27]

सुरत ाब्द योग – कबीरपंथ में स्मृति, ध्यान, प्रेम, रूप आदि अनेक अर्थों में भी सुरति शब्द का प्रयोग हुआ है, और चित्तवृत्तियों के व्यापक अर्थ में भी। आदि पुरुश से उत्पन्न होने के कारण ही कबीरपंथ में शब्द योग का वर्णन मिलता है।

''शब्द हमार दृढ़ हृदय धरहू, निज सुमिरण तुम हमरा करहू।
जो चित सुरति तुम्हारे होइ। तौन वस्तु सिखै सब कोई ।।''[28]

राधास्वामी मत में भी सुरत शब्द योग की साधना प्रणाली अपनायी जाती है। सुरत ही मन को जान देती है, और मन उससे शक्ति पाकर विभिन्न इन्द्रियों के माध्यम से शरीर से काम लेता है।

''राधास्वामी से सतगुरु नहिं, राधास्वामी सा निज नाम ।
सुरत शब्द सम योग नहिं, पाया भेद अनाम ।।''[29]

संत कबीर राधास्वामी दयाल के निज पुत्र थे। वे ऐसे संत यानि कामिल पुरुष थे, जिनको निर्मल चेतन देश में सालोक्य, सामीप्य, सारूप्य और सायुज्य गति हासिल थी। उनके कुछ शब्दों से प्रकट होता है, कि वे सबसे ऊँचे धाम से तशरीफ लाए जो अलख

और अगम के परे है और जिसको राधास्वामी धाम कहते हैं। कबीर साहब अपने सच्चे पिता का पवित्र फ़रमान संसार में पहुँचाने की गरज़ से पहले तशरीफ लाए थे।उन्होंने अपने आने का उद्देष्य स्पष्ट करते हुए कहा है कि –

"कहैं कबीर हम धुर घर के भेदी लाये हुक्म हुजूरी।"[30]

उन्होंने अन्य स्थान पर राधास्वामी नाम को निज नाम घोषित करते हुए कहा –

"कबीर धारा अगम की, सतगुरू दई लखाए।
उलटि ताहि सुमिरन करो, स्वामी संग लगाए।"[31]

सारबचन के एक शब्द में यह पंक्ति आती है –

''साहब कबीर और तुलसी साहब।
दयालमता इन आन चलाई ।।''[32]

निष्कर्श रूप में कहा जा सकता है कबीर पंथ और राधास्वामी मत में निहित दर्शन साधना वा आध्यात्मिक चेतना में बहुत अधिक साम्यता है। संत कबीर से ही कलयुग में संतमत का प्रादुर्भाव हुआ था। कबीर पंथ में गुरु की महिमा, नाम का सुमिरन, प्रेम व भक्ति, माया जीव का वर्णन, सुरत शब्द अभ्यास का वर्णन राधास्वामी मत से बहुत साम्यता रखता है। वे राधास्वामी दयाल की अगवानी से पूर्व उनके प्रकट होने का संदेश लेकर आए थे। तत्पष्चात् राधास्वामी दयाल स्वयं परम पुरुष पूरन धनी स्वामी जी महाराज के रूप में संसार में तशरीफ लाए, और जगत उद्धार की मौज फरमायी, और एलान किया कि जब तक सारी रचना का उद्धार नहीं हो जाता, निजधार वापिस नहीं जाएगी।

संदर्भ

1. परम गुरु महाराज साहब, अमृत बचन, पृ. 2–3, राधास्वामी सतसंग सभा, दयालबाग़, आगरा। राधास्वामी संवत् 178, सन् 1995

2. तत्वार्थ दोहावली, पृ. 312 (पदार्थ काण्ड, ब्रह्मादि प्रकरण) हनुमान साहब, स्वसंवेद कार्यालय, सीमाबाग, बड़ौदा, सन् 1949

3. सर्वज्ञ सागर, पृ. 129–130

4. ज्ञान स्थिति बोध, पृ. 83 लक्ष्मी वेंकटेश्वर प्रेस, बम्बई, संवत् 2009

5. परम पुरुष पूरन धनी स्वामी जी महाराज, सारबचन नज़्म, मंगलाचरन, पृ. 3 राधास्वामी सतसंग सभा, दयालबाग़, आगरा। राधास्वामी संवत् 164

6. मुक्ति प्रकाश ,पृ. 126 मोहनपरि साहब, आचार्य गद्दी बड़ैया, सन् 1969

7. परम पुरुष पूरन धनी स्वामी जी महाराज, सारबचन, षब्द 17वाँ, पृ. 209–210

8. अनुराग सागर, पृ. 11 लक्ष्मी वेंकटेश्वर प्रेस, बम्बई, संवत् 1971

9. परम पुरुष पूरन धनी स्वामी जी महाराज, सारबचन, शब्द 17वाँ, पृ. 161

10. धरम० शब्दावली भेद का अंग षब्द 3 वेलवेडियर प्रेस, प्रयाग, सन् 1947

11. परम पुरुष पूरन धनी स्वामी जी महाराज, सारबचन नज़्म शब्द सातवाँ, पृ. 125–126

12. ज्ञान प्रकाश, पृ. 36 लक्ष्मी वेंकटेश्वर प्रेस बम्बई, संवत् 2010

13. परम गुरू साहब जी महाराज, यथार्थ प्रकाश, भाग – 1, 2, पृ. 46

14. परम पुरुष पूरन धनी स्वामी जी महाराज, सारबचन नज़्म शब्द सातवाँ, पृ. 439

15. परम पुरुष पूरन धनी स्वामी जी महाराज, सारबचन, शब्द 3, पृ. 437–438

16. धरम० शब्दावली भेद का अंग, शब्द 3 पृ. 3 ,वेलवेडियर प्रेस, प्रयाग, सन् 1947

17 परम गुरू साहब जी महाराज, यथार्थ प्रकाश, भाग – 1, 2, पृ. 49

18. धर्म बोध, पृ. 190 लक्ष्मी वेंकटेश्वर प्रेस, बम्बई, संवत् 2009

19. हिन्दी प्रेम प्रचारक, साप्ताहिक संवत् 192, 3 मई 2010, अंक 49 दयालबाग़ प्रेस एवं पब्लिकेशन प्रा. लिमिटेड, दयालबाग़, आगरा।

20. परम पुरुष पूरन धनी स्वामी जी महाराज, सारबचन, शब्द 3, पृ. 322–323

21. परम गुरू महाराज साहब, सरकार साहब, साहब जी महाराज, बचन भाग–2, पृ. 203 राधास्वामी सतसंग सभा, दयालबाग़, आगरा। राधास्वामी संवत् 186, सन् 2003.

22. परम पुरुष पूरन धनी स्वामी जी महाराज, सारबचन, सिफत चौथी , पृ. 19

23. जीव धर्म बोध, पृ. 60 लक्ष्मी वेंकटेश्वर प्रेस, बम्बई, संवत् 2007

24. परम पुरुष पूरन धनी स्वामी जी महाराज, सारबचन, शब्द 3, पृ. 265

25. परम गुरु सरकार साहब, प्रेम समाचार, शब्द 4, पृ. 1 राधास्वामी सतसंग सभा, दयालबाग़, आगरा। राधास्वामी संवत् 188, सन् 2006.

26. धर्मदास शब्दावली, विरह और प्रेम का अंग, षब्द 9

27. परम गुरू हुज़ूर महाराज, प्रेमबानी, भाग–4, शब्द–4, पृ. 92, वेलवेडियर प्रेस, प्रयाग, सन् 1947

28. सर्वज्ञ सागर, पृ. 134, वेलवेडियर प्रेस, प्रयाग

29. परम गुरु सरकार साहब, प्रेम समाचार, शब्द 4, पृ. 61 राधास्वामी सतसंग सभा, दयालबाग़, आगरा। राधास्वामी संवत् 188, सन् 2006.

30. परम गुरु महाराज साहब, अमृत बचन, पृ. 71, राधास्वामी सतसंग सभा, दयालबाग़, आगरा। राधास्वामी संवत् 178, सन् 2006.

31. वही, पृ. 98

32. परम पुरुष पूरन धनी स्वामी जी महाराज, सारबचन, शब्द 3, पृ. 442

Chapter 16

The Nature of Witness Consciousness in Advaita-Vedanta

CHILAKAMARTHI DURGA PRASADA RAO
Department of Sanskrit
Dayalbagh Educational Institute (Deemed University), Agra, India

Abstract

Every major religion and philosophy of the world speaks, often in symbolic terms, about states of consciousness other than those of our ordinary consciousness. According to these teachings, we have the potential to experience qualitatively different levels of perception, awareness and orientation towards ourselves, others and the universe. The first two of these distinct realms of consciousness – sleep and waking consciousness – constitute the normal human condition, our day to day experience. Higher states of being, correlate with fine and subtle levels of reality. In this article, the nature of different levels of consciousness in general and Witness Consciousness in particular, are discussed from the perspective of Advaita -Vedanta

Introduction

Each of the major religions and philosophies of the world speaks, often in symbolic terms, about states of consciousness other than those of our ordinary consciousness. According to these teachings, we have the potential to experience qualitatively different levels of perception, awareness and orientation towards ourselves, others and the universe. The first two of these distinct realms of consciousness – sleep and waking consciousness – constitute the normal human condition, our day to day experience. Higher states of 'being' correlate with fine and subtle levels of reality. In this article the nature of different levels of consciousness in general and Witness Consciousness in particular, is discussed from the perspective of Advaita -Vedanta. Before entering into the subject, the necessity of study of these levels of consciousness is presented hereunder.

It is a natural tendency of every living being to desire happiness and avoid misery. They therefore strive towards that end to the maximum possible extent. But on close observation and personal experience, it is seen that the happiness we acquire in day to day life is subjected to gradation. More over it is always accompanied by some elements of misery. We can even say that there is no pleasure in this world which is not mixed with misery. And the pleasure we get by possessing something will certainly cause misery when we lose it. Even though the joy of heavenly sojourn is pure and not affected by any element of misery, it is also not everlasting.

This being so, it is imperative on the part of the wise to opt for the permanent and absolute happiness. Through the experience of seers and saints, it is known that man can get real and absolute happiness on the realization of his own true nature and this alone is to be the sole aim of human life and there is no higher purpose of human existence than knowing one's own self. The Sastras assert that a man who knows Brahman will achieve the highest good **ब्रह्मविदाप्नोति परम्**

(Brahmavidapnoti param).

Consciousness

All the Upanishads not only establish the Uniqueness of Atman but also assert that nothing else exists. सर्वं खल्विदं ब्रह्म नेह नानास्ति किंचन (Sarvam khalvidam Brahma neha nanasti kinchana) means that the entire universe is nothing but Brahman and there is no plurality in It. Brahman, is the universal spirit and the supreme reality. It is self-effulgent. Being self- luminous, it illuminates everything.

न तत्र सूर्यो भाति न चन्द्रतारकं
नेमा विद्युतो भान्ति कुतोयमग्निः
तमेव भान्तमनुभाति सर्वं
तस्य भासाः सर्वमिदं विभाति। / कठोपनिषत् २ /१५

(*Na tatra suryo bhati na chandratarakam*
Nema vidyuto bhanti kutoyamagnih
Tameva Bhantamanubhati sarvam
Tasya bhasah savvamidam vibhati).

Translation: There the Sun shines not, nor the moon, nor the stars, nor even these lightning flashes; all these shine only after He shines; it is only through His luminosity that all this shines.

The entire creation is the result of movement in consciousness. According to Sankara there is an intelligent principle behind the manifest world which alone can account for the design and purpose of the universe and it is none other than Brahman Itself. Brahman is pure consciousness and it is self-effulgent. It is the light which manifests all objects and all relations between the objects. It is the primordial source of the universe comprising the worlds, the objects in them and the senses and the mind. It has neither inside nor outside and it is a mere mass of knowledge. Brahman, the supreme self, is manifested as Atman, the inner self of all beings. It is neither limited in space and time nor governed by the law of causality. Though it is one and without a second it appears as many to the ignorant. It is the subtle agent that animates the mind, sense organs etc and acquires the characteristics of a knower, knowledge and the known.

Matter, the manifestation of chaitanya at a lower level, can neither know itself nor any thing else. It comes under the known category, Mind. Mind, a comparatively higher level of the manifestation of chaitanya can know matter but it cannot know itself. It is both knower and known. Atman, being the highest level of chaitanya not only knows itself but also every thing else. There is no seer, no hearer, no knower other than Itself. However, It can not be known because a knower of all can not be known by gross mind or senses. He is to be known only by the refined mind after being instructed by a competent and erudite teacher. तद्विज्ञानार्थं स गुरुमेवाभिच्छेत्समित्पाणिःश्रोत्रियं ब्रह्मनिष्ठम्।

(*Tadvijananartham sa gurumevabhigacchet*
Samitpanih shrotriyam brahmanishtham)

Levels of Consciousness

Though the un-manifested consciousness is pure, the manifested consciousness at different levels is impure to different degrees as it is associated with Maya or Avidya. As already stated, we experience three states in our day-to-day life. They are waking state, dreaming state and deep sleep.

We experience consciousness in waking state and we are aware of it. In this state external objects determine the content of our consciousness. It is the state in which mind and sensory organs act as channels for consciousness to flow out and take the shape of the objects under observation. Similarly we are aware of dreaming. Dream consciousness is made up of the same stuff as the waking consciousness, except that its content is not empirically real but a reflection of occurrences experienced in waking state. It is illusory in the sense that, on waking, one realizes the unreality of what is experienced in the dream.

Even though we are not apparently conscious of any experience whatsoever in deep sleep we become aware of the joy we experienced in deep sleep the moment we wake up and reflect upon it. This clearly shows that we are animated by consciousness of the self during that state also. This deep sleep state is characterised by the total absence of all distinctions together with the awareness of the subject and object and the distinction between the two. Apart from these three there is one more state, Turiya, the fourth state, which is neither conscious of the internal world, nor conscious of the external world, nor conscious of both the worlds, nor a mass of consciousness , nor simple consciousness, nor unconsciousness, which is unseen beyond empirical determination, beyond the grasp of the mind, un-demonstrable, unthinkable, indescribable and of the nature of the consciousness alone where all phenomena cease to exist and which remains unchanging, peaceful, auspicious and non dual. The first three states are mutually exclusive in that each exists in its own right to the exclusion of the other two while the fourth is the conscious background against which every thing that happens in the three states . It is as if it is a witness {Sakshin} to all that happens in our conscious life.

Atmaan as Sakshin

The concept of Atman as Sakshin is allegorically expressed in the Mundakopanishad. Atman, albeit one in nature, is described as possessing a dual character. Firstly, the supreme consciousness – through association with the mind and the senses – engages in actions, thereby reaping their sweet and bitter results as Jiva. Secondly there is the consciousness which remains aloof as a pure spectator or witness (Sakshin) who is in essence none other than Jivasakshin identified with Brahman.

द्वा सुपर्णा सयुजा सखाया
समानं वृक्षं परिषस्वजाते
तयोरन्यः पिप्पलं स्वाद्वत्ति
अनश्नन्नन्यो अभिचाकशीति।।

(*Dva suparna sayuja sakhaya*
Samanam vriksham parishasvajate
Tayoranyah pippalam svadvatti
Anashnnannyo abhichakashit)

Translation: Two birds, companions and always united, cling to the self – same tree. One eats the sweet Pippala – fruit, the other looks on without eating.

Here the former refers to the Jivatma, who eats the diverse fruits of many flavours, and consequently experiences the pleasures and pains of life. The latter, who looks on without eating is the Sakshin or Atman, always one with Brahman, ever untouched by Maya in which Jiva is engulfed. He is, at the same time, the controller of both the individual soul and the body and is also the detached witness of their activities. [Swami Nikhilananda on Mundakopanishad-3/1/1]

Swetaswara Upnishad went one step further by stating that the Atman is Sakshin. It regards Him as the supreme deity or consciousness which being all by itself governs the entire Universe. The verse goes like this.

एको देवः सर्वभूतेषु गूढः
सर्वव्यापी सर्वभूतान्तरात्मा
कर्माध्यक्षःसर्वभूताधिवासः
साक्षी चेता केवलो निर्गुणश्च।।

Translation: The one resplendent God is hidden in all beings, all pervading, the inmost self of all creatures, and the overseer of all karmas, dwelling in all beings.

He is the witness [Sakshin], the knower, the Absolute, free from all attributes.{S.U 6/11} Chitsukharya, who established the nature of Atman as Sakshin explains in his magnum opus ' Tattvapradipika' that the self shining nature of Atman as Sakshin, can not be denied because the Shruti says that Atman is self luminous. The sloka runs as follows:

चिद्रूपत्वादकर्मत्वात्स्वयंज्योतिरितिश्रुतेः।
आत्मनः स्वप्रकाशत्वं को निवारयितुं क्षमः।।
– तत्त्वप्रदीपिका

{ *Chidrupatvadkarmatvat*
Svayam jyotiriti shruteh
Atmanah svaprakashatvam
Ko nivarayitum kshamah }
{ Tattvapradipika }

Conclusion

Unlike other branches of knowledge, this knowledge can be acquired through Sadhana on the instruction of a preceptor who has had the experience of supreme reality and that is why it is said in the Mundakopanishad:

Tadvijnartham sa gurumevabhigacchet
Samitpanih shrotriyam brahmanishtham

The same idea is found in the Gita also:

तद्विद्धि प्रणिपातेन परिप्रश्नेन सेवया ।
उपदेक्ष्यन्ति ते ज्ञानं ज्ञानिनस्तत्त्वदर्शिनः ।।

{*Tadviddhi pranipatena*
pariprashnena sevaya
upadekshyanti te jnanam
jnaninah tattvadarshinah.}
{ Bhagavadgita- IV-34}

The Advaita-Vedanta tradition has thus conceived the Sakshichaitanya as the highest level of spiritual consciousness attainable in this life.

Chapter 17

Spiritual Evolution in Relation to Karma - A Comparative Study of Hinduism and Radhasoami Faith

C. TARA SATYAVATHI, C. BHARADWAJ AND PUNEET CHOWDHARY
Indian Agricultural Research Institute, Pusa, New Delhi, India
Rajaborari Estate, M.P., India.

Abstract

Spiritual evolution is the philosophical, theological, esoteric or spiritual idea that nature and human beings and/or human culture evolve along a predetermined cosmological pattern or ascent, or in accordance with certain predetermined potentials. Karma is the concept of "action" or "deed" in Indian religions understood as that which causes the entire cycle of cause and effect. Through the law of karma, the effects of all deeds actively create past, present, and future experiences, thus making one responsible for one's own life, and the pain and joy it brings to him/her and others. The results or 'fruits' of actions are called karma-phala. The karmic principle is the moral law of cause and effect that runs through all spiritual as well as all other aspects of existence. It affects personal lives as one advances in spirituality. It follows a basic principle of harmony, reason and love.

Introduction

The saying goes- "As you sow – so shall you reap" i.e. the results are based on the actions one does. All *karma* or actions, good or bad, produce their result and one cannot get liberation or salvation as long as he/she has to enjoy or suffer the result of any action(s) of his/ her. Man cannot free himself from karma (action) by abstaining from action due to the wandering nature of the uncontrolled mind and thus cannot attain perfection by mere renunciation. *Karma* operates in the spiritual realm as does the law of gravity in the physical world and just as we can be taught to use gravity to our physical advantage; we can also learn to make the karmic principle work for our spiritual growth/ evolution. The intricacies of karma are very hard to grasp and one should understand "akarma", "vikarma" and "karma".

The highest abode mentioned in Hinduism is Parabrahma pada. Other religions like Sikhism did speak of higher levels, Jainism does not speak of any God element in the fate of an individual soul except for its action and association with the karmic particles i.e. pudgals and Buddhism speaks of only liberation of the atman from worldly entanglements and leading a sramanic life for that purpose. The religion which spoke of the highest abode and the spiritual source to be reached is the Radhasoami Faith. In this religion, the scientific basis of keeping track of karmas was also mentioned which is in Manakasa an ethereal layer surrounding us and stores the imprints of the thoughts and actions undertaken. The original spiritual abode can be reached under the guidance of a Guru with an arduous desire in the seeker to reach the same by following the path and procedures of Surat Shabda Yoga. The practice of Surat Shabd Yoga along with the desire to reach the highest spiritual abode i.e. Radhasoami Dham helps in removing the various types of karmas like Kriyamaan Karma, Prarabda Karma and Sanchita Karma along with the Adi Karma which is responsible for the entanglement of the soul in this birth and death cycle. The various stages experienced by the seeker like Jagrat, Svapna, Susupti, Turiya and Turiyatita states are also given in the religious texts. The presence of different spiritual centers in the universe and the corresponding contact centers in the human body are also mentioned in the religious texts of Radhasoami Faith. Also the various lokas or spiritual levels and the description of those regions experienced by the atman during the process of attaining the highest spiritual abode has also been mentioned in the religious literature of Radhasoami faith.

Evolution is both biological and spiritual and the human being is in the midst of a divine process directly touching him and all around him. The spiritual evolution occurring in the individual does not free him from his responsibility for human survival. Thus *karma* and spiritual evolution are important aspects to consider when dealing with the ethical dilemmas and opportunities of lives (Vineeta et al., 2007).

The saying - "**As you sow – so shall you reap**" is applicable from routine day to day activities to the religious goals and ultimate meaning of human life. Man is a social animal and wants the best in every field related to him. With this attitude of achieving the best he has become selfish, self centered and forgotten the duties towards his own people, others and the society at large. This has led to a number of tensions in present day life. The problems that face mankind today and threaten the very structure of humanity are world-problems and not isolated in any geographical area. All these are due to his actions or *karma* as an individual or of the group or the society. *Karma* acts to restore harmony disrupted by the conflict of wills. When individuals interact with each other they set in motion energies, which either separate or unify, and these energies return to them with a force directly proportional to the vitality they were given. Thoughts and actions of humans design their providence: it makes them accountable for their life and for the world in which they live. This is the **Doctrine of Karma**. Spiritual evolution is the process of unfolding universal consciousness through a myriad of forms. It is necessary to understand and appreciate this principle because it affects each one intimately and personally. It directly concerns the present existential situation, the origin and the final destiny of a person as well as the reason for the being to be here right now. (Saxena et al., 2005)

Karma in Hinduism

The concept of karma appeared in Hindu thought during the period 800-200 BC and became widespread during the period considered as "Classical Hinduism" 200 BC - 1100 AD. According to *Brodd Jefferey (2003)* karma is a concept in Hinduism which explains causality through a system where beneficial effects are derived from past beneficial actions and harmful effects from past harmful actions, creating a system of actions and reactions throughout a person's reincarnated lives. As per the Vedas, if an individual sows goodness, he or she will reap goodness; if one sows evil, he or she will reap evil. *Karma* refers to the totality of mankind's actions and their concomitant reactions in current and previous lives, all of which determine the future. However, many karmas do not have an immediate effect; some accumulate and return unexpectedly in an individual's later lives. The conquest of *karma* is believed to lie in intelligent action and dispassionate reaction. Unkindness yields spoiled fruits, called *paap*, and good deeds bring forth sweet fruits, called *punya*. As one acts, so does he become: one becomes virtuous by virtuous action, and evil by evil action. All *kriyamana karmas* become *sanchita karma* upon completion. From this stock of *sanchita karma*, a handful is taken out to serve one lifetime and this handful of actions which has begun to bear fruit and which will be exhausted only on their fruit being enjoyed and not otherwise, is known as *prarabdha karma*. In this way, so long as the stock of *sanchita karma* lasts, a part of it continues to be taken out as *prarabdha karma* for being enjoyed in one lifetime, leading to the cycles of birth and death. A jiva cannot attain Moksha until the accumulated *sanchita karmas* are completely exhausted.

Karma in Sant Mat

According to the Sant Mat philosophy, the surroundings of an entity as also his subjective actions produce impressions on him, which are preserved in *Manakasa*, which is as elastic as ether in creation. Mind, with its four functions, becomes cognizant at the time of recording of the impressions. But when its attention is diverted the previous impressions fade away and pass into the stage of memory. They are never completely eliminated but scrupulously preserved in the old records of *Manakasa*. When we focus our attention on them voluntarily or involuntarily, they are immediately recollected. On close observation of these occurrences of reproduction of these impressions, it can be understood that when the attention is focused on these impressions one acts entirely in accordance with the nature of those impressions, however feeble and unintelligible they are. Secondly, these acts react on *Manakasa* and reinforce the impressions and constitute centres of future action, whenever an attention gets focused on them. These impressions as well as actions done are called *Karmas*. In Sant Mat, there are three types of karmas apart from the initial *Adi karma*. *Adi Karma* does not imply any activity. It is the pre-creational condition of polarization. There were spirit entities in the nether pole, which had a tendency to associate with mind and matter in different degrees.

They assume bodies peculiar to those planes to enable them to associate with the surroundings and enjoy their pleasure. These pleasurable experiences produce a stronger desire to repeat those experiences and make them get entangled in the association of mind and matter. As the bodies assumed in those regions are impermanent and changeable and also infirm, subject to influences of the regions, they experience woe, so the spirit entities thus pay dearly for associating with the mind and matter. Even if our present desires get exhausted, the *Adi Karma*, the root tendency to associate with mind and matter, hurls down the entities once again (Satsangi, 2004).

Table. 1. Types of karmas as per Hinduism and Radhasoami Faith

S.No.	Religion	Source	No. of types of Karma	Name of Karma
1	Hinduism		3	Sanchita Karma
				Praarabdha Karma
				Kriyamana Karma
		Bhagavad Gita	3	Karma
				Vikarma
				Sakarma
		Ashtavakra Gita	3	Sakama Karma
				Nishkama Karma
				Akarma
		Vedas	4	Nitya karma
				Naimittika karma
				Kamya Karma
				Nishidha Karma
		Dharma Shastras	5	Nishkama Karma
				Nishidha Karma
				Kamya Karma
				Asakta Karma
				Anasakta karma
2	Sant Mat: Radhasoami faith	Discourses on Radhasoami Faith	4	Adi Karma
				Kriyaman Karma
				Prarabda Karma
				Sanchita Karma

Spiritual Evolution

Spiritual evolution is not the same as ancestral evolution. It has nothing to do with Darwin's evolutionary theory. *In spiritual evolution, man passes through different stages, each of them having some specific characteristics. Recognizing these characteristics can open the path toward superior levels which leads us to perfection or a higher spiritual bliss which is the summum bonum of life.*

Consciousness is a fruit of evolution and our most prized possession. It sets us apart from the opulent variety of earth-life and puts upon us an onus of responsibility. It takes us on incredible journeys and has given us the gifts of insight and transcendence.

Stages Experienced during Spiritual Evolution as per Hinduism

The different states of consciousness experienced during spiritual evolution are as follows:

1. Wakeful State - The wakeful state is the normal condition of man. The world presents itself to him as it is perceived by his senses. He is outwardly disposed (*BahisPrajna*). In this wakeful state he cognizes external objects through the five sense organs, senses of sight, hearing, taste, smell and touch. He acts with the five organs of action of speech, handling, locomotion, generation and excretion. The five vital breaths form the motive force in the body. The mind is taken in its four aspects of *Manas, Buddhi, Ahamkara and Citta* - mind, intellect, self-sense and thought. Man in this state is led by his desires in diverse ways for the enjoyment of the sense objects. He experiences quickly alternating pleasures and pains because the objects of his enjoyment are transient.

2. Dream State - The dream state is characterized by its internal consciousness or awareness. Man experiences mental states that are reflections of the predispositions and latent impressions caused by his experiences in wakeful state. The soul fashions its own world as in creative imagination. The objects that one enjoys in dreams are internal and subtle. There is no qualitative difference between the experiences of the dream and the wakeful state though there is a little more freedom, on account of the absence of limitations of the physical world. The experience or the subject here is called *Taijasa*. The body instrumental in his experiencer is a subtle body of ethereal nature.

3. State of Deep Sleep -The state of deep sleep is full of bliss and experience of bliss, as all desires have become dormant and no dream is dreamt of. One is just a "man of cognition" there, *Prajnanaghana*. One is said to be *Cetomukhah* at the doorway of thought or mind for one relap ses back into dream and waking states soon. One is just conscious or knower, full of bliss enjoying bliss.

4. State of Self Realization (Turiya State) – In the fourth state of consciousness known as *Turiya*, the *Atman* ceases to be even the source, that is, it is not viewed as the cause of the other three states and it does not relapse into them automatically. It is a transcendental state. In the words of the *Upanishad* "*Turaya* is not that which cognizes the internal (object), not that which cognizes the external (object), not what cognizes both of them, not a mass of cognition, not cognitive, not non-cognitive. The path of self realization or entering into the state of *Turiya* is through the process of withdrawal of the spirit current to its original abode. While doing so the subject passes through the state of *Jagrat, Svapna* and *Susupti* like states and far beyond. "*Omkara*"-*Pranava* is spoken of as the name of the *Brahman* the highest spiritual state. It is said to be consisted of four parts; a, u, m and *Amatra* (zero) corresponding to the four states of consciousness; *Jagrat, Svapan, Susupti, Turiya.*

5. Turiyatita State - One who realizes the Turiya state is Jivanmukta a realized soul, and even while awake, he is detached and aloof as in *Susupti* (withdrawn inwards). The later Upanishads call him *Tatastha*. They also speak of the further state of *Turiyatita*, a state transcending the *Turiya* where the subject is called *Saskin*, the witness, *Nirguna*, devoid of all characteristics. It is the state that is beyond the four, without any reference to them (*Jivadavastham prathamam jagrad, dvitiyam Svapnam, trtiyam Susuptam, Caturtham Turiyam. Caturbhirvirahitam Turiyatitam*). It is significant to note that one who attains that state is also called *Turiyatita* and there is also one *Upanishad* (No. 67) of that name.

Spiritual Evolution in Radhasoami Faith

It is in the scriptures of the Radhasoami Faith written by Param Guru Soamiji Maharaj, Maharaj Sahab, Sarkar Sahab and Sahabji Maharaj, especially, there are clear evidences and description of the higher levels of spiritual consciousness of the *Sant Mat* tradition. According to this religious tradition, there are three Grand divisions of creation: *The Material Region, The Material-Spiritual Region*, and *The Pure Spiritual Region*. The human body is the replica of the Universe and doorways are provided in it. The body is the microcosm and the universe is macrocosm.

There are six *chakras* in the body: *Guda, Indri, Nabhi, Hrday, Kantha* and *Ajna*. Beyond that there is Chidakasa. The next region is spiritual material region corresponding to the mind. Centers provided in the body enables us to establish contact with these regions and they are called *Kamalas*. They are situated between the two lobes of the brain in the Grey matter and six in number. The lower three enable to establish contact with *Sivaloka, Brahmaloka* and *Visnuloka* and beyond that is the *Brahma Pada* with its three divisions of *Virat, Hiranyagarbha* and *Avyakrta*. This highest region is the *Parabrahma Pada* or *Purusottam Pada*. In the terminology of the religion of saints, they are known as: *Sahasdal Kamal, Trikuti, Sunnlok* or *Dasam Dvar*.

The consciousness of *Sahasdal Kamal* and *Trikuti* are said to be the *Turiya* and *Turiyatita* states of Vedic tradition. Then there is a neutral sphere called *Mahasunn* below the Pure Spiritual Region, *Nirmal Chetan Desh* or *Dayal Desa*. In *Dayal Desa*, again we have six sub-divisions: *Bhanwar Gupha, Sat Loka, Anami Loka, Alakh Loka, Agam Loka* and *Radhasoami dham*. Corresponding doorways are situated in the line between the two lobes of the white matter of the brain of man. The consciousness of these different *Lokas* is superior to the consciousness of the lower spheres. It is held in *Sant Mat* that real emancipation of the individual soul is attainable only on reaching the pure spiritual region or *Nirmal Chetan Desa* beyond *Brahmanda*. In this process he has to go through the states of consciousness spoken of earlier. All these are not completely out of the influence of the subtle mind. So until, the spirit enters the regions beyond and traverses to the *Loka* at the top of the region known as Radhasoami *Dham* in the Religion of the Saints, the region of the Supreme Being, it does not shine in its pristine glory and that is the ultimate spiritual evolution an individual soul can reach.

Figure 2: Grand Divisions of Creation as per the Radhasoami Faith

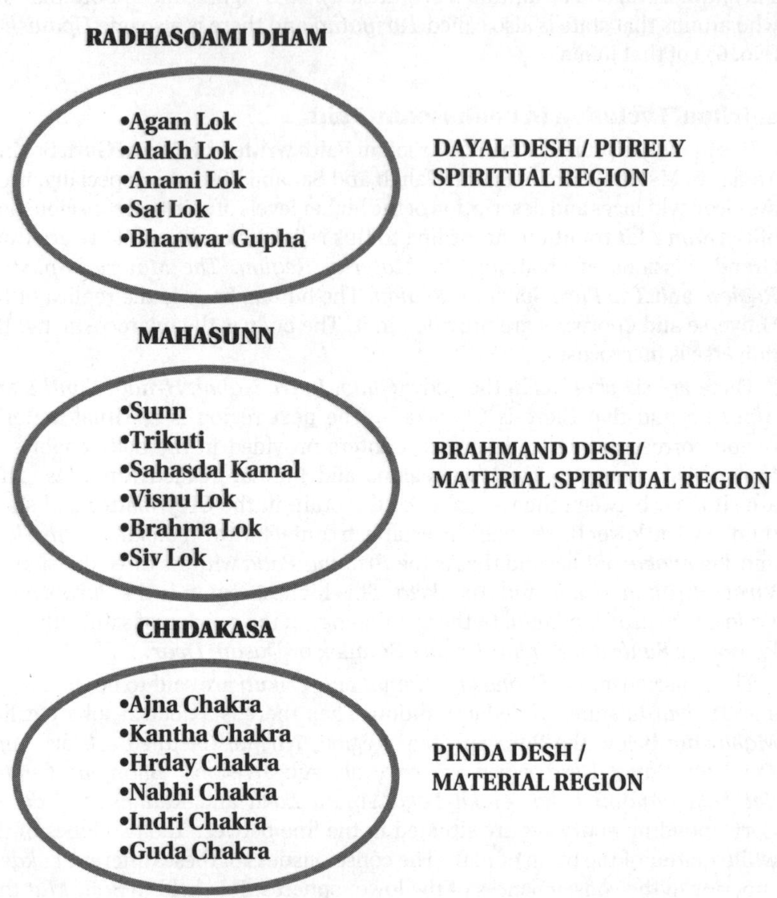

Relation between Karma and Spiritual Evolution: Hinduism

When there is a clear space between you and your body- mind it is not that you are trying to watch this or that, you are simply here. Whatever *karma* is in the mind, whatever *karma* is there in the body or energy, everything has become separate from you. For a few moments, if you can experience this separation through the process of *dhyana*, you know it is possible. If one can make this a part of one's life, *karma* ceases to exist.

If you have an aversion to *karma*, and you are trying to push it away, in the effort to push it away, you end up building more *karma*. Once you come to a living experience that this body is not me, this mind is not me, then there is a different kind of wisdom and understanding in you. **The very process of life is dissolution of karma**. Every living moment of life, if lived totally, enormous amounts of *karma* gets dissolved. Anything and everything that comes has to be experienced fully and intensely. If one experiences every life breath with utmost intensity, then one is liberated from the very process of life and death.

Transmigration or metempsychosis means the soul's going from body to body whether animals, human, angelic or gods. The Hindu theory holds that the soul after death is subject to Karmic Laws and selects gross material body according to its desires and tendencies. The theory of reincarnation or resurrection implies growth and evolution of individual souls from the lower to higher stages of development. The material body is expression of the subtle body. The Gita analyses the nature of *Karma* in an extensive manner. It is necessary to distinguish between *Karma*, Vikarma and Akarma. *Karma* means proper action and Vikarma improper action, while Akarma is inaction. Unless man knows what proper action is and what is improper and also knows how to remain a non-doer while performing action one cannot adopt the path of *Karma* for Salvation which is nothing but the spiritual evolution. Man cannot free himself from doing *Karma*. He cannot even for a moment remain action less. The *Gunas* or attributes of *Prakriti* compel everyone to perform actions.

The great seers of the Upanishads who attained the Atman consciousness or Brahman consciousness chronicled the different levels of consciousness that a man passes through in his life ordinarily, to detailed analysis and distinguished them from the supreme state of religious consciousness that they attained. The Mandukya Upanishad is a veritable thesis on the levels of spiritual evolution i.e. consciousness. There are references to these levels in other texts too, both in the principal Upanishads and in the later Upanishads. They are also described in Yogavasistha and Tantra texts. Asserting the unity of the Individual Soul and the Universal soul - "Ayamatma Brahma" - This self is Brahman.

Our traversing every day through the wakeful, dreamy and deep sleep state of consciousness does not make any difference in our attitudes and dispositions towards life much less in our spiritual or religious status. The mental modifications *Vrittis* and their functions determine the State. Thus any one of these states is not a religiously exalted state. Even the aesthetic experiential state (Rasananda) and the psychedelic states induced by drugs etc., as also the psychical states produced through exercises in courses of our spiritual development are not the religious states since they are not devoid of the effect of desires and their consequences (Kama, Krodha etc.).

So they pull down the self from these levels and associate the self with them and make us ego-centric, egoistic and selfish and engage us in diverse activities of the senses indiscriminately. Hence the clarion call of the Upanishads is to know the essential nature of the self, the subject, to develop self consciousness, "atma va are drastavyah". Thus the question arises: How to know the knower? "Vijnataram are katham vijaniyat?" The subject is different from all that is non-self. It is Pratyagatman - the self in itself is aloof from all the body and the mind. For knowing the self one has to turn his eye inwards (avrtta caksuh) develop the Divya-caksu -

To explain this truth the *Upanishads* give the analogy of a chariot. The self, the *Atman* in the body, is the master of the chariot. The body, Buddhi or intellect is the charioteer, one who drives the chariot. The mind is the reins and the sense organs are the horses. The different objects in the range of the senses are the roads which they traverse. The self, when it is yoked to the mind and the senses is the experiencer or *Bhokta*. The self, as a result of its long association with the mind and senses and the desire for enjoying worldly objects is drawn out and gets entangled with them. This is explained as follows: The *Atman* gets associated with mind, mind with senses and senses with the objects. *Atman* is of the nature of pure consciousness, *Chaitanya*. The current of the *Chaitanya* gets associated with the mind and forms a mental modification, that is, an attention current which is focused on the respective sense objects passing through the sense organs. The attention current is like a fluid e.g. water in an irrigation canal. Flowing through these canals of sense organs it goes to the fields or the sense objects and assumes their form and settles down. This is how we get the knowledge of external objects. The master of the Chariot with an indiscriminate intellect does not attain the Supreme State with such a Charioteer. Not only does he fail to attain emancipation but also gets into the cycles of births and deaths, whereas one possessed of a discriminating intellect and a restrained mind attains the Supreme State and is not reborn. He attains the goal of his spiritual evolution.

Relation between Karma and Spiritual Evolution: Radhasoami Faith

Saints like Kabir Sahab, Guru Nanak, Paltu Sahab, Jagjivan Sahab, Tulsi Sahab and Soamiji Maharaj have spoken of higher regions of creation beyond Para-brahma-pada of the Vedic religious tradition. They stressed on the importance of the practice of listening to the internal spiritual Sound- Anahata Shabda Yoga or Surat Shabda Yoga as the sure means of salvation and taught other holy names besides 'Omkara', namely, 'Sat Nam' and 'Radhasoami'.

Satsang is a Sanskrit word meaning coming together of sanga of those who are seeking the Truth (sat), Almighty, Being or Sat and the Self. A Satsang without truth is waste. The following verse in Bhaja Govindam explains-"*Satsangatvae Nissan gatvam/ Nissan gatvae nirmohatvam/ Nirmohatve nischalatattvam/ Nischalatattve jivanmktih*". From Satsang comes non-attachment; from non-attachment comes freedom from delusion, which leads to self settledness. From this state comes jeevanmukti or true freedom. In the Sant mat if the seeker, who takes refuge in the feet of the Satguru, gets initiated and starts performing spiritual practices, all the kinds of Karmas get eradicated enabling him to reach his original Abode of Pure Spirituality which is the ultimate goal of religion and spiritual evolution. For this the devotee resigns himself to the will of the Lord and conducts himself accordingly, the effects of the actions done by him in the present life do not accrue to him. No new impressions are formed by the Kriyaman Karmas. Even though the effects of the Prarabdha Karmas have got to be experienced by him in the present life there would be a vast difference in the result, i.e. in the amount of pain and pleasure experienced by the devotee.

On account of his engaging in spiritual practices he becomes capable of withdrawing his spirit current inwards and upwards to a certain extent and thus the intensity of his pain and pleasure gets reduced to the extent of his active involvement in spiritual practices. The devotee easily disposes of the *Sanchit Karmas* during his practices. When a devotee traverses the mental sphere in course of his internal journey towards spiritual regions these impressions are manifested by the power of spirit and appear to him as real objects. They detain him for sometime but then he proceeds forward with the help of his Satguru. Thus the effect of *Sanchit Karma* is also nearly obliterated. The devotee thus attains his goal in this life itself eradicating all types of *Karmas* by the Grace of the Supreme Being and Sant Satguru. The worldly desires of a spirit entity are not eradicated by death. The entity is again attracted towards the material plane and is reborn there, in such species as possess a differentiation similar to that of the prominent desire of the entity. This transmigration of an entity from one plane to another is known as *Avagamana*, i.e. coming and going or metempsychosis. As the forces of the Pind and Brahmand have a predominant tendency towards the nether pole, the inherent effort of the spirit entity to liberate itself is ineffective unless it takes spiritual training under an Adept. The devotees surrender to the will of the Lord and depend on His Mauj. They put their faith in the Orders and Will and Pleasure of their Lord and Sant Satguru in all their affairs and feel whatever happens to them is ordained by the merciful Supreme Father. Our past Karmas determines the Kshetra of our life. Suffering may be the effect of our past but `doing' is our most precious privilege. The past is unalterable and done with. It has entered into us and become part of us.

To eradicate the *Adi Karma*, the *Sant Mat* prescribes the most effective of methods. In the same spirit entity, if the seed of desire to reach the purely spiritual region is sown, it would counter act the original tendency for associating with mind and matter. Persons with such a desire for release from this world associate with the Reservoir of spirituality and become seekers and search for true Religion and come to *Sant Mat*, i.e. Radhasoami Faith. The Sant Satguru waters and nourishes the seed to grow into a plant and come to fruition. He makes him direct his attention at the seat of spirit in human body, and ascend to higher regions and ultimately reach the Reservoir of Spirituality.

Conclusion

The concepts and classification of *Karma* and Spiritual evolution vary in different religions. However every religion has related *karma* with ultimate spiritual evolution or consciousness which is the *Summum bonum* of life. Though various classifications of *karma* existed in Hinduism, they were overlapping and often lead to confusion for the followers.

The concept of *Karma* and its relation with spiritual evolution has clearly brought out in the Sant Mat i.e. Radhasoami faith where the path to eradicate the adi karma and how to attain spiritual evolution has been clearly spelt out.

It is clear that the eradication of different types of karmas is possible with the help of *dhyana* or *surat shabd yoga* done under the guidance of a tattvadarsi guru who can guide the seeker/ disciple and help him overcome the major *adi karma* that is responsible for the chaurasi i.e. the cycle of life and deaths. In this religion the scientific basis of keeping track of *karmas* was also mentioned. i.e. *Manakasa* which is an ethereal layer surrounding us and stores the imprints of the thoughts and actions undertaken. This original abode can be reached under the guidance of a Guru with an arduous desire in the seeker to reach the same by following the path and procedures of Surat Shabda Yoga. The practice of Surat Shabd Yoga along with the desire to reach the highest spiritual abode i.e. Radhasoami faith helps in removing the various types of *karmas* like *Kriyamaan Karma, Prarabda Karma* and *Sanchita Karma* along with the *Adi Karma* which is responsible for the entanglement of the soul in this birth and death cycle. One has to develop a strong urge to reach the original spiritual abode from which the *atman* has come and the constant guidance and blessings from the Satguru helps one in reaching it. This is how the spiritual evolution takes place and helps the atman in merging with the original spiritual source of the creation and this is the summum bonum of human life. While nurturing the desire to reach the original abode one has to perform *nishkama karma* as mentioned by Lord Krishna in Bhagavad gita and undertake the day to day activities in this life with full confidence in the guru.

References

Brodd, Jefferey. (2003). *World Religions*. Winona, MN, USA: Saint Mary's Press.

Hefner, Philip. (1993). *The Human Factor: Evolution, Culture, and Religion*. Minneapolis, USA: Fortress Press

Mathur, V, Kumari, M, and Sriramamurti, P. The Karmic Principle: A Bridge between Biological and Spiritual Evolution. *D.E.I. Journal of Science and Engineering Research vol. 14 (1 and 2)*. 237-244.

Satsangee, P. P. (2005) Teachings of Bhagawad Gita and Religion of Saints. In *Theology, Science and Technology: Ethics and Moral Values*. Saxena, P. K., and Chaturvedi, D. K. (Eds.). New Delhi, India: Vikas Publishing House. 23-29.

Satsangi, P. S. [Revered Prof. Prem Saran Satsangi] (2003). Reality and Truth vis-à-vis Wisdom (via Apara Vidya and Para Vidya. Invited talk, International conference of the Association of Asia Pacific Operational Research Societies, August 2003, New Delhi, India. Rep. *Discourses on Radhasoami Faith* (Supplement), Agra, India: Radhasoami Satsang Sabha, Dayalbagh.

Satsangi, P. S. (2004). Karma as Explained in the Various Writings and Speeches of Revered Leaders of Radhasoami Faith, Radhasoami Satsang, Dayalbagh. *Discourses on Radhasoami Faith* (Supplement). Agra, India: Radhasoami Satsang Sabha, Dayalbagh.

Saxena, Arti, Saxena P. K., and Chaturvedi, D. K. (2005). Karmas and Upasana: The Scientific Mantra of Saints. In *Theology, Science and Technology: Ethics and Moral Values*. Saxena, P. K., and Chaturvedi, D. K. (Eds.). New Delhi, India: Vikas Publishing House. 63-68.

Sriramamurti, P. (2005). Progressive Revelation in Religion. In *Theology, Science and Technology: Ethics and Moral Values*. Saxena, P. K., and Chaturvedi, D. K. (Eds.). New Delhi, India: Vikas Publishing House. 360-364.

Chapter 18

Temporal To Ethereal: Spiritual Awakening and Maulana Rumi

RENU JOSAN AND GARIMA KAPUR
Dayalbagh Educational Institute (Deemed University), Agra, India

Abstract
Pierre Chardin, the French philosopher stated, "We are not physical beings having a spiritual experience but spiritual beings having physical experience". Unfortunately, human beings in their mad pursuit of gross materialism and commercialism have forgotten the core of spirituality that lies within. Different religions of the world came into existence with the noble and exalted purpose of developing spiritual consciousness among human beings but, somehow, they all degenerated into mere dogmas, creeds and external forms of worship; which did not serve the real purpose of awakening the soul to the bliss of the higher spiritual regions. The Saints and Fakirs like Kabir Sahab, Guru Nanak Sahab, Tulsi Sahab and Maulana Rumi revived the spiritual practice of worshipping the True Supreme Being internally and revealed the secrets of higher realms of spirituality. Rumi's Masnawi abounds in fables and parables through which he explains spirituality, metaphysics and mystic experience. Rumi has emphasized the importance of true Guru, true Word, true Satsang and unflinching love and devotion towards God. The thrust of the paper lies in exploring the contribution of Rumi towards laying the foundation for the religion of Saints. It is the Sant Mat which will prove to be the bedrock of a better world order and blaze a trail of spiritual enlightenment, panacea for all the ills plaguing the world today.

Pierre Chardin, the French philosopher stated, 'We are not physical beings having a spiritual experience but spiritual beings having physical experience' [1]. Spirituality is our true essence and foundation of our most closely held values. It is spirituality that brings purpose and meaning to life and as we develop it, we grow in wisdom and love. We begin to experience a sense of awe, a sense of connection to all life and a deep reverence for the divine. Unfortunately, human beings in their mad pursuit of gross materialism and commercialism have forgotten the core of spirituality that lies within. The different religions of the world came into existence with the noble and exalted purpose of developing spiritual consciousness among human beings but, somehow, they all degenerated into mere dogmas, creeds and external forms of worship, which did not serve the real purpose of awakening the soul to the bliss of the higher spiritual regions. The words religion and religious have been variously interpreted. Wilfred Cantwell Smith, a Canadian scholar noted for his work on the Islamic tradition defines what it is to be religious, 'He designates first category as cumulative tradition, meaning the religious rites and doctrines and the

---

[1] Qtd. in Alan Shelton, "Find Your Purpose", *The Times of India,* 18 Nov 2007, p17.

second category is of 'Faith', which includes active personal experience of and commitment to God' [2]. Most of the people are the followers of the first category, but it is the commitment to God which holds prime importance. However, this active personal experience of God can only be attained through spiritual practices which enable one to perceive Truth and Ultimate Reality. The Saints and *Fakirs* like Kabir *Sahab*, Guru Nanak *Sahab*, Tulsi *Sahab* and Maulana Rumi revived the spiritual practice of worshipping the True Supreme Being internally and revealed the secrets of higher realms of spirituality.

Maulana Rumi, the thirteenth century Persian mystic was a man of transcendental powers. His inspirational verse speaks with the universal voice of the human soul and brims with exuberant energy, spirituality and passion. Rumi's *Masnawi* abounds in fables and parables through which he explains spirituality, metaphysics and mystic experience. Rumi's *Masnawi* is not a pedantic exposition of the universal mysteries; instead, he communicates in a lucid manner the nature of the True Supreme Being who created higher and lower regions, the supreme importance of *Ibn-ul-waqt* (the living master), the need for discarding old customs, rituals and ceremonies, path of love and the relevance of moral virtues which must be the product of intuition and meditation.

The polarization between microcosm and macrocosm has alienated the human beings from the sphere of spiritual consciousness. It is the teachings of the Saints like Rumi which have always stressed upon the unity and oneness of the two systems and how to progress from the temporal to the spiritual. Different *Yogis* have talked about different techniques of attaining spiritual consciousness leading to different religious traditions but they could not attain level beyond one or two regions of *Brahmand*. The creational process has been explained clearly by most revered Prof. P.S Satsangi Sahab (the eighth revered Guru of the Radhasoami Faith) and He has diagrammatically represented the Universal Consciousness Realization Postulate. However, the diagram presented here is not exactly the same as given in the Supplement in *Discourses on Radhasoami Faith*. In the diagram, corresponding Mohammedan terms for the different regions have been mentioned. Mohammedans call the first three ganglia - Rectum, Reproductive organ and Navel as *Nasoot* and the remaining three Solar Plexus, Throat and the *Nukta-i-Sveda* as *Malkoot*. Similarly, *Sahas Dal* Kamal is termed as *Alam-i-Jabroot*; *Trikuti* as *Alam-i-Lahoot*; *Sunna* as *Alam-i-Hahoot*; *Bhanwar Gufa* as *Hootal-Hoot* and *Sat Lok* as *Hoot*. The Consciousness of Spiritual regions of the three grand divisions of Pure Spirit (*Nirmal Chetan Desh*), Universal Mind (*Brahmand*) and Matter (*Pind*) can not be perceived by physical senses.

The diagram showing the three grand divisions and eighteen sub-divisions of the creation has been given on the following page.

In verse 4291 of Masnawi, Rumi states that "there are eighteen thousand or more divisions of this creation, but these eighteen (thousand) are not within the reach of every eye" [3]. Maulana Rumi has described the three grand divisions of Creation namely *Sifli* (Material Region), *Alame-Akle-Kul* (Universal Mind

---

[2] Lowell W. Bloass, *Theories of Religion*, (New York: The New American Library, 1964) p29.

[3] M.G. Gupta, trans., Rumi, *Masnawi* (Agra: MG Publisher, 1997) p397.

Region) and *Alame-Shahe-Kun-Faqa* (Region of Pure Spirituality). These divisions are further divided into various spheres. The human body is a replica of the pattern existing in the Universe. According to Sufis human body is *Alame Sagir* or the microcosm and the Universe is *Alame Kabir* or the macrocosm.

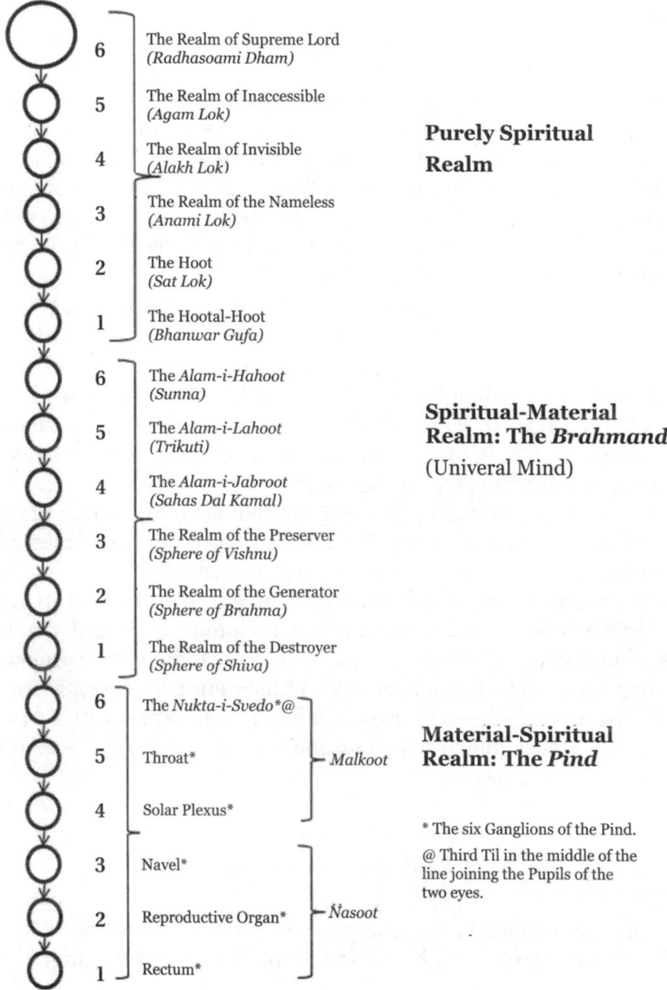

Figure 1: The Three Grand Divisions and Eighteen Subdivisions of this Creation in Spiritual Domain

The six ganglia and the corresponding centres in the grey and white matter of the brain can help us to attain the highest spiritual region, when these centres within the body are activated. The method to be adopted and practised for awakening these centres is "*Surat Shabd Yog*", the practice of uniting the spirit current with the spiritual sound currents. Just as *Brahmand* is an image of the purely spiritual region and Pind is an image of *Brahmand*, so is man endowed with the apertures in the brain corresponding to the regions of *Brahmand* and *Nirmal Chetan Desh*. Somehow, the concept of activating these centres to attain higher spiritual regions was not initiated till the time Saints like Kabir Sahab and others initiated the practice of doing Abhyas from the region of *Sahasdal Kamal*. In Sant Mat, the spirit has to ascend to the higher regions of *Brahmand* and finally reach *Dayal Desh*. It is only then that an individual can be free from the cycle of birth and death and attain state of complete bliss. *Param Guru Huzur Maharaj*, the second revered *Guru* of the Radhasoami Faith, has explained this idea in *Sar Updesh* stating that till the time all the covers enveloping the spirit are not removed, meaning till the spirit does not pass through the third and second regions and reach the first region, a region of Spirituality, the *Dayal Desh*, it will not be separated from its covers, and the process of birth and death, whether soon or late, will definitely continue and spirit will not see vision of *Sat Purusha Radhasoami Dayal*.

In order that one may be able to reach *Dayal Desh*, four tenets have to the strictly followed as expostulated by *Param Guru Huzur Maharaj*. According to the revered *Huzur* one needs true *Guru*, true Word, true Satsang and true devotion to *Guru* for attaining complete salvation. A devotee must have access to an enlightened *Guru*; otherwise it will not be possible to realize the higher realms of spirituality. Some people take recourse to the holy books as a means of attaining salvation but they do not realize that the *Vedas*, the holy *Koran* and the *Puranas* are like laws for regulating the conduct of the people of the world. As stated by the founder of the Radhasoami Faith, the most revered *Huzur Soamiji Maharaj*, "their prime aim is concerned with *pravritti* i.e management and maintenance of the world and they deal with *Nivritti* (salvation) only to a very little extent" [4]. Lord Krishna told Arjuna to go beyond the limits of the Vedas, if he wanted salvation. It is necessary to search for the *Satguru* instead of wasting time in visiting holy places and in reading holy books. The process of achieving salvation becomes easy if one comes in contact with a true *Sant* or *Faqir*. A true seeker should search for the *Satguru* and have love and faith for him. Maulana Rumi has stated:

Chunke kardi zate Murshid ra qabul
Ham Khuda dar zatash amad ham Rasul.[5]

[As you have accepted a particular personality as your *Murshid* (i.e. Guru). You should consider that both God and Prophet are present in him.]

The *Guru* of the age is representative of the Supreme Being and represents all *Sadhs* and Saints. To have a glimpse of the *Guru* who is in communion with the Supreme Being is like having a glimpse of the divine. The prophet himself

---

[4] R.S.S., trans., Huzur Soamiji Maharaj, *Sar Bachan (Prose)* (Agra: RS Sabha, 2005) p61.

[5] Ibid., p41.

declared that God revealed to him that 'I am not contained in the earth or in the sky or even in the empyrean (*Alam-i-Jabroot*), know this for certain, O dear! But curious as it may sound, I am contained in the hearts of the faithful' [6]. The vision of God is not to be found anywhere except in a perfect Saint. It is only here that the true seeker will get vision of the Supreme Being and not in idols, temples or holy places. Emphasizing this aspect Rumi says:

Masjide hast andarun-i-auliya,
Sijdagahe jumla hast an ja khuda.[7]

[There is a mosque within the Saint. The 'Place of Worship' for all is the place where God resides]

In search of a true *Guru*, one should be wary and cautious of false *Gurus*. One may have theoretical knowledge of religious literature, how to make speeches about the details of *Surat-Shabd-Yoga*, and hold *bhandaras*, but this outer strength is different from the inner strength which manifests as true spirituality. A blind man can never lead another blind man. One, who is himself unconscious spiritually, can never make another spiritually unconscious into a conscious being. Elaborating on this Rumi states:

Sadh ka nirkho ankh aur matha, sat ka noor rahe jis satha
Yeh chinha dekh kare pehchan, guru pad ka jin hirday gyan.[8]

[It is necessary to observe keenly the eyes and forehead of a *Sant*, where there is emission of refulgence. This is the sign of true Guru, who has attained the knowledge of *Guru Pad* (i.e. the highest spiritual region).]

It is only true *Guru* who has realized the highest spiritual regions and thus can lead a devotee successfully to *Sat Lok*. Maulana Rumi says, 'If you wish to buy a pomegranate, buy the one which has ripened open, so that its seeds may tell their own tale. Do not go by its appearance only.'[9] The individual salvation is completely dependent on the pleasure of the guru, so, a devotee must search for a true Guru who has access to the higher regions. Emphasising this aspect Rumi states:

Unka haath bahu lamba uncha, sat mukaam ke upar pahuncha
Jo tu sir ko rakha chaye, deen hoy guru sarni aaye.[10]

---

[6] M.G. Gupta, trans., Rumi, *Masnawi* (Agra: MG Publisher, 1997) p290.

[7] R.S.S., trans., Huzur Soamiji Maharaj, *Sar Bachan (Prose)* (Agra: RS Sabha, 2005) p42.

[8] Huzur Maharaj, Sar Updesh, (Agra: RS Sabha, 2006) p31. Hindi translation of Rumi's verses has been done by the second Guru of Radhasoami Faith, Revered Huzur Maharaj.

[9] M.G. Gupta, trans., Rumi, *Masnawi* (Agra: MG Publisher, 1997) p77.

[10] Huzur Maharaj, *Sar Updesh*, (Agra: RS Sabha, 2006) p33.

[Guru has access to the regions above the seventh region. If you want the divine protection then you must humbly find refuge in the lotus feet of guru.]

The holy name i.e. *Shabda* is a great blessing to man but people do not attach any importance to it. Many people are ignorant about the significance of the Word and its repetition. It is to be noted that there are two kinds of names: *Varnatmak* and *Dhunyatmak*. By *Varnatmak* is meant the names used in writing, reading or speaking; while *Dhunyatmak* refers to the names which resound in some region of the creation. The spiritual current of the Supreme Being descended and established its focus in the eighteen centres referred to in figure1 and the force-currents of these centres produce respective sounds. So a sound emanating from the spirit current which issued from the Supreme Being is *Dhunyatmak*. A devotee should engage himself in the practice of listening to the *Shabda* and thereby reach Dayal Desh. Emphasizing the importance of *Shabda, Maulana Rumi* states:

Shabd unche desh ka sun surma.
Jo nida kheeche hain unche ko tujhe,
Jaan veh dhun aayi unche se tujhe.
Sun ke jo avaz jage kaamna,
Kaal ki avaz hain ghar ghalna.[11]

[Rumi says that a devotee should practice listening to that sound coming from higher regions. The sound which pulls you towards higher spiritual regions has come from those very regions but if the hearing of the sound inculcates lustful desires in you, it means it is the sound of *Kal (Satan)*, which is destructive.]

Revered Huzur Maharaj has explained the importance of Shabda by giving a very apt example that of a man getting lost in a forest and on hearing the sound, proceeds in that direction and finally reaches the habitation. It is through the practice of this sound that an individual will be able to reach his final destination. When the spirit is awakened, the devotee gets knowledge of the higher spiritual planes just as a person gets knowledge of the world in his wakeful condition. This is possible only with the repetition of the holy name and contemplation of the holy form. The human body is endowed with the spiritual faculties of a high order and when they are awakened by the repetition of the holy name, the man gets the vision of the higher spiritual plane. Later, the person gets the vision of the luminous form of the *Satguru*, thereby, opening the internal spiritual passage to higher regions. In this regard, Maulana Rumi has stated thus:

Fiqr an bashad ki bakushayad rahe
Rah an bashad ki pesh ayad shahe.
Shah an bashad ki az-khud shah buwad,
Ne ba makhzan ha va gauhar shah buwad.[12]

---

[11] Huzur Maharaj, *Sar Updesh*, (Agra: RS Sabha, 2006) p39.

[12] Sir Anand Sarup Kt., *Yathartha Prakasa* Part I (Agra: RS Sabha, 2007) p11.

[The real *Dhyan* or contemplation of the Holy Form is that which opens up the internal path, the true path is that which leads to the presence of the True Sovereign. The True Sovereign is He who is so in His own right i.e. by virtue of His own high attributes and not one who is called so because of his worldly possessions and treasures.]

Satsang is of prime importance in the attainment of spiritual consciousness. Service of the *Sant Satguru*, listening to and following his precept constitutes external *Satsang*. Internal *Satsang* refers to listening to the sound current, contemplation of the Holy form and reciting the holy name internally without the movement of the tongue. Both are necessary for reaching the higher spiritual regions. Maulana Rumi has stressed upon the service to *Guru* and its positive results:

Ban sake jahan tak tu guru se mukh na pher
Seva kar abhyas kar mat kar tu der.[13]

[Man should not turn himself away from guru instead make utmost efforts to be near him. He should not delay in doing *Abhyas* and service to *Guru*.]

Like the teachings of Radhasoami Faith, Rumi has stressed upon devotion and complete surrender to Satguru. A devotee should develop utmost love and unflinching faith in the holy feet of *Satguru*. Primarily, it is through self effacement that self can mature. In Sufism the annihilation of self (*fana*) is not considered as the negative but as the preservation of the self (*baqa*) in life divine. Maulana Rumi states:

Prem agni apne hirde baliye,
Phikr bhajan aur bandagi ka jaliye.[14]

[A devotee should kindle the fire of love for his Guru in his heart. He should worry only about the recitation of the Holy name and devotion to *Satguru*.]

It is only through the feeling of complete surrender to the *Satguru*, that the negative impulses will be eradicated and the progress towards the final destination will become a smooth path. Maulana Rumi refers to the concept of surrender in Volume I of his *Masnawi* in the form of a story of a fox who surrenders everything to the lion. This complete surrender may not be possible for those who are still drawn towards material gains. The seekers of higher spirituality should take into account the following lines from the most revered Huzur Soami Ji Maharaj's *Sar Bachan, Shabda* (poem):

---

[13] Huzur Maharaj, *Sar Updesh*, (Agra: RS Sabha, 2006) p33.

[14] Ibid., p47.

This teaching is intended for those who are
steadfast in divine love and feel its pangs.
The sensual and the worldly-minded need not
give up their traditional ways.
For, to them their traditional ways are a great
solace and without these they lose all means of guidance.
Our teaching is not meant for them, for worldly
desires have brought about their spiritual ruin.[15]

Some people gloat over their expertise in worldly knowledge and sciences. Such people may attain worldly eminence but not spiritual awakening. Sometimes such people after acquiring worldly knowledge become atheists or critics of religion. Maulana Rumi has a word of caution in this regard:

The empirical, sensory sciences
are like donkey loaded with books,
Or like the makeup of woman's make up.
It washes off.
Don't carry your knowledge load for some selfish reason.
Deny your desires and wilfulness,
and a real mount may appear under you.[16]

The Religion of Saints is focussed on the principle of love and regards love as the highest attribute of the Supreme Being. So the spirit which has emanated from Him is a drop of love. On reaching the heavenly abode, the drop merges into the vast ocean of love and enjoys perennial bliss and happiness. Rumi has very succinctly pointed out that the religion of people who have extreme love for *Satguru* is very different from other religions, as for such people their God is only their true *Satguru*. In the words of Maulana Rumi:

Premiyon ka mat hai sab mat se juda,
Premiyon ka isht hai malik saccha.[17]

In India three ways have been generally followed for attaining salvation viz. *Bhakti Marg* (Path of devotion), *Jnana Marg* (Path of knowledge) and *Karma Marg* (Path of action). It is love for the Supreme Being which forms the epicentre of the *Bhakti Marg*, unlike the method of penance and mortification. Maulana Rumi has emphasised upon the importance of love in the following words:

Ishq veh shola hai jis ghat mein veh roshan ho gaya,
Ek pritam reh gaya aur baki sab jal bhun gaya.[18]

[Once the fire of love has lit up the heart of the devotee, then he is unaware of everything except his lover that is his *Satguru*.]

---

[15] Qtd. in R.S.S. trans., Sir Anand Sarup Kt., *Yathartha Prakasa* Part I (Agra: RS Sabha, 2007) p11.

[16] Coleman Banks, trans., Rumi, *Selected Poems* (Great Britain: Penguin Books, 2004) p5.

[17] Huzur Maharaj, *Sar Updesh*, (Agra: RS Sabha, 2006) p47.

[18] Ibid.

Absorption in a single supreme passion may make the mind so concentrated that all other attachments are transcended and the individual attains union with the Infinite. Krishna's *Raslila* with the Gopis is to be interpreted as the eternal, timeless and spaceless play of God with his own devotees. The devotee has to turn his love and desires towards God. Basically, attempt is to be made by the individual soul to achieve union with God. It is the cry of the flute to go back to its abode (the reed bed) with which Rumi's *Masnawi* opens, 'O man! Hear the flute which in wistful tone complains of being separated from its native place, the reed bed'.[19]

Old religious customs and creeds that have outlived their significance do not help in one's spiritual ascendance. Instead, they prove to be a detriment to the spiritual progress. Maulana Rumi compares such customs with stale, lifeless bread, only retaining its form and grossness and dry thistles which scratch eater's palate and lips. Making the comparison in Verses 4554 - 56, *Masnawi*, Vol I, Rumi says, 'It is like the green thistles which a camel eats, from eating which he gains a hundred benefits and deliciousness, but when their greenness goes away and they have become dry, if that camel eats those very thistles in the forest they would tear into his palate and lips'[20]. Rumi exhorts people to refrain from following old rituals and dogmas. Continuing with comparison of grass Rumi cautions, 'It is now mixed with dust, parched and flesh cutting. O camel! Abstain now from that herbage'[21]. Thus the futility of adhering to worn out traditions and dogmas in attaining access to higher spiritual regions has been very well explicated by Rumi.

Considering the scientific temper of the age, *Acharyas* of Radhasoami Faith have given a very scientific explanation of the spiritual practices. But Maulana Rumi exhorted people to work for their salvation through fables and parables and his teachings have formed the basis of the religion of Saints. Thus it is the teachings of the Saints and *Fakirs* like Rumi, which can redeem mankind almost on the brink of annihilation and devastation. It is the *Sant Mat* which will prove to be the bed rock of a better world order and blaze a trail of spiritual enlightenment, panacea for all the ills plaguing the world today. Let us arise awake and act on the principles enunciated by *Sant Mat* to create better worldliness in order to save humanity from gross and material worldliness.

---

[19] M.G. Gupta, trans., Rumi, *Masnawi* (Agra: MG Publisher, 1997) p1.

[20] Ibid., p422.

[21] Ibid., p424.

Chapter 19

Spirituality And Consciousness in Buddhism

B.V.S. BHANUSHREE
Andhra University, Visakhapatnam

Abstract

Though Buddhism was considered as one of the 'Nastika' systems of Indian thought, it never strictly denied the existence of metaphysical matters. For Buddha, the whole life is in a state of constant flux, which causes suffering. Even Gods cannot escape from these conditions. How can such a realistic and rational philosophy talk about spirituality and consciousness? Does spirituality have any place in Buddhism? How can we interpret Buddha's silence regarding the things beyond? When everything is momentary in life, consciousness is not an exception. Consciousness or vijnana is the one thing, which is carried forward from one birth to another. Yogachara, one of the later Buddhist Schools, developed the concept of consciousness. It is called 'Alaya Vijnana'. They believe that the yogic discipline is required to attain the higher truth. When the mind is clear of all prejudices or illusions, it reflects the truth. Nirvana is the highest goal to reach for any man according to Buddhism. This paper aims to discuss the concepts of spirituality and consciousness and how they have evolved in Buddhism.

Buddhism is a realistic system, with its practical approach in dealing with higher things in life. Buddha maintained silence when he was questioned on the things beyond, such as life after death, eternity of the world, permanence of the soul, and so on. For him these questions are of no use. The truth cannot be known by arguments and discussions. He felt that man has forgotten his real self - he has grasped things other than himself. In so grasping, he has fallen into the endless chain of cause and effect, of *avidya trsna* and karma or ignorance, desire and action, into the chain of *Pratityasamutpada*, the whirlpool of samsara. It is nothing but sorrow to be thus caught in the wheel of birth, death and change; to be merely a helpless thing worked upon by forces outside of oneself.

Truth is not merely a thing to be intellectually known, but also a value to be inwardly realized. Neither intellectualism nor sentimentalism can help us in this process. Nirvana is a great spiritual realization and the ultimate goal of human life, according to Buddhism.

Buddha's silence on the subjects of a permanent self, the nature of nirvana, and his studious disapproval of metaphysical discussion, did not have the results he anticipated. Silence on questions of deep import acts as a spur to speculation. A flood of metaphysical speculation of these forbidden themes ensued. And such speculation without any guidance from the master or his first disciple, and without any guidance from the ancient scriptures, a thousand years later, split up the Buddhist movement into sects upholding views, many of which were clearly considered as heresies in the master's own time.

Buddhism believes that every thing in life is momentary. Whatever be the duration of any state of being, as brief as a flash of lightening or as long as a millennium, yet everything is momentary. All schools of Buddhism agree that there is nothing human or divine that is permanent. *Vijnana*, which passes from life to life, is also a series of individual and momentary consciousness, a regular procession of states. Every conscious state is said to be a disturbance of the stream of being, which is the flow of subconscious existence. Buddhist psychology recognized unconscious life, *Vidhimutta*, which is distinct from waking consciousness, *Vidhichitta*. The two are divided by the threshold of consciousness, the *manodvara*, or the door of the mind.

Later on, this concept of consciousness is developed by *Aryasanga (Asanga)* and his Younger brother *Vasubandhu*, under the school of *Vijnanavada*, or the idealist view of Yogachara.

According to *Yogachara*, external objects independent of consciousness are not intelligible. Since we are conscious of ideas and things together, the two are not different. All the properties we know – length, size, taste etc., are subjective. The apparent phenomena around us are produced by mental operations within us. They appear and disappear like swiftly vanishing clouds. If we ask for the explanation of the actual variety of ideas, the *Yogachara* refers us to the impressions left by previous ideas. Our dream experiences are full of ideas which arise from previous mental impressions without any external objects. Even so, upon awaking, the experience is to be explained. The *Yogachara* traces the activity of consciousness to the beginning-less instinctive tendencies working in it.

The *Yogacharas* are supporters of *Vijnanavada*. They deny the real existence of everything, except *Vijnana* or consciousness. *'Sarvam Buddhimayam jagat'*. The whole world is ideal. Buddhism holds that all that happens is the result of thought and is made up of it. The psychophysical organism, which continues after the death of a man, is said to be created in the matrix by the rebirth of consciousness. Since the *Yogacharas* do not admit to the dependence of consciousness on external objects, and maintain that it is self-subsistent, their view is called *Niralambanavada*. The distinction between material and mental *dharmas* disappears, since all *dharmas* are mental.

The thinking being becomes conscious of its existence and identity of the subject, only by knowing objects. The whole system of facts is placed within the individual consciousness. The *alaya*, with its internal duality of subject and object, becomes by itself, a little world. It is confined to its own circle of modifications. The world of reality is deprived of its independence and reduced to a mere dance of ideas or thought relationships.

The *alaya*, which is a continually changing stream of consciousness, is contrasted with *Atman*, which is immutable, though the *Yogacharas* are not clear about the exact significance of the *Alaya*. It is sometimes the actual self, developing and ever growing. It receives impressions and develops the germs deposited in it by Karma, or experience, and is continually active. It is not merely the superficial self, but the great storehouse of consciousness, which the Yogins find out by meditation. Through meditation and other practices of self-examination, we realize that our waking or superficial consciousness is a fragment of a wider whole. Every individual has within him, this vast whole of consciousness, the great tank, the contents of which, even the conscious self is not fully aware of. Our personal consciousness knows but a small tradition of the sum total of our conscious states, the *alaya vijnana*.

There are indications that the *alaya vijnana* was sometimes used in the sense of the absolute self. It is said to be without any origin, existence, and extinction, *'Utpada sthiti bhanga Varjam'*. It is the permanent background of the endless variety of feelings and ideas, common to all minds. It alone exists; individual, intellectual products are mere phenomena, phases of the *alaya*. All things in the universe are in it. Particular phenomena are manifestations of the *Alaya* according to the number and nature of the conditions. We, in our ignorance, break up this consciousness into several elements.[1]

Mana, the means of knowledge, *meya*, the object of knowledge, and *phala*, the resulting knowledge, are distinctions within the whole of *Vijnana*. Objects arise from the successive modification of mind.[2]

The *alayavijnana* is the fundamental fact of reality, revealing itself in individual minds and things. The distinction between subject and object is a distinction made by knowledge itself within its own fields, and not a relationship between two independent entities as the *vaibhasikas* and the *Sautrantikas* assumed.[3]

The world in space and time appears to be real, because of our imperfect apprehension. Our intellect, though fundamentally free from the modes of subject and object, but due to the succession of unreal ideas or to the beginningless presuppositions, develops diverse distinctions between the percipient and the percept.[4]

According to *yogacharas*, the highest state that transcends all opposites, in which the positive and the negative are one and the same *(bhavabhava Samanata)*, is called *tathata* or pure being. It is also called as *alaya vijnana*, in its dynamic aspect, when it is combined with the principle of individuation or negativity.

Every individual has in him the highest principle bound up with a selfish individuality. Individuality clings to us so long as we are subject to *avidya*. The differences among men are due to the force of ignorance. Alaya or *Citta* is the

---

[1] 'What is of the nature of consciousness is indeed indivisible, but by those whose vision is confused it seems to be, as it were, differentiated into the perceived object, the perceiving subject and the perception itself' Again

"There exists in reality only one thing, and that is of the nature of the intelligent principle of consciousness and its oneness is not destroyed by the varied character of its manifestations".

Sarvbasiddhantasarasamgraha, III, 2-4, taken from S.Radha Krishnan India Philosophy, Vol.1, p.630.

The Lankavatara Sutra Says: "Cittam exists; not the objects; but perceptible by sight. Through objects visually cognized, cittam manifests itself in the body, in one's objects of enjoyment, residence etc. It is called the alaya of men". Quoted by Radha Krishnan, Indian Philosophy, Vol.1, P.630.

Sometimes there is confusion in using the term vijnana to indicate both the changing and the unchanging aspects of mental life. Skandha Vijnana – a phenomenal effect of karma, alaya Vijnana – ever action, continuous, spiritual energy dwelling in all. Ibid: P.632.

Our buddhi is twofold, cognitional and non-cognitional. The former leads to a correct apprehension of truth; the latter, which is dependent on a fundamental insensitiveness, has evolved out of the skandhas, ayatanas and the dhatus (national components of the body), and is the source of avidya and is not an authoritative criterion of truth. Ibid, P.636.

source of objects we perceive and has in it potencies, determined by our past conduct, which are bound to develop. All dharma, pain, pleasure, good and bad conduct, are the outer manifestations of the potential seeds stored in the *alaya*. Some of these seeds are of defilement and so make for *Samsara*. Others are free from defilement and so, tend to liberalism. It is the presence of the transcendental element that helps us to think of higher ideas.

The *Yogacharas* practice Yoga. *Yoga* helps us to acquire intuitive insight. Discursive understanding gives us dependent or empirical knowledge. The metaphysical truth requires a yogic discipline when the mind is clear of all prejudice or illusion; it reflects the truth. Nirvana is the purification of mind, its reiteration to its primitive simplicity or radiant transparency.

References

Chatterjee, A. K. (1975). *The Yogachara Idealism*. Delhi, India: Motilal Banarsidas.

Radhakrishnan, S. (1997). *Indian Philosophy, Vol.1*. Delhi, India: Oxford University Press.

Chapter 20

Mysticism: A Study of the Judaic Tradition

CHHAVI GUPTA
Dayalbagh Educational Institute (Deemed University), Agra, India

Abstract
There is a long-established Jewish tradition of biblical interpretation from a mystical perspective. Jewish commentators since the time of the rabbis, several centuries BCE, discussed the biblical stories and shared their mystical understanding of them. Centuries later, the medieval mystics of the movement known as the Kabbalah also gave complex, symbolic interpretations of biblical texts in order to convey their mystic teachings. They believed that there were several levels of meaning embedded in the Bible, from the literal or contextual to the secret or esoteric. At the deepest level, the entire Torah was seen as a spiritual allegory. The stories that pertain to the creation, and the history of the patriarchs and the ancient Israelites, were also understood as allegories of the soul's spiritual journey and evolution. Jewish mysticism is as old as Judaism. This paper looks into elements of the occult in Judaism which have been found in the Bible, the Talmud, and in the writings of many of their leading figures.

To appreciate the mystic meanings in the Hebrew Bible, it is necessary to look deeply into its language and symbolism. The first book, Genesis, begins with a dramatic account of the creation through the mystic Utterance or Command of God:

> *"In the beginning, God created the heaven and the earth...*
> *And God said, "Let there be light!" and there was light.*
> *And God saw the light, that it was good;*
> *And God divided the light from the darkness"*
>
> Genesis 1:1-4, FBM

From the creation, Genesis moves on to the mythic stories of Adam and Eve and the Garden of Eden, long understood by mystics as an allegorical portrayal of the primal separation of the soul from God and its imprisonment in the physical universe.

The story continues with the episode of Noah and the great flood. (Noah's Ark is the vessel which was built by Noah at God's command to save himself, his family, and the world's animals from a worldwide deluge. God, seeing the wickedness of man, regrets his Creation and resolves to send a great flood to destroy the earth. He sees that Noah is a man "righteous in his generation," and gives him detailed instructions for the Ark. When the animals are safe on board God sends the Flood, which rises until all the mountains are covered and all life that lived on dry land and breathed through its nostrils is destroyed. At the height of the flood the Ark rests on the mountains, the waters abate, and dry land reappears. Noah, his family, and the animals leave the Ark, and God vows to never again send a flood to destroy the Earth.)

When looking at this from a mystical perspective we see:

• Noah and the great flood as the end of one cosmic age and the birth of another.

• The Ark symbolizes the continuity of life through the cosmic cycles of creation, destruc¬tion and re-creation. In another light the Ark is seen as the precursor in offering salvation to mankind.

• Noah is the archetypal Savior of mankind who carries the potential for life from one age to another.

After the period of the flood, the Bible moves onto what can be called early recorded history - the era of the patriarchs and matriarchs. It re¬lates that God commanded Abraham to journey from Mesopotamia, the "land of his fathers", to the land of Canaan (a part of ancient Palestine), and tells of God's covenant (a solemn agreement that is binding on all parties) with him.

The covenant between God and Abraham was an agreement that Abraham would worship only the one Lord. In exchange, God promised that a great and mighty people would issue from Abraham, to whom He would bequeath "a land flow¬ing with milk and honey", if they continued to be faithful to Him.

From a mystical viewpoint, worship of the one God (monotheism) is the worship of the unity that is God. Abraham agreed to teach his descendants this inner worship. In return, God promised to take them to the land of Canaan - the 'promised land', "a land flowing with milk and honey", metaphors for the higher heavenly realms.

Abraham is considered the father of the Jewish religion. Jacob, his grandson, also called Israel, had twelve sons who moved to Egypt where they were at first treated as welcome visitors. Later however, with a change of rulers, Egypt eventu¬ally became unfriendly to them and subjected them to 200 years of forced labour and other hardships.

The Bible relates how Moses was sent by God as their liberator. The revelation experienced by Moses when God called upon him for this task - of the divine Voice issuing from a burning bush that is not consumed has been interpreted by Jewish mystics as a dramatic and graphic account of God reveal-ing Himself in the form of light and sound.

An angel of Yahweh (God) is described as appearing in the flaming bush and God is subsequently described as calling out from it to Moses. God tells Moses to first take off his sandals, due to the place being holy ground. He then tells him to return to Egypt and free the Jewish people.

Jewish interpreters throughout the ages have allegorically interpreted the period of slavery in Egypt and the subsequent exodus thus:

Egypt symbolizes the body, slavery in Egypt is a period of spiritual constriction, the exodus and the forty years of wandering in the desert that followed represent the soul's breaking away from the oppression of worldliness and the beginning of the spiritual journey, and so on.

This symbolic and often mystical interpretation of apparently historical events is characteristically Jewish.

During their wanderings in the desert, the Bible recounts that Moses brought his people to the foot of Mount Sinai where he ascended the mountain and com¬muned with God. God entered into a second covenant with the Israelites. The covenant is symbolized by the Ten Commandments, which Moses carried from the heights of the moun¬tain. Through Moses, God revealed himself to the children of Israel.

Like God's covenant with Abraham, Jewish mystics have taught that this revelation was the experience of God's Holy Name. Climbing the mountain is an ancient Middle Eastern symbol for ascent to the inner spiritual regions. The true Torah or 'revelation' experienced by Moses is thus his inner mystical experience of God, which he tried to convey to the people of Israel. The mystic revelation of God's Name or Word is a theme repeated throughout the Bible.

The Bible speaks of the intense relationship between God and the people of Israel. A pattern emerges in which the people lose faith in God, and God proves His love and protection through a miracle. For although they attested belief in God, whom they called Yahweh (Jehovah), meaning the 'One who is, was and will be', they would consistently lose faith and begin worshipping the deities of the peoples surrounding them. Even while Moses was at the top of Mount Sinai receiving the revelation of the Ten Commandments, the Israelites waiting at the foot of the mountain fashioned a golden calf to worship.

The Ten Commandments, in Hebrew called the 'tablets of the covenant', were placed in a special 'ark of the covenant' which traveled with the Israelites in a mobile sanctuary called the 'tent of the meeting'. According to the Bible story, a cloud of God's glory would hover over the tent, guiding the Israelites on their journeys. The tent and the ark within it were a symbol of God's presence in their midst wherever they journeyed.

Prophecy was a phenomenon known and documented in most ancient Middle Eastern societies. In addition to Abraham and Moses, other biblical prophets include Elijah and Elisha, followed later by Jeremiah and Ezekiel.

References to Elijah in Jewish folklore are many.

One such story is that of Rabbi Joshua ben Levi whose only wish was that he be able to join Elijah in his wanderings. Elijah granted his wish only if he refrained from asking any questions about any of the prophet's actions. He agreed and they began their journey.

- The first place they came to was the house of an elderly couple who were so poor they had only one old cow. The old couple gave of their hospitality as best they could. The next morning, as the travelers left, Elijah prayed that the old cow would die and it did.

- The second place they came to was the home of a wealthy man. He had no patience for his visitors and chased them away with the admonition that they should get jobs and not beg from honest people. As they were leaving, they passed the man's wall and saw that it was crumbling. Elijah prayed that the wall be repaired and it was so.

- Next, they came to a wealthy synagogue. They were allowed to spend the night with only the smallest of provisions. When they left, Elijah prayed that every member of the synagogue might become a leader.

• Finally, they came to a very poor synagogue. Here they were treated with great courtesy and hospitality. When they left, Elijah prayed that God might give them a single wise leader.

At this Rabbi Joshua could no longer hold back. He demanded of Elijah an explanation of his actions.

• At the house of the old couple, Elijah knew that the Angel of Death was coming for the old woman. So he prayed that God might have the angel take the cow instead.

• At the house of the wealthy man, there was a great treasure hidden in the crumbling wall. Elijah prayed that the wall be restored thus keeping the treasure away from the miser.

• The story ends with a moral: A synagogue with many leaders will be ruined by many arguments. A town with a single wise leader will be guided to success and prosperity. "Know then, that if thou seest an evil-doer prosper, it is not always unto his advantage, and if a righteous man suffers need and distress, think not God is unjust.

The biblical story of Elijah's departure is unique. Elijah, in company with Elisha, his disciple and chosen successor, approaches the Jordan. He rolls up his mantle and strikes the water. The water immediately divides and Elijah and Elisha cross on dry land. Suddenly, a chariot of fire and horses of fire appear and Elijah is lifted up to heaven in a whirlwind. This description of his ascent became an important inspiration for later Jewish mystic seekers, who took the account metaphorically, as the ascent of the soul into the inner heavens.

Like Elijah's ascent, Ezekiel's vision of the chariot (as described below) was to serve as a model for Jewish mystics for centuries.

Judaism regards Ezekiel as the third of the Major Prophets. His teachings are dramatic and sensational, particularly the allegory of the fantastic chariot made of six beings - part human, part animal, part angel - vibrating with lights, colours and sounds, in which he ascended to the inner celestial regions, finally reaching the throne of God.

Much of the imagery and style of the biblical prophets reflects the deeper meaning of their words which would only be understood by the true mystic seekers.

It is known that a number of the rabbis of the Talmud were also mystics who practiced meditation. The literature they have left uses images and sym¬bols derived from the vision of the prophet Elisha, who saw his Master, Elijah, rising to the heavens in a chariot of fire, and the experiences of the prophet Ezekiel, who had visions of a heavenly throne and chariot.

These mystics referred to their inner journey as the journey of the chariot, and were thus known as the merkabah (chariot) mystics.

The mystical side of Judaism during the Talmudic period and continuing into the Middle Ages is represented for the most part in the Hekhalot literature. Hekhalot literally means 'palaces' or 'halls'. These works describe the medita¬tion practices of Jewish mystics who were attempting to travel the inner journey through the spiritual regions or palaces on the merkabah (chariot) of light and sound.

Merkabah Mysticism

The expression of Jewish mysticism, referred to as "Merkabah mysticism," focused upon contemplation of Ezekiel's vision of God's chariot (merkabah). This mystical discipline was practiced by the sage Johanan ben Zakkai at least as early as the first century C.E

According to the verses in Ezekiel, the analogy of the Merkabah image consists of a chariot made of many angels being driven by the "Likeness of a Man." Four angels form the basic structure of the chariot. These angels are called the "Chayot" (living creatures). The bodies of the "Chayot" are like that of a human being, but each of them has four faces. The faces are that of a man, a lion, an ox and an eagle. The angel with the face of the man is always on the east side and looks up at the "Likeness of a Man" that drives the chariot. The "Likeness of a Man" sits on a throne made of sapphire.

Jewish biblical commentaries emphasize that the imagery of the Merkabah is not meant to be taken literally; rather the chariot and its accompanying angels are analogies for the various ways that God reveals Himself in this world.

In this chariot they are supposed to ascend to the heavens, where in the dazzling light surrounding them they behold the innermost secrets of all persons and things, otherwise impenetrable and invisible. Recently uncovered Jewish mystical texts also evidence a deep affinity with the rabbinic merkabah homilies which consisted of detailed descriptions of multiple layered heavens (usually seven in number), often guarded over by angels, and encircled by flames and lightning. The highest heaven contains seven palaces (hekhalot), and in the innermost palace resides a supreme divine image (God's Glory or an angelic image) seated on a throne, surrounded by awesome hosts who sing God's praise.

The main interests of all Hekhalot writings are accounts of mystical ascents into heaven, divine visions, and the summoning and control of angels, usually for the purpose of gaining insight into Torah.

Jewish Mysticism (Kabbalah)

One of the most influential of all the Jewish mystical movements is called Kabbalah which attained great influence in thirteenth-century Spain. Kabbalah is a form of rabbinic teaching giving 'hidden' or 'secret' meaning to Hebrew Scriptures. Kabbalah teaches that every Hebrew letter, word, number, even the accent on words of the Hebrew Bible contains a hidden meaning and the methods of interpretation for ascertaining these meanings. Kabbalah literally means 'received' or 'transmitted', implying in¬wardly received knowledge. Most of the works grouped in the Kabbalah impart knowledge concerning the nature of God and the structure of the various realms and levels of the crea¬tion. They do not generally urge a devotional approach in pursuing direct expe¬rience of the Divine. In this sense, Kabbalism is similar to what the Indians call jnana yoga (the yoga of knowledge), while the Sufi or Hasidic tradition is more like bhakti yoga (the yoga of devotion).

The Kabbalah "proceeds through an intricate web of esoteric symbols" and the outstand¬ing book on Jewish esotericism is Sefer Yetzirah ("Book of Creation,"), which came from the Babylonian Jewish community. It is an early meditative and astrological manual which describes the creation as a series of emanations from the one divine Name, Word or Utterance. It outlines a system of meditation through the relationships of numbers, the letters of the Hebrew alpha¬bet and divine names. These methods were used over the centuries by mystics attempting to manipulate supernatural forces.

Jewish mystical exegesis is a method of interpreting the Bible based on the assumption that the Torah itself contains secret knowledge regarding creation and the essence of God. The only way to find these secrets was to know how to decode the text and reveal them.

Focusing on the holiness of the text, mystics consider every nuance of the text to be a clue in discovering divine secrets, from the entire text to the accents on each letter. Once one can find such knowledge, one can use the text in mystical rituals to affect both the upper worlds (heavens) and the lower world (our world). The name of God is considered one of the greatest sources of power and is assumed to be hidden in various forms throughout the text. Much work has been done to try to rearrange the breaks between words to seek out different names for God as well as other aspects of hidden knowledge.

The text was originally considered to be a revelation from God. Assigning numeric values to Jewish letters (giving every word a value) allows one to look for patterns in the text based on those numerical values. Kabbalah appeared in the medieval period and continued into the modern. It is the aspect of Jewish mysticism which is most renowned in modem times, and which is almost seen as a religious movement.

Jewish Mysticism and the Sufis

From the time of Prophet Muhammad in the seventh century, the flourishing Jewish community became integrally associated with Islamic civilization and mysticism. There is a long history of mutual influence between Jewish and Muslim Sufi mystics.

From the eleventh to thirteenth centuries, Jewish mystics quote freely from Sufi mystical writings, which they copied into Hebrew characters. Some Jewish mystics even pursued the spiritual path under the guidance of Sufi Masters, many reading the works of Rumi and Sa'di.

Jewish mystics in the Sufi tradition included Bahya ibn Paquda a Jewish philosopher and rabbi of eleventh ¬century Spain. His book Chovot ha-Levavot, (Duties of the Hearts) deals with the life of the true 'servant', the devotee yearning for the mystical life. Bahya felt that many Jews paid attention only to the outward observance of Jewish law i.e. "the duties to be performed by the parts of the body", without regard to the inner ideas and sentiments that should be embodied in this way of life, i.e. "the duties of the heart".

In the latter part of the thirteenth century, at the time when Theosophic Kabbalah [the primary strand of Kabbalah, aimed at understanding and affecting the divine world] was flourishing, there emerged an alternative Kabbalistic tradition with a different focus. The main exponent of this tradition was Abraham ben Samuel Abulafia who was a revolutionary mystic. He became the founder of the school of "Prophetic Kabbalah"

At the age of thirty-one, at Barcelona, he became subject to visions whereupon he began to study a particular kind of Kabbalah, and received a revelation with messianic overtones. He immersed himself in the study of the Sefer Yetzirah ("Book of Creation") which explains the creation of the world and man based on letter combinations. Letters of the alphabet, numerals, and vowel-points, all became symbols of existence to him, and their combinations and permutations, supplementing and explaining one another, gave him an illumining power. With such auxiliaries, and with the observance of certain rites and ascetic practices, men, he says, may attain the highest aim of existence and become prophets; not in order to work miracles and signs, but to reach the highest degree of perception and be able to penetrate intuitively into the inscrutable nature of the Deity, the riddles of creation, the problems of human life, the purpose of the precepts and the deeper meaning of the Torah.

Experiential Mysticism

Whereas the Theosophic Kabbalist focused their attention on the underlying powers that made up the divine realm, Abulafia turned his attention to cultivating a mystical system that could assist one in achieving a state of unio mystica [i.e. union with God], which he identified as prophecy. He thus called his system "prophetic Kabbalah", though modern scholars have referred to it as ecstatic Kabbalah in so far as it is aimed at producing a state of mystical ecstasy wherein the boundaries separating the self from God are overcome. He became the founder of the school of "Prophetic Kabbalah"

How to Become a Prophet Experiential Mysticism

For Abulafia, prophecy can be attained only when one is in a state of conjunction, a state that can come about only when the soul is freed from the bonds of the body. Thus we have, "The connection of human existence with the divine existence during intellection- until he and He become one entity." The union between human and divine intellects is so complete that in this state the individual can utter with respect to God, "He is I and I am He."

Abulafia's mystical system introduced special techniques in order to bring about this state of conjunction or union (devekut).

The main techniques consisted of:

- letter combination (in three stages: written, oral, and mental) and
- recitation of the divine names, which involved special breathing exercises and bodily postures as well..

Abulafia referred to his "science of letter combination", also identified as the "path of names" as the true account of the chariot [the prototypical Jewish mystical experience derived from Ezekiel's vision of the merkabah.]

Abulafia's Meditation Techniques

In his numerous works Abulafia focuses on complex devices for uniting with the Agent Intellect, or God, through the recitation of divine names, together with breathing techniques and cathartic practices. Abulafia strove for spiritual experience, which he viewed as a prophetic state.

Abulafia suggests a method that is based on a stimulus that continuously changes. His intention is not to relax the consciousness by meditation, but to purify it via a high level of concentration needed for doing many actions at the same time. For this, he uses Hebrew letters.

Abulafia's method includes a number of steps:

- The first step, preparation: the initiate purifies himself through fasting, the wearing of phylacteries (small leather boxes with scriptures written on them, as reminders of their religious duties) and donning pure white garments.
- The second step: the mystic writes out specific letter groups and their permutations.
- The third step, physiological maneuvers: the mystic chants the letters in conjunction with specific respiratory patterns, as well as head positioning.
- The fourth step, mental imagery of letters and human forms: the mystic imagines a human form and himself without a body. Then the mystic 'draws' the letters mentally, i.e. he mentally imagines the patterns of letters. He then rotates the letters and turns them. "And they [the letters], with their forms, are called the Clear Mirror, for all the forms having brightness and strong radiance are included in them. And one who gazes at them in their forms will discover their secrets and speak of them, and they will speak to him. And they are like an image in which a man sees all his forms standing in front of him, and then he will be able to see all the general and specific things."
- During the final step of mental imagery, the mystic passes a succession of four experiences.
    - o The first is an experience of body-photism or illumination, in which light not only surrounds the body but also diffuses into it, giving an impression that the body and its organs have become light.
    - o As the ecstatic Kabbalist continues to practice combining letters and performing physiological maneuvers, he gets the second experience: weakening of the body, in an 'absorptive' manner.
    - o Subsequently, the mystic may feel an enhancement of his thoughts and imaginative capacity. This is the third experience.
    - o The fourth experience is characterized mainly by fear and trembling. Abulafia writes: 'all your body will begin to tremble and your limbs begin to shake, and you will fear a tremendous fear ... and the body will tremble, like the rider who races the horse, who is glad and joyful, while the horse trembles beneath'.
    - o For Abulafia the fear is followed by an experience of pleasure and delight. This feeling is a result of sensing another 'spirit' within his body, as he describes: 'And you shall feel another spirit awakening within yourself and strengthening you and passing over your entire body and giving you pleasure'.
    - o Only after passing these successive experiences does the mystic reach his goal: the vision of a human form, which is closely linked to his own physical appearance and generally experienced as standing in front of

the mystic. The experience is increased when the mystic experiences his autoscopic form (or 'double') speaking- the double begins to talk to the mystic, teaching him the unknown and revealing the future.

Abulafia's ecstatic Kabbalah had an important influence on the history of Jewish mysticism. Jewish mystics in the Sufi tradition emphasized devotion, spiritual inwardness and personal experience of God - their goal being mystical union with God.

I would like to end this paper with the profound observance made by Rabbi Akiba - one of the most well known mystics of the Talmud.

Akiba, noticing a stone at a well that had been hollowed out by drippings from the buckets, said: "If these drippings can, by continuous action, penetrate this solid stone, how much more can the persistent word of God penetrate the pliant, fleshly human heart, if that word but be presented with patient insistency"

References

Bushrui, S. and Massoudi, M. (2010). *The Spiritual Heritage of the Human Race –An Introduction to World Religions.* Oneworld Publications

Hopfe, L. M., and Woodward, M. R. (2007). *Religions of the World 10th Edition*, Prentice Hill: Pearson

Mathews, W. and Wadsworth, T. (2007). *World Religions 5th edition.* Belmont CA, USA: Cengage Learning

Radhasoami Satsang Beas (2003) *A Treasury of Mystic Terms Part 1 Volume 1*, New Delhi: Science of the Soul Research Centre.

Chapter 21

Glimpses of Bhakti and Sufi Consciousness in Radhasoami Faith

PREM KUMARI SRIVASTAVA
Maharaja Agrasen College, University of Delhi, India

Abstract

In this paper, an attempt is being made to problematise the Bhakti and Sufi Consciousness in the Saintly tradition of India with a special focus on Radhasoami Faith. These two movements in the historiography of Indian sociological, cultural and philosophic thought have played a significant role in ushering in a series of changes and shifts of thought in the way God, the almighty was viewed and perceived. On the contemporary register, this significance assumes a much colossal dimension. In an age of doubt, questioning, scientific enquiry and skeptical temper towards religion on one hand, on the other, seeking solace in 'Art of Living' courses and yoga sessions for the 'desired ultimate peace'; why is it that a quietly spiritual, peace-giving solution, a panacea of sorts, is being ushered in by the modern Sant Mat - Religion of Saints? In this paper, I choose to look at the Sufi and Bhakti temper in Radhasoami Faith as one that unifies it with tradition, as also attributes it a uniquely modern scientific temper. The paper emphasizes that the Sufi and Bhakti Consciousness is seminal to Radhasoami Faith and needs to be studied in detail. Towards this end, this research paper will emphasise that Radhasoami Faith is a blending at the highest level of both Bhakti and Sufi consciousness. In fact it is almost a culmination of both. All the positive and nurturing strains of Bhakti and Sufi Consciousness reach its pinnacle and fructify in Radhasoami Faith.

1. Introduction

It is true that the Bhakti and Sufi traditions were widespread in the Indian subcontinent and employed a diverse range of expressions, both literary and linguistic. They also employed the common man's language. Most of them were primarily oral compositions. They also intervened in social and religious reformation and broke away from the rigid institutionalized religious traditions by critiquing the priestly class, its exploitative nature and hypocrisy; emphasizing the direct relationship between the worshipper and God, focusing on the fundamental equality of all human beings irrespective of caste, class, race, gender and religion. Their tradition epitomizes the concept of *fakiri*: complete obliviousness to all social and religious norms. Most scholars agree that the Sufi thought could find a snug place in the Indian Consciousness because the Bhakti sentiment was already there and the two were quite similar in ethos and exposition. (Special emphasis on Adi Sant Kabir, Paltu Sahab, Dadu Dayal, Tulsi Sahab and Maulana Rumi , Ghalib, Rabia and others). Both share important common characteristics such as: the concept of ecstasy and intense love through analogies of Laila Majnu, euphoric singing and dancing as well as total annihilation of the self (*fana*) and merger with the almighty or *Atman*. When Sufism came to India with its features of *fana* and *dhikr* and *sama* (singing and dancing), the doctrines of *tawakhul ala Allah* (total dependence on God's mercy), its emphasis on the role of *murshid* (guide) and its *mashuq-ashiq* (beloved-lover) framework, the common Indian did not find them exotic at all, but similar, if not almost identical, with his own. The question of either accepting them or rejecting them, therefore, was irrelevant to him. The Sufi thought permeated naturally into the Indian national psyche. This was the period when most of the Indian vernaculars were in the formative stages of their growth. Sufi thoughts were so easily absorbed in their literary traditions that now it is indeed difficult to differentiate them from the indigenous sources. Critics like Sisir Kumar Das locate the common metaphor of 'mad lover' in their poetry across India.[1]

2. Historiography of the Two

Bhakti Kala in the North Indian Sant Mat tradition was also called Adikala. The saints compiled the knowledge of Vedanta with emotions and sentiments and took Brahma to the masses. Parshuram Chaturvedi has said that the Saints took the principle of Advaita from the Hindu Darshan, the Karmavada, Janmantarvada and devotional worship from Vaishnavas, Shunyavad, non-violence and the Middle Path from Buddhism, monotheism and brotherhood of man from Islam and the concept of Love for the Lord from Sufis. Most of the Saints were neither very educated nor had they read the epics but they had been born with the knowledge of philosophers. They symbolized the common man. They established a Loka Dharma and spoke mainly of their own religious experiences instead of incomprehensible principles. The names of the Nirguna Bhakti Saints like Adi Sant Kabir, Tukaram, Namdev, Gyaneshvar, Dadu Dayal and Saguna Bhakti Saints such as Surdas, Tulsidas and Mirabai come to our mind of North India.

As far as Sufism is concerned, according to S.K Das: "It is generally believed that the great Sufi mystic Mansur al-Hallaj (b. 858), who was also a great traveller, visited Sindh. From the eleventh century onwards, Sufi saints started exerting their influence on the masses in India particularly in Sindh and Punjab. Within the next two centuries Sufis concentrated in different parts of Northern India. Sheikh Ismail of Bukhara (who settled in Lahore), Ali Hujwari, Sheikh Bhauddin Zakaria Multani, Khwaja Moinuddin Chisti of Ajmer, Khwaja Qutabouddin Bhaktiar Kaki of Delhi, Nizamuddin Auliya – to name a few – all of them flourished between the thirteenth and fourteenth century which coincided with the formative stages of the Bhakti movement in north India and also in certain parts of Sindh. Sufism, though rooted in the Quran, derived much of its inspiration from various sources, some of which were anti-Quranic, including the folk traditions of Arab and Persia. Sufism was also distinguished by features such as the conception of God as love, its approach to God through love, its dependence on God's mercy, and its idea of tawhid and dhikr. Rumi declared, 'Love (mohabhat) and ardent love (ishq) also, are attributes of God.' Das quotes Nicholson who points out that there is Quranic authority for mohabhat

---

[1] Sisir Kumar Das, 'The Mad Lover' *Indian Literature*, vol.XLVII, no.215, May-June 2003, Sahitya Akademi, New Delhi, pp.149-78.

but none for ishq, the key word in Sufi symbolism. Like Bhakti, Sufism was a movement of common people against the rigid and authoritarian centers of power. Sufi mystic poets became popular since they expressed the feelings of ordinary exploited people. They spoke in the language that was understood by the common people.

It was in such a fertile milieu that the Radhasoami Faith was born in 1861. Much has happened since then, but before I discuss that, I would like to quote from the concept note of this international seminar at Dayalbagh Educational Institute (Deemed University) Dayalbagh, Agra (November12-14, 2010) to emphasise that the Sufi and Bhakti consciousness is seminal to Radhasoami Faith and needs to be studied in detail.

The Religion of Saints comprises of the teachings of Saints and Fakirs viz. Kabir Sahab, Tuisi Sahab and Maulana Rumi, culminating in the Radhasoami Faith founded by Param Guru Soami ji Maharaj on the Basant Panchami Day, the 15th of February, 1861 A.D. They taught people to have unflinching faith in the True Supreme Being, the Reservoir of Spirituality, and to worship Him internally by the practice of Sahaj Yoga or Surat Shabda Yoga i.e. uniting the spirit with the spiritual sound current that emanated from the Supreme Being manifesting as Radhasoami, Satt, Om, Lahut etc. at different levels. This practice is to be learnt from the perfect Satguru of the time by developing love and affection for Him.

3. Some Common Characteristics:

It would be interesting to analyse the meeting of the two traditions in Radhasoami Faith. What would also be of interest would be to see where and when this faith moves beyond.

3.1. Eternal Name, Sound and Light

Kabir Sahib, the eternal messenger of the Satya Purush, wanted to pull mankind out of the net of Kala and clearly stated that the Name and Sound is constantly resounding within each Jiva. By concentration, the Surat mingles with this Primordial Sound, becomes one, without any outward actions or rituals. Adi Sant Kabir writes in *Kabir Sakhi Sangrah (KSS)*:

When you forget both your body and mind
And with full love attach yourself to your Master
You will hear the sweet music of the Word
And drink the elixir of immortality.

- p.35: 8 (Lav laagee kal naa parrai)[2]

Adi Sant Kabir also states in the following lines that he has clearly explained the Bhakti Mat.

---

[2] THM 103, unit 3, lesson 4.

Bhakti ka marag jheena re. (Subtle is the path of love!)[3]

In this extract Adi Sant Kabir calls the path of Bhakti (the true path of devotion) as very subtle. It may be compared to a loosely knit garment. [4]

The devotional expositions of saints like **Sant Namadeva (1270- 1350 AD)** a Vitthal Bhakta[5] , **Raidas Sahab (1414 -1540 AD)**[6] **Dadu Dayal Sahab's** (born in 1544 in the Jaipur region of Rajasthan) teachings collectively called Dadu Panth and **Tukaram Sahab's (born 1598 AD)**[7] philosophy helped to strengthen the concept of eternal light and sound of Sant Mat. The following poem of **Paltu Sahab** explains this.

In the sky within is an inverted well, wherein burns a lamp.
.... He who has found a perfect Master—he alone can see it;
To the one without a Master, this flame remains invisible.
From the flame of the lamp emanates a melody,
In trance by an enlightened spirit can it be heard and by none else.
Whoever, O Paltu, hears its tunes, is indeed the most fortunate.

(Part I, Kundli 169 'Ulta kuaan gagan mein.')

The above sentiment is well echoed by Sant Tulsi Sahab in his poem 'Lakhi akaas oundha kuan':

I beheld in the firmament an inverted well,
and was filled with the resplendence of the light within....

(Shabdavali Pt.I, Kundli 16, p.38.)

Further Dadu Dayal Sahab writes,

All are bound by the Word; The Word abides in all.

---

[3] The full poem is given below
Bhakti ka marag jheena re.
Nahi achah nahi chahana, charanan laulina re
Sadhan ke satsang mein, rahe nisdin bheena re
Shabda mein surt aise basey, jaise jal meena re
Maan mani ko yun tajey.jaise teli peena re
Daya chhima santosh gahi, rahe ati adheena re
Parmarath mey deit scir, kachhu bilamba na kina re
Kahein Kabeer mat Bhakti ka, pargat kah dina re

- Kabir: LV p57

[4] In this extract Kabir defines the path of Bhakti and states that the true path of devotion is very subtle.

All arise from the Word, and in the Word do all merge back, sayeth Dadu.

(Sabdein bandhyaa sab rahein, Part 1, Shabda 2)

Read the following selection from the poetry written by the founder of Radhasoami Faith, Shiv Dayal Singh ji known as Param Purush Puran Dhani, Huzur Soamiji Maharaj collected in Sarbachan to understand the importance of eternal light and sound:

Voh sinchen nij paud, hoye bhakt voh per sam,
Phal lagen atise saras, bhoge Satguru mehar se. 33
Karaj kina pur, Sant dhur hirday dhari,
Sur hua man char, nur tur ghat men pragat. 34 (Sortha)

[The Saints themselves water these plants of devotion and after some time those sprouts turn into fully grown-up trees. And then the trees blossom forth and produce very sweet and tasteful fruits and the devotee enjoys those fruits with the Grace of the Satguru.] 33

[Thus the devotee by keeping in his heart the dust of the Feet of the Satguru, i.e. by love and reverence for the Satguru, gains his object. His headstrong mind, which could not be subdued in any way and always pulled the spirit towards the world, now gets crushed and Divine Light and Spiritual Sound manifest themselves within the true devotee.] 34

---

[4] (contd) THM 103, unit 3, lesson 4 The human body is the garment of the soul that performs Bhakti. However the loose garment of the human body gets entangled in Maya and becomes impure. The path is said to be difficult because only when the bodily desires and mind are suppressed and controlled is one able to move forward on this path. A Bhakta should have neither desire for anything nor desire to be without desire. He should try to remain in the company of those who meditate and perform spiritual practices and he should remain completely absorbed doing so becoming saturated in the ambrosia of love. His soul should be deeply embedded in the internal shabda or Word just as the fish moves opposing the motion of water. He should give up honor and wealth just like the teli or oil extractor who takes out the oil and throws aside the husk. He should adopt the virtues of sympathy, forgiveness and satisfaction and surrender himself totally to the Lord. He should not delay in doing actions in service of the Lord.

[5] Sant Namdeva wrote much of his poetry in Hindi and Marathi. He was also the propagator saint of the Baarkari Sampradaya, spreading and propagating his faith from Punjab to the whole of North India. He made a creditable effort to bring together the Saguna and Nirguna Sampradayas and also to enjoin the Hindu and Muslim faiths. Sant Namadeva's collection of Hindi poetry is present in the Granth Sahib. As a young man he was a Saguna Bhakta, but later he became a Nirguna upasaka because of the influence of the Nirguna Panth. His Hindi poetry mainly emphasizes Nirguna thoughts and was presumably written in his later years. He was called Kutumba Kavi because he established Kirtan Sanstha and his Kirtans had a great impact on people and large families began to devote time to Kirtan. He gave the message of true devotion to God. This made him a very popular poet Saint.

[6] He is said to be one of the twelve disciples of Ramananda. His poems gave reference to his Guru being Ramananda. He writes:

'.... Having obtained Ramananda as my Guru,
My faith in God was established...'

[7] It is said that the great Sivaji is said to have come to Tukaram Sahab for blessings. His legacy to the people is his 'Abhangas', which are sung even today. His Gatha is full of entreaties to the Lord to remove the obstacles in his spiritual path.

In Sikhism, the founder Guru Nanak Dev Ji (1469-1539) established the 'Rebabi' tradition. Bhai Mardana, the life long companion of the Guru belonged to a clan of BARDS known in those days as MIRASIS[8]. They would orally recite long poems about the ancestral heritage of love and Bhakti. In the poetry of Bulleh Shah of Punjab, also called the Rumi of Punjab (1680-1759), one witnesses the coming together of the Sufi and Bhakti traditions. He writes:

Masjid Dha Day, Mandir Dha Day
Dha Day Jo Kujh Disda
Par Kissay Da Dil Na Dhawee(n)
Rub Dilaa(n) Wich Wasda

(Tear down the Mosque, tear down the temple
Tear down every thing in sight
But don't (tear down) break anyone's heart
Because God lives there)

(Shabdavali Part.I p.47)

3.2 Imagery of Mad Devotee Full of Ecstasy and Frenzy

According to S.K. Das[9], "The dominating note of Indian religious poetry in the medieval period is that of an ecstasy, a longing of the devotee for union with God and to merge his identity in the Godhead. In no other period of Indian history one finds so many saints and poets in different parts of the country, speaking different languages, practising divergent rituals, belonging to different religious orders, and yet behaving in an almost identical manner in their approach to God." Simultaneously the Sufis also expressed an intense, longing for merger with the Divine. The 'mad lovers' of Sufi poetry belonged to the folk romances that were extremely popular, like Heer Ranja, Sassi Punnu, Laila Majnun etc. In one of the poems of Radhasoami Faith a similar sentiment is expressed:

Hei Guru main tere deedar ka ashiq jo hua...
Laila Ke ishq main Majnun sa Pareshan hua

Similarly, Rumi speaks of the emotional state called ***Haal*** of a Sufi in his religious quest and finds a new symbolism in the ardent love of Majnun for Laila. In the poetry of Radhasoami Faith, we find an echo of this:

Arey man rang ja satguru preet/Hoyey mat aur kisika meet

---

[8] A 'Mirasi' was supposed to be the custodian of 'MIRAS' i.e. The Heritage.

[9] Sisir Kumar Das, 'The Mad Lover' *Indian Literature*, vol.XLVII, no.215, May-June 2003, Sahitya Akademi, New Delhi, pp.149-78.

The "Mad devotee" of both Sufi and Bhakti poetry is completely oblivious to all social and religious norms or rituals in the overwhelming desire to unite with God.

For example in the Kafi7 [10] by Bulleh Shah, the poet wants to free himself of all categories of caste and creed. In his desire to merge himself with the Divine, he transcends all distinctions of religion, caste, class and region.

Says Bulla, I know not who I am.
...Neither I know the secret of religion
Nor am I born of Adam and Eve.
I have given myself no name.
...I belong neither to those who squat,
Nor to those who are given to wandering.

(Translated from the original Punjabi by K.S. Duggal)

The poet's rejection of social and religious distinctions is powerfully expressed in the following verse:

O' Bulleh Shah let's go there
Where everyone is blind
Where no one recognizes our caste (or race, or family name)[11]

The epithet 'mad' is not necessarily a pejorative one in a Hindu religious context. Tagore wrote in an essay 'Pagal' (The Madcap), "the word pagal (mad) is not a term of contempt for us. We admire mad Nimai (i.e. Chaitanyadev) because of his madness. ... and the Sindhi poet Sachal (b. 1739) was also surnamed Sarmast (the intoxicated one) because of his ardent love for God.. Even Kabir, the most restrained of all the poets and saints of the Bhakti period, and a worshipper of the nirguna God, could not escape the frenzy of divine love." He sings in this verse, which is also included in the Granth Sahib:

I am not skilled in book knowledge
Nor do I understand controversy
I have grown mad reciting and hearing God's praises.
O father, I am mad, the whole world is sane

---

[10] Vai as it was called in Sindhi, was a poetic form traditionally used for spiritual themes. It was a musical composition with a distinct rhyme scheme and a refrain at the end of each stanza. Extremely popular among both Punjabi and Sindhi Sufi poets, the Kafi was meant to be sung. Its musicality was a characteristic feature.

[11] *Chal Way Bullehya Chal O'thay Chaliyay*
Jithay Saaray Annay
Na Koi Saadee Zaat PichHanay
Tay Na Koi Saanu Mannay

I am mad
I have not grown mad of mine own will
God hath made me mad...." [12]

The tall saint of the saintly tradition of India, Tulsi Sahab also emphasizes that

Without the guidance of a Master
The way cannot ever be found...

In the poetry of the Radhasoami Faith, in *Sant Bani Sangrah*, there is the symbolism of drinking the cup of Amiras (elixir) to indicate the intoxication emanating from the intense passion of the devotee for the guru. For example:

Pile Pyala ho Matwala Pyala Naam Amiras Ka re
(Drink the cup of Amiras (elixir) and get intoxicated) [13]

True love for the lord comes out like this:

P***us mahina Jara bhari, Karam bharam jyon phus jala ri.*** 1
Jai jal dher hua jab bhari, Prem pavan se turat ura ri. 2

[*It is now the month of Pus and it is extremely cold. Just as people burn straw etc. in winter (to warm themselves), Karmas i.e. all kinds of actions and also bharmas i.e. misconceptions (in the mind) have been burnt. And when ashes rose in heaps, the wind of love blew away these ashes on all sides i.e. true love of the devotee removed all trace of actions and misconceptions.*] [14]

3.3 The Imagery of the Boatman and the Sea

Baul Gaan is a unique expression of Bhakti from Bengal. According to the Bauls [15], a mendicant folk-sect from Bengal, the human soul yearns for an intense mystic love, personified in Baul *gaan* as *maner manush*, 'the man of my heart'. Baul songs express the longing of the human soul to unite with the *maner manush*. The Baul believe that "God" is hidden in the heart of each individual and one has to seek Him out oneself[16]. Read the following:

---

[12] Quoted in Sisir Kumar Das's article.

[13] wherever not indicated, the translations are by the author.

[14] Selections from *Prem Sandesh* [P-52-60].

[15] In Bangla their songs are called baul gaan. Bauls do not believe in any formal religion and do not observe any rituals. They are iconoclasts and humanists who believe in the equality of all human beings whatever caste or creed they may belong to. Their beliefs are a mixture of several traditions, including Hinduism, Sufism, Yoga and Tantra. According to one theory, the Bauls could be the descendants of an Iranian Sufi sect called baal. Another view is that the word 'Baul' is derived from the Sanskrit words vatui and vyakul. The former means "mad" and the latter restless or impatient.Bauls come mainly from the poor and oppressed sections of society. But after being initiated by a guru they step outside the confines of religion and society. Freed from all worldly restrictions they ardently seek the light of love.

I am the boat, you are the sea and also the boatman.
Though you never make the shore, though you let me sink, why should
I be foolish and afraid?
Is the reaching the shore a greater prize than losing myself with you?
If you are only the haven, as they say, then what is the sea?
Let it surge and toss me on its waves, I shall be content.
I live in you, whatever and however you appear.
Save me or kill me as you wish, only never leave me in others' hands.

- Anonymous (Translated from the original Bangla by Rabindranath Tagore)

The poetry of Radhasoami Faith has similar reverberations in some of the following verses from *Ratnanjali* (1st ed 1982, 4th ed 2000):

Guru Dayal Ab Sudhi Lev Meri/Majdhara mein pari ha naiya/Dooban mein nahin deri
(O Merciful Master, think about me now/ the boat is trapped in a whirpool and in no time will be submerged/drowned)

and

Naiya meri bhoorat thi jal mahi
(My boat was getting drowned in the turbulent waters)

and

Aaye bhavjal Naav lagai
(HE came to safely reach my boat to the shore)

and

Bhavjal paar langhay/Tum charnan main baas ho
(HE made me cross the water (ocean) when I sought refuge in HIS feet)

---

[16] Tagore was fascinated by their songs and published them and translated some of them into English. Some believe that in his youth, Tagore knew Lalon Fakir (1774-1891), the renowned Baul. Baul songs have become popular in recent times. Sufi and Bhakti concerts frequently include performances by Bauls. Although this is debatable, among the Bauls it was probably Lalon Fakir's poetry and philosophy that attracted Tagore the most.
Baul singers such as Paban Das, Anando Gopal Das and Purna Das are popular all over the world.

and

Nisdin karo sambhaal/Jab lag beerha paar ho
(When YOU will take care of me everyday only then will my raft be able to cross the waters and reach the shore)

The additional images in Radhasoami Faith are of ***Color*** and ***fana*** that runs through its many compositions. For example

Mere pyare rangeele satguru/Meri surat chuneriya rang do
(My multi-faceted satguru, merge me in your color)

and

Rangeele rang dev chunar hamari,/Aisa rang rango kirpa kar/ Jag mein ho jaye nyaari
(Oh Lord! Color me such with your grace that I become unique and distinctive)

3.4 Image of Washerman

Another important image is that of God as a washerman who will wash away all the devotees' sins. Look at the following example:

Chunar meri maili Bhayee/Ab kape jaaun dhulaan
...Radhasoami dhubia bhari/Pragate aaye jahan

(My body/chunri is contaminated and dirty, where do I go to clean it?... Radhasoami is that washerman who has incarnated on this earth to wash away the sins of the jivas)

(*Ratnanjali* p. 69)

3.5 The Concept of Kripa

The concept of Kripa that the Sufi saints talk about (refer S K Das) also is a recurring image in the poetry of Radhasoami Faith. For example:

Guru mohin lev aaj apna ye/ Ek baat mere nischaye jamti, /aur samaj sab gayi bisraayi/jab lag kirpa guru kin a hoey/koyi na baat ban aayi/

- (*Prem Bilas* Part 1 Shabd 30)

and

Kripa drishti nij meher vrishti/Sab par karo piyare

- (*Ratnanjali* p19)

3.6 Propagation of Secular Spirit

The true Sufi-Bhakti temper is identified by its unique secular spirit. Adi Sant Kabir heralded it and it was taken forward by his lineage.

Hey guru main tere deedar ka aashiq jo hua/Man se Bejaar Surat vaar ke diwaana hua/ Raag aur raagini maine sune antar jaakar/ Mere najdeek huay hindu musalman kafir

and

Yeh satsang aur Radhasoami hai naam/Saran aao hey karmiyon tum tamaam

- (*Ratnanjali* p101-2)

Both the examples are directed towards unison of caste, creed, color and race.

To give just one more example, in *Sant Bani Sangrah*, we find Kabir Sahab's verse metaphorically stating the merger of the Atman with the Parmatman with the imagery of color:

Mere satguru hain rangrej, surat meri rang dali.
(My Lord is a dyer, HE has dyed/colored my soul)

and

har su hai aashkara / Jhahir jahuur tera
har dil mein bas raha hai / jalwa va noor tera

(Every direction is illumined or enlightened by your presence/ every consciousness is enlightened by your aura/every heart is manifest with the aura of your radiance and magnificence)

During the third revered leader, Huzur Maharaj Sahab's time, a Hyderabadi Rakkasa (danseuse) was so influenced by Radhasoami satsang that she sang the following as an example of intense devotion:

Hamne dar parda tujhe, parda nasheen dekh liya

(Oh Lord, the masked, the concealer! I managed to see you bare, in all your glory)

In the *Diary of Sahabji Maharaj*[17] (Part II) Huzur Sahabji Maharaj refers to the visit of Mrs and Mr Mckenzie. Here He refers to these lines by Ghalib:

Dil ko bahlane ko/Ghalib yeh Khyal achchha hai
(The idea is very good to keep oneself amused!)

These are but a few examples of the Sufi Consciousness within the Bhakti tradition. Holi (the festival of colors) and Basant (New Year for Radhasoami Faith and Spring season otherwise) will require a separate discussion and so will the *Barahmasa* (songs of separation enunciated with the help of the 12 months of a year) of the several metaphorical and symbolic representations of the depiction of the acute love between the devotee and the lord.

3.7 Concept of Separation

The intensity of lyricism in Indian religious poetry, too comes from this sense of separation...This is why Radha goes out in *abhisar* on dark rainy nights, Sassi perishes in the trackless deserts and Sohni plunges herself into the rushing tide to meet death. And this is why, Lalla danced bare, Mira left her home, Chaitanya wept, trembled and rolled on the ground of Vrindavan in ecstasy and al-Hallaj danced in his fetters to the place of execution and Rumi celebrated the incident in haunting rhythm:

> ***Sound, drum and fellow flute, resounding Allah Hu***
> ***Dance, ruddy dawn in gladness bounding Allah Hu***
> ***Sound exalted in the centre, O thou streaming light***
> ***Soul of all wheeling planets rounding Allah Hu...."***

Mansur was accused of heresy when he proclaimed *Anal Haq*, which when translated literally means "I am the Truth/ God". In fact Mansur was only announcing his complete merger with the Divine the complete annihilation of his own self (*fana*).

In the years 1930-32, Sir Sahabji Maharaj of Radhasoami Faith, wrote the Hindi/English translation of *Bhagavad Gita* and said, "In my opinion, the basic teachings of Gita is that man should seek the lord in the human form, and when he comes in His contact he should act according to His orders." [18]

Contemplation on the form of the Guru and repetition of the holy name is practiced in a spirit of complete surrender to the Guru in Radhasoami Faith. The Radhasoami Faith teaches Nirmal Bhakti where individual salvation is completely dependent on the pleasure of the Guru. As the goal of Bhakti is to attain both Name and Region (Nam and Dham) the aid of a living Guru is most important. Unlike the early *Sant Mat* tradition, the Radhasoami Faith promises an unbroken succession of Sant Satgurus until the entire creation is emancipated. It states that the Nij Dhar passes from one Guru to its successor who was hitherto His Gurumukh. Paul Brunton in *A Search in Secret India* (1934, 2003 rev.) describing Sahabji Maharaj, the fifth leader of the faith, wrote:

---

[17] *The Dayalbagh Herald* (weekly) Tue, June 29, 2010, week 26, days 1-7.
[18] Sahabji Maharaj. *Bhagavad Gita Ke Updesh* Radhasoami Satsang Sabha, Dayalbagh, 2004.

"…. Nowhere in India, nowhere in the entire world, may I expect to meet his like again." [19]

Another unique feature of Bhakti in Radhasoami satsang is the revelation of the Dhunyatmak Nam i.e. Radhasoami. This is the nearest approach in human speech to the sound accompanying the first spiritual current. The Name and the Named are one and the same i.e. Radhasoami Nam is the Supreme Being Himself. This Name plays an important role in the Bhakti of the Vakta Guru (current Guru). Never before the advent of the Radhasoami Faith on this earth was this Name revealed and the devotees were generally engaged only in the repetition of Varnatmak and rarely Dhunyatmak names of lower Regions.

In fact Bhakti is *Prem* (love) and has been beautifully described through the analogy of Water in this way. The spirit entity in man is like a drop of Love and in Brahma Love is like a wave. At some places Love is like an Ocean as in the Saints and the Supreme Being is an Infinite Reservoir of Love. On account of this difference in the size of Love, worldly desires predominate in human beings and Maya predominates in Brahma. But in Satya Loka, Maya is of no consequence owing to Love being in the form of an ocean. It has become purified there. Maya is completely absent in the Infinite Reservoir of Love i.e. Prime Source of Spirituality. Nothing but Love and Love alone exists there. This reservoir of Love is boundless. It has neither beginning nor end. It is limitless and beyond comprehension. Saints alone and none else can gain access to that Reservoir.

Sarkar Sahab, the fourth Revered Satguru of the Radhasoami Faith had explained "Prema Bhakti" (love and devotion) in one of His Discourses.[20] The Religion of Saints is a religion of Prema Bhakti. Devotion consists in directing one's attention current towards the Holy Feet of the Supreme Lord. This is also known as Sahaj Yoga or Surat Shabda Yoga.

The manner in which God or the Guru blesses and helps a devotee in the process of his attainment of salvation are known as: ***Markata Kishora Nyaya***: God protects and saves the souls as the monkey carries her young to safety, clinging to her body and Marjara Kishora Nyaya: A cat lifts its kitten by the neck and carries it to safety, with no effort required on part of the kitten. God saves the souls in the same manner with no effort required on part of those souls.

The following verses are from *Sar Bachan (Poetry)* of the Radhasoami Faith, and emphasize the importance attached to Guru Bhakti.

Guru ki kar hardam pooja /Guru samaan koi Dev na dooja / Guru Brahma roop dhar aye / Guru Para Brahma gati gaye / Guru Sattanaam pada khola / Guru Alakh Agam ko tola / Guru roop dhara Radhasoami / Guru se barh nahin Anami[21]

---

[19] Brunton Paul. *A Search in Secret India.* Rider, an imprint of Ebury Press, Random House. London. 2003 edition (first published in 1934).

[20] Prema Bhakti from Maharaj Sahab *Discourses on Radhasoami Faith,* Radhasoami Satsang Sabha, Dayalbagh. Revised edition 2008.

Sant Tukaram, Sant Namdev and Sant Dadu, prominent Saints of the Bhakti School, in their own ways, have described the various aspects of saints and saintliness.

The joy of repeating the Lord's Name /Will make us dance and clap /He fondly protects those who surrender to him /He has already liberated countless souls /Who have surrendered to him /And I am sure that he will liberate me too

-(Sant Tukaram Gatha, 2105)

and

The Lord's Name is absolute, the Lord's Name is supreme / Only true and loving devotees realize this, O Nama! Sant Namadeva, Gatha, 680)

A Saint is a veritable ship / In the ocean of the world / Whosoever sits in his company / Is saved, O Dadu

- (Sant Dadu, Gatha, 179)

4. Conclusion

The Bhakti and the Sufi Consciousness has a modern manifestation in Radhasoami Faith. It also has a new language for its Bhaktas. 'Bhakti' entails upon the Bhakta to inculcate the nuances of the following concepts laid down for his own benefit. Only then will he become the mad devotee. A brief glimpse of some of these concepts is given below:

i. The New World Order

The fifth revered leader, Sir Sahabji Maharaj put forth before the Satsang community the concept of 'Aristocratic Democracy' (ARIS-DEMO) as the model for governance. By Aristocrats, He meant 'Spiritual Aristocrats' who would be practitioners of Surat Shabda Yoga and would have an elevated level of consciousness.

ii. Better Worldliness

Better worldliness can be understood as a disposition towards life, by following which, man can achieve the four Purusharthas of Dharma, Artha, Kama and Moksha to attain the status of a Jivanmukta[22] during his lifetime itself. As against the ancient scriptural notion of unworldliness, which started with a prejudice against the religious way of life, Sahabji Maharaj propounded the concept of Better Worldliness: Living in the world comfortably, pursuing the ideal of achieving the highest spiritual goal. Better Worldliness is thus the golden mean between worldliness and unworldliness. It can be seen as a combi-

[21] This Shabda is from Sar Bachan (poetry), Shabd 2, Bachan 18, and Page 322, composed by Soami Ji Maharaj. Describing the supreme status of Guru Maharaj the author says that a Guru should always be worshipped since there is none else of such a high and exalted status, Who having explored Alakh and Agam, has revealed to us the secret of Satnama. The Guru Himself is Radhasoami and there is none other of a higher form un-manifest.

nation of Karma Yoga, Gyana Yoga and Bhakti Yoga, based on a Dharmic way of conduct; a conduct with compassion and forbearance for fellow man, no matter what the nationality, or the color of the skin, religion or caste. Better Worldliness can be explained as a philosophy or a way of life where spiritual pursuits to attain superior consciousness and puritan work ethics make a fine blend. Practicing Better Worldliness would usher in 'Brotherhood of Man' and lead us to an integrated global community.

iii. Fatherhood of God and Brotherhood of Man

Followers of Radhasoami Faith believe in the basic faith of "Fatherhood of God and Brotherhood of mankind." It is based on the principle that service of the human brotherhood far from being a hindrance, in establishing communion with the Supreme Father, is indeed a positive step in that direction.

The aforementioned concepts have a unique resonance with the teachings of Bhakti and the Sufi saints. Prof. Mark Juergensmeyer of University of California, Berkeley, in his well researched book, ***Radhasoami Reality*** says:

"Many in traditional and highly developed area now seek what the adherents of Radhasoami communities have found; a pattern of religious expression and experience that allows them to identify with their cultural past without accepting what they see as its superstitious and greedy excesses, and to embrace modern ways of living without becoming captive to what they perceive as alienating forms of society and sterile forms of thought." [23]

This view is so close to what the Bhakti and the Sufi saints practised and believed in! Finally, Professor Juergensmeyer concludes thus, "...the Radhasoami faith may be a harbinger of the religion of the future, not only in India but elsewhere in the world...."

References

Ahmad, Salim, (2005). The Bhakti Movement. *South Asian Journal, April-June.*

Bashan, K. L. (1954). *The Wonder that was India*. New York, USA: Grove Press.

Bertalanffy, L V.(1969). *General Systems Theory. Foundations, Development, Applications.* New York, USA: George Braziller.

Clothey, F. W. (2006). *Religion in India: A Historical Introduction*. Routledge.

Das, S. K. (2003). The Mad Lover *Indian Literature. vol. XLVII, no. 215, May-June.* New Delhi, India: Sahitya Akademi. 149-78.

Gold. D. (1987). The Lord as Guru: Hindi Saints in the Northern Indian Tradition. New York, USA: Oxford University Press.

Grewal, J. S. (2006). Indigenization of Sufism: The Case of the Punjab. *Religious Movements and Institutions in Medieval India* J.S. Grewal (ed.). New Delhi, India: Oxford University Press. 359.

---

[22] A Jivanmukta is a realized soul who visualizes the entire creation as the children of God and his love for God translates into brotherhood of man.

[23] Mark Juergensmeyer. *Radhasoami Reality – Logic of a Modern Faith.* Princeton University Press, Princeton, New Jersey, 1991.

Juergensmeyer, M. (1996). *Radhasoami Reality*. Princeton, New Jersey, USA: Princeton University Press.

Kaur, K. (2009). Radhasoami Faith: The Sant Tradition. *The Speaking Tree, Times of India*. 24 July Sahabji Maharaj [Sir Anand Sarup Kt.] (rev. ed. 2004). *Bhagavad Gita Ke Updesh*, Agra, India: Radhasoami Satsang Sabha, Dayalbagh.

Klyuev, B. (1989). *Religion in Indian Society - The Dimensions of Unity and Diversity*. New Delhi, India: Sterling Publishers.

Kumar, Chauhan and Bodh Prakash (2005). *Cultural Diversity, Linguistic Plurality and Literary Traditions in India*. New Delhi, India: Macmillan India Ltd. (Edited for the Department of English, University of Delhi).

Maharaj Sahab [Pt. Brahm Sankar Misra Sahab] (2009). *Discourses on Radhasoami Faith*, Agra, India: Radhasoami Satsang Sabha, Dayalbagh.

Param Purush Puran Dhani Huzur Soamiji Maharaj [Shiv Dayal Singh Sahab]. *Sar Bachan (poetry)*. Agra, India: Radhasoami Satsang Sabha, Dayalbagh.

Radhakrishnan, S. (Rev. edns. 1994). *Indian Philosophy I and II*. New Delhi, India: Indus Publications.

Sahabji Maharaj [Sir Anand Sarup Kt.] (1957). *Selections from Prem Sandesha*, Agra, India: Radhasoami Satsang Sabha, Dayalbagh.

Sangari, K. (2006). Mirabai: The Female Voice and Oral Compositions. *Religious Movements and Institutions in Medieval India*. J.S. Grewal (ed.). New Delhi, India: Oxford University Press. 228-254.

Saxena Arti, Saxena P. K., and Chaturvedi, D. K. (2005). *Theology, Science and Technology: Ethics and Moral Values*. New Delhi, India: Vikas Publishing House.

Singh, R. (2010). A Grand Convergence. *The Speaking Tree.. The Times of India* New Delhi edition. December 12, P. 3

Sinha. N. (1998). *Bhakti Sutras of Narada*. Delhi, India: Munshiram Manoharlal Publishers.

______(1998). *Shandilya Sutram*. Delhi, India: Munshiram Manoharlal Publishers.

Souvenirs - Radhasoami Satsang 1861-1961 (reprint 2001). Agra, India: Radhasoami Satsang Sabha, Dayalbagh.

Srivastava, P. K. (2006). The Culture Conundrum: Can it be popular? *Yearly Academic Journal*, Kalindi College, University of Delhi.

Swami Tapasyananda (2003). *Bhakti School of Vedanta*. Chennai, India: Sri Rama Krishna Math.

Tart, C. T. (1975). *States of Consciousness*. New York, USA: E.P. Dutton and Co.

THM 203 *Sant Mat: Religion of Saints II*. Unit 5: 4

VI

Means of Attaining Higher Levels of Spiritual Consciousness

Chapter 22

आध्यात्मिक ज्ञान के ऊँचे स्तर को प्राप्त करने के साधन

SWAMI KADAMANAND
Radhasowami Parmanand Ashram, Delhi

मेरे सतगुरू परमसन्त श्री प्रीतानन्द जी महाराज ने, मुझे दीक्षा देते समय कुछ परहेज बताए, नाम बताया, सुमरिन, भजन, ध्यान का तरीका बताया, आसन व स्थान के बारे में बताया, कुछ शौंक दई और कहा कि बेटा मैंने जो करने को कहा है वह अवश्य करना, लेकिन जो मैंने अपने अनुभव बताए हैं उनको मत मानना, स्वयं अनुभव करना और उन्ही को सही मानना, मैंने ऐसा ही किया।

1ण परहेजः–

पद्ध पर धन धूल समान समझना, अपनी खुद की नेक कमाई से अपना व अपने आश्रितों का भरण पोषण करना।

पपद्ध चाल–चलन में मनसा, वाचा एवं कर्मणा सूचा रहना।

पपपद्ध कोई किसी किस्म का नशा नहीं करना।

2ण शौंक :–

पद्ध पूरा सन्त समर्थ सतगुरू करना व स्वयं गुरूमुख शिष्य होके रहना।

पपद्ध बुरी संगत से बचना, सन्त, साध व गुरूमुख शिष्यों से ही सम्बन्ध रखना।

पपपद्ध भौतिक, मानसिक व आध्यात्मिक, सात्त्विक आहार ग्रहण करना।

पअद्ध भजन, ध्यान व साधना का स्थान व समय निश्चित रखना

अद्ध साधना की निरन्तरता भँग नहीं होने देना।

अपद्ध ध्यान के लिए प्रतिदिन कम से कम ढाई घण्टे का समय देना।

अपपद्ध सतगुरू के प्रति पूरा भाव व भरोसा रखना व सूची नियत से सतगुरू की आज्ञा का पालन करना।

अपपपद्ध गुरू वाक्यम सेवा, सतगुरू की आज्ञा का पालन व उनकी शौंक पर अमल करना ही उनकी असल सेवा है, सँगत से कसी प्रकार की सेवा व भेंट अपने लिए स्वीकार नहीं करना।

पगद्ध तन, मन व वचन से अकर्ता रहते हुए शुभ, सात्विक कर्म करना व सोचना।

गद्ध विषय–वासना रहित होकर रूचि व लगन से साधना करना व जीवन जीना।

गपद्ध सतगुरू का कृपा–पात्र व अधिकारी शिष्य होकर रहना।

गपपद्ध नाम सुमरिन व सतगुरू का ध्यान आठों पहर रहना चाहिए।

गपपपद्ध सबसे समभाव रखना व संगत को अपनी सन्तान समझना।

गपअद्ध खुले ह्दय से प्रेम व सत्य ज्ञान बाँटना।

गअद्ध कहनी व रहनी एक रखना, छुपाने लायक कुछ भी नहीं होना चाहिए।

गअपद्ध बिना गुरू की आज्ञा के गुरूवाई नहीं करना, गुरू की आज्ञा होने पर भी, गुरू वाई करते हुए भी अपने आपको गुरू का शिष्य व सेवक ही समझना व संगत का भी सेवक ही समझना।

गअपपद्ध हमेशा सबके हित की सोचना व करना।

गअपपपद्ध हर हाल में सतगुरू व कुल मालिक के भाणे में रहना।

गपगद्ध सँयमी, सरल सादगी पूर्ण व दिखावा एवं आडम्बर रहित रहना।

गगद्ध सतगुरू की नकल नहीं करना, उनसे हर हरकत, कर्म एवं बात का खुलासा करवा सकते हो।

साधना के दौरान कुछ अनुभव

1ण ध्यान में चाहे अनचाहे साधक दूसरे ग्रहों में जा सकता है।

2ण साधना के दौरान सिद्धियाँ स्वयंमेव आ जाती हैं।

3ण साधना द्वारा हम पिछले जन्मों में जा सकते हैं लेकिन सतगुरू ने ऐसा करने से मना किया हुआ है, अनचाहे भी कभी कभार ऐसा हो सकता है।

4ण सन्त सतगुरू होनी को अनहोनी कर सकते हैं।

5ण सतगुरू हर समय व हर परिस्थिति में अपने शिष्य/शिष्याओं के साथ सहायतार्थ रहते हैं व उन्हें कभी अकेला/बेसहारा नहीं छोड़ते।

6ण सतगुरू गुरूमुख को भौतिक रूप से वहाँ न होते हुए भी दर्शन दे सकते हैं, बात कर सकते हैं, चेतावनी/सहायता कर सकते हैं।

7ण सतगुरू ऐसे चमत्कार कर सकते हैं जो सम्भव नहीं लगते व ना कभी देखे व सुने हों।

8ण सतगुरू अपने शिष्य/शिष्या को दुखी या कष्टमय सहन नहीं कर सकते।

9ण सतगुरू सन्त किसी से भी नाराज नहीं होते, चाहे कोई उनसे कैसा भी व्यवहार करे, ना ही वो किसी का अनिष्ट सोचते व ना ही करते हैं।

10ण सन्तों का क्रोध केवल दिखावा व हितकारी होता है।

11ण सन्त सतगुरू अपने शरणागत को अपना सब कुछ दे सकते हैं, यहाँ तक कि अपना जीवन भी।

12ण सन्त सतगुरू के सभी गुण कोई नहीं गिना सकता।

13ण सतगुरू चाहे जिसको जीवन दान दे सकते हैं।

14ण सन्तों की कुल मालिक सुनता व मानता है व प्रकृति भी बस में होती है।

15ण सन्त सतगुरू की अपनी सँगत के प्रति दया–मेहर चोला छोड़ने के बाद भी ज्यों की त्यों बनी रहती है।

16ण सन्त को पहचान पाना असम्भव है, वे कोई बाहरी दिखावा, भेष, केश पहचान ;स्ंइसमद्ध नहीं रखते।

17ण गुरू के बिना, ज्ञान सम्भव नहीं, उनकी दया के बिना साधना नहीं हो सकती।

18ण सतगुरू चाहे तो शिष्य/शिष्या को एक ही जन्म में पार कर सकते हैं, उनके

लिए कुछ भी असम्भव नहीं, वे पूर्णरूपेण समर्थ होते हैं, फिर भी वे अपने द्वारा किए गए किसी का कार्य का श्रेय खुद को नहीं देते, वे इसे अपने सतगुरू/कुल मालिक की मौज मानते हैं, मालिक भी सब दया सन्तों के माध्यम से ही करते हैं।

19ण परमात्मा न्यायकारी है, वे भेदभाव या मेर/तेर नहीं करते।

20ण साधना के दौरान साधक को अद्‌भुत शक्तियाँ अनायास ही प्राप्त हो जाती है, साधक समाधि के बाद बहुत कुछ परिवर्तित हो जाता है।

21ण साधक समाधि में सूक्ष्म रूप से कहीं भी जा सकते हैं।

कुछ तथ्य

1ण कुल मालिक :– वैसे तो परमपिता परमात्मा की आज तक कोई भी पूर्ण व्याख्या नहीं कर सका व ना ही सम्भव है, फिर भी उसके कुछ–एक गुण जो सर्वविदित हैं, यहाँ लिखे जा रहे हैं, जैसे :– निराकार, रँगहीन, रूप व आकृतिहीन, सर्वव्यापक, सर्वज्ञ, समर्थ, न्यायकारी, आदि व अन्तहीन, अजन्मा, सर्वशक्तिमान, चेतन, शाश्वत, अखण्ड, एकरस, अपरिवर्तनशील, सच्चिदानन्द सब रचना का कर्ता, धर्ता व हर्ता।

2ण आत्मा का कोई अस्तित्व नहीं, आत्मा व परमात्मा एक ही हैं, परमात्मा का जो हिस्सा (अँश) जीव में कार्यरत है उसको आत्मा कहें तो कोई एतराज नहीं है वह परमात्मा ही, वह परमात्मा से अलग नहीं हो सकता, जैसे परमात्मा की कोई सीमा नहीं, उसी प्रकार उक्त कही गई आत्मा की भी कोई सीमा नहीं, इस प्रकार सबकी आत्मा एक, जैसे सबका मालिक एक, इसी प्रकार पाँचों तत्व भी सबके एक।

3ण हर एक जीव की वस्तु कुल मालिक को व्यक्त कर रही है, सबसे उसी का प्रकाश, शक्ति, गति व चेतना कार्यरत है।

4ण दो शाश्वत वस्तुएँ एक साथ वजूद में हो ही नहीं सकती।

5ण जीवों का शरीर भवसागर में एक भँवर तुल्य है जो कुल मालिक की शक्ति गति, प्रकाश व चेतना को उपयोग कर उसी को व्यक्त कर रहा है, यह आकार, बनावट, कार्य व गुणों में भिन्न हो सकता है, यह एक कोशिकायुक्त या असंख्य कोशिकायुक्त हो सकता है।

6ण मृत्यु, जीव के शरीर का कार्य करने में असक्ष्म होना है, परमात्मा/आत्मा का अभाव नहीं। भैतिक शरीर बेकार होने पर सूक्ष्म, कारण, महाकारण, केवल्य या हँस शरीर कार्य करने लगते हैं।

7ण जीव का सँस्कार व शरीर रहित होना ही मुक्ति है।

8ण अनहद शब्द ग्रहों (सूर्य, ग्रह, उपग्रह आदि) की गति के कारण उत्पन्न ध्वनि के कारण उत्पन्न होता है, यह आहत शब्द है अनाहत शब्द नहीं।

9ण साधना के दौरान अनुभव होने वाले स्थान, स्थान नहीं बल्कि स्तर है, शब्द भी हमारी साधना के दौरान, एकाग्रता के स्तर के कारण भिन्न–भिन्न सुनाई देते हें, शब्द लक्ष्य नहीं, बल्कि एकाग्रता की नाप है सत्यलोक से आगे शब्द गुप्त है।

10ण साधारण मनुष्य की श्रवण शक्ति 2000 कम्पन प्रति सैकेण्ड से 20000 कम्पन प्रति सैकेण्ड होती है। साधना से यह श्रवण शक्ति अत्यधिक बढ़ जाती है जिसके कारण अनहद शब्द सुनना सम्भव हो जाता है।

11ण पारस पत्थर, कल्पतरू इत्यादि मिथ्य है, इनका असलियत में कोई अस्तित्व नहीं।

12ण दो भिन्न–भिन्न वस्तुएँ एकाकार नहीं हो सकती जैसे पानी व मिट्‌टी, आत्मा व परमात्मा।

13ए उस सूक्ष्मतम अणु की प्राप्ति के पश्चात् जिससे सब तत्व बने हैं, रसायनशास्त्र का अन्त आ जाता है व उस शक्ति की प्राप्ति के पश्चात जिससे सब शक्तियाँ उत्पन्न होती है भौतिक–शास्त्र का अन्त आ जाता है।

14ए सकल सृष्टि एकसाथ कभी विनाश को प्राप्त नहीं होती, ग्रह, उपग्रह, सूर्य नित बनते बिगड़ते रहते हैं, रचना भी प्रवाह से अनन्त है। हमारा कुछ भी अलग नहीं हवा, पानी, अग्नि, आकाश व मिट्टी, आत्मा, परमात्मा, रचना में कुछ भी स्थिर नहीं यहाँ तक कि हमारा शरीर भी स्थिर नहीं व अलग नहीं, निरन्तर रूप से हमारे शरीर के अवयवों का आपस में आदान, प्रदान व बनना–बिगड़ना जारी रहता है।

15ए रचना में हमारे जैसी अनन्त पृथ्वियाँ हैं जिन में हमारे से कुछ उन्नत भी हैं।

16ए अध्यात्म विद्या का कोई अन्त नहीं यह भी परमात्मा की नाँई अन्तहीन है।

Chapter 23

How Brain Gains Access to Self-Conscious Mind and Beyond: Convergence of Concepts of Neuroscience and Radhasoami Faith

VIJAI KUMAR
Dayalbagh, Agra, India

MOHIT SINHA
Dayalbagh Educational Institute (Demmed University), Agra, India

Abstract

The paper discusses the means of communion of microcosm through human brain to different states of consciousness of the macrocosm and the mechanism by which it gains access to self-conscious mind. The evolution of brain, the instrument of consciousness and cognition, has paralleled the evolution of mind and "... the substances are evolving and all evolution is taking place including the evolution of mind". (Most Revered Prof. P.S. Satsangi Sahab). There are two groups of theories to explain human consciousness. The first of these propounds that "mind and consciousness are identical to the operations of the brain or, at least, to some of these operations". Rene Descartes is regarded as the father of the second set of theories. He espoused the concept of two forms of substances, 'res extensa', the physical substance occupying space, and 'res cogitans' the thinking substance and thus inaugurated the concept of "dualism". We present a concept on the basis of modified dualism, which describes on the basis of neuroscience the mechanism by which the brain communicates with self-conscious mind. There is an arrangement of vertical chains of neurons, the columns or modules, through the whole depth of cerebral cortex orthogonal to its surface, which, in structure and function, comprise the basic cortical units. According to Eccles there are parts of the brain which actively communicate with the self conscious mind through these columns (modules),of the cerebral cortex. These parts can be called the liaison brain, which may be regarded as an aperture providing a two-way communication channel with self-conscious mind. The "liaison brain" described by the neuroscientists, we feel, may be likened to an aperture which provides access to the self conscious mind just as the 12 apertures in brain graciously revealed by Param Guru Maharaj Sahab provide a means of communion with the higher regions i.e. Brahamanda and the Nirmal Chetan Desh. There is thus a convergence of concepts of neuroscience and Radhasoami Faith.

Prologue

Sir Sahabji Maharaj the Fifth Most Revered Sant Satguru of the Radhasoami Faith has stated that: "We may doubt a hundred things and dispute a thousand, but we dare not refuse to admit that we are living beings."

We go a step further and say that we dare not refuse to admit that we are living beings with consciousness, which is one of the fundamental, possibly the most fundamental, characteristic of human species. This characteristic is an evolutionary novelty (Dobzhansky 1967).

The highest state of consciousness is a property inherent in the Supreme Essence. Sant Mat or Religion of Saints clearly speaks of ascent of the spirit and its attaining to different states of spiritual consciousness in its course (Sriramamurti 2005). We have attempted to scientifically explore how brain communicates with the self-conscious mind and the similarity of this concept to the means of communion of microcosm through human brain to higher states of consciousness as revealed in the Radhasoami Faith.

Evolution of Brain and Mind

The mind has passed through three stages of evolution – the Episodic Culture of Homo Australopithecus and living apes, the Mimetic Culture of Homo erectus and Mythic Culture of Homo sapiens (Donald 1991).

The evolution of human brain, the instrument of cognition and consciousness, has paralleled the evolution of human mind. It has also evolved in three main stages:

1. It's ancient and primitive part, the core, reptilian brain. It is represented in human brain by the structures at the top of the spinal cord including brain stem. It controls body functions, which are required for sustaining life.

2. Next evolved the mammalian brain by addition of new functions and new ways of controlling the body and new dimensions to living above the repetitions evolved. Autonomic nervous systems and hypothalamus for control of life preserving functions, mechanism of storage of experience based memories and reactions and generation of feelings about events too evolved in this phase.

3. In the third phase, mammalian brain became human brain by addition of massive grey matter, the neo-cortex, which forms about 85% of the human brain mass. The uniqueness of prosimian and human brain being this expansion of neocortex.

According to **Most Revered Prof. P.S. Satsangi Sahab** "the rest of the evolution is continuing to take place i.e. their [spirit entities] bodies are evolving, the substances are evolving and all evolution is taking place including the evolution of mind."

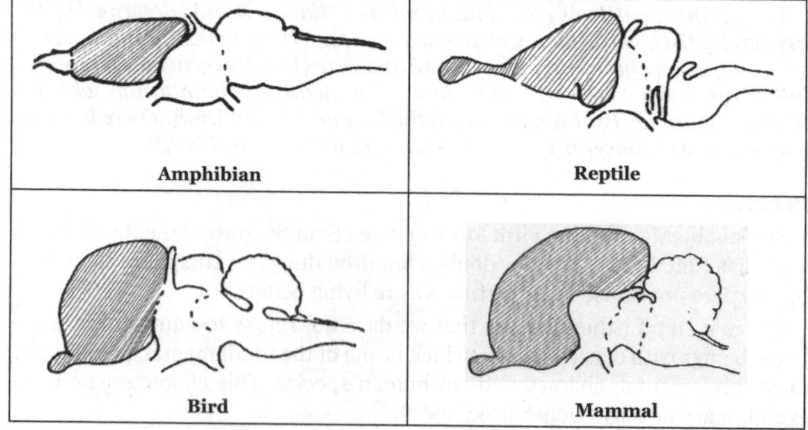

Moving up the ladder of evolution, there is a massive increase in the number and complexity of connections among the neurons of animal brains.

Functionally, the most important step in evolution happened when the simple nervous system with its subsystems exchanging signals in an insulated way developed into a complex nervous systems with re-enterant dynamics in which enormous number of signals are integrated within a single neural process, the dynamic core. In such a system, signals from different modalities and memory combine to form scenes – it is a remembered present (Edleman 1989). At this stage the information acquires a new potential – that of subjectivity. In other words it is information for somebody; in short it becomes consciousness itself.

The evolution of brain, the instrument of consciousness and cognition

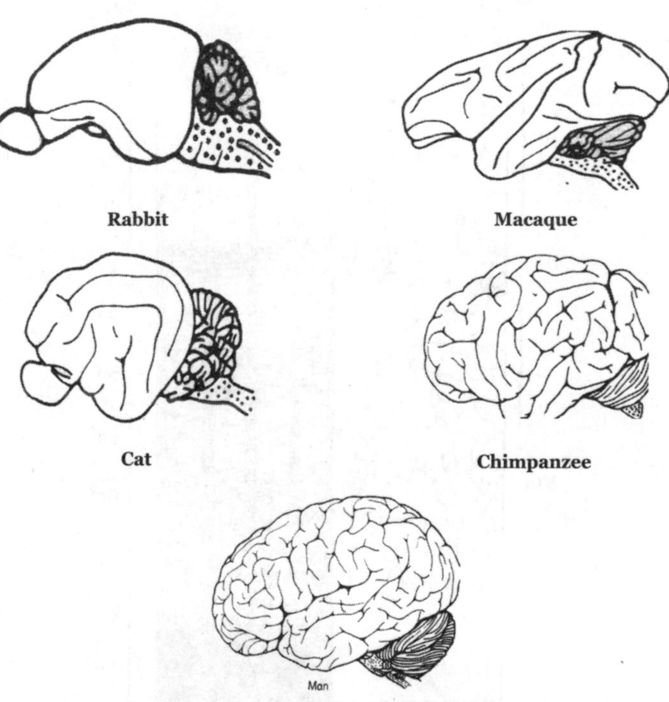

Some mammalian brain using the same scale

In most parts of the cerebral cortex, there is horizontal lamination of nerve cells (neurons) into six layers. But whatever localization of function and specialization of cerebral cortex may exist, it exists over two-dimensional cortical spaces and not layer by layer in the third dimension also.

Besides the horizontal lamination of the neurons into six layers, there is an arrangement of vertical chains of neurons through the whole depth of the cortex forming columns orthogonal to the cortical surface. The cortical neurons of small sharply defined areas, which form columns or modules, exhibit an approximately similar response to specific afferent inputs and have similar properties. Close neighbors at 100 m distance in the horizontal division begin to show differences in response.

The column is a complex organization of cells. Szentagothi (1969) has evolved the concept that in both structure and function, the column or module is the basic cortical unit. Mount castle (1978) has broadened the concept of column into different units based on size and function.

Fine structure of cerebral cortex (diagrammatic)

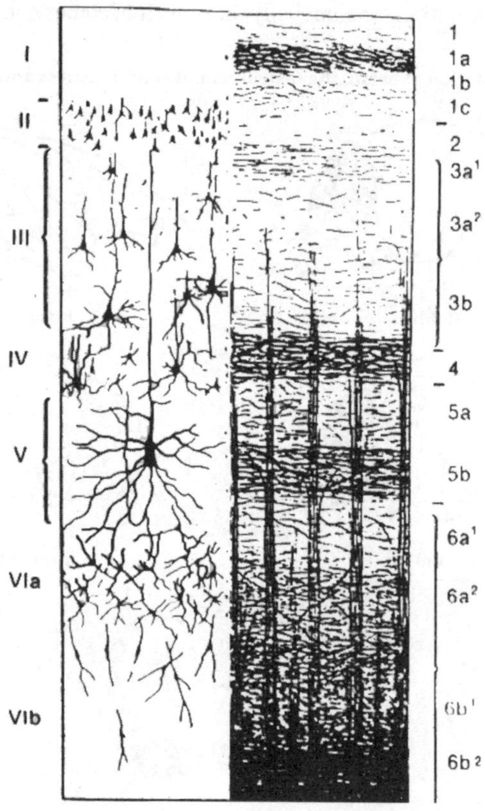

I. lamina zonalis

II. lamina granularis externa

III. lamina pyramidalis

IV. lamina granularis interna

V. lamina ganglionaris

VI. Lamina multiformis

The total Number of Cortical Columns is estimated as 50 – 100 million/ hemisphere. These are vertical to the surface and 3 mm long and 0.1 to 0.5 mm across. The columns are complex organizations of many specific neuron types and comprise of input, and output channels. These structural and functional units of cortex contain 1000 to 100,000 neurons each, generally up to 10,000, which have unitary existence. It maybe noted that excitatory level in a module is communicated to other cortical modules from moment to moment. There is continuous interaction between the columns. Many of the neurons constituting the columns are inhibitory and produce an inhibitory action on their adjacent columns. Each column attempts to dominate other modules and vice versa.

COLUMNS OR MODULES

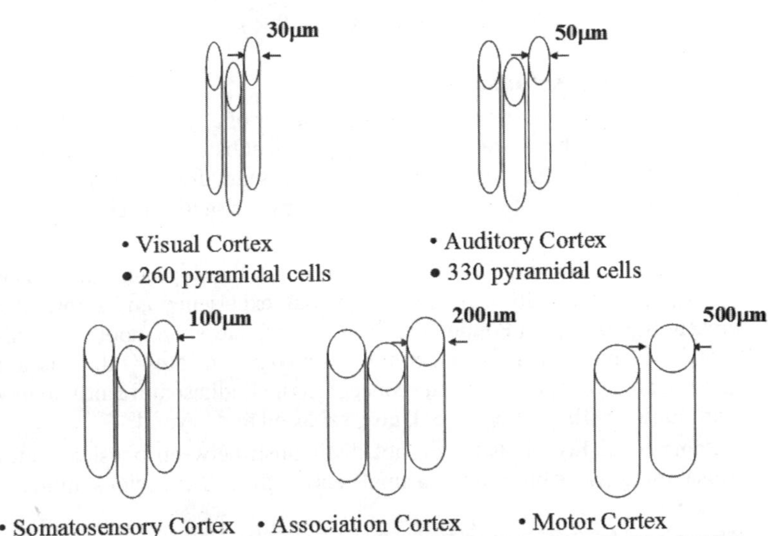

Summary of the functional units of various parts of the cortex – the columns. (Based on Norman D-Cook, 1986)

Theories of Consciousness of Relevance to the Study: The Materialistic Hypotheses

In so far as our present study is concerned, we may consider two groups of theories to explain consciousness. The first of these which the philosophers and scientists have taken to today has a materialistic stance, namely that the "mind and consciousness are identical to the operations of the brain or, at least, to certain of these operations" (Edelman and Tononi. 2000).

It espouses that there is nothing else beyond the brain circuits, going so far as to believe that once we understand the working of the brain sufficiently well the concept of consciousness will disappear. According to these neuroscientists and neuro theologists, it is the amazingly complex material structures of brain and body that gives rise to dynamic processes and meaning. We don't have to assume any other thing – other worlds, spirits or exotic unproven forces e.g. Quantum Gravity. Cerebral cortex is sufficient for self-awareness.

Other materialists believe that consciousness emerges form physical events in the brain but is not reducible to these.

Riding on the waves of modern neuroscience discoveries the materialists recall that:

The Brain – is wider than sky –
For – put them side by side –
The one the other will contain
With ease – and You – beside

(Emily Dickinson 1830 – 1886)

Dualism & Consciousness

Rene Descartes can be regarded as the father of a second set of theories. He distinguished between res extensa' – physical substance with spatial extent – and 'res cogitans, thinking substance and thus inaugurated dualism. He argued that 'res cogitans' is unique to humans and gives rise to consciousness.

Cartesian two-world concept was a landmark development in philosophical concept and generally explained all of our experience and knowledge. We present the concept of Popper and Eccles (1977), based on modified dualism, to explain the mechanism by which the brain communicates with consciousness of mind and compare it with the concept in the Radhasoami Faith on means of communion with the Region of Universal Mind and beyond.

Popper and Eccles (1977) do not distinguish between physical, astral and causal mind states but refer to a single entity, the self-conscious mind.

Three-world Concept of Popper

Popper, as recalled by Eccles, has proposed the concept of three worlds that comprise all existents and all experiences (Eccles, 1970).

World 1 is the world of physical objects comprising both living and non-living entities, including human brain, which acts as a selective channel for the flow of information.

World 2 is the world of states of consciousness and mental states that each one of us knows at first hand for oneself only.

By contrast, **world 3** is the world of knowledge in the objective sense, and as such has an extremely wide range of contents.

The three worlds may not be separate at all but reflect aspects of a deeper truth about the world as a whole, which is at present unknown. The "three world" concept of Popper, however, still remains to be universally accepted.

Roger Penrose (2005), interestingly, has proposed a relationship of the physical, mental and Platonic – mathematical forms of existence as 3 separate worlds. Everything in the universe, he believes, is governed in completely precise details by mathematical principles. Our own physical actions the volitional conscious acts would be entirely subject to such ultimate mathematical control, where control might ultimately allow for some random behavior governed by strict probabilistic principles.

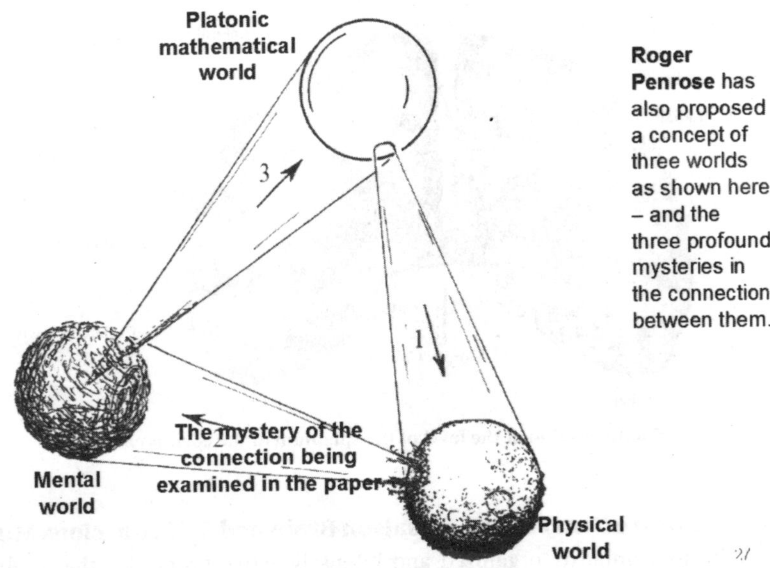

(After Roger Penrose 2005)

Self-conscious Mind and the Liaison Brain

Our conscious experience arises in only one part of our body, the highest level of the brain – and even then when brain is in the right state of dynamic activity (Adrian 1947 cited by J.C. Eccles 1970). The receptor organs and their associated neural pathways provide the only channels of communication by which the brain can sense events in the external world.

According to Eccles there are parts of the brain, which actively communicate with the self-conscious mind through the columns of the cerebral cortex. These constitute the liaison brain. It is inconceivable that the self-conscious mind is in liaison with single nerve cells or neurons. The liaison brain is superimposed on the neural machinery in all its performance at certain sites of the cerebral hemisphere, where effective interactions with the self-conscious mind, both in receiving and in giving takes place. It is believed that only a minute, specialized, zone of the cerebral hemispheres is in liaison with the self-conscious mind at a given time.

The essential feature of the hypothesis is the active role of the self-conscious mind in its influence on the neural machinery.

In the commissurotomy patients this is restricted to the dominant hemisphere but normally there may well be some liaison areas of the brain in the minor hemisphere.

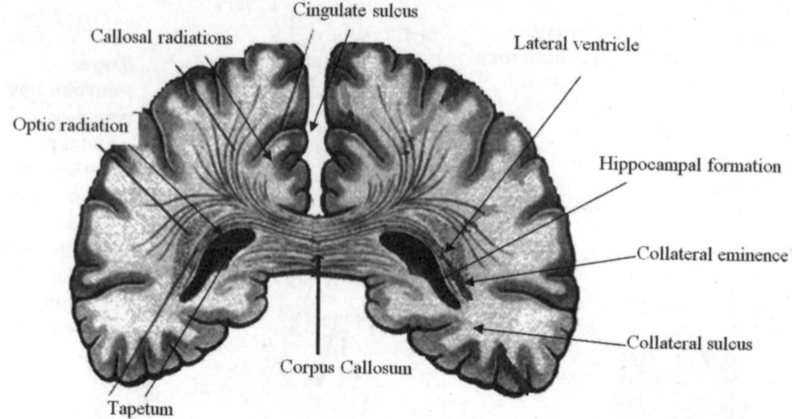

A frontal section at the level of the splenium of the corpus callosum

Mechanism of Interaction of Liaison Brain and Self-conscious Mind

With its complexly organized and intensely active properties the cerebral cortex module could be a component of the physical world (World 1) which is open to the self-conscious mind (world 2) both for receiving from and giving to. Further, not all modules in the cerebral cortex have this transcendent property of being open components of the interface.

In this context each module may be considered a radio transmitter – receiver unit – a vastly complicated electronics circuit. The interface units would be restricted to the liaison brain and that too when they are in the correct level (state) of activity.

Diagrammatically the open and closed and partly open modules are shown in the following image:

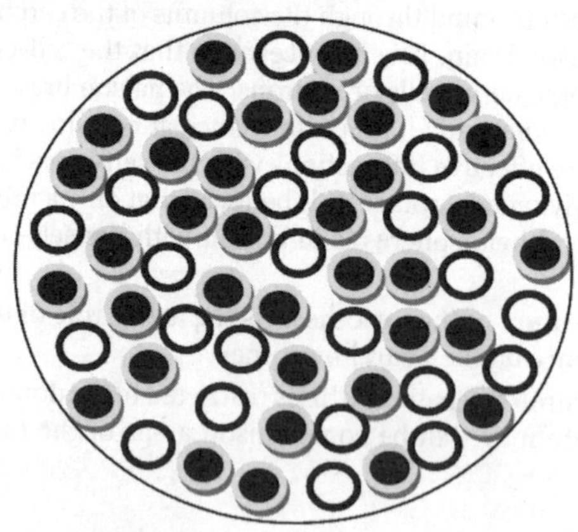

Pattern of open and closed modules of cerebral cortex

The self- conscious mind directly communicates with the open module and via the association and intercolumnar fibres causing inhibition and excitation of others and may result in opening up others.

The self conscious mind can scan the activity of each module of liaison brain- or at least those tuned in to its present interest and thus builds-up its experience from moment to moment. It is an essence of this hypothesis that the relations between self-conscious mind and the cortical modules are reciprocal, the self-conscious mind being both an activator and a receiver.

Secondly, the liaison brain comprises a large part of the dominant hemisphere, particularly the linguistic areas, the poly-modal sensory areas the ideational areas and a large area of pre-frontal lobe.

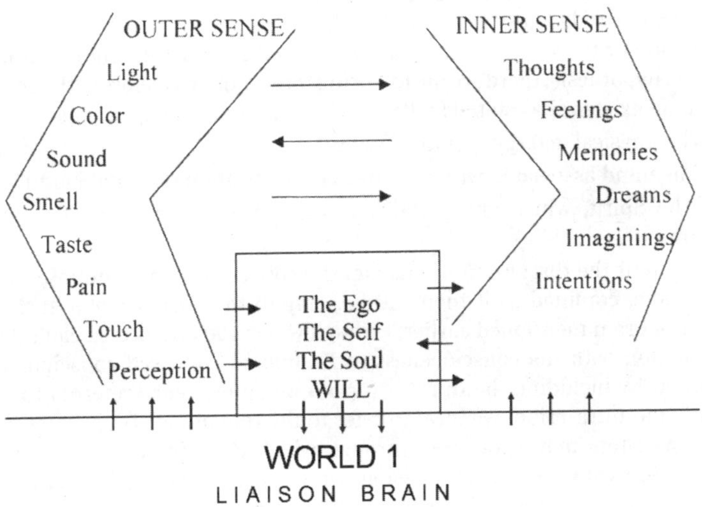

Liaison Brain as a Brain Aperture

Param Guru Maharaj Sahab (1909) has graciously revealed that "In the fissure between the two lobes of the brain there are twelve apertures, which provide the means for communion with the six sub-divisions of Brahmanda and with the six sub-divisions of the purely spiritual region. The apertures pertaining to Brahmanda are to be found in the grey matter, and those pertaining to the purely spiritual region, in the white matter. .... The innermost quarters within those apertures, by means of which the microcosm is associated with Brahmanda and the purely spiritual regions, are of supreme importance. .... Similarly, the innermost localities of the apertures of the brain, referred to, will have to be sought for holding communion with the higher spheres, and for eventually gaining access into the regions of Brahmanda and those beyond them".

Convergence of Concepts of Neuroscience and Radhasoami Faith

The liaison brain, we propose, may be likened to the apertures referred to in the "Discourses" through which microcosm can be in communion with the second Grand Division or Brahmanda. The openings in columns and modules of liaison brain are functionally similar to these apertures.

There thus seems to be a convergence of the concept of the liaison brain as discussed above which provides an opening, an aperture as it were, to the self conscious mind and the apertures as revealed by the Masters of the Radhasoami Faith and explained by Param Guru Maharaj Sahab in the "Discourses".

While the scientific concept of liaison brain and the self conscious mind is based on "dualism", we have to go beyond the Cartesian dualism of absolute distinction between mental and material substance in which the defining characteristic of matter is to be extended, to occupy space, and the defining character of mind is to be conscious, to understand the ultimate source of consciousness.

On the basis of the teaching of our Masters, we believe that there is a more refined and subtle entity than mind, which is the seat of consciousness. This is ultra-mind or the spirit of Sant Mat. It is encased in human mind. Contrary to dualism hypothesis, there are the following three, not two factors in the economy of human existence as stated by Param Guru Maharaj Sahab, namely:

1. The physical, energy – matter frame
2. The mind associated with the internal constitution or "antahkaran" and
3. The Spirit, which gives vitality to other two and referred to above as "ultramind".

If we limit the discussion to dualism the concept we have proposed will be incomplete, confined as it then will be, only to the six apertures in the grey matter of brain mentioned earlier, through which the microcosm can establish communion with the consciousness of Brahmanda and self conscious mind. However, by including the third factor of human existence referred to above, namely the-ultra-mind, we have to refer to the remaining six apertures which lie in the white matter of brain through which the microcosm can establish communion with the six sub divisions of purely spiritual region. The picture of the economy of the human microcosm as revealed in the Discourses on Radhasoami Faith will in this way be complete.

References

Cook, Norman D. (1986). *The Brain Code*. London, UK: Methuen & Company.

Dickinson, Emily (1976). *The Complete Poems of Emily Dickinson*. No. 632. Johnson, Thomas H. (Ed.). Boston, USA: Back Bay Books.

Dobzhansky, T. (1967). *The Biology of Ultimate Concern*. New York, USA: New American Library.

Donald, Merlin (1991). *Origins of the Modern Mind: Three Stages in the Evolution of Culture and Cognition*. Cambridge, MA, USA: Harvard University Press.

Eccles, J.C. (1970). *Facing Reality: Philosophical Adventures of a Brain Scientist*. Berlin, Heidelberg, Germany: Springer-Verlag.

Edleman, G.M. (1989). *The Remembered Present: A Biological Theory of Consciousness*. New York, USA: Basic Books.

Edelman, C..M. and Tononi, G. (2000). *A Universe of Consciousness*, p.5. New York, USA: Basic Books.

Maharaj Sahab [Pandit Brahm Sankar Misra Sahab] (1960). *Discourses on Radhasoami Faith.* Agra, India: Radhasomi Satsang Sabha, Dayalbagh.

Penrose, Roger (2005). *The Road to Reality: A Complete Guide to the Laws of Universe.* New York, USA: Alfred A. Knopf.

Popper, Karl and Eccles, John C. (1977). *The Self and Its Brain: An Argument for Interactionism.* Berlin, Heidelberg, Germany: Springer-Verlag.

Satsangi, P.S. [Revered Prof. Prem Saran Satsangi] (2006). Discourse Delivered in Satsang on 8th October, 2006, *The Dayalbagh Herald*, Tuesday, January 9, 2007.

Sriramamurti, P. (2005). Science of Spiritual Consciousness - the Super Science. Presented at the Seminar on Better Worldliness, Dayalbagh Educational Institute, Deemed University, Agra, India.

Szentagothi, J. (1969). Architecture of the Cerebral Cortex. Jasper, H.H., Ward, A.A. and Pope, A. (eds.). In *Basic Mechanisms of the Epilepsies*. Boston, USA: Little Brown.

Chapter 24

Challenges in Developing Science of Spirituality and Consciousness

RAVI K. SINHA
New Delhi, India

Abstract
This note traces the progress made in development of the science of consciousness and immense challenges confronting it. It focuses on the limitations of current scientific methods in dealing with consciousness encountered in quantum mechanics. Most scientists dismiss consciousness under the approach of "correct predictions are all one needs for all practical purposes, (FAPP)".They ignore what the eastern religion systems have been teaching for three millenniums about Maya, universal connectedness etc. The note highlights the need for a third revolution in scientific thinking similar to the dramatic course corrections in the scientific world after Copernicus's findings about motion of celestial bodies in the sixteenth century and the overtaking of the classical physics after the discovery of quantum mechanics. The Religion of Saints is the most scientific religion on earth. 'Discourses on Radhasoami Faith' by Param Guru Huzur Maharaj Sahab gives a scientific exposition the faith (based on then known concepts of science) that is unparalleled. The recent expositions by Most Revered Dr. Satsangi Sahab take the work of Maharaj Sahab forward with links to current state of science. His systems engineering background, sharp critical skills, wide and deep knowledge of sciences, very high intellect and wisdom combined with highest spiritual connections provides for a unique opportunity to the world to understand spirituality underpinned by science.

In researching for this paper I was intrigued to learn that inclusion of consciousness in scientific enquiry has faced huge road blocks in the last 300 years. I have decided to focus on the historical perspective of linkage between science and spirituality and the swings it has been through and to examine why science has come to dominate the world view.

Many thinkers feel that science is on the verge of another revolution perhaps bigger than the Copernican Revolution or the overturning of Newtonian physics by Quantum Mechanics. It may be that we are at a unique point of history of science and mankind when we might witness demolition of long held assumptions about the nature of science.

Copernican Revolution

Till the 16th and 17th century there were many inaccurate assumptions that held back the development of modern astronomy. One of the assumptions was that the Earth was the centre of the Universe.

Nicolas Copernicus, an unlikely revolutionary, challenged that assumption. In 1543 Copernicus published his treatise The Revolution of Celestial Spheres where a new view of the world was presented-the heliocentric model where the earth revolved around sun. This reluctant revolutionary set in motion a chain of events that would eventually produce the greatest revolution in thinking that Western civilization has seen. His ideas remained rather obscure for about 100 years after his death. But, in the 17th century the work of Kepler, Galileo, and Newton would build on the heliocentric Universe of Copernicus and produce the revolution that would sweep away completely the ideas of Aristotle and replace them with the modern view of astronomy and natural science. This sequence is commonly called the Copernican Revolution.

Ironically, this revolution led to another orthodoxy taking hold and therein lie the seeds of another potential revolution.

The modern world view that began to take shape in the 17th century was the result of a revolt against a system of thought that had come to seem repugnant. This new world view emphasized the empirical and reductionism. It separated the objective – which can be viewed by all – from the subjective which is viewed in the privacy of one's own mind. There were good reasons to concentrate on the objective and an important reason being to avoid a territorial clash with the institutions of religions.

The scientific became equated with reliably measurable, excluding a vast realm of human concern which was discounted as "subjective" or "metaphysical". This orthodoxy is now under challenge and we may be witnessing a new era of reunion of metaphysics and science.

It is probable that we are going through another profound change comparable to Copernican revolution. At the heart of it is a challenge to the prevailing knowledge authority system. It may be a time for reunion of science and metaphysics. Willis Harman in his book Global Mind Change says metaphysics has two quite different meanings in common usage. The first meaning refers to a branch of philosophy comprising ontology, dealing with the questions "what is reality?" and "how did it come to being?" and epistemology concerned with the question "how do we know?" The second meaning is the study of transcendent, the contacting of the reality that lies beyond the 'physical'.

In the first sense of the meaning of the term metaphysics, one can think of three different kinds of implicit metaphysics:

- M-1 - Materialism asserts that the basic stuff of universe is matter–energy. We learn about reality from studying the measurable world. All phenomena are products of their interactions of matter and energy.
- M-2 - Metaphysics is dualistic. Dualism asserts that the universe also contains "mind", which cannot be reduced to matter or energy, and is responsible for consciousness.
- M-3 - The third metaphysics finds that the ultimate stuff of the universe is consciousness. Consciousness is primary and matter–energy arises in some senses out of mind. Ultimately the reality behind the phenomenal world is contacted, not through the physical senses, but through the deep intuition. Consciousness is not the end product of material evolution; rather consciousness was here first!

The fundamental revolution that might be happening especially in the western society could be termed as shift of dominant metaphysics from M-1 to M-3.

In this context, it is useful to recall the quantum enigma which shows how physics has encountered consciousness. Quantum mechanics postulates particles as probability distributions with following characteristics:

- The "measurement problem"
- Entangled pairs
- Wave/particle duality

The quantum enigma, conventionally call the "measurement problem" appears right up front in the simplest quantum experiments. Though the enigma has confronted the physics for eight decades or more, it remains unresolved. Quantum theory tells us that observing an object to be some place causes it to be there. An object can be in two or many places at once–even at far distant places. Its existence at the particular place where it happens to be found becomes an actuality only upon its observation. It also tells us about entangled pairs i.e. an observation of one object can instantaneously influence the behaviour of another greatly distinct object – even if no physical force connects the two.

Another feature involves "quantum superposition" or wave particle duality. Components of isolated small scale systems can exist in different states or locations simultaneously. This is contrary to our perceived macroscopic world in which objects have well defined positions and are decidedly concrete. The problem is the transition-why and how does microscopic quantum superposed states become classical and definite in the macro-world? This problem is called quantum state reduction, or collapse of the wave function and it may be the key to both consciousness and reality.

Is Consciousness Purely Physical?

Traditional materialist view tends to regard consciousness as purely physical. Physical explanations have had extraordinary success elsewhere in science. However, increasing numbers of physicists are asserting that consciousness is necessary to bring the universe into being. Objects emerge from a transcendent possibility domain into the realm of physical manifestation when (non-local) consciousness "collapses the wave function". Consciousness is being viewed as an aspect of the "unbroken wholeness" which is the source of all existence. Positing consciousness as a more fundamental aspect of reality than space-time or matter-energy may be necessary in order to resolve the many paradoxes inherent in materialist interpretations of quantum mechanics.

It is interesting to recall the views of Evan Harris Walker from the book Physics of Consciousness. He tries to demonstrate how quantum physics reveals deeper truths about the consciousness and the universe. Walker argues that the consciousness is a property of electrons 'quantum tunnelling' through the brain. In other words electrons in atoms are all the time blipping out in one location and blipping back in at another location without ever crossing the space in between. This means particles in every atom of our body are disappearing and reappearing all the time. Apparently this is not a wild theory. Quantum tunnelling has been experimentally verified. One implication of this theory is that Consciousness and Will are defined as electrons tunnelling in and out of our space–time and bouncing back and forth inside our scalp as a standing wave while skipping across our brain's neural net to convert possibility into reality. The choice for what would be real is made between the quantum of time the electrons disappear and reappear. This also implies that mind or consciousness itself is not physical. Only the hosting hardware of our brain is physical.

Conclusion

I would like to emphasize that we may be on the cusp of another scientific revolution perhaps bigger than the Copernican revolution when the science would acknowledge and incorporate consciousness in its scope. Methods would be found to pursue scientific investigation of consciousness. We may live to see what may come to be regarded as a golden period of science when it goes through another revolutionary change in its world view and fundamental assumptions.

Dayalbagh is perhaps the only place on earth in present time where science and spirituality come together in a very powerful way under the guidance of Revered Dr Satsangi Sahab.

I find myself to be extremely fortunate to be associated with the Religion of Saints i.e. Radhasoami Faith. It is perhaps the most scientific religion on earth. In Discourses on Radhasoami Faith, Param Guru Maharaj Sahab gave scientific exposition of the faith based on the then known concepts of science. The recent expositions by Revered Dr Satsangi Sahab take the work of Maharaj Sahab forward with appropriate links to the current developments in Science. His systems, engineering background, sharp critical skills, wide and deep knowledge of sciences, super intellect and wisdom combined with highest spiritual experiences provides for a unique opportunity to the world to understand spirituality underpinned by science.

Chapter 25

Religion of Saints (Sants) - Radhasoami Faith: Pathway to Evolution of 'Complete'/ Holistic Science

RAJIV SINHA
DCM Shriram Consolidated Limited, India

Abstract

The proposition in this paper is presented in two parts: a) The nature and practice of the Radhasoami Faith, which renders it ever contemporary and modern and b.) The potential of the Faith to unify the objective science with the subjective experience leading to evolution of "Complete Science" and a unified approach to studies of consciousness. The first Part is an attempt to understand the manifested nature and the unique values of the Radhasoami Faith as well as the underlying principles and logic, which make It ever contemporary. The second Part examines how the current scientific inquiry continues to strictly adhere to facts/ideas that can be proven using physical experimentation i.e. objectivism while keeping itself sanitized from the experiential or the subjective domain. There is contradiction here as even some widely accepted scientific results have not been established through the physical approach route. The billions of dollars poured into the Large Hadron collider in the chase of elusive fundamental particle is but one recent example. The Radhasoami Faith, on the other hand, has an experiential approach to these questions, providing a way forward. Could the Radhasoami Faith be the bridge to unify these two streams?

The Radhasoami Faith as a Contemporary Religion

The Radhasoami Faith manifests an extraordinary quality of timelessness: It is as relevant and as fresh and modern in 2010 as it was in 1861 or 1910. The Faith is inclusive and thus reinforces the ever present social need for harmony in the current times. To put forth the arguments in favour of this notion, we may touch upon some salient areas:

It is a faith in which, without denying, or belittling other religions or faiths, it fully explains their relative reach from the perspective of spiritual realization. The followers of other faiths can realize/ experience different 'Dhams' or levels without any judgment call made, conflict or evocation of negative passions.

The Radhasoami Faith unambiguously defines the Object of Religion as attainment of Supreme Bliss .It then goes on to uniquely detail the path for each devotee to attain this spiritual goal and Ultimate Union with this Supreme Element. Yet the Faith shuns orthodoxy, rituals, cults and any kind of self-deprivation practices. I quote Most Revered Dr. Prem Saran Satsangi Sahab: **"Radhasoami Faith teaches us that one should earn spirituality while performing ones' duties in this world" and "that we should lead a life of 'Sanyas' as a householder."**

It promotes the concept of "better worldliness" and enshrines the principles of inclusiveness and welfare of communities. One of the paths by which a better world is evolving is with emphasis on complete education, thus physical, mental and spiritual education works as a means to help the Jiva in his journey.

By postulating the axiom of "Fatherhood of God and Brotherhood of Man" it very simply, yet powerfully provides a rationale for human existence and gives guidance for managing one's life. It envisages and promotes an egalitarian society – the very imperatives societies at large desperately want.

It even focuses on the urgent needs of the community at large, and beyond its followers, by being somewhat of a torch bearer. It is creating simple yet effective solutions, given its limited resources, in the areas of education and medical service.

The Faith teaches values which are basic and timeless for a peaceful and meaningful co-existence i.e. seva, tolerance, co-operation, hard work, eco friendliness, frugality etc. It in fact gives ample opportunities to devotees for 'Seva', along with instructions in *Bhajan* and *Dhyan*, in order to mould them into perfect agents for spiritual advancement and help them on this journey.

The Radhasoami Faith encourages the spirit of enquiry and discovery by laying core emphasis on high quality and value based education. In fact '*education and more education*' is seen as essential even in the journey towards realizing spiritual goals. Yet this is done with a broad based content embracing modern scientific education -vastly different in nature from the approach in a Seminary, Madrasa or an Ashram.The Faith also adapts to and utilizes contemporary technology effectively to better connect with followers. E- Satsang, which is the live telecast of prayer sessions held in the presence of the Spiritual Adept, is a recent example.

The presence of a Living Sant Sat Guru is an enormous blessing providing as it does a fountain of solace and Guidance for the seekers. The Sant Sat Guru's timely and objective Pronouncements continually provide Interpretation and Guidance to deal with the unique nature of contemporary life styles and pressures.

Pathway to the Evolution of a 'Complete'/Holistic Science

The Radhasoami Faith has the potential to unify the objective sciences with the subjective experiences leading to the evolution of a "Complete Science" and a unified approach to studies of consciousness. We may also examine here, how current scientific inquiry continues to strictly adhere to facts/ideas that can be proven using physical experimentation i.e. objectivism while keeping itself sanitized from the experiential or the subjective domain. There is a contradiction here as even some widely accepted scientific results have not been established through the physical approach route. The billions of dollars poured into the Large Hadron collider in the chase of the elusive fundamental particle is but one recent example. The Radhasoami Faith, on the other hand, has an experiential approach to these questions, providing a way forward. Could the Radhasoami Faith be the bridge to unify these two streams?

The Faith is unique as it is revealed on principles of sound reasoning and explanation even though the Exposition is Experiential.

It encapsulates the spirit of scientific enquiry – hallmark of current civilization – while exposing the limits of scientific rationality and the reach of current scientific knowledge and physical experimentation. It effortlessly amalgamates the state of current scientific knowledge be it the age of physics in 1907 or the continuing evolutions in quantum mechanics in 2010!!

It lucidly and logically reveals how "the spirit-force is the source of prime energy "and that the source of spirit is the true Supreme Being". (Discourses on Radhasoami Faith). It, in fact, succinctly highlights the gap between science and spirituality rather than denying one over the other. Significantly over the years the gap seems to have narrowed and there is a glimmer of realization amongst a few prominent scientists that the limits to unraveling the fundamentals of matter may require transcending the boundaries imposed by the current 'Vidya". This is further discussed below with examples.

From the Age of Aristotelian Reason ("Aristotle's writings on science are largely qualitative, as opposed to quantitative"- Wikipedia) commencing in fourth century BC, the human intellectual progress primarily sprang from subjective reasoning, logical deduction and the recording of observed phenomena. Over the subsequent centuries the voice of reason got covered under the opaque film of extreme religious beliefs, dogma and myths. By the dark Middle Ages even the torch bearers of science like Galileo were denounced to the Inquisition. Interestingly a quote attributed to him reads: "God wrote the universe in the language of mathematics" (Galileo). The pendulum had swung to one extreme.

This led to cry for reform and the spirit of scientific enquiry started to manifest itself through giants such as Francis Bacon, Leibniz and Newton etc.

In the following centuries, objective science gradually started occupying centre stage as the early breakthroughs provided enormous benefits to man in fields ranging from health to locomotion. There was nothing that science could not make possible. Thus over the past few centuries "subjectivity has been progressively excluded from the practice of science, leaving an essentially secular analytical paradigm (Robert Jahn)". We lost sight of the fact that experiential and inspirational learning was the other wheel piloting the progress along with objective experiments and theories. Science became sterile. The pendulum had now swung to the other extremity. Perhaps the scientific community has dug itself in an egotistical hole! Yet there are prominent figures from this community who no longer deny the need to examine the subjective if we have to move forward. More voices are being heard.

Science confines itself to reductionism. Yet the study of Psychology, considered to be an objective attempt to understand human consciousness, largely uses experiential or qualitative explanations to interpret the behaviour. Then should the postulates developed by the likes of Sigmund Freud, Carl Jung etc. be treated as illusions since these cannot be consistently established through experimentation? In a lighter vein, perhaps the next best seller by Richard Dawkins will thrash Freud and the practice of psychiatry!!

In a programme lasting over three decades (1979-2007) the Princeton Engineering Anomalies Research (PEAR) Laboratory under Dr. Robert G. Jahn studied the Science of Subjectivity by carrying out experiments to study the interaction of human consciousness with sensitive physical devices. Their premise was that any movement towards incorporating subjectivity into our scientific journey would mean acknowledgement of consciousness as a reality.

Through many experiments they concluded that, I quote "operator consciousness is capable of inserting information, in its most rudimentary objective form, namely binary bits, into the physical random number generator, by some anomalous means that is independent of space and time ------- Any attempt to set forth a theoretical model to complement such experimental data in a traditional scientific dialogue is an awesome epistemological task."

They went on to conclude "It is not unfounded, therefore to hope that the same exquisite consciousness that has so brilliantly conceived and refined its science of the objective, and that has at the same time so fully experienced and celebrated the subjective dimensions of its life, **can now finally integrate these complementary perspectives into a super-science of the whole, wherein consciousness will stand as full partner with its cosmos in the establishment of reality.**" Amazingly, going way beyond the above experiments, here at Dayalbagh we were advised to "study the effects of spiritual force-field directly on a base electro-magnetic field produced in the neighbourhood of a meditationist due to different stages of meditation". Thereafter unique experiment carried out in Dayalbagh in 2007 **"gave us some qualitative appreciation that as spirituality increased, the randomness (of Random Number Generator) reduced"!**

Though Quantum mechanics has been now studied over 100 years yet is, frustratingly for physicists, still only partly resolved. There are mostly interpretations of observed phenomena –perhaps in the realm of subjectivity!! John C. Mather of NASA, a noble laureate and the man behind deploying COBE satellite to study evidence of the physical Big Bang , recently expressed it well "The wonderful thing is that we don't know ,a conceptual breakthrough is needed." We have yet to conclusively establish whether the string theory , now with 'twistors' as postulated by Roger Penrose , finally succeeds in unifying all the particles and forces observed and the nature of space. Perhaps our self-imposed limitations of objectivism make us blind to the linkages with the realm of insight/intuition and experiential learning. There is almost a hard wired response to negating any impulse to find solutions by also considering the subjective realm!

It is here that the Religion of Saints manifests itself and provides a uniquely reasoned transition from the objective to the region of consciousness. In fact the three Grand Divisions so well explained in the Radhasoami Faith clearly define the continuum from Physical to the Mind and finally to the Plane of Spirituality thus establishing coexistence rather than a schism between the physical and the spiritual.

The revelations by the Param Sant Sat Gurus in fact show the bridge between scientific progress and the beginning of spirituality by logically establishing how the human form is precisely a microcosm of the Macrocosm.

Defining the spheres of 'Apar Vidya' – the current scientific knowledge – and 'Par Vidya' – as the pathway to spirituality, It is providing both a catalyst and direction to explore/ experiment ways to make the leap from pure scientific rationality to the universe of spirituality and finally to the Ultimate Reality. The Faith defines, in an analogous way, that Apar Vidya has in it the seeds to lead to Par Vidya, Concepts first brought out by the Most Revered Dr. Prem Saran Satsangi Sahab.

Though based on Experiential Revelations, It meticulously details the nature of the Spiritual Regions, the description of lower division, the location of Brahmand and 'And' while creating the linkages between these Regions of the macrocosm as reflected in microcosm in the human form.

From the times of Kabir Sahab the 'the first to come " and 'the son of the true Almighty, Supreme creator, Radhasoami", (*Discourses on Radhasoami Faith*) the Teaching of Saints have been consistent and in unison till the full Revelation by Param Guru Soamiji Maharaj.

Perhaps with such Guidance, the scientists/ intellectuals will be able to comprehend that the Region of Spiritual Consciousness exists beyond objective knowledge. Once the gap is understood to be transpersonal, intuitive and experiential, but not experimental- or even mystical! – the nature of spiritual consciousness will be realized. Thus, directionally Radhasoami Faith can provide the basis for studies of spiritual consciousness in a multi –disciplinary paradigm incorporating the objectivism of science with the subjective. Thus here need not be an 'either or' syndrome between science vs. spiritual consciousness and subjective knowledge, but rather a close integration for extending frontiers of our understanding.

There are also initiatives such as the University of Arizona, Tucson's 'Toward a Science of Consciousness' Conferences held annually which attract many scientists exploring such duality. An eminent mathematical physicist such as Roger Penrose hypothesized that quantum mechanics plays an essential role in the understanding of human consciousness(Ref: Emperor's New Mind) and his subsequent work with Stuart Hameroff to develop a biological analog of a quantum computer carries this forward(Ref. Shadows of the Mind)

It is, however, the extraordinarily reasoned structure of the "Discourses on Radhasoami Faith" that provides great clarity as to how the approach and practice of Radhasoami Faith is finally the way forward for human kind.

This has been expanded with a superbly detailed and explicit rendering of the structure of the Creation by the Most Revered Dr. Prem Saran Satsangi Sahab using the state-of-art scientific concepts of systems theory and quantum theory!!

There are a number of Sects of Radhasoami Faith totaling 30-35 lakh followers. Yet the basic Explanation and Revealation made by Param Guru Soamiji Maharaj is unchangeable and timeless and provides the connecting glue.

As Jivas we can only pray that one day we will experience that the boundaries imposed by the seemingly unbreachable scientific postulates such the Heisenberg Principle and the laws of irreversible Entropy may in fact be limiting only in the physical plane and as the knowledge advances and breaches the chasm between objectivism and first person experiential reality, the information content will overwhelm uncertainty and lead us to Ultimate Reality or Truth – under the Benevolent Guidance of Param Sant Sat Guru.

Science, by thus incorporating both the objective Apar Vidya and the subjective Par Vidya will then be truly 'Complete'. The quantum theory will then have its final resolution!!!

Finally, in words of Einstein, "Science without religion is lame; religion without science is blind", The Radhasoami Faith provides the continuum!

References

Jahn, R. G., and Dunne, B.J. (1997). Science of the Subjective. *Journal of Scientific Exploration*. 11.

Maharaj Sahab [Pt. Brahm Sankar Misra Sahab] (1960). *Discourses on Radhasoami Faith*. Agra, India: Radhasoami Satsang Sabha, Dayalbagh.

Chapter 26

Awakening Spiritual Consciousness

PAMI DUA
Delhi School of Economics, University of Delhi, India

ANITA KHETERPAL
Dayalbagh Educational Institute (Deemed University), Agra, India

Abstract

Spiritual consciousness is the light of all lights, foundation of all cognitions and the only Ultimate Reality. At the individual level it can be awakened and raised in three stages: first, by learning the art of meditation; second, by bringing about a personal transformation through meditation and ethical living; and third, by completely surrendering oneself at the Lotus Feet of the God Almighty or a perfect Guru. At the global level, the attainment of inner peace via raising spiritual consciousness at the individual level generates radiation and vibrations of love, tranquility and compassion resulting in human unity and universal love and in the feelings of Fatherhood of God and Brotherhood of Man.

Introduction

Many of the world's greatest thinkers, philosophers, saints, mystics, and founders of religion have spent their lives in the quest for permanent and everlasting peace, happiness and tranquility. The writings of many saints and mystics indicate that true happiness can be found within, by transcending physical consciousness and exploring spiritual regions. More and more people are trying to adopt the spiritual path in their pursuit for true and eternal happiness.

In fact, a deeper study into each religion reveals several mystic experiences described by the saints and spiritual adepts. Disciples are taught to rise above physical consciousness and explore spiritual planes by separating their consciousness from the physical body and traversing higher regions of consciousness or spiritual consciousness. Here, ***physical consciousness*** refers to our awareness of our body, our mind and the world around us whereas ***spiritual consciousness*** means becoming conscious of the soul and God within us. Spiritual consciousness is thus the consciousness at the level of the soul, independent of our body and mind.

We are, in fact, more than our body and mind. We are actually a soul, a conscious entity which inhabits the body. The soul is a part of the Over soul or God; it is of the same essence as God. The soul is what enlivens the body. When the soul leaves the body at the time of death, the body dies. But the soul does not die; it is immortal. Thus, we continue to exist even after the demise of the mortal frame. However, we do not have to wait until our physical end to realize the life at the level of the soul. The unbounded joys, exhilaration and inner peace and bliss that come from attaining spiritual consciousness can be experienced and enjoyed by anyone who wishes to develop this consciousness during their lifetime.

Steps to Awaken Spiritual Consciousness

There are four main steps towards awakening spiritual consciousness as follows. The first three are at the individual level while the fourth relates to the global level. Progress on this path can be achieved with the Grace and Mercy of the perfect Guru or Master.

1. The first step towards increasing spiritual consciousness is learning the art of meditation.

2. The next step is to achieve personal transformation so that we can lead a life in the world that can increase our spiritual consciousness. It involves living a life in such a way that our consciousness remains centered in our soul while we are attending to our worldly duties and responsibilities. This means that we develop spiritual qualities such as truthfulness, purity, humility, selfless service and nonviolence. This personal transformation can happen through meditation and ethical living.

3. The third step to spiritual consciousness is to completely surrender oneself at the Lotus Feet of the God Almighty or the perfect Guru. This stage can be interpreted as the epitome of personal transformation. At this stage, intellect has no role to play.

4. Once inner peace and personal transformation are achieved, a person would radiate love and compassion. This would in turn, contribute towards the attainment of outer peace and the dissemination of human unity and universal love resulting in the feelings of '*Fatherhood of God and Brotherhood of Man*'.

Each of the above steps is examined in more detail below.

1. Meditation

Meditation is the means by which we can separate our soul from the body and the world outside, and merge with God, the ocean of all-consciousness. It is the process of inverting our attention from the outer world and the body to focus on the doorway that leads to spiritual dimensions, the third eye, which is the highest *chakra* in the body. Through meditation, we can rise above our physical consciousness and discover the wealth of spiritual regions within and experience oneness of our soul with God and thus attain spiritual consciousness. Spiritual consciousness can be termed as all-consciousness. In other words, it is awareness of everything there is to be known and through meditation we gain access to this infinite source of wisdom.

Through the spiritual journey, the soul regains its original bliss and consciousness, which we have forgotten since the soul is environed by the body and mind and the illusion of the world.

The spirit or soul of man (*Atman* or *Surat*) is an emanation from the Supreme Being and the outer expression of the soul comprises 'attention', which is dissipated in our body and exits into the world via the five senses, viz., sight, hearing, smell, taste and touch. To rise from physical to spiritual consciousness, we have to withdraw our attention from the world outside and concentrate it at the seat of the soul. In the world, the soul is asleep until we awaken it spiritually with the help of a perfect Guru. It is only then that we become conscious of our true Home. What we believe to be consciousness in this world is merely a sleeping state compared to the consciousness experienced in the spiritual realms.

Meditation by *Surat Shabd Yoga* has been described as follows by Revered Gracious Huzur Professor P.S. Satsangi Sahab, the eighth Sant Satguru of the Radhasoami Faith:

"...if one meditates and practices what we call 'Surat Shabd Yoga' that is, the union of spirit force (current) with the sound current from the reservoir of the spirit force, then we have a communication channel (passage) available for the spirit force (current) to reach its reservoir by travelling up this sound current flowing back to the spiritual reservoir. The spirit force makes a journey within one's own human self (being) without going anywhere in the outer world so as to witness the Ultimate Reality at the highest level."

The process of withdrawing the soul from the body during meditation is the same as that which we undergo at the time of death. *"The primary difference is that when we leave the physical body at the time of death, a 'silver cord', which connects the soul with the body, breaks, and the soul, cannot return. But during meditation, the silver cord does not break and we can return to the body at will*[1]*"* (Sant Darshan Singh ji Maharaj).

Practicing meditation facilitates personal transformation that helps to focus our spiritual consciousness in our soul while undertaking our worldly responsibilities. As such, the process of meditation and awakening of spiritual consciousness does not eliminate the worldly problems of life, but provides us with a new angle of vision and perspective as we rise above the physical world into regions of peace and tranquility. The experience of inner intoxication and bliss helps us to become somewhat oblivious to our problems and sufferings and hence helps us to progress even further on the path of spiritual consciousness into realms of higher and higher consciousness and attain self-knowledge and God-realization.

2. Personal Transformation through Meditation and Ethical Living

After learning meditation, the next step towards spiritual consciousness is to achieve personal transformation so that we can lead a life in the world that increases our spiritual consciousness. This transformation can be achieved through meditation and by following the path of ethical living. The process of meditation helps to purify our soul. It helps us to counteract the negative influences in the world. We become less attached to worldly desires and the negative habits sparked by worldly attachments slowly fade away. We experience a personal transformation which involves living our life in such a way that our consciousness remains centered in our soul while we are attending

---

[1] Extracted from "*The Wonders of Inner Space – Mystic Talks*" by Sant Darshan Singh ji Maharaj.

to our worldly duties and responsibilities. This means that we develop spiritual qualities and ethical virtues such as humility, tolerance, compassion, love, kindness, forgiveness, honesty, purity, sincerity, simplicity, selfless service, respect, obedience, justice, cooperation, responsibility, hard work, courage, integrity, unity and nonviolence.

Personal transformation is an individual's journey within himself, a journey he undertakes when his soul is ready for the ascent to the higher domains. It is a journey of self awareness and an acceptance of one's weaknesses and strengths, of understanding one's beliefs and opinions. This self knowledge helps the individual to work on himself, so he can balance his weaknesses with his strengths, thus assisting him to purify his thoughts and deeds. The journey of the soul towards purification of our actions leads to personal transformation which enables us to live an ethical life with proper values, thereby kindling our ascent of spiritual consciousness.

During the journey of the spirit force within the body it is pulled down by various temptations and external forces and energies which detract our minds from the internal journey. We may be discouraged and impatient with the process and the progress. Resistance of the body, bodily habits, deep rooted mental tendencies, and intellect may produce obstacles in the practice of meditation. As described in Sar Bachan (Prose) composed by the August Founder of the Radhasoami Faith, Param Purush Puran Dhani Param Guru Huzur Soamiji Maharaj, "The roots of Kama, Krodha, Lobha, Moha and Ahamkara and the dirt of Asa and worldly desires are in the heart." As long as our attention is focused on the world around us, our physical body, and our constant stream of thoughts, we are unable to withdraw our sensory currents to the seat of the soul. However, for personal transformation to occur, the direction of the spirit force should be upwards.

We therefore need to understand what impedes the ascent of the spirit to higher domains and how we can overcome these obstacles. We can consider the human body as comprising three elements, viz., the physical body, the mind and the spirit. The fact is that the mind and the body are the main obstacles towards the ascent of the spirit to the higher domains.

The role of the mind and the body in impeding the rise of the spiritual force and the ways to overcome obstacles for engineering personal transformation through meditation for attaining higher spiritual consciousness is explained as under.

Obstacles in Mediation Related to the Mind and Body

Mind

It is noted in *Sar Bachan (Prose)* that "*Man's mind is just like an elephant in rut and goes in whatever direction it likes and the jiva is dragged behind*". The way to bring about deep spiritual change is to work at allowing the highest part of us, the divine force to become the dominant force in our life. This is possible by controlling the mind. In the process of controlling it, we make a conscious contact with the divine force within us. This facilitates the process of personal transformation.

Factors that affect the mind are as follows:

- **Mind chatter:** The mind's job is to keep us tied to the outer world. It will try to produce one thought after another, a constant flow of mind chatter. As long as our soul is identified with the mind it will also be dragged to the worldly temptations. The force of the mind is one of the greatest hindrances on our path back to God. It will keep accumulating more and more karmas to our already full storehouse.
- **Emotions, memories of past actions and depression:** Emotions are the reaction of the body to the mind. Emotions can be in the form of lust, anger, dissatisfaction, and restlessness. Past memories can lead to an explosion of emotions during meditation. Depression and melancholy also arise during meditation owing to previous samsakaras, bad company and ill health.
- **Ego:** The mind lives in a delusionary world of self importance and self absorption. The ego becomes the all important factor in our lives. In the Holy words of Param Guru Maharaj Sahab, the third Revered Sant Satguru of the Radhasoami Faith "As long as the veil of "I" and "You" continues to exist, the Supreme Lord remains invisible ....Every association with the world is false, i.e. covered with veil.[2]"
- **Lack of faith or doubt in the existence of God** and the lack of desire to meditate is a common ailment of the mind.
- **Lack of time:** The mind tends to blame everything and everyone else for the lack of time to meditate.
- **Temptations of worldly and materialistic desires** are the excuses that the mind makes in order to avoid the path of ethical values and spiritual upliftment.
- **Social Environment:** During meditation, the distractions from our daily life, our profession, our business and financial uncertainties and distractions from family, friends or interpersonal relationships obstruct our ascent to higher regions.

Physical Body

The human body is a temple, a replica of the spiritual regions, and it is in the human form that we are able to reach the Higher Domains. The body is an instrument for attaining self-realization. Factors that affect the body include the following:

- **Poor Health or Disease:** A sickly, dilapidated body stands in the way of meditation. This is a hindrance in the path of the meditator because it draws the mind again and again to the physical body and makes it difficult to keep it directed inwards.
- **Laziness leading to sleepiness and drowsiness:** Laziness, half-sleepy state, excessive sleep, mental inactivity, etc. are the products of

---

[2] Extracted from "*Selected Bachans of Param Guru Maharaj Sahab*", Radhasoami Satsang Sabha, Dayalbagh.

inertia. Some people have an apparently healthy physical body but lack nerve power so that they always feel below par and disinclined to take up any work requiring prolonged exertion. Whatever the cause of fatigue, it acts as an obstacle because it undermines all efforts to practice Sadhana.

- **Faulty Diet:** Eating too much, consuming unhealthy food, drinking alcohol or other intoxicants reduce concentration.

How to Overcome Obstacles to Achieve Personal Transformation

Self awareness and self analysis are major milestones to personal transformation. Once we have understood our goal of reaching the Almighty in this lifetime, we are able to use discrimination to make choices which will help our soul reach its eternal goal.

The most important step towards personal transformation is learning to control the mind. Param Guru Maharaj Sahab gives an example of 'Conquering or Controlling the Mind' as follows:

"When lightning flashes brightly and clouds thunder or some ferocious animal comes in front or some great calamity or trouble comes, the mind of man gets terribly shaken. If these conditions do not produce any effect on the mind of a person, that person can be said to have conquered his mind.[3]*"*

The methods for overcoming the obstacles of the mind and body in the process of meditation include the following:

Control of the mind

Higher consciousness is associated with exceptional control over one's mind and will power, leading to profound personal transformation and subsequently leading to spiritual growth and enlightenment. To meditate successfully the mind must be still. Some suggestions for controlling the mind are as follows:

- **Repeat the Holy Name:** To keep the mind still, disciples of the Sant Mat are taught to repeat the Holy Name at all times.
- **Make Satsang and Satsang activities the focal point of life:** The key to overcome the temptations of the worldly and materialistic desires is to follow the motto of "*simple living and high thinking*" prescribed by Param Guru Huzur Mehtaji Maharaj, the sixth Revered Sant Satguru of the Radhasoami Faith, and not be swayed by the evils of consumerism, materialism and unnecessary glamour. This can be achieved if the Satsang culture is deeply embedded in our lifestyles so that it becomes the focal point of our lifestyle. This would happen if while performing worldly activities, we continuously remember the advice of Param Guru Huzur Mehtaji Maharaj that "*Remember your Lord Almighty and begin every work with His Name in your heart or on your lips.*"

---

[3] Extracted from "*Selected Bachans of Param Guru Maharaj Sahab*", Radhasoami Satsang Sabha, Dayalbagh.

With Supreme Grace, a conscious effort can be made to discipline our lifestyle so that we are able to devote time to Seva, Satsang and Abhyas and remember the mandate of Revered Gracious Huzur Professor P.S. Satsangi Sahab that:

'Sab dukhon ka ek elaaj, satsang, seva aur abhyas'

In this manner, our minds will always be occupied with Satsang and Satsang related activities and we would be able to protect ourselves from distractions and temptations of worldly life. The advice of Param Guru Huzur Mehtaji Maharaj can be followed that "*Never throw yourself in environments wherein your heart and mind may get excited and you may not be able to control them.*"

- **Adopt 'Better Worldliness':** 'Better worldliness' can be the essence of our life which is, to quote Revered Gracious Huzur Professor P.S. Satsangi Sahab, "*characterized by a life-style in which the attributes of spirit will also have the fuller expression along with the attributes of body and mind' and we should 'engage regularly in community service, and spiritual practice for ascension of intuitive consciousness.*" We should follow neither the path of 'unworldliness' nor that of 'pleasure seeking worldliness'. Instead, "*we must pursue the ideal of better worldliness in consonance with the teachings of Satsang, in which, alongside physical development and mental development, Spiritual development may also take place; that is there may be a balanced all round development.*"
- **Be Detached from Worldly Activities:** Detachment is an inner state of calmness and being uninvolved on the emotional and mental planes. Real detachment means inner strength, and the ability to function calmly and with full inner control under all circumstances. A detached person is not harassed and hassled, and can do everything with concentration and attention, thus ensuring successful outcomes of his actions. Guru Nanak has said that we should be like the lotus flower which stays in the water and is yet unaffected by it. To quote Maharaj Charan Singh ji[4],

  "Only attachment creates detachment. Detachment does not create any attachment."

- **Fear of the Guru and others:** Some kind of fear may be desirable for the correction of the mind. Param Guru Huzur Maharaj, the second Revered Sant Satguru of the Radhasoami Faith, in the scripture, Prem Patra Part V lists the fear of the Guru, of one's cast, relations and friends, of one's honour, of death and pain, of Government officers, of family deities and of life after death. Regarding professional life, Param Guru Sarkar Sahab, the fourth Revered Sant Satguru of the Radhasoami Faith noted that "*......the*

---

[4] Extracted from "*The Master Speaks*" by Maharaj Charan Singh ji of Radhasoami Satsang, Beas.

strictness and the pressure by officers keep the mind under restraint[5]".

- **Study religious books:** Doubt and lack of faith can be removed by Satsang, study of religious books, good thoughts and reasoning.
- **Develop love for the Guru.** Strong distractions and obstacles of the mind and body are caused when the mind is not ready for meditation, when the intellectual area of the mind is overpowering. For this, we need the Grace, Mercy and Blessings of a Guru, whose *darshana* will give us the extra power to move awareness permanently out of the areas of distraction. He will help us to move out of the intellectual areas of the body and change the energy flow within our body.
- **Follow Ethical Living and Adopt Religious Code of Conduct:** Personal transformation is also feasible if we follow the underlying simple code of conduct of the Radhasoami Faith of virtue and vice; virtue being all such thoughts and acts that lead one nearer to the Supreme Lord, while vice is all that leads one away from the Lord.

Pursuit of meditation and ethical living are stepping stones to the highest domain. A conscious effort has to be made to weed out the ethical lacunae of mind and body before we can reach personal transformation and self awareness. In the Holy words of Param Guru Huzur Sahabji Maharaj,

"*Good ethical behaviour can be acquired if one has right understanding and can also be acquired by following the teachings of religion.*"

- **Believe in the Power of Now:** A small and effective technique is "*Living in the moment*". Here we have to make an effort to consciously rise above the thoughts and fears of the past and the uncertainties of the future to be present in the now. The stillness of the mind and the freedom from the nonstop chatter of the thoughts will help to break the major obstacle in the path of meditation. We have to understand that:

"*Past is history, future is a mystery, and present is a gift.*"

- **Inculcate an Attitude of Gratitude:** One of the biggest hindrances to achieving success in meditation is the negative thoughts resulting from the failures and downsides in our life. Developing an attitude of gratitude has a positive impact on the way we think and feel. It is an acceptance of the situation as it is, leading to peace and gratitude.
- **Selfless Service to Mankind:** True selfless service is an expression of love. It encompasses helping more than our own physical family – it includes all humanity, without any expectation of reward or appreciation.

---

[5] Extracted from "*Selected Bachans of Param Guru Sarkar Sahab,*" Radhasoami Satsang Sabha, Dayalbagh.

- **Maintain a Healthy, Physical body:** A healthy vegetarian diet and a disciplined life with proper physical exercises help in controlling the mind. Drugs and intoxicants which dull our mind and lead to laziness and drowsiness should be avoided.

The real essence of attaining higher levels of spiritual consciousness and personal transformation is to surrender oneself to the Sant Satguru as described in *Sar Bachan (Prose)*, an extract of which is given below:

"Two tigers are pursuing this Jiva and these are: (i) Kala and (ii) Mind. As long as both of these are not killed, no progress in paramartha can be made and there is none else, except the Satguru, who can kill them. Hence he alone who surrenders himself to the Sant Satguru will be able to overcome them and he alone would go beyond the Region dominated by them."

3. Complete Surrender

Complete surrender to the *Will* and the *Mauj* of the Supreme Being facilitates the awakening of spiritual consciousness. It is the path of placing ourselves entirely in the hands of the Sant Satguru, and whatever happens, nothing should shake our faith in Him. Only the Sant Satguru knows the turns and twists on the spiritual path, and He alone can help us to traverse this path. Surrendering ourselves at the Lotus Feet of the God Almighty implies that we stop applying our intellect. Surrendering does not mean simply resigning ourselves to whatever is happening. It is a much higher stage where we accept the Sant Satguru or Master as the doer in our life.

Complete surrender is possible when the process of personal transformation is complete in all respects. Adopting the path of complete surrender helps us to reach our destination more easily.

The concept of complete surrender is fittingly described by Param Guru Huzur Sahabji Maharaj, the fifth Revered Sant Satguru of the Radhasoami faith as follows:

"Whatever Radhasoami Dayal is pleased to give, we must accept with an open mind. If He makes me a king, I will sit on the throne in a way that no king ever sat before, and if He makes me roll in dust, I will roll and roll in such a way that no beggar ever rolled before."

If we are able to unconditionally surrender ourselves at the Lotus Feet of the God Almighty, we have attained the epitome of personal transformation. At this stage, we radiate kindness, love, affection and compassion to all who cross our paths. Our inner peace and harmony generates outer peace and universal love.

4. Inner and Outer Peace and Attainment of Human Unity, Universal Love and Global Peace

Increasing spiritual consciousness via meditation, personal transformation, and subsequently complete surrender at the Lotus Feet of the God Almighty can have far reaching effects.

In the Holy words of Sant Rajinder Singh ji Maharaj[6] :

"*When we rise above body-consciousness during meditation, cross the planes of creation and reunite with God, we become completely filled with peace and harmony. Not only do we live more happy and balanced lives, receiving the joy of God's love, but we also radiate peace and joy to those around us. We see all other people, indeed all life forms, as part of God. Once we see the divine Light of God and realize that Light is in all people and creatures, we never again hurt anyone, speak harshly, or think ill of anyone. ....We experience peace within, and the world becomes peaceful because its inhabitants are peaceful.*"

Furthermore, "*A transformed world transforms the cosmos. ....When people of all religions and nations experience this transformation; we will see the morning of the Golden Age. We will respect all; strife and hatred will disappear from our planet, and peace will reign.*"

Thus, the attainment of inner peace via raising spiritual consciousness is the key to human unity and universal love resulting in the feelings of *Fatherhood of God and Brotherhood of Man*. Through meditation and personal transformation, we can become ambassadors of God's love. Once we have attained our union with God, human unity and global peace will become natural by-products.

Conclusions

In the Holy words of Param Guru Huzur Sahabji Maharaj,"*Providence has located within human body, a special spiritual faculty, and it is the exclusive function of religion to teach man all about that faculty. When that faculty is developed in us like our other physical and mental faculties, we shall be able to perceive Truth and realize Ultimate Reality in the same manner as we perceive and realize the sun with our physical eyes.*"

The four methods and or stages of raising spiritual consciousness starting from the individual level to the level of all mankind have been explained in this paper. At the human level, we can describe various ways of achieving spiritual consciousness. The reality is that nothing can be achieved without the *Mauj* or *Will* of the God Almighty or the perfect Guru. We can only try to meditate and thereby bring about a personal transformation but our efforts would be futile without Grace and Mercy of the God Almighty or the perfect Guru. To quote from *Sar Bachan (Prose)*.

---

[6] Extracted from "*Discover the Divine Within You*" by Sant Rajinder Singh Ji Maharaj, Head of Sawan Kirpal Ruhani Mission.

"One's efforts and Lord's Mercy both go together. One cannot make any effort without the Lord's Mercy and if one does make any effort, the Lord will not show His Mercy."

The essence of increasing spiritual consciousness is to pray most humbly at the Lotus Feet of the God Almighty or the perfect Guru that He may shower Grace and Mercy and make us worthy of receiving His Blessings and Grace so that we may progress on the path of attaining higher and higher levels of spiritual consciousness.

We may also pray that Grace and Mercy may be showered on all mankind so that the entire world may be engulfed in higher levels of spiritual consciousness such that globally, we may submit the prayer of Param Guru Huzur Sahabji Maharaj, the fifth Revered Sant Satguru of the Radhasoami Faith and the August Founder of Dayalbagh that:

"Let us live like humble servants of the Supreme Father, let us live like dutiful children of the Supreme Father and let us love each other like earnest devotees of the Supreme Father."

References

Huzur Maharaj [Rai Bahadur Salig Ram Sahab] (1960). *Prem Patra Part V*. Agra, India: Radhasoami Satsang Sabha, Dayalbagh.

Maharaj Charan Singh (1973). *The Master Speaks*. Punjab, India: Radhasoami Satsang, Beas.

Maharaj Sahab [Pt. Brahm Sankar Misra Sahab] (1982). *Selected Bachans*. Agra, India: Radhasoami Satsang Sabha, Dayalbagh.

Param Purush Puran Dhani Huzur Soamiji Maharaj. [Shiv Dayal Singh Sahab] (2005). *Sar Bachan (Prose)*. Agra, India: Radhasoami Satsang Sabha, Dayalbagh.

Sarkar Sahab [Kamta Prasad Sinha Sahab] (1983). *Selected Bachans*. Agra, India: Radhasoami Satsang Sabha, Dayalbagh.

Sant Darshan Singh ji Maharaj (1988). *The Wonders of Inner Space – Mystic Talks*. India: Sawan Kirpal Publications.

Sant Rajinder Singh ji Maharaj (2006). *Discover the Divine Within You*, New Delhi, India: Penguin.

Chapter 27

Spiritual Consciousness and Universal Love: Sant Mat Philosophy

GUR PYARI MEHRA
ONGC, India

Abstract

Spiritual Consciousness is a condition of being consciously in touch, not only with other souls but with Cosmic Consciousness, God and the Divine Mind. The secret of God's mystery is Love which originates in the original unmanifest Infinite Consciousness. Love alone bridges the great gulf between the finite and the infinite. Reason and logic end within the realm of the mind, but love is the symphony of the soul, and its radiant tones resound throughout all creation. This paper describes the nature of Spiritual Consciousness, Spiritual Joy and the Principles of Surat Shabd Yog – the shortest and farthest path into one's inner space, which is the path of love and surrender, taught by the Saints. It further presents the importance of Guru Bhakti, Satsang, Sewa and Abhyaas as described in the teachings of the Radhasoami Faith.

Introduction

सुरत प्रेम की बुंद अकथ इसका ब्योहारा

अंशी प्रेम भंडार प्रीति उस अगम अपारा ।

The only Sara Vastu (True substance) in this world is Prema or Love. Love is a vibration of the Spirit. It is eternal, infinite and undecaying. Physical love is passion or Moha or infatuation. Universal love is divine love. Cosmic Love, universal Love are synonymous terms. Universal Love terminates in Advaitic unity or oneness or Upanishadic consciousness of seers and sages. Hafiz, Kabir, Nanak, Tulsi Sahab, Mira, Gouranga, Tukaram, Ramadas, all have tasted this universal love. Sant Kabir Sahab expressed it as

"पी ले प्याला हो मतवाला प्यला नाम अमीं रस का रे"

Everyone has within him the reservoir of love for Lord, but it is concealed under the dirt of worldly desires. This dirt can be removed through Satsang, devotional practices and *Vairag*. It is only when one has achieved purification of his mind that the Love for Lord is engendered in his heart.

पोथी पढ़ पढ़ जग मुआ, पंडित भया न कोय,

ढाई अक्षर प्रेम का पढ़े सेा पंडित होय ।

The Spirit as Consciousness

Spiritual Consciousness is a condition of Being consciously in touch with not only other souls but with cosmic consciousness and God. It is at this spiritual plane that we transcend the limitations of our emotions, feelings, and thoughts, and instead gain a new unified perception of life. The spiritual plane can be reflected in our lives at first as silence, light, and intuition. At more advanced levels it is expressed as a unitary consciousness, where all conflicting thoughts, ideas, events, and life circumstances are reconciled into a greater harmony. The gateway to higher levels of consciousness is our heart.

Our day to day activities are generally governed by the conscious, subconscious and unconscious mind. The spiritual element of consciousness is least familiar to us and remains distant or subconscious to our daily existence. Spirituality is inner joy of life or higher frequency of consciousness. When the conscious mind catches even a glimpse of spiritual essence one feels the joy and excitement. Spiritual Consciousness has various levels. The joy and bliss that is experienced at the highest level of Spiritual Region is so great that one is lost in ecstasy and words fail to describe the intensity of self absorption and love.

Universal Love and Sant Mat

Universal Love is beyond any form of human love, including human true love and it encompasses everything. According to Sant Mat philosophy:

The spirit is the ***Ansh*** of Supreme Being. It is internally tied down ***to indriyas, tattvas*** and ***mind*** and externally to worldly objects, family and kinship. Kabir Sahab described that all worldly pleasures and enjoyments are transitory and false:

यह दुनियां दो रोज की, मत कर या से हेत,

गुरू चरनन से लागिये, जो पूरन सुख देत ।

Tulsi Sahab in his Bani conveyed that being encased in the human body the spirit is suffering from all kinds of miseries, except for those who have true love in the Holy Feet of the Satguru:

कोई तो तन मन दुखी, कोई चित्त उदास,

एक एक दुख सबन को , सुखी संत को दास ।

No individual can safely traverse the inner path without the aid of an unerring guide. The Guru has been placed on a pedestal even higher than God. In Bhakti, at the highest level of surrender, the ego of the devotee totally vanishes after which the spirit blissfully enjoys oneness with the Lord:

जब मै था तब हरि नही जब हरि तब मैं नहिं,

प्रेम गली अति सांकरी जामें दो ना समाय ।

The shortest and the farthest path into the inner space is through Surat-Shabd Yoga.

Universal Love and Spiritual Progress in the Radhasoami Faith

The Supreme Being Merciful Radhasoami is the reservoir of Love. The Spirit which is His Ansa or current is also love. Hence as long as Love is not engendered in the Spirit, the Spirit cannot establish contact with its Reservoir.

The Supreme Creator or Being has the features of Supreme Intelligence, Bliss, Energy and Luminosity. It does not have any form or any Shape.

राधास्वामी प्रेम के निज भंडारी, राधास्वामी प्रेम से रची रचना री।

सत चित आनंद यह गुन भारी, और चौथे परकाश अपारी।

ये चारों मिल प्रेम कहा री, प्रेम धार के अग ये चारी ।

Love or affection is but another name of the force of attraction i.e., (Quvat-i-Jalba). It is on account of this force that the entire creation which has come into existence through the combination of small particles and atoms is being maintained and it is also on account of this force that all the bodies i.e., all forms in the creation are being maintained and are carrying out their functions. If there was no love, friendship would not exist and one would not apply their mind to any work.

The region of *Sat Lok* and *Such Khand* is a very elevated region and is the Darbar of Saints. There are three other regions above it which were not formerly revealed by any Saint. Param Purush Puran Dhani Merciful Radhasoami Dayal, on account of his great Compassion for the Jivas has now clearly described these regions and also mercifully revealed the Secret of the Highest Region.

Surat Shabd Yoga, is the yogic practice of uniting Atman or Surat with the sound currents which accompanies all emanations of the Spirit Current.

If you repeat the Mystic word "**Radhasoami**" not by the external tongue, nor the tongue of the mind, but by the tongue of the Spirit, then you can hear the sound more clearly. It will work out in the form of a crescendo and this musical sound will attract and take you to the higher regions. In this way one can - the pilgrim Spirit can make its journey upwards in stages, till it finally reaches the Supreme Being.

As long as the spirit does not cut or loosen the bonds which have grown up with its physical, subtle, and causal bodies i.e., body, mind and sense organs and does not turn towards it's original abode after discarding the impure regions pertaining to Pind and Brahamand,and does not go beyond the Brahmandi mind, the knot between spirit and matter would not be loosened.

Spiritual Progress through Love in the Holy Feet of the Satguru

It is not possible for the spirit to return to its original abode without the grace of a perfect preceptor or Satguru. It is desirable for all that they should first offer prayers in the Holy feet of the Satguru and then engage the spirit in the contemplation of the holy form. The pleasure of Satguru can be achieved through humility and submission.

जब गुरू से हुआ गहरा प्यार ,शब्द भेद तब मिलिया सार ।

सतसंगी सब प्यारे लागें गहिरी प्रीति परस्पर पाले ।

दया भाव जीवन में आवे सुरत अंस घट धट नजरावे ।

Initiation is the process by which the power of the master removes the veil shrouding the inner eye, inner ear and freezes the Karma .The initiated devotees are known as "प्रेमी भाई और प्रेमिन बहन"

The Karmas of everyone who sincerely develop love for the Holy Feet are to be eradicated, and in this process one has to undergo some suffering. An increase in eagerness, yearning, uneasiness, worry and love are indicative of the gift of Grace and Mercy by the Satguru Merciful Radhasoami Dayal,

This vairag or detachment from the world and Anurag, i.e., love for the Satguru and the Lord can be engendered in the association of the Satguru or Sadh. When the love ripens, Adhikari Jeeva turns inward and engages in Spiritual Practice and gets Internal Joy.

Amrit Bachan Of Param Purush Puran Dhani Radhasoami Sahab Regarding Love

This path is the Path of Love and Love cannot be attained without Satsang.

One should First of all develop Love for the Satguru. One cannot achieve anything without the help of the Satguru of the time.

Whosoever has Love for the Satguru and Faith in him would be able to contact Shabda.

Both the things i.e., devotion to the Guru and the World cannot be accomplished at the same time.

Unless one has to some extent such eagerness, love and faith (as mentioned above), it is very difficult to traverse the path internally or to receive any revelation of the glory of the Lord, because as long as some eagerness, love and faith do not fill one's path, his spirit, mind and senses would not get concentrated and would not apply themselves to the practices nor would he get any joy in them.

As long as one does not act according to the orders of saints, the mind cannot be purified.

The Love of the Lord is necessary both to enable one to surrender himself to the Lord and to perform one's practices. He alone who has a true desire to reach the Supreme Being can subjugate this capricious mind.

The condition of the Jeeva is such that whatever efforts he may make, he cannot move up from the plane of the mind and he comes down again and again. The Form of Satguru helps the devotee in ascending within one self. (जो कुछ करें, करें गुरु प्यारे जीव निवल क्या कार कमाये)**.** One cannot achieve anything without the help of the Satguru of the present time.

Satsangis are fortunate to have the opportunity to join this faith where they can enjoy Spiritual Experiences of the highest order:

दयालबाग में जो गतिविधियां हो रही हैं ये उसी तरह की हैं जो दयाल देश में होती हैं । – – – – जैसा हुजूर साहबजी महाराज नें फरमाया है यह नर्दुमपरस्ती नहीं है , यह किसी मनुष्य की पूजा नहीं है । आप सतगुरू के मन या शरीर की पूजा नहीं करते। आप सतगुरू के मन या शरीर में निहित सुरत जो राधास्वामी दयाल से जुड़ी हुई है उसकी पूजा करते हैं । तो यह राधास्वामी दयाल की पूजा है, भक्ति है जो हमारा सतसंग सिखाता है ।

पर यह स्थूल रूप से प्रारम्भ होती है तो आप सतगुरू के प्रति प्रेम और प्रतीति दृढ़ करते हैं धीरे धीरे यह सूक्ष्म होता जाता है।

निर्गुण भक्ति करना वैसे असंभव है पर यह तरीका जो राधास्वामी दयाल ने अख्तियार किया कि सगुण भक्ति से आरम्भ करके आपको निर्गुण भक्ति तक ले जाते हैं तो आप वहां तक पहुंच पाते हैं।

The entire spiritual journey is propelled by love and a desire to approach the Supreme Father. This love and faith are also granted by Him, and one day he would grant His fullest love and faith. When the love of the Lord gets fully enshrined in the higher mind, it then begins to grow and it would also then be more or less permanent.

In other words, the extent to which the desires and impulses of worldly things are reduced would correspond to the extent that the desire for Parmarth become strong, and then one would apply himself internally with purity and ease in practice. This would lead to the experience of more and more bliss and joy.

A true devotee prays for the gift of Love Only:

प्रेम दात गुरू दीजिए मेरे समरथ दाता हो।
प्रेम रंग भीजत रहूं ए नित तुम ही धियाता हो ।

References

Huzur Maharaj [Rai Bahadur Salig Ram Sahab] (1960). *Prem Bani*, Part-4, Shabd 10, 81 and 141. Agra, India: Radhasoami Satsang Sabha, Dayalbagh.

Huzur Maharaj [Rai Bahadur Salig Ram Sahab] (1958). *Prem Patra*, 148. Agra, India: Radhasoami Satsang Sabha, Dayalbagh.

Huzur Maharaj [Rai Bahadur Salig Ram Sahab] (2009). *Prem Updesh*, 38. Agra, India: Radhasoami Satsang Sabha, Dayalbagh.

Huzur Maharaj [Rai Bahadur Salig Ram Sahab] (2009). *Prem Updesh,* 3. Agra, India: Radhasoami Satsang Sabha, Dayalbagh.

Maharaj Sahab [Pt. Brahm Sankar Misra Sahab] (2004). *Discourses on Radhasoami Faith (with supplement).* Agra, India: Radhasomi Satsang Sabha, Dayalbagh.

Param Purush Puran Dhani Huzur Soamiji Maharaj [Shiv Dayal Singh Sahab] (1998). *Sar Bachan* (Prose), Shabda 7. Agra, India: Radhasoami Satsang Sabha, Dayalbagh.

Param Purush Puran Dhani Huzur Soamiji Maharaj [Shiv Dayal Singh Sahab] (1998). *Sar Bachan* (Prose), Shabda 65. Agra, India: Radhasoami Satsang Sabha, Dayalbagh.

Sahabji Maharaj [Sir Anand Sarup Kt.] (1997). *Prem Bilas,* Shabd 68, 92. Agra, India: Radhasoami Satsang Sabha, Dayalbagh.

Sahabji Maharaj [Sir Anand Sarup Kt.] (1997). *Prem Bilas*, Shabd 15, 19. Agra, India: Radhasoami Satsang Sabha, Dayalbagh.

Sant Bani Sangrah. 66. Agra, India: Radhasoami Satsang Sabha, Dayalbagh.

Sant Bani Sangrah. 74. Agra, India: Radhasoami Satsang Sabha, Dayalbagh.

Singh,G., and Kashyap,V. *Kabir Dohawali.* Agra, India: Sadhana Publication.

Chapter 28

Surat Shabda Yoga is the Only Means to Attain Highest Spiritual Consciousness

SARAN PYARI ROY
Dayalbagh Educational Institute (Deemed University), Agra, India

Abstract
In modern times of extreme materialism and suffering, i.e., Kalyuga, we have been blessed with incarnations in the form of Saints who have revealed the highest level of spiritual consciousness and the means to attain it. This meditational method is called Surat Shabda Yoga, i.e, the art of harmonizing one's spirit with the spiritual sound currents of higher regions.In this paper, an effort has been made to emphasize the importance of this technique to achieve the highest objective by highlighting, (i) the universality of this approach propagated by various Saints, and that (ii) the sound current sustains the creation at different levels of existence and is the true form of the Sant Satguru (Shabda Guru) – the exalted spiritual teacher and preceptor of the time, who is in communion with the highest region. Satsang and seva help in this endeavour by developing the right outlook, peace of mind, detachment and lightening the burden of karmas.

Introduction

ईश्वर ने मनुष्य को सृष्टि में सभी जीवों से श्रेष्ठ बनाया और उसमें विवेक शक्ति (wisdom) और अन्य उच्च कोटि की शक्तियों का समावेश किया कि जिनके जागृत होने पर वह अपनी चैतन्य शक्ति का विकास कर इस जड़ जगत के ऊपर स्थित चैतन्य लोकों के सुखों का आनन्द ले सकता है।

इस संसार में केवल दो वस्तुएँ हैं। जड़ और चेतन, मानव शरीर व मन तो समय व काल अनुसार नाश हो जाता है।

"If all those components of our body, which are subject to change, be removed from our body then the immutable essence which would be left behind is our real self, our vital force, our surat, our spirit." साधारण जीवन में हम जिस चेतन शक्ति से दैनिक कार्य करते हैं उसमें और आध्यात्मिक चेतना में बहुत अन्तर है क्योंकि मेरे ''अंह'' का ज्ञान का संबध मस्तिष्क से है न कि आत्मा से ।

"Spirit is different from the conscious self or "I" in us. The conscious self in ordinary humanity is the mind, which like physical body receives life and vitality from the spirit. The spirit is life giving and vitalizing principle in man. It is the creator and sustainer of the universe." (Page 3, Writings & Speeches, Param Guru Huzur Sahabji Maharaj.")

अतः स्पष्ट है – आत्मा ही शरीर व मन को जान देती है।

''सुरत प्राण शक्ति या जान के जौहर का एक केन्द्र है कि जहाँ से धारें निकल कर शरीर और मन को जान देती है।'' (पेज 13 अमृत बचन, परम गुरु साहब जी महाराज)

परन्तु मानव इस जौहर को तभी देख सकता है जब आध्यात्मिक साधना द्वारा अन्तः चक्षुओं को जागृत किया जाये। आत्मा का वास्तविक रुप सत्त चित्त आनन्द है। और तन व मन के

बंधनों से मुक्त होकर दसम द्वारे के पास पहुँचती है तभी वह अपना असली रुप देख सकती है। उस समय जब उसे अपने अस्तित्व का ज्ञान होता है वही आध्यात्मिक चेतना है।

"There are a number of other centers ....that gifted ones obtain flashes of intuition and peeps into the mysteries of spiritual planes. Among these centres there is one known in the language of adepts as "Dasma dwara" the tenth door. Which if energized produces spiritual consciousness and opens the way to the mansion of the supreme spirit. (Page 6, Writings & Speeches, Param Guru Huzur Sahabji Maharaj.".)

Meditation of Holy Names and Mantras

पुराने समय में आध्यात्मिक चेतना के विकास के लिए अभ्यासी मूल चक्र यानि गुदा चक्र से अभ्यास शुरू करते थे कोई अष्टाँग योग यानि प्राणायाम जिसमें सांस रोकना पड़ता है करते थे और दूसरे अभ्यास मुद्रा हठ योग, आदि भी प्रचलित थे। पंतञली महाराज ने भी योग सूत्रों में मंत्रों के जाप करने की विधियाँ बताई है। हिन्दू धर्म में गायत्री मंत्र और साम मंत्रों को विषेश महत्व दिया जाता है इसी प्रकार पवित्र नाम ओंकार का सुमिरन करने की साधना द्वारा आध्यात्मिक चेतना के विकास का मार्ग बताते हैं। विभिन्न आध्यात्मिक स्थानों के अधिष्ठाताओं तक पँहुचने के लिए विभिन्न नामों का जाप आवश्यक है।

किन्तु बाद में संत मत का प्रारम्भ हुआ और उन्होनें ब्रहम और पारब्रहम से आगे सत्तलोक व 'सत्तनाम' 'सार शब्द' का बखान किया और सुरत–शब्द मार्ग का प्रचार किया।

''थोड़े से नाम पूरे और सच्चे संतो के और सच्चे साध फ़कीरों के जो पिछले 700 वर्ष में प्रकट हुए यहाँ लिखे जाते हैं। कबीर साहब, तुलसी साहब, जगजीवन साहब, गरीबदास जी, पलटू साहब, गुरुनानक, दादू जी, तुलसीदास जी, नाभा जी, स्वामी हरिदास जी, सूरदास जी और रैदास जी और मुसलमानों में ऐसे शम्सतबरेज़, मौलवी रूम, हाफिज़ सरमद, मुजहिद। इन साहबों के बचन बानि देखने से हाल उनकी पहुँच और स्थान का मालूम हो सकता है। (पृष्ठ 253, यथार्थ प्रकाश, भाग 1व 2)

कबीर साहब ने भी सुरत–शब्द योग को आध्यात्मिक चेतना के विकास का उत्तम साधन माना है।

कबीर साहब ने जिस आध्यात्मिक चेतना का गहन अनुभव किया वह तीन लोक से कहीं उच्च चैतन्य मंडलों की चेतना थी–

''तीन लोक नौखड में, गुरु ते बड़ा न कोई, ।
करता करै न कर सके गुरु करे सोई होई'' ।।
(संतबानी संग्रह, भाग 1 पृष्ठ 8)

कबीर साहब ने जिस गुरु की महिमा का वर्णन किया है वह साधारण गुरु का शरीर नहीं है अपितु शब्द गुरु की भक्ति है।

''गुरु हमारा गगन में, चेला है चित्त मांहि, सुरत शब्द मेला भया बिछुडत कबहुं नाहि।।
सुरत समानी नाम में, नाम किया परकास, पति बरता पति को मिली पलक न छोडे पास ।।
(संतबानी संग्रह पृष्ठ 7,18)

कबीर साहब के अनुसार शब्द की धारा ही परम शक्ति से हमारा सम्पर्क करा सकती है।

शब्द की धार (Nada Current) लाखों कोस दूर गुरु से हमारा प्रतिपल मेल करा सकती है यदि हम अपनी सुरत (spirit) उसमें लीन कर लें।

"लक्ष कोस जो गुरु बसें दीजे सुरत पठाय, शब्द तुरी (घोड़ी) असवार होय, छिन आवे छिन जाय"।।

(संतबानी संग्रह भाग 1 पेज–4)

कबीर ने सम्पूर्ण सृष्टि के उच्च स्थानों त्रिकुटी, पारब्रहम, सुन्न, महासुन्न, भँवर गुफा, सत्तलोक, अलख,व अगम लोक और अनामी पुरुष जो इन सब स्थानों का स्वामी है उसे प्राप्त किया और ओंकार, ररंकार, सोहंग, सत्तनाम, शब्द को भी अन्तर में परखा। उसका मार्ग दोनों आँखों के पीछे तीसरे तिल (Third eye) के भीतर तिल से बताया जैसा कि उनके निम्न पद से स्पष्ट होता है।

"है तिल के तिल के तिल भीतर बिरले साधु पाया है,
चहुँ दल कमल त्रिकुटी साजे ओकार दरसाया है।
ररंकार पद सेत सुन्न पद षट्दल कमल बताया है,
पारब्रहम महासुन्न मझारा सोई निःछर गाया है।
भँवरगुफा में सोहंग राजे मुरली अधिक बजाया है,
सन्तलोक सन्तपुरुष बिराजे अलख अगम दोऊ भाया हैं
पुरुष अनामी सब पर स्वामी ब्रहमाण्ड पार जो गाया है।।"

(यथार्थ प्रकाश, भाग–3 पेज 252)

चेतना के विकास हेतु गुरुनानक ने सुरत शब्द योग की महिमा का वर्णन किया है । यह नाम भी परम शक्ति से उत्पन्न निरन्तर गूंजने वाला सत्तनाम शब्द है जो रचना का आधार है और इसका रास्ता भी मनुष्य के घट में भीतर गुप्त केन्द्रों व द्वारों से होकर ही है।

"पंच शब्द तेह पूरन नाद, अनहद बाजे अचरज बिस्माद।।"

(यर्थाथ प्रकाष– 3, पृष्ठ 45)

गुरु नानक जी कहते हैं कि सतगुरु की महिमा अपर अपार है । गुरु के चरणों में सिर झुकाकार दीनता, प्रेम से उनसे घट का भेद लेना चाहिए तभी आध्यात्मिक चेतना का विकास सम्भव है।

"बिनवन्त नानक गुरूचरन लागे बाजे अनहद तूरे।
अनहद रूप अनाहद बानी, चरनसरन जे बसत भवानी।

उल्ट कँवल अमृत भरे एह मन कितहुँ न जाय।
अजपा जाप न बीसरे, आदि जुगादि समाय।।"

(यर्थाथ प्रकाश, 1, 2 पृष्ठ 19)

सुरत आत्मा परमात्मा में सुरत शब्द योग द्वारा रत होकर ही परम सत्य का ज्ञान व परम सुख प्राप्त कर सकती है। और उच्चतर आध्यात्मिक चेतना प्राप्त कर सकती है।

तुलसी साहब के अनुसार संत कलयुग को बहुत अच्छा समझते हैं क्योंकि इसमें बड़े संत स्वयं जन्म लेकर जीवों को तारते हैं।–

"कलयुग संत बड़ा ठहरावे। संत उतरि पिय घर से आवें।।
नाम डोरि दे सुरत लखावें। सुरति डोर जीव पिय घर जावे।
सब संतन कलु बड़ा बताया। यामें जीव अपन पै पाया।।"
(पृष्ठ 112, रत्न सागर, तुलसी साहब)

"सत्तलोक सत्तपुरुष का करे सुरति से ध्याना।
सत गगन ऊपर चढ़े, जहँ सतगुरु अस्थाना"।।
(रत्न सागर पेज 140)

सत्तनाम की प्राप्ति के लिए हमें अपने चित्त को उलट कर अपनी सुरत को सतगुरु (शब्द गुरु) का ध्यान कर वापिस परम सत्य के पास जाना चाहिए।

"सूरज बसे अकास में, किरनि भूमि पर बास,
जो अकास उल्टे चढ़े, सो सतगुरु के दास,
अलल पच्छ का अंड ज्यों, उलटि चले अस्मान।
त्यों सुरति संत सजन की, आठ पहरे गुर ध्यान ।।

राधास्वामी मत को संत मत भी कहते है। राधास्वामी मत के अनुसार भी सुरत–शब्द योग आध्यात्मिक चेतना के उच्चतम विकास का एकमात्र साधन है। प्राचीन समय में अभ्यासी मूल चक्र या गुदा चक्र से अभ्यास करते थे परन्तु राधास्वामी मत में यह अभ्यास छठे चक्र सहस दल कमल से कराया जाता है और अष्टाँग योग यानि प्राणायाम करना साधारण लोगों के लिए बहुत कठिन है । राधास्वामी मत में सहज योग अर्थात् सुरत–शब्द योग जारी किया गया। इस मत के अनुसार परम पुरुष पूरन धनी स्वामी जी महाराज साहब ने–स्वयं राधास्वामी दयाल ने निज धाम से इस संसार में जीवों के कल्याण के लिए आने की मौज फरमाई । अतः राधास्वामी धाम से निज धार जीवों के उद्धार के लिए यहाँ आई । और सब जीवों का उद्धार करके ही वापिस जायेगी। इस मत में जीवित गुरु अर्थात् वक्त गुरु की भक्ति की जाती है। जब एक गुरु गुप्त होतें हैं तो वह निज धार दूसरे गुरु में समा जाती है इस प्रकार यह निज धार निरन्तर भक्तों की संभाल के लिए इस संसार में जारी रहती है।

परम गुरु हुजूर सरकार साहब ने फरमाया है।–

"शब्द नाम महज़ आवाज का नहीं हैं। शक्ति जब तक गुप्त है, अनाम और अरुप है। शक्ति जब प्रकट होती है तो शब्द स्वरुप है और वही शब्द उसका निज नाम और निज रुप है। कुल मालिक या परम शक्ति ने जब अनाम और अरुप दशा प्रकट करने की मौज की, तो वह आदि शब्द स्वरुप होकर दरसा । वही शब्द उस मालिक का निज रुप निज नाम हुआ वही शब्द राधास्वामी शब्द है।.......वही धार गुरुधार या निजधार है वही सदा उद्धार के काम को जारी रखती है। (प्रेम समाचार, पेज 21, 27 परम गुरु हुजूर सरकार साहब)

राधास्वामी मत के अनुसार शब्द ने ही सारी सृष्टि पिंड, ब्रहमांड़ और निर्मल चेतन देश की रचना की।–

"शब्द ने रची त्रिलाकी सारी, शब्द से माया फैली भारी।

शब्द ने अखण्ड़ ब्रहमाण्ड रचा री, शब्द से सात द्वीप नौखण्ड बना री।
शब्द ने गुन तीनों और परजा धारी, शब्द से धरनि आकाश खडा री।
शब्द ने जीव और ब्रहम किया री, शब्द से चाँद और सूर भया री।
शब्द सुन महासुन्न सँवारी, शब्द ने चौथा लोक करारी।
शब्द ही घट घट करे पुकारी, शब्द फिर अलख अगम से न्यारी।
शब्द से खाली कोई न रहा री, शब्द सब ठौर ठिकान भरा री।।''

(सारबचन नज्म पेज 109)

''सिवाय मनुष्य चोले के ओर कोई देह इस देश में ऐसी नही है जहाँ पर चैतन्य की कार्यवाही प्रकट हो। अलावा इसके नर शरीर की महिमा रचना भर की सब किस्म की देहों से इस वजह से बहुत भारी है कि इसमें छः चक्र पिंड के कारकुन है, चूँकी यह ब्रहमांड के 6 कमलों की छाया है इसलिए जो द्वारे ब्रहमांड के 6 कमलों के इस देह में है वे पूरे कारकुन हो सकते हैं और चूँकि ब्रहमांड के 6 कमल चैतन्य धाम के 6 पद्म के अधीन और छाया है, इसलिए वह भी 6 पदम अभ्यास से पूरे जगाय जा सकते हैं। इस तौर पर इस मनुष्य षरीर को मालिक की रचना का कामिल और पूरा नमूना बनाया है। इसमें यह कुदरत है कि अठारह द्वारे, जो आदि से अन्त तक की रचना से मिले हुए हैं कारकुन किये जा सकते हैं''।

(प्रेमसमाचार, पृष्ठ 27, परम गुरु हुजूर सरकार साहब)

''यह इंसान का जिस्म इत्तिफाकिया अमर नही है बल्कि किसी कायदे कानून से बनाया गया है । देखो सूरज लोक से जो धारा आती है वह एक छोटा सा सूरज पैदा कर देती है। इसी तरह वहाँ से धार आयी उसने भी इंसान का जिस्म बनाया आलमें सगीर ;डपबतवबवेउद्ध की कारवाई आलमें कबीर (Macrocosm) की कारवाई के मुताबिक है। जब यह सत्य है कि मानव शरीर में उच्च लोकों से आध्यात्मिक संबध बनाने की सुविधा है तो सुरत शब्द योग द्वारा ही संभव है।

"for uniting the spirit force with the sound currents, which accompany the various emanations of spirit currents for attaining increasing levels of consciousness ranging from macrocosm of the universe and in the microcosm of the human frame. The meditation practice begins by concentrating full attention at the seat of the spirit midway between the pupils of the two eyes repeating internally one of the mystic names- OM, Rarang, Sohang, Sat and Radhasoami] So that the spirit gets kinetic and attunes itself, as if it were in resonance, progressively with the characteristic sound- currents (musical notes) emanating from higher and higher sub-regions." (System movement, Autobiographical retrospective, page162, Prof. Prem Saran Satsangi)

आध्यात्मिक साधना में यदि हम ऊँचे घाट –ह्रदय घाट से ऊपर उठकर कंठ या छठे चक्र से आन्तरिक रुप से चेतन नाम का सुमिरन करें तो हमारा पूरा व्यक्तित्व (Personality) ही बदल जायेगा। और हमारी दशा ऐसी होगी कि जैसे किसी अँधेरी कोठरी से निकल अन्तरिक्ष में आ जाये । तब आत्मा को अपने में और सम्पूर्ण विश्व में एक समान शक्ति का बोध होगा।–

If you leave this plane and ascend to higher ones a new personality will be born in you and entirely new consciousness will be born in you and after traversing the intermediate spiritual plane, you will finally reach the plane of that centre which as soon as it is energized will give the experience that what ever you want occurs outside you then you feel that the consciousness of that which is in you and that what is outside is the same. Both beat with the same rhyme. There is perfect harmony between the two. It appears as if personality of both, is one and the same. In fact you become aware that you are an extension of the consciousness of Nature. (Writings & Speeches of Param Guru Huzur Sahabji Maharaj, Page 285).

चेतन शब्द का रुख अन्तर्मुखी है चूँकि चेतन शक्ति की क्रिया अन्तर्मुखी और आकर्षक है इसलिए उससे जो शब्द उत्पन्न हुआ उसका असर भी रचना पर अन्तर्मुखी और आकर्षक होना चाहिए। जितने भी चेतन शब्द रचना में हैं, उन सब के अन्दर से दोनों विशेषतायें मौजूद है और इस बजह से उन शब्दों के सुनने से अभ्यासी की सुरत का बड़े जोर के साथ खिंचाव अन्तर की जानिब होता है। और यह अभ्यास बाकायदा तौर पर करने से सुरत ऊँचे मंड़लों की जानिब, जहाँ से वे चेतन शब्द जारी होते हैं खिंच या चढ़ जाती है। यही वजह है कि सुरत शब्द अभ्यास सुरत की चढ़ाई करने का उच्चतम साधन माना जाता है।

''राधास्वामी मत में जो भक्ति ओर साधन के तरीके सिखलाऐ जाते हैं वे तीन अंगों को जगाने वाले अलहदा आध्यात्मिक साधन यानि रुहानी अमल है।

1. सुरत की जबान से यानि तवज्जुह की धार से चेतन नाम का सुमिरन करना।
2. वक्त गुरु स्वरुप के चेतन रुप का ध्यान व सतसंग करना व सतगुरु सेवा।

सतसंग अन्तर और बाहर चेतकर करना चाहिए गुरु से दृष्टि से दृष्टि मिलानी चाहिए क्योंकि गुरु के नेत्रों से निकली चेतन धार का प्रकाश हमारे अन्तर तक पहुँच सके। सच्चे भक्त को निष्काम करनी करना चाहिए। स्वार्थ भाव से की गई सेवा में सेवा का फल नहीं मिलता।''

''गुरु आज्ञा से जो शिष करई, सो करतूत भक्ति फल देई।.''...........

''सतगुरु सेवा जिन करी, हिरदय चिन्ता धार। छूटत ही सो पहुँचिया, साहब के दरबार।।''

3. चेतन शब्द का श्रवण करना।

(अमृत बचन, पेज– 46, परम गुरु हुजूर साहब जी महाराज)

राधास्वामी मत के अनुसार राधास्वामी नाम का उच्चारण करने से मानव ह्दय पवित्र हो जाता है। तथा अच्छे संस्कार पड़ते हैं और आध्यात्मिक चेतना में उच्चतम वृद्धि होती है इसलिए राधास्वामी नाम का सुमिरन निरन्तर करते रहना चाहिए–

''याद रखो राधास्वामी नाम से बढ़कर कोई विद्या नही, कोई सम्पत्ति नहीं, कोई शक्ति नहीं, इसे अपने अन्दर इतना अराधो कि इसका सुमिरन करते ही सद्‌गुरु स्वरुप आपके सामने प्रकट हो जायें। निष्चय कीजिए कि आपके सब दुःख व कष्ट निवारण हो जायेगें। आपके सब कार्य सिद्ध हो जायेगें। न इस जीवन में कोई दुःख, न मरते समय कोई कष्ट। आपके लिए मार्ग साफ हो जाता है। यह है वह अनमोल रत्न अर्थात् राधास्वामी नाम जो प्रत्येक सतसंगी को प्रदान किया गया है।'' (परम गुरु हुजूर साहब जी महाराज,हिन्दी प्रेमप्रचारक 5 नवम्बर 1934)

राधास्वामी नाम सृष्टि के कण–कण में विद्यमान है। और क्योंकि यह समस्त सृष्टि के सर्वोच्च धाम निज धाम का शब्द है सुरत को निज धाम तक पहुँचा सकता है क्योंकि रचना के प्रत्येक मंडल व उसके उप मंडल से होती हुई यह पिंड में ठहरी है और इसका इज़हार प्रत्येक मंडल में प्रतिपल स्वतः ही हो रहा है यह नाम एक Master key जैसा है।–

"Any mystic name can enable the spirit force through spiritual practice to ascend up to the level of consciousness of the sub region of its origin accordingly. Radhasoami the original mystic name of the supreme creator is the one like a master key sound which can enable the human spirit to attain the highest level of consciousness, commensurate with the attainment of absolute truth or ultimate reality of the supreme creational plane." (System Movement, Autobiographical Retrospective, Gracious Huzur Prof. P.S. Satsangi Sahab).

A comparison of different yoga forms is as shown in the following Table.

Yoga	Key feature	Origin (Divine/ Human)	Highest Realization	Observation
Hatha Yoga (Hatha Yoga Pradipika)	More Stress on Physical Purification	Shiva/Swami Swatamarama	Union with Universal Mind	Highly Dangerous, mistakes can disrupt physical and mental well being
Ashang Yoga/ Pranayam (Yoga Sutra of Patanjali)	Comprehensive with stress on Moral, Ethical and Mental Purification	Hiranyagarbha / Patanjali Maharishi	Brahman Realization, Union with Universal Mind	Virtually Impossible to follow correctly in Kalyuga
Surat Shabda Yoga (Sant Mat of Huzur Soamiji Maharaj)	Travel through higher regions with the aid of Spiritual Sound	Radhasoami Dayal/Huzur Soamiji Maharaj	Realization and Union with Radhasoami Dayal, fountainhead of Pure Spirituality	Simplest with no side effect. Starts from 6th *Chakra* where other yogas reach with difficulty

संत मत के अनुसार सुरत शब्द योग ही उच्चतम अध्यात्मिक चेतना प्राप्त करने का एक मात्र साधन है:

सुरत शब्द कमाई करना, सब जतन दूर अब धरना
यह सार सार सब गया, संतन मत भाष सुनाया।

(सारबचन, पृष्ठ 385)

स्वयं परम पुरूष पूरन धनी स्वामी महाराज ने फरमाया है–

'सुरत शब्द कमाई से मन बस में आवेगा और सिवाय इसके दूसरा कोई उपाय मन को निष्चल और निर्मल करके चढ़ाने का आकाश के परे इस कलियुग में निश्चय करके नहीं है।' (सारबचन, पृष्ठ 5)

There is thus a duality of spirit force. The uniting faculty of the spirit-force is the spiritual sound- current and the center-forming faculty of the same force constitutes the spirit current. The sound is the active form and the spirit is the focus form of the same force. The sound attracts and the spirit forms the reservoir.

Conclusion

In conclusion, the Pure Spiritual Region by definition cannot have anything other than pure spiritual energy. The only way to reach such a region is through a purely spiritual manner. The only such way is the spiritual sound current which is the active form of the same force whose focus form is the spirit. Any other medium including prana or mind control cannot exist in the purely spiritual region and are limited to the lower strata of the region of Universal Mind and can take the Jivatama only upto this limit. This also correlates with the fact that the medium was introduced by Deities which belonged to this region of Universal Mind.

Chapter 29

Karma, Gyana & Bhakti: Pillars to Attain Higher Consciousness

PRANITA JAISWAL
Central Institute of Post Harvest Engineering and Technology
Ludhiana, India

DAYAL JAISWAL
Vimarsh The Consultancy Group
Gurgaon, India

Abstract

One of the few elements that world religions share is the assertion that human beings do not live in harmony with the Ultimate Reality. In other words, humanity does not manifest its purpose of existence. Life is a far cry from the ideal claimed by religion, so that humanity needs salvation from its present condition. And in the current scenario the best way to proceed on the path of emancipation is to do karma (duties) without desire, with mind focus on the ultimate reality- the supreme power.

Introduction

All involuntary and voluntary activities of human beings are directed towards avoidance of pain and acquisition of pleasure. Man acquires necessary means and paraphernalia to satisfy his desires. Discovering that no amount of paraphernalia would satisfy his desires, he began to enquire into the real nature of things around and that of his own self. Discovering that the most valuable thing in the world is his own self he began to understand own true nature and 'religion' thus came into existence. A strong acquisitive impulse arose to turn inwards and seek the super bliss, called Param Purushartha, the Supreme Goal of Life. Thus the greatest goal of human life became 'Moksha' meaning deliverance, emancipation and liberty or 'rid off' of something undesirable, i.e. cycle of rebirth and attachment to world.

However, with more involvement in perplexities of world, he gradually became ignorant of his true self. The problem is with his consciousness. His salvation is in attaining that original state of lost consciousness. So, salvation is a matter of perception or realization that, "You are already one with God; you just have to perceive or realize this fact. Perceiving, in this context, is not a cognitive activity". It is not a matter of intellectually knowing or logically deducing that we are God, but rather transcending this cognitive rational consciousness and experiencing a 'higher' state of expanded consciousness which is believed to be God and our true self.

The various ways explained by the realized souls for attainment of God has three basic pillars – Karma, Gyana and Bhakti. Gita one of greatest spiritual guide of all times describes that those inclined towards activity or service to mankind through work, is Karma Yoga; those inclined towards devotion, Bhakti

Yoga and intellectually inclined can veer towards Jnana Yoga. Karma, Jnana and Bhakti Yoga are the Trinity of Yoga Philosophy for attainment of ultimate objective i.e. unification of human Soul with the Ultimate Reality, i.e. 'Salvation' or 'Mukti'. Acquisition of factual information for achieving the above-mentioned goal is knowledge or Jnana. However, just superficial knowledge cannot help to accomplish the goal; on the contrary, it leads to pride or Ahankara. One must act in accordance with the gathered knowledge. The physical movement for translating an idea into practice is action or 'Karma'. The anxious wait with an internal urge is devotion or Bhakti. These Yogas are like the rungs of a ladder extended to the doorway to salvation or Moksha, the rungs being Karma Yoga, leading to Jnana Yoga, leading to Bhakti Yoga. A living Tattvadarshi Guru helps the Devotee by aligning the ladders, so that the disciple can keep his goal in focus. Karma and Jnana have their importance in so far as they are auxiliary to Bhakti, while Bhakti is indeed the doorway to Moksha.

The meaning of salvation in world religions lays stress on three important aspects - the resources needed for attaining salvation, the actual way of getting saved and the meaning of being saved. Concerning the first two aspects, some religions claim that salvation can be attained by using only inner human resources. They demand the use of meditation, accumulation of wisdom, asceticism, rituals, good deeds, etc. Other religions state that humans need only Grace of an external personal agent. This agent can be God, a bodhisattva, an avatar, etc. One's duty is to recognize the impossibility of being saved by one's own efforts, and therefore accept Grace unconditionally. There are also combinations of these two ways.

There are important distinctions to be mentioned concerning the meaning of salvation from an eternal perspective. The monotheistic religions state that barrier between humans and God is sin. Salvation means removing this moral barrier and restoring a personal communion with God, which will endure forever. Pantheistic religions consider the human self to be one with the impersonal Ultimate Reality, and therefore humanity's problem is epistemological. Salvation means liberation from ignorance and the fusion of the impersonal self with the Absolute, of knower with Known. Other Eastern religions, such as Buddhism, see salvation as an illumination, namely the discovery of and conformity of oneself with an eternal law that governs existence. Dualistic religions state that two opposed forces of good and evil rule our worldand see salvation as a return to an initial angelic state from which souls have fallen into a physical body. Likewise, Guru Nanak Sahab of the Sikh faith, enjoined upon men to make effort to reach 'Sachchkhanda' (Sat Loka of the Sant Mat). Radhasoami faith talks about Dayal desh and importance of practicing Surat Shabd Yoga along with the Grace of Sant Satguru to reach there. Kabir Sahab was the first to identify these levels and was thus called Adi Sant.

A Synthesis of Karma, Gyana, Bhakti: Current Scenario

One of the few elements that world religions share is the assertion that humanity does not manifest its purpose of existence. Life is a far cry from the ideal claimed by religion, so that humanity needs salvation from its present condition.

Developments in science and technology are increasingly revealing the workings of the brain and are attempting to understand human consciousness. For an integral approach to knowledge one has not only to be guided by instinct, intelligence and reason but also by intuition which results in higher sensibilities which can only be nourished by literature, arts and religion. These are unfortunately looked down upon and not accepted by scientists as relevant means of acquiring knowledge.

The human body consists of three elements, the body, mind and the soul; and therefore, for an all-round and balanced development of man, the development has to be in all of the three faculties, (1) Physical, (2) Mental and (3) Spiritual. While the first two, are gross, it is the Spiritual faculty which is of the highest order and helps man retrace the path of the Spirit to its Origin and experience what unbounded and everlasting peace and bliss is. Religion shows the way to Spiritual development.

Bhakti is said to be the doorway for emancipation but as per my understanding all these ways (Karma, Gyana and Bhakti Yoga), are interrelated. Involvement in one leads to another. Hence all the three paths are equally important and treading on any one of these paths involuntarily leads to the other. The core is that one should have the yearning, the craving to reach and to tread on the path of emancipation and understand that the pleasures and enjoyments that are perceived in this world, have their source (reservoir) in our spirit, soul or the Jivatma. So if one is engaged in the path to the Seat of the Spirit then without much effort or distraction, pleasures of the higher order can be enjoyed without assistance from inwardly directed senses of perception for as long as one remains there. Further, since the Spirit is just a drop of its Eternal Reservoir, it can very well be imagined what bliss can be experienced upon reaching The Ultimate Reality which is a boundless ocean of happiness and Eternal Pleasure.

So in current scenario, when people are so much involved in the perplexities of world that most of them do not even think of salvation,, the best way to proceed / tread on the path of emancipation would be the karma marga i.e. to perform duties without desire. One can not escape from the fruits of ones action. As is said by Most Revered Prof. Prem Saran Satsangi Sahab that:

"Karam jo tu karega wahi bhogna padega"

Conclusion

In this world where everything is illusory, perishable and of a transient nature, the living being is perplexed by pains and sorrows and desires peace and pleasure and do not have an understanding of real pleasure. Enjoyment experienced by sensory organs is thought of as pleasure. Man therefore remains entangled in the pursuit of these illusionary pleasures of his senses which are of a transient nature and is forever in search of real and lasting pleasure.

Thus at this juncture, when people are entangled in maya-jaal of prakriti, one can not focus on performance of meditational practices as mind is involved with day to day loss and gains, sorrow, happiness and stray thoughts which, as a matter of fact, involve oscillation of attention and diversion of the mind to irrelevant objects. This shifting of attention, off and on, from one object to another is inimical to progress in *Dhyana*, And bhakti is not something that one can be forced to perform, it is an emotion which develops automatically, yet at the same time if one can perform day to day activities (Karma) without desire then with passage of time slowly one will develop detachment and with the Grace of Lord be involved in bhakti/devotion. As said by Param Guru Huzur Sarkar Sahab, 4th Revered Sant Satguru of Radhasoami Faith, Dayalbagh:

"Sumiran karni, dhyan hai karni, shabd shravan sab karni
Satsang karni, seva karni, bhakti bhav sab karni".

Chapter 30

Nirakh-Parakh: Means of Achieving High Level of Spiritual Consciousness

SUMIRAN SATSANGI
American Express, Gurgaon, India

Abstract

The present paper explains the importance of Nirakh Parakh in our every-day life to attain high level of Spiritual Consciousness. By consciousness we mean our level of perception about ourselves and the world around us. The higher the perception, the greater the consciousness. Nirakh is keeping a constant watch on activities of one's mind and the sense organs, And Parakh is whenever mind or sense organs tend towards improper, undesirable and unnecessary activities, thoughts or objects to have it involved in proper and useful deeds and thoughts. It is more important for a person who wants to attain High level of Spiritual Consciousness to see that his precious time is not wasted in useless thoughts or deeds .Only by constantly engaging in this activity, day by day he would be attaining higher and higher levels of Spiritual Consciousness. The paper attempts to explore the importance of Nirakh Parakh by comparing nature and behaviour of a person , who has control over his mind and sense organs and is at higher level of Spiritual Consciousness with the one who enjoys pleasures of his senses, and lets go his mind in undesirable and improper activities.

Introduction

By consciousness we mean our level of perception about ourselves, the world around us and the ultimate truth. The higher the perception, the greater the consciousness. Those who had spiritual experiences have noted that their state of awareness i.e. their consciousness, has been elevated beyond the norm, enabling that person to experience existence from a whole new perspective. The term Spiritual Consciousness refers to a Unitary Consciousness, where all conflicting thoughts, events and life circumstances are brought into a greater harmony. This gives rise to an inner consciousness that is at peace with itself.

Higher Consciousness is generally regarded as a developed state of Consciousness in Which, aspects of the mind, such as thought, perception and attention are improved, refined and enhanced. It is usually associated with transcendence, spiritual enlightenment, and union with the divine. Spiritual Consciousness can be acquired only by awakening of Spiritual Consciousness within us by the impact of the spiritual force currents on the subtle nerve-centres within the brain. And for that it is necessary that one should withdraw his attention from the physical plane and concentrate it on the subtle centres of the brain referred to.

Ultimate Goal of Existence

We all should be aware of our ultimate goal of existence and that is to realise the ultimate truth, or reach the highest region of consciousness where there is total bliss and nothing else. Truth, Reality and Wisdom- Truth is the ultimate reality or ultimate region, Reality is our perception about truth. Wisdom is how much we are in conformity with truth. Hence the goal of every person should be to raise ones spirit upward and upward, gradually reaching the ultimate region and realise the ultimate truth, i.e. attaining high levels of Spiritual Consciousness with time and reaching the ultimate destination where Truth, Reality and Ultimate wisdom become one and the same. Thus gradual upgradation of Spiritual Consciousness is necessary to attain the ultimate Wisdom or realise Ultimate Consciousness.

Nirakh Parakh

Nirakh Parakh means to be aware of what you are doing at all times and have control over-

- One's Thoughts
- One's Actions
- One's Words
- One's Sprit- (Inner self) or 'Atman'

Thus it means to keep a constant watch over whatever we are doing-

Thoughts which are coming in our mind, words we are speaking, actions we are doing at any point of time, and our soul or 'Atman' should always remain connected to the Supreme God. It is really very important to have control on your ' Mind' and sense organs - this is what Nirakh Parakh is.

Nirakh is keeping a constant watch on activities of one's mind and the sense organs. Parakh is whenever mind or sense organs tend towards improper, undesirable and unnecessary activities, thoughts or objects, to have it involved in proper and useful deeds and thoughts. It is necessary to take care of one's time. It is one's duty to see that his time is not spent uselessly and that his mind and senses are kept under restraint i.e. the impulse for improper and useless activities and objects does not arise.

In the words of His Holiness Param Guru Sahabji Maharaj, 5th Revered Sant Satguru of Radhasoami Faith, Dayalbagh-

"It is only when a person cultivates a habit of watching the activities of his mind that he can resist its influence. Otherwise, the mind is liable to slip on being flattered, like the foot on a greasy surface. Indeed how nice it would be if only people were as anxious to mend their ways, as they are to hear themselves praised!"

Nirakh Parakh - Some Practical Tools/Scales

- Comparing the traits of Gurumukh Vs Manmukh
- Introspection/Retrospection/Self Examination
- Spiritual Positioning
- Comparing the traits of Gurumukh Vs Manmukh

Characteristic of Person with High level of Spiritual Consciousness (Gurumukh) Vs Person with Low level of Spiritual Consciousness (Manmukh)

It is important to know what is the difference in the behaviour of two persons, one who is in constant effort to raise his level of Spiritual Consciousness and thus try and control his sense organs by constantly engaging in Nirakh Parakh and one who has no control on mind and sense organs, and thus remains at lower levels of Spiritual Consciousness.

In the characteristics discussed below Gurumukh is someone who has control over his mind and sense organs and is at Higher level of Spiritual Consciousness, While Manmukh is one who enjoys pleasures of his senses, and let go in his mind in undesirable and improper activities. Each person can use this scale to do his or her Nirakh Parakh and thus judge about one's own condition on the basis of some of the points given below:

1. In all his Spiritual acts, the aim of the Gurumukh is to secure the pleasure of the Supreme Being or God; a Manmukh however, seeks his own pleasure in all he does.

2. A Gurumukh endures hunger and thirst, so that his Spiritual activities may be performed properly, a Manmukh takes delight in eating and drinking, like brutes.

3. A Gurumukh is always thoughtful and has fear, a Manmukh daily multiplies his bonds and desires. He is fearless and careless.

4. A Gurumukh does not fear anybody except God, a Manmukh is afraid of all but the God.

5. A Gurumukh has no expectation from anybody but God, a Manmukh expects from everybody excepting God.

6. Gurumukh sacrifices riches for spiritual benefits, a Manmukh barters spiritual benefit for wealth, he does not mind if he can secure wealth at the expense of Spiritual benefit.

7. A Gurumukh performs takes care that he doesn't commit any sin by his thought, speech or deed, and repents for the same, a Manmukh commits sins and rejoices.

8. A Gurumukh acts with deliberation and patience, a Manmukh acts thoughtlessly in a frenzy.

9. A Gurumukh is absorbed in spiritual and useful activities, a Manmukh sleeps and slumbers and waste his time.

10. A Gurumukh is contended and thankful for what the Lord has granted him, a Manmukh is dissatisfied, greedy and ungrateful. For this reason he is always unhappy and displeased.

11. A Gurumukh does not use abusive language, a Manmukh usually utters abusive language and is not ashamed of it.

12. A Gurumukh's speech is soft and gentle because it is always imbued with the sublimity and praises of God, a Manmukh's speech is bitter because it always indulges in the good and evil things of the world

13. A Gurumukh's heart is more tender than a flower, a Manmukh's heart is harder than stone.

14. A Gurumukh is a well wisher, a Manmukh is selfish.

15. A Gurumukh is taciturn, truthful and not easily offended, a Manmukh is talkative, easily grieved and false.

In the words of His Holiness Param Guru Sahabji Maharaj-

"Overeating, oversleeping and being overactive in connection with worldly duties are inimical to spiritual progress. A devotee should, therefore, be always on his guard that he does not, even unconsciously, place himself within the power (influence) of these enemies."

Doing Introspection/Retrospection/Self Examination Every Day

Continuous Introspection- During the day, we can try and control the activities of mind which tend to always wander and indulge in improper activities by

a) Repetition of Holy Name and Contemplation of Holy Form while doing all our worldly tasks- eating, talking, walking etc.

b) Before indulging in any of the task in which you are not sure of as to proceed or not - ask yourself - 'Will the Supreme Being would be happy with my action' and if you think the answer is 'Yes' go on with your action, else do not proceed with the same.

During Satsang while listening to discourses and Shabdas we must listen the same carefully with attention and try and relate ourselves with the Path or Shabda as to where we stand.

Positioning

One should at night before sleeping or whenever possible should self examine.

Where did one made mistakes, did he or she was able to kept senses under control or did one allowed one's senses to wander fearlessly and thus felt disconnection with Supreme Creator, and thus could not find peace and inner happiness.

'Summe up at night what thou hast done by day;
And in the morning what thou hast to do.
Dresse and undresse thy soul; mark the decay
And growth of it; if, with thy watch, that too
Be down then winde up both; since we shall be
Most surely judg'd, make thy accounts agree.'

- George Herbert,
The Temple -The Church Porch

'We should every night call ourselves to an account: What infirmity have I mastered to-day? what passion opposed? what temptation resisted? what virtue acquired? Our vices will abate of themselves if they be brought every day to the shrift.'

- Seneca (Lucius Annaeus Seneca)

Before sleeping at night, one should try and analyse whether love for Supreme Being in one's heart has increased or decreased. By keeping an eye on his

'Daya' and 'Mehar' (Grace and Mercy) one comes to know of Supreme Being's immense love, grace and mercy on each one of us, one's affection and love for Supreme Being increases and one comes more closer to God with this increase in Spiritual Consciousness.

Nirakh Parakh and Increase in Spiritual Consiousness

Now how does doing Nirakh Parakh everyday by the above means lead to increase in Spiritual Consciousness? In the below pictorial diagram it has been tried to answer this question.

Let's start from smaller circle inside to outer circle. We all do several tasks and activities everyday, which can be referred to as "Daily Karmas". By doing Nirakh Parakh of these 'Karmas" everyday through the methods mentioned above we are able to:

i) Differentiate between Right and Wrong

ii) We learn our own vices.

iii) We are able to have control on our sense organs

With the above comes "Righteousness", "Humility" and increase in love for Supreme Creator who is the protector of all, and thus increase in Spiritual Consciousness

Increase in Spiritual Consciousness

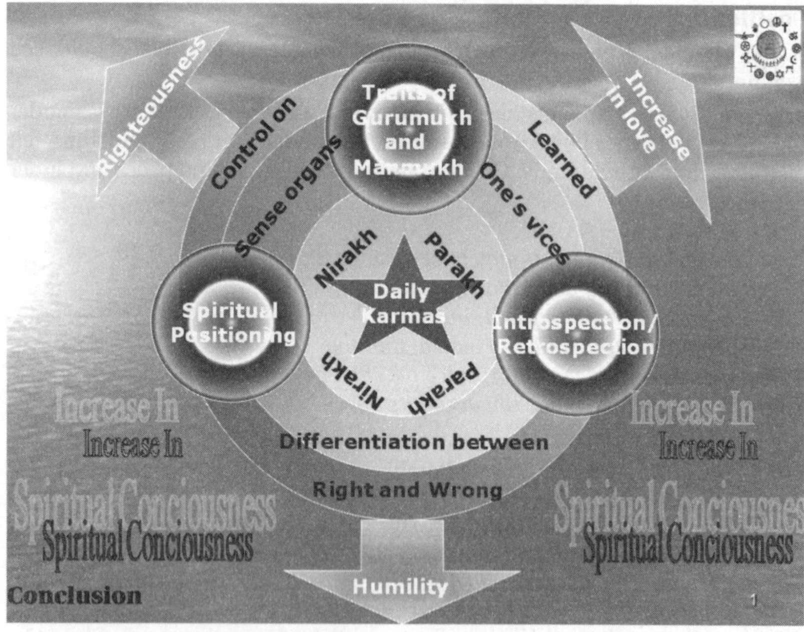

Nirakh Parakh actually plays a very important role in all levels of Spiritual Consciousness. At every level a person can check for himself, whether one is pursuing the right path or not. By doing Nirakh Parakh of whatever spiritual benefits he is getting, i.e. how much peace he is experiencing, how much love for Supreme Father he has gained, he can know his spiritual status as to where he stands. Thus Nirakh Parkh would make him judge all this himself, see as to where he is lacking, and also help him try and improve upon his current condition. It is more important for a person who wants to attain High level of Spiritual Consciousness to see that his precious time is not wasted in useless thoughts or deeds.To keep control on senses so that they do not think of any useless thoughts or deeds. Only by constantly doing this activity, that day by day he would be attaining higher and higher levels of Spiritual consciousness. Supreme Lord has kept everything in this world according to some rules and regulations. Whoever is intelligent can understand it through Nirakh Parakh and can easily pursue his aim of attaining higher and higher level of Spiritual Consciousness.

References

Huzur Maharaj [Rai Bahadur Salig Ram Sahab] (1963). *Prem Patra Part II*. Agra, India: Radhasoami Satsang Sabha, Dayalbagh.

Huzur Maharaj [Rai Bahadur Salig Ram Sahab] *Bachans*. Agra, India: Radhasoami Satsang Sabha, Dayalbagh.

Sahabji Maharaj [Sir Anand Sarup Kt.] (2004). *Table Talk*. Dayalbagh, Agra: Radhasoami Satsang Sabha.

Satsangi, P.S. [Revered Prof. Prem Saran Satsangi] (2003). *Reality and Truth vis-à-vis Wisdom via 'Apara Vidya' and 'Para Vidya'*, International Conference of the Association of Asia-Pacific Operational Research Societies. New Delhi, India.

Chapter 31

आध्यात्मिक चेतना के उच्च स्तरों को प्राप्त करने का एक साधन–रङ्ग

Rang: A Means of Attaining Higher Levels of Spiritual Consciousness

AGAM KULSHRESHTHA
Dayalbagh Educational Institute (Deemed University), Agra, India

Abstract
Rang is a mode of singing. To arouse spiritual consciousness, it is an important device. Sant Tulsi Sahab directed to sing Doha, Soratha, Gazal etc in Rang or Rangat genre in the Ghat Ramayan. He has used Rang to describe Sahasdal Kamal to Agam Lok. At some place, it also denotes the higher level spiritual power or spiritual consciousness. The term Rang is found in Sanskrit Shiksha Granthas whose creation was done long ago from saint literature. Rang is also popular in sufi music. It's a kind of quawwali. People sing quawwali for the unison of their souls with the Almighty through the path shown by their Pir or Chishti. Rang is sung one or two days before or after an Urs when some offering is made at a Dargah or Tomb. According to sanskrit Shiksha Granthas the colour of Rang is SHABAL which means Rang Biranga (consisting of many colours). As per such granthas, singing of Rang enables a person to see the colourful nature of God. Saints in their Banis (Recitals) gave the message of the Prem Rang. The absorption of all Rangs is in Nirmal Prem Rang. Thus Rang is in its existence from the vedic period to Saint literature. Its recitation is an important device as a means of attaining higher levels of spiritual consciousness.

लौकिक दृष्टि से रंग (ब्वसवनत) एक सामान्य सा शब्द है किन्तु आध्यात्मिक दृष्टि से इसका अर्थ गूढ़ है। कबीर, सूर, तुलसी आदि संतों ने रङ्ग शब्द के दार्शनिक अर्थ को स्वीकार करते हुए आत्मा को परमात्मा के रंग में रंगने की बात कही है।

कबीर साहब कहते हैं–

रांम नाम रंग लागौं कुरंगत होई।
हरि रंग सौ रंग और और न कोई।।

यहाँ हम जिस रंग की बात कर रहे हैं, वह रंग गायन की एक विधा है। यह रंग गायन– विधा आध्यात्मिक चेतना के उच्चस्तरों को प्राप्त करने का एक सहज साधन है। संतों में संत तुलसी साहब ने सर्वप्रथम स्पष्ट रूप से रंग–गायकी का कथन किया है। ऐतिहासिक दृष्टि से यदि हम देखें तो सर्व प्रथम संस्कृत शिक्षा–ग्रन्थों में रंग का उल्लेख है। वैदिक वर्णमाला में त्रिशष्टि (63) वर्ण है जिनके स्वर, व्यञ्जन और अयोगवाह ये तीन भेद होते हैं।

<u>अयोगवाह</u>

अयम			यम
: विसर्जनीय	।	ᳲ	ह्रस्व
˘‸ जीह्वामूलीय	।	✕	दीर्घ
˘‸ उपध्मानीय	।	ँ	अनुनासिक चिह्न
˙ अनुस्वार	।	ळ	यह अक्षर

संस्कृत शिक्षा ग्रन्थों में रंग, अनुनासिक को कहा गया है। मुख सहित नासिका से बोला जाने वाला वर्ण अनुनासिक होता है पाणिनीय शिक्षा में रंग की उत्पत्ति नासामूल से बताई है–

> नस्त उत्पद्यते रंगः कांस्येन समनिस्वनः।
> मृदुष्चैव द्विमात्रः स्याद् वृष्टि मां 2 इव दर्शनम्।।[(1)]

रंग की एक मात्रा ह्रदय में, आधी मात्रा मूर्द्धा में और आधी मात्रा नासिका में रहती है।

> ह्रदये चैकमात्रस्त्वर्द्धमात्रस्तु मूर्द्धनि।
> नासिकायां तथार्द्धं च रङ्गस्यैव द्विमात्रता।।[(2)]

षिक्षा ग्रन्थों में वर्णमाला के रंगों का भी कथन हुआ है जैसे स्वरों का वर्ण शुक्ल तथा स्पर्शों (व्यञ्जन) का वर्ण कृष्ण कहा गया। इन्हीं ग्रन्थों में रंग को शबल[(3)] वर्ण का कहा गया है।

इस प्रकार संस्कृत शिक्षा ग्रन्थों में रंग को अनुनासिक (अयोगवाह–यम) कहा है। रंग का उच्चारण स्थल 'नासिका' है। नासिका का सम्बन्ध प्राण से होता है। रंग के उच्चारण में वायु लोहे के गोले के समान स्थान का पीडन करता है[(4)] प्राचीन मन्त्रद्रश्टा ऋषियों ने रंगादि विधियों में मन्त्रोच्चारण द्वारा नासिकादि स्थल विशेशों में झंकृति अथवा वायुपीडन द्वारा उच्चस्तरीय चैतन्यता की ओर रूख एवं एकाकार का वैज्ञानिक प्रयास किया।

अमीर खुसरो कव्वाली के जनक कहे जाते हैं। कव्वाली तथा रंग में अत्यन्त समानता है। वस्तुतः रंग, कव्वाली का एक प्रकार कहा जा सकता है। कव्वाली का आयोजन उर्स के अवसर पर होता है। उर्स पर उन सूफी संतों से यह मानकर प्रार्थना (कव्वाली) की जाती है कि वे अल्लाह के करीब है और जीवित (अमर) हैं और अब वे हमारे लिये दुआ करें कि हमारा भी इस दुनिया से निज़ात होवे।

कव्वाली का एक प्रकार रंग है । रंग उर्स के एक या दो दिन आगे या बाद में गाया जाता है तथा इस रंग गान के साथ कोई भी वस्तु सूफ़ी संतों के सामने पेश की जाती है और कुबूल फरमाने को कहा जाता है। इस अवसर पर रंग गान होता है। वैसे तो रंग कभी भी गाया जा सकता है किन्तु उर्स के अवसर पर रंग गान से विशेष कृपा होती है। इस प्रकार रंग (कव्वाली) गान द्वारा सूफ़ी सन्त जो कि मालिक के रंग में रंगकर जीवित है (विलास कर रहे हैं), उनसे प्रार्थना की जाती है कि वे सूफ़ी भक्तों के लिये भी उसके रंग में रंगने की प्रार्थना करें। सूफ़ी सन्त श्वेत वस्त्र धारण नहीं करते तथा बाह्य दिखावे एवं सजावट से परहेज़ करते हैं। वे सूफ़ियाने रंग में रंगे होते

हैं तथा हरे एवं पीले वस्त्र धारण करते हैं।

कार्य से कारण का ज्ञान होता है। घट से मृदा का तथा फल–फूल से उनके कारण ा बीज का। सूफ़ी संतों के हरित पीत वस्त्र भी सम्भवतः हरित पीत प्रकाश की ओर संकेत करते हैं। सारबचन में कहा है–

अंडन शोभा बरनूँ कैसी,
सब्ज सेत कोई पीत वरन सी।[5]

जो रंगोच्चारण, शिक्षा ग्रन्थों में द्विमात्रिक था वही सूफी रंग गायकी में मध्यमलय में हो गया। संतों में सर्वप्रथम संत तुलसी साहब ने घट रामायन में दोहा, सोरठा गजल रेख्ता आदि को रंग विधा में गायन करने का स्पष्ट निर्देष किया है। उन्होंने रंग के स्थान पर रंगत शब्द का प्रयोग किया है जैसे दोहा रंगत सोरठा[6] गजल रंगत हिन्दी[7] आदि। कबीर साहब ने भी रंगत, कुरंगत[8] आदि शब्दों का प्रयोग किया है। रंगत शब्द का हिन्दी अर्थ भी रंग ही है[9] साधन ही से चक्रों के अन्तरी ख़वास जगते हैं।[10] रूहानी ताकत अर्थात् चेतनता जगाने की सुमिरन, भजन आदि अनेक युक्तियों के समान संत तुलसी साहब ने रंग गान रूप साधन से आत्मा के उच्च आध्यात्मिकता की ओर रूख़ का कथन किया है।

संत तुलसी साहब ने रंग विधा का प्रायः दो प्रकार से प्रयोग किया है। प्रथम दोहा रंगत सोरठा गान द्वारा सुरत (आत्मा) के सहस दल कमल (आकाश या अम्बर) तथा गगन (त्रिकुटी) के प्रकाश के रंग में रंगने का तथा दूसरा होली के साथ रंग का कथन है।

निम्न दोहा–सोरठा छन्दों में रंग गायकी के रूप में अम्बर तथा गगन तक का कथन है।

बूझै कोई संत। आदि अंत जानै लशी।[11]
परचै परम प्रकाश। जिन आकाश अम्बर चखी।।

ग ग ग ग

लशि प्रकाष पद तेज। सेज गवन गढ़ गगन में ।[12]
पति पिया प्रेम विलास। तुलसी दास दस गिरा में।।

षिक्षा ग्रन्थों में रंग के वर्ण का भी कथन है। वहाँ स्वरों का वर्ण षुक्ल, स्पर्षों (व्यञ्जनों) का कृशण रंग माना है तथा रंग का वर्ण षबल है। षबल का अर्थ है चितकबरा या रंग–बिरंगा तथा 'षबल' के कथन से परम तत्त्व के रंग–बिरंगे स्वरूप का कथन है। सारबचन में कहा है–

पचरंगी फुलवारी निरखो।
दीपदान घट भीतर परखो।।[13]

पुराणों में होली (प्रह्लाद की कथानुसार) का विस्तृत उल्लेख प्राप्त होता है तथा परवर्ती काल तक होली में रंग की बरसात भारतीय संस्कृति का एक महत्त्वपूर्ण उत्सव हो गया। ब्रज की होली विष्व प्रसिद्ध है जिसके लौकिक और दार्षनिक दोनों पक्ष हैं।

सन्त तुलसी साहब ने होली तथा धमार आदि गायकियों का कथन घट रामायन में किया है। संगीत में जब होरी या होली नामक गीत को धमार ताल में गाया जाता है तब उसे धमार कहा जाता है। धमार गायन में प्रायः ब्रज की होली का वर्णन होता है। धमार में दुगुन, चौगुन, बोलतान आदि का प्रयोग होता है। यह एक कठिन गायकी है।

संत तुलसी साहब ने एक स्थल पर होली और रंग का एक साथ प्रयोग किया है– कि कर्मों का कुम्भ फूट गया। सुरत ऊपर के लोकों में पिया परमात्मा को देखती है तो लिपटने लगती है और बढ़ते–बढ़ते वह अगम लोक के धनी के रंग में रंग जाती है। सुरत होली खेलते–खेलते गगन से अगम लोक तक चढ़ जाती है।

तुलसी सतगुरू अगम लशाई। लैकी लगन लश लोक सिधाई।[(14)]
दुःख सुख दोष शोक सब छूटा। कलसा कुंभ करम का फूटा।।

होली गायकी के छन्दों के पश्चात रंग गायकी (दोहा रंगत सोरठा)3 में संत तुलसी साहब सुरत के सूर होने अथवा सुरत की उच्च स्तरीय रूहानी ताकत या आत्म चेतना की पुष्टि भी करते हैं।

प्रिये लाल मत मूर। सूर सुरति अस विधि भई।[(15)]

सारबचन में भी बारहमासा में कहा है–

अब छुट गया मेरा सब कुसंग।
मैंने पायो अद्‌भुत आदि रंग।।[(16)]

ग ग ग ग ग

ग्रेषस हुजूर प्रेम सरन सत्संगी साहब ने होली 2009 के स्पेशल सत्संग के अवसर पर फरमाया–

....................जब मैं ध्यान में बैठा तो मैंने पाया कि होली तो आज बड़े धूमधाम से ऊँचे धामों में मनाई जा रही थी और वहाँ जो संगत थी वह बहुरंग होली खेल चुकी थी और फूलमाला से सुसज्जित बैठे हुए थे। यह हाल सहसदलकमल से लेकर राधास्वामी धाम तक था। रंग में अन्तर है। रंग अधिक शोख़ हैं नीचों के धामों में। अधिक सूफ़ियाना हैं ऊँचे के धामों में। बहुत अधिक रूहानी हैं राधास्वामी धाम में।[(17)]

संतों ने अपनी बानी में रंग गायकी द्वारा संसार के विविध रंगों से छूटकर निर्मल प्रेम रंग में रंगने के लिए सन्देश दिया। अस्तु ! यह रङ्‌ग गायकी शिक्षा ग्रन्थों से संतसाहित्य तक फलीफूली, जीवन्त रही। शिक्षा ग्रन्थों में जो रङ्‌गोच्चारण द्विमात्रिक था, उसका गान सूफ़ी एवं अन्य संतों ने मध्यम लय में किया। ब्रह्माण्ड के समस्त व्यापार भी मध्यम लय में ही होते हैं।

राधास्वामी सत्संग के पाठों की लय भी प्रायः मध्यमलय है। कव्वाली भारतीय सूफियों का भक्ति सङ्‌गीत है। रङ्‌ग उसका एक प्रकार था। दयालबाग में इस वर्ष में ग्रेशस हुजूर जी की आज्ञा से राधास्वामी सत्संग के एक सौ पचास वर्शों के उपलक्ष्य में कव्वालियों का आयोजन हो रहा है।

रङ्ग का व्युत्पत्ति परक अर्थ है–रज्यति अस्मिन्(18) अर्थात् जो इसमें अर्थात् परम तत्त्व में रंग दे। परम तत्त्व में रंगने के लिए वैदिक काल से लेकर संत साहित्य तक 'रंग' गायन रूप साधना अथवा उसका अभ्यास किया जाता रहा। अभ्यास से ही निर्भयता, मधुरोच्चारण एवं लक्ष्य की सिद्धि होती है। (19) इस प्रकार चक्रों के अन्तरी ख़वास जाग्रत करने का एक सहज साधन है 'रंग' गायन। इस रंग विधा से वैदिक ऋषियों ने परम तत्त्व के शबल या रंग बिरंगे या शोख़ (चटकीले) रंग में, सूफी सन्तों ने सूफ़ियाने रंग में तथा अन्य संतों ने निर्मल प्रेम रंग में रंगने के लिए अपनी–अपनी वाणियों में सन्देश देते हुए जीव का संसार से निज़ात पाने हेतु उच्च आध्यात्मिक की ओर रूख़ कराया। इस प्रकार रंग गायकी आध्यात्मिक चेतना के विविध स्तरों को प्राप्त करने का एक सगुण, सुलभ एवं सहज साधन है।

संदर्भ–सूची

पाणिनीय शिक्षा 29 इसके अतिरिक्त नारदीय शिक्षा 1/8 माण्डूकी शिक्षा 113 में भी ऐसा कहा गया है।

पाणिनीय शिक्षा 28

याज्ञवल्क्य शिक्षा उ० – 2 तत्र स्वराः शुक्ला.........

पाणिनीय शिक्षा 5/1

सारबचन पृ० 538

घट रामायन, लखनऊ 1896 पृ० 91, 127

घट रामायन, लखनऊ 1895 पृ० –120

रांम नांम रंग लागों, कुरंगत होई/हरि रंग सौ रंग और न कोई (कबीर ग्रन्थावली पृ०161 पद 215)

रंगत–स्त्री हिन्दी (1) रंग/वर्षा (2) दशा (3) अवस्था

नालन्दा अघतन कोष पृ० 754

अमृत वचन परम गुरू महाराज साहब पृ० 38

घट रामायन, दोहा रंगत सोरठा पृ० 9

घट रामायन, दोहा रंगत सोरठा 6, पृ० 11

सार वचन पृ० 533 तथा 701

घट रामायन, पृ० 318 होली –2

घट रामायन, पृ० 318 दोहा रंगत सोरठा 107

सार बचन– बसन्त व होली, षब्द पहला कड़ी 7, 12, 13, 14, 15, 24, पृ० 839,

प्रेम प्रचारक सोमवार 20 अप्रैल 2009

आम्नायात् प्रपदो भवति प्रपदो भवति निर्भयः।

निर्भयो मधुरो भवति माधुर्यात् सिद्धिमाप्नुयात्।। (माण्डूकी शिक्षा 151)

रज्यति अस्मिन्– पुं० रंङ्ग, अनुनासिक्य (व्याकरण में), Nasal Modification of a vowel-sanskrit Hindi English Dictionary By Surya Kant Headrabad 1975

Chapter 32

Means of Attaining Higher Levels of Spiritual Consciousness

SHYAM SINGH
Lucknow, Uttar Pradesh, India

Abstract
It seems like we toil all our lives for a promised paradise yet it constantly eludes us. Humans endeavor to attain happiness but are left with certain hollowness instead. This paper aspires to explain that it is upon attaining higher levels of consciousness that happiness can be had. The human body has been programmed for this purpose and is capable of understanding the Ultimate Truth.

Introduction

First of all what is consciousness? In general terms when we are not sleeping, we are in what is called a conscious state. It means our conscious state keeps us in a kinetic state. Consciousness is defined in three states i.e. (i) Conscious (ii) Semi-conscious and (iii) Un-conscious.

But truly speaking this consciousness is due to which we are counted as alive, is governed and derived from Spiritual Consciousness i.e. Consciousness of the Spirit, which is spiritual consciousness and it has its own levels - either upwards or downwards. The lowermost level of the spirit is nothing but virtually Hell where pain dominates. The uppermost level of the spirit is Heaven where only pleasure remains.

All of our thoughts and acts, in our life, are targeted to acquire pleasure not sorrow. But if one analyses his actions, then all our thoughts & deeds, targeted to acquire pleasure, bring only sorrow. This happens because at lower levels of spiritual consciousness, where the being normally operates, both pure and coarse matter exists. So for acquiring pleasure alone (without sorrow combined with it) one will have to ascend upwards to attain a higher level of spiritual consciousness. This raises the following questions –

1. Who needs to attain higher levels of spiritual consciousness?
2. What is needed to attain higher levels of spiritual consciousness?
3. What is consciousness and spiritual consciousness?
4. How does one attain higher levels of spiritual consciousness?

It would not be out of place to define here - “Who Am I?” We are human beings. We need to attain higher levels of spiritual consciousness because it is only in a human body where apertures are present to attain higher levels of spiritual consciousness and no other creature has these apertures. Thus the goal of our existence is the highest one and not simply to eat, drink, and be merry (not forever). The very fact that nature has bestowed upon human beings, the most highly developed intellect and powers to enable them to seek God, which alone distinguishes them from other beings.

So let us try to answer the question "Who am I?" The answer is I am a human being? A Human being is a three-tier system comprising of:

1. **Body (Coarse Matter)** containing ten senses (5 perceptive and 5 voluntary)
2. **Mind (Subtle Matter)** containing –
   - **'Mann'**- which creates DESIRE;
   - **'Buddhi'** – INTELLECT, which suggests the options to fulfill desire and is guided by SELF;
   - **'Chitta'** – which ACTs on the suggested option;
   - **'Ahamkar'** – I/Self which gets satisfied when suggested action is positively accomplished.
   - This Mind is known as **"Antahkaran Chatustya"** or "Inner-Self".
3. **Spirit (Ethereal Matter)** which is embedded in our Body and makes Body and Mind, kinetic and alive.

The Body, along with its senses, is like hardware, The Mind is like the Operating System, operating various applications/senses for gaining knowledge and performing acts and the Spirit is like a Battery fitted in a specific slot on the Mother Board of the Central Processing Unit, which also works on regulating and maintaining Time & Date i.e. AGE even when the System is on shutdown. This battery is also discharged in its own time. So is our Battery - The SPIRIT (Soul, Atman).

We now come to next question - what is the need of attaining higher levels of spiritual consciousness? This is required as it is the prime target of all human beings. In the words of Param Sant Kabir Sahab –

"Vriksha kabhun nahi phal chakhen, Nadi na sanchay neer,
Parmarath ke karne, Sadhun dhara Sareer"

The first line of this couplet says that tree does not eat its fruits and river never collects its water but human beings live only for fruits and collection, indicating involvement and attachment in material world. This does not seem to be the purpose of human life, which is the best creature in this creation, created by The Lord.

The second line of this couplet says that this human body is provided for "Parmarath" i.e. Param+Artha, means to attain the Highest Meaning, actually Thyself. No doubt "Swarth" i.e. "Swa+arth", means Meaning of Oneself ie to know oneself. It is essential and imperative to know Oneself first and only then Thyself can be understood and one can know Oneself by concentrating his Attention Current, which is focused outward, internally and to Higher levels. It may be mentioned here, that today we mean "Swarth" as self-desires and fulfillment of these desires by whatever means. However, this is not true.

Paramarth leads to permanent bliss - communion with the Supreme Creator and liberation from the sorrow of birth, death and re-birth which is nothing but permanent sorrow. To achieve everlasting pleasure and relief from pain, one must make efforts for achieving Parmarath – the only way to attain higher levels of spiritual consciousness. To know "Param+arth" one will have to forget "Swa+arth". If Swarth (I-ness) remains there will not be Parmarath (High-ness).

There is a need to attain higher levels of spiritual consciousness because the purpose of our life in human form is not to indulge in sensual pleasure but to attain the creator where everlasting pleasure & happiness reigns.

The ONLY means to achieve Higher Level of Consciousness is our SPIRIT. The Spirit that is our real consciousness is of the Lowest Order in this creation, but it does not mean it is impertinent, because it is a particle of that energy which created the Universe and makes our Mind & Body kinetic and keeps us alive. All of our actions are due to this spirit and its current and it is this force which makes us feel conscious. The consciousness, which we have due to our spirit, is a particle of the reservoir of all consciousness which is the highest spiritual consciousness. Thus, the quality and character of the reservoir and its particle remain the same, therefore by holding the particle situated in our body i.e. Spirit, we can ascend to the highest level, whence from the Spirit had originally descended.

Consciousness can be recognised by way of a filter/logic that is used by us when we make any decision. If it is governed by the "Self" then it is only consciousness and if the filter/logic used is "Moral" then it is spiritual consciousness. Whatever we think and practice through the filter of Self, results in benefiting oneself or at best his family, friends & relatives only. But if the filter of Morals is used, then it will benefit all and the fruits also will be everlasting.

While, consciousness may be positive, any decision made out of it will certainly not be beneficial to all and its result may also not be favourable to all. But any decision made out of spiritual consciousness will surely be beneficial to all and this is where we become either honest or dishonest. If one's logic in the making of a decision is 'Moral' then one will remain honest and truthful. When one is acting at the behest of Spiritual Consciousness, the Thoughts & Deeds are governed by 'Morals'.

Consciousness is that which enables us to be active but a current of consciousness in the form of our Attention flows downward and outward and gets absorbed in the material world. Yet when it is turned inwardly, it is strengthened and tends to be spiritual. When consciousness spreads in each & every particle of our body, it gets concentrated on its seat and it becomes spiritual consciousness and as & when it ascends, the level attained is the level of spiritual consciousness. In other words, when our attention current is diffused, it is simply consciousness but when it is collected and concentrated on the seat of the spirit, it works as an instrument of spirituality, which is spiritual consciousness.

Hence the significant step is to ascertain the process for reversing the action of diffusion of the Spiritual Current, which is within us in the form of our Attention Current.

As clearly said by Param Sant Kabir Sahab –

"Vriksha kabhun nahi phal chakhen, Nadi na sanchay neer,"

The essence of this line is one must do his/her Karma selflessly without any expectation and not get involved needlessly in worldly affairs, which means more than the essential required limits. When this is followed and practised in everyday life, one will be able to know the "Param+Arth" i.e. Highest Spiritual Consciousness and a continuous effort of the seeker and Mercy of the Master will ultimately bring success i.e. we achieve the aim of human life.

A higher level of spiritual consciousness can be attained through breaking the bondages of the Body, Senses, Five Elements, Inner-self (Antahkaran), Trigun-SAT, RAJ & TAM. Yet before coming to the Body there are bondages outside the body also and they are Kith & Kin, Social Norms, Wealth & Property, Family and Prestige.

The aforementioned bondages are alive only due to "I-ness" and if there is "I-ness" there will not be "High-ness". The bondages are due to one's own "I" having components of Desire, Anger, Envy-Affection, Ego, and Greed etc. This "I" is nothing but a shadow of the spirit as in cloudy weather the moon is not visible above the clouds but there is a bigger hollow image in the cloud, which gives the impression that there is a moon above the clouds. This hollow image is nothing but our "I".

This "I" or "Ahm" can be subdued, by practising in our day-to-day life, five Basic Elements i.e. Truth, Honesty, Humility, Obedience and Love (Sacrifice). Only when "I" is subdued, can the control of bonds be loosened. This can be achieved by restricting the attention to the bonds only to the extent needed for sustaining our body.

It may also be mentioned that Discipline plays a vital role in subduing the Mind. Discipline is not a set of rules for a particular time & space as generally understood. For attaining the highest level of Spiritual Consciousness, Discipline stands for 24 hours a day (all time & space) Regularity, Punctuality, Moderate Thought & Behaviour governed with Moral Values at all levels i.e. Material, Physical, Mental, & Spiritual.

Our Spirit provides energy through the attention current to our Mind, in oreder to think, and to our Body, in order to act, and if there is no attention current attached to any particular component of our body then it will be latent and in the same way the mind & body will be latent.

In view of this, it is clear that "Spirit" (Surat, Rooh, or Soul) is of paramount importance in this creation as it sustains each & everything and gives life to every animate and inanimate object. Nothing can exist without the Spirit. In our body the Spirit works through our Attention Current, which is almost always flowing outwardly. Hence all the activities in this world are performed. This continuous outward flow of the spiritual current weakens us physically & mentally.

Thus, by reversing the flow of attention current from flowing outwardly, the total energy is concentrated inwardly and moves upwardly towards the seat of the spirit. When the Attention current is, thus, cut-off from all the coarse matter, it gains strength and is able to stay at the seat of the Spirit by *Sumiran* (repetition of Holy Name) and *Dhyan* (Contemplation of Holy Form). It is the only means of attaining higher levels of spiritual consciousness that in The Religion of Saints, it is known as "Surat Shabd Yog" or "Sahaj Shabd Yog". This is not a difficult process if one has a simple and self-less mind and devotes himself to the Holy Feet of the Supreme Father.

The above topic has also been depicted in the cone shape. The Cone shape is adopted with a view that the top point of the Cone is Omni-potent, Omniscient & Omni-intelligent which has zoomed out up to the base of the Cone.

When we look at the circumference of the Cone base, we find that on each and every point of the circumference, as mentioned in physics, two forces are acting upon us i.e. centrifugal and centripetal force. Our desires work as centripetal force, which brings sorrow to us.

When we practice to have control over our Senses and Inner-self with moderate behaviour and thought, then it brings stability to us on the point of the circumference where we stand. This strength comes from Satsang and Seva.

The important act of Parmarath is to apply centripetal force on us by way of 'Prem', 'Preeti' and 'Pratiti', which leads towards Centre of the Cone's base and then ascending perpendicularly towards the top point of the Cone with the celestial tune of the last abode. Thus, the whole knowledge spread over the circumference of the Cone's base zooms in to a focal point i.e. Centre of the circumference. This point within us is known as 'SURAT' and our body comprising of all the senses, is the circumference. Further, as it is elevated from the Centre-point, the elevation process starts and knowledge is also enhanced, purified and precise; it can be described as Meeting with Truth and later on Ultimate Truth.

Chapter 33

Self-Surrender (Sarangati) Leads to Higher Consciousness

SANDEEP GUPTA
Dayalbagh Educational Institute (Deemed University), Agra, India

DHARAMPAL SATSANGI
Dayalbagh Educational Institute (Deemed University), Agra, India

Abstract
Fundamental to esoteric metaphysics is the Law of Unity which derives from the fact that a spectrum of consciousness underlies all existence. Depending on spiritual evolution it assumes varying grades from Vaikhari to Madhyama to Pashyanti to the ultimate known as Para or Super Consciousness. Corresponding to these grades of consciousness are sound and vibration that envelope the entire existence. Super Consciousness with its un-manifest sound and vibration is referred to as God and the Sant Satguru is its manifest form. Connecting the Manifest and Un-manifest is the Cosmic sound called 'Naada' or 'Shabda' extending like a ladder from the Sant Satguru (The Manifest) to God 'The Super Consciousness' (The Un-Manifest). Seek refuge in Sant Satguru, catch hold of 'Shabda' by His Grace, and reach God 'The Super Consciousness', rung by rung.

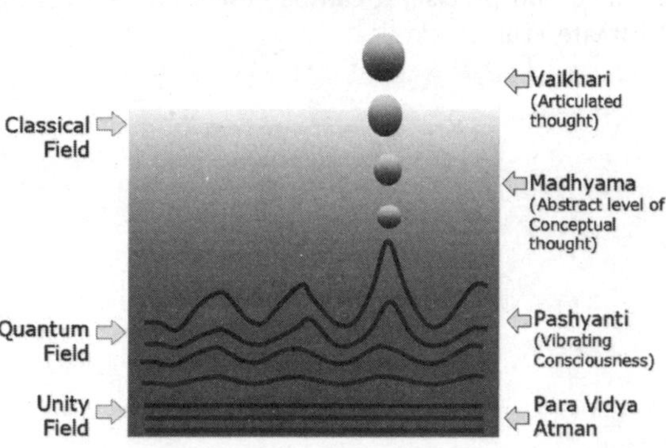

Fundamental to esoteric metaphysics is the Law of Unity which derives from the fact that a spectrum of consciousness envelopes all existence. Our being is divided into four layers of consciousness. As we speak this is the last (fourth) layer called *Vaikhari* which means "fruition", i.e. flowering. But even before we speak a word it becomes manifest as a feeling, as an experience; that is the third stage called *Madhyama*, "the middle." But even before something is experienced inside, in a latent form and we cannot experience it ordinarily unless we are very meditative and have become so totally calm that even a stirring in the seed which has not sprouted yet, can be perceived; it is very subtle. This is called *Pashyanti* which means "looking back", looking to the source; and is the second layer. And beyond that is our fundamental being out of which everything emanates. That is called Para which means "the transcendental" or Super Consciousness.

These states of consciousness correspond with the four states known technically as *jagrat, svapna, susupti*, and *turiya* - or the wakeful state, the dreaming state, the dreamless state, and the transcendental state.

Each level of consciousness corresponds to a level of existence, and its cosmic sound and vibration. One's own experience of them depends upon the refinement of one's consciousness. It takes one of realized consciousness (Para consciousness) to experience the full range of existence and it is Sant Satguru who can comprehend all the four stages.

The Law of Unity Consciousness

Following from this perception, esoteric thinkers next saw that the entire cosmos is a manifestation of the underlying un-manifest consciousness, and the manifest takes form from the formless un-manifest, and continues to be sustained by it. The manifest cosmos cannot be differentiated from the underlying un-manifest consciousness, and accordingly they have concluded that existence has three fundamental aspects: (1) the manifest consciousness (the cosmos), (2) the un-manifest Super Consciousness, and (3) the unity of these two. Esoteric thinkers perceived that it is all three together, which constitute the Law of Unity Consciousness.

Spirituality, as defined by the esoteric thinkers, is an engagement with the un-manifest Super Consciousness. It is not predicated on rituals or dogma, rather, it is an experience which comes out of direct perception and leads to the goal where the separate manifest and un-manifest aspects of consciousness merge back into a unity. United, humanity then becomes a living aspect of the Law of Unity Consciousness, of which "*Fatherhood of God and Brotherhood of Man*" is the natural outcome.

Sant Satguru as Manifest and Un-manifest

In the Sant Mat Philosophy, Sant Satguru is the manifest form of the formless Un-manifest Super Consciousness. He is available for perception of the senses, for the feelings of the mind, and for the understanding of the intellect. That, which is not available for any one of these instruments of cognition, is considered as the un-manifest and is mainly for understanding and philosophizing. Lord Krishna says in the Gita:

The foolish think of Me, the Un-manifest, as having come to manifestation, not knowing My higher, immutable and peerless nature. ..... [Gita 7:24]

Since ages, man has been striving to reduce the gap between himself and God. There are two ways of doing this: One way is to elevate humankind towards Divinity, and the person who achieves this state is believed to have attained perfection. The second way is to bring the un-manifest God to human level in the manifest form of Sant Satguru. Here, Divinity manifests itself for the sake of humankind, so man can relate to Him, concentrate his attention on His form and love and worship Him.

Spiritual evolution through self-surrender is typically eastern whereas the western perspective is based on the concept of a messenger and hence is necessarily more formal. Followers of the Bhakti tradition and the Sufis are more comfortable with the idea of Sant Satguru as God manifest who comes to the devotee for an intimate relationship. Love for God becomes authentic when one is assured of His love for us. In the Bhagavad Gita, it is Lord Krishna Himself who first tells Arjuna: "*You are dear to me*", which enabled Arjuna to surrender.

The Radhasoami Faith gives the assurance that following its teachings, a devotee shall attain the final Abode (Super Consciousness) within four lives. As has been said in the Scriptures of the Radhasoami Faith:

एक जन्म गुरुभक्ति कर जन्म दूसरे नाम
जन्म तीसरे मुक्तिपद चौथे में निज धाम [Sar Bachan (poetry), pp 176]

Translation: The first life is for devotion to the Sat Guru, in the second, one should practice contemplation of the 'Shabda', in the third life the consciousness level of the devotee ascends to Mukti Pad (Sunn Loka), and in the fourth life he reaches the Final Abode.

Note: The lives here refer to stages in the ascendance of consciousness. An earnest devotee can transcend more than one stage in one physical life.

Self Surrender (Saranagati) for Consciousness Elevation

Once we recognize Sant Satguru as the manifest form of the Un-manifest God, and the entire phenomenon of creation as the descent of consciousness with the primordial Sound in various sound forms in between, suddenly, the entire creation is filled with 'That', and "Thou art that", rRoelh .

Originating from the un-manifest and projecting through to the manifest is a continuous spectrum of consciousness based on the layers of Karmik sheaths that make Super Consciousness and its primordial sound assumes different forms as it travels through the varying mediums of mind and matter to make contact with the manifest. The primordial sound (Shabda), therefore, while assuming different forms, serves as an unbroken link between the two Principles - one without form (i.e. Super Consciousness) and the other with-form (Sant Satguru).

Seeking refuge in the Sant Satguru is to latch on to His consciousness in a spirit of humility and help-less-ness until the Guru manifests within the devotee as Shabd Guru. Once manifested, the Shabd Guru takes charge, so to say, of onward ascendance of consciousness to the formless Super Consciousness (un-manifest). This is the final Abode of the Spirit, wherefrom, having reached once, there is no return. This has been described in the Scriptures of the Radhasoami Faith, thus:

गुरु बल काल करम सिर फोड़ूँ
माया की फाड़ूँ चदरिया हो
जोत रूप लख त्रिकुटी धाऊँ

चंदा की निरखूँ उजरिया हो

....

राधास्वामी चरन जाय फिर परसूँ
मिला पद अमर उजियारा हो -----------[Prem Bani IV, pp66]

Translation: Describing the ascendance of the Spirit Current the author says that with the strength of the *Guru* I set aside *Kaal* and *Maya* and proceed to have audience with the Cosmic Light. Moving further on I pay obeisance at the feet of Radhasoami and thus reach my Eternal Abode of Super Consciousness.

On this journey, as a devotee evolves into higher states of consciousness, he hears 'different' Sound forms which really are a variation of the primordial Sound itself. Saints have declared that there is actually no difference between the 'Shabda' and the Lord Himself. As Christ has said:

"*In the beginning was the Word*
and the Word was with God
and the Word was God
and the word became manifest."

The statement implies that the universe is nothing but an expression and manifestation of the Divine. God is not in the universe but the universe is God. Whether something is manifest in the physical, astral or causal world, animate or inanimate, seen or unseen, perceived or unperceived, it all constitutes God as Sound or 'Shabda'.

Param Sants in the *Radhasoami* tradition have revealed the primordial Sound form as Radhasoami, which reverberates in the entire Cosmos. Its various forms, as it transcends through different layers of consciousness to take its manifest form in the Sant Satguru, are *Sat, Soham, Rarang*, and *Om*. Sant Satgurus have laid great emphasis on contemplation (*Surat Shabda Yoga*) after taking refuge in the Sant Satguru, for the latent power of the primordial sound becomes manifest through its repetition (*Jaap*) as *Shabd Guru*, and the subconscious layers of mind are awakened. The devotee '*catching hold*' of the 'Shabda' gradually ascends from lower levels of consciousness to higher levels, on way to Super Consciousness. Scriptures of the Radhasoami Faith say:

शब्द डोर निज घर से लागी
चलो चढ़ पकड़ रसरिया हो .... [Prembani Part IV pp 66]

Translation: Catch hold of the ropeway of primordial sound attached to the Ultimate Abode, and reach the Eternal Home.

It is further said:

स्वामी मेहर बिचार बचन धीरज अस बोले
सुनहु भेद अब सार कहत हूँ तुमसे खोले

....

जे बड़भागी जीव मिले सतगुर से आई
चरन कमल सिर धार रहे तिन माहिं समाई
तिनकी सुरत लपेट शब्द में इक दिन धुर घर
सहजहि दें पहुँचाय मेहर से प्यारे सतगुर -------- [Prem Bilas I to IV, pp 101]

Translation: Those who have been lucky enough to find the Sant Satguru and have taken refuge in Him; their Spirit, guided by the primordial Shabda will easily reach the Final Abode one day.

Quality of Devotion

Devotees often feel dejected when even after practicing devotion to the Sant Satguru for an extended period they do not feel the ecstasy of *Saranagati*. This is a condition that is experienced by all earnest devotees and indicates that the bounds of lower level consciousness have not yet been completely transcended. According to the Scriptures of the Radhasoami Faith complete surrender and true Saranagati comes only after one crosses the limits of body, mind and intellect, by developing intense love and faith in the feet of the Satguru. This leads to firm belief, and humility develops; and humility is the pre-requisite to *Saranagati*.

Epilogue

Sant Satguru is the manifest form of the un-manifest Ultimate Reality and surrender to Him is the easiest way for manifestation of Shabd Guru within the devotee. The Shabd Guru then leads the devotee to higher realms of consciousness until it reaches the un-manifest Super Consciousness.

References

Huzur Maharaj [Rai Bahadur Salig Ram Sahab] (1983). *Prem Patra, Parts I-III*. Agra, India: Radhasoami Satsang Sabha, Dayalbagh.

Lal Sahab [Dr. Makund Behari Lal Sahab] (1986). Bachan at Murar, *The Dayalbagh Herald,* December 2. Agra, India: Radhasoami Satsang Sabha, Dayalbagh.

Maharaj Sahab [Pandit Brahm Sankar Misra Sahab] (2004). *Discourses on Radhasoami Faith.* Agra, India: Radhasoami Satsang Sabha, Dayalbagh.

Param Purush Puran Dhani Huzur Soamiji Maharaj [Shiv Dayal Singh Sahab] (1980). *Sar Bachan (Poetry)*. Agra, India: Radhasoami Satsang Sabha, Dayalbagh.

Sahabji Maharaj [Sir Anand Sarup Kt.] (1980). *Prem Bilas Parts 1 to 4.* Dayalbagh, Agra: Radhasoami Satsang Sabha.

Sahabji Maharaj [Sir Anand Sarup Kt.] (2006). *Writings and Speeches of Param Guru Sahabji Maharaj.* Agra, India: Radhasoami Satsang Sabha, Dayalbagh.

Swami Chinmayananda (2001). *Srimad Bhagvad Gita.* Chapter III. Mumbai, India: Central Chinmaya Mission Trust.

Chapter 34

Survival of the Fittest: Achieving Higher Levels of Consciousness

ANJU SRIVASTAVA
Dayalbagh Educational Institute (Deemed University), Agra, India

SANJAY SRIVASTAVA
Dayalbagh Educational Institute (Deemed University), Agra, India

Abstract

In this paper we elicit a new dimension to the term 'survival of the fittest', a term popularly used in the theory of evolution and explicate its relevance for the survival of human race in the light of achieving higher levels of consciousness – a meaningful survival.

Introduction

In 1859, Charles Darwin set out his theory of evolution by natural selection as an explanation for adaptation and speciation. The concept of fitness is central to natural selection. Broadly, individuals who are more "fit" have better potential for survival, as in the well-known phrase "survival of the fittest" – the individuals who best adapt to the environment are the ones who will most likely survive. They possess variations that give them a selective advantage. It is pertinent to mention two related terms in the context of evolution – Neo-Darwinism, and Social Darwinism. Wikipedia defines these terms as follows: (1) Neo-Darwinism is a term used to describe the 'modern synthesis' of Darwinian evolution through natural selection with Mendelian genetics, the latter being a set of primary tenets specifying that evolution involves the transmission of characteristics from parent to child through the mechanism of genetic transfer, rather than the 'blending process' of pre-Mendelian evolutionary science, (2)

Social Darwinism is a pejorative term used for various late nineteenth century ideologies which, while often contradictory, exploited ideas of survival of the fittest. In sociology it has been defined as a theory of social evolution which asserts that "There are underlying, and largely irresistible, forces acting in societies which are like the natural forces that operate in animal and plant communities. One can therefore formulate social laws similar to natural ones. These social forces are of such a kind as to produce evolutionary progress through the natural conflicts between social groups. The best-adapted and most successful social groups survive these conflicts, raising the evolutionary level of society generally (the 'survival of the fittest')."

Evolutionary thought, however, extends beyond the study of life. If we can coin a term – spiritual fitness – it should be defined as the higher and purer form of fitness which one should acquire for the evolution of a better world. The characteristics of spiritual fitness are in contrast with the fitness defined in the Neo-Darwinism, or in the Social Darwinism One does not acquire it by competing and struggling with others; rather one has to struggle with oneself to attain it.

Struggling with oneself implies struggling with one's own mind (*mann*) which is an important teaching in the Religion of Saints as emphasized in the following lines:

Mann Maro Tan Ko Jaro
Indri Ras Bhog Bisaro
(Sarbachan (Nazm), page 364, print year 1998)

Karni Karo Mar Mann Dalo
Indriya Rok Duwara
(Sarbachan (Nazm), page 650, print year 1998)

By definition, spiritual fitness should have different degrees and it does. One can surely deduce that the higher degrees of spiritual fitness can be acquired by achieving higher levels of consciousness. In Hindu philosophy *Turiya* and *Turiyatita* refer to higher levels of consciousness in the increasing order. A few relevant definitions of consciousness follow.

Consciousness – The state of being aware; collective thoughts and feelings of an individual or an aggregate of people. The evolution of consciousness involves the expansion and deepening of the individual and group's potential for thought, understanding and awareness.

(The evolution of spiritual consciousness: interface between integral science and spirituality, past and emerging, page 336, 2004)

Consciousness is called *Prajna* in Sanskrit – It is awareness in its fullness – pertaining to a certain level. It is also a great term in Buddhist tradition. It is made out clearly that the sole purpose of all the spiritual exercises is the elevation of the human soul to those levels of consciousness.

(Lecture Notes, THM 201, Unit 4: Lesson 2, page 11, 2008)

The Religion of Saints and Spiritual Fitness

We may wonder and question the extent of the ultimate level of consciousness and the process by which it can be achieved in order to acquire the highest degree of spiritual fitness. The Religion of Saints or Radhasoami Faith has pointed out the ways to achieve the highest and the purest level of consciousness – higher than *Turiya* and *Turiyatita*. It is this level of consciousness which can make an individual capable of acquiring the highest degree of spiritual fitness. A brief description of the philosophy of the Religion of Saints follows.

In the last few hundred years, starting from the advent of Kabir Sahib, who is considered *Adi Sant*, we have a succession of great Saints whose teachings are uniform in nature and are collectively called the *Sant Mat* (the Religion of Saints). *Kabir Sahib, Guru Nanak*, the founder of Sikhism, *Tulsi Sahib, Soamiji Maharaj*, the founder of the Radhasomi Faith, are the great names among them. Some of the *Sufi Fakirs* like *Sams Tabrej* and *Maulana Rumi* are also reckoned among them. These saints speak of higher levels of spiritual consciousness above *Turiya* and *Turiyatita*. They taught the practice of listening to spiritual sounds or Holy Names of *OM*, *SATNAM*, and *RADHASOAMI*, the repetition of which is the only means of salvation. This is referred to as *Anhad Shabd Yoga*, *Surat Shabda Yoga* or *Sultan-ul-Azkar*. The Radhasoami Faith is explained in the most scientific way in 'Discourses on Radhasoami Faith, Param Guru Maharaj Sahab 3rd Revered Sant Satguru, Radhasoami Faith, Dayalbagh, Pub. R.S. Sabha, Dayalbagh, Agra, 1960.

(Lecture Notes, THM 201, Unit 1: Lecture 2, page 7, 2008)

However, one cannot progress in the direction of achieving higher and purer spiritual fitness without a living Sant Satguru as described in the Radhasoami Faith, as evident from below

According to the Radhasoami Faith, the Supreme Being has blessed the human body with certain latent faculties, by awakening of which, the spirit entity can establish contact with different regions of the Creation. The development of these faculties should be the aim of a man's life. The Supreme Being has also been pleased to ordain the advent on earth, from time to time, of holy and awakened Souls from the highest regions, fully conversant with the secrets of the latent human faculties and the practical methods of awakening them, in order to help *Jivas*, to attain salvation. In the Radhasoami Faith, they are described as Sant Satgurus. Now their advent is a line of perpetual succession. The founder of the Religion was Param-Purush Puran Dhani Soamiji Maharaj. The Faith lays down that in order to awaken the spiritual faculties; one has to become the disciple of some competent and accomplished teacher. In the Radhasaomi Faith the Sant Satguru is such a teacher.

(Lecture Notes, THM 201, Unit 1: Lecture 2, page 8, 2008)

A person with good *sanskars* (imprints left on the subconscious mind by experiences in this and previous lives) can only seek the refuge of Sant Satguru as per the Radhasoami Faith. A complete love towards Sant Satguru is of paramount importance in this Faith. Thus an individual with good *sanskars* can achieve the highest level of consciousness and therefore the highest degree of spiritual fitness by developing a true love towards the Supreme Father/Sant Satguru and by obeying His orders and mandates with full devotion. The beauty of spiritual fitness lies in its positive impact on society and the whole human race. Individuals with higher spiritual fitness not only make themselves fit for their meaningful survival in this world and beyond, but also support and benefit others in the population rather than competing with each other within a population for their survival – in other words, they work towards achieving the aim of Fatherhood of God and Brotherhood of Man. Such individuals together may be termed as a superior human race – a race which is also concerned for the welfare of the whole world – a race which will conclusively make a better world. It is worth quoting the following words of Param Guru Sahabji Maharaj, 4th Revered Sant Satguru, Radhasoami Faith, Dayalbagh, in this context:

> "Religion is the greatest gift of God to humanity and is also the most ancient friend of man, in the coming future it will prove itself to be the

saviour of human race." "From Religion I mean the spiritual light that purifies and illumines the human heart, that elevates and expands the human soul and that makes it possible for the human mind to realise the Fatherhood of God and Brotherhood of Man.

(Vishva Ke Vividh Dharma, page 5, 2004)

References

Dayalbagh Educational Institute (Deemed University) (2004). *Vishva Ke Vividh Dharma*. Agra, India: DEI, Dayalbagh.

Gulick, Donna (Spring 2004). The Evolution of Spiritual Consciousness: Interface between Integral Science and Spirituality, Past and Emerging. *World Futures* 60 (4), 335 – 341.

Maharaj Sahab [Pandit Brahm Sankar Misra Sahab] (2004). *Discourses on Radhasoami Faith*. Agra, India: Radhasoami Satsang Sabha, Dayalbagh.

Param Purush Puran Dhani Huzur Soamiji Maharaj [Shiv Dayal Singh Sahab] (1998). *Sar Bachan* (Nazm). Agra, India: Radhasoami Satsang Sabha, Dayalbagh.

VII

Scientific Perception Studies

Chapter 35

Radhasoami and the Future of Religion

MARK JUERGENSMEYER
University of California, Santa Barbara, USA

Abstract
This paper examines the prospect of finding a truly global religion. One which will not be anchored to the past but will steer towards a future where science and religion can finally form a nexus and realize that they need not be mutually exclusive. It aims to find a future global religion which is not tethered to dogmatism and ritualism but is liberal and pragmatic. It aims to find a future global religion which is not custom oriented to any particular community but suitable for humanity at large. This paper aims to illustrate that the Radhasoami faith is just such a religion.

India's first Prime Minister Jawaharlal Nehru came to Dayalbagh shortly after India's independence and said that he has heard of the marvelous accomplishments of Dayalbagh and he wanted to come and witness it with his own eyes. He did and he was impressed and I am impressed also. The Radhasoami tradition has changed at least outwardly in a 150 years since its inception and of course its central truths remain intact. But a 150 years ago there was simply a sadhu camp across the road where Soami Bagh is now located. According to Master Anand Swarup the spot where DEI now stands was all mounds of dirt and pits and an awful sight. It was then renovated and made into this magnificent location, this garden of Soami Dayal, this garden of Mercy. So, extraordinary things have happened. And in many ways of course the Radhasoami tradition has come out of the Indian context, it has come out of the particular character of those masters who have molded it.

So, the question for me and also the question for you as a scholar of the study of world religions is "Do we think of Radhasoami as a local tradition or as a global religion?" And I want to present its position in these brief remarks. The Radhasoami Faith is a global religion and this conclusion is based on three points; first of all, its universality. The great sociologist Max Weber once categorized religious traditions according to their universality, the religions of universal salvation. He set world religions according to particular peoples and places. Judaism for example and Hinduism, in both religions, they depend upon a relationship to a particular people and a particular place. Christianity which grew out of Judaism and Buddhism that grew out of Hinduism were universal religions. They took some of the ideas from the original tradition but they made it universal, available to everyone. And the same of course is true with the Radhasoami tradition. Ideas and practices may be familiar with or lifted out of the Indian context and made available to anyone, anywhere. They can be practiced by people of any background, any religion, any social location, in any part of the globe.

It reminds me of the fact that while in Delhi a couple of years ago, I went to a clothing shop to buy some shirts to take back to the United States. I saw behind the clothing merchant a picture. And I immediately recognized the picture as one of the masters in the Radhasoami tradition and asked him a question. "How is this picture different from the pictures of Shiva or pictures of Krishna?" The other people in the shop looked shocked but looking at me, the merchant smiled and said, "Oh! I do not know Shiva, I do not know Krishna. I can't get to know them without a priest, without a ritual. But you see this Master? I know Him and He knows me. And there's nothing between Him and me except His love". What a remarkable thing! He did not need all of the trappings, a ritual, place and priest, all of the conventional edifices of religion to become a direct disciple in His Master's love. So there is universality in Radhasoami.

The second point that I am going to make in favour of Radhasoami as a global religion is its post-secularism. Now, in the modern world, especially after enlightenment in Europe and America an attempt was made to separate religion from the secular world. The two were thought to be totally and entirely separate boxes. Religion was supposed to be encapsulated in a little corner of the world so that it would not intrude on secular life. At this moment of what is called post modernity when some of the assumptions of modern rationality are being challenged, sometimes intellectually, sometimes politically on the streets with resurgence movements around the world. An attempt however, is being made to rethink that kind of sacred division and try to look for elements of morality and spirituality, within sacred life, to look for rationality and the clarity of order that can also be found within religious traditions. But I submit to you that this has been a part of the Radhasoami tradition from the very beginning when science and the soul were seen to be not two different things but part of the same thing. I mentioned earlier that one promotes now not *other worldliness* but rather *better worldliness*.

Again, I have a story to illustrate this point. I was talking with a professor in India, a scientist who I knew to be a satsangi and I said to him, "You know in my university in the United States, it is often very difficult to admit your religion among your colleagues. They will think somehow you are less intellectual, you are less rational, and you are less scientific". I said at the same time, many people within certain religions are very frightened of science. They are afraid that the scientific laws, the scientific approach will intrude and destroy it. There are Christians who are afraid of theories of evolution, theories of science that will undermine religion". I said, "How do you deal with this division? How do you deal with the fears as a religious person of science, and as a scientific person with religion?" Then he looked at me and he smiled. He said, "What is there to fear? As a scientist I am seeking the truth. As a satsangi, I am seeking the truth! There is only one truth. There are different ways to look at it, but there is only one truth. What is there to fear? There is no difference between me as a scientist and me as a satsangi". And that said, we realize that the truth is one and there is nothing to fear in the spiritual quest and there is nothing to fear in the scientific quest.

We are all in some ineffable way trying to approach a deeper sense of reality. A reality that cannot be seen because after all where will science be if we already knew everything that there was to be known? The mystery of science is that there is a mystery of the reality in this world. The mystery of religion is that there is a mystery of reality in this world. So it seems to be that in post-secularism, Radhasoami has already shown that it is a global religion. There is the emphasis on the future. Most religious traditions are deeply embedded in the past. They look towards the great scriptures, the great teachings, the great masters who walked long ago on this earth, of the great legends that were really beyond any kind of historical calculation. But with the Radhasoami tradition of course, this is never entirely the case. Of course there is a great tradition to be recalled but the sense of mastery is with us.

There is a present day sense of - as one of the satsangis from the United States tried to explain why she was so taken with the Radhasoami message. You know when I was in SUNY and was a Christian, we learned about biblical times. And I tried to imagine what it could be like so long ago. She said here, among the master, I am living in biblical times. I am in biblical times. So the sense of spirituality and spiritual knowledge, and spiritual truth are very much about - being a part of the present. This is deeply a part of the Radhasoami tradition and beyond that of course it is a part of the future. Again we can see this on the walls of REI Hall - the virtue that Dayalbagh has proclaimed; there is an extraordinary reason why Nehru came here, not just to see what Dayalbagh achieved but to see India's future, to see what India could become. Because the Radhasoami community is in some extraordinary way an alternative society, a visionary society, a society of the future but one in which you could live in, one you could be in, that you can experience. Social reality and a social sense of the future is also a part of the Radhasoami teachings.

I know of no other religious tradition where the name of the tradition is also the name of the highest order of reality that one works towards and aspires for in the future. So the very name Radhasoami suggests the future towards which one seeks to aspire on one's spiritual journey. Again I have a story to illustrate this fact. When I was living in India I would often stay on the mounts in Mussoorie, where there is a wonderful programme in Hindi. Since a voice troubled me to master Hindi, this gave me an opportunity to focus on it this summer. It happened that one of my neighbours were a lovely couple from Britain who would come to India to be close to their master in the Radhasoami tradition. They would bring me over tea, we would talk and I knew that the time was coming when they had to leave India. Their passport and visa were expiring so people expected them back in England. I knew that they had no job when they returned, and they had no solid plans, so I said to the wife, "Kate, aren't you anxious about or aren't you fearful about the future? Aren't you afraid that you don't know what's going to happen to you all through your way?" And she said, "I am a satsangi. I know what is going to happen to me all through my way. And I know how I am going to get there. Well I don't always know what is going to happen between now and then. But that's not very important, isn't it?" I said, "Well, I guess you are right. I mean if your sense of future is much more grand than what you are going to do next year when you return in England, then you really have much more of a sense of your trajectory; trajectory of life". So, it seems to me that this future orientation both socially and in Radhasoami teachings are yet another thing that convinces me that Radhasoami is a global religion.

Here's a go, I was privileged to work on a book Radhasoami Reality that you have mentioned, and since then I have worked on many things so I thought that I should review what I wrote before coming to join you, and I was surprised to discover that my closing words in the book echoes in the notes that I prepared to give you in my remarks today about how the Radhasoami tradition really speaks to the global future. These are my concluding sentences. It seems to me that Radhasoami's central notion that the truth and the authority can be embodied in a person, that transformation of the self accrues for the purification of the perception of energy. That love in the community can be experienced in the dispersion, that social service is based on personal commitment and the time and place have ultimate centres.

These fundamental ideas in the Radhasoami tradition each contain features of modern and in some cases even post-modern religion. As such the Radhasoami religion may be a harbinger of the religion of the future, not only in India but elsewhere in the world where modernity, modern life, global life is perceived with a certain amount of suspicion because many in the highly developed world now seek what the adherence of the Radhasoami communities have already found. A pattern of religious expression and experience that allows them to identify with their cultural past without accepting what they see as superstitious gaudy excesses. And they embrace modern ways of living without becoming captive to what they perceive as alienating forms of society and still affirm a frugal life style. And I believe these are the elements that describe the Radhasoami's future as a global religion, so I join you in celebrating the Radhasoami religion's glorious past but also its existence as a global religion in the future.

Chapter 36

Systems Approach to Consciousness

PETER H. ROE
Department of Systems Design Engineering, Faculty of Engineering
University of Waterloo, Waterloo, Ontatio, Canada

Abstract

There can be a plausible model of a civilization, with the idea that an input to the various subsystems that involved spiritual awareness would be necessary for peaceful progress.[1] The idea of developing this model is attempted in this paper following a series of steps that involve:

- ***Establishing a pair of complementary variables that satisfy the continuity and potential principles, such that one variable sums to zero in circuits (the through variable and the other sums to zero at points (the across variable)***
- ***Characterizing the various identified subsystems as multi-terminal components, with relations among their through and across variables***
- ***Formulating a system graph, etc.***

However, the properties of human nature which were identified in the model as being major influences on the development of particular forms of civilization, namely cooperativeness and competitiveness, do not have the characteristics necessary for the complementary variables of a graph-theoretic model, so that the model development would not be directly concerned with the theme of spiritual consciousness, so this paper is framed against this approach.

Introduction

It is certainly true that meditation can produce the serene feelings that lead to cooperative attitudes, and when people are awakened spiritually, whole populations can be sufficiently conscious to produce peaceful societies. Nonetheless, religious fervour can and does produce the opposite results, as can be seen in many conflicts through history to the present day.

How then should a professor of systems engineering approach a seminar sponsored and attended by eminent scholars of comparative religion? It is with a measure of trepidation and humility that I will bring up a few ideas which may be obvious to an Indian, but which are less so in the West. I am clearly a North American of European origin, specifically an Anglo-Irish Canadian, and this is the background of my contribution to SPIRCON 2010.

Spirituality, Religion and Meditation: Preliminary Distinctions

Spirituality is that innate property of the human race that causes us to yearn for knowledge of powers greater than ourselves, provides a hope for insight

[1] Peter H. Roe, Inaugural Address, SPAWSYS 2008, DEI, Agra, India.

into the reasons for our lives and leads us to search for purpose for humanity and the whole of existence – it is at the core of every person's being.

We must therefore understand that at least a germ of the spiritual lies within each human being. Even further, every person alive has had, or will have, an experience of some kind that leads to an awareness of this innate characteristic. Moreover, we must acknowledge that spirituality is an essential precursor to religion of whatever form.

Religions are the gathering together of certain aspects of spirituality into coherent forms of belief and faith in humanity's attempts to understand the unknowable. The ancient religions harnessed spirituality and attempted to explain the world as known in their times and places. For example, the dwellers of valley of the Nile saw the annual flooding of their valley, which continually enriched their land, observed the variation of the suns rays according to season, and formed their religion which ascribed all power to the sun God. This religion lasted for some thousands of years, through the Pharaonic period, until further knowledge about the climatic cycles and the relationship of the sun to its planets became available.

Some religions survive changes in scientific knowledge. Their origins continue, but become understood as myths, parables and allegories which serve to illuminate and enrich the sets of beliefs and doctrines that surround them. For example, it is difficult to believe the literal truth of the story in Judeo-Christian[2] scripture of the formation of the first woman from the rib of the first man on earth; in the same way, we cannot take as literal history the adventures and misadventures of *Sita* in the Ramayana[3]. Today, we treat these as allegorical.

Of course, there are also relatively modern religions, an example being the Baha'i faith, founded in Persia in 1863. The Baha'i[4] religion is monotheistic and its followers believe in the ultimate unity of all religions; they are also ardent believers in (eventual) world peace.

As we have stated, spirituality is a precursor in humanity to all religions and all religions rely on spirituality to assert their essence. Accordingly, true followers of any religion need to achieve consciousness of their own spirituality.

Meditation is a means of achieving spiritual consciousness. It is neither spirituality nor religion, but is a process, used particularly in the Eastern religions, but also in Christianity, for transcending the worldly and secular and thereby achieving the inner peace that allows an individual's spiritual essence to come to the forefront of his or her mental consciousness. Meditation, whether practiced by Buddhists, Hindus or Christians, could perhaps be described as a way toward uncovering the inner meaning of faith.

Faith is a step beyond belief. A detailed discussion of the relation between faith, belief and reason is beyond the scope of this presentation.[5] One can

---

[2] The Holy Bible, Book of Genesis, Chapter 2.

[3] Ramayana as translated by C. Rajagopalachari, Bhavan's Book University, 1958.

[4] For information, see http://www.bahai.org.

[5] See, for example, David Wisdom, *Kierkegaard on belief, faith, & explanation*, Columbia University

believe something, using one's intellect, despite it being impossible to prove. I summarized, for instance, some arguments for the existence of an almighty, purposeful creator in an article for the journal, *Literary Paritantra* (Systems)[6], but it is an act of faith to extend that belief to a manifestation of the almighty here on earth. Thus, my personal faith is that God was incarnate in a man called Jesus and appeared on earth some 2000 years ago. It is faith that leads Muslims to prayer; it is faith that imbues the followers of the Bab; it is faith that reinforces the worshippers of Krishna.

Spiritual Consciousness through Meditation

All the great religions of the world agree that meditation is a path toward spiritual awareness. The strongest proponents of following this path are those in the subcontinent, but this way is not closed to others.

What is meditation? It is, as we have already said, a means of reaching that inner calm that helps to become a part of the divine. When we achieve that state, let us call it spiritual consciousness, we will be able to hear that "still small voice of God" which disperses fear, bringing trust, serenity and repose. This is something that can be learned. There is a book by Jon Kabut-Zin[7] which teaches the Buddhist way for meditation. It teaches people in the West how to set about meditation and achieve this peace.

H.K. Kesavan points out that "even the interim benefits of spiritual meditation are quite attractive." In more detail, he says:

"Once one commences the spiritual journey with recourse to the daily experience of the higher state of consciousness, however fleeting it may be, one develops the habit of keeping up with the pleasant practice for its own sake without consciously looking for the distant goal ... The rejuvenating process itself lends, most assuredly, ever increasing charm to life in general and, consequently, provides a great deal of internal contentment. When the sun rises in the morning, one looks forward eagerly to the meditative process, and the tranquility experienced invariably has the effect of spilling over to the rest of the day. ... As time progresses and as the practice matures along with other aids to experience, whatever intellectual doubts that creep in from time to time will gradually melt away of their own accord, and the proverbial meandering mind will propel itself, more often than not, to a state of complete stillness and total tranquility. All this internal transformation is likely to take place with a minimum of effort. It is as if the mind were returning to its natural state of deep rest without the least necessity of any internal guidance or external control, very much like the homing instinct of birds."[8]

Christian Meditation[9] differs from Hindu and Buddhist meditation in a number of ways. For instance most forms of Christian meditation emphasize

---

[6] Peter H. Roe, *Creation, the Universe, and Systems*, Literary Paritantra (Systems), Vol. 1 No. 1 & 2, pp 25-28.

[7] Jon Kabat-Zinn, *Full Catastrophe Living*, Bantam-Dell, New York, 1990.

[8] H.K. Kesavan, *Science & Spirituality – A Hindu Perspective*, 1st Books, Waterloo, Ontario, Canada, 2003.

[9] See, for example, http://en.wikipedia.org/wiki/Christian_meditation.

contemplation of a religious object, a cross, a bible, or some other symbol, rather than the repetition of a mantra (OM). However the Benedictine[10] monk, John Main[11], taught the use of the mantra, Maranatha, an Aramaic word that can be translated as "Our Lord, come!" Thus he was in consonance both with the Eastern methods and with the idea that Christian meditation is devotional, rather than a means of opening and concentrating the mind to perceive the soul and the almighty within oneself.

Spiritual Consciousness through the Senses

Meditation is a way of putting aside the senses of sight, sound, touch and smell to make the mind free and tranquil, thus bringing awareness of the spirit, but is not the only path to spiritual fulfillment.

If spiritual awareness is only reachable in this way, there would be no point in building the masterful buildings – temples, cathedrals, mosques – whose very sight inspires awe in the mind of the beholder. It matters little whether the visitor is an adherent of the faith of the builders of these remarkable edifices; upon entry under the right circumstances, the immediate sense of wonder can simply, if only for an instant, bring the mind 'face-to-face' as it were, into communion with the almighty.

On a smaller scale, but still available to multitudes at a time, are such things as the Nandi on the Mysore hills, the statue of Jesus above Rio de Janeiro and the bronze Buddha of Kamakura. Again, they evince spiritual consciousness among observers. Moreover, personal objects can have the same function. The amulets carried by the ancient Inuit (Eskimo) people of Northern Canada, the beads fingered by Roman Catholic Christians, the prayer wheels of Tibetan monks, all fall into this category.

Man-made objects need not be specifically religious to evoke spiritual reactions. An example is the famous painting, Guernica, by Picasso, of a village in Spain that had been bombed in the Spanish civil war of the 1930's.[12]

Nature itself can be awe inspiring both on a grand scale and in the small. A double rainbow seen through the window of a train, the magnificence of the view of a mountain peak, the extent of a prairie horizon, the shimmering of the aurora borealis, the quiet of a corner in a flower garden – all these can produce moments in which a person can become conscious of the inner spirit that yearns for the presence of the creator.

Special events in a person's life, especially those charged with emotion, can themselves produce a heightened awareness of the inner spirit. A ritual of passage from childhood to adulthood, for example the bar mitzvah of the Jewish faith, or the confirmation of vows made by adults for an infant, a wedding or a funeral, all fall into this class. But such special occasions are not the only ones

---

[10] The Benedictine Order is part of the Roman Catholic church, the largest sect of Christianity.

[11] John Main was the inspiration behind the foundation, in 1991, of the World Community for Christian Meditation; he died in 1982 at his monastery in Montreal. For information on the WCCM, see http://www.wccm.org.

[12] *Guernica* was initially exhibited in July 1937 at the Spanish Pavilion at the Paris International Expostion It is now in the Museo Nacional Centro de Arte Reina Sofía, in Madrid.

– seemingly chance occurrences can produce the same result.

The sense of smell can also be spiritually awakening. The profound feelings induced by the fragrance of early spring in a northern woods, and even the odour of natural fertilizer spread on a farmer's fields can be enough to evoke the feeling of closeness to the creator of the universe.

Music can be deeply spiritual. From the chants of monks to the huge sounds of orchestral works, with all manner of songs, choirs and musical instruments, it is almost impossible to find individuals who have not had spiritual inspiration from music.

The sounds of nature also awaken spiritual consciousness. The song of a bird can uplift the spirits; the wind whistling through the trees and the sound of waves breaking on a rocky coast – all such things are sources that lead the mind to transcend the limits of workaday living.

Conclusion

I do not wish to leave out the written word as a pathway to heightened spirituality. Profound study of the holy books of one's religion, or of the great works of philosophy, is a major means for improving one's knowledge, searching one's spirit, and enlarging one's faith. The combination of sight, sound, touch and smell found in many religious ceremonies is an extremely powerful agent of spirituality. And to this, one can add meditation. If a person can experience glorious events and regularly practice meditation, such an individual can truly arrive at a level of spiritual consciousness hardly attainable by other means.

Chapter 37

Spirituality of the One System: Dimensions of Time and Space

JACK ELLIS
Professor Emeritus in Environmental Studies York University, Toronto, Canada

Take the understanding of the East
And the knowledge of the West
And then seek.

- G.I. Gurdjieff

Abstract
In recent decades, research in systems concepts and systems understanding has expanded the range and depth of how we understand our world. However, most systems research has been directed to quantification of various phenomena and their interrelationships. With few exceptions this effort has bypassed the philosophical, dialectical and spiritual modes of understanding that have been pursued by mankind since the dawn of humanity. But in India, principally at DEI Dayalbagh, a spiritual dimension of systems theory is being nurtured and developed and a spiritually based model of man and the macrocosm is being created. It is this concept that may hold the greatest potential for achieving a blending of the understanding of the East with the knowledge of the West. The ultimate reality of systems theory is that there is only one system. This paper attempts to explore the implications of this fact for human spirituality: that the microcosm (man) and the macrocosm (Supreme Being, universe) are one. It will touch on how mankind as Homo sapiens has expressed this reality over eons of time, and how it must encompass potentially unlimited dimensions of space. It will explore how the realization of one system might be attained, and how its expression in great religions of the world may not be as estranged from it as may appear from the general view of their practices.

Introduction

The following quotation by George Gurdjieff (1866 -1949), a Russian mystic and spiritual teacher, sums up the motivation behind this paper:

Take the understanding of the East
And the knowledge of the West
And then seek[1].

It is, of course, impossible to wrap up the complete "knowledge of the West" and "the understanding of the East" in one single paper, but various elements

---

[1] G. I. Gurdjieff, as quoted in Peter Ouspensky (1949). In Search of the Miraculous: Fragments Of An Unknown Teaching, New York: Harcourt Brace.

of both will be discussed and related to one another.

Systems theory and systems analysis has been a flourishing field of knowledge in recent decades. Great progress has been made in quantitative modeling of physical systems and of non-physical systems, including social, economic and ecological systems.

All of these efforts have, of necessity, addressed bounded systems. That is, some closed portion of reality has to be selected for the system to be analyzed and results obtained.

The bigger question is: *what happens when one wishes to consider an open system?*

The Space Dimension: The Universe?

Every machine or organism that one wishes to study is connected to its operating environment. This, in turn, is connected to its economic setting, its natural and built environment, and to its social and political setting. Each such setting is connected beyond the field, factory or enterprise into a whole community, which is connected to a nation, which is part of a global entity – our planet Earth.

And planet Earth is part of a solar system, influenced not only by its own star, the Sun, but by a host of interplanetary and interstellar bodies and phenomena. The system, therefore, goes right to the boundaries of our universe. This thought raises the question: *what is the universe, really?*

Much of modern cosmology uses quantum theoretic concepts to postulate that the universe is, ultimately, information[2]. Seth Lloyd, a Professor of "Quantum Mechanical Engineering" at the Massachusetts Institute of Technology, even claims to have calculated the informational content of the universe. He also likens the universe to a quantum computer, and he and some other thinkers[3] claim that the universe is a quantum computer.

Another thought is the universe really an *illusion*, or are we actually living inside some *simulation*? Such a concept can be traced back in western thought to Parmenides and Plato, and in eastern thought to the *Advaita Vedanta.*

And where did the universe come from? The Christian Bible says: "In the beginning was the Word and the Word was with God, and the Word was God.[4]" Vedic religion, including the *Radhasoami* faith, claims this 'Word' is the current of sound or current of consciousness or prime current of spirituality which issued forth from its source, the Supreme Being. It is this current that has produced light, energy, matter and all other forces in our universe.

What do we find when we search for these ingredients of our universe? Despite all the advances in astronomy and stellar measurement over the past

---

[2] See, for instance: Lloyd, Seth (2006). *Programming the Universe: A Quantum Computer Scientist Takes On The Cosmos.* New York: Alfred Knopf, or
Rosenblum, B. and F. Kuttner (2008). *Quantum Enigma: Physics Encounters Consciousness.* New York: Oxford University Press.

[3] Such as Vedral, Vlasko (2010). *Decoding Reality: The Universe As Quantum Information.* Oxford: Oxford University Press.

[4] John, I-1.

several centuries, these studies show that all of the galaxies, stars, planets, and other physical objects that we can detect make up only 0.04% of the total mass-energy of our universe. Intergalactic gas accounts for a further 3.6%. Some 22% is thought to be constituted by 'dark matter' and the remaining 74% by 'dark energy'[5]. This 'dark' 96% is the subject of much research and speculation.

Dark matter was postulated in 1934 by Fritz Zwicky to make the measurements of orbital velocities of galaxies and galaxy clusters agree with the mass required by theory. Dark energy is considered to be the source of energy required to account for the observed increasing rate of expansion of our universe[6].

Is our universe the only one that exists?

Some cosmologists and other thinkers postulate the possibility of several, perhaps many, other universes, '*multiverses*' or perhaps parallel universes, that may exist alongside our own reality[7]. Whether there are such universes or not, it is clear that at the macro level *the system* is infinite! And what is at the micro level? Each component of an organism, machine or device is made up of smaller parts, each of which consists of one or more materials. These materials are comprised of molecules, structured from atoms. And each atom is comprised of a bewildering possible combination of particles. These in turn are comprised of elementary particles; quarks, leptons, bosons, and so on.

It is quite a paradox that the *largest* machine man has ever created – the Large Hadron Collider at CERN, near Geneva – is intended to detect the most *infinitesimal* of sub-atomic particles, including perhaps the elusive Higgs Boson - the one some physicists call the "God particle"[8]. At least, that is about where the present state of western particle physics takes us.

Thus it is clear that at the micro level *the system* is also infinite. There is only one system.

The Time Dimension: Co-Evolution of Mankind and Spiritual Religion

The spirituality of human beings in human societies is the key to spiritual development in and of the universe. In considering the potential for most humans to grasp and integrate the '*one system*' spirituality, we note that the spiritual concept of our being in unity with the '*one system*' has quite a long history.

To give some time perspective, it is believed that the first life forms on this planet emerged about 4,000 million years ago[9]. The first organisms that use

---

[5] Kowalski, M. and D. Rubin (2008). "Improved Cosmological Constraints from New, Old and Combined Supernova Datasets". *The Astrophysical Journal.* Chicago, University of Chicago Press, 686: 749–778.

[6] P. Peebles and B. Ratra (2003). "The cosmological constant and dark energy". *Reviews of Modern Physics* 75: 559–606.

[7] See, for instance: Tegmark, Max (May 2003). "Parallel Universes". *Scientific American.* or J. Schmidhuber (2002): "Hierarchies of generalized Kolmogorov complexities and nonenumerable universal measures computable in the limit". *International Journal of Foundations of Computer Science* 13(4):587-612.

[8] Lederman, L. and D. Teresi (2006) *The God Particle: If The Universe Is The Answer, What Is The Question?* New York: Mariner Books.

[9] The source references for the following discussion of general evolutionary timelines are given in http://en.wikipedia.org/wiki/Timeline_of_human_evolution, retrieved on 12.09.2010.

oxygen appeared only about 2,400 million years ago. The first multi-cellular organism, a sponge-like creature, appeared 600 million years ago. Not until about 265 million years ago did the first mammal-like creatures emerge. Between 85 and 65 million years ago the first primates appeared. During the following eons various branches of apes and monkeys roamed the earth until about 15 million years ago, when the branch of great apes known as *hominidae* split off.

Some 7 million years ago, the first of several lines of erect humanoids emerged[10]. During the period from 800,000 to 500,000 years ago, the brain size of hominid species increased by at least three times. The path of further evolution leading to *Homo sapiens* is still the subject of much anthropological research and debate, but brain size evidently peaked about the time the first archaic *Homo sapiens* appeared.

Spiritual awareness and, in particular, spiritual self-awareness, requires a brain that is large enough to formulate religious and philosophical ideas[11]. Much of the expansion of the evolving hominid's brain took place in the neocortex; the area of the brain responsible for language, emotion and self-awareness. These higher order cognitive functions are necessary for human spirituality to occur. In chimpanzees the neocortex occupies 50% of the brain, whereas in modern humans it occupies 80% of the brain[12].

Even in pre-literate hunter-gatherer societies which constructed few lasting structures or monuments, spirituality is in evidence. Certain practices still prevalent today among aboriginal cultures all over the world are evidence of this[13]. For instance, most hunting cultures require that a prayer be said before taking an animal for food or clothing. Many cultures also have prayer rituals for harvesting plants, whether gathered individually or harvested as a crop.

While most bands and small tribes of humans (and possibly even pre-humans) expressed their spirituality through supernatural belief of some kind, the use of burial rituals is perhaps the earliest evidence we have of specifically spiritual religious activity. Ritual burials with grave goods clearly show that the particular society possessed a spiritual awareness of life and death and also believed in an afterlife[14].

The earliest ritual burials that have been credibly dated were discovered during the early 1930s at Mount Quafez in Israel. Remains are dated at 80-120,000 years old. The skulls found there show characteristics of Neanderthals as well as of modern *Homo sapiens*[15].

---

[10] The Smithsonian Institution has compiled a graphic presentation of human evolution as it is presently known, with references, available at http://humanorigins.si.edu/evidence/human-evolution-timeline-interactive, retrieved on 12.09.2010.

[11] Ehrlich, Paul (2000). *Human Natures: Genes, Cultures, and the Human Prospect.* Washington, D.C.: Island Press. pp. page 214.

[12] Dunbar, Robin. (2004). *The Human Story.* London: Faber and Faber.

[13] Shapiro, Warren (1998). Ideology, History of Religion and Hunter-Gatherer Studies, *J. Roy. Anthrop. Inst.* 4 489-510.

[14] Lieberman, Philip (1991). *Uniquely Human.* Cambridge, Mass.: Harvard University Press.

[15] Lewin, Roger; Foley, Robert A. (2004). *Principles of Human Evolution.* Malden, MA: Blackwell Publishing. pp. 385.

The oldest large site clearly constructed for religious purposes was discovered in 1995 at a place in southern Turkey called Göbekli Tepe[16]. Estimated to be 11,500 years old, its discovery caused a major upheaval in our thinking about the history of civilization[17], since it dates from a period where society was not yet sedentary, but survived as hunter-gatherers.

The area of this site is huge. Excavation of the lower stratum so far has revealed four circular or oval structures ranging from 10 to 30 metres in diameter. Geophysical surveys indicate that there may be 16 more. These stone structures are dated well before the Mesopotamian cultures built what previously were believed to be the first religious structures.

The cultures that eventually did emerge in Mesopotamia and also in Ancient Egypt developed into hierarchically structured theocracies wherein the king or other rulers were both political and spiritual leaders, justifying their political power through divine authority. In Egypt, the Pharaohs became to be considered actual divinities.

In societies without a written language, religious and spiritual ideas had to be communicated orally, and societal ideas were limited to those contained in the collective memories of members of the society. The invention of writing about 5000 years ago in either Sumeria or Ancient Egypt allowed larger amounts of concepts, ideals and rituals to be recorded and shared over generations of time[18]. The first religious texts that we have today are thought to be the Pyramid Texts from ancient Egypt, dating to between 2400-2300 BCE[19].

Many pre-literate societies around the world did construct ritual monuments that demonstrate an explicit concept of human connection to the universe. Some of these are huge and have lasted until this day. Typically these monuments took the form of a circular array of stones or timbers, although many formed lodges or even tunnels. Nearly all of these religious structures are oriented toward astronomical or astrological features, although the passage of time has hidden the exact configuration in some cases. A good overview can be found in the Wikipedia articles on Henges and Megaliths[20].

Henges are most prevalent in the British Isles, Stonehenge is the best known. This site has been dated as early as 8,000 years BCE, when an early wooden circle was erected. Its various additional rings and stone structures are believed to date from between 3000 BCE to 2200 BCE. Many other stone and wooden structures with evident religious functions have been found in other parts of Europe, including Ireland, France, Germany, Belgium, Spain, Portugal, Italy and Malta. Their estimated dates of construction range from about 5000 BCE to 1200 BCE. All in all, discoveries of what have been referred to as "*archae-*

---

[16] Badisches Landesmuseum Karlsruhe (ed.). (2007). *Vor 12.000 Jahren in Anatolien. Die ältesten Monumente der Menschheit.* Stuttgart : Theiss.

[17] "The World's First Temple", Archaeology magazine, Nov/Dec 2008 p 23.

[18] Pyysiäinen, Ilkka (2004). Holy Book: The Invention of Writing and Religious Cognition. i*n Magic, Miracles, and Religion: A Scientist's Perspective.* Walnut Creek, CA: AltMira Press.

[19] Allen, James (2007). *The Ancient Egyptian Pyramid Texts.* Atlanta, Ga.: Scholars Press.

[20] http://en.wikipedia.org/wiki/Henge, http://en.wikipedia.org/wiki/Megalith.

oastronomical" structures have been found in some 25 countries[21], including, of course, India's Jantar Mantar and Gyara Sidi.

The world's most famous site of this nature is undoubtedly the Great Pyramid of Giza in Egypt, which was completed about 2650 BCE, then being over 146 m tall and weighing some 5.9 million tonnes. The interior of the pyramid comprises a fairly intricate complex of chambers, tunnels and shafts. Two shafts emerging from the king's burial chamber are aligned with particular stars in the northern and southern skies, their attributed purpose being to facilitate the passage of the king's soul to its appropriate place in the afterlife[22].

Along the route of cultural and spiritual development, the concept of *oneness* of the supreme spirit with the entirety of the universe began to be lost. Religious spirituality began to be expressed through rote worship of multiple manifestations, often known as *gods*. This occurred in the *dharmic* religions of eastern societies as well as in western religions of societies such as the Minoans, Greeks and Romans.

While elite leaders such as priests seem to have retained an inner knowledge and awareness of the unity of all gods, the average member of the society typically did not. The rise of Abrahamic religions based on monotheism perhaps could have been a movement to - as it were - *re-unite* religious spirituality in a focus on the one. But the advancing complexities of the societies professing these religions resulted in a more hierarchical form of society, and of the religions themselves.

Through the middle ages (5th to 15th Centuries CE) and afterwards, some more or less secret societies seem to have retained an awareness of the spirituality of the one, through ritual, symbols and esoteric inner knowledge, sharing this only with small numbers of carefully selected initiates. The full range of such societies cannot be addressed here, but some better known examples include the Pythagorean from the era after about 500 BCE to the Freemasons and Illuminati, who exist to this day[23]. Some current Christian theological writings express the concept of eventual resurrection of all souls in spiritual bodies in a heaven, using methods and language of modern physical cosmology[24].

The architecture of most churches, temples and other places of worship – certainly, the most famous ones – is usually designed to draw the eye and the thoughts of worshippers *upwards*, presumably towards the supreme deity – although the primary attention is often focused on some intermediary such as a saint or a portion of holy script. In the more elaborate places of worship, there is often an explicit attempt to inspire in the beholder a sense of awe and wonder, which psychologists know is similar to an intense spiritual feeling.

---

[21] See, for instance: http://en.wikipedia.org/wiki/List_of_archaeoastronomical_sites_by_country.

[22] Jackson,K. and J. Stamp (2002) *Pyramid: Beyond Imagination*. London. BBC Worldwide Ltd, pp. 79 & 104.

[23] For example see: O'Meara, Dominic J. (1989) *Pythagoras Revived: Mathematics and Philosophy in Late Antiquity*. Oxford : Clarendon Press. Stevenson, David (1988). *The Origins of Freemasonry: Scotland's Century 1590-1710*. Cambridge: Cambridge University Press. Israel, Jonathan (2002). *Radical Enlightenment: Philosophy and the Making of Modernity*. Oxford: Oxford University Press.

[24] Taylor, Frank (1997). *The Physics Of Immortality: Modern Cosmology*. New York, Anchor Press.

The idea that a strong feeling of spiritual connection may be inspired by the body's response to a rush of some hormone is the basis for recent research into the possibility that there could be something called a '*God gene*'. The hypothesis is that people who are seen as "spiritual" possess this gene to a greater extent than others who are not so prone to spiritual feelings[25].

The suggestion that religion is somehow genetically "hardwired" into human beings is, not surprisingly, controversial. One genetic factor claimed to predispose those bearing it to interpret peak emotional episodes as spiritual or religious revelation is thought to be the VMAT2 protein encoded by the SLC18A2 gene[26]. VMAT2 stands for 'vesicular monoamine transporter 2', which is a protein that carries neurotransmitters such as dopamine, serotonin, etc. from cellular cytosol into synaptic vesicles. Persons found to have impaired VMAT2 function often suffer from anxiety and depression, and are more susceptible to conditions such as Parkinson`s Disease[27].

It is the *synapses* in the brain that enable our neurons to make connections and form circuits in our central nervous system. That is how we control our body, think our thoughts, store information and make decisions. The adult human brain is estimated to contain from 1014 to 5 × 1014 (100-500 trillion) synapses[28]. Every cubic millimeter of cerebral cortex contains roughly a billion of them[29]. The human brain is a most remarkable creation, and develops with astonishing speed after conception[30]. Just 16 days after a sperm has buried its head into an egg, the beginning brain emerges in the form of the neural plate. This is a single layer of cells, which develops from the outer layer of the embryo called the ectoderm, and gives rise to the entire nervous system.

At about three weeks of life, the neural plate buckles in the middle and the sheet of cells curves together to form a tube. Each end then closes so that the neural tube somewhat resembles a cylindrical cardboard carrier used to mail posters. After the tube has closed - one of the critical points of brain development - the single layer of cells begins to divide rapidly. The neural tube expands and, between the fourth and seventh week after conception, a series of five vesicles, or sacs, appear at the front end of the tube. These will become the major portions of the brain.

If you were, say, a lizard, that is about all the brain you would get. You would have no cortex, or outer layer that, in humans, is the seat of higher thought.

After conception of twenty-six weeks, the human brain is producing more than 50,000 neurons every second. Those neurons migrate outward, assembling the different regions that will allow us to walk, to talk, to remember our mother's

---

25 One book recently on the best-seller list is: Wright, Robert. (2009). *The Evolution of God*. Boston: Back Bay Press.

26 Hamer, Dean. (2004). T*he God gene: how faith is hardwired into our genes*. Garden City, N.Y: Doubleday.

27 Little KY, Krolewski DM, Zhang L, Cassin BJ (January 2003). "Loss of striatal vesicular monoamine transporter protein (VMAT2) in human cocaine users". *Am J Psychiatry* 160 (1): 47–55.

28 Drachman D (2005). "Do we have brain to spare?". *Neurology* 64 (12): 2004–5.

29 Alonso-Nanclares L, Gonzalez-Soriano J, Rodriguez JR, DeFelipe J. (2008). Gender Differences in human cortical synaptic density. Proc Natl Acad Sci U S A. 105(38):14615-9.

30 Lagercrantz H, Hanson M, Evrard P, Rodeck C (eds) (2002) *The newborn brain. Neuroscience and clinical applications.* Cambridge: Cambridge Univ. Press.

voice. The spinal cord connects to the cerebral cortex, the region of the brain responsible for higher thought processes, something that must happen for us to be aware of our surroundings. A newborn's brain has 20 billion neurons and a trillion synaptic connections, and the foetal brain must create a profusion of brain cells during intrauterine life — about 250,000 each minute — to reach this scale.

Thus, we can see that right from their birth human beings evidently are well equipped to think, to reason, to experience emotion, and - most importantly - to grow spiritually. The question is: why do not more of the human population grow to realise the ultimate degree of spirituality - that we are one with the one system?

Implications of "One System"

I believe that we all must absorb the truth of the foregoing statement, and it should become part of the consciousness and spirituality of all individuals in all societies. The question is how can this goal be achieved - or at least, approached? Can we simply proclaim widely the fact that there is only one system, and that we as human beings are a part of it - even that we are it - and hope that this will become widely followed and change our destiny? Probably not! The world is too vast and most people are too pre-occupied with their daily lives within their own societies to extend their consciousness much beyond their physical horizon. They cannot reach the needed discipline and lifestyle to realize just how intimately they are joined with the universe and the supreme entity it includes.

Leaders of the *Radhasoami* faith community, including the present one, Rev. P. S. Satsangi, have shown how it can be approached within the faith community[31]. It certainly would benefit the world if this consciousness could be extended as far as possible. Beyond such a community, however, I am optimistic that the conscious awareness of the fact that *there is only one system* can be taught. It can be an underlying axiom of a great diversity of academic courses – on literature, in science, on philosophy. It can also be imparted by certain practices of meditation and mind/body control.

The practice of yoga to attain physical control of the entire body and the senses can lead towards realization of the ultimate reality. Appropriate practice of meditation can enhance the functioning of the parasympathetic nervous system that calms the mind and brings it into an enhanced state of consciousness.

If and when people absorb the concept that *there is only one system* and let it become at least a part of their consciousness, their actions inherently will tend to be less self-centered and more system-oriented. Intuitively they will see: *"As above, so below"*.

---

[31] Satsangi, P.S. (2006) *Systems Movement: Autobiographical Retrospectives.* International Journal of General Systems, Vol. 35, Issue 2, 2006, P 127 – 167 or Satsangi P.S. (2008) "On Systems Modelling of Macrocosm and Microcosm in the Domain of Spiritual Consciousness", Vision Talk at the Inaugural Function of International Seminar on Spiritual Awakening: A Systems Approach to Address the Civilizational Crisis (SPAWSYS 2008).

Chapter 38

At the Infinity

LAXMIDHAR BAHERA
IIT Kanpur, India

Abstract
The concept of infinity has been used in Mathematics, Physics and many scientific disciplines, although the concept remains vague. This paper enumerates many examples to clearly delineate what is infinity and what is not infinity. Cantor's idea of countable and uncountable infinity has been revisited. It is shown that the notion of part and whole does not exist at infinity. The problem of creating an entity called 'INFINITY' will be discussed. The Vedantic interpretation of infinity is provided with a broad outline of the approach to the subject in the discussion.

Introduction

Many a times when we study and conduct investigations, we experience the world. This knowledge is only at the level of experience whether the meter needle is showing 5 amps, 10 amps, or the electrons spin up or down, it's all experience. We do not see or do not have the ability to enter into the reality of existence and see it physically. All that we perform is the act of *seeing* or using our sensory perception and then there is an unhidden process that creates a sensation and we feel the experience. This is all we have or are capable of. Within this experience as a human being, we try to see unity in diversity. So with this in mind, let's see what this infinity is.

What is Infinity

Many of the times, we think a big number is infinity, but it isn't, it is just a large number. We can increase this number but it still remains, just a large number. Like in the case of factorial 999999 - we can go on like this, but *still* just large numbers. What about the total number of sand particles on the planet? Or, for that matter, how many molecules constitute the planet earth? A physicist would probably sit down and try to compute the diameter and density of Earth, at least within the upper bound. Even though, it has a finite structure, it appears to us as being infinite. Similarly, a bigger question would be the number of photons emitted by all the luminaries across the universe - impossible to calculate! But again, can we say it is infinity? If we ask the cosmologist, he would not be sure because of the ongoing debate over whether the universe is closed or open. If we consider the universe as a closed system, then by the analogy of the theory of *finite*, one may say, this is simply a very large number. It is certainly not infinity. The moment we consider the universe as open, it doesn't have a boundary, it's ever expanding, so then we cannot be sure of what the answer is.

Some of the mathematical notions we normally use or students make a mistake with is 1/0. Actually, mathematically, this equation is wrong. I can only divide two natural numbers. Zero is not a natural number. So it cannot be divided. Thus, it is mathematically invalid.

Another example would be that everybody thinks – 1/∞ (infinity) is correct, but infinity is not a natural number. If 'n' is a natural number, then n+1 is a natural number. Infinity (∞) is a natural number. ∞+1 should be a natural number but ∞+1 is the same as ∞. So 1/∞ is not actually a valid operation.

Everybody, from physicists to biologists, use: $\lim_{x \to 0} 1/x = \infty$.

By stating this – one may assume that they have created infinity but yet again, *merely a large number*. Nobody can actually create infinity.

Now let us see which has a greater number of points on it - the small line segment whose length is 1cm, 10cms or a line of infinite length? Of course, before George Cantor (around 1850), nobody had an answer to this, But after his postulation, people recognized that all these lines have the same number of points, whether it is the small line or the bigger one.

Yet, why should we be interested in infinity? In the case of the scientist, philosopher or sociologist, unless he has the ability to capitulate to our environment, he cannot make any claims about it. The same stands true for infinity - can we recreate it? For example when we talk about atoms, electrons, molecules; we first recreated electricity, recreated a fan, and recreated a variety of systems based on these principles. Then we started making assumptions about it. Similarly, if we want to really talk about infinity, first let's ask the question, can we recreate infinity? Before we even think about recreating infinity, let us look at some mathematical problems that we are dealing with, particularly irrational numbers, e, π, √2, which don't have an exact value. It's amazing how we can draw a line of 1mt, another line of 1mt at a right angle, but we cannot *exactly* compute the diagonal. It's just beyond our comprehension. Similarly in the case of π, we can't write its exact value because the more you expand it, the more it expands. It's an unending structure. So is the case with √2. The notion then is that although we have never created infinity, it is in front of us in a variety of ways.

Cantor's Argument

If we look at not only Galileo and George Cantor but our Indian traditional saints, everybody acknowledged infinity. The Pre-Cantor view was that infinity was a very large number. So there was potential infinity and actual infinity. People didn't think there was actual infinity. So, what Cantor stated was a revolution of sorts. Cantor said, it is God who is really the *infinity*. This belief of his brought on a great deal of mockery, even his own teacher vilified him. In fact he entered into an absolute depression because his colleagues criticized him over his conception of actual infinity. The logic he put into the concept of infinity was finally accepted by a great mathematician called Hilbert when he presented his 17th unsolved problem to look at the cardinality of the real number system.

One of Cantor's central arguments was that if we did not accept infinity then √2 doesn't exist as well as π. These concepts are however, a part of our day to day life. So how can we say that π doesn't exist, √2 doesn't exist and e doesn't exist? Hence, infinity must exist. Apart from this, he talked about the hierarchy of infinity, countable infinity, and uncountable infinity. Without going into too much detail, we see that the set theory that mathematicians use came from Cantor and the fundamental concept is that two sets are equal if you can find a one-one correspondence between set A to set B. Like for example A, B, C and 1, 2, 3; they are of the same size because I can find a correspondence. People didn't believe this is an infinite set before Cantor. Cantor tried to make others believe that this is actually an infinite set because in the case of 1, 2, 3, 4, 5, 6 up to 10 etc - you go on adding till there was always *still one more*. So he used this logic to show that this set should be seen as a whole, not as a process of counting which appears to be finite process. As a whole, this is an infinite set. Now, if I take the odd numbers out of this natural set; all the even numbers are left. So now, which is larger - The parent set which has both odd and even numbers or the second set with even numbers? The beauty was that in his argument he established a one-one correspondence. You take one element from the original set and equate or find a corresponding one from the other set, and thus find a one-one correspondence from counting. Because of this, he established that even numbers, natural numbers and normal parent natural numbers are of the same size.

The astounding feature of Cantor's infinity (shown at the level of infinity) is that there is no difference between the part and the whole. I can't actually say that the part is different from the whole, which we normally assume. Not only can you go ahead with perfect squares, like a series of perfect squares, 12, 22, 32, 42 but these are the same size as 1, 2, 3, 4, 5. So the whole being greater than the part is not valid. If you look at rational numbers, you can see, - 1/1, 2/1, 3/1.....these are all rational. This is actually a series of natural numbers. Now if you go on like this, we find that this is another infinite series. So it seems that the rational numbers have to be much larger than the actual parts, which are the natural numbers. But Cantor refuted this and said that they are actually the same. We can count 1, 2, 3, 4, 5, 6, 7, 8, 9, 10 and so forth. This means that there is an infinite of infinite series. We can go on counting them and when we are counting, we are again generating an infinite series 1, 2, 3, 4, 5, 6.... So we are once again creating a natural number series. What he actually showed us is that even a rational number; the series of rational numbers and a set of rational numbers are all the same size as that of only natural numbers. Now Cantor made a very potent statement after this proof of his. He said that he saw it but didn't believe it. Now if we see this in its entirety and in the case of real numbers – from 0 to 1. How do I count? After 0 what should be counted? 0.1, 0.01, 0.001, 0.0001, 0.00001, 0.000001. Where should we start? So in a layman's language the real numbers are uncountable because of the irrationals included in them. A real beginning from 0 to 1 consists of both rational and irrational numbers but the irrationals don't follow any laws. They are infinite and hence the cardinality of real numbers. Cantor's argument on infinity is inspirational but did Cantor actually recreate infinity? He simply visualized that infinity existed. He couldn't create it. If we simply go on counting 1, 2, 3, 4, 5, 6 we can go on counting for millions, billions, trillions and zillions of years. Yet you still can't reach an end. That means infinity cannot be created. Cantor simply discovered that there exists a mathematical infinity and that in the mathematical realm, there is infinity. One of the aspects that one should wonder about is if this infinity could ever be recreated? Can we start from 1 and reach infinity or is infinity always infinity?

Theological Perspective of Infinity

In theology we ask the same question. Can anybody become God or will God always be God? Some people still like to argue and say that one can become God. But my view or my faith is that God is always God. We will always remain infinitesimal. Uncountable infinity was talked about by *Arjun* when he saw the *Virata* form of *Krishna* in the battlefield of *Kurukshetra*, where he said I see no beginning, no end and no middle. He also said if thousands of millions of suns were to appear, the totality of refulgence will fail in front of the radiance coming from this *Virata* form. Another example of infinity is when *Mother Yashoda* opened the mouth of Krishna on the complaint that Krishna is eating mud. *Mother Yashoda*, on opening the mouth of *Krishna* saw the entire cosmos. Not only that, she observed inside his mouth – the view of her looking inside his mouth. So again, here is a concept of infinity where there is no inside or outside. Like in the case of the finite - suppose we say that a house is finite - we say it has an inside and an outside. But when I talk about infinity, it doesn't have an inside or outside, there is no difference. This is like the famous *vedantic* a phrase from *Ishopanishadic* invocation:

Om

Purnamadah Purnamidam
Purnat Purnamudachyate
Purnasya Purnamadaya
Purnameva Vashishyate

This talks about infinity again. But the beauty of this particular verse is that the complete whole that is emanating from the original complete whole is also complete. Another example is that half of the mother's cell and half of the father's cell combines to form one cell. And in that one cell all the information is there and through cell division we have teeth, hair, skin, nostrils and kidneys – a myriad of cells coming from that one original cell. So complete and perfect! This particular process; the natural process that infinity has set-in, is its own creation and it cannot be duplicated. No power or effort can duplicate this effort.

Srimad Bhagavatam

There is another case of infinity. There was a great *rishi* called *Markandeya* who lived for many years. He asked this question – if in every 4.3 million years, only one jiva or soul gets perfected and goes back to God or to the spiritual world through this process of creation which has been going on continuously from the scale of eternity, it appears that infinite souls should go back. Then why do we still have an infinite amount of souls in this world? So the concept of infinity troubles very saintly people or *rishis* like *Markandeya* rishi also. There is a prayer *Brahmaji* made to *Krishna* 5000 years ago and this prayer is very famous because it is in *Srimad Bhagavatam*, 10th Canto, 14th Chapter, 7th Verse. Brahmaji while glorifying Krishna, says, in times to come, learned philosophers and scientists might be able to count all the number of atoms on the earth, particles of the snow and perhaps even the molecules radiating from the sun, the stars and other luminaries, but among these learned men who could possibly count the unlimited transcendental qualities possessed by You, the Supreme personality of the God, who has descended upon this earth for the benefit of all living entities! So the idea is that although infinity has been used in many scientific disciplines, it is still a concept that is still not properly understood.

The Vedanta and Science

The Vedanta talks about infinity. Research leads to self-realization as well as perfection. It will be interesting to deal with this concept while taking some cues from the *Vedanta*. But being a scientist, my sincere appeal is that science must develop whilst taking cues from Vedanta because scientific concepts will become highly enriched. If you look at modern science - it does not talk beyond position, whether it is current or otherwise, whether it is ammeter needle or some measurement needle. Even the greatest physicists have said that physics does three things - it measures, *position, position and position*. But if you look at our experience, it does not lie within space only but semantics. From semantics comes the notion of consciousness. If semantics is not understood, then the idea of consciousness is not understood properly. To develop upon this, the idea of the five elements and the object of the five senses which create information has to be brought into science. Then science will accommodate ethics, morality or the principle of universality within it. At the moment science doesn't have a role of ethics within it.

Chapter 39

The Material, the Psyche and the Spiritual

A.K. MUKHOPADHYAY
All India Institute of Medical Sciences, New Delhi, India

Abstract

Science, at present, works within the boundary of the universe that in turn is determined by the boundary of the cerebral cortex. Twentieth century's science followed the initial formulation of two independently successful theories of physics, relativity and quantum mechanics, thus the theory of very large and very small respectively. Einstein's starting point in science was when Space, Time and Matter got together. According to him, Matter distorts the geometry of the dynamic manifold of Space Time, and the warping of Space and Time is gravity. The Quantum Principle stands on the phenomenon of absolute discontinuity. Energy in its smallest possible quantity is released as, and behaves as a 'quantum'. In the context of time and space the smallest measurable time in Planck's scale is 10-43 second and space length is 10-33 cm. It is worth remembering that, till date all the scientists' efforts to find the common ground of their origin has been greeted with little success.

Introduction

There is a great divide between spirituality and science, psyche and the soma. We could compare it to the sky and the earth, it is a divide between the non-local and local science. In science, the object of exploration is matter. In spirituality the object of exploration is consciousness. In science, the tools are the mind and intelligence. In spirituality, the tool is the self. Science deals with local players. Spirituality deals with non-local players. Now what are these local players? They are matter, energy, space, time and information. Our time begins with birth and death, whether this refers to the individual or the universe. Space is limited by the velocity of light and horizon of the black hole and the energy spectrum we deal with is between the absolute zero and the super force. As far as local theories are concerned - there are three theories, the theory of relativity, quantum theory, and the quantum field theory - each has their limitation. Problems of singularity are the problems of relativity. The Quantum theory has the problem of measurement and the Quantum field theory has the problem of infinity.

There are five non-local players which spirituality deals with. They include consciousness, the mind, life principle, the self and information. Why do we call it a non-local science? It is due to the fact that all of these players have a standard operative procedure for their individual mechanics and their joint mechanics. There are variants and constants which regulate their mechanics in the non-local realm. The moot question is how the non-local family can behave within a confined state? Consciousness which is non-local, which cannot be localized - still, gets confined to the brain. The mind which is non-local can be confined to the brain. But information has a transcendental aspect and a non-transcendental aspect which we can measure. So the local science has its players and the non – local science has its players with the probability that information is the connecting link between the two.

In the textbook, Principles of Neural Science edited by none less than the Nobel Laureate Eric Kandel, we would be able to observe a picture of a person from a PET scan with an obsessive compulsive disorder where, you would see the redness in the left side which is the head of the caudate nucleus and another picture showing the medicated therapy as well as one showing the head of the caudate nucleus, after medication - the redness has disappeared. And after psychotherapy nothing has been given - nothing material, and yet same redness has again disappeared. Thus we conclude that the mind affects matter; the psyche, the non-local players are affecting the local players. But what is this psyche? Is it the mind? Is it the soul? Or is it consciousness – or the self being? Is it this that deals with phenomenology? Or is it just an information processing system? Is this similar to the scenario of six blind men exploring the elephant! All of the above are true but partially right.. I suggest that all these are five integral ingredients of psyche.

Consciousness, Self, Mind & Private Facets of Self and Information

Consciousness – does it do anything? Is it a noun or a verb? A doctor's consciousness disappears or ends at the intensive care unit or the operation theatre and a patient becomes conscious after an unconscious state. Eric Kandel defines consciousness; as the ability of the individual to respond appropriately to environmental stimuli. So if we put a jogi under the PET scanner or NMR scanner to investigate consciousness within his brain – the big question would be - is consciousness confined merely to the brain?

There are problems with neuro-centric consciousness. What happens if the brain is not there? What is it in brainless animals? What is it in plants? What is it in matter? Should the brain or consciousness create an intelligent response to stimulus. Does nature have any brain or intelligence? We are familiar with the picture of Ganapathi. He has the head of an elephant and the body of a human being yet he expresses himself with the consciousness of a human being.

So where is consciousness? Does it lie in the brain or in the body? The Ganpathi is an unusual combination of animal brain experiencing human consciousness. In fact, animal, human and divine consciousness are simultaneously being expressed. Consciousness is like a spider which weaves a web but is itself outside of the sheer of the net.

So we may deduce that consciousness can be brain confined, brain trapped, brain encased and yet there is a consciousness in nature. This is the brain-independent consciousness and connecting the two is the self-consciousness. It is a great journey from brain confined consciousness to nature consciousness. In spiritual parlance we can call it the jivatma, atma and the paramatma.

Now, what is the self? The Self is a particulate consciousness, the operational unit within the system. It is the operational unit of consciousness within the system. And this individualized unit of consciousness involutes within the system. Now there are two views. One is the emergent theory, the Neural Network Theory that emerges from the brain; the other theory is the Downward Causation Theory in which - from unconditional consciousness it is informed to work within a system, informed that it is individual from unconditional consciousness but it has to behave within the given constraint, however, it is the bridge between the brain-bound and the brain-independent consciousness.

Coming to the third element of psyche, the mind. The mind does not exist in monism; whether in material monism or in consciousness monism. The mind comes only with duality. The mind cuts the conscious system into two. Sri Aurobindo said "The mind is that which cuts consciousness into two", and the end of the mind is the beginning of consciousness. The mind is defined as an organ, the mind works as an organ of communication between two conscious systems. If we think we have one consciousness as the brain-bound consciousness, then the brain-independent consciousness extends even beyond the universe, multiple universes etc. So we have several layers in between the two consciousnesses.

We see the space-time bound world, and then there is a void which is interstellar space, then we have inter-galactic space and that is inter-universal space. So we have an apparent void, we have a great void and we have a divine void. And then there is tunneling here. The outer tunnel, inner tunnel and there are frequency zones. So there are seven strata structures of the mind. This is the classical consciousness of the mind, and is the non-dual or advaita consciousness from which multiple universes are born.

Now lets consider the private facets of self. The self is a particulate consciousness, an operational unit of the whole system - Akash Chetana and the Ghat Chatana. Now when this becomes separated from universal consciousness, the self, the five phenomena - it is born - so it has a new life but one day it has to merge again with universal consciousness - so there is death; it has a conditioned existence - which is due to the ego and during its conditioned existence it wants to share its properties - love, and it also desires for the continuity of the self - that is sex. So life, death, love, ego, sex, are five aspects that are put in one biological integration centre (Dynamic Web of Supra-Cortical Consciousness, Mukhopadhyay, 1987).

Where Freud merely remained confined to the sexual aspect, Maslow talked about life and the necessity of life but it was Jung who brought the collective unconsciousness synchronicity into focus. Sri Aurobindo from India, emphasized on the physical experience or material experience of death while alive. He said unless you experience death in totality while you are alive your psyche does not become conducive for the divine. All spiritual leaders have gone through this death experience knowingly or unknowingly and finally their psyche has beome conducive for the divine. Nowadays the whole world has become obsessed with sex and the ego. This is all you see on television. In all spiritual realms love is life. But what is separating is the death. So we have to integrate all five. And we can put it in a different way. This is a depth phenomenology; this is the surface phenomenology of the material world. This is the depth phenomenology of the mind and consciousness and this is the elementary phenomenology. Life, death, love, ego, sex – kām, prem, ahankār, jivan and mrityu.

What is information? A new concept of information is that information has a dual (aspect); it has a transcendental aspect and non-transcendental aspect. It is bipolar. It is the objective pole with which the scientists work and it has a subjective pole. But Shannon's definition is brilliant - "information is that which reduces uncertainty". The perceived and conceived uncertainty could be elevated by an appropriate input of information. Now information mechanics and psychic mechanics are inextricably connected. The psyche is an informational hub. Without information the psyche is vacuous. So we can bring out a model in which you see the classical world, and then you go to the quantum world and quantum mechanics. Mechanists are silent on two points, quantum void and quantum discontinuity. Free will is start of a wheel in which you have to traverse through all five phases.

When Swami Vivekananda says "I am a voice without a form" what does he mean? He probably means he is an embodiment of divine information. Also he hints that information is prior to form. Here I propose that information is a form inside. Form, space and time are brought out by the mind by the inside out phenomena. When the form is released in space and time this form may again go the mind as an idea, image and process and is being processed in the mind and the energy comes and this energy goes to the neurons. You may have a split atom or molecule but it is still an information split. I am splitting information into form and energy. Now this energy will be information based energy different from matter based energy, solar energy, atomic energy. This is actually happening in the brain. How is it happening - we do not know.

The mind is sensitive to information. The self is sensitive to phenomena and consciousness is sensitive to the process of surrender. This is very important. You do not access consciousness unless you surrender. You cannot access consciousness with information. You cannot access consciousness with phenomena. Information acts on the mind, phenomena acts on the self. Information also acts on the self to some extent; This is the root of all spirituality and religion. It is a fool proof methodology. The surrender of the brain-bound consciousness to the consciousness is nirguna. The Quran says all prophets' final religion is unconditional, active and a total surrender to God's will. The one word in Arabic language for this process is Islam and a person who does this is a Muslim. The Bible also says Matthew 11:28-29, "Come to me, all you who are weary and burdened and I will give you rest. Take my yoke upon you and learn from me for I am gentle, humble in heart, for you will find rest for your soul". Bhagavadgita also says so – "sarva-dharman parityajya; mam ekam saranam vraja; aham tvam sarva-papebhyo; moksayisyami ma sucah!"

So, we work with the mind and intellect but the mind is driven from behind by the Chitta. And the intellect is driven from behind by the ego. And this makes the antahkaran chatushtay - the self in the system-bound consciousness is buried inside it. What we have to do is dig out the self, out of this system-bound consciousness. And then we have to look at the subsystem-independent consciousness. This may be a Guru, God, or a Mantra. Then you connect the self with the system-independent consciousness – this is when you are the real driver of this antahkaran chatushtay. Your self has surrendered to God. As Shri Krishna explained to Arjuna – "mayy eva mana āshatsva mayi buddhim nivesaya; nivasisyasi mayy eva ata ūrdhvam na samsayah!" If you give your the mind and intellect to me, surely you will live within me. And then if you even kill, the responsibility is Divine's!

References

Mukhopadhyay, A.K. (1987). *The Dynamic Web of Supracortical Consciousness*. New Delhi, India: S.K. Mukhopadhyay.

Chapter 40

Religion: A Scientific Perspective

P.N. TANDON
National Brain Research Centre Society, AIIMS, Delhi, India

Abstract
Traditionally, religion and science are considered to be two distinct fields of thought and enquiry. Though some scientists contend that the two cannot co-exist, others believe they have linked destinies, since search for truth is the motivating force behind both. Nobel Laureate, Charles Townes, acknowledged that God was a "Source of Strength" during his discovery of the laser. According to him, "Science wants to know the mechanism of the universe, whereas, religion wants to know the meaning. The two cannot be separated". In contrast to this, a 1981 statement of the US National Academy of Sciences proclaimed, "Religion and Science are separate and mutually exclusive realms of human thought".Recent years have witnessed a revival in interest in attempts to reconcile rational enquiry (science) and spiritual conviction (religion). Thus, a study of belief (or faith or religion) in all its forms has recently become a very hot topic among scientists, particularly the cognitive scientists and philosophers alike. A large number of books like "Born to Believe: God, Science and the Origin of Ordinary and Extraordinary Beliefs" by Andrew Newberg and Robert Waldman (2007); "The Soul in the Brain: The Cerebral Basis of Language, Art and Belief" by Michael R Trimble (2007); "The quest for the Spiritual Neuron" by Jacob Abraham (2004), an earlier paper by Roger Sperry (1995) "A Search for Beliefs to live by consistent with science" have kept this debate alive. An attempt is made to present some of the recent deliberations, on the subject primarily by renowned scientists.

Introduction

I, by training and profession, was a neurosurgeon till a few years ago who thought I knew something about the brain but also realized that there is so much more to learn about the brain than what we knew. After handling the brain for 30-40 years to deal with its physical problems caused by injury or disease progressively over the years, I got interested in the complex problem of brain-mind relations in brain and consciousness and I still continue to be a student of this fascinating subject. Therefore, one of the purposes of coming here was to learn from such distinguished people. However, since I have been asked to do so, I take the opportunity to share with you some of my thoughts on the subject. I will try to express where we started and where we are in our efforts to understand this complex subject.

Historical Perspective

It is not surprising that the mind has been a subject of study for eternity. As far as we have recorded literature on any civilization, there have been references to the study of mind. Many people believe, and certainly most of the Western scientists start their talk about this complex subject by quoting the Greek scholars Galen, Plato, Aristotle, Hippocrates and others as if they were the first to study this subject. They do not realize that this has been a subject of great intuitive and logical studies in this country, India. We lost track of much of this valuable knowledge but in this audience, there are scholars who have been studying these resources and bringing out the nuances of these for people like us. One of them is Professor Mukhopadhyay for whom I have great admiration; then we have Dr. Sangeetha Menon. Just to mention a few examples for the Indian resources, the Taittiriyopanishad classified consciousness at different planes: the physical consciousness, the psychic consciousness and the beatitudinous consciousness. In contrast to that, at a very basic level, which I think the modern scientists will have no difficulty in accepting, is the Mandukopanishad which describes four states of consciousness - jagriti, that is awake, swapna, that is dreaming, Susupti, that is deep sleep and Turiya or the non-dual thoughtless state. Today, the modern scientific community finds it difficult to comprehend the concept of the state of Turiya. "Whether we agree with these concepts or not is a different issue, but the fact that they thought of all this goes to reflect how much intellectual exercise had gone on in this area. Again the literature is so vast and it is far beyond me even to attempt to briefly summarize the essence of it. I only wish to point out that it has been a subject of study for more than several millennia.

In the context of mind, one of the most quoted authors of the West is Descartes, who considered the body and the soul as two distinct entities, and went so far as to localize the point of interaction between the two to the pineal gland. I do not know of anything that has been more highly quoted than a single diagram of his interpretation of the brain and mind relationship in which the mind was supposed to be in the pineal body and the brain only concerned with sensations. Notwithstanding the utter improbability of such a hypothesis, it introduced the concept of dualism and a trend for a reductionist approach which has dominated so much the thinking of Western philosophers and scientists alike.

Lessons from Recent Studies

In any case, the most important question that arises in one's mind is: if consciousness is the function of the brain, does it have a seat in the brain? Can brain mechanisms explain consciousness in its entirety? Now, this word "entirety", is what caused the greatest trouble for people like us. What is entirety? Is entirety in the terms of what the philosopher thinks, what the religious sages think or only in terms of what little literate clinicians like me think? If we could just remove that word "entirety", I would easily say, yes, the brain mechanisms explain consciousness as I understand it. I will come to that in a second. There are other unresolved questions too, such as: Are consciousness and mind synonymous? What is mind? Is the brain the organ of mind? And so on. Now if you take up an unsolved question and try to solve it, it is wise to convert it into simpler propositions. Therefore, having worked as a clinician and caring for patients with brain disorders affecting their consciousness by morning, evening and night; it became essential for us to develop a working definition of consciousness and its gradation. To us, the clinicians, consciousness *is the ability of the person to be aware of his/her environment, to be aware of himself or herself and to have volition.* These are three major components and this is how we tested our patients by checking whether he recognized the people around him, knew who he was, where he was, whether he remembered what day of the month it was, could recall his life-events from memory. Similarly if we asked him to lift his arm and lift his leg, was he able to do that. That was very simple and we quickly gave mathematical numbers to it so that we could predictably grade his state of consciousness.

It is not surprising that, in our attempts to resolve any problem at a given moment of human existence, we go only as far as our tools will permit. That is no doubt a very simplistic view. In any case initially, we had no tools and therefore we used our brains and we had what is written in the Upanishads and Vedas and what Aristotle and Hippocrates talked about. These thinkers had no tools. They of course had their minds and their observations and their intuition and their ability to logically develop some hypotheses. Progressively, various sciences developed and we started to utilize them and study the same subject - mind and consciousness (from different standpoints). Therefore, a whole group of people developed theories of mind and consciousness. There were those who believe that consciousness is a unitary state, and those who believed that the brain and mind and consciousness are two different things, and there were mystics who believed in only one consciousness that was the state of Brahman or Ananda. Surprisingly, all mystics, irrespective of the culture they belonged to, have described the same experience in different languages but with identical characteristics. That means there must be some commonality in this experience. Hence, whether I believe in it or not, I would not like to dismiss this as irrelevant for any study on consciousness. However, as we moved from religion to philosophy, from philosophy to psychology, from psychology to neurology, from neurology to cognitive science and today to a combination of all these approaches to study, we find the emergence of behaviorist, functionalist, mentalist, pan-psychiatrist, parallelist and emergent materialists from time to time who provided their own interpretation of the subject. It only depicts that you can go only up to the limits of your capability at a given moment of time and that applies not just to the individuals but equally to collective intellectual bodies.

Before I discuss what constitutes consciousness, let me tell you what is mind to us. Mind is what reflects the mental activity. What is mental activity? It implies anything that goes on between the sensory input and motor output. I see somebody. That is a sensory input. But that I recognize him, that I have an emotional response associated with it, that I have will power to decide whether I shall go and shake hands with him or whether I will turn around and look the other way around, I, then act accordingly; all that goes on is mental activity reflected in the mind. Campbell in 1980 concluded that consciousness is not identical with the brain or mind. It is that which witnesses changes which occur in the brain and mind. Surprisingly, a similar conclusion was arrived at after prolonged discussions between a most outstanding neurophysiologist of the last century, John Eccles, and a philosopher K. R. Popper. They sat together, debated for days and brought out a book "The Self and Its Brain" (Popper and Eccles, 1977) and came to an astounding conclusion: that "the unity of conscious experience is provided by the self-consciousness mind and not by the neural machinery of the liaison areas of cerebral hemisphere". William James (1892), the father of the American psychology, said that consciousness is not a thing, but a process. I think that is a correct statement even today. It is not a thing; it is not a material thing. He added that everybody knows what consciousness is until he tries to define it. And I can tell you that having devoted the last 10 years specifically to the study of this subject, I have no better definition than what I gave you. But that is too simplistic; a definition as Prof. Mukhopadhyay would say does not cover its entirety. It does not cover its entirety because we are incapable of handling that entirety. Somebody who is more capable may like to join hands with us and see whether we can expand our horizons.

Let me attempt to elaborate a little further as to the various components of consciousness. Awareness, attention, cognition, discrimination, memory, responsiveness, volition are at least some of the definable constituents of the unitary state of consciousness. Consciousness is not attention or memory or anyone of these individually, including awareness. It is a combination of all of these and this is why it is so complex. Since they could not be quantified, earlier we had problems to study them scientifically. We have come to a stage where each individual component referred to can now be studied quantitatively as I will illustrate during my talk.

Since this audience may have people who have no idea of what the brain looks like, it is recommended to see a picture of a human brain as exposed during an operation. The cerebral cortex is divided into frontal lobe, parietal lobe, occipital lobe, and temporal lobe. The cerebellum is the brain stem. When you split the brain in two halves, you get to see the bundles of fibres which connect one half of the brain to the other half. I do not need to go into the details of all this. The building blocks of the brain are the nerve cells (neurons), supporting cells (glia) and fibre bundles. The neurons are interconnected to form neuronal circuits or networks. Each neuron is connected to 100 to 1000 other neurons. The junction between the neurons is not in continuity. There is always a gap between the projections from one neuron to the other neuron. This is called a synapse. Charles Sherrington, a Nobel Laureate and neurophysiologist, said that consciousness is a phenomenon of synaptic activity. Many others believe today that consciousness is a phenomenon which is the result of the connecting networks functioning synchronously at a given time.

As late as 1966, and even later than that, Sperry (1966), a distinguished neurobiologist, eloquently stated that we were having problems with understanding consciousness, because the inner sensations, feelings, concepts, mental images and the like cannot be weighed or measured, photographed or spectrographed or chromatographed or otherwise recorded or dealt with objectively by any known scientific methodology. That is a little less than 40 years ago. I will try to illustrate that the situation has changed dramatically so that at least some of them can now be photographed, even spectrographed, though they may not be chromatographed.

Let me digress a bit. One of my teachers is Dr. Wilder Penfield from Montreal, who studied brains of conscious human beings during surgery for epilepsy and meticulously recorded every single response following gentle electrical stimulation. Towards the end of his scientific life, he thought that he would like to answer the question which has been a matter of great concern to everyone:

what is mind; are brain and mind the same or two different things? The last scientific book that he ever wrote was *The Mystery of Mind* (Penfield 1975). I will suggest that those who are interested in the subject should read it. Here I quote his conclusion:

From my own part after years of striving to explain the mind on the basis of brain action alone, I have come to the conclusion that it is simpler (and far easier to be logical) that one adopts a hypothesis that our being does consist of two fundamental elements - the brain and the mind.

Wald (1979), another outstanding biologist, argued that consciousness is not a part of the universe of space and time, of observable and measurable quantity that is amenable to scientific investigation. You see this was as late as 1975 and 1980, still the feeling was that we cannot study it scientifically, and therefore we leave it to the philosophers who can understand it probably better than we do.

There were others who felt that it never will become possible to identity physically the presence or absence of consciousness, much less its contents. I can quote the names of many in this regard. One of our most outstanding and most respected physicists, Dr. D.S. Kothari, said:

Atom or brain belongs to the external objective world of space-time and matter-energy. Self or mind belongs to the internal subjective world. The subjective (mental) world is not describable in terms of space-time and matter-energy concepts. Self or mind, therefore, lies outside natural science (Kothari 1980, pp. 1-28).

This was in 1980. Twenty years ago, people were still thinking that they cannot tackle the subject scientifically. I, with all humility, tend to disagree with this and would like to illustrate in the next part of my presentation, where we are. As I mentioned at the outset, I am not, for one moment, saying that we have solved the problem of the mystery of mind or of the brain-mind relationship or the mind-consciousness relationship. But we now have the tools with which each of its components that I referred to earlier can at least be studied scientifically. On the basis of our own studies and the recently emerged new information, in my Presidential address to the Indian National Science Academy, I concluded that:

On my own part I am convinced that the mystery of consciousness is inexorably linked to the mystery of the brain, this mystery is more likely to be resolved, if ever it does get resolved, (that shows my uncertainty, my not being too confident) by a holistic approach to study the brain as it was becoming possible now through investigations of the human beings (Tandon 1993).

Three to four days ago, I gave a talk at the Indian Science Congress Association in a symposium entitled From Molecules to Mind. The title of my talk was 'Demystifying Mind'. I am trying to demystify, but I'm neither trying to say that the mystery is solved nor trying to make light of the complexity of the problem. As a clinician, I saw so many clinical syndromes which have a bearing on the subject. I have just chosen a couple to illustrate. Patients with Korsakoff psychosis, for whom we know where the lesion is, a person has loss of memory. But if you meet one, you will find him a jolly good fellow, he talks to you, confabulates in answer to your questions. Five minutes later when you meet him, he asks you who you are and when you say that you met him just a few minutes ago, he exclaims that he has never, met you in my life. This is what we call a cocktail-party syndrome. Even without a brain lesion under the influence of some toxic substances, one can behave as if he neither has awareness of self or his environment, but for all practical purposes he appears as a normal 'conscious' human being. As per the definition of consciousness that I referred to earlier, such a person cannot be considered to be conscious. Similarly a person with a lesion in the brainstem no bigger than half a centimeter in diameter has no perceptible voluntary movement in his body. When you talk to him, he listens, he sees you, but he has no means to responding to you and you take it for granted that he is unconscious. But the moment he recovers that capability, he can tell you everything that happened to him during that period when you thought he was not conscious. Thus his ability to control his expression voluntarily, which is one component of the working definition of consciousness, could be misinterpreted as loss of consciousness.

There are a number of such syndromes which create problems for establishing a fool-proof definition of consciousness. For example, global amnesia is another. During an episode of global amnesia a Professor giving a talk, like me here, suddenly starts fumbling, not knowing what he is doing and he even wonders aloud "what's the matter, what's the matter, what has happened". When questioned, what is wrong with him, he declares "I am alright". Informed that he was giving a lecture, he says, "No, I am not giving any lecture".Is he conscious or unconscious? At least, he has no memory of all this even when he recovers. Study of patients with well-defined lesions in the brain has provided a wealth of information on various aspects of consciousness.

Two of the most classical cases are as such. A person had a knife injury. The knife went through the face and the base of the skull into a very vital area of the brain, resulting in at least one aspect of his conscious functioning, especially in respect to recall of past memory being affected. Another patient who was operated upon for epilepsy had one temporal lobe including the hippocampus removed. I have removed hundreds of temporal lobes. We know removal of one temporal lobe does not result in any discernible deficit. Based on such assumptions, somebody removed both sides. This person had no capability of recording any ongoing experience even though his IQ test was perfectly normal. His behavior appeared perfectly normal. He was a draftsman and he would go, sit and do his drafting work perfectly well but when you asked him after five minutes what he was doing there, he has no idea of what he was doing. Was he conscious or unconscious? These are the kinds of questions that started to creep up in our mind. There are beautiful descriptions of these patients who have been studied endlessly by psychologists and imaging specialists using latest techniques of brain imaging. Analysing the data thus generated starts to provide new insights on brain function and its correlation with behaviour.

There may be yet another example. We had virtually removed one half of this young boy's brain. He never lost his consciousness as a result of this. He was of course totally paralysed on the opposite side i.e. left side and he needed a support to walk. This shows, we could remove large chunks of brain without impairing consciousness. Thus one sided removal or injury to any area of the cerebral hemisphere, even whole of it, does not abolish conscious thinking. It may change the contents of awareness, interfere with voluntary act, render less effective planned action, deprive the patient of word symbols, but he still thinks and weeps and sometimes laughs also at his own self if not at others. Is he conscious or not? Another case of a little tumor in an area of brain and removing that tumor one had to go through the whole brain. There is a tiny little structure in the brain called the fornix and if by any mistake in removing this tumor, one damages this structure, the person loses all recent memory. It is now obvious that memory is not necessarily equivalent to consciousness but certainly is an important component of consciousness.

I am only trying to give these examples to illustrate how valuable insights can be gained not only about brain function but about consciousness from the study of such patients. In yet another way, one could study the same phenomenon. During surgery for epilepsy on conscious patients under local anesthesia, gentle electrical stimulation of the temporal cortex in some patients activated the past record of the stream of consciousness. Limited to the duration of the electrical stimulation, the patient re-lived all that he had been aware of, and also an earlier experience of which was laid down initially. No doubt this could not be achieved in every patient submitted to such stimulation. But the evidence provided by these few patients as if there was a cinematographic or video recording of past experiences in the brain would strongly support the contention that the brain is an important organ responsible for our consciousness.

As a part of the management strategy, surgeons introduce electrodes into the human brain to record electrical activity (electro-corticography). These studies are carried out for treatment of a patient's disease but while doing that we utilize the opportunity to study the electrical activity, and response to stimulation. By these observations we can safeguard the interest of that patient and future patients, at the same time obtain valuable information about functional localization in specific regions of the brain. With more recent technology, similar information can be obtained from the surface without putting anything inside the brain, by doing, electro-magnetographic recording. Thus recording can be obtained from well-defined areas of the brain even in the depth. Simultaneous recording can be done from many areas when the person is carrying out a voluntary act or a psychological exercise. This is done in real time, and during that period the patient's experience can be co-related to activity in specific regions of the brain.

During the last 15-20 years, CAT scan, magnetic resonance imaging (MRI scan), functional magnetic resonance studies (fMRI), Single Photon Emission Computerized Tomography (SPECT), magneto-encephalography (MEG), provide non-invasive methods of studying anatomy, physiology, chemistry of discrete regions of the brain in fully conscious, thinking and performing individuals. It is now becoming possible to do such studies even in infants.

Let me show some examples to illustrate how even higher mental function can now be studied. It has become possible to see which part of the brain is activated while the person is hearing words, or when the person is seeing words, or when the person is speaking words and when the person is generating words. When a person is shown some nonsensical symbols of which nobody knows what they are, one part of the brain is active. Next when some English alphabets which cannot be pronounced as a word were shown another region was activated. When shown a word that has no meaning, the activation is at a different site. And yet another region is activated when a recognizable word is presented.

There are other ways of studying functional localization using fMRI. Utilizing even more sophisticated modern technology of electro-magnetography, using SQIDs (Superconducting Quantum Interference Devices) on the surface of the skull, not on the brain, one can study in real time, things that are happening in the brain during such processes, as memorizing or doing mental mathematics.

In this manner it has been possible to delineate the parts of the brain that get activated during anger, happiness, fear and sadness. Carried out under certain specific circumstances with inherent limitations, there are still technological problems, which need to be sorted out to improve these results. But there is a difference in localization between happiness and anger and for that matter between anger and fear. One can thus get information from a variety of techniques, not just one technique, for the same function because some give us very good anatomical resolution, whereas others give us functional information. Some can only be interpreted when we have collected data over several seconds, while others can give us data which are in real time. All this information needs to be integrated into one unified concept.

Even more complex behavioral traits have been studied like identifying the areas of the brain involved in persons addicted to cocaine. Consistently we find higher activity in the basifrontal region and medial aspect of the frontal region. The change after he has been treated is so obvious. Addiction is a major societal problem today in the world. If we start to understand the basic mechanism underlying this, even if we leave aside the philosophical aspect of consciousness, and look at the practical aspect, we can derive immense benefits.

From the data that have been collected, we start to find out that the left hemisphere deals with reasoning, problem-solving, spoken and written language, mathematics and science. The right hemisphere is supposed to be more dominant in women and accounts for insight, imagination, art, awareness, hearing, melody and pattern recognition. Study of patients following surgical procedures that disconnect two halves of the cerebral hemispheres suggests that the two sides can be independently conscious.

The brain imaging studies of more complex mental functions in health and psychopathological states have revealed the areas of brain involved with emotions. There are illustrations that demonstrate the areas of the brain showing activity in a patient who was in a panic state, or another one who was in a manic stage of manic depressive psychosis, quite different from when he was in a depressive phase. We are inclined, maybe wrongly, to believe that this part of the brain is linked to this particular aspect of a person's emotion or mental function.

Notwithstanding this voluminous information already available and being added to everyday, the question whether we are nearing identification of the neural mechanism underlying consciousness, leave aside mind, remains unanswered. We no doubt have piecemeal information about the various elements that we believe give rise to the unitary subjective experience of consciousness or self awareness. Yet many questions remain unanswered. The foremost amongst these are:

i) Does demonstration of neural activity in a part of the brain reflect a mere association with a particular mental phenomenon or a cause for it?
ii) How is the activity in widely distributed areas of the brain even for simple sensory function integrated to provide a comprehensive experience?
iii) Are there specific mechanisms or specific circuits responsible for this integration?
iv) Can the same mechanisms explain phenomena like "mystic experiences", "hypnotism", "out-of-body experience" and such others so vividly described by large number of persons from diverse background?

No doubt there are many more such questions. The purpose of this presentation, I must acknowledge, was only to demonstrate the current scientific approaches used to study this subject and our present state of knowledge about them. I hope this presentation will stimulate scholars from other disciplines, gathered at this seminar to come together on this difficult journey to unravel the mystery of mind and consciousness.

Take this very simple thing- vision, which is the most studied perception system. You see in the eye, it goes to the brain, goes to the back of the brain. It does not go as a full total picture. Different parts of the brain are involved in different functions. For instance, colour for this part, for the depth of the subject, if the subject is moving the position that is the distance from you to the object and different parts of the brain are analyzing that information differently. So, I am breaking down the whole image into pieces. What is connected to what? I don't see only colour or position, I see the object. We still do not know the answer. There are at least 40 areas of the brain which are involved in the simple task of visual functioning, the most studied.

Consider a cup of coffee. You may think that a cup of coffee is only an object, that it has length, breadth, shape, size and colour. No. A cup of coffee arouses many other sensations in you. It arouses the sensation of smell, warmth, the shape, even the sense that this coffee comes out from the coffee beans and as I have often said it might also remind you of the company that you had when you had a special cup of coffee. That moment of time might be the most pleasant moment of your life which you recall with all its intensity and emotion combined together. So, it is not just a cup of coffee and each component, as you see, involves different parts of the brain. Therefore, the question is what brings it together.

The matter doesn't end with this. Daily routine is the mundane aspect of our existence. Sri Ramakrishna said, " ...in the depths of meditation there arises the consciousness of the impartite, the indivisible Reality. Body is forgotten, mind ceases to function -there remains pure consciousness". Shri Ramakrishna is not alone. Many saints in diverse cultures have come to a similar conclusion. All that I have said so far has nothing to approach the answer to this question as of today. The very eminent, distinguished physicist Erwin Schrodinger said that the whole world is a project of the one undivided cosmic consciousness and each of us is an integral part of it. These are philosophical questions dealt with by scientists and non-scientists equally but still not within our ability to grasp them in hard core data.

I close by saying that my conclusion remains unchanged after 10 years. There are enough unexplained observations which need to be resolved before the answer to the internal question of brain, mind and consciousness can be found. No doubt this question is difficult but the past could be made easier and better illuminated if the neuro-biologists take along with them the natural scientists, the psychologists and the philosophers on this journey.

References

Campbell, A. (1980). *Seven States of Consciousnes*. London, UK: Victor Gollancz Ltd.

James, W. (1892). *Textbook on Psychology*. London, UK: Macmillan.

Kothari, D. S. (1980). Atom and Self (Meghnad Saha Lecture 1978). In *Proceedings of Indian National Science Academy*, 46A. I-28.

Penfield, W. P. (1975). *The Mystery of Mind: A Critical Study of Consciousness and the Human Brain*, Princeton. NJ, USA: Princeton University Press.

Popper, K. R., and J. C. Eccles. (1977). *The Self and its Brain*. Berlin, Germany: Springer Verlag.

Sperry, R. W. (1966). Mind, Brain, and Humanist Value. *Bull Atomic Science* 22. 2-6.

Tandon, P. N. (1995). Concepts of Consciousness: Brain-mind Relationship. *Decade of Brain* India/USA Research. In Mental Health. Kaslow, S. B., Murthy, S. Srinivasa, and Coelho, C. V. (Eds.). 17-22.

Tandon, P. N. (1999). Exploring Consciousness! *Neurobiological Approaches in Scientific and Philosophical Studies on Consciousness*. Menon, S., Narasimhan, M. G., Sinha, A., and Sreekantan, B. V. (Eds.). Bangalore, India: NIAS.

Tandon, P. N. (2000). Theme Address - Round Table discussion on Consciousness in *Proceedings of the Round Table on Consciousness*, Oct 12-13, *National Brain Research Centre Symposia Series-I*, National Brain Research Centre, Gurgaon, India, 17-22.

Tandon, P. N. (2001, 1993). Consciousness: Clinical and Beyond (Presidential Address, INSA, December 30, 1992, New Delhi, India), Indian *National Science Academy*, B 59. 5-51. Reproduced by Indian Institute of Advanced Study, Shimla, under their Dissemination of Knowledge Series.

Wald, G. (1979). Life and Mind in the Universe. In *The Evolution of Consciousness*. Gandhi, K (Ed.). New Delhi, India: National Publishing House. l-16.

Chapter 41

Indian Spiritual Teachings and Quantum Physics

SUBHASH KAK
Oklahoma State University, Oklahoma, USA

Abstract

This paper provides an overview of Indian spirituality and its consideration of the problems of consciousness, freedom, sin, and meaning. It will compare ideas of Indian spirituality with that of quantum physics, and show that in both the universe is best viewed from the complementary perspectives of physical structure and observers. It will be argued that improbable coincidences corroborated in literature support the view that non-material entities have independent existence. But such evidence, just like first person accounts of spontaneous scientific discovery, cannot be conclusive for establishing that the world of ideas has independent existence. Nevertheless, such accounts justify the investigation of the relationship between the nature of our minds and conceptions of the universe. It is argued that the nature of knowledge is recursive which is grounded on the structure of our minds and universe. The relationships of the visions of the cosmos in the arts and sciences, which arise from the equivalence between the outer and the inner realities of a culture, are discussed.

Introduction

The Vedic texts from ancient India (approx. 3000–1000BCE) claim to be ātmavidyā, "science of self" or "consciousness science." The most ancient of these is the cryptic Rig-Veda. But prose commentaries, called the Brāhmanas and the Upanishads that appeared in the centuries following the Vedas; provide a framework to decode its narrative, establishing its central concern with consciousness. Until recently, the question of consciousness was considered to lie outside of the scope of science and, consequently, the Indian texts on the subject were not properly examined. Scientific attitudes toward consciousness have changed due to the recent advances in neuroscience and because modern physics and computer science must confront the question of the observer. In the Vedic view, reality is unitary at the deepest level since otherwise there would be chaos. This reality is called Brahman (neuter gender). Brahman engenders and, paradoxically, transcends the mind/matter split. It is identical to consciousness at the cosmic scale and it informs individual minds. Turning focus to the very nature of the mind provides insight about consciousness.

This paper deals with the problem of how we reconcile spirit and matter which is after all the central theme of spirit, spirituality and consciousness. It's very difficult for one to deal with consciousness from a scientific perspective for a variety of reasons such as since consciousness is not an object unlike what sciences normally do, that is deal with objects. Therefore, how do we construct a theory of it? Consciousness cannot be looked upon as an entity that can be studied and on which experiments can be performed. There is a split or there are two different ways to look at this problem. Given that science has already mastered the outer world to a great extent, we have harnessed the power that the world forces, outer forces present to us and which can be use for our development, our outer development. We have come now to a frontier which is the frontier of our inner world, of our inner cosmos where we seem to be powerless in many ways to proceed. Now should we try to make material models of our inner world? It appears using logic such models will fall short because such models would at best be like shadows of the cave of Plato trying to find what reality is, from that display or filth work of the shadows in the cave. A lot of science which is a part of our educational curriculum is of course reductionist and materialistic. That goes back all the way to Newton and successors to Newton. But there is one element of modern science, namely quantum theory, which is not quite reductionist and this paper relates how quantum theory provides us certain perspective which first of all is quite consistent with the insights that we have received from mystical tradition everywhere and from what the Sant Mat for example tells us indirectly through its Sandhya Bhasha where you use a paradox to convey a much deeper concept.

There are some fundamental connections that exist between this tradition of the spirit that we have from India and modern science itself. Not everybody would be aware that Erwin Schrödinger the Austrian Physicist who is one of the two creators of quantum theory and quantum theory as we know is at the basis of chemistry, which is at the basis of biology, which is at the basis of all wonderful achievements that technology has given us in the last one hundred years. So Erwin Schrödinger in his autobiography which he wrote in his 60s claimed that the fundamental insight that he obtained in the 1920s, which made it possible to make the jump beyond classical theory to quantum theory came to him out of one of the Upanishadic Mahavakyas namely "*Ayam Atma Brahma*" that "this Atman is the entire Brahman". This entity which is within us, is able to comprehend the entire cosmos. And this gave him the idea of using the concept of a super positioned state which when we look at it and when we interact with it, collapses to one of the different possibilities.

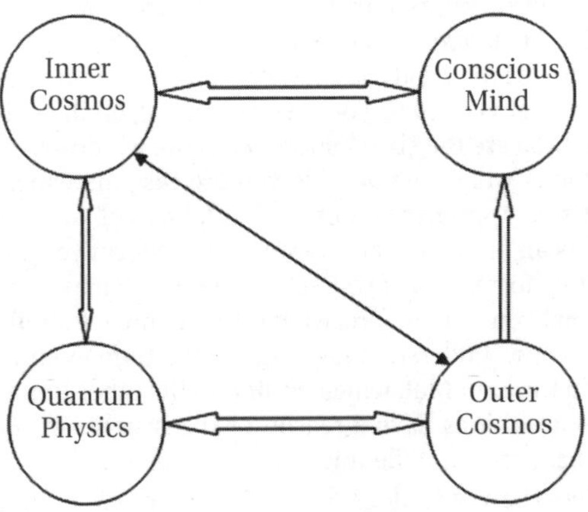

In the schematic of Figure given above, it is indicated that if quantum theory describes processes for the outer cosmos, consciousness does so for the inner cosmos. Since quantum theory must ultimately underlie the processes in the inner cosmos, it appears that for the sake of symmetry it should be possible for consciousness to influence the outer cosmos.

So there is a link between Indian spiritual tradition and modern science itself. This doesn't mean that modern scientists accept to imply that the kind of extra-Aristotelian logic should therefore be used in order to understand our inner world. In spite of all of this pre-history, modern science remains fundamentally reductionist and therefore the models that people propose related to the nature of our mind and spirit continue to be fundamentally material and if they are material, one would imagine that there would be limitations that these models would have.

The foundations of the various traditions that we have within India are related to the nature of this spirit. There are three fundamental ideas. One is an idea which you see in Maharaj Sahab's book, the idea for equation between microcosm and the macrocosm. In Sanskrit which is called "*Yatha Pinde Thatha Brahmande*" and "as in the cell so in the cosmos". This is one element.

The second element is that all ordinary knowledge is fundamentally limited and leads to paradox. In the Upanishads this is described as you're approaching *paroksha*. In fact there's this great statement that "Paroksha Priya ivahi Devah" that the God's love is what is paradoxical. This really means that we comprehend the outer world with the senses we have and apply logic to it. We always use logic because of our conscious mind, which is a classical apparatus or instrument or "*antahkaran*". This instrument utilizes a model like framework or logical framework which, however, leads us to a paradox. This paradox is described as "*apara-para split*" in the Upanishads. Whatever is described by ordinary language is apara knowledge or lower knowledge which will eventually lead us to a paradox. This is why we as individuals, live in the magic box, a magic box with six walls and these walls form the window on the non-apprehendable or the infinite or the transcendent. Each of the six walls provides a certain perspective. If you are looking at your tradition that is *purva mimansa* of whatever tradition you have. If you are looking at the structure of language, that is the *nyaya*, if you are looking at the structure of matter, that is *vaisesika*. If you are looking at the creation, that is *samkhya*. If you are looking at the synthesis, that is *yoga*. If you are speculating on the entire cosmos, that is Vedanta. So these are the six perspectives or six windows. Since they look in different directions what they provide you are insights which appear contradictory and it's that apprehension of the limitations of your knowledge, which presents itself as an epiphany, allows you to transform yourself. This is called the *yagna* or transformation of yourself where which makes it possible for you to go beyond what you were before, what limited understanding you had before on to a much deeper understanding. This is the fundamental understanding which we find in the Sant Mat, which we find in the other Indian traditions that we have, which traditions have a reason of the insights of the *rishis* and the *sants* over the past several millennium.

Now, what does the sceptic do and who is the sceptic? A sceptic is the one who has been educated in the formal university education. All the formal university education is of course based on the reductionist paradigm that you can reduce everything to a certain foundational axiomatic system. It's like going back to the word as the literal thing and not having a deeper insight. People getting education in schools and universities, whether in India or in Europe or the United States of America, shall be taught that the physical world is all there is. And therefore the question arises how we then convince somebody who believes the reductionist view of reality, that there's something more. This is a question that comes up. Now, within our own personal experience each one of us is convinced that the transcendent exists. Because we have seen the transcendent in our experience at sometime or the other, sometimes looking at the sunrise or sunset or in our relationships that we may have with nature, with friends, relatives and so on. However, our experience of transcendent may not be sufficient to convince others who are told that the only way to see things is as matter. It's because of this that there is a crisis that we face in the world where people feel, especially in the West, that this is the only attitude (i.e. all things are matter) worthy of being promoted and hence is, as such, promoted. People feel that they are nothing more than their bodies and if they are to die one day, then what is the life worth for?

What is the value of life? and what we have? These two clubbed together is what we have from the mystics, who are our teachers and from ourselves because each one of us is potentially a teacher, each one of us has to apprehend the infinite at some point of time in ourselves, that there is something to experience which cannot be reduced. But this has also been communicated down to us through certain hints and one of those hints is this whole idea of number 108, you know you have 108 beads in the *japa mala*. So what is this number 108 so central to the Indian experience that all religions, that have risen in India, value this number? And this number is then made a part of the practice that one has 108 names of the Gods or the Goddesses or the divine or 108 *teerth sthans* and so on. And what we discovered in our study of these traditions is that in reality 108 is a symbolic, *prateekatmak*, a symbolic representation of the universe. This is because the sun and the moon are 108 times their respective diameters from the earth which is why their angular size is about the same. Modern science has also shown us that the very size of the sun is 108 times the size of the earth and this then is a hint which is provided to us that look this micro-macro equation, the equation between inner sun and the outer sun, is captured in this number 108. Now of course you can always say that this is just a coincidence and that's what somebody who is from the materialistic background would say, it's just a coincidence and it may very well be a coincidence. But still it's absolutely astonishing and that's what it is!

In the nineteenth century the whole question of where does knowledge emerge was taken up by some scholars in Europe and in particular a scholar named Jacque Hadamard from France who was a physicist and mathematician. He wrote to a hundred different leading scientists of the day and said please tell me honestly what state of mind were you when you made your important discovery. They wrote back and their predominant answer was that "look I was actually not deliberately thinking about the problem I came by the solution spontaneously" which goes counter to the reductionist view that what you do is you gather up information, then you do certain combinatory analysis on this and suddenly a new insight emerges. He said no. Most people said that's not what happened. For example we have heard of Kekule and the structure of benzene. He claimed that in a dream he saw these six snakes each holding the tail of the other, right? And this is how this seems to emerge from if one were to accept it, our insights, our most wonderful achievements don't come from us, don't come from our phenomenal mind, but seem to come from somewhere else. But where do they come from? You could not have a material model that here is this cosmos and there is something beyond this solar system and somehow we are connected to that space and that's where the information is and we are getting it. Because, it does not do justice to what it is. That would then still mean that we are all material particles separate from each other and besides how will we explain where and why would we get connected with it?

Well, we do have other evidence from neuroscience and many of you may have read the work of Oliver Sacks a well known neurologist from New York who has written books such as "The Man Who Mistook his Wife for a Hat" and so on where he speaks of his experiments with savants. The savants who are profoundly retarded and have cognitive problems are still able to do things which are absolutely impossible to fit into the computer model of the brain or into a model of consciousness where all that we are doing in our life is gathering information and having gathered this information we have certain abilities with which we comprehend reality. This is a model at the basis of modern education that what you need to do is to take a young person and fill him with a lot of information and facts and somehow then you would be able to be creative. This is counter to the ancient view that mind is not a vessel to be filled but a fire to be lit and that fire is not separate from one individual to another. Oliver Sacks, a physician to many individuals, tells in one of his stories that a profoundly handicapped young person who had no schooling who could not even read and count was playing with a box of match sticks. The box opened up and as the matches fell he said 118. Oliver Sacks counted the match sticks and they were exactly 118.

The question is, is there something more to it than just a coincidence? There is of course the most remarkable of these coincidences which tells you that there ought to be truly something. The great minister in the court of Vijayanagara empire, namely Sayanacharya, in his commentary on the Surya Hymn of the Rigveda mentions that "O Surya or Sunlight, you who travel at the speed of 2202 *yojanas* in a half a *nimisha*" and this is 700 years ago before there were any tools to speak of, any speed to be associated with sun or sunrays but both *yojana* and *nimisha* are standard units. Just 20 years ago people wondered what these numbers might be. They made calculations and found that this was exactly equal to the speed of light. To clearly claim that Indians knew what the speed of light was 700 years ago is not credible because we did not have those tools and this was not a part of the scientific framework as existed in the *pathshalas* and amongst the *jyotish* families that lived in India. So what this indicates is that just as creative scientists and other creative people claim that their greatest discoveries seem to come from outside, likewise what the scientist actually does is to get connected to the transcendent which is not outside in a physical sense, outside of our solar system to which we are somehow getting access. The transcendent interpenetrates this entire cosmos, interpenetrates this reality and when we get connected to it, then we have access to what is extraordinary.

Schrödinger, in another book that he wrote called "What is Life" (a collection of his lectures which he delivered in Ireland) which influenced Francis Krick, the discoverer of the structure of DNA, said that if you really think about it, there cannot be a multitude of minds. The idea of multitude of minds is something that has emerged in the West in the last 200-300 years. He said, he thought that the only resolution to the problem of consciousness, and this is Schrödinger, the creator of quantum mechanics writing, he said, was the Indian idea or the *Vedantic* idea that there is a single consciousness like the outer sun and the consciousness of each one of us is like the water in a different pot which reflects this light. It's because of our association with ourselves which makes us think that light is coming from the pot. While in reality this light is coming from outside and is getting reflected from the pot. Now this idea of a single consciousness and its multitude of reflection solve a lot of problem and are fundamentally consistent with quantum theory. In quantum theory the two points of departure are firstly, that reality at its deepest level is a super position of all possibilities. Secondly when you approach this system of all possibilities and make a measurement with your phenomenal mind you can access only one of the many different possibilities when you are limiting yourself from all to a single one. That what one could claim is where uncommon insight comes from or where our understanding comes from, is the phenomenal training through discipline, through what are called *sanskars* and through *sanskars* we obtain an ability to look at reality in a particular fashion and neuroscience of course agrees with that. But eventually this way of looking at reality in a particular way also limits the possibilities that exist. Therefore ultimately in order to have the spiritual insight you must transcend this *sanskaras*. This is described in the Zen tradition for example as saying that when you see the Buddha, you must kill him. So that whatever formal framework that he had come up with must then be abandoned and it's only then you would be able to obtain that astonishing insight.

To conclude then, what binds it all together is reality which, we have to accept, cannot be understood by the use of mechanical models; that reality is something transcendent which captures the mystery of consciousness. It's extra-terrestrial, it's not a force, it interpenetrates. But our brains have a structure like a receptacle which gets the ability to comprehend certain aspects or apprehend certain aspects of this reality and for that you do need a spiritual practice and other intellectual discipline. Therefore both the material and the spiritual are viewed as two complementary sides of this reality. Just like the bird needs two wings to fly, similarly the material and the spiritual are required to lead us from our ordinary understanding to the deeper understanding where all of us are one.

Chapter 42

Spirituality, Consciousness and Behavioural Health

C. TULSI DASS
Deva Center, Varanasi

C. DEEPIKA DASS
New Heights Public School, Varanasi, India

Abstract

In the 21st century Globalization, Spirituality, Consciousness and Mental health have become much talked about terms around the world. The Eastern religions propose their own definitions and religious practices to give expression to these words whereas western thinkers, philosophers and religious people have defined them according to their own convenience. A comprehensive review of literature shows a large amount of subjective expression of beliefs and values pertinent to the society and culture. This gives a view that there are no universal definitions of Spirituality and Consciousness. This is also true with the scientific definition of mental health today. Authors would like to stress that despite differences in eastern and western models of thinking, a common ground can be observed in the behavioral health and cognitive thinking and feeling pattern of its spiritual seekers. Through this experiential paper the authors would like to throw light on these behavioral and cognitive thinking patterns from the field of applied psychology, psychiatry and eastern yogic practices.

The thrust of my last 25 years of work, or the nucleus of my work was on the promotional Aspects of the Mental Health Status of an Individual, away from the "diseased" based health preventive model. Most of the preventive strategies are mainly oriented to "population at risk" rather than promoting the normal healthy individual lifestyles for a healthy future. I conducted empirical researches in the area of Relaxation Response, Bio feedback and self regulation therapies, which are well recognized tools of modern day psychotherapies (Singh, R., Oberhummer, 1980, Das, 1985). During the course of my last 25 years of work, I came across a number of Monks and followers of Christianity, Buddhist monks of high caliber, Religious pundits, Philosophers, Fakirs, Satsangies of Radha Soami faith, Bahai faith, Naga Sadhus who gave me some idea of spirituality, consciousness, the religion of saints and specially the role of the Sant Sat Guru (the spiritual master) in alleviating the suffering and making us aware of our spiritual entity and its direction. Within the normal routine of scientific enquiry, where objectivity and the cause and effect phenomenon along with duplication of experiment is of profound importance, subjective and philosophical constructs are of no meaning. Consciousness studies, religion of saints, self-realization and subjective introspective reports are some of the "challenges" of modern day science.

Before the 19th century, such philosophical concepts were under metaphysical enquiry, where subjective and introspective reports were accepted as a source of knowledge. When psychology in the early years of the 20th century, attempted to become an objective science, with redefining "behaviorism", the subject of "consciousness" disappeared more or less completely from the scientific enquiry (Guzaldere, 1995). Only at the end of the 20th century, did consciousness force itself into the scientific agenda. This time, it was taken up by objective psychology, evidenced based medicine and hard sciences like Neurophysiology, computer sciences and even physics. The study of consciousness almost became a study of inter disciplinary subjects and integral psychology was one prominent force.

A deep knowledge about consciousness, its awareness and the process of "self realization" of the soul or spirit also came from spiritual traditions, saints and sages from Indian traditions, who specialized for thousands of years in the exploration of inner worlds and after achieving realization themselves, passed this knowledge on to the common man for his upliftment. This became a major source for modern scientific enquiries. These saints and sages, who came under the Religion of Saints not only proposed the theoretical framework but also gave practical and psychological guidelines to study the technology of awareness and consciousness (Revered Prof. Satsangi Sahab, 2004, Sriram Murty, 1987, Bahm, 1961, Prabhupada, 1972, Vivekananda, 1974, Uduppa, 1976).

India is a vast country with its one billion people living harmoniously in diverse cultural religious and spiritual backgrounds. India is a Multi Cultural, Multi Religious Country having 18 major languages, 6400 castes and sub castes, 6 major religions, 1600 minor languages and dialects, 52 major tribes, 6 main ethnic groups, 29 major festivals, 7 union territories and 28 states. On the brighter side, our country can look forward to the benefits arising from globalization and scientific advancements like cyber advancements, information explosion, space technology, nuclear power generation and efforts currently on to become a superpower. However, on the not so bright side, we are still fighting with the problems of population explosion, health and hygiene and newer diseases such as HIV, super bugs, the pollution of water, the sanitation crisis, illiteracy, religious misconceptions, taboos/evil practices, poverty/caste wars, religious fanaticism, crime and corruption etc. All these evils are still rampant in society.

Spirituality and resilience are an integral component of everyday life of the individual. Resilience is an unusual word, which means, the capacity of a person or a social system to live well and to develop positively in a socially acceptable way despite difficult circumstances.

Let me also confess here, that there are no more distinctions between eastern and western civilizations and cultures, as was in the past. Globalization and rapid advancements in electronics and information flow have created one culture and one World Order. A psyche however has emerged, which is full of Type A personality traits (heart attack prone) - aggressive, highly competitive, egoistic, pleasure seeking and materialistic and perpetually short of time.

More recently, I was on a tour of European countries, from Holland to France to Switzerland to Germany. One of the common elements I found was that everybody was always in a great rush, as seen in the case of an emergency.

When I asked a European friend of mine about his need for hurry, he mentioned that he was getting late for lunch and that was his tension. This phenomenon is now visible in India too, due to the mixing of cultural values and adoption of a western style of living. A large number of people are suffering from some kind of stress and tension either physical (psycho somatic problems), psychological (anxieties), social (addiction to alcohol and other substances, marital disharmony) or even economical, leading even to suicides. People are confused and even opting for costly medical-cosmetic treatments, or adopting pseudo philosophies and techniques of health and happiness to alleviate their pain and suffering. It has became a common trend in larger cities to associate oneself with so called religious priests or monks and follow their philosophy and methodologies to relieve stress. Even on the academic and research level, one of the editorial articles in the journal of clinical psychological research points out that most articles are focusing on 'pessimism' and not on 'optimism' or 'hope'. It points out that in the last three decades of the 20th century, journals published 46000 papers on depression and only 400 empirical articles on joy and optimism.

People are striving and aspiring for peace and happiness through religious communes and pseudo philosophies and methods, leading to more problems and forgetting the age old wisdom and heritage of saints and sages. The need of the hour is to alleviate the suffering of humanity. The 17th century was known as the age of enlightenment, the 18th century as the age of reasoning, the 19th century as the age of progress and the 20th century as the age of anxiety. Now, the current 21st century is definitely the age of confusion, fears, future anxieties and psychosomatic stress.

The Spiritual element, as one of the strong components of the overall health model, is now very well accepted by social scientists. WHO defines health as "a state of complete physical, mental, social and spiritual well being". Spirituality, spiritual development and behavioral aspects have now been well recognized in the circles of psychologists and psychiatrists. In fact, now it is a well documented truth that spirituality is an experience having implications on one's physical and psychological functions and spiritual ideas can be effectively used as a variable in modern psychotherapies to enhance positive growth and well being in willing individuals (Rangaswamy, 1994). There is a panorama of ancient literature which suggests the various ways of enhancing happiness and subjective well-being. Meditation (Carrington & Ephron1975, Vahiya, et. Al.1975, Vigne1995), Walsh 1981, in the field of stress management (Sawada & Septoe, 1988), increasing internal focus (Marlette et. Al. 1984) Karma Yoga (Singh et al 1980 1982), increasing self-actualization (Alexander et al 1991, Das T, 1985).

From time immemorial, Indian wisdom, thoughts, scriptures, philosophies and treaties recognize the fact that through modern scientific temperament one can play a powerful game with external environment and may have some more materialistic advancement, test-tube babies, artificial rains, Neurogenesis, in the name of "scientific achievements" leading to more pleasure and more dominance over the nature. However, the real happiness and awareness leading to consciousness was forgotten, as this required change in human being himself rather than outside world. Spirituality is a soul searching inward journey with awareness and consciousnes and gradually the scientific temperament is accepting the fact that "A sound body has a sound mind and a sound mind is the seat of sound Spirituality."

The foundations of spiritual science are based on the realization that our sensory experiences can only give us partial knowledge; and for the knowledge of the absolute truth, we need some other senses. After years and years of sadhna (doing spiritual practices) the saints realized in their brain's latent inner senses that the world was entirely different from what they had constructed by the knowledge of physical senses. Pursuing the inner path further and further, they discovered even more hidden senses or centers. They found a nerve centre in their brain which, as soon as it became kinetic, revealed to them the ultimate reality. This knowledge was called Apara Vidya and when obtained through higher senses – Para Vidya or transcendental knowledge. According to one of the Param Gurus of the Radhasoami faith, Huzur Sahabji Maharaj:

"The greatest discovery that has been made or that shall ever be and the highest truth that has been communicated to humanity or that shall ever be, is that there is nothing higher or nobler than Atman. There is no truth higher than God and no enjoyment higher than God realization."

Swami Ram, one of the greatest yogis of 21st Century and Founder of Himalayan Institute of Yoga once said "You physical scientists believe that there is a brain in our body whereas we believe there is a body in our brain".

In this way, we can say "WE ARE OUR BRAIN". It is the brain which is the creator of the creation. It has a universe outside and a universe within itself (Bio feedback and Dr. Green researches 1970's)

An interesting parallel element can be observed in one of the rapidly advancing tools of psychotherapy known as Neuro Linguistic Programming (NLP). The "Neuro" part relates to Neurology and the way in which our brain processes the information that we receive from our five senses – seeing, hearing, feeling, tasting and smelling. The "Linguistic" part relates to the use of language systems – symbolism, metaphors as well as spoken words – to code, organize and attribute meanings to our internal representations of the world. The "Programming" is about the way in which our experience is coded, stored and transformed to create habits and "programs" – similar to how software runs on a PC. One of the principle pre-suppositions of NLP is "the Map is not the reality". This metaphor is at the heart of NLP in the same way that a menu is not a meal, and an orchestral score is not a piece of music, so the experience we have of the world is not the world itself. The "Map" is your mind or your own perception and physical world is different from your Map. Many people believe their internal Map to be the true representation of reality, when in fact it is not so but it is just an interpretation of reality. NLP believes that while we experience the world though our five senses which are stimulating our brain we also, in order to cope with information, delete, distort and generalize a lot of information and the remaining data is filtered and added with our past experiences of values and beliefs.

An interesting parallel can be drawn when experts of neuro linguistic programming such as Robert Dilts states that "life, the mind and body are one system." He states that our bodies, our societies and the universe form an ecology of complex systems and sub systems all of which interact with and mutually influence each other. He further states that the universe is a system made up of galaxies and planets. Society is a system consisting of cultures and sub cultures made up of people. The human body according to them is a great example of a system in action. The mind and body are thought of as one system, each directly influencing the other. You cannot isolate just one part of the system. Equally, when you change one aspect of a system, you will have in some way changed the rest. When working on your own issues, or with other people, you need to be aware of the wider systems or the ecology that will be involved.

Thus the role of an indigenous system of medicine particularly various forms of Yoga can be very distinctive and unique in our culture due to special demographic characteristics of our population. The author of this paper holds the view that in our noble efforts to help our poor masses, we should not be bound by suffocating restrictions attempted by alien systems of medicines. Rather we should try to develop a system or a program, which can have the ingredients of both the eastern and western system of techniques and which can be culturally tailored, to suit the needs of our population.

Indian thought and spirituality has something to offer to the whole world. Here, I would like to point out some of the ancient methods, which are suitable in our culture to alter the internal state of the human being:

- From our Vedas and Upanishads- the chanting of sounds, the role of Sat Guru and Vakt Guru.
- From Bhagavad-Gita – the concept of Karma Yoga as a work culture.
- From Ramayana and other holy scriptures – simple stories to motivate children towards values.
- From Patanjali Yogasutra- Various "do's" and "don'ts" of daily living, food and the benefits of vegetarianism, postural exercise and various methods to increase the attention, contemplation, concentration and osteopathic health of an individual.
- From Ayurveda – Methods to promote longevity.
- From Jainism - Promotion of vegetarianism.
- From Buddhism - Vipasana and the middle path of living to decrease stress and tensions of daily living (very well utilized in cardiac stress management programs).
- From Sufism – Methods to develop the inner self.
- There are also some cults and movements like Sikhism, Tibetan scriptures which have suggested an effective way of living, and the promotion of the Holistic Health of an individual.

There are certain belief systems upon which the abovementioned spiritual philosophies are operational. Ancient Indian wisdom states that one has to have strong faith and belief in these "rational beliefs" to have health, happiness and wellbeing. For example:

• I believe in the divinity of the Vedas and other spiritual scriptures. These primordial hymns are God's word and the bedrock of Sanatana Dharma, the eternal religion which has neither beginning nor end.

• I believe in one, all-pervasive Supreme Being who is both immanent and transcendent, both Creator and Unmanifest Reality.

• I believe that the universe undergoes endless cycles of creation, preservation and dissolution.

• I believe in karma, the law of cause and effect by which each individual creates his own destiny by his thoughts, words and deeds.

• I believe that the soul reincarnates, evolving through many births until all karmas have been resolved, and moksha, spiritual knowledge and liberation from the cycle of rebirth, is attained through awareness and realization. Not a single soul will be eternally deprived of this destiny.

• I believe that divine beings exist in unseen worlds and that temple worship, rituals, sacraments as well as personal devotionals create a communion with these devas and Gods.

• I believe that all life is sacred, to be loved and revered, and therefore we must practice ahimsa.

• I believe that no particular religion teaches the only way to salvation above all others, but that all genuine religious paths are facets of God's Pure Love and Light, deserving tolerance and understanding.

My point of view through this theoretic empirical paper, is not to turn the wheel back to the spiritual reality of the Stone Age and to forget about scientific laws of experimentation, but I would like to emphasize that, if one is trained to control or modify his internal make up without getting frustrated, depressed or getting aggressive, with the above mentioned techniques, then a high success rate at behavioral and mental health can be achieved. Definitely, this is something of a humanistic approach, which may not counter terrorism in the outside world, but it will definitely counter terrorism of the internal world of human beings leading to everlasting peace, happiness, and love.

References

Alexander, C. N. and Rainforth M. V. et al, (1991). Transcendental Meditation, Self-Actualization, and Psychological Health: A Conceptual Overview and Statistical Meta Analysis. *Journal of Social Behavior and Personality*, 6. 189-247.

Bhat, V. K. and Srivastav, O. N. (1974). *Hindi Adaptation of the Middlesex Hospital Questionnaire. Unpublished M.D., thesis*. Department of Psychiatry, IMS, B.H.U.

Carrington, P. and Ephron. (1975). H.S. Meditation as an Adjunct Psychotherapy. In *New Dimensions in Psychiatry*. Arietri, S., and Chrzanowski, G. (Eds.), .261-292. New York, USA: Wiley.

Chinmayananda Swami. (1958). *The Bhagavad-Gita*, 1, 2, 3. New Delhi, India: Mrs. Shila Pusi.

Das, T. (1985). An Experimental Behavioral Analysis of Generalization of Relaxation Response.

Unpublished thesis, 1, 101.

Hollingshed, A. B., and Redlich. (1958). *F.C., Social Class and Mental Illness: A Community Study*. New York, USA: Wiley.

Lake, A. et. al. (1979). Biofeedback and Relaxation in the Management of Migraine. *Journal of Applied Behavior Analysis, 2*. 122-140

Marlatt, C., Pagano, R. and Ross, R. (1984). Effect of Meditation and Relaxation Training upon alcohol use in male social drinkers. In *Meditation: Classic and contemporary perspective*. Shapiro, D., and Walsh, R. (Eds.). 105- 120. New York, USA: Aldine.

Maharaj Sahab [Pt. Brahm Sankar Misra Sahab] (2009). *Discourses on Radha Soami Faith*. Agra, India: Radhasoami Satsang Sabha, Dayalbagh.

Park, J. E. and Park, K. (1977). *Text Book of Preventive and Social Medicine*. Jabalpur, India: Banarasida Bhandot Publishers.

Phillips, D. and Judd, R. (1978). *How to fall out of love*. Boston, USA: Houghton Miffin Co.

Prabhupad, S. A. C. (1972). *Bhagavad-Gita As it is*. London, UK: Collier Macmillan.

Rangaswami, K. (1994). Spirituality and Psychotherapy. *Indian Journal of Psychology*, 21, 1.

Satsangi, P. S. [Revered Professor Prem Saran Satsangi] (2009), *Reality and Truth vis-à-vis Wisdom via Apara Vidya and Para Vidya*, Discourses on Radha Soami Faith. Agra, India: Radhasoami Satsang Sabha, Dayalbagh

Singh, R. and Oberhummer. I. (1980). Behavior Therapy within Settings of Karma Yoga. *Journal. of Behavior Therapy and Exp., Psychiatry*, 2, 135-141.

Sriramamurty, P. (1987). *Levels of Religious Consciousness – Upanishads, Gita and The Religion of Saints*. Bhartiya Vidya, Vols 45-47.

Swada, Y. and Steptoe, A. (1988). The Effects of Belief of Meditation Training on Cardiovascular Stress Responses, *Tr. of psychophysiology*, 2, 249-257.

Udapa, K. N. (1976). *Manual of Science and Philosophy of Yoga*, Varanasi.

Vanistendael, S. (1998). *Growth in the Muddle of Life*. Geneva, Switzerland: International Catholic Bureau.

Vahiya, N. S., Doongzi, D. R. and Jeste, D. V. (1975). Value of Patanjali Concepts in the Treatment of Psychoneurosis. In *New Dimensions in Psychiatry*. Arieti, S. and Chrzonowki, G. (Eds.). (293-304), New York, USA: Wiley.

Vigne, J. (1995). *Indian Wisdom, Modern Psychology and Christianity*. Varanasi, India: B.H.U.

Walsh, R. (1981). Meditation. In *Handbook of Innovative Psychotherapies*. R. Coursing (Ed.) 470-488, New York, USA: Wiley.

Watson, P. J .and Workman, E. A. (1981). The Non–concurrent Multiple Baseline Design across Individuals Design. An Extension of the Traditional Multiple Baseline Design. *Journal of Behavior Therapy and Experimental Psychiatry*. 12, 257-259.

Wolpe, J. (1982). *The Practice of Behavior Therapy (3rd ed.)*. New York, USA: Pergamon Press

Chapter 43

Relationship between Consciousness and Different Levels of Karma

VINEETA MATHUR AND K. MAHARAJ KUMARI
Department of Chemistry, Faculty of Science
Dayalbagh Educational Institute (Deemed University), Agra, India

Abstract

Every day actions called Kriyaman karmas affect an individual's consciousness resulting in the existing state of being or an experience. Karmas are of two types good and bad, good defined as those which take one closer to the Supreme Being and bad defined as those which make one distant from the Lord. A study was conducted on the relationship of consciousness of 110 participants to five everyday karmas. The aim of the study was to find out which of these karmas were higher level karmas and enhanced consciousness. Statistical analysis using Pearson's correlation methods and Factor Analysis using SPSS PC + version 6 was done. The results clearly showed a relationship between higher consciousness and the good karmas taken up for the study. The karmas taken up for the study were further identified as Nishkam karmas and Kamya karmas.

Consciousness, a perceived characteristic of the spirit emerges as awareness when one is one's own observer. According to Indian philosophical traditions consciousness has two aspects: the transcendental, which is a result of intuition (*para vidya*) and the phenomenal achieved by cognition (*apara vidya*). Humans have the ability to realize reality in itself as consciousness (Rao, 2005). *Consciousness (C)* can be a state of being or an experience. By will, by thought and by action a man affects and is affected by his surroundings. When the mind withdraws itself from sensory processes by conscious choice it is able to access direct knowledge of what consciousness is and when the mind empties itself it partakes in pure consciousness experiencing ultimate realization. Higher consciousness results from a state of dynamic equilibrium and peace of mind resulting in permanent happiness (Kaw, 2000).

Kriyaman karmas are every day actions or *karmas* performed in the current life since birth. The consequences are experienced in this life or in future lives as the fruits of actions. The Hindu concept of *karma* which has no direct equivalent in Western religions holds significant implications for human well-being (Dalal & Pande, 1988; Hill and Pargament, 2003). Well-being is constructed out of three components: i) life-satisfaction ii) positive affect and iii) low negative affect (Krishna Mohan, 2001). *Kriyaman karmas* may be either good or bad. Good *karmas* are deeds done without desire, for the sole purpose of meeting the Lord and are recognized by the saints as good for *parmartha* (Ultimate Truth). Bad *karmas* are selfish deeds performed for personal worldly good. According to saints this is prohibited and must be avoided for the benefit of *parmartha* (Satsangi, 2004). A deed (*karma*) which brings one closer to the Feet of the Lord is the best while the bad deed takes one away from the Lord by developing attachment for the world and increasing desire. A deed which brings comfort to a living being is good; if it results in pain for the living being it is bad (Satsangi, 2004).

This study proposes that elevated consciousness, empowerment of mind and general well-being of the human entity is the outcome of good *kriyaman karma*. Out of the broad spectrum of *Kriyaman karmas* few are studied viz. spirituality(S), intuition (I), compassion (Co), righteousness (R) and possessiveness (P). These variables are used as markers to study the effect of *Kriyaman karmas* on the consciousness (C) of the human entity.

The Variables SICoRP:

Spirituality (S), a belief in and reliance on a higher power, is partially distinct from religiousness and together with positive ideology elevates one's consciousness. Definitions of spirituality given by scholars include phrases such as feeling connected, believing in a power outside of one's self, searching for a purpose in life, experiencing a numinous quality, and moving towards personal wholeness (Canda, 1995; Ganje-Fling & McCarthy, 1996; Decker, 1993; King et al., 1995; Krishnamohan, 2001). In the context of this study spirituality includes concepts of transcendence, a universal religion, individual spiritual experiences, meditation techniques, concept of better worldliness and spiritual beliefs leading to higher consciousness.

Intuitive knowledge is achieved by transcendental experience and is a gift of God. The variable Intuitiveness (I) is the key to liberation and includes intellect, reflectiveness, inner strength and understanding one's self. In Indian tradition intuition and reflective attitude are important in elevating intellect and thought process, increasing inner strength, wisdom and one's potential to achieve an ultimate balance that will free one's spirit from this plane. Intuitive knowledge can be used to explore and examine one's own strengths and weaknesses. Intuitiveness is a light which illuminates understanding so one must listen to one's intuition. It is the link to oneself and to the universe (Moore, 2002).

Compassion (Co) is defined as being moved by the suffering of others and having the desire to alleviate suffering. Compassion is a form of empathy, bliss. The variable 'Co' includes a deep and abiding sense of service to all, love for mankind, humility and altruism. Humility is a form of egoless happiness. In a person, compassion and humility regulate common emotions like gratitude, tolerance, acceptance of all life has in store and hope and comfort in difficult times.

Righteousness is always doing what is virtuous. It is the way in which Nature's laws are created and manifested. The variable righteousness (R) includes integrating forces at work, morality, duty, service, power of judging right from wrong, sense of direction, self-discipline in eating and beneficial health behaviours.

Possessiveness (P) stands for the visible power of wealth, exercising control over dear ones, other humans as well as material things. The variable includes egoism, attachment, selfishness and thinking of oneself as the doer of all deeds.

These are all negative traits which result in the individual becoming a materialistic person. This is the gross form of awareness leading to thoughts of worldly possessions, food and other matters far removed from spirituality.

For this study the above mentioned karma variables are together referred to as SICoRP (spirituality, intuitiveness, compassion, righteous attitude and possessiveness) and are used to study the relationship of *Kriyaman karmas* to human consciousness in the respondents.

Method

A study was conducted in which 110 adult, literate participants from all walks of life were given a questionnaire designed to investigate how consciousness relates to different karmas. Sixty questions were used in the study of consciousness levels as related to *karmas* like spirituality, intuitiveness, compassion, righteousness and possessiveness of the human being. The respondents were asked to answer on a five point scale choosing from five options, Definitely Yes, Yes, Maybe, No, Definitely No. The response scale is 1 (Definitely No) to 5 (Definitely Yes). Questions measuring human consciousness are based on topics such as transcendental experiences and issues of faith of men conforming to their mental dispositions etc.

The assessment of spirituality is assessed by questions relating to belief in Fatherhood of God and brotherhood of man, reincarnation and *karma*, and importance of spirituality in life. To measure the intuitive power of adults the questionnaire has questions on intellect, inner strength, and alleged abilities or talents of individuals. The study of the variable compassion and humility consists of questions on well-being of people, compassion for those in trouble and issues related to modesty and tolerance. Questions, related to the variable of righteousness and duty, are asked on strengths that promote integrity in life, on personal opinions of moral issues, texts that inspire and on self-discipline. Respondents are also asked questions on possessiveness of dear ones and selfishness towards personal possessions.

The data obtained was used for correlation and factor analysis studies.

Results and Discussion

The mean values and standard deviations for the karma variables and consciousness of the entire sample population (N = 110) are as shown in Table 1.

Table 1 - Means and S.D of Variables

	S	*I*	*Co*	*R*	*P*	*C*
Mean	24.34	34.2	34.21	29.14	25.51	21.74
S.D	10.7	7.4	5.8	6.3	10.4	11.3

The large values of standard deviations could probably be because of varied sample comprising of people from all walks of life. This study evaluates using Pearson's correlations, how the five specific karmas (SICoRP) of the study correlate with human consciousness (C).

Table 2 - Correlations between Consciousness and Karmas for Respondents

Karmas	***Consciousness***
Spirituality	0.51**
Intuitiveness	0.45**
Compassion	0.51**
Righteousness	0.41**
Possessiveness	-0.43**
	(** signifies p<.001)

Table 2 shows Pearson's correlations for five karmas and consciousness. Significant higher correlation between karma of spirituality and consciousness (0.51) indicates that higher spirituality results in higher consciousness. Correlations for karma of intuitiveness and consciousness (0.45) are also significant. Earlier studies have similarly demonstrated that by working more on one's intuitiveness or "gut feelings" one can increase consciousness (Rogers and Wiseman, 2006). Pearson's correlations for karma of compassion and consciousness (0.51) are significant. Similar findings are reported in an earlier study on compassion in which those who are conscious of the needs of others wanted to help others in their needs (Newberg and Iverson, 2003). Significant correlations are also seen for karma of righteousness and consciousness (0.41). This suggests that morality and ethics is a prerogative of the group. Spirituality and intuition, both good karmas have significant correlations with consciousness indicating that they result in higher consciousness and those who have higher consciousness are more compassionate and righteous. Only correlations for karma of possessiveness and consciousness (-0.4327) are negative though significant, suggesting that possessiveness is probably a lower karma conflicting in nature to consciousness.

Table 3 - Factor Analysis of Variables

	Factor 1	Factor 2	Factor 3	Communality
Consciousness	.60	.43	-.34	.67
Spirituality	.90	.13	.04	.83
Intuition	.68	.17	-.32	.60
Compassion	.33	.70	-.24	.65
Righteousness	.09	.90	-.07	.83
Possessiveness	-.15	-.17	.95	.95
Eigen Values	2.9	1.4	1.1	
% Variance	48.7	14.1	12.5	
Cumulative %	48.7	62.7	75.2	
Predicted level of karma	Nishkam karma Self-less karma	Nishkam/Kamya karma Self-centered / Self-less karma	Kamya karma Self- centered karma	

Results of factor analysis carried out on the data of respondents reveal three factors which contribute to 75.2 % of total variance of data. Factor I, having loadings on consciousness, spirituality and intuitiveness indicates that since spirituality and intuitiveness are both good karmas they are related to higher spiritual consciousness. The *karmas* contributing to Factor I are self-less *karmas* and may be called *Nishkam Karmas*. Similar results are seen in studies done on spiritual life contributing to higher consciousness (Wesson, 2008). Factor II groups together righteousness and compassion indicating that some in this group go about their daily duties for themselves and with concern for others (not for the Lord). Karma of morality, duty, service, judgment, sense of direction and self-discipline are contributing factors and may be called self-centered karma. However it is observed that many in the group are particular about helping those in need and doing what is right. Loadings on consciousness are also moderate. This indicates that these are habitually performed and recollected daily karmas of the group related to moderate levels of consciousness. So, probably Factor II is a mixture of self-centered and selfless karmas and is therefore attributed to both *Nishkam and Kamya karma*. Only a mind which is free from worldly conflicts knows that its duties are to be performed with a spiritual mission to enjoy happiness (Verma, 1998; Roccas, 2005). Other studies report that divine righteousness has the potential to open doors to fullness of integrated life for all people involved (De Wet, 2005). Possessiveness karma comes out separately as Factor III and it does not show any loading of good karmas or consciousness. This indicates that possessiveness is a selfish Karma and Factor III may be called *Kamyakarma*.

Factor analysis was carried out by the principle component method using the SPSS PC + version 6 software, on the data collected, to find out the kind of karmas which group together with consciousness. An attempt was made to determine the factors contributing to the correlations of karma variables and their consciousness outcomes. The composite karma variables spirituality, intuitiveness, compassion, righteousness and possessiveness are included in the data base and are seen to be associated with the consciousness of human being. The analysis identifies the percentage of factors that contribute to total variance. The grouped loadings in each factor could be attributed to different levels of karma. These results are presented in table form, but only loadings > 0.5 are considered statistically significant.

Conclusion

Manifested consciousness is not always aware of itself in an optimum manner and exists at different levels of awareness. There seems to be a direct and positive correlation between the levels of karmas and the level of consciousness attained. Higher consciousness is attained by those who perform karmas which take an individual closer to the Lord and are called Nishkam Karma. Such karmas have higher objectives such as peace of mind and dynamic equilibrium. Karmas performed with discretion in every day life are a mixture of Nishkam and Kamya karmas. People with lower consciousness perform Kamya karmas which are lower karmas with selfish thoughts of material gains and possessions.

References

Canda, E. (1995). Existential Family Therapy: Using the Concepts of Victor Frankl. Families in Society: *The Journal of Contemporary Human Services*. 76. 451-452.

Dalal, A. K., and Pande, W. (1988). Psychological Recovery of Accident Victims with Temporary and Permanent Disability. *International Journal of Psychology*. (23). 25–40.

De Wet, F. W. (2005). The Disintegration of Life in a Polarized Society: Surprised by the Integrating Power of Divine Righteousness. *The International Journal of the Humanities. 5(2). 173-180.*

Decker, L. R. (1993). The Role of Trauma in Spiritual Development. Special issue: Trauma and Transcendence. *Journal of Humanistic Psychology*. 33. 33-46.

Ganje-Fling, M. A. and McCarthy, P. (1996). Impact of Childhood Social Abuse on Client Spiritual Development: Counseling Implications. *Journal of Counseling and Development*. 74. 253-258.

Hill, P., and Pargament, K. I. (2003). Advances in the Conceptualization and Measurement of Religion and Spirituality: Implications for Physical and Mental Health Research. *American Psychologist*. 58. 64–74.

Kaw M. K. (2000). *The Science of Spirituality*. Delhi, India: Full Circle Publishing,

King, M., Speck, P., and Thomas, A. (1995). The Royal Free Interview for Religious and Spiritual Beliefs: Development and Standardization. *Psychological Medicine*, 25. 1125-1134.

Krishna Mohan, K. (2001). Spirituality and Well-being: An Overview. *Consciousness and Its Transformation*. Cornelissen, Matthijs (Ed.) Pondicherry, India: SAICE

Moore, D. L. (2002). *On Karma and Karmic Astrology*.

Newberg A. B., Iversen J. (2003). The Neural Basis of the Complex Mental Task of Meditation: Neurotransmitter and Neurochemical Considerations. *Medical Hypothesis*. 61(2). 282-291.

Rao, K. R. (2005). Consciousness Studies: Cross-Cultural Perspectives, Jefferson, NC, USA: McFarland and Co. Inc. Publishers.

Roccas, S. (2005). Religion and Value Systems. *Journal of Social Issues*. 61(4). 747—759

Rogers, P., and Wiseman, R. (2005). Self-Perceived High Intuitiveness: An Initial Exploration. *Imagination, Cognition and Personality*. 25(2). 161-177.

Satsangi, P. S. [Revered Prof. Prem Saran Satsangi] (2004). *What is called Karma?* Discourses on Radhasoami Faith with Supplement. Agra, India: Radhasoami Satsang Sabha, Dayalbagh

Verma, S. (1998) The State of a Healthy mind: The Indian World View. *Journal of Indian Psychology*. 16 (2). 1-9.

Wesson, K. A. (2008). *Brain Basics for the Teaching Professionals*. Science Master, Part II.

Chapter 44

A Fuzzy Model of Consciousness and the Soul Hypothesis

RUCHI KULSHRESHTHA
Department of Chemistry, L.M. College, Jodhpur, India

MOHIT KULSHRESHTHA
BSNL, Jodhpur, India

Abstract

The ancient Indian scientists or Rishis developed a scientific theory of consciousness. How the ancient theory corresponds with modern studies in areas of psychotherapy and consciousness– has been dealt with in this paper. More importantly, starting from a fuzzy model of mental consciousness proposed by Rishis, we explain in this paper, why and how the soul-consciousness, unveiled by meditation, is integrated into the therapeutic solution prescribed by Rishis. The related theoretic aspects are substantiated by presenting a unique case study of Socrates.

Introduction

If fuzzy means talking in terms of qualitative variables rather than exact numerical quantities then the Rishis can be credited with a fuzzy formulation describing the condition of any mental or physical system by referring it to three basic modes of nature called as gunas. This trimodal fuzzy model of nature underlies the psychological analysis of Rishis and in this paper we have not only evaluated it by applying it to a clinical vignette as example but also succeeded in deriving a basic postulate of a popular school of psychodynamic thought, the transactional analysis pioneered by Eric Berne. Thus firmly footed fuzzy model of consciousness has been shown to be competent enough for purposes of mental consciousness analysis and also for logically measuring the rise of consciousness, consequent upon continued meditative practice. In fact, as shown in the work, the soul hypothesis can be logically built upon this model.

Finally, a verification of the soul hypothesis is pursued giving parallels between the soul described in the Gita and the Daemon described in writings of contemporaries of Socrates.

A Fuzzy Model of Consciousness

Many researchers have scientifically studied neurobiological effects of meditation. The techniques of meditation may differ but consistent findings include:

- Activation of fronto-parietal neural networks related to sustained internalised attention.
- Activation of limbic and left frontal brain areas in relation to positive emotions.

- Biochemical changes suggestive of positive affect.

How come no Rishi, no mystic ever talked about neurobiology in relation with meditation? That above changes will be registered due to meditation is sufficiently but summarily conveyed in language of science of Yoga in the following way:

- Meditation leads to pre-dominance of Sattwa in the practitioner [5].

According to Indian books, sattwa, rajas and tamas are three essential modes of cosmic force; the sattwa is that force of nature which translates into quality as happiness, harmony and light. Equilibrium is the keyword for sattwa. Therefore, the 'relaxation response' [6] linked with meditation is but a manifestation of sattwa. The happiness-causing release of dopamine [7] is just a manifestation of sattwa. Likewise, where in [8], the investigators note that meditation leads to efficient brain mechanisms for engaging into and then disengaging from target stimuli in response to task demands, a Yogi would simply say that meditation lends to intelligence the ability to see "the law of action" and "the law of abstention from action" as noted in the Gita Chapter 18; Verse 30 for sattwic intelligence.

The other two gunas or qualitative powers may now be defined. The rajas is the force of kinesis and translates in quality as struggle and effort, passion and action; tamas is the force of inconscience and inertia and translates in quality as obscurity and incapacity and inaction. Mental consciousness is not cast entirely in the single mould of any of these three modes of the cosmic Force; all three are present in everyone and everywhere. There is a constant combining and separation of their shifting relations and interpenetrating influences, often a conflict, a wrestling of forces, a struggle to dominate each other. So, a dominant mode may often be identified at a given point of time.

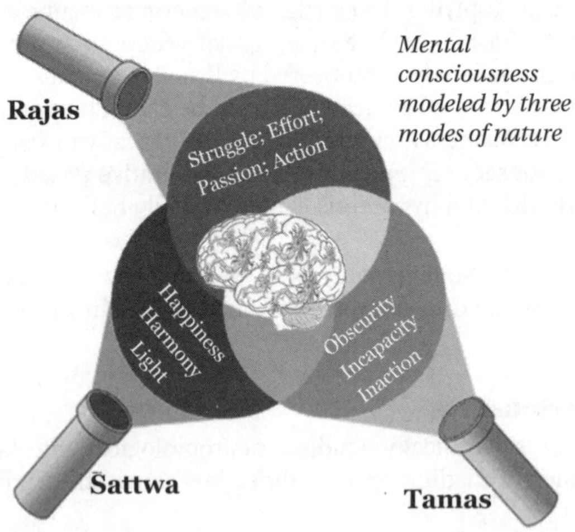

Mental consciousness modeled by three modes of nature

We may now define the fuzzy rules which capture operational mechanism of human psyche. The first rule says: If rajas is depressed – say, in favour of sattwa – then tamas pours in to occupy its place. As an example of this rule, consider the following vignette picked from [9]: "Nasima, a 16-year-old girl from a close family, became unable to go back to school after a half-term break. She felt too afraid of the other girls. Her parents were concerned and took her to an adolescent centre for help. It emerged that Nasima had become deeply confused in adolescence and feared what was going on in her mind. Her fear of becoming a sexual adult was so great that she felt compelled to remain childlike, frozen in time and stuck to her mother. After initial work at the centre, which gave her hope that she could be helped, she went into analysis." In this vignette, we see that when desire or rajas is suppressed in favor of childlike attachment or platonic love i. e sattwa, the incapacitating mode of tamas pours in and Nasima is unable to attend to her school. So, the mental process is seen to have conformed to the fuzzy rule we have cited above. Now, the aim of psychotherapy must be to so adjust the proportion of the three gunas, that the tamaso-sattwic position of Nasima turns into either rajaso-sattwic or better to predominantly sattwic, thus allowing her to be able to attend school while also coping with new feelings arising as a part of her adolescent development. A second rule may be expressed as: If sattwa is depressed – say, to promote rajas – then tamas pours in to occupy its place. This rule explains the basis of why people play games [10]; games are repetitive patterns of interaction among people, comprising of complex series of transactions which at the face appear to have only an overt, social meaning but in actuality have a covert, psychological meaning. In transactional analysis [10] a basic concept is that people play games to avoid perceived risks of intimacy and that a game has an ulterior motive in form of a psychological payoff– a feeling such as guilt, depression or anger. Now, there is governing by a psychological payoff which is rajasic temperament as rajas binds by desire for fruit of action. Further, the suppression of intimacy is depressing the sattwa – truthfulness and goodness embodied in intimacy characterize sattwic mode. And, the result of sattwic suppression is locking of people in unconscious deals of games i.e. they are gripped by tamas which is characterized by unconsciousness and incapacity to come out of the repetitive compulsion of the game. So, a basic postulate of the psychology of human relationships is seen to follow in straightforward manner from the fuzzy rule at hand.

From above discussions, we find that the Rishis adopted a kind of fuzzy modeling to capture the states of consciousness just as modern scientists employ for complex systems. The triguna or trimodal theory based on intense observation and scientific testing is not just some kind of jugglery of metaphysical ideas but a masterpiece of Rishis because it sufficiently though qualitatively in linguistic variables conveys the states of consciousness and dynamic aims of a therapy.

Psychotherapy as per Rishis

Modern psychoanalytic theory retains psychic determinism [11] as a fundamental concept. This means that psychoanalysts acknowledge that our internal experience, our behaviors, our choice of romantic partners, our career decisions, and even our hobbies are shaped by unconscious forces that are beyond our awareness. What is beyond conscious awareness may be ascribed to nature. So, Rishis noticing this determinism of nature put it in this way that the force and propulsion of three modes (discussed in previous section) come from nature and not from ego.

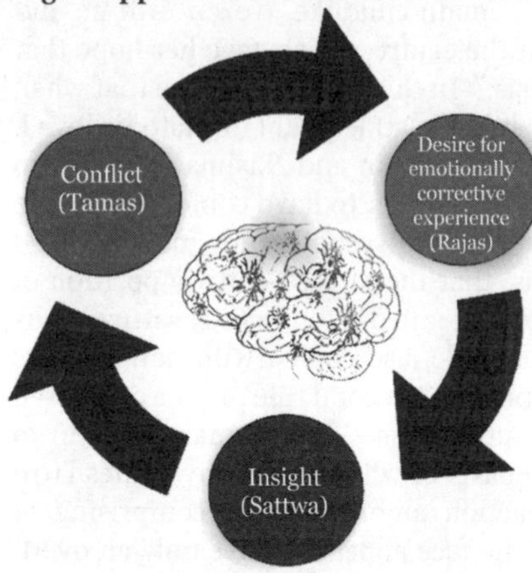

The ego subject to three modes is inflicted with binding and limiting action of the modes. For example, in the clinical vignette of previous section the sattwa has bound Nasima by over attachment to goodness of platonic love, this the analyst has worded as: "...she felt compelled to remain childlike, frozen in time and stuck to her mother". We see that even the best of three gunas, the sattwa, can have such a limiting effect. So, Rishis researched for a psychotherapy which, instead of merely adjusting man comfortably within the field of gunas (or modes), actually and ultimately frees him from the binding effects of the three gunas. They found that ego alone cannot free itself from the binding of gunas. If life of man is examined long enough then as modern psychoanalysts would also agree the three modes of tamas, rajas and sattwa would be seen to effect a mechanical repetition of the same sequence, in order of their one-to-one correspondence, of conflict, desire for emotionally corrective experience and insight (like from transference interpretation [11]) resolving a given conflict, but would not let man become free of their triply binding and limiting action.

In the previous section, we have seen that meditation can enhance sattwic quality. The sattwa dominates but does not bind if one persists in meditation. This means meditation is just the key we are looking for. Rishis noted that meditation unveils a consciousness which is not bound by three modes of nature and which can govern optimally the say of a guna in steering the life of man. They attributed this consciousness which is master of the modes – not just a helpless subject like ego – to soul and prescribed their psychotherapeutic solution: act from right consciousness by switching in the say of soul through meditation.

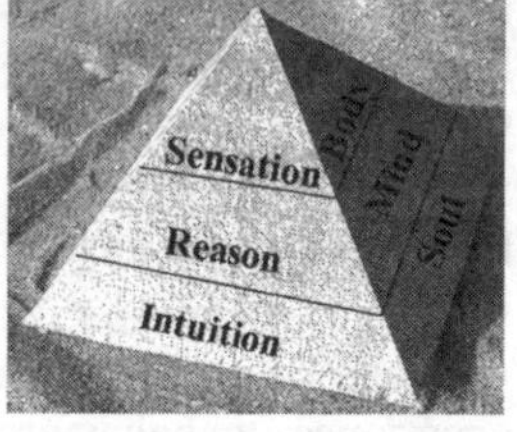

Experts in hypnotism often experiment successfully in establishing the presence of a superconscious aspect of human psyche. For example, in an experiment [12] conducted by the psychology major, Carl Sargent, at the University of Cambridge, the subjects under hypnosis guessed a Zener card, drawn randomly by another person seated at a different place, on an average more than twice as correct as subjects in the normal waking state. The super consciousness thus follows in same manner as Freud proved the unconscious in his hypnotic experiments.

Rishis meditated and saw that intuitions of super conscious nature are opened to man by meditation. Just as sensation is to the body or reason is to the mind, the intuition is to the soul. This soul-born discrimination or intuition is the key factor in psychotherapy of Rishis.

Socrates: A Case Study

Even if one person throughout history has experienced in the conscious state the soul-faculty of intuition then it is worth framing a hypothesis of the soul and testing it with meditation as a method for unveiling this soul-faculty. We know that such a person does exist in history and in fact had to die because of his innocent sharing with people of his soul-communion experience. If one doubts the rational condition of mentality of this person then it may be offered that his style of questioning and reasoning has been highly recommended for use in psychotherapy [13]. The case of Socrates and his Daemon stands unparalleled throughout history in proof and promise of soul-guidance [14].

Most remarkably, the characteristic features of the Daemon examined and compiled, for example in [15], correspond fairly well with the account of the soul given in the Gita. For example, in the Gita we find that the soul is the giver of sanction (Chapter 13, Verse 23) to nature for its activity and the Daemon also, as the keyword to his interaction with Socrates, is a consenter for his acts. This is evident from an excerpt from Apology where Plato's Socrates tells: "It began in my early childhood– a sort of voice which comes to me; and when it comes it always dissuades me from what I am proposing to do, and never urges me on." Here's another excerpt from writings of Xenophon, "As for my claims that a divine voice comes to me and communicates what I must do, how in claiming this am I introducing new deities?" Similarly, Plutarch writes that the Daemon can sanction Socrates' own decisions. Now, if at all the Gita is right in stating that the soul has the role of a sanctioner then it must be understood in the same way as the Daemon did for Socrates. That the Daemon is not a mental or neural phenomenon can be verified if an instance of its intuitive power is found in historical writings.

So, we consider this account by Plutarch: "More and greater things you may learn from Simias, and other companions of Socrates; but once, when I was present, as I went to Euthyphron the soothsayer, it happened, Simias, as you remember, that Socrates was going up to Symbolum, and the house of Andocides, all the way asking questions, and playfully attacking Euthyphron. When, suddenly standing still, and making us to do the same, he pondered with himself for some time. Then, turning about, he walked through Trunkmakers' Street, calling back his friends that walked before him, affirming that it was because of his daemon. Many turned back, amongst whom I, holding Euthyphron, was one; but some of the youths, keeping on the straight road, in order, as it were, to disprove the daemon of Socrates, took along with them Charillus the piper, who came with me to Athens to see Cebes. Now, as they were walking through Sculptors' Street, near the court houses, a herd of pigs, covered with mud, met them; and, being too many for the street, and running against one another, they upset some that could not get out of the way, and dirtied others ; and Charillus came home with his legs and clothes very muddy; so that often, in merriment, they would remember Socrates' daemon, wondering at its constant care of the man, and that Heaven kept such a particular watch over him." From this account we find that the daemon has intuition ascribed to him, a super conscious faculty of perceiving directly without needing any external neurosensory data has been verified and this precognitive extrasensory perception

(ESP) of Socrates is "because of his daemon". Clearly, no subtle auto-associative operations of neural memory can explain the precognition or ESP demonstrated in this anecdote.

Plato, a disciple of Socrates, in his Laws writes: "Kronos gave our communities as their kings and rulers, not men but Daemons, beings of diviner and superior kind just as we still do the same with our flocks of sheep and herds of other domesticated animals. We do not set oxen to manage oxen, or goats to manage goats; we their betters in kind, act as masters ourselves. So the god, in his kindness to man, did the same; he set over us the superior race of Daemons." Now, this treatment of Daemons matches well with the treatment given to the soul in Gita which declares (Chapter III; verse 10): 'God created all communities with divine sparks i.e. souls and then told them to evolve and grow in the soul-guidance and to fulfill all their wishes by uniting ultimately their egos with their souls.'

Similarly, the Daemon does not have any gender nor does he grow old in keeping with the eternal principle for the soul (Chapter 15; verse 7 of Gita). And, why does Socrates follow him, not doing what he himself wishes? Though a psychiatrist may diagnose the symptoms of split-personality etc., but a Yogi would say that: 'Socrates developed intuition by meditating in previous life and with this faculty opened, acting not from egoistic intelligence but from spiritual guidance, he fulfilled the Karma Yoga of Gita (Chapter 2, Verse 50) in his birth as Socrates.' Finally, when judged with penalty of his life, the spiritual temperament of Socrates did not let him feel imbalanced or in mourning because as a signal from his Daemon he knew that death is not necessarily a poor or bad experience and in fact, may be a good one. This, again, is in keeping with Gita's one of chief propositions (Chapter II; verse 13) that a self-composed man does not allow himself to be disturbed by death because just as ego sees physically changing state of body from boyhood to old age similarly the soul perceives death to be a process merely of change of bodily clothes. This living demonstration of exact coincidence between theory in Gita and practice by Socrates is a powerful example in favor of the science of consciousness developed and gifted by Rishis.

Conclusion

The correspondence between ancient theory of consciousness and modern approach to psychological analysis and therapeutic prescription has been discussed. We have noted the efficacy and maturity of the model of mental consciousness postulated by Rishis by matching the implications of this model with the findings of modern researchers. Just as modern psychotherapy works by raising the consciousness of a patient using, say, transference interpretation [11] similarly with the aid of meditation, Rishis achieve freedom from faulty mental mechanism. However, a comparison has shown that Rishis, instead of simply comfortably adjusting for a while within the field of triply binding and limiting modes of nature, argue for total freedom. The ego with its defense mechanisms is incompetent to handle effectively its subjection to the three modes whereas the soul has a promise for granting release from crippling or hampering play of the three gunas. And, meditation is a way to realize the kingdom of the soul.

References

Aftanas and Golocheikine. (2001). Human Anterior and Frontal Midline Theta and Lower Alpha Reflect Emotionally Positive State and Internalized Attention: High-resolution EEG Investigation of Meditation. *Neuroscience Letters*. 310 (1). 57-60.

Benson, H. et al. (1974). The Relaxation Response. *Psychiatry*. 37. 37– 46.

Berne, E. (1968). *Games People Play*. Harmondsworth, UK: Penguin.

Davidson, R. J., and Lutz, A. (2007). Buddha's Brain: Neuroplasticity and Meditation. *IEEE Signal Processing Magazine. September*. 172-176.

Gabbard, G. O. et al. (2005). *Oxford Textbook of Psychotherapy (First edition)*. Oxford University Press.

Kjaer, T. W. et al. (2002). Increased Dopamine Tone during Meditation-induced Change of Consciousness. *Brain Res Cogn Brain Res. Apr 13(2)*. 255-9.

Lazar, S. W. et al. (2000). Functional Brain Mapping of the Relaxation Response and Meditation. *NeuroReport* 11. 1581-1585.

Leudar, I., and Thomas, P. (2000). *Voices of Reason, Voices of Insanity: Studies of Verbal Hallucinations*, Routledge, 25-27.

Lou H. C. et al. (1999). A 15O-H2O PET Study of Meditation and the Resting State of Normal Consciousness. *Human Brain Mapping*. 7. 98-105.

Manning, H. E. (1872). The Daemon of Socrates. *The Royal Institution*. Jan. 26.

Milton, J. et al. (2004). A Short Introduction to Psychoanalysis. Sage Publications, 3.

Newberg, A. B. et al. (2001). The Measurement of Regional Cerebral Blood Flow during the Complex Cognitive Task of Meditation: A Preliminary SPECT Study. *Psychiatry Research: Neuroimaging. 106*. 113-122.

Overholser, J. C. (1993). Elements of the Socratic Method: I. Systematic Questioning. *Psychotherapy*. 30. 67-74.

Sahabji Maharaj [Sir Anand Sarup Kt.] (2009). *Diary of Sahab Ji Maharaj (Part III)*, Agra, India: Radhasoami Satsang Sabha, Dayalbagh, 32-33.

Chapter 45

The Science of Spiritual Consciousness

RAVINDRA SRIVASTAVA
BSES, Delhi, India

Abstract

Science is a systematic method of gathering knowledge and organizing it into laws and principles; Spiritual Consciousness is the spirit force and its reservoir. Hence, the subject means to analyze the characteristics, nature, tendencies, working principles, acts and manifestations of the spirit force in a scientific manner. Science deems that all the activities in the world are due to Force (Energy). We, in our study, will establish that the spirit is nothing abstract but is a Force (Energy) and dominates all other (i.e. electrical, magnetic, nuclear, chemical, biological etc) forces of nature. It will also be established that the modus operandi of the spirit force is fundamental, and, all the other aforesaid forces (a) owe their origin to the spirit force and (b) their working principles are a replication of the principles adopted by the spirit force during its manifestation. An analogy will be drawn between the principle of operation of the spirit force and material forces. The 'Creation of Cosmos' by the process of Spiritualization of the spirit force with an insight into the intricate concepts viz. 'Object of Creation', 'Birth of Time' and 'Origin of Ego' will be the core of the study. It will be shown that upon manifestation of The Prime Force, the sound produced was 'Radhasoami' and its four component parts 'Ra' 'Dha' 'Soa' & 'Mi' are indispensable for overcoming the meshes of Time (kala) Coverings (karmas) and Ego. Our study will also envisage - (a) the objective of the spirit force; (b) the impediments encountered in the achievement of its objective; and (c) the remedial measures required to overcome the impediments.

What is Spiritual Consciousness (The Spirit Force?)

It is well known that all the animated actions and desires are directed towards attaining pleasure and avoiding pain. We feel pleasure and pain in a wakeful condition only. In the states of deep slumber or trance, there is no feeling of pleasure or pain. This means, there is "something" in the wakeful condition which becomes inoperative in the slumber and trance states. This "something" is known as the sensory current, and the spirit is a group or cluster of innumerable sensory currents. Its concentration causes pleasure and distraction leads to pain. Since concentration (inward tendency) of the spirit leads to pleasure, and attaining pleasure is the inherent desire of all beings hence it can be deduced that the nature of spirit force is inward.

Attributes of the Spirit Force

(a) *SAT* - Self Existent- the spirit is self- existent and does not need anything for its existence unlike the body and mind which depend on other entities like food and thought.

(b) *CHIT* - All Intelligent -can perceive and comprehend every event irrespective of time and space.

(c) *ANAND* - Blissful - a state much higher than those achieved by body and mind in the form of happiness, delight and ecstasy.
(d) *PRAKASH* - luminosity - which is devoid of any limitation imposed by the presence of a medium.
(e) *PREM* - Merger - is the highest form of attraction when the entity comes into unison with its source.
(f) *AKARSHAN* - Attraction rather than diffusion.
(g) *SHAKTI* - Pure Energy - without any contamination and which does not dampen or dilute on usage and indulgence.

The Spirit is a Force (Energy) and is Dominant over All Material Forces

Postulate 1- Principle of Action of Force

"Every Force acts from a higher plane, through a medium and manifests at a lower plane". The table below depicts this principle as observed by various material forces

Type of Force	Its State at Higher Plane	Medium	Its State at Lower Plane	Manifest-ation	Deduction
Electro-magnetic Radiations	Sun	Photons	Radiations	X rays, TV etc	EM radiation is a force
Heat Energy	Specific heat	Disinte-grated state of molecules	Heat	Warmth	Heat is a force
Spirit	Trance Disembodied	Body and Mind	Moving and thinking faculty	Pleasure and pain	Spirit is a force

Similar to material forces, the spirit too follows the 'principle of action of a force' hence should be deduced as a force (energy).

Postulate 2- Law of Conservation / Distribution of Energy

"The Total Energy of a system is always conserved, and upon manifestation, its sum total is distributed in various other forms of energy". For instance, the total spirit energy in the case of a man, a flower and a stone is equal or conserved. Its distribution however varies according to the level of intellect, fragrance and hard outer body. In the case of a man, a major part of the spirit-energy is utilized in intellect, and less in fragrance and hard body shell. The converse is true for a flower and a stone. In all, the distribution of spirit energy varies but its sum total remains constant. Hence, similar to the material forces, the spirit too abides by the law of conservation / distribution of energy, hence should be deduced as a Force.

Postulate 3

Unlike material forces whose manifestation stops when the medium is removed, the spirit force on the contrary, depicts a higher degree of manifestation when the medium is removed. For example – Intellectual faculties of the spirit enhance during the trance and disembodied state when the medium of physical body and mind are at rest or absent.

Postulate 4

Spirit Force makes all other forces live – All the material forces (chemical, biological etc.) aid the growth of body and mind as long as the spirit is present. Once the spirit departs, these material forces start disintegrating the body. This indicates that it is the presence or absence of the spirit force, which renders all the material forces as active or inactive.

Hence, the postulates conclusively prove that the spirit is a Force (Energy) and dominates all forces.

State of the Spirit and its Reservois, Prior to Creation (Adi State)

In the *Adi* state, the Supreme Force was in a state of self absorption (*Shunya Samadhi*) and all the energy was like a 'single mass'. In this domain of the "single mass", the energy was 'locked' within the innumerable points i.e. the energy was in an un-manifested form. This convergent state or the state of withdrawal of energy resulted in a neutral zone between the two planes - the plane to which the energy was withdrawn and the plane from which the energy was being withdrawn. In effect, there existed an eternal polarization in the Supreme Force (single mass) leading to concentration and depletion of the Prime Energy at the two poles. The content which caused this polarization was the original amount of infinite spirituality at the positive pole and infinitesimally low amount of spirituality at the nether pole; the two poles can be compared to a cloudlet in the infinite sky. This state of eternal polarization is similar to the polarization observed in a bar magnet with concentration and depletion of magnetism at the two poles with a neutral zone between them (Figure 1). Also, due to the enormous attractive capability of the positive pole there was a perpetual kind of suction or withdrawal of spirituality from the negative to the positive pole. This is done by means of subtle lines of force composed of innumerable points acting in the same direction as a united link. These points were not trifles but were the spirit entities (Surat / *Atma*) which were in comatose condition due to their individual coverings. But they were connecting the two poles through their innermost quarters and forming a primeval / united link between poles or the spirits i.e. the spirits were transferring or conducting spirituality from the negative to the Supreme Positive Pole. At this juncture there was an upheaval or commotion in the Prime Source which led to the potential (latent) energy turning kinetic.

It is a well known fact that energy, when it turns kinetic, manifests itself through currents and two distinct sounds are produced as a result of commotion. In the state of *Adi*, due to continuous withdrawal, the difference of spirituality between the poles increased further. It led to the rise of The Prime Spiritual current (with the sound *Radha*) in a fashion similar to that observed in the breakage of dielectric strength and consequent flow of current between electric poles. This was preceded by an upheaval in the Prime Source (with the sound *Soami*). Thus *Radhasoami* was the Prime sound which was produced when the

Prime Energy manifested from potential to kinetic form.

In *Adi*, due to the united link (Figure 2) the Supreme positive pole was ever-connected to all the spirit entities and was ever-cognizant with the densest and coarsest parts of the negative pole. The innermost spirituality of the spirits was ever -awake because of their linkage to the Positive Pole. Also, The Prime Sound (*Radhasoami*) when manifested itself, was impressed or stamped in the innermost quarters of each spirit entity, because all spirits were inter-connected just like beads of a rosary through a thread. Contrary to the united action, there was an individual action (Figure 2) of the spirit entity due to its original coverings which led to the generation of a 'sense of distinctness from the Prime Source'. This sense of duality (*dwait*) was the genesis of Ego (*Ahankar*). The Primeval Form (*Adi roop*) of the Prime Force was elliptical and convergent. This is substantiated by the fact that the phenomenon of 'ellipsoid nature with convergent tendency' is visible in all other force- centers of nature also, may it be the motion of electrons round the nucleus or that of planets around the sun. The nascent form of all the forces is elliptical (viz. sun, nucleus, embryo etc) and convergent.

Note- *The Modern day Quantum Theory bears huge resemblance to the Adi phenomenon. The Self absorption state of Adi is similar to the GUT symmetry of Quantum Theory. The Supreme Positive pole being analogus to the unchangeable Quantum potential; the omnipresent field between the poles can be compared to the 4 quantum fields; and the spirits to the elementary particles like quarks, bosons. The Sound of Radhasoami signifies the first big bang.*

Reason for Variety and Uniqueness in Creation

During *Adi*, the spirits due to their respective coverings were placed at differential locations between the two poles or were 'viewed or perceived' differentially by the Supreme Pole. This gave rise to variety in creation i.e. the farther the spirit from the positive pole, its life form is grosser. The different species, different morphological characteristics, different music tunes, different colours etc are all due to their different level of proximity to the positive pole during *Adi* (Figure 3)

Similarly, every spirit is unique in itself. As shown in Figure 3, the spirits were located between the poles similar to the points between magnetic poles. It is a characteristic of magnetic lines of force that only one tangent can be drawn at a point. Every being in the creation is unique due to his DNA, finger prints, and biometrics so his position as a spirit entity between the poles was unique during *Adi*.

Why Was Creation Obtained (Gracious Object of Creation)

During *Adi*, The Supreme Being was in a state of absolute bliss with infinite amount of spirituality. The spirit entities at the nether pole were lying in comatose covers and were totally unaware of the refulgence, and bliss enjoyed at the positive pole. The Supreme Being, in order to bestow upon the comatose spirits of the nether pole, ordained creation so that the individual coverings of these spirits are removed and they attain an equi-spirituality state as of The Supreme essence. It is pertinent to note that the objective of flow of electric current is similar - to bring, both the poles at equi-potential state.

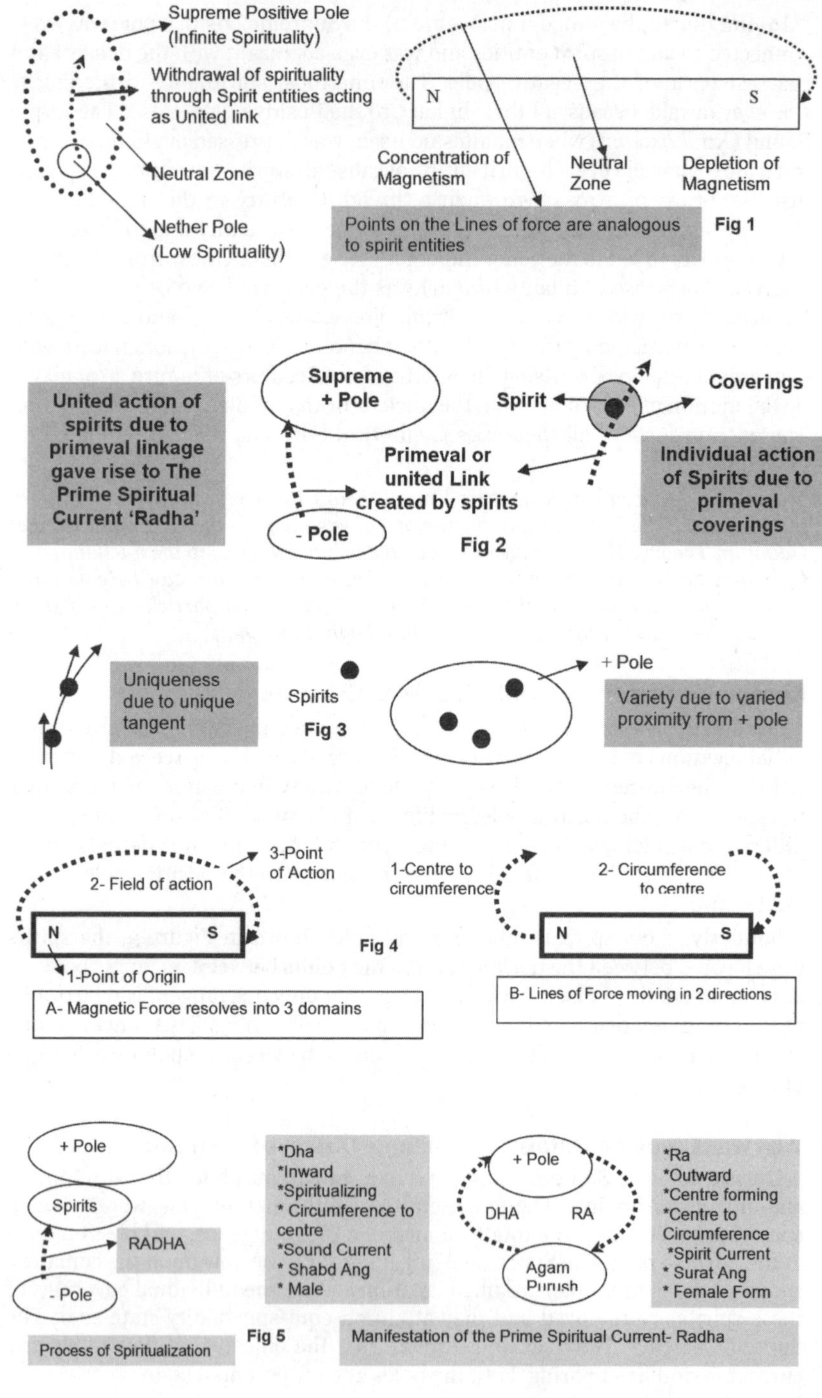
Supreme Positive Pole
(Infinite Spirituality)
Withdrawal of spirituality
through Spirit entities acting
as United link
Neutral Zone
Nether Pole
(Low Spirituality)
N
S
Concentration of
Magnetism
Neutral
Zone
Depletion of
Magnetism
Points on the Lines of force are analogous
to spirit entities
Fig 1
United action of
spirits due to
primeval linkage
gave rise to The
Prime Spiritual
Current 'Radha'
Supreme
+ Pole
Spirit
Coverings
Primeval or
united Link
created by spirits
- Pole
Fig 2
Individual action
of Spirits due to
primeval
coverings
Uniqueness
due to unique
tangent
Spirits
Fig 3
+ Pole
Variety due to varied
proximity from + pole
3-Point
of Action
2- Field of action
N
S
1-Point of Origin
Fig 4
A- Magnetic Force resolves into 3 domains
1-Centre to
circumference
2- Circumference
to centre
N
S
B- Lines of Force moving in 2 directions
+ Pole
Spirits
RADHA
- Pole
Process of Spiritualization
*Dha
*Inward
*Spiritualizing
* Circumference to
centre
*Sound Current
* Shabd Ang
* Male
+ Pole
DHA
RA
Agam
Purush
*Ra
*Outward
*Centre forming
*Centre to
Circumference
*Spirit Current
* Surat Ang
* Female Form
Fig 5
Manifestation of the Prime Spiritual Current- Radha

Process of Spiritualization

We have also seen in Article 4 and Figure 1, that the spirit force behaves similar to a magnet. The first characteristic of The Prime Energy resolving into three domains (Figure 4) led to the formation of 3 Grand divisions - *Nirmal Chetan* (point of origin), *Bramhand* (field of action) and *Pind* (point of action). The second characteristic (outward-inward) of the Prime spiritual current as shown in fig 4, led to the formation of 6 sub-divisions in each , thus a total of 18 regions in the entire macrocosm were created by the process of spiritualization (fig 5) of The Prime energy .i.e. "*Radha*". It carried the entire spirit mass of the nether pole to the Supreme Positive pole for spiritualization or purification, and in the return path created a focus or presiding deity and *loka* (region) in which the spirits were located through its spirit component (outward / centre forming / *Surat ang -Ra*). Its sound component (inward / spiritualization / *Shabd ang- Dha*) pulled the spirits back to the source. The two components of 'Radha' (Adi Surat) were preceded by the original upheaval *'Soami' (Adi Shabd)* having *'Soa'* and *'Mi'* as outward–inward components. At this juncture it is pertinent to mention that the outward and inward components of the spiritual current were commingled only up to the 5th region (*Satlok*).

After *Satlok* the creational current encountered friction due to gross and subtle matter of the nether pole, hence the two components of the creational current, from *Satlok* were cast off as independent or un-commingled currents of *Kala* and *Adya*, which respectively manifested as the male and female forms in the lower regions of *Bramhand* and *Pind*. Each lower region thus created was characterized by a presiding deity and a distinct sound. It is worth mentioning that since the spirit descended from the topmost *loka (Radhasoami)* via the other *lokas*, hence it carried with it, the various sounds (*Sohang, Rarang, Om* etc) produced en route. Thus, all the spiritual sounds are vibrating in the innermost quarter of each presiding deity and each spirit entity of the entire creation.

Macrocosm and Microcosm

Just as the Prime Force created the Macrocosm with 18 divisions, the spirit force which has the same essence as the Prime Force replicated the act and created the Microcosm comprising of the Spirit, Mind and body with 6 apertures each in the physical frame, grey matter and white matter of the brain to perceive the material and spiritual world.

Creation of Time (Kala), Origin of Ego (Ahankar) and its Offshoots

The creational current on account of continuous engagement in creation, encountered friction and observed dilution in its steadiness. It thus wavered or turned vibrational, consequently giving rise to the concept of frequency and hence to the creation of time (*kala*). The circular, cyclic (go-return) and repetitive nature of Time and its centrifugal-centripetal tendencies are observed in innumerable activities viz 'blood flow from heart to body & back to heart, the movement of planets around the sun, the gas cycles, the alternating current, the wheel etc. Spirits of *Bramhand* and *Pind* on account of their being located below *Satlok* thus fall in the region of *Kala* and are subject to the cyclic nature of time including Metempsychosis (*Avagaman*).

We have also seen in article 4 and Figure 2 that the individual coverings over spirits as opposed to their united action produced the concept of duality (feeling of being distinct from the Supreme essence) or Ego. It is this very happening that did not allow the spirits with 'sense of distinctness' to be located in the purely spiritual region. With the Prime Source getting kinetic, this seed of Ego (*Ahankar*) too got kinetic and made the spirit feel as a living and moving force, thus leading to the origin of Desire (*Kaamna*). This desire, when met resistance led to the creation of Anger (*Krodh*). Overcoming this resistance, was followed by the engenderment of a feeling of attainment of the wanted object which resulted in Avarice (*Lobh*). Finally the feeling of clutching the attained object created attachment (*Moha*).

Component Parts of the Prime Sound (*Radhasoami*)

During *Adi*, the spirit entity between the poles was observing two forces of opposite nature. The extraneous force trying to create positive and negative poles in the single mass (refer article 4) and secondly the creational force trying to restore this polarization. The spirit entity was thus under a state of tremor and the sound produced was *Ra* (which represents tremors). Next, the individual tremors of all the spirits joined in tandem and produced a smoother sound *Dha*.

Preceding this, was The Prime Commotion in the elliptical and convergent form of the Supreme Force which was respectively characterized by the production of sound *Soa* (representing ellipsoid form) and sound *Mi* (representing inward convergence). The spirit by pronouncing *Ra* (gross sound) casts off the gross covers of Pind. Repetition of *Dha* (smoother sound) enables the spirit to get rid of the subtle covers of *Bramhand*. Sound *Soa* (elliptical) makes the spirit, encircle the circumference of the purely spiritual region and repetition of sound *Mi* (convergence) pulls the spirit to the base of action i.e *Radhasoami* region.

Objective fo the Spirit Force, Impediments Encountered and The Remedial Measure

The objective of the spirit force to reach its reservoir, is marred by the impeding forces of *kala* (Time), *karma* (coverings) and *Ahankar* (ego), which in turn led to descent of the spirit through the sound currents of *Kala* and *Adya* (ref article 7). Basic scientific laws enunciate that in order to overcome any impeding force, a redemption force which is higher in magnitude and opposite in direction is required. Hence to overcome the aforesaid impeding forces, the redemption force should be a sound current in upward direction. What sound other than the Prime Sound Radhasoami accomplishes this? This Supreme sound when manifests in Human Form (the superior most in entire creation) is known as the *Param Sant Satguru* and He is the only means of spiritual elevation. The Human Form prescribes the method of Surat -Shabd Yoga (Spirit -Sound merger) and connects the downward flowing spirit, to the internally resounding upward directed spiritual sounds by (a) *Sumiran*- which leads to withdrawal of spirit towards 6th *Chakra* (b) *Dhyan*- which makes the spirit stable at the 6th *Chakra* and (c) *Bhajan-* which makes the spirit ascend and merge with the internally resounding *Shabda*. He owns the devotee and by various methods like sacrament, external association (*Satsang*), revealing His form at higher regions during meditation, injects spirituality which cast off the coverings and purify the spirit. This enables the devotee traverse the spiritual path leading to The Prime abode. The process of eradication of *karmas, kala,* Ego adopted by The Redemption Force is depicted below

KARMA / TIME / EGO	GENESIS or REASON FOR ORIGIN	MEANS OF ERADICATION
Kriyaman Karm	performed in current life cycle	by renouncing the desire for results of the actions performed
Prarabdh Karm	performed in immediately preceding life cycle	by miniaturized afflictions
Sanchit Karm	accumulated actions of previous cycles	by Injecting spirituality at higher planes during meditation
Adi Karm (Asa)	due to primeval propensity of the spirit to associate with matter and to flow downwards	by engendering within the spirit, desire (Birah) to reach the Prime abode
Ego (Ahankar)	Sense of Distinctness; Pseudo notion of considering oneself, instead of Supreme Being as the fountainhead of all energy and doings	by providing series of failures i.e. increasing dependence (Saran) on Prime source and by inculcating humility (Dinta)
Time (Kala)	Creational current getting wavered (article 9)	by the 4 component parts of The Prime Shabd (article 11).

Conclusion

Spirit is a Force (Energy) and the most dominant one. *Radhasaomi-* The Prime Sound is the creator, sustainer and the redeeming force. *Surat Shabd Yoga* is the only means of spiritual elevation and *Param Sant Satguru* is The Only one who can carry the redemption of the spirit entity.

Chapter 46

The Evolution of Spiritual Consciousness: Interface Between Integral Science and Spirituality

BRIJARAJ SINGH
Dayalbagh Educational Institute (Deemed University), Agra, India

Abstract

The Science of Consciousness is essentially the study of the non-material world. It is the study of metaphysical phenomena that, for the most part, are not subject to the theories and laws of Newtonian-Cartesian science. However, the human implications of the results of studying consciousness, beyond the physical realm, are immense. This article outlines the spiritual principles shared by Integral Science and the emerging Integral Spirituality. It includes a brief overview of past changes in spiritual consciousness, the role of science in the current shift, and why various beliefs are coalescing into a new Integral Spirituality. The author then explores the causes and possible effects of these changes, concluding that the motivations and transformations must come from a synthesis of all fields.

The Evolution of Spiritual Consciousness: Interface Between Integral Science and Spirituality

In recent years, a new dialogue between various members of the scientific and spiritual communities has helped fuel a rocket-like acceleration of a new spiritual consciousness. The growing number of mind-body-spirit conferences and classes at medical schools from Harvard to Duke Universities, are a sign of this New Consciousness. Science appears to be verifying what people have intuited to be true and linking it to solid empirical theory. Lay seekers from both sides of the aisle who want to understand, define, and experience the energetic world hungrily consume books with applicable scientific theory.

Integral science adds a new level of understanding. Here, humanity is a collaborative learning species built of, by, and into a creative and awesomely ordered energy cosmos whose patterns and principles still guide us. We are a brilliant myth-making species that evolves by pooling information, creating mental maps (worldviews, etc.), and changing our behavior based on insights from all of the above. Yet, the cosmos' workings are still largely beyond our ken.

This new stage of spiritual consciousness, therefore, incorporates a wide range of scientific discoveries and thoughts, yet its essence is also being discovered in new translations of ancient writings such as The Nag Hammadi Library; The Dead Sea Scrolls; and early Roman historical journals on Christianity. The resulting synthesis integrates a wide range of existing spiritual/religious traditions such as Judaism, Christianity, Islam, Buddhism, Taoism, and Goddess and native traditions such as Huna from the Hawaiian Islands, and Native American wisdom from Alaska to South America. The combination suggests practical solutions to many personal and global dilemmas.

Humanity originally developed the concept of spiritual consciousness to explain its relationship to the Cosmos, the Planet, and other living beings. Our desire for a feeling of connection to the Greater Ordering Oneness (Goerner, 1999) still drives our search and helps define the results. The current definitions of spirituality tend to be limited to beliefs and experiences of Oneness in a mystical, non-physical form. Today's synthesis of scientific and spiritual consciousness is providing a more solid pathway to fill the same longing for connection that humans have pursued since the first person worshipped the sun or the moon.

Working definitions of the concepts explored in this article are:

- **Consciousness**—The state of being aware; collective thoughts and feelings of an individual or an aggregate of people. The evolution of consciousness involves the expansion and deepening of the individual and group's potential for thought, understanding, and awareness.
- **The Greater Oneness**—The Wholeness and Essence in all that is—which is always larger than current words can define; that which creates and maintains patterns and order in the Universe.
- **Integral Spirituality** —The melding of explanations/discoveries from Integral Science and long-standing insights/truths from many existing spiritual belief systems and traditions.
- **Religion**—a structured set of beliefs that usually establishes a cosmology, spiritual practices, and rituals, often based on the tenets, experiences, and stories of a specific teacher. Religion differs from spirituality in the degree of concreteness versus pursuit. This article will not attempt to compare the emerging stage of consciousness with the world's many religions.

Integral Science and Spirituality Share the Following Beliefs/Principles

- Energy is invisible, incorporeal, creative, and omnipresent, while also being physical, natural, and empirically discernable.
- Energy flow moves seemingly separate bits of matter in recurring and predictable patterns.
- Energy plus fundamental forces form a single, inseparable fabric that binds and envelops all things in a universal, comprehensively connected weave and an unfathomably intricate Design.
- This combination produces a universal creative force that permeates, guides, and develops all things in the Cosmos. Although the full meaning of its movements is beyond human understanding, all is lawful and orderly underneath.
- This creative force also acts like an "absolute mind" with a built-in compulsion to evolve to healthier, more functional forms and patterns when possible. This pursuit is also built into every facet of the whole. For example, when healthy cells are placed next to unhealthy heart cells, the poorly functioning cells improve their performance.
- Because this Universal Creative Force creates a fractal universe, it also produces an "as above, so below" reality where that which we observe on higher

levels we also see on lower levels. Whether we examine anatomical examples of fractal embedding in the physical body or whether we examine the psychological behavior of children of schizophrenic mothers, we see the same holographic image of the original pattern playing out in its component parts.

- It also produces an "as within, so without" reality where that which we observe within a structure is indicative of that which we expect to observe outside the structure. We observe the psychological effects of submerged patterns affecting surface realities in both the pressure dynamics of plate tectonics and abusive adult anger that results from an abusive childhood.
- Similarly, that which we send forth comes back to us. In spiritual teachings this is variously called the law of circulation, the law of karma, or the law of cause and effect. The Golden Rule reflects the same principle in Christian spirituality, whereas in Buddhism the teaching is that the degree of suffering results from the degree of resistance to life as it is. In modern times we see the principle in pollution that comes back to haunt us in ill health and global warming.
- Because we are interconnected with everything and follow the same Universal principles, we are responsible for our interactions with all of the above.

Causes of Today's Shift in Spiritual Consciousness

Historically, the evolution of spiritual consciousness is driven by intense pressures inside and outside the society, as well as from failing social structures. Currently, stressors in education, politics, communications, economics, and health, as well as personal needs for security, peace, and happiness, are producing an accelerating demand for practical solutions to apply personally, locally, and globally in this multifaceted, worldwide crisis.

As I see it, the engine driving today's shift in consciousness is desperation and despair—along with the flip side of desire for hope, greater inner peace, and the reflection of that peace in the world. Historically, whether one is looking at changes in society or the spiritual evolution within the life of an individual, the most common motivator is emotional crisis: terminal disease, personal terror in a war-zone, a near-death experience, or some other major crisis. Occasionally, a major consciousness change begins with an uplifting transformative experience, such as Astronaut Dr. Edgar Mitchell's epiphany when viewing Earth from outer space, which led him to a lifetime mission to bring science and spirituality together to seek answers to the unanswered questions. As he says, "The story of my life ... is an account of being hit on the head with astonishing experiences, which drove me to find an explanation" (LORA 2004). In our society, people are starving for meaning in the chaos, for patterns in the mess, for hope in any area of modern life from politics to ecology to personal stability. Their desperation sends them searching for new ideas in science, poetry, ancient traditions, mystical experiences, and more.

Because humanity lives by its models and myths, another impetus for today's changing spiritual consciousness is that we have outgrown many modern stories and heroes. Their inadequacy is driving people to seek new practices, definitions, and paradigms in order to find replacements. (Thus, as Joseph Campbell [1996] explains, one of mythology's main functions is "to reject or reconcile consciousness to existence.") Yet, while today's spiritual impetus is seeking new myths, it is also reclaiming older ones and trying to unite spiritual insights with "scientific" grounding.

Emerging Spiritual Beliefs

Among the many emerging spiritual beliefs are:

- Current myths focus primarily on humanity's relationship to the outside world, the new myths need to emphasize the way humans experience themselves and relate to each other, as well as to the larger web of which they are a part.
- There are patterns (or laws)—that are palpable in form and that exist in the interaction of molecules, cells, species, planets, and more—that give us insight into the greater picture. Both scientific and spiritual perceptions suggest that there is, in fact, a Oneness that creates order in the physical universe, as well as in the less clearly visible realms.
- This Oneness is not anthropomorphic; it does not have a gender and is not separate from us, nor are we separate from the Oneness. Quite possibly, this Oneness is still expanding and creating through its creations and by its nature.
- Life contains mystery. As far as we know in this stage of evolution, there are no final, perfect, and despotically correct answers. Since there are better and worse answers, however, we must keep our minds open to new refinements.
- Individuals crave greater inner peace and simplicity in their personal and professional lives. In order to achieve these elements of spiritual growth, they must change the attitudes and methods they are using.
- Every individual comes into the world with a complex list of beliefs derived from mass consciousness, both personal and historical. These thoughts form a fractal web of tenets woven throughout our lives and the lives of others. In our integral world, we need to re-examine and transcend the limitations and errors of thoughts inherited from family lineage, society, religions, and so on. Our greatest challenge is to figure out which of our "thought trails" really do lead to food, and which lead to dead-ends or toxic traps. For instance, we are now hopefully learning that imbuing the Great Ordering Oneness with angry and judgmental traits serves merely to justify our own self-destructive violence against others.
- Because current beliefs are built on interpretations of stories, today's scholars are examining the accuracy of translations of "sacred texts" and considering how their historical and sociological context affects interpretation. At the same time, metaphysicians are using archetypal interpretations of characters in classic texts such as The Old and New Testaments, The Bhagavad Gita, and gods and goddesses of Greece and Rome to help re-think traditional understanding. For example, Mary can be seen as the Divine Feminine and Joseph as the Masculine Principle that embodies faith.
- Integral spirituality believes that the human mind can bridge large distances by drawing on the profound, holographic nature of all information in the universe—as well as the simple sequential physical stimulus path from one brain to another. Events like distance healing and empathic communication can be explained in terms of individuals tapping into the wave "interference"

patterns of this vast information web.

• Because human beings use thought to change all aspects of themselves and society, thoughts also have power. They produce actions, events, and changes in the life of the individual and the collective. For example, if I envision my husband as a powerful decision maker, then my thoughts change my actions in ways that empower that belief. If I ground my life on a steadfast belief and constantly remove obstacles within myself, then people and things that support that belief will be drawn toward me. These simple truths support the profound concept that we magnetize the results of our beliefs.

• Similarly, because thoughts have an effect and everything affects everything else, we have a definite responsibility for the decisions we make, positions we take, and the footprints we leave behind.

• Like all effective evolutions, this new stage of consciousness seeks to "include and transcend" prior stages, building on the authentic role of long-standing principles and practices while moving into greater understanding and improved functioning.

• Integral Spirituality is moving toward "inclusiveness" in place of dualism. For example, Eastern and Western religions are coming together in a new balance, and Integral thinkers are seeking balance between the Feminine and Masculine Principles. Likewise, the evolving spirituality incorporates opposites such as the light and the dark, the yin and the yang, the "right way" and the "wrong way."

Integral Science and Integral Spirituality also suggest that traditional moral and ethical systems reflect principles of a learning universe. Every great nation and religion has added new insight to our understanding of how to live together peacefully and synergistically. Moral and ethical systems represent preserved lessons about which kinds of principles and behaviors work and which do not. Yet, over time, advocates of dominator culture tend to reduce such lessons to dogmatic doctrines and dictatorial judgment and to distort them to suit dominator sensibilities. Because dominator culture also emphasizes control of society by the few, authorities (in church and state) also tend to stifle learning by declaring all deviations from their belief system wrong (heretical) and often illegal.

Joining the concepts that (1) the universe has (in some sense) intrinsic moral laws, and (2) that our true nature is about the learning, significantly shifts the context of moral debate. Instead of focusing on control and infallibility, the integral age emphasizes the process of continuing movement toward and refinement of that which serves the highest good. While Integral Science and Integral Spirituality reject the idea of a final "doctrine," they support the concept of better and worse. Thus they do not eliminate morals and ethics, but gives them flexibility according to societal and individual knowledge through experimentation and evolution. While there will always be disagreements about which idea or way of life makes more sense, because the goal is to "include and transcend," these conflicts revolve around integrating and improving, not around winning or losing.

In summation, Integral Spirituality emphasizes our relationship to all aspects of creation, including each other. Rather than an anthropomorphic God, we honor the "God Everywhere", the "God-in-All," and the wisdom in all belief systems. The real error in thinking is to believe that one's view or system is infallible or that reality can be encapsulated in a single box.

Integral Spirituality emphasizes the wisdom to know that we do not know everything, but can know better. As Buddhism exemplifies, this new spirituality will focus less on defining that "which is too big to define" and even cease to name "It," as Judaism does, because any name or definition implies limitation. Thus, the Great Ordering Oneness is all-inclusive; its totality is found in all its parts, yet it is always more than those parts. This understanding puts no limit on what we can become or what we can understand.

Today, escalating demands in politics, education, economics, spirituality, medicine, and daily life (to name a few) invite science and spirituality to combine forces. Public demand is building for science to help bridge the schism between physical and spiritual evolution. In putting more emphasis on energy, Integral science puts less emphasis on physical matter and corporeality. This opens new avenues by which we can incorporate such spiritual teachings as life after death, reincarnation, and more. Yet, spirituality is being called to move beyond its comfortable assumptions and models as well. These combined understandings confirm the compatibility between spiritual principles of action for the highest good of all and the principles of ecological and evolutionary health, balance, harmony, and happiness.

Integral Spirituality recognizes patterns or laws rising out of the Great Oneness. It honors those who recognize these patterns intuitively, as well as those who recognize them empirically. Visionaries and leaders in science and spirituality need to come together to conceptualize and actualize the changes needed for our planet and humanity. Yet, personal spiritual questioning and growth is also crucial to the change at hand because society only changes when numerous individuals change themselves. Personal responsibility becomes a vital part of the integrated new paradigm of spirituality, humanity, and science. Because we are a collaborative learning species that is fully interconnected with that greater web, it is our responsibility to take action to save the planet, as well as our personal quality of life.

Understanding the principles by which the Universe operates helps clarify our responsibility as humans on this planet. Our society is surrounded by dangers that could lead to eventual extinction of most of life on this planet. These are dangers that we humans have caused. Problems such as pollution, poor education, crumbling communities, uncared-for populations (elderly, child, etc.), adulterated food, plus shrinking social and economic well-being, do not stop at national borders. Thus, individuals and societies are searching for better answers. In response to human misery, human beings all over the world are creating a new vision, a new mission. Men and women in science and spirituality, along with those in all other fields of thought, need to unite to create concepts and methods that not only give birth to this new paradigm, but put it into action.

References

Campbell, J. (1996). *Inward Journey*. San Anselmo, CA, USA: Joseph Campbell Foundation (Audio Collection)

Goerner, S. (1999). *After the Clockwork Universe: The Emerging Science and Culture of Integral Society*. Edinburgh, UK: Floris Books.

Kuhn, T. (1970). *The Structure of Scientific Revolutions*. Chicago, IL, USA: The University of Chicago Press.

Lora, D. (2004). The Way of an Explorer. *Shift: At the Frontiers of Consciousness*. New York, USA: Artists Rights Society (ARS).

Chapter 47

Measurement of Mental and Physical Consciousness in Surat-Shabda-Yoga using Computerized Digital EEG System

FATEH SINGH
Guru Nanak Hospital, Mumbai

PREM KUMAR SINHA
Dayalbagh Educational Institute (Deemed University), Agra, India

Abstract

The basic element of Radhasoami Faith is Surat-Shabda-Yoga. In this research study EEG, ECG, SBP, DBP and Heart Rate was recorded in Bio-Medical Engineering Laboratory, D.E.I. Faculty of Engineering, Dayalbagh, Agra before, during and after Sumiran-Dhayan-Bhajan practice on selected subjects of age between 35 to 95 years. However in this research paper, only combination of static (artifact-free EEG) and dynamic analysis of EEG data recorded by Computerized Digital EEG System is presented. Changes in all the four types of Brain waves: Beta, Alpha, Theta and Delta were analyzed. The analysis clearly showed that after Sumiran-Dhayan-Bhajan practice there was a considerable increase in Theta wave activity and high increase in the Delta wave activity which indicates that the brain of the subjects becomes deeply focused thus resulting Higher Level of Mental Consciousness. The significant decrease in Beta wave activity indicates lesser anxiety and mental tensions.

Introduction

At the end of the 20th century, contemporary science considers itself capable of answering the ultimate secret of nature, that of consciousness. Like the shadows on the wall of Plato's cave, neurophysiologists, psychologists, bio-medical engineers and other scientists investigate the problem from their own points of view, but the answer must be one and as unique as consciousness itself. How can one use EEG, a crude measure of the temporal activity of 1010 neurons, to study the subtle phenomenon of consciousness? To paraphrase the words of the gestalt psychologist Kurt Goldstein, if consciousness appears on points of contact between organism and environment, then EEG, MRI and Positron Emission Tomography might be the tools of choice. Deepak et al [3] concluded that meditation improves clinico-EEG measures in drug-resistant epileptics. Bhatia et al [2] discussed the electro-physiological evaluation of Sudarshan Kriya. The relation between EEG and gross neurophysiological changes in states of consciousness (alertness vs. sleep, sleep phases, coma, epileptic seizures, etc.) has been well-established and analyzed [1,4,5,6]. Mahesh Yogi [7] did lot of studies on Indians and Americans performing Yogic Meditation (YM) and Transcendental Meditation (TM).

In the Radhasoami Faith, the Supreme Being manifested Himself on earth as Param Purush Puran Dhani Soamiji Maharaj, who revealed the secrets of creation and methods for achieving salvation. In this faith, adherents are enjoined to (i) attend Satsang of the Satguru to develop love and faith in the Supreme Being, and obtain purity of heart and mind, (ii) to perform Seva (selfless work) as per His orders to obtain the pleasure of the Lord and to achieve a stable mind, and (iii) to practice Surat-Shabda-Yoga i.e. uniting of the Spirit with the Spiritual Sound Current that emanated from the Ultimate Reality. This spiritual practice is to be learnt from the Perfect Satguru of the time by developing affection and love and, therefore, faith in Him.

In this research study, EEG, ECG, SBP, DBP and heart rate (HR) was recorded in the Bio-Medical Engineering Laboratory, D.E.I. Faculty of Engineering, Dayalbagh, Agra, before, during and after *Sumiran-Dhayan-Bhajan* Practice on selected subjects of Radhasoami Faith. This research paper presents only the analysis of EEG data recorded by Computerized Digital EEG System. An electroencephalogram (EEG) may be done to:

- Watch brain activity while a person is doing meditation.
- Diagnose epilepsy and see what types of seizures are occurring. EEG is the most useful and important test in confirming a diagnosis of epilepsy.
- Check for problems with loss of consciousness or dementia.
- Help find out a person's chance of recovery after a change in consciousness.
- Find out if a person who is in a coma is brain-dead.
- Study sleep disorders, such as narcolepsy.
- Watch brain activity while a person is receiving general anaesthesia during brain surgery.
- Help find out if a person has a physical problem (problems in the brain, spinal cord, or nervous system) or a mental health problem.

Functional Anatomy of the Brain

The human brain has the following parts: (i) cerebrum, (ii) cerebellum, and (iii) brain stem. Each part has its own functions. The cerebrum performs functions like thinking, learning, creativity, five senses, memory, emotion, problem-solving, and decision-making. The cerebellum receives messages from most of the muscles in our body. Then it communicates with other parts of the brain, and sends messages about movement and balance back to the body. The brain stem regulates the heart rate, breathing, swallowing, blinking, digesting etc., and controls the basic functions of the brain. It comprises the pons, medulla oblongata. The right and left hemispheres of the brain appear to produce different brain functions. The right hemisphere seems to be much more spatial, creative, analogical, holistic and non-logical. The left hemisphere is active in linear, logical, practical, rational and time-oriented. The brain, a masterpiece of God's creation, has an inherent electrical potential which is generated within itself and distributed throughout the body. Activities of the brain can be studied through the use of x-rays, EEG (Electro-encephalogram), CT scans (Computerized Tomography), MRI Scan (Magnetic Resonance Imaging), PET scans (Positron Emission Tomography).

Brain Waves

The electrical potential generated by the brain is measured by specialized equipment called electro-encephalograph (EEG). The EEG shows four types of patterns called brain waves. These waves are rhythmic in nature. They occur independently on each side of the brain. In certain instances, both sides of the brain waves are in synchronization. During *Sumiran-Dhayan-Bhajan* practice and deep relaxation, the left and right brain wave patterns occur together. Bio-medical engineers and scientists now believe that synchronization makes greater brain power available, enabling the learning of large amounts of information very quickly, high creativity and emotional self-control.

There are four types of brain waves:

(i) Beta waves, which occur at a frequency of 13 to 25 cycles per second, are mainly seen in intense mental activity like talking, speaking, doing work, solving problems etc. They are also seen during tension.

(ii) Alpha waves, which occur at a frequency of 8 to 12 cycles per second, are seen in states of quiet and resting alertness. These also indicate a state of relaxation. These waves form at the diffuse thalamo-cortical system in the mid-brain. Mostly, these areas have the functions of learning, memory, consciousness and abstract thinking etc. They are most intensely recorded in the occipital region of the brain.

Benefits of alpha waves:

- The more alpha waves generated, the greater the benefit.
- There is synchronization of the right and left sides of the brain.
- Increase in alpha waves helps relieve anxiety, and reduces stress-related disorders.
- Result in a relaxed, concentrated state of mind leading to greater alertness.
- Strengthens the immune system, leading the body to heal faster.
- Associated with a state of high creativity, which leads to peak performance.
- Effective for reprogramming inner conscious levels.

(iii) Theta waves, which occur at a frequency of 4 to 8 cycles per second, are commonly observed in young children, during emotional stress in adults, particularly during periods of disappointment and frustration. They occur in many brain disorders, and are most frequently recorded over the parietal and temporal regions of the brain.

(iv) Delta waves, which occur at a frequency of 0.5 to 4 cycles per second, occur in the state of deep sleep and also in very serious organic brain diseases. They occur strictly in the cortex region of the brain.

Brain waves can be assessed in the following eight different ways, depending on the parameters that need to be studied or analyzed:

Brain Waves (B.W.), Single Amplitude Map (S.A.P.), Tn Map (T.M.), Frequency Map (F.M.), Frequency Spectrum (F.S.), Progressive Amplitude Map (P.A.M.), Progressive Frequency Map (P.F.M.) and Frequency Tabular Analysis (F.T.A.)

Materials and Methods

Subjects

Eleven physically and mentally healthy, devoted and willing satsangis, seven males and four females, of age between 35 to 95 years, participated in this research study as subjects. They were all adherents of the Radhasoami Faith, living in Dayalbagh or nearby. The subjects had no history of neurological or psychiatric disorders, and none of them were on any medication at the time of experiments. The subjects were told not to eat or drink foods that had caffeine (such as coffee, tea, cola, and chocolate) for 8 hours before the test, and were asked to shampoo their hair and rinse it with clear water the evening before of the test. The subjects were also advised not to put on any hair conditioner or oil after shampooing.

Experimental Set-up

In this research study, EEG was recorded on the selected eleven subjects in the Bio-Medical Engineering Laboratory, D.E.I. Faculty of Engineering, Dayalbagh, Agra before, during and after *Sumiran-Dhayan-Bhajan* practice, using 24-channel MEDICAID WINDOWS XP- based Computerized Digital EEG System NEUROPAGE PLUS NP-2400P and obtained 22 channel EEG with common (average) reference. In this system the delta, theta, alpha and beta frequency bands of EEG activity can be separated, analyzed and presented in easily- understood colour graphics display. Frequency Mapping shows the prevalence of each of the four frequency bands and their distribution across the scalp. While spectral mapping shows the prominency of frequency at each individual electrode placed on the scalp, amplitude mapping shows accuracy in tracing the quick movement foci across the scalp by graphically showing subtle amplitude distribution changes. Electrode positions were adopted according to International 10-20 System of electrode referenced to the linked ear lobe electrodes (Fig 1). Montage 1 [FP2-F8, F8-T4, T4-T6, T6-O2, FP2-F4, F4-C4, C4-P4, P4-O2, FP1-F7, F7-T3, T3-T5, T5-O1, FP1-F3, F3-C3, C3-P3, P3-O1, Fz-Cz, Cz-Pz, , EMG, ECG] and Ag/AgCl electrodes were used with impedance less than 5kW. The filter settings were as: High Filter (HF) 70 Hz, Low Filter (LF) 1 Hz- 3Hz. Sensitivity was taken as 5 μV- 7 μV. MEDICAID NP-2400P Software was used for Digital EEG analysis.

EEG was recorded separately before, during and after the *Sumiran-Dhyan-Bhajan* practice session for a minimum of 900 seconds in each period. Subjects were in a relaxed state with eyes closed, and had no activity apart from the mental effort. Subjects had no physical contact. The total experiment took approximately 55 minutes, including preparation of the subject.

Results and Discussion

Topographic head maps showing the distribution of the various brain rhythms on the scalp are shown below. Delta wave activity depicts higher levels of consciousness; theta wave activity shows mental consciousness while alpha wave activity gives a picture of physical consciousness. Beta wave activity gives an idea of specialized regions.

The result clearly showed that the alpha wave activity was very high at all the electrode positions before *Sumiran-Dhayan-Bhajan* practice, thus verifying that the subjects had high levels of relaxation in general. The EEG analysis of all the subjects clearly showed that, after *Sumiran-Dhayan-Bhajan* practice, there was a considerable increase in the theta wave activity and high increase in the delta wave activity, which indicates that the brains of the subjects became deeply focused, resulting in higher levels of mental consciousness (Fig 3). It was interesting to note that the simultaneous increase of these wave activities was maximum along the midline brain region. Also, in almost all the subjects, in the temporal region there was maximum increase in alpha wave activity and maximum decrease in beta wave activity.

The EEG analysis of all the subjects also clearly showed that after *Sumiran-Dhayan-Bhajan* practice, in the midline brain and fronto-parietal regions, there was a very small or insignificant decrease in the alpha wave activity while, more or less right through the entire hemisphere, there was noticeable decrease in the beta wave activity. The voltage maps of a subject are shown in FIG 2 after *Sumiran-Dhayan-Bhajan* practice.

Conclusion

In this research paper, the EEG of selected subjects of Radhasoami Faith were recorded in the Bio-Medical Engineering Laboratory, D.E.I. Faculty of Engineering, Dayalbagh, Agra before, during and after *Sumiran-Dhayan-Bhajan* practice. The experimental results and analysis clearly showed that, after *Sumiran-Dhayan-Bhajan* practice, there was a significant increase in theta wave activity and high increase in the delta wave activity in most regions of the brain, indicating that the brain of the subjects became deeply focused resulting in higher level of mental consciousness. The significant decrease in beta wave activity indicates lesser anxiety, mental tensions and excitement in almost all the subjects.

Sanctified and inspired by the Holy Practice as told by our Worshipful Param Theologian, we bow at Their Lotus Feet always in the unassailable confidence that They would grant us Their Grace and Mercy to fulfil all Their Mandates, all by Themselves. The entire community of devotees awaits with folded hands of prayer to dedicate itself at Their Beloved Holy Feet for Their Service to realize the Fatherhood of God and Brotherhood of Man.

References

Basr, (ed.), (1988) *Dynamics of Sensory and Cognitive Processing by the Brain*, Berlin, Germany: Springer Verlag.

Bhatia M., A. Kumar, N. Kumar, R. M. Pandey and V. Kochupillai (2003) Electrophysiological Evaluation of Sudarshan Kriya: An EEG, BAER, P300 study, *Indian Journal of Physiology and Pharmacology*, Vol. 47, No. 2,157-163

Deepak, K.K., S. K. Manchanda and M. C. Maheshwari, (1994) Meditation improves clinicoelectroencephalographic measures in drug-resistant epileptics, *Biofeedback and Self Regulation*, Vol. 19, 25-40

Gevins, A. and A. Rå1¦ond, (Eds.) (1987) *Handbook of EEG and Clinical Neurophysilogy, Vol.1: Methods of analysis of brain electrical and magnetic signals*, Amsterdam, Holland: Elsevier Science Publishers.

Lopes da Silva, F.H., W.S. van Leeuwen and A. Raimon, (Eds.) (1986) *Handbook of EEG and Clinical Neurophysilogy, Vol.2: Clinical applications of computer analysis of EEG and other neurophysiological signals*, Amsterdam, Holland: Elsevier Science Publishers.

Rael, B., Cahn and J. Polich, (2006) *Meditation States and Traits: EEG, ERP and Neuroimaging Studies*, Psychological Bulletin, Vol. 132, No. 2, 180-211,

Mahesh Y (1963) *The science of being and art of living*, New York:Penguin Books.

Figure 1 - EEG Electrode Placement

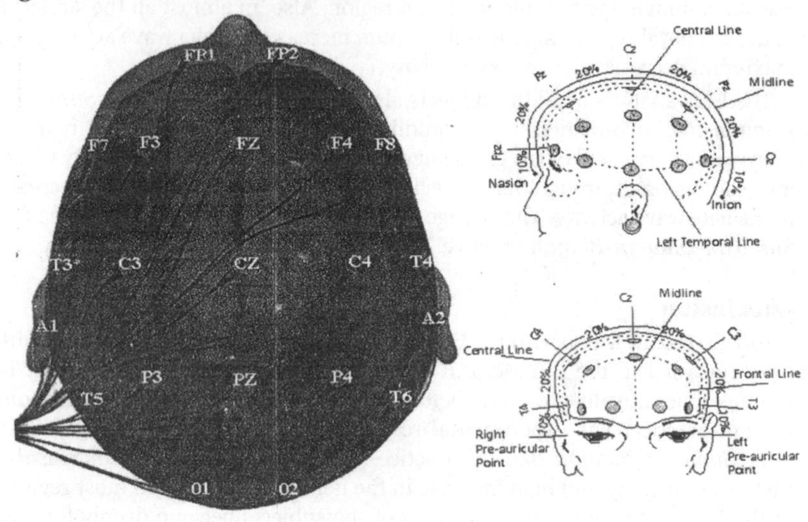

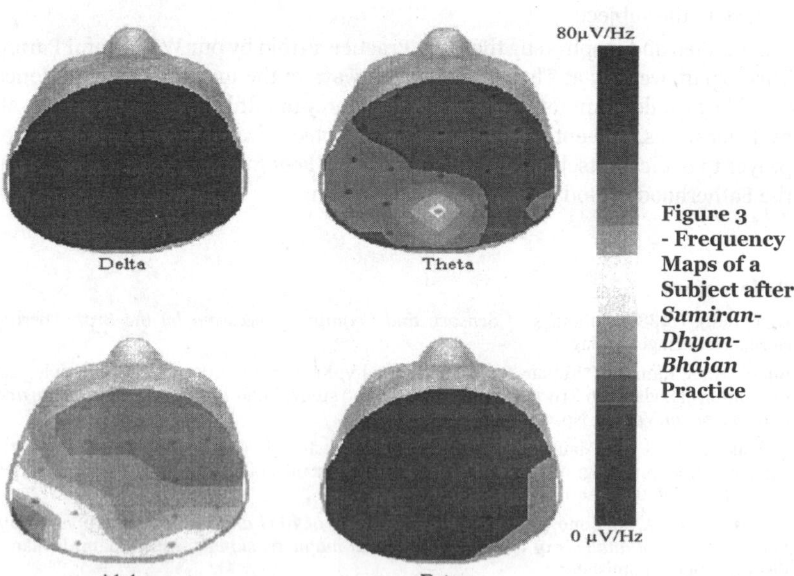

Figure 3 - Frequency Maps of a Subject after *Sumiran-Dhyan-Bhajan* Practice

Figure 2 - Voltage Maps of a Subject

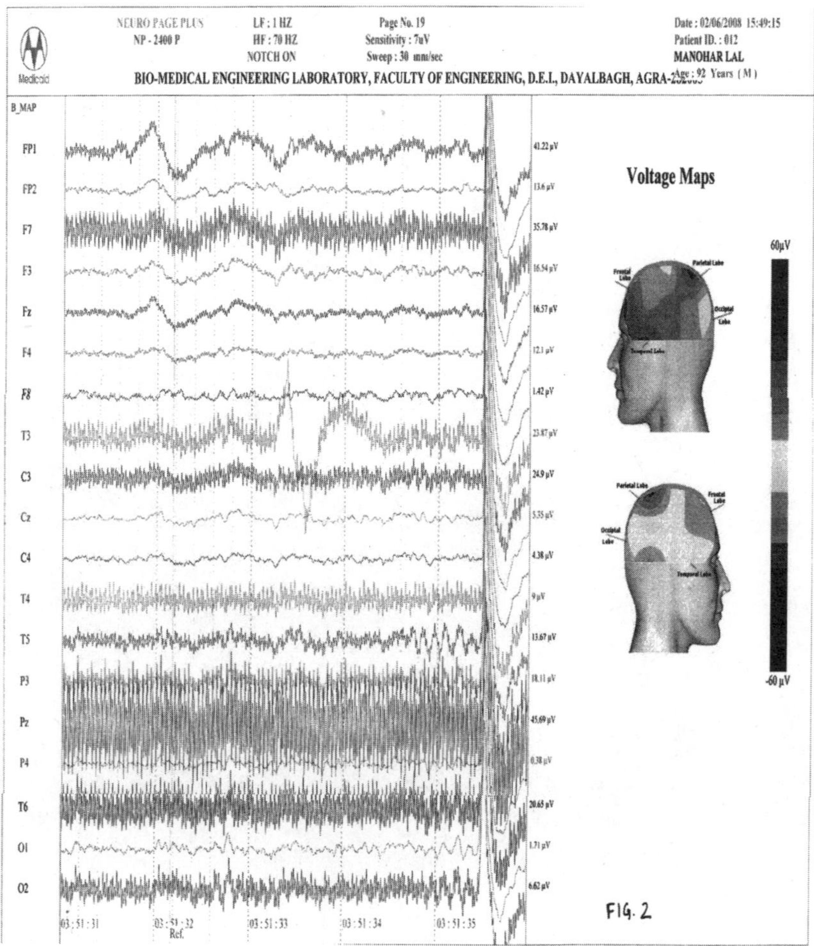

VIII

Sant Mat / Radhasoami Faith: States of Spiritual Consciousness

Chapter 48

'Sant Mat' the Religion of Saints and Consciousness Studies

P. SRIRAMAMURTI
Dayalbagh Educational Institute (Deemed University), Agra, India

Abstract

The Spiritual Essence that is the Originator, Sustainer and Absorber of this Universe has the attributes of Truth, Absolute Reality, Highest Level of Consciousness, Supreme Bliss, Refulgence and Love and it is called 'Chaitanya'. It is also the essence of man, the microcosm. The Rishis, Sants and Param Sants revealed this Truth progressively, i.e. Brahman, Para Brahman, Satt and Radhasoami. Scientists studying emergent systems speak of transcendental systems inclusive of the ecstatic states of consciousness realized in the extant religions. The concept of Spectrum of Consciousness too tries to include these religious states. The Science of Human Possibilities is also taking into account the human potential of realizing the highest level of Spiritual Consciousness attained by seers and Sants. The meeting point of these two approaches is to be seen as a red-letter day ushering in an era of an experiential and experimental Science of Spiritual Consciousness.

Consciousness: Religious and Scientific Perception

Truth, Absolute reality, highest level of Consciousness, Supreme Bliss, Refulgence and Love are being realized to be the attributes of the Spiritual Essence that is the Originator, Sustainer, and Absorber of this entire creation. This essence is 'Chaitanya' or 'Supreme Consciousness' of the Primeval Spirit Force in creation and also the essence of man. Man is microcosm, the Cosmos in miniature while the creation is Macrocosm. Thus, as in man who has three dimensions of physical body, intelligent mind and essence of Spirit there are three dimensions of Physical Matter, Universal Mind and Supreme Reservoir of Spirituality in the creation. While, these dimensions are progressively revealed by, Seers and Sages, Prophets and Incarnations, Sants and Param Sants, the scientific enquiry too is trying to comprehend this reality as progressively emergent systems e.g. Subatomic Systems, Physical Systems, Bio-Systems, Psychological and Cultural Systems, and Transcendental Systems. The meeting point of these two approaches is to be seen as a red-letter day in the history of mankind ushering in an era of experiential and experimental Science of Spiritual consciousness.

Religion and Consciousness

In the religious traditions, Supremacy of Spirit is taken axiomatically. Higher levels of Spiritual Consciousness are sought to guide the lives of men and human societies. In effect, we see that it did not matter whether it is the East or the West, Hindu or Semitic. The essentials of mystical experiences that they had have all been one, interacting, exploring and influencing each other. The finest blend has evolved in the teachings of the 'Sants' and 'Fakirs' like Kabir Sahab, Guru Nanak, Maulana Rumi, Soamiji Maharaj. They included the Buddhist, Jain and Christian, Islamic traditions in their mystical dialogue and integration of theory and practice.

Scientific Enquiry

Consciousness, in the scientific enquiry, is taken as awareness of all kinds of outside world, self-awareness and absolute awareness of all. In Indian tradition, the word *Chaitanya* connotes it. However, *Chaitanya* has farther and deeper implications and overtones than the word 'Consciousness'. We may call this Science of Consciousness - "*Chaitanya Vijnan*" . Consciousness is mainly the attribute of spirit, though mind and matter, as covers thereof in human embodiment partially reflect that attribute in them. Some philosophers speak of the dichotomy of Spirit and Matter, Purusha and Prakriti, but it is seen that Matter too came out of Spirit Energy ("*Ātmanah Ākasah Sambhutah, Akashad vayuh, Vayoragnih, Agnerapah, Adbhyah Prithivi*"). The creational process described in Upanishads and Sant Mat clearly sets forth this truth. Scientific investigations are also underway demonstrating how spirit influences mind and mind influences matter. Studies in the area of interface of brain and mind, mind and spirit which are prevalent in Yoga and Mystic traditions of all religions are becoming subjects of scientific investigation. Practical religionists and serious scientists are coming together to study these phenomena. Psychologists and social scientists are looking for an awakening in man, a spiritual awakening that can alone resolve the civilization crises, individual and societal and establish a new world order of 'Fatherhood of God and Brotherhood of Man'. In this context, I believe it is the pursuit of Consciousness Studies in the light of 'Sant Mat' – Radhasoami Faith, assumes great importance and becomes imperative.

Consciousness Studies are coming to the forefront of scientific inquiry, and these are interdisciplinary. Consciousness Studies are generally directed towards dream state, near death experience, eschatology, pathological states of awareness states of stress and relief and extended to contemplative states. Neuro-physiology and Neuro psychology deal with brain functions, sensations, feelings, thoughts and emotions. Questions arise: Is mind the product of resolution of electro-chemical reactions in the brain? Does brain influence mind or mind influence brain? What is Soul or Spirit? Para psychical phenomena like telepathy, clairvoyance, and psycho kinesis are studied with designed experiments. Phenomena and faculties of mind mentioned in Yoga texts of various traditions are also subjected to scrutiny. Drug induced psychedelic states, worked up states of consciousness attained by mesmerism, autosuggestion etc., too are being studied. They all come under the purview of Jagrat, Svapna, and Sushupti – conditions of brain and lower mind. Subjects who attained higher states of Turiya and beyond are neither available for objective tests nor interested in such inquiry leading to skepticism in scientists in the existence of such higher states of consciousness. There are a few Yogis who demonstrated these Siddhis to some chosen audiences. Studies in contemplative states of meditations and prayers are also afoot to prove their efficacy and they are being resorted to for stress relief and other therapeutic purposes. Yet modern science is to design experiments and apply them to study higher states of Samadhi experiences mentioned in the mystical teachings of religions, as there are very few such subjects who are available for enabling conduct of these tests.

Mystical States

Mystical states attained by religious men are elaborately described in the esoteric teachings of various religions. Methods to understand and test the attainment of practitioners and Gurus are also given in them. The seeker, when searching for a true Guru has to examine the Guru for his attainments and Guru who wants to guide his disciple has to assess the progress and attainments of His disciple and take him forward. For this purpose, several signs of attainments are given in the texts, which serve like the modern methods of matrices and questionnaires, observations and experiments. On recognition of a 'Sant' it is mentioned that He is one who is full of compassion for all without any distinction, guiding them towards their salvation. Other modern methods like the Random Number Generation, Magnetic Resonance Imaging etc. can be adopted to detect the subject's progress.

संत नहिं परखे बोल और चाल।
संत इक देखें अंतर हाल।। 26
दया जिव निस दिन पाले संत।
बहुत जिव भार उठावें संत।। 21

...........Prembilas S-91, (21& 26)

Studies in Religious Consciousness

There are studies of philosophers, Eastern and Western, which also have discussed this topic at length. While the Eastern view regards Consciousness as an independent source making subjective awareness possible, the Western approach favors the view that consciousness is merely a quality of certain brain and mental states. However, all the spiritual traditions of the world in fact assert that cortical processes alone cannot result in subjective awareness. It is the light of Consciousness of Spirit that shines on the objects and makes them subjectively realized (tasya bhasa sarvamidam vibhati). Mind is the medium and gateway between consciousness of spirit and the objective world. It is the product of conjunction of spirit and matter. 'Normal awareness is the result of projection of spiritual currents through the medium of mental attentions focused on external objects. When it is projected on to mental modifications, it perceives mental objects. If it is concentrated on internal centers, it has Self Knowledge, Knowledge of the Knower progressively travelling inwards from Pseudo subjects to the Subject in the Purely Spiritual Region.

Modern Scholars: Philosophical and Scientific View Points

Some modern scholars have proceeded on exploratory researches on consciousness from both the philosophical and scientific view points. The nature of it, pure consciousness, which not only knows all objects but also itself is explained on the basis of Indian Yoga and philosophical texts. According to the paradigm of investigation given in the Taittiriya Upanishad, the Pure Spirit, the knower, is covered with five sheaths – Kosas – Annamaya Kosa, the body, the material sheath on the surface, the Pranamaya Kosa, bio-energy sheath of vital airs, the Manomaya Kosa, the mind cover of sensory knowledge; the Vijnanamaya Kosa – the cover of higher mind of intelligence and discrimination of buddhi, Anandmaya Kosa, the cover of reflected bliss of spirit in the deep sleep. The spirit characterized by Chit, pure consciousness, is beyond these sheaths.

The Kathopanishad gives a somewhat different paradigm. In III-13, it says that a man of subtle intellect sees the self within himself by following the said means of its attainment. He would withdraw and merge his attention focused on senses in mind. That mind he merges in intelligent self and that intelligent self, in the universal consciousness, and that universal consciousness in the peaceful Self of Pure Consciousness. In this process the pseudo subject gradually shifts to real subject as has been succinctly explained in Drik- Drsya-Viveka by Sankaracharya –

रुपम् दृश्यम् लोचनम् दृक्
तत् दृश्यं दृक् तु मानसम्।
दृश्या धीवृत्तयः साक्षी
दृगेव न तु दृश्यते।।

"Form is seen by eye, the seer; that eye is seen by the mind – seer; the modifications of the mind are seen by the eternal seer, the Atman, the eternal Sakshi; The Atman is always the seer but never the seen."

Origin of Universal Consciousness

Prof. P.S. Satsangi has given a framework for scientific investigations into Consciousness in the following manner with the unique paradigm enunciating the nature of Esoteric Macrocosmic Creational System and the corresponding Microcosmic System, Prof. P.S.Satsangi gave the Fundamental Spiritual Axioms as follows:

The origin of the creation is an infinite spiritual energy source or reservoir known as the Supreme Creator or Being. Each constituent element of it (mono spiritual pole), known as the spirit force possesses prime-energy. All other forces of nature (mental or physical) have been evolved by the association of this spirit force with the media of different kinds (mental or physical).

Pre-creational postulate: *In the pre-creational condition, the Supreme Creator (the original infinite spiritual energy source or reservoir of all spirit forces) was in a state of absolute self-absorption (i.e. completely potential energy state). (However, there existed an infinite positive pole of spirituality at the top and a negative or lower or nether pole of low order spirituality at the bottom).*

Creational Postulate: *In the fullness of time, there was such a vast potential difference in the spirituality that there was a huge commotion or upheaval in the Supreme Creator (something like 'Big Bang' at the physical level). It was a manifestation of prime energy in a kinetic form by means of a process like magnetization. This resulted in the flow of the first great spiritual current "Adi Chetan Dhar" from the region of the Supreme Creator nearest to the negative pole towards the positive pole as inward spiritual Sound Current and then returning to the negative pole as an outward spiritual current. The sound that accompanied the vibrations in the spirit emanations constituting the "Adi Chetan Dhar" and the great upheaval in the Supreme Creator resembled – "Radhasoami" closely in the articulate speech.*

Universal Consciousness Realization Postulate: *Yoga (uniting) of Surat (Spirit force) with Shabda (Spiritual Sound Currents) is the means taught in the Religion of Saints for achieving union with the creator. Any mystic name Niranjan, Om, Rarang, Soham, Sat, Radhasoami would enable the spirit force through spiritual practices to ascend to the region of its origin. But Radhasoami is the Original mystic name, the master key that enables one to attain the highest level of Consciousness, through the intermediate steps, which is commensurate with the attainment of absolute truth or ultimate reality or Supreme Creator.*

Consciousness Levels Explained: Intensity of refulgence and subtlety of sounds has been the criterion by which, different levels of consciousness are distinguished. Analogies are given such as the brightness of candle flame, rising sun, moon and sun and further myriads of suns and moons. The music of gong, percussion instruments, string instruments, wind instruments, and so on is given analogies of sounds. As the sounds are heard in trance, their expression in articulate speech nearing the spoken language of the revealing saints varies. But the great teachers have also given their correspondence in clear terms thus emphasizing the truth that the internal path being the same, the pursuit of the reverberating primeval internal sound from the lower centers to that of its origin in the Pure Spiritual Regions. Sarbachan Bachan 25- Shabda2 substantiates this – explaining the states of consciousness in detail.

जग जाग्रत भौ दुःख मूल।
सुपना भी दुख सुख सूल।।
सुषपति कुछ घर आराम।
वह भी नहिं ठहरन धाम।।
तीनों में भरमत आठों जाम।
पूरा नहीं कहीं बिसराम।।

कर दया भेद बतलाया।
तुरिया पद मारग गाया।।
तुरिया से आगे बरना ।
फिर उस से आगे चलना।।
तिस के भी परे लखाया।
उसके भी पार सुनाया।।
तिस परे और समझाया।
कुछ आगे और बुझाया।।

वहाँ से पुनि आगे भाषा।
निज धाम मुख्य यह राखा।।

सतगुरु फिर भेद बतावें।
अब खुलकर तोहि सुनावें।।
तुरिया पद सहसकंवल में ।
तिस आगे चढ़ त्रिकुटी में।।
दस द्वारा सुन में खोलो।
फिर महसुन्न चढ़ तोलो।।
चढ़ भंवरगुफा तब आई।
फिर सत्तनाम पद पाई।।
वहां से भी चली अगाड़ी।
हुई अलख पुरुष दरबारी।।
जाय अगम लोक को लीन्हा।
लीला सब वहां की चीन्हा।।
राधास्वामी धाम लखाया।
अब यही ठीक घर पाया।।

Sarbachan B25, S2

Translation:-

The wakeful state is a source of fear and pain and the dream state too is full of pains and pleasures. The deep sleep gives some relief but does not last long. One passes through these three states daily with no rest. The Satguru took pity on the Jiva and disclosed the secret of the fourth state and the way to attain it. He described the state beyond and also the one beyond that. He showed the state still beyond and also one further. He explained the state beyond and made known the one beyond that. Telling about the further state, He spoke of His Original Abode (The region of Param Sants) --- The Satguru disclosed the secret in clear terms. The fourth state is in Sahasdal Kamal. The next state is up in Trikuti. In Sunn, the Tenth Gate of Saints opens. One goes up to the Mahasunn from there. Above that come Bhanwargupha and then the abode of Sat Nam. Going further up from there, the Spirit goes in front of Alakh Purush. Goes further to Agam Lok and sees the splendor thereof. Finally, the Sant Satguru showed the Region of Radhasoami, which is rightly, the Original Abode.

We may compare this with the Shabdas of Kabir Sahab to establish their correspondence:

कर नैनों दीदार महल में प्यारा है।।
कर नैनों दीदार यह पिंड से न्यारा है।।
..............................कबीर शब्दावली भाग 1

है तिल के तिल के तिल भीतर बिरले साधू पाया है

Kabir Sahab quoted in Yathartha Prakasha II P.302

The modern holistic studies in Human Possibilities, Spectrum of Consciousness and Emergence of Transcendental Systems can be made inclusive of higher states of Consciousness that have been revealed by Rishis, Munis, Buddhas, Prophets, Sufis, Sants and Param Sants. The researchers so far have considered and included the states of Consciousness of practitioners of Yoga techniques known in the extant major religions but not those of Sufis, Sants and Param Sants. I believe that our deliberations here will, to some extent draw the attention of distinguished scholars to the attainments of these explorers of higher levels of Spiritual Consciousness.

References

Graves, M. (2008). *Mind, Brain and Elusive Soul – Human Systems of Cognitive Science and Religion*, Ashgate Science and Religion Series.

Huzur Maharaj [Rai Bahadur Salig Ram Sahab] (2008). Catechism – 'Prashnottar' Q & A. Agra, India: Radhasoami Satsang Sabha, Dayalbagh.

Maharaj Sahab [Pandit Brahm Sankar Misra Sahab] (2009). *Discourses on Radhasoami Faith*. Agra, India: Radhasoami Satsang Sabha, Dayalbagh.

Sahabji Maharaj [Sir Anand Sarup Kt.] (1997). *Prem Bilas*, Shabd 19, 21, 26. Agra, India: Radhasoami Satsang Sabha, Dayalbagh.

Satsangi, P.S. [Revered Prof. Prem Saran Satsangi] (2010). Applied Systems Research for Better Worldliness. Proceedings of Joint International Conference on Applied Systems Research and XXXIII National Systems Conference (ASR-NSC 2009), 27-29 November, 2009. New Delhi, India: Tata McGraw Hill Education Private Ltd.

Seminar Proceedings. (2002). *Philosophy and Science: An Exploratory Approach to Consciousness*. Kolkata, India: Ramakrishna Mission's Institute of Culture, Gol Path.

Seminar Proceedings. (2004). *Life, Mind and Consciousness*. Kolkata, India: Ramakrishna Mission's Institute of Culture, Gol Path.

Seminar Proceedings (2006). *Consciousness: A Deeper Scientific Search*. Kolkata, India: Ramakrishna Mission's Institute of Culture, Gol Path.

Wilber K. (2002). *The Spectrum of Consciousness*. Delhi, India: Motilal Banarsidass.

Chapter 49

Religion of Saints: Levels of Consciousness

ANAND MOHAN
Dayalbagh Educational Institute (Deemed University), Agra, India

S.L. KAYASTHA
BHU, Varanasi, India

Abstract

Consciousness is ordinarily thought of as a state of awareness. The fascinating and intriguing complexity of consciousness needs deep understanding of the higher realms of spirituality. The interface between awakening of spiritual faculties of man and developing inner consciousness of self is related to the realization of truth, the ultimate reality. Truth is the highest virtue but higher still is truthful living. This helps in self-realization and experiencing higher states of consciousness. However, true, long-term practitioners of transcendental meditation performed with patience and perfection, are rare. The internal practice of Surat Sabda Yoga in the Radhasoami Faith and the Religion of Saints has always provided simple means and ways to attain higher levels of consciousness.

Introduction

The Religion of Saints comprising teachings of Saints and Fakirs like Kabir Sahab, Tulsi Sahab and Maulana Rumi, culminated in the Radhasoami Faith founded by Param Purush Puran Dhani Soamiji Maharaj on the auspicious Basant Panchami Day, the 15th of February, 1861 A.D. They taught people to have unflinching Faith in the True Supreme Being, the Reservoir of spirituality and to worship Him internally by the practice of Sahaj Yoga or Surat Shabda Yoga i.e. uniting the spirit with the spiritual sound current that emanated from the Supreme Being manifesting as Radhasoami, Satt, Om, Lahut etc. at different levels. This practice is to be learnt from the perfect Satguru of the time by developing love and affection for Him.

Spirit is the highest truth that has ever been discovered and there is nothing higher or nobler than spirit, the Atman, and the Reservoir of spirit force activating spirit, mind, and body is God. There no truth higher than God and no enjoyment higher than God Realization. The Sat, Chit, Anand, Prem, and Prakash are reflected in truth, consciousness, bliss, love and refulgence. The individual spirit confined in human being is enveloped by covers of physical body and mind. However, providence has provided within the human body a special spiritual faculty which when developed enables one to perceive Truth and ultimate Reality. It is the exclusive function of religion to teach all about that faculty and help man in awakening the hidden senses and nerve centres in the brain and show the way in which they can be made kinetic by sound practice.

These spiritual practices have been the essential teachings of all religions which are, unfortunately, not being pursued nowadays. The Religion of

Saints not only revived the practices but also gave out secrets of higher realms of spirituality telling them about the corresponding nerve centres in human brain and stressing the need of awakening them and undergoing training under the adept, who has himself awakened all the hidden senses. This religion has proved to be the science of spirituality, nay the science of ultra-transcendental spirituality – the Para Vidya par excellence, and is called the 'Religion of Saints' or 'Radhasoami Faith'.

Understanding Consciousness

With only a few exceptions, consciousness is presumed to be the most complex and baffling of human properties, exceedingly difficult to define and investigate. It is not only the most common and most complex but also the most puzzling of all states. The realm of mystic experiences and theological issues converge at consciousness studies. Everyone is conscious yet no one can quite agree about precisely what consciousness means. Dictionaries define consciousness as awareness of one's own existence, sensations, thoughts, surroundings or 'contents of mind'. Consciousness is an elaborate rite of passage into everything that makes us 'human'. The study of human consciousness is the study of ourselves in the deepest meaning of word. The scope of recent researches on consciousness studies has extended beyond the conventional areas of psychology, neuroscience, physics, philosophy, artificial intelligence and even social, cultural, ethical and religious issues. The whole gamut of multidisciplinary approach to consciousness studies is to break artificial barriers between specialties so that they learn to familiarize with the work from outside their own field with greater confidence. There is good reason to believe that consciousness is not only caused by neurobiological states but actually it is the neurobiological state. As Francis Crick, co-discoverer of the molecular structure of DNA in 1953, has suggested, "you, your joys and your sorrows, your memories and your ambitions, your sense of personal identity and free-will, are no more than the behaviour of a vast assembly of nerve-cells and their associated modules", and yet it is some unknown aspect of brain activity. Both awareness and consciousness occur automatically. An individual's will neither makes them happen, nor prevents them from happening. According to Edelman, consciousness is closely tied to homeostatic value or an organism's ability to maintain internal biological harmony. Inspite of very real difficulties we dream of understanding consciousness gradually rather than suddenly, and we are now coming closer to discovering how we know that we know[1].

Reality is much bigger than it seems. The part of the universe we cull is a merest tip of the iceberg. The brain with its complex and intricate structure has over 11 billion specialized nerve cells or neurons with over 100 billion inter-connections and is still not entirely understood by neurologists. One must also consider the ethics of tinkering with the organ from which all ethical reflections arise.

Nevertheless, the true practitioners of cultivation of consciousness are

---

[1] Damasia, Antanio R. 1998. Clean consciousness: a celebration of mankind's exploration of unknown. TIME: Special Issue: 49-51

restricted to a very narrow band of long-term practitioners of transcendental meditation, referred to as 'Saints' or 'Sant'. Saints have been most conscious about the ultimate reality, God. Kabir Saheb, Tulsi Saheb, Guru Nanak Saheb and many others have practised the Religion of Saints. Guru Nanak Ji emphasized the repetition of 'Nam' for attaining Salvation and practising good deeds in Grihasth Ashram. 'My religion consists of a humble admiration of the illimitable superior spirit who reveals Himself in the slight details that we are able to perceive with our frail and feeble minds' (Saint Augustine). Perfection is attained through true understanding, infinite patience and precise attention to detail. The power of detachment is a great wealth and the power of devotion is an asset. We should work for such true wealth.

Social Reformers Versus Attainment of Consciousness

The essence of religion is a living faith in spirit and man's capacity to assimilate it. The central fact of religion is the existence felt within us of an abounding inner life which transcends our consciousness. We feel certain powers moving within us, we know not what, we know not why. These vague intuitions, these faint dreams are the far cries of the universal dwelling in us and the function of religion is to make our souls sensitive to the universal. In man alone does the universal come to consciousness. He alone is aware that there is a universe, that it has a history and may have a destiny[2].

To have religious men as components of the society makes all the difference in the life of that society. We have been fortunate enough to have a selected band of dedicated social reformers on our soil. With the passage of time they have transformed our society with revolutionary changes which witnessed the attainment of social consciousness of definite level.

In this series, Swami Dayanand was a reformer of religious prejudices and practices. Swami Vivekanand was also a saint who organized Ramakrishna Ashram that provided food and shelter and medical help to the needy. Swami Vivekanand found his spiritual development in the sewa of Daridra Narayan. The tall personalities like Malaviya ji and Gandhi ji helped to establish institutions for education and liberation from bondage. Gandhi ji found his spiritual progress in service of poor and freedom from the exploitation of foreign bondage. Malaviya ji always preached truth and harmony. "Speak truth, think truth, continue your studies throughout life. Be just and fear none. Fear only to do that which is ill and ignoble. Stand up for right. Love to serve your fellow men. Love Motherland. Promote public weal. Do good whenever you get a chance for it"[3].

न त्वहं कामये राज्यं, न स्वर्गं न पुनर्भवम।
कामये दुःखतप्तानां प्राणिनां आर्ति नाषनम्।।

'I have no desire for kingdom or heaven, or even liberation from cycle of births and deaths but I do desire to remove the hardships of my fellow- men

---

[2] Damasia, S.Radhakrishnan, Address, Twenty First Convocation, B.H.U., 17.12.1938

[3] Mahamana Malviya Ji, Address, Second Convocation, B.H.U., 26.01.1920

being tortured by miseries' (Mahamana Malviya ji).

Even the enlightened scientists have lighted the lamp of spirit. Ramanujam looked for spiritual advancement in his mathematical expressions. He observed, "An equation has no meaning unless it expresses the thought of God". Ramanujam thought intuitively. He was a vegetarian and worshiped his family goddess Namagiri Lakshmi even in Cambridge. Albert Einstein expressed, "Faith is to believe what we do not see. The reward of faith is to see what we believe". "We can be confident that action which is in accord with a few basic beliefs cannot be wrong and can atleast testify to the values we need to cultivate. These are beliefs that the human race is a family, that it has inherited a place on earth in common and its members have an obligation to work towards sharing it, so that none is deprived of the elementary needs in life and all have responsibility to leave it un-degraded for those who follow" (Gilbert F. White, eminent environmentalist).

'The Supreme Being wanted to be many. The urge for self dispersal is at the root of creation. It was through that kind of creative urge that Prafulla Chandra became many in the minds of his pupils by diffusing himself and thereby reactivating himself in many younger minds. But this would hardly have been possible unless he had the capacity to give himself away fully'[4].

Consciousness: Dayalbagh Way of Life

Param Guru Huzur Dr. Lal Sahab has explained how economy and discipline would help in self-control and self-scrutiny, and true faith and love and self-surrender in His Lotus Feet would develop and then the path to spiritual development becomes easy. "Your way of life also changes that makes you humble in an easy way (Saral Upay)". As stated earlier, love and firm faith (*Priti and Pratiti*) will be developed, when a Satsangi surrenders with humility in HIS Lotus Feet. Only then would a Satsangi become eligible to perform 'Arti' (आरती करने के लायक) and all difficulties will be removed and there will be steady progress in spirituality. Satsangi should remain steady and alert all the time, lest the whirlpool of mind knock him down with attachment and worldly illusion. It is clear that the culture of consumption does not lead to peace of mind and cleanliness of environment. This world is not ours. It is God's world.

Radhasoami Satsang, Dayalbagh has always provided simple means and ways of complete development. Every Satsangi should take advantage of these facilities[5].

There are seven layers in our existence, viz., body, breath, mind, intellect, memory, ego, and the self. The first six are subject to change. The physical body changes over time. The mind oscillates between past and future, likes and dislikes. The intellect is caught between agreement and disagreement, memory experience, gain and loss. The sense of belongingness depends on the extent of our ego. The antidote to ego is being natural. This can happen with

---

[4] Ravindra Nath Tagore (Quoted in P.C. Ray's biography by J. Sengupta, National Book Press)

[5] Kayastha, S.L. Simple ways of complete development in Radhasoami Satsang, Dayalbagh – *The Dayalbagh Herald*, 5 February, 2008 week 6, Radhasoami Samvat 190 40.3-5

spiritual practices. What does it mean to transcend body consciousness? When you move from your limited identity and enter the unbounded consciousness even for a few moments, it energizes and rejuvenates you. The phenomena of moving beyond the limited identity of body, form, shape and location is transcending body-consciousness. The journey is from external world of sensory perceptions and objects to the infinite space within and it is that sound which leads to reality, Sat and Radhasoami Dham. This needs constant practise and devotion that is provided by an adept, who himself has awakened all the hidden senses. Consciousness is Chetna (चेतना). This has to be experienced (अनुभूति), and developing inner (अन्तर्चेतना) consciousness of the self with such direct experience that only then can one know the divine creator, the spirit, the Atman and Parmatman– "that is the reservoir of spirit force".

Radhasoami faith was founded by Param Purush Puran Dhani Huzur Soami Ji Maharaj on the Basant Panchami Day the 15th February 1861. The teachings are simple and are conveyed to the seekers on the advice of Sant Satguru in first and second Updesh. It envisages concentration at the vital point (between the eyes) and contemplation of the Holy Form of Sant Satguru. This gradually leads to vital spiritual regions with the help of sound that is vibrating in the upper regions. Param Purush Puran Dhani Huzur Soamiji Maharaj lived in a small place in Panni Gali, Agra, where HE performed these spiritual practices and on the request of HIS dear disciple Param Guru Huzur Maharaj, HE revealed the practice of contemplation of Holy Form and Spiritual Sound to all. It attracted many devotees to the Radhasoami Faith. However, the selected ones who devoted themselves wholly to the worship of the Gracious Feet of Sant Satgurus succeeded them as Gurus, namely Huzur Maharaj, Maharaj Sahab, Sarkar Sahab, Sahabji Maharaj, Mehta ji Maharaj, Dr. Lal Sahab and Prof. Satsangi Sahab. Spirit is the noblest and highest truth. There is no truth higher than God realization. The religion of Saints thus revived the practices of true spirituality and also imparted secrets of higher spirituality, informing about corresponding nerve centres in the brain and stressing the need of awakening them. In this way the 'Religion of Saints' is in fact the 'Science of Spirituality' or 'Para Vidya' which constitutes the vitally essential practices of the Radhasoami Faith. With love, (Prem) a devotee would awaken his consciousness and enjoy Sat, Chit, Anand that is true reality, consciousness and bliss. The levels of consciousness vary from devotee to devotee. Param Guru Huzur Maharaj observed "The more you love the Supreme Father, the more His Mercy and Grace will attend you in all your work"[6].

Levels of consciousness vary from person to person, according to attainment of higher and higher realms of spirituality and in the humble submission defying subjective or objective comparison. Undoubtedly, science and technology in the new millennium have expanded their range and scope. Falling in line with the above milieu, active groups of optimistic scientists extend support for duplicating the operation of the mind on a computer mediating a quantum role in brain functions. However, as the instinct for spiritual life is in human nature,

[6] Param Guru Huzur Maharaj (rev. edn. 2005) in *Pilgrims Path* No.28 P.57, Radhasoami Satsang Sabha, Dayalbagh, Agra.

it is most likely that ethical-spiritual dimension, in conjuncture with intellectuals of science, may facilitate to resolve in future the uninterrupted continuity of science in search of creation of universe, consciousness, the ultimate truth that apparently seems to have pushed mankind towards the limits of knowledge. In this crusade towards the final frontiers of knowledge where the last pillar of science culminates at religion, we will have to wait and see what rewards future will bring.

Chapter 50

Unprecedented and Merciful Revelation of the Complete Spectrum of Spiritual Consciousness in the Radhasoami Faith

SUKHDEV ROY
Dayalbagh Educational Institute (Deemed University), Agra, India

Abstract

Over the last thousand years, the material world has been blessed with the advent of Sants who have propagated the devotional path and gradually revealed higher levels of spiritual consciousness. The beginning in this period can be traced from the time of various Sufi mystics and Faqirs that include Shams-i-Tabrez and Maulana Jalal-ud-din Rumi in the 13th century, in Central Asia cum Indian subcontinent, who initiated the exposition of higher realms of spiritual consciousness i.e., beyond Brahmanda, the Region of Pure Spirit. Sant Kabir who incarnated in India in the fifteenth century disclosed the higher realms in more detail and the highest realm in a relatively concealed manner. He is considered as the first incarnation from the highest spiritual region and the true initiator of Sant Mat - the pristine path of spirituality.

During the 15th-19th century, there have been many Sants who have incarnated to spread its teachings such as, Guru Nanak, Paltu Das ji, Jagjivan Sahab and Tulsi Das ji and other spiritual adepts which include Surdas ji, Dadu Sahab, Dariya Sahab, Garib Das ji, Dulan Das ji, Hari Das ji and Raidas ji. They advocated the Bhakti Marg, devotion with love to the Sant Satguru of the time through Surat Shabda Yoga, i.e., the art of harmonizing the spirit with the spiritual sound current. Param Purush Puran Dhani Soamiji Maharaj, the August Founder of the Radhasoami Faith, incarnated in 1818 and mercifully revealed the Radhasoami Region - the highest region of spiritual consciousness.

His advent marked an unprecedented revelation of the complete spectrum of spiritual consciousness. In an extremely lucid, clear and detailed exposition, He mercifully described the gracious object, structure and manifestation of Shabda throughout creation and established the science of spiritual cosmology. He mercifully not only disclosed the Radhasoami Name, which is the Shabda of the Supreme Being that sustains the entire creation, but also explained a simple method to attain the highest region and merge in the Supreme Being. His teachings while maintaining continuity with the traditions of Sant Mat, provided additional enlightenment of the final objective, salvation, the proper method for its attainment and highlighted the importance of the Sant Satguru, the special entity in communion with the Radhasoami Region and carrier of the Prime Spiritual Current. This merited the formation of Radhasoami Faith as a distinct movement of Sant Mat. His exquisite detailed description of the various forms of existence in different levels of spiritual consciousness, amazingly, also includes a numerical estimate of their grand magnitude. Subsequently, His successors further elaborated His revela-

tions and made them more accessible to larger masses according to the needs of the time.

In this paper, a humble effort has been made to highlight (i) the limited understanding of western science of consciousness and the importance of developing an integral worldview, (ii) the universality of the teachings of various Sants, with respect to different levels of spiritual consciousness, (iii) the distinct contribution of Param Purush Puran Dhani Soamiji Maharaj and His successors, in describing the various features of the different higher levels of spiritual consciousness, and (iv) to create a map of the entire spectrum of spiritual consciousness based on the Radhasoami Faith.

Introduction

Consciousness has been the subject of study from time immemorial. It is the central issue in the quest to comprehend Truth, Ultimate Reality and God. "Consciousness" derives from the Latin word '*conscientia*' which primarily means moral conscience. However, over time, it has been associated with different meanings, which are based on the education and background of a person. Consciousness has been used by philosophers to describe the functional interaction of a person with the world, especially social and political interaction, and also to describe a person's moral conscience. Philosophers have defined it in terms of two principal components: firstly phenomenal consciousness which consists of our experience with things laid out in space and time, sensations, emotions, thoughts, etc., and secondly access consciousness, which involves the processes that act on the things in experience.

Phenomenal consciousness is much like the "perceptual space" of psychological and physiological research. It is the many simultaneous events that become the space of experience in general and it is now a legitimate target of scientific research. The human mind with its inquisitive, rational, logical and externally directed attributes to understand Truth and Reality, a branch of activity called science, has been trying to determine the basis of conscious experience, its location, and how it works, whereas, the philosopher attempts to ascertain the form of things in phenomenal consciousness. Does phenomenal consciousness directly experiences things in the world beyond the body, is it brain activity based on things in the world and internal processes — a sort of virtual reality — or is it some spiritual or other phenomenon?

Explanations of consciousness fall into four broad categories, (i) that attempt to explain the empirical experience called consciousness with scientific theories, (ii) that seek to find some way in which consciousness could be explained by digital computers, or (iii) by nineteenth century materialism by redefining or eliminating experience, and (iv) that regard consciousness as inexplicable or supernatural.

Modern science with its focus on understanding reality by observing and measuring physical phenomena in nature has been jolted by intriguing new discoveries over the last century that reveal the role of consciousness in the outcome of a measurement. To sum it up in the words of Werner Heisenberg, the Nobel Laureate in Physics, "*what we observe is not nature itself, but nature exposed to our method of questioning*" [Heisenberg, 1963].

Although the currently accepted view of modern molecular science empowered with quantum physics is that the substrate of consciousness emerges as a property of an ever increasing computational complexity among neurons, it is still one of the major unsolved and poorly understood problems in biology. Over the years, advances in scientific studies of psychology, psychometrics, behavioural sciences and cognition have developed an understanding of human consciousness in terms of intelligence. The definition of intelligence has long been a matter of controversy, with emotional and spiritual intelligence having been proposed recently. However, a universally accepted theory of the mind, self or psychology is still a subject of research.

Religion on the other hand, has addressed consciousness from the spiritual perspective. Although various states of consciousness based on the spirit, mind and body have been mapped in the great religious and spiritual traditions since ancient times, the advent of various incarnations of Sufi Faqirs and Sants over the last thousand years, mercifully revealed the higher states of spiritual consciousness and the means to attain them. Param Sants *Kabir Sahab, Guru Nanak Sahab, Paltu Das ji, Jagjivan Sahab* and *Tulsi Sahab* and described various stages of spiritual refinement and emphasized the importance of following the Surat Shabda Yoga – the art of harmonizing with spiritual sound currents, under the expert tutelage of a living Guru. With the incarnation of All Merciful Soamiji Maharaj, the August Founder of the Radhasoami Faith, this movement got a tremendous boost. In the most lucid description, He most graciously explained all aspects of creation in detail and for the first time clearly described the highest spiritual dimension.

It is clear from the teachings of Sant Mat that like the electromagnetic spectrum, consciousness establishes a multiplicity of aspects as it transcends time and space and manifests itself in different spheres, thereby making disparate religions and disciplines speak to a different wavelength of awareness. Establishing the complete spectrum of consciousness helps in integrating Science and Religion (primarily western and eastern approaches), to form an integral worldview and to achieve the main objective of life. It is a great blessing for mankind that All Merciful Soamiji Maharaj, revealed the full spectrum of spiritual consciousness to help souls attain their true abode and salvation.

Integral Worldview of Reality

Developing an integral worldview of reality based on the commonalities derived from various branches of human knowledge and experience, which includes both science and religion, the creative modern thinker Ken Wilber defines the great holarchy as shown in Fig. 1.

According to this traditional view, physics that deals with matter inanimate is at the lowest level, giving us insights into the most basic and crudest working of nature. Physics is superseded by biology that concerns with understanding living organisms, which in turn is superseded by psychology, the study of humans the most advanced life form and the human mind with its various attributes. These three branches of science are encompassed by religion involving theology and mysticism. There is a jump in the levels of hierarchy. Modernity differentiated art, morals and science and let each pursue its own truths. Wisdom lies in developing an integral approach that integrates the great nest of being with the differentiations of modernity and hence, seamlessly integrates religion and scientific realms and worldviews. Thus, science with exterior realities and religion with interior realities should develop alongside each other and not one on top of the other. They would provide correlative facets of interior and exterior spiritual realities paving the way for an acceptable unified theory of reality.

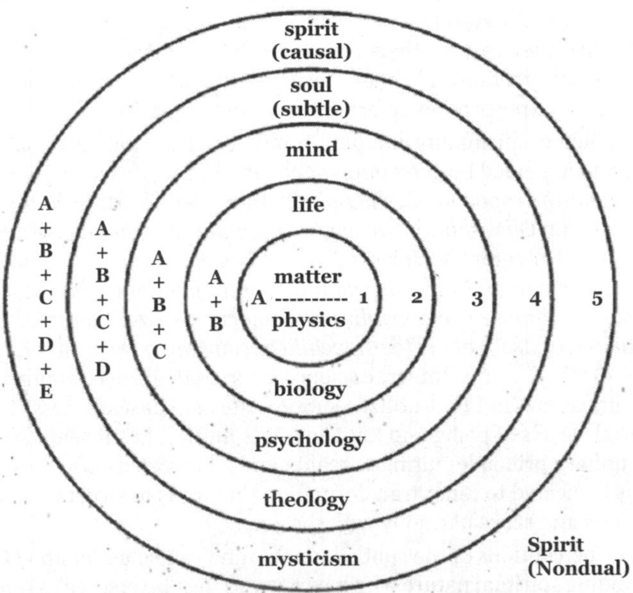

Fig. 1 The great holarchy. Spirit is both the highest level (causal) and the nondual grounds of all levels (Wilber, 2004)

Establishing the highest objective of science to be Truth, it is useful to classify narrow sciences as the "hard sciences", dealing with matter, inanimate and animate, i.e., physics, chemistry and biology, although they also use a number of tools that are not empirical, such as mathematics and logic (which are inner realities). The broader sciences not rooted in the exterior, physical, sensorimotor world, but are concerned with interior states and qualitative research methodologies, are "*human sciences*" or the "*soft sciences*", which involve, psychology, sociology, anthropology, linguistics, semiotics and the cognitive sciences. All of these attempt to use a scientific approach to the study of human consciousness.

A methodology applicable to develop the unified theory of reality, scientific inquiry can in general be defined based on the generalized empirical method with a three stage knowledge validation, (i) Injunction, i.e., to know something, it is necessary to do something, an experiment or an actual practice; (ii) Apprehension, illumination or experience, i.e., once an experiment is performed, one is introduced to a series of experiences brought forth by the injunction, technically known as data. Hence, we can have physical experiences (physical data), mental experiences (or mental data), and spiritual experiences (or spiritual data; and (iii) Communal verification, i.e., we check the validity of the experiences or evidence with others who have also seen the evidence, a community of peers.

Hence, deep spirituality involves the direct investigation of experiential evidence disclosed in the higher states of conscious development that involve, psychic, subtle, causal and nondual (Fig. 3). The methodology is as followed by general science. They rely on specific social practices or injunctions (e.g. contemplation); they rest on their claims on data and experiential evidence; and they constantly refine and check these data in an enlightened community, which is why they are correctly referred to as "contemplative sciences".

Science, religion/spirituality and philosophy search for the universal unitary principle and are guided by perception of beauty. Pythagoras attributed beauty to "*the harmony of proportions*", whereas, Plotinus identified it with "*the eternal splendour of the 'One' shining through the material phenomena*". Michael Talbot, in "The Holographic Universe", describes all of material creation as a "*ripple...a pattern of excitation in the midst of an unimaginably vast ocean" and "despite its apparent materiality and enormous size, the universe does not exist in and of itself, but is the stepchild of something far vaster and more ineffable.*" (Talbot, 1991). Integral science or sacred science, applies generalized empirical method that utilizes subtle states of consciousness. It recognizes multiple levels of being and knowing. It is unitive, i.e., it searches for the universal unitary principle- ultimate reality and all knowledge is related to the whole. It is dedicated to inner transformation that leads to structure change in consciousness and seeks harmony with the One.

Hence the perceptions of the subtle human mind can be understood to be (i) an all pervading spiritual nature which permeates the universe, (ii) a numinous presence underlying, enfolding, and shining through the forms of the cosmos, (iii) a creative presence in which we "live and move and have our being" and (iv) a translucent splendour of the One shining through the material phenomena. All life, coexisting together at the same time, is both matter and space: movement and stillness sound and silence, light and darkness. As we have seen earlier, the wave/particle duality (Non-Locality) means that everything is joined or connected together. This duality also means that objects that appear to have seemingly opposite properties are of the same substance but in a different form or density of a vibrational level.

In the Lankavatara Sutra from "Buddha Speaks", "light and shade, long and short, black and white, can only be experienced in relation to each other; light is not independent of shade, nor black of white. There are no opposites, only relationships."

Another example of this polarity principle is found in sound harmonics. Fields may be anharmonic on one level but harmonic on different levels. Anharmonic would be like plucking a guitar string and allowing it to vibrate freely. The sound and the frequencies of the corresponding vibration are no longer exactly in the same frequency ratio. Harmonics, is the vibration multiples of the same frequency. The Taoists also viewed the dynamic interplay between the polar opposites as yin and yang. These pairs of opposites share a polar relationship where the two poles are dynamically linked to the other and found throughout nature.

This idea of implicit unity of all opposites can be extremely difficult to accept. However paradoxical it may seem to some, Eastern philosophies have always considered this as essential for attaining enlightenment to go 'beyond earthly opposites,' and in China the polar relationship of all opposites lies at the very basis of Taoist thought. *Thus Chuang Tzu says, The "this" is also "that." The "that" is also "this."... That the "that" and the "this" cease to be opposites is the very essence of Tao. Only this essence, an axis as it were, is the center of the circle responding to the endless changes"* (Capra, 1983).

This ancient wisdom of duality is the essence of the Tao. It also appears to be the essence of physics. Alan Watts, a philosopher, writer, speaker, and expert in comparative religion and best known as an interpreter and popularizer of Asian philosophies for a Western audience claimed, "*Every explicit duality is an implicit unity.*" Heraclitus the Greek philosopher also realized that all opposites have a unity and relativity. "*The way up and down is one and the same", and "God is day-night, winter-summer, war-peace, satiety-hunger.*"

Science and religion also represent a complimentary pair of polar opposites residing within a highly complex paradox. If we view these opposites as the ends of the light spectrum, we have a diverse range of human culture and ideals. These cultural dimensions in this range quantify the ideal of "unity of diversity", biologically, ecologically and sociologically. The full magnitude of the paradox disappears in the light of diverse duality. In the words of Hazrat Inayat Khan, "*Life starts with the knowledge of diversity, but the awareness of unity is the pinnacle of life.*"

Werner Heisenberg, observed, "It is probably true quite generally that in the history of human thinking, the most fruitful developments frequently take place at those points where two different lines of thought meet. These lines may have their roots in quite different arts of human culture, in different times or different cultural environments or different religious traditions: hence, if they actually meet, there is, if they are at least so much related to each other that a real interaction can take place, then one may hope that new and interesting developments may follow" (Heisenberg, 1963). Hence, an integral worldview can be formed by looking at points where both science and religion meet.

The Mystical Experience

Religion, spirituality and mysticism have since time immemorial, provided an altogether different worldview that not only describes the higher states of consciousness and spiritual dimensions, but the physical creation as well. Various traditions exist that describe different methodologies and techniques to develop the spiritual faculties in the human frame that lie beyond the senses and pertain to the reflections of the higher spiritual dimensions, to comprehend reality. The spectacular progress of science and technology from the industrial revolution, led to a strong shift in the application of mind and senses in the outward physical world, for physical comfort and welfare, resulting in a neglect of the esoteric sciences and an incomplete, paradoxical, fictitious and confusing understanding of reality. Several leading scientists, when confronted with the deep understanding of nature through the scientific approach realized the importance of integrating other branches of human experience and unity of knowledge.

In the words of Albert Einstein, "*The most beautiful emotion that we can experience is the mystical. It is the sower of all true art and science. He to whom this emotion is a stranger ... is as good as dead. To know that what is impenetrable to us really exists, manifesting itself as the highest wisdom and the most radiant beauty, which our dull faculties can comprehend only in their most primitive forms- this knowledge, this feeling, is at the center to true religiousness." Wolfgang Pauli, the Physics Nobel Laureate observed that "The integration of opposites, including a synthesis embracing both rational understanding and the mystical experience of unity, is the mythos of our current age.*" [Jammer, 1974].

Every observation can be interpreted at multiple levels of significance. Each level of significance is internally consistent, factual, logical, objective and gives no evidence of higher levels. Although lower levels of significance have no factual error and feign complete understanding, true significance is missed leading to an impoverished view of reality. There are different levels or qualities of consciousness, with a continuum of states of consciousness ranging from gross/ordinary to subtle/contemplative. These can thus be associated with multiple levels of significance. Reality emerges as a cross section of human consciousness and the transcendent possibility domain, with each level bringing forth a world. There are thus multiple levels of reality from gross (physical) to subtle (nonphysical).

Franscisco Varela, the Chilean biologist, philosopher and neuroscientist who together with his teacher Humberto Maturana, is best known for introducing the concept of 'autopoiesis' to biology, states that "*It is important to note that these levels of subtle mind are not theoretical; instead they are delineated rather precisely on the basis of actual experience, and they merit respectful attention by anyone who claims to rely on empirical science... An understanding of these levels of subtle mind requires a sustained, disciplined, and well-informed meditation practice. In a sense, these phenomena are open only to those who are willing to carry out the experiments, as it were. That some form of special training is needed for firsthand experience of new realm of phenomena is not surprising... But in traditional science, such phenomena remain hidden from view, since most scientists still avoid any disciplined study of their own experience, whether through meditation or other introspective methods.*" (Varela, 1991,1999, Varela and Shear, 1999).

The attributes of subtle experiences are essentially the same in different cultures. They are direct, nonconceptual experience, beyond words, concepts and dualities, transverbal, transrational, and nondual. They are developed through meditation/contemplation and are not shaped by language, concepts and cultural forms. The real transcends, surrounds, and overflows our miserable categories. It fleshes out the skeleton of scientific theory and provides an interpretation (at a higher level of significance) for the "empty symbols" of science.

His Holiness Sir Sahabji Maharaj, the Fifth Revered Leader of the Radhasoami

Faith and the August Founder of Dayalbagh, proclaimed that "*...Truth which we all so much love, can never be comprehended with physical instruments of science, nor can Ultimate Reality which we so much adore, be realized with the mental effort of philosophy. Providence has located within the human body a special faculty and it is the exclusive function of religion to teach man all about that faculty. When that faculty is developed in us like our physical and mental faculties, we shall be able to perceive Truth in the same manner as we now perceive and realize the sun with our physical eyes. And when this takes place, you will be both astonished and amused to find that Truth-the goal of science, Ultimate Reality-the goal of philosophy, and God-the goal of religion, are but three names of the same Supreme Essence.*" (Sarup, 1935).

His Holiness Maharaj Sahab, the Third Spiritual Leader of the Radhasoami Faith explicitly laid down an exhaustive exposition of enquiry and methodology based on scientific principles into the seemingly complex issues of existence, evolution, object and sustenance of life, reality and the spiritual dimension, to dispel any misgivings about true religion (Misra, 1909). His Holiness Professor P.S. Satsangi Sahab, the present Spiritual Leader of the Radhasoami Faith, has most graciously recently extended the physical systems theory as a rudimentary modelling framework for "*complete*" creational system including not only physical processes, but also "*esoteric*" mental and spiritual processes (Satsangi, 2003).

In the Religion of Saints, all the secrets of this creation are considered to be proof of the teachings of Saints, which includes science. In the magnanimous words of His Holiness Sarkar Sahab, the Fourth Revered Leader of the Radhasoami Faith, in '*Prarthana*', in Prem Samachar (Ratnavali, 1939),

जेती है मनुश्य की विद्या जेती मर्म रचना की ।
करें सिद्ध सब संत बचन को नित नवीन दे साखी ।। 68 ।।
सुरतवन्त अनुरागी प्रेमी निरपक्षी चितसीला ।
रग रग तार तार रचना में परखें प्रीतम लीला ।। 69 ।।
अन्ध घोर अस्थूल भूल भ्रम खान जो रचा पसारा ।
वाही में अस भक्तन झलके अद्भुत नूर अपारा ।। 70 ।।

Levels of Being and Knowing

We are familiar with different states of consciousness, the basic ones being waking, dreaming and deep sleep. Each state is characterized with different experiences. The more focused our attention is on a particular state, the more awareness and understanding we develop pertaining to the activities we perform in that state. For instance, in the wakeful state, we are able to perform a task better, in a more efficient manner, or we succeed in our objective by concentrating more on a given task.

The great wisdom traditions (Christian, Hindu, Islamic, Buddhist, Jewish Kabbalah, Sufi and Sant Mat) maintain that the three natural states of consciousness actually contain endless spiritual wisdom and spiritual awakening, which can be attained through proper training. An interesting feature about our states of consciousness being is that they come and go, although stages of consciousness are permanent. For instance, once a child develops through the linguistic stages of development, the child has permanent access to language. It isn't present one minute and gone the next. So once, one stably reaches a stage of growth and development, one can access the capacities of that stage. What can inherently be inferred is that in the course of life, our respective evolutionary paths, there are different stages of development. One can consider the stages of moral development, which are classified as egocentric, ethnocentric to worldcentric, or visualize these three stages as body, mind and spirit. The *chakra* system is another view of the different stages of consciousness and energy available to human beings, which exist in a set hierarchy, with physical, relational and spiritual dimensions (Wilber, 2005).

The entire spectrum of consciousness or the codification of direct experiential reality that has been consensually validated and is essentially universal, can be envisioned in Fig.2.

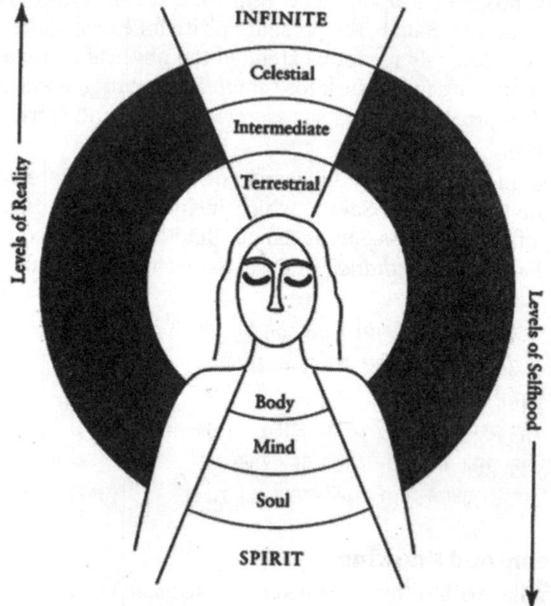

Fig. 2 The Great Nest of Being (Smith, 1992; Wilber, 2004)

Figure 2 is a simple summary of the traditional religious worldview found virtually the world over which recognize some version of body, mind, soul and spirit. The different levels of selfhood are considered as body, mind, soul and spirit, each of which identifies with a corresponding level of reality, i.e., body with terrestrial, mind with intermediate, soul with celestial and spirit with infinite.

Modern Scholars: Philosophical and Scientific View Points

A comparative diagram of the different levels of selfhood and reality propounded in the great religious traditions has been shown in Fig. 3. Plotinus, for example, held the traditional Great Chain of Being as a general unfolding from matter to body to mind to soul to spirit, to be both ontological levels of being and chronological levels of individual development.

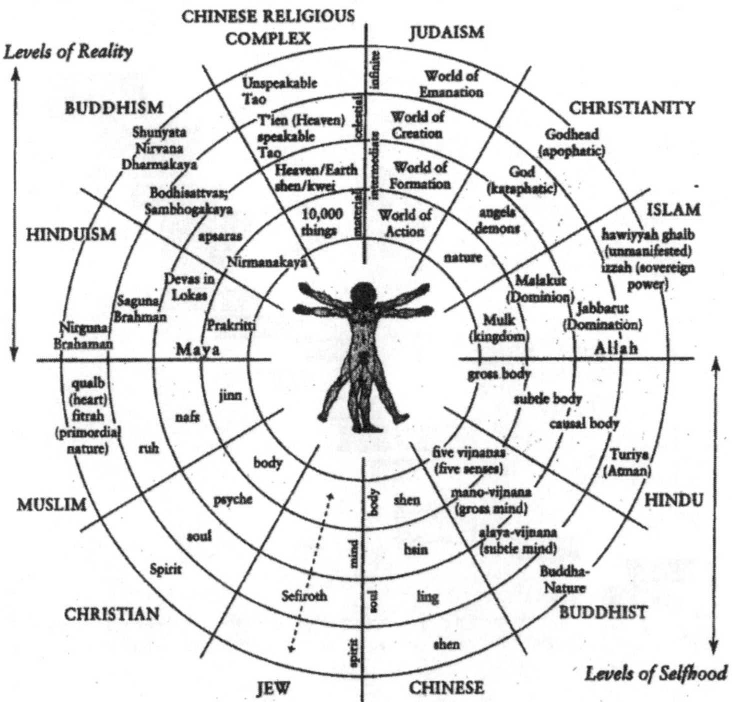

Fig. 3 The Great Nest in various Traditions (Wilber, 2004)

Although only four levels have been shown, most traditions have richer and more detailed maps as well. Especially the Religion of Saints or the great tradition of Sant Mat describes in profound detail the different levels of reality in exquisite detail encompassing all the levels ever disclosed. It maps reality into three grand divisions with each division comprising of six sub-divisions as shown in Fig. 3 (Singh, 1884a,b, Ram, 1893, 1948, Misra, 1909, Satsangi, 2003). The basic essence is that reality is understood to consist of several levels or waves of being and knowing.

Higher States of Consciousness Revealed by Sants

Interestingly, an examination of the teachings of various Sants who graced the events and propagated Bhakti movement in the 15-18th century reveals great commonalities. The periods of various Sants and Sufi Faqirs have been shown in Fig.4.

Their emphasis was on the following:

- Contemporary Sant Satguru
- His Satsang
- Bhakti Marg: Devotion to Him with unconditional love and selfless service
- Surat Shabda Yoga, i.e., the practice of concentration on sound currents
- Salvation on attaining the region of pure spirit : Nirmal Chetan Desh

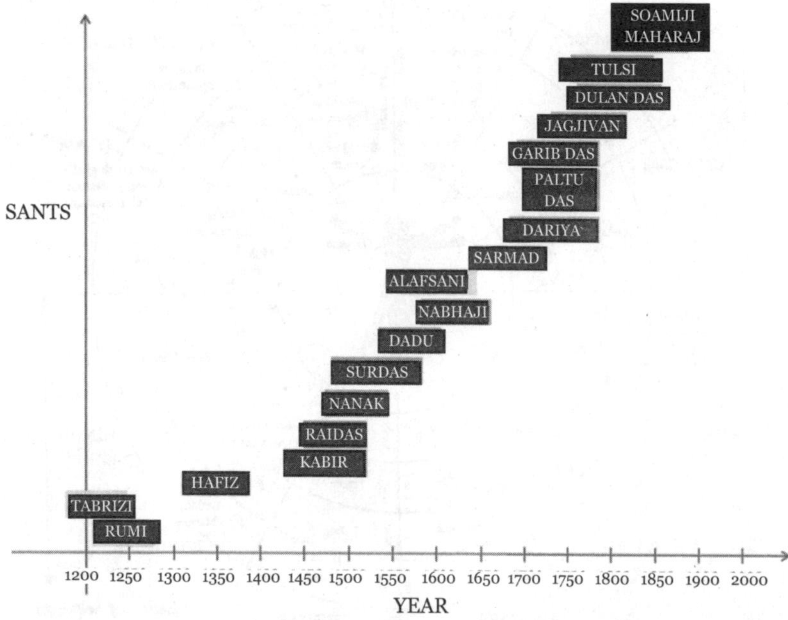

Fig.4. Period of some of the prominent Sants and Sufi Faqirs in the last 1000 years

The language used by all of them has been a simple and contemporary language with use of common north Indian words in common usage. The poetry, verses and hymns composed by all of them reflect common feelings and emotions. The names of higher planes of spiritual consciousness, their references and description and the Shabdas and sound representations in the material world are also similar. This is evident from the following few Shabdas and verses of some of the great Sants:

Sant Kabir Sahab

Sant Kabir Sahab has beautifully described the various spiritual regions and sounds in detail, in the following Shabda:

कर नैनो दीवार महल में प्यारा है ।।टेक।।

काम क्रोध मद लोभ बिसारो, सील सँतोप छिमा सत धारो ।
मद् मांस मिथ्या तजि डारो,
हो ज्ञान घोड़े असवार भरम में न्यारा है ।।1।।
धोती नेती बस्ती पाओ, आसन पदम जुगत से लाओ ।
कुम्भक कर रेचक करवाओ,
पहिले मूल सुधार कारज हो सारा है ।।2।।
मूल कँवलदल चतुर बखानी, कलिंग जाप लाल रँग मानो ।
देव गनेस तहँ रोपा थानो, ऋध सिध चँवर ढुलारा है ।।3।।
स्वाद चक्र शटदल बिस्तारो, ब्रह्म सावित्रो रूप निहारो ।
उलटि नागिनी का सिर मारो, तहाँ सब्द ओंकारा ।।4।।
नाभी अश्ट कँवल दल साजा, सेत सिंघासन बिस्नु बिराजा ।
हिरिंग जाप तासु मुख गाजा, लक्ष्मी सिव आधारा है ।।6।।
द्वादस कँवल हृदय के माहिं, जंग गौर सिव ध्यान लगाई ।
सोहं सब्द तहाँ धुन छाई, गन करैं जैजैकारा ।।7।।
दो दल कँवल कंठ के माही, तेहि मध बसे अबिद्या बाई ।
हरि हर ब्रह्मा चँवर ढुराई, जहँ ऋंग नाम उचारा है ।।7।।
ता पर कंज कँवल है, भाई, बग भौंरा दुइ रूप लखाई ।
निज मन करत तहाँ ठकुराई, सो नैनन पिछतारा है ।।8।।
कँवलन भेद किया निर्वारा, यह सब रचना पिंड मँझारा ।
सतसँग कर सतगुरु सिर धारा, वह सत नाम उचारा है ।।9।।
आँख कान मुख बन्द कराओ, अनहद झिंगा सब्द सुनाओ ।
दोनों तिल इक तार मिलाओ, तब देखो गुलजारा है ।।10।।
चंद सूर एकै घर लाओ, सुशमन सेती ध्यान लगाओ ।
तिरबेनी के संध समाओ, भोर उतर चल पारा है ।।11।।
घंटा संख सुनो धन दोई, सहस कँवल दल जगमग होई ।
ता मध करता निरखो सोई, बंकनाल धस पारा है ।।12।।
डाकिनी साकिनी बहु किलकारें, जम किंकर धर्म दूत हकारें ।
सत्त नाम सुन भागें सारे, जब सतगुरु नाम उचारा है ।।13।।
गगन मँडल बिच उर्धमुख कुइया, गुरुमुख्ख साधू भर भर पीया ।
निगुरे प्यास मरे बिन कीया, जा के हिये अँधियारा है ।।14।।
त्रिकुटी महल में बिद्या सारा, घनहर गरजें गजे नगारा ।
लाल बरना सूरज उँजियारा, चतुर कँवर मँझार सब्द ओंकारा है ।।15।।
साध सोई जिन यह गढ़ लीन्हा, नौ दरवाजे परगट चीन्हा ।
दसवाँ खोल जाय जिन दीन्हा, जहाँ कुलुफ रहा मारा है ।।16।।
आगे सेत सुन्न है भाई, मान सरोवर पैठि अन्हाई ।
हंसन मिलि हंसा होई जाई, मिलै जो अमी बहारा है ।।17।।
किंगरी सारँग बजै सितारा, अच्छर ब्रह्म सुन्न दरबारा ।
द्वादस भानु हंस उकतयारा, खट दल कवल मँझार सब्द ररंकारा है ।।18।।
महा सुन्न सिनध बिशमी घाटी, बिन सतगुरु पावै नहिं बाटी ।
ब्याघर सिघ सरप बहु काटी, तहँ सहज अचिंत पसारा है ।।19।।
अश्ट दल कँवल पारब्रह्म भाई, दहिने द्वादस अचत रहाई ।
बायें दस दल सहज समाई, यों कँवलन निरवारा है ।।20।।

पाँच ब्रह्म पाँचों अँड बीनो, पाँच ब्रह्म निःअच्छर चीन्हा ।
चार मुकाम गुप्त तहँ किन्हों, जा मध बंदीवान पुरुश दरबारा है ।।21।।
दो पर्बत के संधा निहारो, भँवर गुफा तें संत पुकारो ।
हंसा करते केल अपारी, तहाँ गुरन दर्बारा है ।।22।।
सहस अठासी दीप रचाये, हीरे पन्ने महल जड़ाये ।
मुरली बजत अखंड सदाये, तहँ सोहं झनकारा है ।।23।।
सोहं हद्द तजी जब भाई, सत्त लोक की हद पुनि आई ।
उठत सुगंध महा अधिकाई, जा को वार न पारा है ।।24।।
पोड़स भानु हंस को रूपा, बीना सत धुन बजै अनूपा ।
हंसा करत चँवर सिर भूपा, सत्त पुरुश दर्बारा है ।।25।।
कोटिन भानु उदय जो होई, एते ही पुनि चंद्र लखोई ।
पुरुश रोम सम एक न होई, ऐसा पुरुश दीदारा है ।।26।।
आगे अलख लोक है भाई, अलख पुरुश की तहँ ठकुराई ।
अरबन सूर रोम सम नाहीं, ऐसा अलखा निहारा है ।।27।।
ता पर अगम महल इक साजा, अगम पुरुश ताहि को राजा ।
खरबन सूर रोम इक लाजा, ऐसा अगम अपारा है ।।28।।
ता पर अकह लोक है भाई, पुरुश अनामी तहाँ रहाई ।
जो पहँचा जानेगा वाही, कहन सुनन तें न्यारा है ।।29।।
काया भेद किया निर्बारा, यह सब रचना पिंड मँझारा ।
माया अवगति जाल पसारा, सो कारीगर भारा है।।30।।
आदि माया कीन्हीं चतुराई, झूठी बाजी पिंड दिखाई।
अवगति रचन रची अँड माहीं, ता का प्रतिबिंब डारा है।।31।।
सब्द बिहंगम चाल हमारी, कहें कबीर सतगुरु दइ तारी ।
खुले कपाट सब्द झनकारी, पिंड अंड के पार सो देस हमारा है ।।32।।

In the above poem He refers to a region beyond Agam Loka, which is Anami (Nameless).

In the following verse, Sant Kabir Sahab refers to the Radhasoami Region in a concealed manner.

कबीर धारा अगम की, सतगुरु दई लखाए ।
उलट ताहि सुमिरन करो, स्वामी संग मिलाए ।।

According to the verse, He advises to repeat the word "धारा", from Agam after transposing it and joining with the word "स्वामी", which leads to the word "राधास्वामी".

In another verse Kabir Sahab says,

अगवानी हम आइया ले सतगुरु सन्देष ।
पाछे सतगुरु भी आयँगे पूरे साज समेत ।।

"I have come in advance with the Message of the Satguru. The Satguru Himself will come afterwards in all His glory and grandeur and provided with all the facilities for the spread of His Message." It is evident that He revealed the grand spectrum of spiritual consciousness albeit with a concealed revelation of the highest region.

Param Guru Maharaj Sahab, the Third Revered Leader of the Radhasoami Faith, explained the origin and the importance of the Supreme Name "Radhasoami", "*The imitation in articulate sound of the first spiritual current, which is the beginning and the cause of all creation, is 'Radha', and the imitation of the wave or commotion that gave rise to this prime current is 'Soami'. The true holy name or the supreme mantra of the origin and source of all spirituality in creation is 'Radhasoami'; and when the true Supreme Being thus manifested Himself as Creator and evolved the creation, the wave and currents announced Him as Radhasoami in the vast region of spirituality first evolved. This true name is present everywhere in creation, and can be heard at the innermost plane where the spirit current is acting.*" (Misra, 1909, 2004).

Most Revered Satsangi Sahab, has further generalized the physical systems theory to elucidate the esoteric spiritual systems theory framework, by formulating this as the pre-creational and creational postulates (Satsangi, 2007):

"*<u>Pre-creational Postulate</u>: In the pre-creational condition, the Supreme Creator, the Infinite Source of Spirit Energy was in a state of absolute self-absorption. It was a completely latent potential energy state. However, there was an eternal polarization with an Infinite Positive Pole of Spirituality at the top and a negative or lower pole of a lower order of spirituality at the bottom.*

<u>Creational Postulate</u>: In the fullness of time there came to be such a vast potential difference in spirituality between the two poles that there was a huge commotion or upheaval in the Supreme Creator comparable to the 'Big Bang' in the physical plane. It was a manifestation of the Prime Energy in a kinetic form creating a "quantum" force field of spiritual action or a process of spiritualization similar to magnetization. As a result the first great spiritual current known as "Adi-Chetan-Dhar" issued forth from the region of the Supreme Creator which was nearest to the negative pole and proceeded away from the positive pole as an outward focus or Centre-forming Spiritual Current, and then returned to the positive pole as an inward spiritualizing sound current, completing the circuit. The sound that accompanied the vibrations in the spirit emanations of "Adi-Chetan-Dhar" and the great upheaval, when articulated, became "Radha-soami"."

Sant Guru Nanak

Guru Nanak describes the glory of the Shabda in the following three verses:

नौ दर ठाके धावत रहाये। दसवें निज घर बासा पाए।।
ओथे अनहद शब्द बजहि दिन राती। गुरमति शब्द सुनावनियाँ
बिन शब्दे अन्दर आनेरा। ना वस्तु लहे न चूके फेरा
गुरु हत्थ कुंजी होर ते दर खुल्ले नाही। गुर पूरे भाग मिलावनियाँ।।

बीना शब्द बजावे जोगी, दर्शन रुप अपारो। शब्द अनाहद सो सहुराता नानक कहे विचारो।

पंच शब्द तेह पूरन नाद, अनहद बाजे अचरज बिस्माद।।
ँदज क्कन ँइ
जीम विससवूपदह ँइकं सेव कमेबतपइमे कपमितमदज समअमसे व बिवदेबपवनेदमेरू

दादू देखा मैं प्यारा अगम जो पंथ निहारा ।।टेक।।
अश्ट कँवल दल सुरत षब्द मैं, रूप रंग से न्यारा ।। 1 ।।
पिंड ब्रह्मंड और बेद कितेबे, पाँच तत्त के पारा ।। 2 ।।
सत्तलोक जहँ पुरुश बिदेही, वह साहिब करतारा ।। 3 ।।
आदि जोत और काल निरंजन, इनका वहाँ न पसारा ।। 4 ।।
राम रहीम रब्ब नहिं आतम, मोहमद नहिं औतारा ।।5 ।।
सब सन्तन के चरन सीस धर, चीन्हा सार असारा ।। 6 ।।
ँदज क्तपल ँइ

Sant Dariya Sahab describes 'Banknal' and 'Bhawjal' a synonym for 'Bhanwargupha', in the following Shabda:

दरिया दरबारा खुल गया अजर किवाड़ा ।।टेक।।
चमकी बीज चली ज्यों धारा, ज्यों बिजुली बिच तारा ।
खुल गये चन्द बन्द बदरी का, घोर मिटा अँधियारा ।। 1 ।।
लौ लगी जाय लगन के लारा, चाँदनी चौक निहारा ।
सूरत सैल करे नभ ऊपर, बंकनाल पट फारा ।। 2 ।।
चढ़ गई चाँप चली ज्यों धारा, ज्यों मकरी मक तारा ।
मैं मिली जाय पाय पिय प्यारा, ज्यों सरिताा जलधारा ।। 3 ।।
देखा रूप अरूप अलेखा, लेखा वार न पारा ।
दरिया दिल दरवेष भये तब, उतरे भवजल पारा ।। 4 ।।

Sant Paltu Sahab

Sant Paltu Sahab describes the higher levels of spiritual consciousness where sounds of 'flute' and 'Sohang' resound after piercing through the 'Tenth Door':

बंसी बाजी गगन में मगन भया मन मोर ।।टेक।।
मगन भया मन मोर महल अटवें पर बैठा ।
जहाँ उठे सोहंगम षब्द षब्द के भीतर पैठा ।। 1 ।।
नाना उठें तरंग रंग कुछ कहा न जाई ।
चाँद सुरज छिप गये सुखमना सेज बिछाइ ।। 2 ।।
छूट गया तन ग्रेह नेह उन ही से लागी ।
दसवाँ द्वारा फोड़ जोत बाहर होय जागी ।। 3 ।।
पलटू धारा तेल की मेलत हो गया भोर ।
बंसी बाजी गगन में मगन भया मन मोर ।। 4 ।।

Sant Tulsi Sahab

Sant Tulsi Sahab describes the state of 'Sunn' with 'Sohang' sound beyond that of 'Trikuti' with 'Om' sound, in one of his Shabdas from Ratna Sagar, Pg. 138.

"सुन हिरदे यह भेद निनारा । सो का जाने वद विचारा ||
षब्द षब्द में अंतर भाई जो हम कही वेद नहिं पाई ||
और षब्द वेद बतलावे। त्रिकुटी मद्ध माहि से आवे ||
ओंकार के पार ठिकाना । जहँ है सुन्न षब्द अस्थाना ||
सो कहं संत षब्द सुख दाई। सो महिमा वेद से कहीं पाई ||
अंडा सुन्न में सैल कराई । सो वो षब्द परखिया भाई ||
ओअं सोहं जाप सुनावा। सो सब यह माया पर भावा ||
वह तो षब्द सुन्न के माहि, उलट चढ़े अधर घर माहि ||
सो बूझे यह बाँक बयाना। सतसंग में कोई सज्जन जाना ||

Dulan Das Ji

Sant Dulan Das ji describes the glory of 'Trikuti' and 'Alakh' in the following Shabda:

तू काहे को जग में आया, जो पै नाम से प्रीति न लाया रे ||टेक||
तृश्ना काम सवाद घनेरे, मन से नहिं बिसखया रे |
भोग बिलास आस निस बासर, इत उत चित भरमाया रे || 1 ||
त्रिकुटी तीरथ प्रेम जल निर्मल, सुरत नहीं अन्हवाया रे |
दुर्ममति करम मैल सब मन के, सुमिरि सुमिरि न छुड़ाया रे || 2 ||
कहँ से आयो कहँ को जैहै, अन्त खोज नहिं पाया रे |
उपजि उपजि के बिनसि गये सब, काल सबै जग खाया रे || 3 ||
कर सतसंग आपने अंतर, तज मन मोह औ माया रे |
जन दूलन बल बल सतगुरु के, जिनमोहि अलख लखाया रे || 4 ||

It is interesting to note that Dulan Das ji was the Chief Disciple of Sant Jagjivan Sahab, who lived in the 18th century A.D. has in his poem said,

साँईं तेरो गुप्त मर्म हम जानी, कस करि कहौं बखानी !
ष्c स्वतक! ट ींअम बवउम जव ादवू व जीम `मबतमज ंइवनज ल्वनतेमसफि भ्वू बंद ट वचमदसल हपअम पज जव वजीमतेघ्ठ प्ज पे विससवूमक इल जीम अमतेमए
निज घर है वह अमग अपारा, जहाँ बिराजै स्वामी ।
ताके परे अलोक अनामी, जाको रूप न नामी ||

"The Region where our Lord abides in all His Glory is inaccessible and Limitless. And beyond that is the Abode of the Supreme Lord, which has no form and no name and that Abode is Loka, i.e., it cannot be said to be a Loka." It can be inferred that Dulan Das ji was told by Sant Jagjivan Sahab about the existence of a region higher to the Sat Loka as referred by Him in the following verse:

निज माता सीता सोई राधा, निज पितु राम सुवाती ।
दोउ मिलि जीवन बंद छुड़ाया, निज पद में दिया ठामी ।।

"The Supreme Mother Sita (that which has moved like a straight furrow, perhaps meaning a current) is Radha and the Supreme Father Ram (i.e., Who pervades everything) is Soami. These two together have released the Jivas from bondage and granted them abode in the Region of the Supreme Lord." The usage of the words राधा and स्वामी and the function they are stated to perform, evidently refer to the Supreme Lord Radhasoami. In the verse that follows, Dulan Das has explained his own authority for making the above statements:

दूलन दास के साँई जगजीवन, निज सुत जक्त पठानी ।
मुक्ति द्वारा की कूँजी दीन्हीं, ताते कुलुफ़ खुलानी ।।

Dulan Das ji has ended with the verse:

दूलन यह मत गुप्त है, प्रगट न करौ बखान ।
ऐसे राखु छिपाय मन, जस बिधवा औधान ।।

'All this is secret and should not be told openly to the people. In fact, it should be concealed as carefully and well as a widowed woman conceals the fact of her pregnancy.' It could be the reason why Dulan Das ji did not speak out more explicitly, although it can be reasonably be justified that Jagjivan Sahab knew that the Name of the Supreme Lord was Radhasoami and He might have told his Gurumukh disciple about it (Dass, 1967).

With the complete detailed description of the various levels of consciousness described by Param Purush Puran Dhani Soamiji Maharaj, mercifully revealing the True name of the Supreme Being as '*Radhasoami*', and further elucidated by His successors, the various levels in the three grand divisions, with each division forming six sub-divisions, alongwith their characteristic features, such as Shabda, sound, deities and corresponding Sufi nomenclature, can be arranged in the following tabular form.[Singh, 1884a,b]

Param Purush Puran Dhani Soamiji Maharaj mercifully gave exquisite description of the higher states of spiritual consciousness by describing the detailed features of the following regions (Singh, 1884 and 1938).

1. Sunn

- Greater Luminosity than Trikuti
- Numerable Mansarovar-Ponds of Nectar
- Beautiful Flowers and Gardens
- Blissful Dancing Spirits
- Eating subtle very sweet spiritual things
- Musical Ragas and Raginis resounding everywhere
- Waterfalls of Nectars
- Platforms of diamonds, rubies and jewels
- Plants of jewels, pearls
- Jewels studded fishes in ponds, whose glitter attracts the heart

	Spiritual Regions	Deities	Shabda	Sound	Sufi	Status	Descrpt. - Other Religions	Emanations	Incarnations
Region of Pure Spirit Dayal or Nirmal Chetan Desh	Radhasoami	Radhasoami	Radhasoami			Param Sant/ Satguru			
	Agam Loka	Agam Purusha							
	Alakh Loka	Alakh Purusha							
	Anami Loka								
	Sat Loka/Sach Khand	Sat Purusha/ Adi Purusha	Sat Shabda/Maha Nad/Sar Shabda, Sat Naam, Sat-sat, Haq-haq (5th Shabda)	Bagpipes (Bina)	Hoot			From below Sat Loka, first Niranjan (Kala Purusha-dark current with a blue tint), then Jyoti or Adya current-(greenish yellow hue) to form Brahmanda	
	Bhanwar Gupha (whirling vortices)	Sohang Purush	Word of Sohang Purusha	Flute	Hutalhoot				
Para-Brahma Super Causal Beyond Mind	Mahasunn		Four shabdas & five stations hidden		Hahoot	Sant			
Universal Mind Brahmanda (as in Vedas) Causal Plane — Pure Nirguna	Sunn/Dasam Dwar/Atma Pad/Region of Para-Brahma (kamal of one dal)		Word of Parbrahma, Rarang	Sarangi, Sitar	Arsh-e-Azim/Alam –e-Lahoot	Sadh, Mahatma			
Pure Sagun Creation	Trikuti/Gagan/Region of Brahma/Pranav/Maha Akasa (kamal of four dals)	Pran Purusha/ Brahma-Om/Khuda-e-azim/Brahmandi Mana	Om, Hu-Hu	Roaring Clouds, Thunder-Drum like		Yogeshwar	Holy Vedas Holy Koran Adi Purana of Jains	Subtle Matter/Maya/Sakti/ Chaitanya Prana (Jyoti/Adya known here as Maya), three gunas (Sat, Raj, Tam), five tattvas in subtle form	Rama, Krishna, Yogeshwaras-Vyasa, Vasishtha, Rishabh Deva of Jains
	Sahasdal Kamal/Arsh Set Shyam of eight dals (eight petalled lotus)	Niranjan Jyoti/Nij Mana Siva Sakti/ Lakshmi Narayana/ Narayana Jyoti/ Syam Sunder/ Arsh/Khuda, Isvara		Bells and Conch	Nij Mana, Jabroot	Yogi		Tanmatras (five senses) of the tattvas (sense organs in tangible form), Pranas, (vital airs-prana, apana, vyana, udana, samana), Prakrities (25 in no.), Chidakasa	Incarnations of 2nd grade, Auliyas, Yogis
Region of Anda (Astral Plane)	Vishnu								
	Brahma								
	Shiva				Nukota-i-Subeda				
Regions of Pind (reflections of higher regions, 6 chakras) — Gross Sagun Creation	1st Chakra: Tisra Til (behind two eyes) (two dal kamal)	Paramatma, God, Brahma			Malkoot				Prophets, incarnations, Valis, Yogis, Siddhas
	2nd Chakra : Kantha Chakra, Throat (sixteen dal kamal)	Durga		Pashyanti, Madhyama, Baikhari (at Tongue)			Virata form of God actually refers to Sahas Dal Kamal, Atma Pad reflection of Sunn	Pranas, Desire	
	3rd Chakra : Heart Centre/ Solar Plexus (twelve dal kamal)	Pindi (subtle body of man) Mind						Image of Siva Sakti focused here, regulation of body: thoughts, feelings	
	4th Chakra: At Navel eight dal kamal	Vishnu-Lakshmi		Para Bani	Nasoot			Nourishment of Body, source of lower pranas (vital airs)	
	5th Chakra : at Reproductive Organ (6 dal kamal)	Brahma-Savitri						Vitality to Physical Body, passions	
	6th Chakra : At Rectum (4 dal kamal))	Ganesa							

Hell, Dals : Virttiyan (tendencies) and currents; Triloki = Set of Pind, And and Brahmand

Fig.4. Spiritual Architecture and Cosmology according to the Radhasoami Faith

- Numerable Glass Palaces inhabited with extremely purified, blissful white spirits
- Extremely picturesque
- Devoid of coarse matter

2. Maha Sunn

- Extremely large ground
- Almost endless expanse of Darkness
- Four unrevealed secret places
- Numerous spirits sent off from the Supreme Being's court
- There are resting places for these spirits
- No suffering, they keep doing their own work in their own light
- Are not blessed with the Vision of Supreme Being and are uneasy/perturbed
- Those spirits who happen to see the Sants taking spirits from the lower regions to upper regions, are blessed by the Sants, who get them pardoned and get them called near the Supreme Being

3. Bhanwargupha

- Whirling vortices
- Spirits keep swinging there
- Everywhere in the surroundings are innumerable bright spiritual centres
- Sohan-Sohan, Anahu-Anahu shabdas are always resounding
- Spirits and white spirits are immersed in the bliss of these sounds
- Smells of Sandalwood, different perfumes
- Numerous melodies of flute

4. Sat Loka

- Extremely large
- Sound of Sat-Sat, Haq-Haq coming out of the Bina
- Dimenion of Trees : crore crore yojana
- Crores of suns and moons on the trees instead of flowers and fruits
- 1 padam (10 lakh arab) palang area (1 palang = 1 triloki)
- Golden and silver canals full of nectar
- Gigantic trees laden with crores of suns and moons
- Numerable spirits enjoying on these trees
- Gigantic gardens
- Satpurusha : Each cell intensely illuminated > cores of suns and moons
- His eyes, nose, ears, face, hands and feet refulgent with light
- White Spirits see Satpurusha and hear the bina and eat nectar

5. Alakh Loka

- Area greater than Sat Loka
- Alakh Purusha much more refulgent with light
- Alakh Purusha : Each cell intensely illuminated > Arab, Kharab suns
- 1 sankh area (1 crore arab)
- Arab Kharab suns in one cell of Alakh Purush

6. Agam Loka

- Area greater than Agam Loka : Maha sankh
- Extremely large body of Alakh Purusha much more refulgent with light
- His body spans crores of sankh in dimension
- White souls have wonderful forms
- Bliss is also wonderful

7. Radhasoami

- Infinite, Indescribable
- Anami Purusha
- Radhasoami Shabda's sound described as "Bhanwar kare gunjar"

Most Revered Satsangi Sahab has recently described the Supreme Name's sound to be that of a fine, subtle and divine resonating Bina.

Param Purush Puran Dhani Soamiji Maharaj mercifully has also described the dimensions of the various higher regions of spiritual consciousness as shown in Fig.5 (Singh, 1884 and 1938).

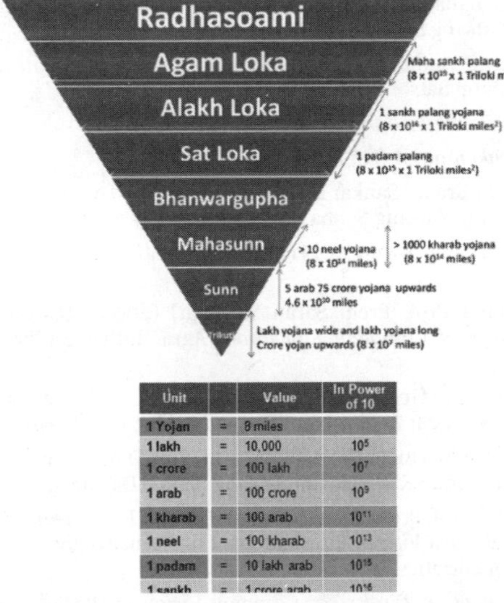

Unit		Value	In Power of 10
1 Yojan	=	8 miles	
1 lakh	=	10,000	10^5
1 crore	=	100 lakh	10^7
1 arab	=	100 crore	10^9
1 kharab	=	100 arab	10^{11}
1 neel	=	100 kharab	10^{13}
1 padam	=	10 lakh arab	10^{15}
1 sankh	=	1 crore arab	10^{16}

Fig. 5. Numerical estimates of higher spiritual regions given by Param Purush Puran Dhani Soamiji Maharaj

Conclusion

With the merciful revelation of the Supreme Being as "*Radhasoami*", the True Name as "*Radhasoami*", and the grand object of creation and its detailed process, the complete spectrum of spiritual consciousness has been established in the Radhasoami Faith with unprecedented clarity. It enables the comprehension of the glory of the Supreme Being, the grand scale of creation on our low plane of existence. This would certainly provide the impetus for mankind and the myriad of life forms to attain absolute salvation and ultimate enlightenment.

Acknowledgement

The author expresses deep gratitude in the Lotus Feet of Most Revered Professor P.S. Satsangi Sahab for His highly enlightening discourses and divine inspiration. He is also grateful to Professor P. Sriramamurti for his kind encouragement and helpful discussions.

References

Capra, F. (1983). *The Tao of Physics*. London, UK: Flamingo.

Dass, S. (August 8, 1967). Radhasoami Name. *The Dayalbagh Herald*. 5, 8. Radhasoami Satsang Sabha, Dayalbagh.

Feuerstein, G. (1987). *Structures of Consciousness: The Genius of Jean Gebser - An Introduction and Critique*. Lower Lake, CA, USA: Integral Publishing.

Gebser, J. (1985, 1991). *The Ever-Present Origin*, (Trans. Noel Barstad & Algis Mickunas). Athens, Greece: Ohio University Press.

Heisenberg, W. (1963). *Physics and Philosophy*. London, UK: Allen and Unwin.

Huzur Maharaj [Rai Bahadur Salig Ram Sahab] (1960). *Prem Patra*. Agra, India: Radhasoami Satsang Sabha, Dayalbagh.

Huzur Maharaj [Rai Bahadur Salig Ram Sahab] (1960). *Radhasoami Mat Sandesa*. Agra, India: Radhasoami Satsang Sabha, Dayalbagh.

Huzur Maharaj. [Rai Bahadur Salig Ram Sahab] (1976). *Catechism and Exalted Precepts*. Agra, India: Radhasoami Satsang Sabha, Dayalbagh.

Jammer, M. (1974). *The Philosophy of Quantum Theory*. Wiley.

Khan, I. (2000). *Awakening: A Sufi Experience*. Tarcher.

Maharaj Sahab [Pandit Brahm Sankar Misra Sahab] (2004). *Discourses on Radhasoami Faith*. Agra, India: Radhasoami Satsang Sabha, Dayalbagh.

Sahabji Maharaj [Sir Anand Sarup Kt.] (1935). Convocation Address, Agra University, India, Nov. 23.

Satsangi, P.S. [Revered Prof. Prem Saran Satsangi] (2005). *Discourses on Education in Dayalbagh - A Vision of Complete Education*. Agra, India: Radhasoami Satsang Sabha, Dayalbagh.

Param Purush Puran Dhani Huzur Soamiji Maharaj [Shiv Dayal Singh Sahab] (1938,1884). *Sar Bachan (Poetry)*. Agra, India: Radhasoami Satsang Sabha, Dayalbagh.

Param Purush Puran Dhani Huzur Soamiji Maharaj [Shiv Dayal Singh Sahab] (1959,1884). *Sar Bachan (Prose)*. Agra, India: Radhasoami Satsang Sabha, Dayalbagh.

Satsangi, P.S. [Revered Prof. Prem Saran Satsangi] (2003). *Reality and Truth vis-à-vis Wisdom via 'Apara Vidya' and 'Para Vidya'*. International Conference of the Association of Asia-Pacific Operational Research Societies. New Delhi, India.

Smith, H. (1992). *Forgotten Truth: The Common Vision of World's Religions*. (pp. 62). San Francisco, USA: Harper.

Talbot, M. (1991). *The Holographic Universe*. New York, USA: Harper Collins Publishers.

Varela, F., Thompson, E., and Rosch, E. (1991). *The Embodied Mind: Cognitive Science and Human Experience*. Massachusetts, USA: MIT Press.

Varela, F. (1999). *Ethical Know-How: Action, Wisdom and Cognition*. Stanford, USA: Stanford University Press.

Varela, F., and Shear, J. (Eds.) (1999). *The View from Within: First Person Methodologies in the Study of Consciousness*. London, UK: Imprint Academic.

Wilber, K. (2004). *Theory of Everything*. Boston, USA: Shambhala Publications.

Chapter 51

Sant Satguru
The Only Means of Attaining Highest Spiritual Consciousness

SATYA SRIVASTAVA
Department of History, Mahila Collge, Lucknow

Abstract

Higher consciousness means consciousness of a human being who has reached a higher level of evolutionary development and who has come to know reality more accurately. This evolution is brought about by application of spiritual knowledge to the conduct of human life, and of mental proficiency brought about by spiritual practices. Man is entirely incapable of achieving this state of higher consciousness by himself. He needs a Master, a Sant Satguru for this purpose. Amongst the three faculties of man – physical, mental and spiritual - the last one is often ignored and not developed, in spite of the fact that the spirit force is the only static Truth, and it's reservoir is Supreme Being Himself. The human body is bestowed with a special spiritual faculty which when developed enables one to realize the Ultimate Truth. Religion of Saints, having reached its culmination in Radhasoami faith, and having a Sant Satguru at its core, propounds the way to achieve this state. Moral restraint and meditation are the basic requirements. In this discipline, the inspiration of the Master or a Sant Satguru is indispensable.

Introduction

"Anything that we are aware of at a given moment forms part of our consciousness, making conscious experience at once the most familiar and most mysterious aspect of our lives." [1]

Higher consciousness, also called super consciousness is used to denote the consciousness of a human being who has reached a higher level of evolutionary development and who has come to know reality more accurately. This evolution is what is brought about by the application of spiritual knowledge to the conduct of human life, and of mental proficiency brought about by spiritual practices. Man is entirely incapable of achieving this state of higher consciousness. He needs a Master, a Sant Satguru for this purpose.

Amongst the three faculties of man – physical, mental and spiritual - the last one is often ignored and not developed, in spite of the fact that the spirit force is the ***only static*** Truth in this ephemeral world and its reservoir is God Himself – The Ultimate Truth. Paul Brunton repents that, 'The majority of men will die

[1] Searle (1995)

without caring and without knowing whether life has a meaning or no meaning; whether man has something divine in him or is a mere skin-bag of flesh, blood, bones, nerves, and muscles. They are strangers to themselves.' [2]

Nothing is nobler and more enjoyable than acquiring knowledge of Atman – realizing God with in us. The human body is bestowed with a special spiritual faculty which when developed enables one to perceive the Ultimate Truth and Ultimate Reality. Religion of Saints having reached its culmination in Radhasoami faith and having a Sant Satguru as its core, advocates the way to achieve this state.

Sant Satguru – The Only Means of achieving Highest Consciousness

Sahabji Maharaj has brought out that it is stated in the *Puranas* that whether it was Vyasya or Vashishtha, or whether it was Shesh or Mahesh, whether Parasar or whether Yogi Narad, or Shringi Rishi – they all were mistaken and confused. They did not realize the Ultimate Truth. None of them came to know about the purely spiritual region i.e. Dayal Desh or the Ultra Transcendental region.[3] Reason – ***they did not have true guru to guide, protect and encourage them***. For *achieving spiritual consciousness, moral restraint and meditation are the most important tools for the purification of the mind.* In this discipline, the inspiration of the Master or a Sant Satguru is indispensable. ***"Pritham sidhi hai Guru-Bhakti, Guru Bhakti bin kaaj na ratti, Pirtham sidhi bhakti Guru ki, Dusar sidhi bhakti Naam ki, Guru-Bhakti bin Shabad mein pachate, So bhi maanush murakh jaan."*** [4]

How to Find and Recognize a True Sant Satguru

Only when and if the Sant Satguru Himself condescends to give His introduction to a *jiva*, can the *jiva* come to know about Him and receive the gift of love from Him. Huzur Soamiji Maharaj has given one definite characteristic of a true Sant Satguru in His book Saar Bachan, ***"Guru soi jo shabd sanehi, Shabd bina doosar nahin sei"***[5] ***"Shabd kamaave so Guru poora, Unn charnann ki ho jaa dhura"***[6]

Sahabji Maharaj has stated other ways of identifying a Sant Satguru[7]. Some of them are;

- In loving Him, love for the Supreme Being is automatically developed.
- One who by His *'drishti'* alone energizes your spirit.
- One who comes to know about your problem, without you telling Him, and also suggests remedy for the same.
- One, who on a prayer from His devotee, changes adverse weather conditions, making cool winds blow when it is very hot etc,

---

[2] Brunton (1970)

[3] Sahabji Maharaj (1957), *Yathartha Prakasa*

[4] *Sar Bachan*, quoted in, *Yathartha Prakasa*, pp. 7, 253

[5] *Sar Bachan*

[6] ibid

All saints emphasize that it is only in human form, that deliverance from the cycle of birth and death can be obtained. A human form is one for which even gods pine – for it is only in human form that Satguru bhakti can be performed and salvation achieved. "Kaun kare aarat Satguru ki, Brahmadik taras rahein hain, Mili Nahin yeh padvi".[8] Pious deeds may lead to an abode in heaven. But heaven does not give eternal bliss. It is only a short respite from pain and suffering. After the merit of the individual's good actions is exhausted, he may be thrown into the fires of hell or given birth in the lower species.

The reason for this is that the Human body is a perfect microcosm of the whole macrocosm and has within it all the doors of all the three grand divisions of creation – *pind, brahmand* and the ultra transcendental region or *'Dayal Desh'*. The *chakras* of the ganglia in the human body are the replica of the physical world. The *kamals* represent the *brahmand*, and the *padams* represent the ultra transcendental region, at the end of which is the Supreme Being.

There are six apertures in the grey matter of the brain to view *Brahmand* and there are six apertures in the white matter of the brain to view the ultra transcendental region or *Dayal Desh*. Thus, the human body encompasses within itself the whole route which leads to the Supreme Being and which can be traversed ***during one's lifetime only with the help of a Sant Satguru*** who has himself achieved the highest abode. Thus a jiva can seek redemption from the bondage of birth and death and achieve *moksha*.

The Sant Satguru of Radha Soami faith, being the very ansh, of Huzur Radhasoami Dayal and having descended from Radhasoami Dham, the highest level of the highest grand division of creation[9] is conversant and capable of guiding and taking the individual spirit forces who seek His protection, to the highest spiritual region of creation ie. Radhasoami Dham, within their individual human frames, through *Surat Shabad Yog*. Thus highest form of spiritual consciousnes ***can be and is*** bestowed by the Sant Satguru of Radhasoami faith.

The Radhasoami Faith teaches one to hear the Radhasoami sound internally during *Surat Shabda Yoga*, as a result of which one can be spiritually elevated to the highest spiritual region. In the Radhasoami Faith, the Prime commotion is also known as *Adi Shabda* and the Prime Spiritual Current as *Adi Surat*. *Rãdha* is the name of the *Adi Surat* and *Soami* is the name of *Adi Shabda* of the Supreme Abode. ***"Rãdha Adi Surat ka Nam, Soami Adi Shabda Nija Dham"***[10]

Radhasoami faith stresses on the necessity of withdrawing consciousness from the nine portals of the body and bringing it to the tenth portal or eye center. Entering through this door with the grace and company of the Master is

[7] Param Guru Maharaj Sahab, Param Guru Sarkar Sahab, Param Guru Sahabji Maharaj Ke Bachan, (2003), Dayalbagh, Agra: Radhasoami Satsang Sabha

[8] *Sar Bachan*, p. 558

[9] For Theory of Creation see – Huzur Maharaj Sahab (Pandit Brahm Shankar Misra), Discourses On Radhasoami Faith, with Supplement, Dayal Bagh, Agra, 2004; Huzur Prem Saran Satsangi Sahab: Autobiographical Retrospectives, International Journal of General Systems, 2006 Taylor and Francis.

equivalent to 'dying while living'.

Tulsi Sahab has also explained the practice of Surat Shabd Yoga, ***by moment gather thy soul and hold it at the Eye Center. Cleanse thou the mirror of thy mind and catch the Divine Melody with thy soul; if thy longing is keen, thou shalt pierce the veil and attain the quintessence. Indeed, O Tulsi, thou shalt then behold the radiant dust of the lotus feet of thy Master.***[11]

How can one sit so still, repeat only holy name and think of God constantly? The answer is only by falling in love. So the secret of *Surat Shabd Yoga and of mysticism is not necessarily practice and more practice, but love.* **To be so devoted to one's Lord that nothing can stand in the way.....this and nothing else is the truth of Sant Mat.** As Rumi says, "*Only from the Heart, Can you reach the sky. The rose of Glory, Can only be raised in the Heart.*"

Help Rendered By Sant Satguru in Radhasoami Faith

Benefits of Contemplation of the Form of Sant Satguru

Radhasoami Faith has prescribed contemplation of the form of the Sant Satguru for spiritual practices. Param Guru, Maharaj Sahab brings out, "Unless the form of the adept of the purely spiritual or the 1st division of creation be contemplated, a development of the spirit force detached from the association of the universal mind will not be possible. Contemplation with affection of a Param Sant, evokes spiritualism of his face and features into the devotee. Saints have access to all the subtle planes of the various spheres they have traversed and gained access to. They accordingly become cognizant of the contemplation of their forms, as soon as the devotional practice of *dhyan* is performed and accord necessary help to the devotee. This assistance is always accorded in an imperceptible form during *'Dhyan'* (practice of contemplation). But a devotee with some experience recongnises that help in the spiritual concentration produced at the spirit center by such help. To strengthen faith and to simulate fresh impulse an adept however allows devotees at times to get glimpses of His Astral form."[12]

Benefits from Sant Satguru's Darshan

The most important thing to look for in Radhasoami faith is Sant Satguru's benign and merciful *drishti* and His *darshan*. Once a person comes before the Sant Satguru his salvation is just a matter of time. ***"Khed mite Guru daras se, Aur na koi upaye,"***[13] Sant Satguru's *darshan* helps to eradicate the bad karmas of many births, making a *jiva* suitable for the performance of *Surat Shabd Yoga*, which puts him on the road to salvation. The Sant Satguru of

---

[10] Discourses, p.17

[11] Tulsi Sahib, *Shabdavali*, Pt. I, Kakahra 7, p. 25

[12] Discourses, pp.43-44

[13] Sar Bachan, p.637

Radhasoami faith is Omnipotent, Omniscient and Omnipresent. He should not be considered a human,***"Guru ko maanush mat kaho, maanush unki deh, Antar ke jab pat khulen, darsein purush videh"***[14]

Benefits of the Influence of Sant Satguru

The mind has a tendency to flow outwards. The purpose for which saints take birth is to free *Jivas* from the entanglements of *Manas* and *Maya* and to lead them towards union with *Parmatman.* The method is to seek shelter in the feet of one's *Satguru* and to attach one's mind to the Name or Word as taught by the *Satguru.* The Spiritual Name resides within the *Satguru* at all times. Therefore, He is able to divert the mind and attention of His devotees and enjoin it with the Name. When the devotee moves on the path taught by the *Guru*, he attains the state of meditation easily and is freed from the desires of the world.

Radhasoami faith is a practical religion. It is not confined to just reading the scriptures and instructions of the leaders as is done in other religions. Aim of Radhasoami faith is the realization of the True Supreme Being while living and access to His august presence. For this internal practices have to be performed daily which ultimately result in control of one's mind and body and which also help in awakening a jiva's spiritual faculties thereby making him fit enough for union with the Supreme Being.***"Dil Ka Hujra Saaf kar, Jaana ke aane ke liye, Dhyan gairon ka utha, uske bithane ke liye"***[15] Devotion and love for Satguru is the only way to perform these spiritual practices successfully. Hence the importance attached to Satguru Bhakti in Radhasoami faith.

As the Satguru in Radhasoami faith has complete control over His sense organs and His heart is always full with love of Supreme Being, the seeker, by living in His company and by imbibing His influence begins to have an intense desire to keep his mind and sense organs in control, to direct his attention towards the Supreme Being and to awaken love and devotion towards Him. Gradually the devotee ceases to attach any importance to worldly supports and help and begins to rely only on the help and grace of Supreme Being, like his Satguru. Under the loving care of Satguru the *rajoguni*[16] and *tamoguni*[17] tendencies of his nature gradually disappear and he develops the *satoguni*[18] tendencies of his Master and Teacher. Each day as love for Satguru increases in his heart the form of Satguru remains ever-present in his heart and he is able to perform the spiritual practices of *Sumiran* and *Dhyan*, quite successfully.

Practical Help Rendered by Sant Satguru During Meditaton

The meditation practice of the Sant tradition is a combination of Bhakti (love

---

[14] Prem Bilas, p.198

[15] Tulsi Sahib, Sant Bani, quoted in *Tulsi Sahib-Jeevan Updesh aur Vani*, Radhasoami Satsang, Beas, Amritsar,1993 p. 44

[16] Attributes which originate from or lead to the qualities or mood of *rajogun* - energy and activity or passion mood.

[17] Attributes which originate from or lead to qualities or mood of *tamogun* - darkness mood.

[18] Goodness mood or mood of righteousness.

and devotion) called *Surat Shabda Yoga* -- inner Light and Sound Meditation working with the Third Eye Center, the Seat of the Soul.

However, the condition of the devotee at the *sixth chakra*, in the beginning is like that of the newborn child. It is not possible for his mind and spirit to remain concentrated at that center for sufficient time. The mind and spirit current keep dropping down towards lower centers again and again and the devotee is in a state of perpetual struggle. The Sant Satguru comes to the devotee's aid in such moments of weaknesses and increases his spirituality by occasionally projecting His own spiritual current towards the devotee and focusing it at the seat of the devotee's spirit. Huzur Sahabji Maharaj says that then, "as a miniature of the real sun shining in the sky comes into existence on the ground below, when a ray of the sun is focused through a convex lens, in the same manner, the Spiritual Form of the Sant Satguru manifests itself internally in smaller size at the seat of the devotee's spirit, when the spiritual current of the Satguru is focused at that centre."[19] With this manifestation of Satguru within the devotee, his mind and spirit are completely withdrawn to his *sixth chakra* and tend to move to higher regions, always receiving help from the Satguru in his inward journey.

When there is sufficient increase in the spirituality of a devotee at any particular internal centre, his spirit attains the state of complete wakefulness at that centre and with the help of the internal *Shabd*, gradually the devotee attains the highest stage of spiritual development and finally becomes one with the True Supreme Being.[20]

Professor Prem Saran Satsangi Sahab, present Sant Satguru of RadhaSoami faith at Dayalbagh, while explaining the various levels of consciousness and their accompanying sounds, made an open offer to the entire humanity, ***"So, I offer you as proof, experiencing of these higher spiritual regions (through meditation) and seeing the scientific basis from which the whole creation has evolved."*** [21]

Benefits of Sant Satguru's Satsang

The personal spiritual influence Sant Satguru is immense and it becomes especially manifest when he is conducting divine service for spiritual training which in Radhasoami Faith is Satsang. It is a training class for practical spiritual instructions and for devotional practice.[22] During *Satsang* the presence of the Sant Satguru dispels a devotee's ignorance to a great extent and the sacred and serene rays emanating from His purely spiritual form helps the devotee in the *Satsang* to realize his shortcomings and also feel remorse for them. Those who perform spiritual practices regularly are virtually held by hand and are guided by Sant Satguru in their inward journey during *Satsang*, and they also at times

---

[19] Yathartha Prakasa, p.12

[20] Ibid, p.13

[21] Prem Saran Satsangi Sahab (2004) *Supplement to Discourses On Radhasoami Faith*, Dayalbagh, Agra: Radhasoami Satsang Sabha, p.12

[22] Discourses, p. 63

experience exquisite emotional ecstasies within themselves. The entire holy service of Satsang is one of engrossing rapture for the devotee. As Kabir Sahab has said, ***"Moorakh jan koi maram na jaane, Satsang mein amrit barse"***[23]

Help by Sant Satguru at the Time of Death [24]

One does not realize the importance of Sant Satguru during his lifetime. However, as Sahabji Maharaj says that when at the time of death Sant Satguru appears in all His glory and magnificence, and helps a *jiva* to tide over this most difficult time, then only one realizes Satguru's true worth. Even if a devotee does not remember Him, the Sant Satguru, fulfilling His commitment of protecting the *jiva* and of keeping his *laaj* (honour), appears at the last moment and takes His *jiva* away. A devotee of Sant Satguru in Radhasoami faith is promised,

- Salvation in maximum of four *janams*.
- Of getting human form only, after every birth, so that one can perform bhakti of Sant Satguru and work for his redemption.
- Freedom from the agents of *Kaal*. They *will* come at the time of death but will keep standing afar. Even during lifetime, *Kaal Purush* can accord punishment to a satsangi only after taking permission from the Sant Satguru.

Every second, every moment of his life a devotee receives Sant Satguru's grace and mercy and keeps getting astonished as to why, he, a virtual bagful of vices is so blessed and keeps thanking the Almighty for his good luck and fortune. As Sahabji Maharaj writes, ***'Saat sindh jo massi Karen, lekhan bankat payen, Raain diwas lekhak banein, gun augun likhe naa jaaein'.***[25]

References

Brunton, P. (1970). *The Inner Reality*. London, UK: Rider.

Maharaj Sahab [Pandit Brahm Sankar Misra Sahab] (2004) *Discourses on Radhasoami Faith, with Supplement*. Agra, India: Radhasoami Satsang Sabha, Dayalbagh.

Maharaj Sahab [Pandit Brahm Sankar Misra Sahab], Sarkar Sahab [Kamta Prasad Sinha Sahab] and Sahabji Maharaj [Sir Anand Sarup Kt.] (2003). *Maharaj Sahab, Sarkar Sahab and Sahabji Maharaj Ke Bachan* Part-II. Agra, India: Radhasoami Satsang Sabha, Dayalbagh.

Param Purush Puran Dhani Huzur Soamiji Maharaj [Shiv Dayal Singh Sahab] (1993). *Sar Bachan*. Agra, India: Radhasoami Satsang Sabha, Dayalbagh.

Sahabji Maharaj [Sir Anand Sarup Kt.] (1957). *Yathartha Prakash*. Agra, India: Radhasoami Satsang Sabha, Dayalbagh.

Sahabji Maharaj [Sir Anand Sarup Kt.] (1997). *Prem Bilas*. Agra, India: Radhasoami Satsang Sabha, Dayalbagh.

Sahabji Maharaj [Sir Anand Sarup Kt.] (2003). *Param Guru Sahabji Maharaj Ke Bachan*. Agra, India: Radhasoami Satsang Sabha, Dayalbagh.

---

[23] ibid, p.65

[24] *Param Guru Sahabji Maharaj ke Bachan,* (2003) Dayalbagh, Agra: Radhasoami Satsang Sabha, 136, 137,172

[25] Prem Bilas (1997), p.189

Satsangi P.S. [Revered Prof. Prem Saran Satsangi] (2004). *Supplement to Discourses on Radhasoami Faith*. Agra, India: Radhasoami Satsang Sabha, Dayalbagh.

Satsangi, P.S. [Revered Prof. Prem Saran Satsangi] (2006). Autobiographical Retrospectives. *International Journal of General Systems*. Taylor and Francis.

Searle, J. (1995). *The Oxford Companion to Philosophy*. London, UK: Oxford University Press.

Tulsi Sahib. (1993). Sant Bani, quoted in Tulsi Sahib - *Jeevan Updesh aur Vani* p. 44. Beas, India: Radhasoami Satsang, Beas.

Chapter 52

Emergence of Higher Levels of Consciousness

ASHARANI NARANG
Dayalbagh, Agra, India

Abstract

The object of man's life is the attainment of Lord's Abode and this is to be achieved by elevating the spirit from its seat in the human body with the aid of the spiritual current which is perceived as sound internally to the region of pure spirit which alone is the region of perfect emancipation and salvation. The secret of devotional practises can be learnt either under direct instructions from the Sant Satguru who is the communion with the Supreme Being or under His orders.The devotional practises are as follows:1) Repetition of the Holy Name at the seat of the spirit in the human body.2) Contemplation of the Holy Form of the Sant Satguru at the seat of the Spirit.3) Sound practice which consists of concentrating attention at the seat of the spirit and establishing contact with the current of Shabda i.e. The Spirit force which is self existent, intelligent, blissful and refulgent.This faith gives us knowledge about science of transcendental, ultra transcendental consciousness far beyond the reach of science. But its foundation is scientific. The method of Surat Shabda Yoga i.e. the method of uniting the spirit current with the sound current is the most powerful and beyond the reach of modern science.

Emergence of Higher Levels of Consciousness

The object of man's life is the attainment of Lord's Abode and this is to be achieved by elevating the spirit from its seat in the human body with the aid of the spiritual current which is perceived as sound internally to the region of pure spirit which alone is the region of perfect emancipation and salvation. The secret of devotional practises can be learnt either under direct instructions from the Sant Satguru who is in communion with the Supreme Being or under His orders.

The devotional practises taught are given below:

Repetition of the Holy name at the seat of the spirit in the human body.

Contemplation of the Holy Form of the Sant Satguru at the seat of the Spirit.

Sound practise which consists in concentrating attention at the seat of the spirit and establishing contact with the current of Shabda i.e. The Spirit force which is self existent, intelligent, blissful and refulgent.

This faith gives us knowledge about science of transcendental and ultra transcendental consciousness far beyond the reach of science. But its foundation is scientific. The method of Surat Shabda Yoga i.e. the method of uniting the spirit current with the sound current is the most powerful and beyond the reach of modern science. However for realizing experimental knowledge through scientific methods, the Surat Shabda Yoga is the only means.

It is said that realizing one's own Atman is a kind of attaining salvation. Radhasoami Faith says that in this way Atman gets purified. Considering that Atman is presently in the deep-rooted bonds of Kaal and Maya , the Surat Shabda Yoga, that is the practise of uniting the spirit current with sound current, is the only means for releasing the Atman from such bonds. There is no other way.

The Surat Shabda Yoga is the firm bed rock on which the strong foundation of Radhasoami Faith rests. Satsang and Seva too are inseparable parts of Radhasoami Faith.

The Saints have divided the entire creation into three divisions:

(i) Nirmal Chetan Desa i.e. the Region of the Merciful, where there is no trace of Maya and where the entire creation is spiritual i.e. of Chaitanya Spirit.

(ii) Pure Chaitanya and pure Maya Desa, where Maya manifested itself and the creation of Bramhanda, i.e. the manifestation of Brahma.

(iii) Pure Chaitanya and gross Maya Desa, where the creation consists of Gods,human beings and living organisms of four classes.

The creation of forms which exist in the second and third divisions would be destroyed sooner or later and therefore these two divisions are not fit for the stay of a devotee who seeks true salvation because stay in these divisions, either by merging with the Form of the Deity or with the Formless Deity of any religion, cannot last forever. In other words after sometime the spirit will have to rise and be reborn assuming some body and undergo pain and pleasures pertaining to that body. This is why Merciful Radhasoami and all the Saints have stated that as long as the spirit does not reach the Nirmal Chetan Desa i.e. the Region of Sat Purusha Radhasoami, it cannot achieve true salvation i.e. the cycle of birth and death would continue.

In the Religion of Saints, Mukti or salvation signifies becoming one with the Lord. There is some custom or other in every nation of the world that in order to express one's affection and love for another person; they touch each other's bodies with some part of their bodies. For example, some people shake hands, some people rub each other's noses, some people touch each other's lips and so on. In fact, by means of these practises the jivatmas of these people try to come into contact with each other through some part of their bodies, but the coarse part of the body becomes an obstruction and the contact thus established between these persons is purely temporary and superficial. One can understand from this that if the covers of body and mind are removed from over a particular spirit and that spirit reaches the August Presence of the Supreme Lord, the condition would be that on a one side a drop of spirit, full of love, moves towards the Supreme Lord, and on the other side, the infinite ocean of spiritual energy, in which waves of love rise again and again, turns His attention towards the loving spirit. In these circumstances, what else can happen except that the spirit would try to get merged and get lost in the Supreme Lord and the Supreme Lord would try to absorb the spirit and ultimately the spirit would become one with the Supreme Lord. When the object of the Radhasoami Faith is the attainment of such Mukti or salvation, it becomes the duty of all of us that we should try to firmly take the steps which have been prescribed for the attainment of this invaluable wealth and we should try to become one i.e. harmonize with our Satguru. How can the person who does not possess the ability to become one with the Personality which has become one with the Supreme Lord, become one with the Supreme Lord? It is evident that this ability can be acquired by changing our ways and by engaging in devotion.

Saints often explain to us that the relationship of the Saints with the Lord is like that of waves with the ocean. A wave rises from the ocean and again merges back into the ocean. Similarly if you throw anything to the waves, the waves will take it to the bottom of the sea and it remains merged with the waves at the bottom of the sea. How can it return to the waves of the ocean ? The Masters instruct us in Spiritual Practice by which we can merge into the waves of the ocean. They are already merged into the Lord so we also become a part of the Lord. Jesus said "The father is in me and I am in the Father". So when we become 'He' the Saint who has already merged into the Father, we also become the Father. It is just through this channel that we can cross the domain of Kaal, but as long as we remain in his domain we cannot get release from birth and death. Real love and devotion for the Lord through His Saints and the waves of His ocean alone can take us back to the Lord.

It was stated that if the covers of the body and the mind are removed from over the spirit of a man, the result would be that the spirit, on getting release from all physical and mental suffering and from the effects of gross and subtle forces of nature and from all kinds of restraints put upon it by the body and the mind, would manifest itself in its pure spiritual form and would freely behave in its own real attributes which are self-existence, all-intelligent, bliss and light and if this spirit may establish contact with the Supreme Lord who is the Reservoir of Spirituality, its condition would be like that of the drop of water which, after separation from earth, reaches the ocean.

When by the grace of a true master we are brought into the magnetic field of the word or logos, it pulls us towards itself and draws us upwards to the Lord. With the help of its sound we must find the direction of our true name.

It is this true Word or Name that is essential in attaining liberation and it is found within the body. Unless we search for it within ourselves, join ourselves to it and completely merge in it, we can never obtain salvation.

Guru Adhar Das says:

It is the true Shabd
That brings true honour
In the court of the Lord;
Without devotion to Nam
No one can gain salvation.

Guru Adhar Das says:

They who know not shabd
Are blind and deaf;

Why did they came at all
Into this world?
Without Shabd
There is utter darkness within
One neither finds the precious thing
Nor escapes from the rounds
Of birth and death.

Christ says in the Bible, "*If ye continue in my word, then are ye my disciples indeed and ye shall know the truth and the truth shall make you free.*"

Kabir Sahib says:

Just as a stock of hay
Is reduced to ashes by a single spark
So are all sins consumed
The moment Nam enters the heart

Soamiji Maharaj says:

"*Shabd destroys the accumulated karmas. Shabd merges one in the ocean of Shabd.*
Earn, O friend, with earnest effort
The boundless wealth of Shabd;
Through Shabd achieve a victory over kal.
See the abode of Shabd within;
Through Shabd itself, behold the Beloved.
Shabd will erase the impressions of karmas,
And Shabd will enable you
To merge with Shabd.
Without Shabd, all knowledge is false;
Without Shabd, all contemplation is hollow.
O ignorant man, do not let go of Shabd;
So declares Radhasoami, the Lord.

Guru Adhar Das says:

"*The seeker once attached to the Guru Shabd, is never parted from it. He effortlessly merges with Truth.*"

Christ says in the bible, "*He that hearth my word – hath everlasting life and is passed from death into life.*" "*Blessed are they that hear the word of God, and keep it.*"

Guru Nanak says that "*the Truth is above all; its practice is superior to all other practices.*" The spiritual value of Nam-bhakti, devotion to the Word, far exceeds that of any other religious practice.

When the Lord bestows His Grace, He does so through the Saints. Actually, He Himself comes in the form of a human being and awakens in us love for the Lord. By devotion to the Name He merges us in Him.

Guru Amar Das says:

By His grace we find a true Guru,
Who teaches us the practice
Of attaining the soul to the Shabd.

Christ says in the Bible, "*Ye have not chosen me, but I have chosen you and ordained you that ye should go and bring forth fruit.*"

It is only in the human body that God can be realized. If, therefore, we train ourselves, with the help of a true Adept, to withdraw the currents of mind and soul from the nine apertures of the body and focus them at the eye centre, we can contact 'Nam' which can result in perfect peace and bliss, both here and in the higher realms. We are then like an accomplished bride who is honoured for her attainments, both in her own house and that of her parents-in-law. Knowing that this world is full of pain and grief where not even kings are happy, it is only proper that we turn to the region of 'Nam'. "Nam is the antidote for all ills, and all sins doth it wash away." If we want real peace we must search for it within ourselves. Unless we merge in that light, unless we become a part of that light about which Christ said, "If thine eye be single thy whole body shall be full of light." Unless we see that light within us, unless we merge into that light we can never get peace.

Kabir says that God can be met only after death is raising all false hope. If one has met the Lord in one's lifetime he would meet Him again after death otherwise he will be consigned to the region of Yama. In other words, if one has not met the Supreme Lord in his lifetime, he will not meet Him afterwards. One should meet the Supreme Lord in his lifetime.

Death overtakes all. Blessed are those who die daily while living, that is to say, they have learnt to vacate the body during their lifetime through Surat Shabda Yoga and to contact the Master 'within'. Such souls are the happiest brides, for they have realized their Lord in this very life and have thus consummated their union. "True Wisdom hath he in whom Nam abideth and who has been united to Nam. Never again is he separated from it and in his True Home doth he find abode."

We must seek Him, who alone is permanent and unchangeable. This Supreme Creator, the Final Cause, One without a second, is Nam, Shabd or 'Sach' (Truth). He is also called the Heavenly sound. He cannot be comprehended with intellect, for intellect is limited and He is limitless. He is beyond the reach of mind and reasoning, which actually bar spiritual progress by raising senseless doubts and misgivings. The poor and the lowly, who have simplicity and innocence, advance on the Path distinctly faster. No man ever achieved spiritual progress by a process of logic. "Neither by contemplation nor by intellectual discourse, can we realize Him." The only way to do so is to seek a true Master and follow his instructions implicitly. Once we contact Nam, we leave the phenomenal world with its pain and sorrow behind and enter into the world of Bliss. There is no substitute whatever for Nam. All other methods – recitals, penances, pilgrimages – are utterly futile. They keep us confined to the domain of duality and illusion and its eternal wheel. "In Kalyuga, Nam alone doth sustain. Save Nam all else is false and vain."

Formerly, it was as though the owner of the house (our body) was asleep and the house was at the mercy of five thieves - lust, anger, greed, attachment and ego or pride (ahankar). Now that the owner has woken up, the thieves have run away. Huzur Baba Sawan Singh Maharaj Ji used to say "when a soul 'wakes up', the five thieves go out and inform the owner of the house that the place is now too hot for them to survive there and they have to leave." Kabir also said to annihilate the five perversions and be attached to Nam. So long as the five enemies have control of the house, the soul is a helpless prisoner. They leave it only when the owner means business and will tolerate their presence no longer. The Elixir of Shabd, which is the life-giving Nectar for the soul, acts as a poison for these thieves. They run away and the corresponding virtues take their place. Thus lust goes and its place is taken up by continence, anger is replaced by forgiveness, with avarice comes contentment, and egotism and pride are replaced by discrimination and humility. The mind, which hankered after trifles and whose desire to possess knew no bounds, becomes still and contended. The soul, becoming free from all entanglements, heads towards its real home. Holding on to the Melody of Nam, by the Grace of the Master, it completes the journey of months in a matter of days. The sense world now appears as an alien country and the regions inside as its native land.

Guru Amar Das says:

Without Nam
There is no admittance
To the Lord's Court;
You will be harassed
By the messengers of death.

In no uncertain words
The Master urges you, O brother,
To attach yourself to the unstruck melody,
For there is no way other than that of Shabd;
Without the Shabd there is no liberation
From the vessel of the body.

It is also stated that just as there is movement in the atmosphere when we move our hand and a sound is produced from the air which is present on all sides as a cover over the hand, this sound is quite different from the sound produced by the movement of our mind (the movement which caused are hands to move), similarly the Shabda which emanated on the first manifestation of the Supreme Energy of the True Supreme Being, is different from the Shabdas emanating from the covers over that Supreme Energy. If the Shabda produced from the Supreme Energy is likened to the sound produced by the movement of the mind, then the other Shabdas i.e. Niranjan, Om, Sohan etc would be likened with the sound produced by the movement of the hand in the air, because the matter of the regions from where these Shabdas manifested is functioning as the cover over the prime spirit current in the same manner as the air surrounding the hand acts as a cover for our hand.

The true Satguru acts like a magnet. The magnet first of all arranges the iron filings that enter its magnetic field and then it draws the iron filings to itself. As the iron filings come nearer and nearer the magnet, they come more and more under the influence of the magnet so that they finally come into contact with the magnet and are magnetized i.e. both the iron filings and the magnet become one. Similarly, the Satguru, with the current of His spirituality gives our jivataman light and corrects the tendency of our spirit. Under the influence of His spiritual currents, our spirit is drawn towards Him and when it comes into contact with Him now and then, new spirituality is awakened within us. The day our spirit is fully harmonized with His spirit, permanent contact of our spirit with the current on which the spirit of the Satguru came down to this earth and with whose support it is staying here would be established and as that current is inclined to move towards the Supreme Lord, the inclination of our spirit too would move towards the Supreme Lord and when that current would become one with the Supreme Lord, our spirit shall also become one with the Supreme Lord.

Just as one has to use one's eyes in order to have darshan of the sun, similarly in order to have Darshan of the Supreme Lord, one has to awaken the internal eye which is located within man's body. It is with the help of this eye that the Darshan of the Supreme Lord can be obtained. According to the teachings of the Radhasoami Faith however, it is as much possible for a man to perceive God as it is possible for a man with eyes to perceive the Sun, but we must first learn the location of the eye with which God can be perceived and to awaken it and then permit the Divine rays permeating the universe to impinge on it. People do talk of the sixth sense, the divya chakshu or the divine eye, but few indeed care to appreciate and put to use this one of greatest gifts of Providence. The downward tendencies and outward propensities of the mind are so strong in man that, to many, it appears an impossible task to undergo even the preliminary training that is necessary to check its enormous drain on their spirituality in order to render them "spiritual enough" for proceeding with the experiment. Ordinary spiritual currents flowing in our bodies when focused internally by the practise of spiritual exercises, becomes tremendously powerful like the diffused rays of the sun passing through a convex glass. When a devotee is able to focus his attention at the proper centre sufficiently well, he begins to feel that a new faculty of perception is developing within him. The internal experiences that he obtains subsequently through this new faculty strengthen his faith in the success of the experiment and spur him on to proceed to the next higher spiritual centre or *chakra*. Each new *chakra*, on becoming kinetic evolves within him and a new consciousness, altogether different from what he experienced at the previous centre, and he realizes that a higher and more spiritual personality is awakened at each new stage. Ultimately, the stage is reached when the *chakra* or centre with which God-perception is possible, becomes kinetic.

In merging with the Supreme Being, our consciousness is separate. You are separate. You are not conscious of your consciousness. You just merge. Even in worldly love, you are so absorbed in the beloved that you do not even think about where you are or what you are. The spiritual merging is much more fascinating, absorbing, it is much more sublime and nobler. The bliss of merging into the Supreme Being cannot be expressed in mortal language. There is no thought of individuality, consciousness or anything else. It is all love, all bliss, for in merging we become the Supreme Being and He is All, He is everything.

The Lord is one. When we merge back into him we become the Lord. We become a part of Him. A drop of water has its own identity when it is in the mud. When it leaves the ground by means of evaporation, it still has its own identity separate from the ground and separate from the cloud. But when it merges back into the cloud, it becomes the cloud. That minute part of the cloud becomes the cloud by merging into it. When we love the Lord we do not like to remain away from the Beloved. We lose our identity when merged and yet retain our identity when separated. For example if you merge the flame of a lighted candle into the flame of a fire, can you differentiate whether it is the flame of a fire or the flame of the candle? When you take the candle away from the fire, you have an independent individual flame, but when you take it back into the fire, it merges into the fire and is no longer a mere candle light. Similarly the soul merges into the Lord.

With the Lord's Grace we obtain the company of Saints. With their Grace we learn the secret of uniting our soul with the sound current, the Word or the Name. Once the mind becomes fond of listening to this 'Voice of God', it turns away forever from the world and all worldly objects. The sweetness of this inner spiritual melody makes everything else seem tasteless or bitter. Compared with its enchantment, everything else seems dull and uninteresting. The possession of diamonds naturally causes one to lose interest in coloured shells. In the same way, the sweetness of the inner melody makes this world lose its attraction and turns the mind towards God. One's love for the world comes to an end and love for God takes its place.

Guru Amar Das says:

Whatever is, is by His will;
By His will we find the Guru
Who fills our mind with love for Shabd.

It is important to note here that, by spirit, we do not mean "the conscious self" or the "I" in us. The conscious self in ordinary humanity is the mind which, like the physical body receives life and vitality from the spirit. The spirit is the life giving and vitalizing principle in man. It is the creator and sustainer of the universe. Although permeating the whole creation and every particle of our body and every quarter of our mind, it is yet so subtle that it is beyond the reach of the mind and senses. It is for this reason that the delicate and powerful instruments, invented by science, become futile in the quest of the ultimate truth. The realization of the spirit is a condition or state of consciousness of the highest and purest order. The spiritual consciousness is independent of every kind of external stimulus. To attain it, all the activities of the physical senses and the mind have to be brought to a stand-still. Otherwise, it is not possible to shut off the influence of external stimuli. In other words, the road to the ultimate truth lies inwards and not outwards, and man stands in need of being put on this road and helped and guided till he reaches the goal i.e. realizes the spirit – the ultimate Truth.

In addition to the different centres localized by the scientist, there are a number of other centres situated in the fissure between the two lobes of the brain. It is on the excitation of one or other of these centres that the gifted ones obtain flashes of intuitions and peeps into the mysteries of the spiritual planes. Among these centres, there is one known in the language of the adepts as the Dasam-Dwara (the tenth door), which, if energized, produces spiritual consciousness and opens the way to the Mansion of the Supreme Spirit. The road leading from the state of the dream state to deep slumber and so on to the states of trance, ecstasy, death etc on which men move to and fro all their lives without any conscious effort on their parts, is thus the road which leads to the portal of spiritual consciousness and to the Mansion of the Supreme Spirit. This is the road on which the seeker after Truth must be put and helped and guided till he reaches the goal, i.e. realizes the spirit – the ultimate Truth.

In the state of Moksha there is the Supreme Being and there is also the individual spirit entity. The knowledge obtained there by the spirit entity will be a state of consciousness experienced by the entire spiritual constitution and it cannot be described by a term like feelings. It is not easy to form even an idea of what spiritual consciousness is. On the highest spiritual plane there is on the one hand the Supreme Being – an infinite ocean of spiritual energy in a kinetic state sending infinite spiritual currents. On the other hand is your Atman, a drop from the ocean of spiritual energy. Infinite spiritual currents from the Supreme Being impinge on the atman, producing in the latter a condition of tremor, in consequence of which the individual spirit begins to vibrate in unison with the most powerful currents which beat on it from all possible directions. It is in fact inconceivable that the individual spirit which is an emanation from the Supreme Being should not become one with the Latter, when like a novice it enters the mansion of the Highest. Throw anything into salt, and after a time it will be converted into salt. When a piece of wood is thrown into burning fire, water is first evaporated from it and then it becomes a burning fire itself. It is in this wise that the atman begins to vibrate with the Supreme Being.

We may also take into consideration the experience of the state of ecstasy. In this state, in the words of St. Theresa, "while the soul is asleep as regards earthly things, it is awake to the things of heaven." "It is true," she says, "that if anyone asks me how is it that, while our faculties and senses are as much suspended (in their operation) as if they were dead, we are able to hear and understand anything. I can only answer that this is a secret which God has reserved, with many another, to Himself." "The understanding," she adds, "stays its discursive operations, but the will remains fixed in God by love; it rules as a sovereign."

When the devoted Satsangi, after crossing the second division, proceed further, his spiritual form would also became subtle and more subtle and spiritual and his contact with the forms of the first division which are really more formless than the formless beings of the second division would be established by means of this spiritual form of his. Thus according to the Radhasoami religion love and devotion would continue up to the region of the Merciful Lord i.e. up to the first division and this worship and devotion is known as Bhed

Bhakti i.e. devotion with a difference and the relationship of the master and the servant would continue throughout. When the devotee would come into contact with the original abode i.e. meet the real Formless Being, his devotion would be Abheda Bhakti. i.e devotion without any difference and the loving devotee on reaching there would develop such power that whenever he so likes, he could become one with the Formless Being and whenever he likes he could separate himself from Him and have the pleasure of His Darshana. Such is the high status that can be attained by a loving devotee of the Radhasoami Faith. This power was never attained by any devotee of any other religion in the lower region where they merged in the formless being nor can it be attained by them as long as they do not perform the practices after learning the method of practices of Merciful Radhasoami.

The form that the spirit energy takes when it is in commotion and when it ensues forth as current is the Nij Shabda or the Supreme Name. The object of the Radhasoami Faith or its teachings is to help man establish contact or connection with this Shabda. In order that contact with this Shabda is established one needs to have the required degree of purity and subtlety. When contact of any spirit is established with the Prime Shabda, the spirit under its influence would get freedom from the bonds of the body and the mind and get into touch with the source of that Shabda, i.e. with the Region from which the Shabda originally emanated because this Shabda is most attractive. If this Prime Shabda is pronounced in human language, the Shabda representing the current will be 'Radha' and the Shabda representing the commotion would be 'Soami.' This is the reason why 'Radhasoami' is said to be the real name of the True Supreme Being.

The Abode of the Soami i.e the Supreme Being is very wonderful and only Radha i.e. the Prime Spirit current has access to it and that current alone can see it and nobody else can reach there. The beauty of that region is beyond comprehension and is infinite and indescribable and there the Radhasoami name is present in an un-manifest form i.e. the sound of the Radhasoami name resounds there in an extremely subtle form. Nobody can get admission into that Region without the Grace of Supreme Lord.

It is absolutely impossible to express one's gratitude to the Supreme Being, Merciful Radhasoami for the easy method of salvation that He has in his Great mercy, revealed to the Jivas in the present times, and which can be followed without renouncing ones family or profession. This method of Surat Shabd Yoga is so very effective that if one follows it a bit carefully the world and its pleasures can exert little influence on him. On the contrary he would get purified day by day and attain the Original Abode one day while at the same time, he would enjoy the world with greater relish and delight than worldly people do and the poisonous effect of that enjoyment shall not touch him.

References

Ayyar, A.S.P. (1949). *Layman's Bhagavad Gita*. Mumbai, India: Bhartiya Vidya Bhawan.

Huzur Maharaj [Rai Bahadur Salig Ram Sahab] (1958). *Prem Patra*. Agra, India: Radhasoami Satsang Sabha, Dayalbagh.

Huzur Maharaj [Rai Bahadur Salig Ram Sahab] (2009). *Prashnottar*. Agra, India: Radhasoami

Satsang Sabha, Dayalbagh.

Maharaj Charan Singh. *The Master Answers*. Punjab, India: Radhasoami Satsang, Beas.

Maharaj Charan Singh. *The Path*. Punjab, India: Radhasoami Satsang, Beas.

Maharaj Sahab [Pandit Brahm Sankar Misra Sahab] (2009). *Discourses on Radhasoami Faith*. Agra, India: Radhasoami Satsang Sabha, Dayalbagh.

Mehtaji Maharaj [Gurcharan Das Mehta Sahab] *Selected Bachans of Param Guru Huzur Mehtaji Maharaj*. Agra, India: Radhasoami Satsang Sabha, Dayalbagh.

Pandit Ram Sharan. *Sant Tulsidas*.

Sahabji Maharaj [Sir Anand Sarup Kt.] (2006). *Writings and Speeches of Param Guru Huzur Sahabji Maharaj*. Agra, India: Radhasoami Satsang Sabha, Dayalbagh.

Sahabji Maharaj [Sir Anand Sarup Kt.] (2009). *Diary of Sahabji Maharaj Part I,II & III*. Agra, India: Radhasoami Satsang Sabha, Dayalbagh.

Sardar Bahadur Maharaj Jagat Singh. *The Science of the Soul*. Beas, India: Radhasoami Satsang.

Sarkar Sahab [Kamta Prasad Sinha Sahab] *Selected Bachans*. Agra, India: Radhasoami Satsang Sabha, Dayalbagh.

Souvenir. (2011). Agra, India: Radhasoami Satsang Sabha, Dayalbagh.

Chapter 53

Means to Attain Higher Levels of Consciousness

SHRADDHA PRASAD
Dayalbagh Educational Institute (Deemed University), Agra, India

Abstract

Consciousness is an intense positive energy capable of orchestrating a sea change in one's life. Higher levels of consciousness hold the key to true happiness. This paper examines the path and method to attain these higher levels. The devices required are the body, mind and soul. Man is innately a spiritual being so the harmony in his life cannot be fulfilled by material gains; he needs to reunite with his true inner self.

Introduction

Religion brings about spirituality with an inherent flame of consciousness that brings Unity with the Lord. Religion is a conviction with a set of tenets to follow with discipline, knowledge, honesty and in earnest. Consciousness, which is a part of higher form of religiousness, is a simple topic; however man has made it complex with the use of technical jargons and empirical calculations. Consciousness is an intense positive energy that encircles man and when activated leads to clairaudience that is intuitive, clairvoyance that is visionary, and clairsentience that is prophetic. It results from touch, sound, light, vision to emancipation. The language of consciousness is speechless, warm, helpful, achievable and real. Ironically men from all walks of life with varied professions have tried to decode consciousness in their very own way, like the philosophers state it as an experience, scientists with space and time, medical professionals with alertness and responsiveness, psychologists with subjectivity, change, continuity and selectivity, and religion with the highest form of knowledge, god-knowing and an unknown state of ecstasy leading to humbleness, tranquility and equanimity. It shows how vast is its offering that is not only true, but comprehendible and doable. Man just needs to gauge the obvious with the proper instruments present within him and then get enthralled in the reservoir of Supreme Force. Consciousness is the ability to perceive a relationship between oneself and his environment, which is possible only through the expression of love. Those with elevated levels of consciousness exhibit only love as Consciousness is Love Personified and perceives the warmth of this hidden flame within him.

Devices needed to activate consciousness are body, mind and soul. Body being the vehicle, mind the motor and soul is the driver. And the essential tools to catapult man are, religion as the ignition, spiritualism the fuel, consciousness thus activated acts as the accelerator that decelerates when mind intervenes, intuition as the GPS instrument, cruise control as the transcendent ideas and final destination is Unity with the Source or redemption. Man is aware that all problems are caused by the mind and desires arising from it. He also knows that it is not easy to control the mind and keep it effectively away from desire. He realizes when consciousness is inactive then the mind overpowers and becomes the master controller entrapping spirituality and giving the owner the liberty to decide the next course of action. The dawn of consciousness is possible only when man realizes his worth and develops a desirable way of thinking and living and by not letting his mind yield to unwarranted subjects. He needs to control his mind when in some sort of fear, pain, excitement or anxiety, a state of emotional distress that overpowers his distinguishing persona. This fearful state takes man away from reality and even under slightest provocation, subjects his demeanour to anger, or being tearful, haughty and rude. It is opposite to the state of being bright and cheerful, which even under the gravest of provocations will remain calm, pleasant, and soul enriching, a state of the controlled mind.

The mind has two drivers, the soul and senses. When the driver is the soul it activates intuition, giving rise to intuitive knowledge, which is positive and spiritual. However when the driver is the senses then it results in worldly attractions leading to kaam (lust), krodh (anger), moha (affection), lobh (greed) and ahankar (ego). The master of the mind is the soul and the slaves of the mind are the senses. When consciousness remains idle it gets converted into mass equivalent resulting in anger, abuse and throwing of tantrums, inflicting pain on to oneself and others. Since everything is made of energy hence igniting consciousness is not an arduous effort, bringing piety to a doable reality. The property of energy is to move and produce two fold movements, inward and outward. When inwards then it is spiritual elevation and when outwards it is towards worldly materialistic attractions. The inward flow of energy can be hindered by an inflated feeling of pride of being superior to others, called an ego. The ego is innate with oneself and is dominant. It lies dormant at the time of a man's birth. However, man who has the ability to activate the ego makes it reach such levels whereby ego takes over and governs man beyond a reasonable control.

The best way to control the ego after controlling one's mind is to consider the ego as a visitor and treat it with due respect and humility while maintaining one's calm, contemplating on the spiritual name or energy and meditating as and when possible. It is best advisable to admire ego as a known asset but that of the neighbour's. Stress, another attribute, is caused by actions or situations on psychological or physical demands over a period of time. A certain amount of both physical and mental stress is required for normal and healthy growth to increase productivity and quality. However when not managed properly, stress can lead to chaos, needing to be addressed. Man should train to distance himself from situations that cause unpleasantness and return when the situation eases. It is healthy to agree to disagree rather than to win a worthless argument. All this alertness can come only when one makes an effort to activate his consciousness levels. Self-esteem and self-respect are advisable as it helps build positivity and develops mutual love and respect for all living things.

One can overcome deep-rooted deterrents with the practice of meditation. The great way of entering and developing within this stage is through performing a ritual, where deep forces are introduced in a controlled way. If entry to this stage comes suddenly then it may result in a spiritual emergency, which at times may be hard to distinguish from psychosis and thus needs careful handling.

When one moves on to the level of the spirit he has to leave behind the symbol and ritual and the use of meditation becomes the prime method. Renunciation of the previous stage can be painful and difficult; however, when in the deep water of spirituality, such comfortable warmth of the previous stage becomes less significant. It is safer to start meditation at a spiritual school with others and then gradually move from a common meditational base to an exclusive one, simply because the energy generated by the congregation when everyone prays and meditates together is much higher than the energy he or she can generate on their own. This abundant energy thus generated transmits into one another by charging a few, igniting another few and leaving the rest in awe to revisit the temple of energy and earn esoteric peace and warmth.

The practice of meditation is the inner path leading to a growth in consciousness. This growth leads the conscience to play its role and declare the sense of right and wrong, enabling man to become a deft decision maker. Man needs to render devout services to The Lord and His mankind, through his tan (body), man (mind), dhan (resources) and surat (soul). His preeti (love) and pratiti (faith) has to be profound, failing which he may not be able to reach the higher levels of consciousness. He may attain certain lower levels of consciousness as the ego continues to play its role till the Universal Mind. While focussing on controlling the likes of body, mind and resources, the man needs to render service through his spirit. Rendering service through the spirit is by far the most superior form rather than offering services through the body, mind and resources, which no doubt are essential but fail to reward redemption. When a man performs service through his spirit he gains energy emanating from the Supreme Reservoir enabling him to transcend from one Loka (spiritual plane) to another and ultimately uniting him with the Supreme. Such transitions are possible only when man controls the likes of his body, routes the focus of his mind, optimally cum effectively makes use of the available resources, and ardently senses the benign presence of his soul. Besides man and hard-work are synonyms, thus fostering positive energy does not seem an arduous effort, bringing piety to a doable reality and building an aura around oneself.

Possessing mere belief in any worldly or spiritual doctrine is termed as faith - that transports man from reality to his belief through the spiritual current named as consciousness. Likewise an atheist or non-believer of God too believes in some doctrine, which expresses his views after certain deliberations and through an imperative evaluation process. This involves scrutiny through the process of theology, which is a link with consciousness thus providing sufficient enough reason to transport the reviewer to the realms of spiritualism. It should be borne in mind that no information, for or against spirituality is irrelevant as such inferences are possible only when some force directs a believer or non-believer to reach his desired conclusion. This force can be under any name or as the Supreme Force acts as a guide, appearing to be larger than the reviewer, suggests all men bear consciousness and cannot be devoid of redemption.

The Brain, Mind and Consciousness plays a distinct role in a man's life. The Brain decodes the received information without any manipulation whereas the Mind is a flow with an ability to act, analyse and manipulate as and when required, hence needs control. The Brain is a system whereas the Mind is a process that analyses information in an apparatus called the brain. The Brain knows, the mind understands, the body practices and the soul intuits. The Brain is a perpetual learner that needs continuous information for growth in knowledge to deepen his understanding, and The Mind has the ability to reason and interpret knowledge to differentiate understanding by using processes. The Brain is a direct computation of perception and the Mind is the awareness of consciousness that only a man possesses. Besides analysis and interpretation, the mind has another positive aspect to introspect and retrospect that enables a man to gauge his actions and reactions to improve his future deeds, a process helpful in building consciousness. When a man contemplates beauty, goodness, justice, and peace, he gets intimations of harmonious unity with the spiritual domain. Meditation acquaints his spiritual body with the reality in which it subsists. He then discovers a definite force assisting his best efforts and efforts of all. Man finds consciousness as his unfailing friend and guide that is positive, constructive, directive and in a forward movement of spiritual evolution. The other means to attain higher levels of consciousness are through progressive awareness, critical thinking, and building self-confidence. The Mind thus plays a pivotal role in the growth of consciousness.

The Body or good health is managed through the conditioning of the mind. It is judged by how one perceives and reacts to a given situation and what quality of information does he share. Good health is not only by being in a congenial ambience or by the nature of work assigned to him. It has a varying perception with a vast paradigm. A man may be in the best ambience and company but the sort of information he is discussing, becomes critical. If he thinks ill and shares the same, he can never improve his health, even if he is working in green fields or in a swanky office. Only when he is mentally, emotionally and intellectually healthy can he then enjoy the benefits of nutritious food, good education, family, friends and company of his co-workers. This way his personality will turn positive, otherwise all his goodness turns to garbage and consciousness eludes him. It is only when a healthy mind and body are in sync, that it leads to transpersonal philosophy and turns the persons ideal beyond the individual self.

Man is a spiritual being and lives in a world made by humans. Achieving worldly pursuits gives a man a very positive impetus in his growth of levels of consciousness, like making money or having luxurious things and being a part of this world, are some examples of personal fulfillment. Therefore there is no reason to apologize for enjoying the material gifts given to man as long as material comforts do not engulf man's supreme entity and make him forget the prime reason of his birth. If his levels of consciousness are present, he for sure will know where to draw the line. If a man spends his entire life chasing the worldly fleeting rewards and does not work towards his return journey he is sure to fail in his prime mission.

Truly one should set priorities and awaken his best self to remain as number one. Failing which a struggler always struggles and ends up with empty hands, be it in a worldly or spiritual domain. There will be times when a man may begin to crumble and a stage of enormous upheaval and change is likely during which he needs to pause as it is the time of a very beautiful personal growth.

It is like stating, the caterpillar may be experiencing the darkness of cocoon, but guess what is really happening? "A butterfly is being born". Or to say, "The night is darkest before dawn". While citing the example of a butterfly or dawn, one connotes its radiance, beauty, vibrant colours and lightness providing grace and subtlety. Also when a butterfly flaps her wings others enjoy its beauty and glide. So does dawn spread its freshness, provides purpose and bequeaths a reason to live again. Likewise when consciousness expands then man breaks away from his mental, physical, and emotional bonds and his mind transcends beyond limitations. He finds himself in a new, great and wonderful world. Dormant forces, faculties and talents become alive and man discovers himself to be a humble and greater person than ever before.

When one begins to discover truth he realises how much power he wields. He becomes aware and wants to explore more. There will be times when a seeker receives new learning with heightened awareness leading him to restlessness and confusion but it is the beginning of a consciousness that will lead him to a ticket, to board the boat that will catapult him to the Reservoir of sacredness. To be able to swim a man should be quick and alert in his endeavours or else he may sink. While he is in an ocean, he will swim if he clutches on to wood but will surely drown if he holds on to iron. Wood is the Lord with an intrinsic flame and Iron is the world. As man travels deeper in water he faces greater problems and a feeling of sinking is present but the net result is as rewarding as the current pulling him is consciousness, the father figure. Man may appear to be confronting with more worldly obstacles and achieving less of worldly success however such external confrontations lead to equanimity within him. This internal cleaning process exterminates the acquired negativism earned from the lowest region of Creation. The thicker the layer of impurity, complex is the cleaning process necessary to do cutting, cleaning and easing an inward flow of consciousness.

Once when man elevates his consciousness levels he then cannot stoop to the level of manipulation. He accepts whatever is the result and takes it in his stride with the 3P's - patience, perseverance and positivity. Man's thoughts, which are part of his mind, possesses a power which when poured with positivity, grows stronger affecting his attitude, expectations, behaviour and actions, which is constructive. He improves his creative visualization, concentration and spiritual growth. He enjoys meditation at any clean quiet place and does not need to isolate himself at a secluded place. A man with full grown consciousness is then a walking, talking and thinking being like his Supreme Father. Each man has the potential to achieve the Absolute, however very few are able to do it as man has an innate tendency to turn complacent upon achieving a certain amount of success rather than build on it, especially in the field of spirituality.

Man can be a beneficiary as he possesses all the attributes for his spiritual growth and is the source too to activate consciousness, which is the only ingredient for redemption. To attain consciousness he has his body to work with, his mind to think and chart his growth, and his soul to assist in his distinct mission. Besides, man has both worldly and spiritual instruments to grant him a wholesome life as the world furnishes him with worldly content and religion with spiritual content. Achieving in spiritual discipline does not seem improbable especially when a man is used to putting in arduous efforts in accomplishing his worldly goals. It takes him more than 30 years of real hard-work to become the CEO of a worldly organization, whereas in spiritualism he is a born CEO with his body, mind and soul as a complete organization. Though both worldly wealth and spiritual abundance have the same goals - to maximise with similar challenges, reality suggests that man has no choice but to excel in an organization that belongs to him by birth. If he does fail to chart his spiritual success he then lacks vision and a man without vision is sure not to succeed in his spiritual endeavour.

The cultivation of unitary awareness provides inspiration and energy to reconcile all opposites within daily life. The connection is shown below in the diagram. The outer circle penetrates from all directions with cross-lines and represents harmony at the dualistic level of the self with five modes of activity, which is necessary for a complete and balanced way of living and to attain consciousness.

Diagram of the Qualities of the Ideal Person in Equilibrium

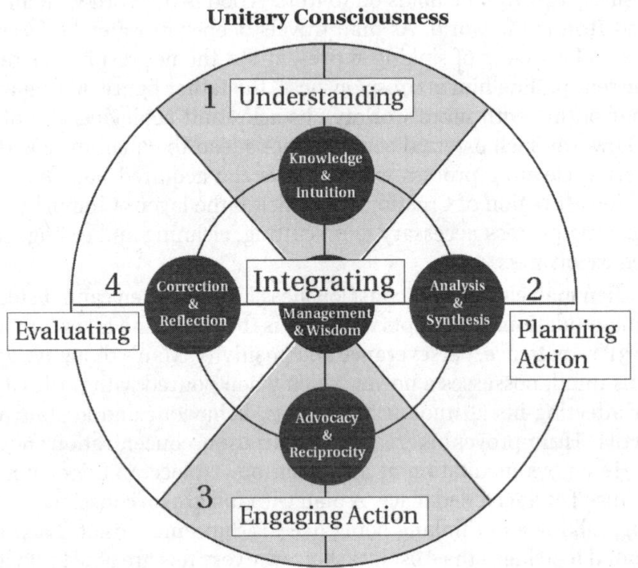

Modes of Activity	***Constituent Qualities***
1. Understanding	Knowledge & Intuition
2. Planning Action	Analysis & Synthesis
3. Engaging Action	Advocacy & Reciprocity
4. Evaluating	Correction & Reflection
5. Integrating	Management & Wisdom

The **first mode** of activity - Understanding requires Knowledge and Intuition. Both are complementary and mutually supportive to be converged for intuitive insights. The **second mode** is Planning Action on how to act in an appropriate manner in any situation. Planning involves Analysis and Synthesis. Analysis examines alternatives and consequences in a logical, empirical manner, identifies cause-effect relations to predict outcomes of decisions. Synthesis brings together alternatives with explicit assumptions and understanding for a complete plan to emerge. The **third mode** is Engaging Action. Each action has a reaction and thus should be charted out by understanding and planning. The converging of actions should be based on Advocacy and Reciprocity. Advocacy is a commitment to the group and Reciprocity is the person engaged in action to be aware of the perspectives and needs of other people and beings, with one's moral commitments. The **fourth mode** is Evaluating, an ongoing process of considering the results of actions as they occur. It involves the interaction of Reflection and Correction. The person needs to reflect upon his actions and its consequences. Reflection should arise from a mind that is clear, peaceful, and rooted in unitary consciousness. The reflective person considers all the modes of activity complemented by correction of errors giving an insight into the quality and success of one's actions. Correction changes the course of one's actions whenever necessary. An ideal person is not rigidly fixed in any plan and flows with changing circumstances. The **fifth mode** is Integrating, an ongoing process of linking, regulating, coordinating and organizing all modes of activity and thus has a central place in the diagram. Integrating needs both Management and Wisdom. Management organizes and supervises all activities, and Wisdom guides one to take actions that do not seem practical, yet it may be more profound and beneficial. It follows intuition or intuitive know-how that visits in a very subtle form and can be mistaken for self-talk or a mere thought. Man with elevated consciousness can discern its presence and find intuition as steering his onward path. To be able to enjoy and develop as an ideal person, try to overcome ego. Also try and attain success and bliss in most endeavours by practicing all modes of activity daily.

Quick recall: Means are a standard to surmount the challenges of life, Levels of consciousness are exalted and friendly to achieve, and Emancipation is an assured result fulfilling the purpose of one's birth.

Chapter 54

Means of Attaining Higher Levels of Spiritual Consciousness

ANJALI NIGAM
Whiteswan Consulting Group, Agra, India

AJIT NIGAM
Railway Board, Delhi, India

Abstract

The common bridge between spirituality and religion is altruistic love – regard for and devotion to the interests of others. In this respect, the basic spiritual teachings of the world's great religions are remarkably similar. In religion this is manifested through the Golden Rule, also called the Rule of Reciprocity – 'do unto others as you would have them do unto you' – which is the basic teaching and ethos of Radhasoami Faith and also common to all major religions. From this perspective, spirituality is necessary for religion but religion is not necessary for spirituality. Consequently, workplace spirituality can be inclusive or exclusive of religious theory and practice. The authors have therefore made an attempt to create a management model based on 'Spiritual Leadership', which would urge our managers of today to actually initiate themselves into connecting with their internal self and thereby facilitating them to use their internal powers for maintaining better relationship with self through which they will be able to manage their worldly relationships better, resolve conflicts, be more effective as team workers, manage time lines thereby driving self to attain worldly and spiritual goals, i.e. balancing 'Swartha' and Parmartha'(teaching of Radhasoami faith) together for a more fulfilling as well as emotionally and spiritually motivating lifestyle, leading to higher personal and professional effectiveness. In the trainings that are conducted for the corporate managers and students, techniques that help participants in achieving this objective are used.

Introduction and Background

Radhasoami Faith: a torchbearer for the 'New World Order- Achieving Higher levels of Spiritual Consciousness through 'Better Worldliness'

The common bridge between spirituality and religion is altruistic love – regard for and devotion to the interests of others. In this respect, the basic spiritual teachings of the world's great religions are remarkably similar. In religion this is manifested through the Golden Rule, also called the Rule of Reciprocity – 'do unto others as you would have them do unto you' – which is the basic teaching and ethos of Radhasoami Faith and also common to all major religions. From this perspective, spirituality is necessary for religion but religion is not necessary for spirituality. Consequently, workplace spirituality can be inclusive or exclusive of religious theory and practice.

Spiritual Leadership and its Relevance for Corporate Managers

The authors have therefore made an attempt to create a management model based on 'Spiritual Leadership', which would urge our managers of today to actually initiate themselves into connecting with their internal self and thereby facilitating them to use their internal powers for maintaining better relationship with self through which they will be able to manage their worldly relationships better, resolve conflicts, be more effective as team workers, manage time lines thereby driving self to attain worldly and spiritual goals, i.e. balancing '*Swartha*' and '*Parmartha*'(teachings of Radhasoami faith) together for a more fulfilling as well as emotionally and spiritually motivating lifestyle, leading to higher personal and professional effectiveness. In our trainings which we conduct for the corporate managers and students, we use techniques which help participants in achieving this objective to some extent.

Testing the Spiritual Leadership Model

We have been testing the model under study for the last 3 years on various corporate managers across India and recently we tested it in Japan, this October 2010, on participants from various nationalities including Japan, China, Mongolia, Philippines and the Vietnam. The results have been very encouraging. The technique called the 'Visualization Technique' was used and the participants were guided through the facilitator using oral guidance, with Indian Classical Music and the spiritual sound of 'OM' as a base. The results showed total disconnect from the worldly thoughts, a total sense of peace and calm. The participants reported to be feeling much more connected to their own self, happier and reportedly felt peace and joy which they had never felt before. The technique was used for 3-5 minutes each time.

(The results for the participants from these Asian Countries were very encouraging, with very good feedback. We trained two consultants for conducting these workshops in Japan).

The idea behind is to facilitate these managers in striking a chord with their internal selves, whereby realizing the universal peace and joy while feeling the worldly problems as just superficial and looking at them detachedly and trying to solve them with a 'detached positivity' leading to and realizing their innate capability for connecting with the divine reservoir of happiness. This has lead to better management at the workplace and home with an objective and value based approach leading to a balance in '*Swartha*' (worldly) and '*Parmartha*' (Spiritual) duties being fulfilled leading to 'Universal Brotherhood' and 'Better Worldliness', due to fall in biases and prejudices in personal and professional lives.

Teachings of Radhasoami Faith as a Rationale for the above

Quoting once again... *the common bridge between spirituality and religion is altruistic love – regard or devotion to the interests of others. In this respect, the basic spiritual teachings of the world's great religions are remarkably similar. In religion this is manifested through the Golden Rule, also called the Rule of Reciprocity – 'do unto others as you would have them do unto you' – which is the basic teaching and ethos of Radhasoami Faith and also common to all major religions.* The universe the 'Macrocosm' and the individual spirit 'Microcosm' are one and hence the universe starts responding to the individual's good deeds with positive reinforcements.

The individual self i.e. the spirit entity is the microcosm and is a miniscule part of the whole universal macrocosm, is a bundle of values and beliefs, in turn nurtured by the religion. In our case, Religion of Saints, i.e. Radhasoami Faith, that teaches us to live a life of peaceful co-existence, happiness through selfless service, humility and brotherhood. The attempt is towards 'creating a state of Better Worldliness' where all peacefully co-exist and the Universal law of 'Fatherhood of God and Brotherhood of man is established, hence this model for universal managerial application.

The human body has all the doors and similar levels as in the case of the universe. Kabir Sahib says...'*yeh to ghar hai prem ka, khala ka ghar nahin...* 'achieving salvation is only possible in this human body. Hence, the internal connection with the true self, leads to achieving higher levels of consciousness and thereby facilitating the individual to appreciate and practice 'Fatherhood of God and Brotherhood of Man', i.e. working with a 'detached attachment' for better worldliness with peaceful co-existence, and '*Vasudhaiva Kutumbakam*', working and living in this world, doing all duties without getting lipta or involved, in other words... '*tan chale par man nahin bahahi...*'.

As per the *teachings of Radhasoami Faith, which is the performing of 'swartha with Parmartha', balancing both worldly and spiritual domains, i.e. detachedly performing one's worldly duties while getting spiritual re-enforcements through internal practices of 'surat shabda yoga' and trying to achieve higher levels of 'spiritual consciousness'*. Connecting with the internal self through meditational practices whereby increasing one's level of 'spiritual consciousness, leads to lesser accumulation of *Adi Karmas*, as per the 'Karma Theory'.

The Resultant 'Spiritual Leadership'

When ones energies are diverted from the world and its worldly objects, while doing all duties, when one does not think himself to be the '*karta*' or the 'doer', no further karmas are accumulated. In the religion of Saints, when the individual performs '*Surat Shabda Yoga*' as in Radhasoami Faith, the urge to be one with the supreme being, while trying to concentrate at the seat of the spirit and listening to the internal sounds, helps in nurturing the mystic body and hence elevation of the level of consciousness, takes one's mind away from the outer worldly things which in turn helps in non-accumulation of *Adi* karmas.

...'*through our experiments in the corporate sector, and use of Visualization Technique we are trying to facilitate the corporate managers, in striking a connection with internal selves while helping in self-discipline through control of the senses, mind and emotions*'.

Everyone has a Mystic faculty even though it is in a hidden form and in various stages of development. Nurturing and developing this faculty leads to elevation of consciousness.

Achieving Higher Level of Spiritual Consciousness

Mysticism deals with transcendental and peak experiences in the field of consciousness as an expansion of normal consciousness. Humans have the hidden potential for awakening higher levels of consciousness which is not a physiological or psychological phenomenon. Hence it is beyond sense perception and reasoning and manifests inwardly. It is associated with bliss of an extraordinary intensity culminating in the ecstasy of an experience of union with God - the Supreme Source of Consciousness and Spirituality. The scriptures of extant religions contain a number of descriptions of such elevated states of consciousness.

These states are attainable by balanced self-discipline, control of the senses, mind and emotions that are inconceivable to most of the people. True mystics are wise and balanced human beings—never fanatical, self-seeking or emotionally excessive. Mystics do not employ theology or reasoning for attaining that state. It is also the principal characteristic of the greatest philosophers and founders of religions like Plato, Echart, Lord Jesus, Prophet Muhammad, Seers of *Upanishads*, and Saints. Mystical experience stirred their whole being and led them on their noble missions in their lives giving supreme happiness to them, and their followers.

Model for the Study

Below is the model for the present study.

Individual, the Microcosm, and the mystic being, is a part of the whole universal macrocosm, and is a bundle of Values and beliefs nurtured by Religion e.g. Religion of Saints- Radhasoami Faith. Radhasoami Faith which helps imbibe value based ethos of living, i.e. *adhyayan* (education), *seva* (Selfless Social Service), *vyayaam* (physical exercise) for children and satsang (spiritual congregation in the presence of the Sant Satguru or the spiritual Adept), seva (selfless service to mankind) and *abhyaas* (spiritual practice by contemplating the divine form at the seat of the spirit or hearing of the internal sounds) for adults, for alleviating the spirit to higher spiritual regions, i.e. facilitating in the flow of energy from the lower to the upper echelons i.e. from Pind to Bramhmand and further to Pure Spiritual Region- Dayal Desh

As mentioned above, the faith further teaches all to adhere and balance *Swartha* (worldly) and *Parmartha* (spiritual) duties simultaneously for achieving higher levels of spiritual consciousness to attain salvation while living in this body, guided by the Sant Satguru in Physical form.

The above leads to a resultant higher level of spiritual consciousness, due to the unification of 5 *indriyas*, and the *mann* and *chitta*, leading to their reins being in the hands of the spirit entity, the Pure Self (which can now command obedience from these 5 bhootas, also *mann* and *chitta*, leading to the 3rd eye of Intuition being opened- and the Pure Self getting connected to the macrocosm- the ocean of spirituality- the original abode of the spirit entity.

Radhasoami Faith, the New World Order & Spiritual Consciousness

Fifth Revered Sant Satguru of Radhasoami Faith Sir Sahabji Maharaj put forth before the *Satsang* community Aristocratic Democracy (ARIS-DEMO) as the model for governance. By Aristocrats, He meant '*Spiritual Aristocrats*' who would be practitioners of *Surat Shabda Yoga* and would have an elevated level of consciousness. For it would only be such persons who would have true love for the Lord and compassion for His entire creation, that would treat all on an equal footing. And it will only be such noble men who would be true practitioners of universal brotherhood, *Vasudhaiva Kutumbakam*.

According to the followers of Radhasoami Faith the concept of '*Arya Nagar*' was a dream of Sahabji Maharaj and Dayalbagh is proclaimed as the embodiment of that dream. The institutions of Dayalbagh are the training grounds for 'Supermen', performing together the duties of Brahmin, Kshatriya, Vaishya and Shudra. The *Sant Satguru* is Himself present in Dayalbagh as an ideal example of 'Superman'. It would not be long before *Satsang* culture will be viewed by the world as a new, ideal *Sanskriti* or Culture, which may be termed as the *New World Order*.

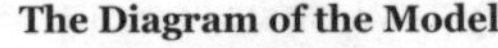

The Diagram of the Model

The resultant control over the 5 indriyas, mann, chitta, leading to their reins being in the hand of the spirit entity, the Pure Self. Therefore higher level of consciousness is achieved leading to the 3rd eye of intuition being opened - and results in the Pure Self getting connected to the macrocosm - the ocean of spirituality - its original abode.

The living ethos leads to a pure way of living coupled with 'Surat Shabda Yoga' facilitates in the flow of energy from the lower to the upper echelons, i.e. from Pind to Brahmand and further to Pure Spiritual Region - Dayal Desh, i.e. reaching higher levels of spiritual consciousness.

Radhasoami Faith - Value based ethos of living - addhyan, seva, vyayam for children and satsang, seva and abhyas for adults.

Swartha and Parmartha, guided by the Sant Satguru in Physical Body.

Individual the Microcosm, and the mystic being, is a part of the whole universal macrocosm, is a bundle of values and beliefs nurtured by Religion, e.g. Religion of Saints - Radhasoami Faith

Better Worldliness and Higher Levels of Spiritual Consciousness:

Followers of Radhasoami Faith believe that by following the *Satsang* Culture, one inculcates the ideal of *Better Worldliness*, following which, man can achieve the four *Purusharthas* of *Dharma, Artha, Kama* and *Moksha* to attain the status of a *Jivanmukta* during his lifetime itself. A *jivanmukta* is a realized soul who visualizes the entire creation as the children of God and his love for God translates into brotherhood of man, thereby helping him to realize higher consciousness levels.

Better Worldliness can be explained as a philosophy or a way of life where spiritual pursuits to attain superior consciousness and puritan work ethics make a fine blend. In olden days, seats of learning were mainly religious institutions. Religious education dominated the curriculum. Religious way of life which is unworldly was considered the ideal. In the changed conditions worldliness took the place of unworldliness...

Sahabji Maharaj, the Fifth Revered *Sant Satguru* of Radhasoami Faith, propounded the concept of *Better Worldliness*. Living in the world comfortably, one should pursue the ideal of achieving the highest spiritual goal. Better Worldliness is thus the golden mean between worldliness and unworldliness that is advocated in *Satsang*.

To put it another way, Better Worldliness can be seen as a combination of Karma Yoga, Gyana Yoga and Bhakti Yoga, based on a Dharmic way of conduct; a conduct with compassion and forbearance for fellow man, no matter what the nationality, or the color of the skin, religion or caste. Practicing Better Worldliness would usher in 'Brotherhood of Man' and lead us to an integrated global community.

Fatherhood of God and Brotherhood of Man

Followers of Radhasoami Faith believe that Dayalbagh is the new torch-bearer with the basic faith in Fatherhood of God and Brotherhood of mankind. It is a concept underlying the new experiment of combining religious activities with social, educational and industrial effort in Dayalbagh. It is based on the principle that service of the human brotherhood far from being a hindrance, in establishing communion with the Supreme Father, is indeed a positive step in that direction.

Teachings of the Satsang and the Satsang Culture aim at elevating the level of consciousness. Human consciousness is awareness in its fullness which increases progressively as the human Spirit ascends to higher levels of spiritual consciousness and determines our attitude and disposition towards life.

The philosophy of the Radhasoami faith highlights higher states of consciousness which can be attained through *Surat Shabd Abhyaas*, and once achieved; bring about a permanent change of consciousness and disposition towards fellow beings in the Lord's creation. One should thus learn not only to develop intellectual faculties, but to also control the lower appetites of man and satisfy his higher cravings with the help of religion.

It is only after one attains higher states of consciousness that he truly visualizes all of humanity as under the fatherhood of the same one God. And it will only be after that, that he will be persuaded to practice brotherhood of man in its true sense. The teachings of Satsang and the Satsang culture aim at a gradual elevation of consciousness, and in this sense is a flag bearer in the evolution of an equitable society of the future.

Yasya deve para Bhaktirytha deve tatha gurau
Tasyaithe kathita hyartha prakasante mahAtmanah

(To him, the wise, who has deep devotion to the Lord and has devotion to the *Guru*, these teachings, when told would shine, that is, bear fruit!)
(*Svetasvatara 6-230*)

References

Maharaj Sahab [Pandit Brahm Sankar Misra Sahab] (1960). *Discourses on Radhasoami Faith.* Agra, India: Radhasoami Satsang Sabha, Dayalbagh.

Levels of Religious Consciousness – Upanishads, Gita and Radhasoami Faith. (1987). Bombay, India: Bhartiya Vidya Bhavan.

Sahabji Maharaj [Sir Anand Sarup Kt.] (1957). *Yathartha Prakash*, Part-II. Agra, India: Radhasoami Satsang Sabha, Dayalbagh.

Chapter 55

States and Levels of Consciousness

V. NARSIMHA RAO
Visakhapatnam, India

Abstract

In this paper we will aim to explain the process of the development of consciousness. Consciousness is present in varying degrees in different individuals. The achievement of higher levels of consciousness is possible if one is able to develop dislike for the worldly pleasures and consequently inculcate deep attachment for his Religious adept. The widely known stages of consciousness are the wakeful state, dream, deep sleep and Turiya and most of the religions stop at that. The turiya state corresponds to the 4th Loka of brahamand. The religion of saints has described higher levels of consciousness beyond these states.The Jivatma, upto the Turiya state, is still blended with fine quantities of mind & matter. However, as the soul moves beyond the Turiya state, it separates from mind & matter and enters the pure spiritual region. With this the attraction to the ocean of spirituality or The Supreme Being goes on increasing and the soul moves up and finally merges into the infinite ocean of spirituality. Consciousness is mainly Downward Causal by the Will of the Supreme Being and Upward Reciprocal by the devotee. All other states of consciousness lie in between these two. This highest level of pure spiritual consciousness is the abode of the Supreme Being. This can be attained only with true devotion to the Sant Satguru who is the manifest form of the merciful Supreme Being.

Introduction

The Faculty of self perception is termed as consciousness. This state can't be found in the mineral kingdom as the Spirit in them is dormant. In the vegetable kingdom also the spirit is dormant but it exhibits its state of life by flourishing in branches, leaves flowering, bark casting and seed forming etc. In the animal kingdom functional consciousness is present in a lesser degree e.g. there are beautiful tender leaves on the tree and a goat wants to eat them. However it can't cut the branches of the tree and eat the leaves. Only a man can do that. Thus, till a man cuts the branches and feeds the goat, it has to wait. Human beings possess, mind, thinking power etc, and act accordingly. In human beings, life can be defined as the process of development of consciousness. This consciousness varies in degrees in different individuals, as all human beings are not of the same state. This consciousness develops as age advances i.e., from child hood till the end of life.

Exoteric and Esoteric Consciousness

Some individuals possess empirical or exoteric consciousness. They simply depend on their senses. They absorb whatever knowledge is provided by the senses as it is e.g. his eyes acknowledge the green colour in leaves, he will receive this information and think no further. But a man who has developed scientific faculties will acknowledge through his senses that the leaf is green because it can't absorb green color and emits it - so the leaf is green. In the same way the man who leads an empirical life, sees life as an ordinary thing. Whatever experience he gets in the world, he will merely receive it that way and thus shall eat, drink, seek progeny, seek financial status, name or fame. Therefore, he will lead his life experiencing the joy and worries which come his way and die as an ordinary being. As long as he lives, he will always strive hard for attaining peace and happiness. The happiness he gets in the material plane is of trivial value. The happiness he gets here is short lived and even if he gets it repeatedly - he shall not be satisfied. He will go on searching for happiness through other means.

But a man having esoteric consciousness acknowledges the statements of sages of yore, men of wisdom and high intellectuals, great Rishis and values life as a gift of God. He knows that life is not meant for eating, drinking and producing offspring. He starts thinking about why life has been bestowed by God and probes deeper into it while beginning to think about Atma and Parmatma. He strives hard to get self realization or self consciousness which is endowed with concepts, perception and experiences of higher consciousness. He feels unhappy on seeing that human beings are grounded in the mill stones of mundane wishes. Hence he tries to enrich his life by probing into religious matters which aids him to ascend to higher levels of Consciousness. By gaining in the development of consciousness and with inquisitive knowledge he will naturally compare his mundane life with that of spirit consciousness and God consciousness. Thus, in order to improve his spirit consciousness, he will depend on persons in whom higher consciousness has already developed e.g Sages, Mahatmas, Gurus etc and will try to emulate them.

Higher Consciousness through Worldly Detachment

In order to enrich life with higher consciousness, man has to develop a dislike or detachment towards the world and become religiously conscious. The grade/ degree of enrichment depends on the extent and degree of losing bonds with the world. There is an example in the writings of Moulana Rumi, a sufi saint. Once, a king fell in love with a lady. He gave a lot of money to her family, brought that lady to his palace and made her his queen. In a short time the lady became ill. The reason of illness couldn't be detected by any medical expert and day by day her condition deteriorated. The king went to the masjid and prayed to Allah for hours together and he prayed and prayed with closed eyes. As soon as he entered into the slumber mode, an old man appeared in his thoughts and said, tomorrow a Hakim (medical expert) sent by me will come to your palace. He will solve the problem.

The next day, as destined, a Hakim came and met the king. The king narrated his love for the lady and about her illness. The Hakim while counseling the lady came to know that she was in love with a goldsmith at a certain village. Now he knew the reason of her illness. With the permission of the King, he arranged to bring that particular goldsmith to the palace. The lady and the Goldsmith were allowed to move in together. Soon the lady regained her health and started moving joyfully. Then after a few days the Hakim started giving a kind of Sarbath (sweetened drink) to the Goldsmith daily which was laced with a slow poison. As the days passed on the goldsmith started loosing the glow & glamour on his face and was slowly stamped with a deathly pallor. As the health of the goldsmith worsened by each passing day, the lady also slowly developed a dislike towards the goldsmith. In this way the lady soon became detached from the love of the goldsmith.

So, let us consider that the goldsmith is the world and the lady is our mind. Hence, when the attachment with the world diminishes and dislike develops for the world, the attachment to the Religious Adept increases.

Stages of Consciousness

When the consciousness of the Soul and Spirit is once affirmed in a man, he will come to acknowledge himself to be one of with the eternal Divinity. He will find, to his great astonishment, that his limited Ego-centric self has vanished and by gaining spiritual consciousness, he will slowly place himself at the Feet of a Spiritual Adept for furtherance of achieving the desire of getting 'Darshan'(vision) of the Lord. Slowly with the blessings of a Spiritual Adept, his level of consciousness will start rising from wakeful to dream, deep sleep and the fourth stage of **Turiya** i.e in the 10th loka from the bottom of Pind loka or 3rd loka of Brahmand.

Consciousness in the wakeful state is under the control of the jiva and he can act according to his thoughts. He can be good or evil. It depends upon his will, either he can perform philanthropic deeds, religious deeds or he could be a robber or murderer. Though this state is quite difficult, a Jiva with Will can act as per his mind without getting drifted away by the senses. In the dream state, however, the limitation of the three dimensions and the thought process is not there. The Jiva will be free; he may do as per the impressions ingrained in the depth of his mind. He may enjoy or feel perturbed according to the situations in his dream. But when he enters into deep sleep or **Shushupthi**, consciousness will depend upon his past karmas & past actions. He may feel some peace there but for a short time. So, the Jiva, can do whatever he wants to only in the wakeful state, though "**Jagrat AWASTHA**" is also a troublesome state. If he mends or turns his life towards the religious mandates of the saints - while in a wakeful or **Jagrat state** he may see the fruits of it in his dream and deep sleep state. However, the Jiva constantly oscillates in these three states without any peace or rest.

The fourth stage of consciousness is **Turiya** in **Sahasdalkamal**, the 4th Loka of Brahmand. Very few people witness this **Turiya**. Some of the religions end here and some end at Trikuti. However, saints have opened the way beyond Trikuti into higher regions of Spirituality. The secrets of higher Lokas beyond Trikuti have been revealed by Saints, especially, in the Radhasoami Faith and the way is clearly opened to all devotees who wish to go higher than the mental ego by following the Surat Shabd Yoga path under the discipleship of the Sant Satguru. This Surat Shabd Yoga leads beyond Turiya and it is the 5th level of consciousness as per the statements of Saints. It is called Chitanavasta.

Attainment of Moksha (emancipation) through Higher Consciousness

At Trikuti, consciousness is not fully spiritual as it is a stage of Brahmanda. Even at this stage the Jiva is in a dual state because the soul is blended with the mind and is called Jivatma. Param Guru Huzur Sahabji Maharaj answered a question put by a devotee about what is meant by "Jivatma - He explained that as we know - when two gases of Hydrogen and Oxygen are mixed a third substance is formed. The third substance is an entirely different one. Similarly the spirit mixed with the mind produces a third substance known as Jivatma. Atma is **CHETAN** and mind is **JAD**. But the combination of these two produces a substance which is neither CHETAN NOR JAD. It is JIVATMA. It is the mind energized by the spirit developing into Jivatma that obtains all knowledge and is responsible for all actions in this plane. This combination is called JAD CHETAN". When once the Soul goes beyond Trikuti, the bond of the mind with the Soul is broken. The mind will remain at Trikuti because it is the representative of Kala Purusha which is forbidden to go beyond Trikuti. The Soul then enters into the dominion of Sunnalok/ Manasasarovar and reaches nearer to the stage of Moksha. It gets rid of the admixture of mind, matter and all impurities and ultimately it exists by itself. The Soul, rid of its duality, gets freedom.

Hitherto, imagine the Atma like a feather attached to thousands of mounds of weight, which now has got rid of that weight and has become even lighter than a feather. It gains increased spirituality and consequently moves towards the reservoir of infinite spirituality. The consciousness that the soul gets is pure spiritual consciousness and as it proceeds further, the spiritual consciousness increases and subsequently when it merges in the Supreme Being it attains the consciousness of the Supreme Being. This is the condition of Moksha- Param Guru Huzur Sahabji Maharaj explained it like this " the Surat forgets itself and gets absorbed while doing Darshan of the Supreme Being and this can never be understood by the mind which is always restless like a monkey. Drops of water in the ocean are never tired of the ocean and the rays of the sun are never tired of the Sun, similarly the Surat or Atma whose essence is the Supreme Being will feel at home there. The mind wants rest and food, so does the Atma, but her rest and food are the Darshan of the Supreme Being. She would therefore never like to run away from God. In the state of Moksha, the Surat will be attracted towards God and God will attract the Surat. When there is mutual attraction the question of separation or repulsion does not arise. A piece of paper can remain away from a fire but as soon as it is thrown into the fire it becomes fire and thereafter the paper cannot be separated from the fire. Similarly, when the Atma gets communion with God, it merges into God and the Surat & God become one; there is no question of separation". This is the ultimate stage of consciousness for which all should aspire.

Spiritual Consciousness: Beyond the Karma Theory

A great saint, Rishi Kakabhushnda by name, has written 'talapatra', some 5000 years ago. He had narrated certain points which are nearer to the Radhasoami Faith. 1) He wrote that after 5010 A.D., various religious and spiritual changes will occur. 2) Man who has been living for thousands of years with inner slavery to Karma will find a new way of Yoga to get rid of the Karma Theory. 3) A new yoga will be revealed to him by a Master (Satguru). Man, unlike previously i.e. who used to take many births to get Siddhi will soon be released within 10 years through this new yoga. He will get Siddhi or Moksha or emancipation, by practicing this new yoga. There will be no doubt in this. 4) This new yoga starts from Sahasdalkamal and he can't use this Yoga Shakti on his own accord. This yoga shakti shall be under the control of the Loka Guru (Jeevit Guru). The normal yoga practice starts from the Mulaadhar *Chakra* at the Rectal Ganglion and goes up to Sahasrasar. In these lower *chakras* or the ganglia, the center solar plexus will be first awakened and it will be difficult for the practitioner to control its effect. But in this new yoga spiritual practices start from Sahasrasar. Whatever trials he may make, the power of Yoga will work only to the extent it is needed for him. A Yog Sadhak cannot exert himself to increase or decrease or to improve more or less as it will not be in his control. This power will act according to the wishes of the Lok Guru or Master. 5) The effect of this new yoga shall not be meant for personal emancipation but for the emancipation of mankind. In this penance man can't wish for his emancipation alone because it will be a selfish motive. The Vishwa Guru will make him do 'Seva' of mankind compulsorily.

In order to awaken the higher degree of Spiritual Consciousness one has to surrender to the Satguru of the time, with body, mind and soul because the Satguru is the extension/incarnation of the Supreme Being. Param Guru Sahabji Maharaj, the 5th Revered Leader of Radhasoami faith explained "the Spirit of an ordinary man is asleep. The energy is potential like heat in a piece of coal. The heat energy should be ignited, made kinetic, and then only is it useful to man. Spiritual energy has two functions 1) "Rachanatmak Ang i.e creational function 2) "Bhodhnatamak Ang" i.e Intellectual function. Number 1 is visible in all living things. Number 2 is latent. But in the Satguru, the No 2 function is Kinetic. Through the means of that function the Satguru's Spirit is in direct communion with the Supreme Being. The Satguru's body to all appearances is like our body, but there is a peculiar and rare arrangement in Him....."

Hence, surrender to the Satguru is a must to overcome all the obstacles that come our way. Until and unless He blesses us and leads us to higher stages, it is not possible to ascend on our own accord. His help and support at every stage is most essential to the devotee.

Downward Causal and Upward Reciprocal Consciousness

Coming to the point of grades/levels of consciousness, in my view there are only two main types of consciousness. The action of the first one is downward and the action of the second one is upward.

The first manifestation of consciousness took place in the Pure Spiritual Region. In that there was a wish manifested that all the spirits at the Feet of the Supreme Being which were deprived of the majesty, grandeur, luminosity of the Super positive pole should be surcharged with higher spirituality and all the spirits be absorbed at the fountain head of the region of the Supreme Being. In an invited talk at the International Conference of the Association of Asia Pacific Operational Society dated 08.12.2003, Gracious Huzur Prem Saran Satsangi Sahab while answering the question of a member stated that. In the pre-creational condition the Supreme Being was in a state of Shunya Samadhi, absolute self-absorption and there were lower orders of spirituality in the nether pole or lower pole or negative pole and He wanted these spirit forces, which were in comatose condition, unaware of the existence of The Supreme Being to have the bliss of full communion or correspondence with the Supreme Being. And, therefore, it became necessary to create this Great Commotion, transport the spirit forces of lower spirituality into the region of the Supreme Being, accept as many of them as possible within His own region, directly under the His purview but, when it was not possible to galvanize (spiritualise) the others (sufficiently). He had no choice but to create Brahmanda and then the material plane; and then He found that these spirit forces have been denied the bliss and permanence and radiance of the realization of the Supreme Being, then as we all know incarnations started coming to this world and they tried to raise them to a higher spiritual plane and this is the reason why the Supreme Being did that. It was for the ultimate good so that these spirit forces which were in comatose condition would become fully conscious of His presence and partake of the full bliss, intelligence and energy of the Supreme Being.

In a similar way the other religions also confirmed this fact. For instance in the Hindu religion Aetreya Upanishad says "Saeekshet Lokaan Sruja" i.e. He thought himself let me create worlds and the desire to know His Leela. The Bible says - let there be light and there was light. The Kuran says Kun, in Satsang it is through Mauj that a commotion was created.

So the effect of the first consciousness was turned downwards and to be appropriate I call it Mercy *personified consciousness*. The second one is upward consciousness and I call it *reciprocative consciousness*. In this context it is necessary to mention here that once Param Guru Huzur Sahabji Maharaj said that a Jiva can't do any thing on his own accord in religious matters but he can only reciprocate "The Lord Showers Mercy on the Jiva and the Jiva will reciprocate it by doing Bhakti". In Bhakti or devotional consciousness there are three grades 1) Priti 2) Pratiti 3) Prem. Out of the three stages, as per Param Guru Sahabji Maharaj's bachan, the first is Prateeti that is having belief and the second is Preeti that is having faith and third is Prem. One has to pass from the first to the second and the second to the third i.e., Prem and in the level of Prem also he should reach the level of Gurumukh consciousness.

This Gurumukh consciousness is illustrated by an anecdote – once a seeker came to Kabir Sahab and asked what is Gurumukh Awastha or state of Gurumukh. He said I will show you. He called his consort '*Loee*' and asked her to search for the Dharki (weaving shuttle) while hiding the shuttle behind his back. His Consort had seen it and in spite of that, she started searching for the shuttle. After few minutes Kabir Sahab said to her when it was dark - don't you have the sense to light a lamp and then search? He said this even though it was day light. But His Consort did not reply and lighted a lamp and started searching, after a few minutes when she did not find it, He took out the shuttle from its hidden place and showed it to her saying don't you have eyes to see that it is behind my back. She prayed to Kabir Sahab to excuse her for her all faults. Then Kabir sahib said to the seeker, this is what is called the state of Gurumukhta. Man has to develop such a state of devotion towards the Satguru, and then only will it be called real love.

Creational Levels of Downward Causal Consciousness

The manifestation of the First Consciousness was mercy personified and it created Brahmand in six subdivisions and the higher three divisions of Parabrahma 1) which corresponds to the latent consciousness in the deep slumber of a man and this is called *Parabrahma Pad* or *Avyakta Purush* or unmanifest. 2) Hiranyagharbha corresponding to the consciousness in a dream state 3) *Virat Swaroop* (manifested mass) corresponding to consciousness in the wakeful condition of man. Then Niranjan Brahma has created three currents/forces a) Creative force (Brahma) b) Maintenance force (Vishnu) and c) Destructive Force (Shiva) for the creation, maintenance and destruction of the **Pind loka** or material regions (totally in 6 subdivisions). All these were created in order to accommodate the spirits according to their states and to purify and make them fit to go back to the pure Spiritual Region. The Second reciprocal Bhakti consciousness, for the first time in the true sense, was manifested through the prayer by Param Guru Huzur Maharaj. "*Satguru se Karoon Pukari Santan Mat Kije Jaari*"– I pray to the Satguru, that He may be so pleased as to ordain that the religion of Saints spread far and wide and the salvation of Jivas may thus take place.

Prior to the advent of Soamji Maharaj (the 1st revered leader of Radhasoami faith), the Jiva was incapable to pass Trikuti and get real emancipation in the true sense. When Soamiji Maharaj, the Incarnation of Radhasoami Dayal, opened the gates of the Pure Spiritual region and this Mercy Personified form of consciousness was reciprocated by Param Guru Huzur Maharaj by doing true Bhakti of His Lord and in turn taught us about true Bhakti, true devotion and true Seva.

Conclusion

It is worthwhile to consider here that when elders shower love on the young it is called affection and it is also shows Mercy. If the younger shows love towards elders and does any service for them, it is called Seva. Similarly, the Supreme Being wanted to shower mercy in order to take all the Souls (Jivas) to His abode, which were till then, denied of this bliss, permanence, radiance and realization of the Supreme Being. So this may be termed as LOVE PERSONIFIED CONSCIOUSNESS to serve the whole creation that was separated from its source and with its compassionate process of cleansing from its impurities and then to absorb the whole creation into its original source. Hence, this process was bestowed on mankind in the form of seva of His devotees which in turn is conceived as the seva of the Lord, as the Lord wishes to uplift all the jivas to His Pure Spiritual region.

In my opinion, in between these two main types of consciousness, the other five types of consciousness are observed. The Jiva behaves in wakeful, dream, deep sleep, Turiya at Sahasdal Kamal, the fifth state is the Chetan State of consciousness. To attain this Chetan state of consciousness, the Jiva has to approach a True guru who has reached the Pure spiritual region. After knowing the secrets of Surat Shabd Yog he starts doing spiritual practices and slowly and steadily ascends to higher spheres of spirituality wherein he hears the mystical sounds like A Bell, Conch, Mridang, OM etc. and ultimately reaches Sunna Lok which is the next higher region above Trikuti. Here consciousness of the soul becomes pure, having no tendency to mix with matter and mind and only one consciousness or faculty of getting absorbed in the pure spirituality remains. Param Guru Huzur Maharaj speaks about the condition of the soul at that point of Moksha. "In that condition our pure spirit with no sheaths or covers shall be able to enjoy free, unrestricted and unobstructed play of her inherent attributes viz. Sat Chit, Anand and Prakash and that ocean of spirituality also vibrating in harmony with us will add His attributes of Param Sat, Param Chit, Param Anand and Param Prakash". So this is the higher spiritual consciousness which we all are to strive hard to achieve under the shelter of the Sant Satguru.

A diagram on "States and Levels of Consciousness" is provided on the following page.

STATES AND LEVELS OF CONSCIOUSNESS

PURE SPIRITUAL REGION:
Mercy Personified Consciousness

Sunna Loka
Corresponding to latent consciousness in deep slumber or trance of man

Trikuti – *Brahma Presiding Deity*
Corresponding to consciousness in dream state of man

Sahasradal Kamal
Corresponding to consciousness in the wakeful state of man

Vishnu
Consciousness to maintain creation of Pind

Brahma
Creative Consciousness of Pind

Siva
Destruction Consciousness of Pind

Human Being
Consciousness of trance or Dheerga Shushupti

Consciousness in dream state

Consciousness in wakeful condition

For getting highest happiness/highest Consciousness adopts religious activities i.e. Bhakti

For getting highest happiness/highest Consciousness adopts religious activities i.e. Bhakti

PRATEETI (belief)

PREETI (immense faith)

PREM (Love)
Reciprocal Consciousness under the guidance and blessings of Satgugu

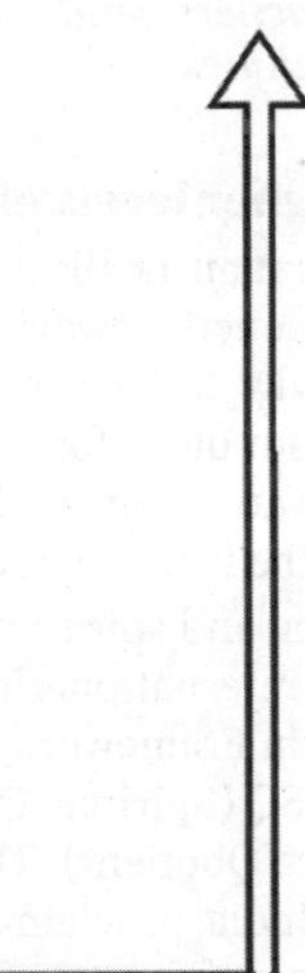

Surrenders to Satguru and practices Surat Shabda Yoga

Consciousness in Wakeful State

Consciousness in Deep Slumber

Turiya consciousness at Sahasradalkamal

Becomes one with the consciousness of Sunn thus acquiring status of Hamsa / Hamsinis

Enters into realm of pure spiritual region and merges into the ocean of spirituality and attains the highest spiritual consciousness

Chapter 56

Enhancing Spiritual Consciousness: An Educational Model for the Undergraduate Level

SOAMI PIARA SATSANGEE, NANDITA SATSANGEE, SARLA PAUL AND NEHA SHIVHARE

Dayalbagh Educational Institute (Deemed University), Agra, India

Abstract

The vision of education is to develop the latent potentialities of man – body, mind and spirit. Unfortunately, our present education system deals with just the first two aspects and that too in a deficient way. This leads mankind to the edge of the precipice. The need of the hour is to reconstruct the educational superstructure giving it a strong foundation of spiritual education. It has been found that a high spiritual quotient leads to improved functioning of the emotional and cognitive domains, thus contributing to the well being of the individual and the society at large. Realizing the importance of development of spiritual consciousness, various universities and departments are now running courses to promote spiritual development including the Oxford and Cambridge Universities, Akamai University, Maharishi University and Dayalbagh Educational Institute. This paper proposes a model of Spiritual Education based on the three S's of Spiritual Education: Satsang-cum-Surat Shabda Yoga, Seva, Sahyog-Sangathan propounded by the renowned systems scientist, educationist and spiritual leader, Prof. P.S. Satsangi. It consists of a specification of six components of the educational system: focus (goals); content; syntax (process and structuring of education); social system (roles and relationships of teachers, students, etc.); support system (resources needed); evaluation and feedback.

Emergence of Higher levels of Consciousness

The history of human civilization bears testimony to the development of varied human tendencies swaying from superstitious religiosity to liberal humanism and finally to keen rationality. Despite this massive progress we remain engaged in our quest for balance, perfection and lasting happiness with a shifting focus towards spirituality and values. These tendencies have been vividly reflected in the field of education too.

The need for moral and spiritual education has been increasingly recognized both at national and international levels. The National Policy of Education – 1986 (National Curriculum Framework, 2005. p. 34) in India has stressed the development of a strong SQ (Spiritual Quotient) and EQ (Emotional Quotient) along with IQ (Intelligence Quotient). The widely acclaimed Education Commission (1964-66), Govt. of India, proclaims that 'Man's knowledge and mastery of outer space and of his own self are out of balance. It is this imbalance which mankind must seek to redress' (Government of India, 1966 p.39). In pursuance of this need the Commission has included among the fourfold National Objectives of the education System the 'Development of Fundamental, Social, Moral and **Spiritual Values**'.

At the International level, Dr. Bevan Morris (2008) while expounding the system of Consciousness Based Education, being practiced at Maharishi University, USA, enumerates a number of its advantages. He holds the view that 'Consciousness - Based Education develops coherent brain functioning, bringing holistic benefits to all aspects of the students' life' and that the 'level of consciousness acquired by a student directly determines the quality of knowledge that any student can gain'. Further, it unfolds the 'unbounded creative potentiality of the students and gives them the experience of deepest inner bliss and peace'. Thus, a high level of spirituality leads to high emotional maturity which promotes high cognitive faculties which in turn have an impact on the social and physical well being of the individual. Thus, a high SQ has an elevating effect on the EQ and IQ of the learners. Students with a balanced and holistically developed personality will create a better society and a better world order. Moreover, various research studies have shown that Consciousness - Based Education (closely aligned to other forms of education like 'Character' education and 'Value' education) leads to a number of personal and societal gains. A survey of 176 schools adopting such education showed 77% decrease in discipline problems, 68% increase in attendance and 64% decrease in vandalism (Townsend, 2004). The spiritual potentiality of the human personality has been recognized by philosophers, saints and modern scientists alike. His Holiness Sir Sahabji Maharaj has explicitly stated that "providence has located within the human body a special spiritual faculty . . . When that faculty is developed in us like our other physical and mental faculties, we shall be able to perceive Truth and realize Ultimate Reality in the same manner as we perceive and realize the Sun with our physical eyes" (Discourses on Education in Dayalbagh: A Vision of Complete Education, 2005). Many acclaimed physicists and scientists have also verified the presence of an "omnipotent spiritual force field" pervading the entire cosmos.

The Concept of an Educational Model

A teaching model as visualized by Joyce and Weil (1996) specifies the process and conditions of classroom teaching. It consists of four fundamental elements viz.:

a) Focus – the objectives of teaching

b) Syntax - the procedure of teaching

c) Social System – the roles and relationships of students, teachers and other school personnel

d) Support System – the resources needed.

This model being a 'teaching' model concerns itself with process of classroom teaching alone. As such it needs to be broadened to include the wider concept of an entire educational system. The modified educational model that we propose consists of the following modified and supplemented elements or components.

a) **Focus**: refers to the goals and objectives of the entire educational program

b) **Content**: specifies 'what' is to be acquired and learnt in order to accomplish the objectives.

c) **Syntax**: addresses the issue of 'how' to impart the content in order to reach the desired goals. It includes a description of the process (activities) and structuring of the total environment employed to achieve the goal. It may also indicate philosophical, psychological and pedagogical principles to guide the teacher.

d) **Social System**: pertains to the social environment within which learning is to take place. The chief component is the student-teacher roles; their relationships and norms of inter personal behaviour.

e) **Support System**: specifies the resources needed for achieving the goal.

f) **Evaluation and Feedback**: refers to the assessment of the effectiveness of the education model so as to know to what extent we have achieved the desired goals.

A Proposed Educational Model for Enhancing Spiritual Consciousness

Spiritual Consciousness has been widely discussed and variously defined by psychologists, philosophers, scientists and religious exponents. However, in the context of the present model the notion of spiritual consciousness consists of the following essential features:

1) A heightened awareness of oneself and ones surroundings;
2) A sense of detachment;
3) Manifested feelings of fraternity, co-operation, responsibility, commitment, service, discipline, self-sacrifice, empathy, consideration;
4) Experiencing an upliftment of the spirit (experience of internal sound and light of different realms of spirituality) (Roy, S. 2007);
5) Experiencing of internal peace and bliss;
6) Experiential knowledge of ones relationship with the macrocosmic all pervasive reality.

There are two broad approaches to incorporating a new component like spiritual consciousness in the curriculum. The first approach is to frame a separate course in the area concerned and offer it as a compulsory or optional subject. The second approach is to integrate the basic elements of the new component into all curricular subjects and areas. The present model visualizes the use of both these approaches.

A detailed framework of the proposed model along the six dimensions mentioned earlier is given below.

Component I - Focus: The basic goals of the model are:

1) To orient and create an awareness among the students regarding spiritual consciousness;
2) To motivate the students to enhance their levels of spiritual

consciousness;
3) To provide a suitable environment for nurturing spiritual consciousness;
4) To integrate the fundamental principles and practices of spiritual consciousness into all curricular and co-curricular areas;
5) To enable the students to practice activities for enhancing their spiritual consciousness;
6) To enable the students to apply the benefits of enhanced spiritual consciousness for individual and collective benefit (better worldliness and universal brotherhood).

Components II & III - Content and Syntax

These two components of the model are closely related to each other and hence are being discussed together. Before elaborating the details of content and syntax, certain pedagogical principles must be kept in mind for effective transaction of the content and syntax.

Basic Pedagogical Principles

According to the recent trends in pedagogy, sound acquisition of learning objectives should be based on the following principles:

1. **Participatory and Constructive Learning:** Learners should not be passive recipients of knowledge imparted by the teacher but active participants in the process of discovering, constructing and achieving the learning outcomes whether related to knowledge or values or spirituality (Novak, J., 1993; Glaserfeld, E. Van, 1989; Osborne, R.J., 1985).

2. **Holistic Learning**: Recent advances in neuroscience have revealed the interdependence of motor, emotional, and cognitive functions of the brain (Damasio, 2003; Le Doux, 1996). Integrating all aspects or domains of the human personality – cognitive, affective, psycho-motor and transcendental consciousness leads to holistic and more effective learning (Neilson, 2005).

3. **Restraint from Indoctrination**: Conventional methods of indoctrinating the teachers' point of view must be avoided at all costs as this runs contrary to the principles of liberal and democratic learning. Indoctrination According to Tan (2004), indoctrination consists of three basic ingredients which are its drawbacks: (a) One is told what to do or think, (b) provided with no reasons and (c) given no alternatives. Hence, teachers, especially in the areas of inculcating values and higher consciousness, must provide reasons and explore alternatives as far as possible.

4. **Experiential Learning**: Experiencing first - hand knowledge which is aimed at is especially essential while enhancing spiritual consciousness and fostering related values. Hence, the teaching of theory should be simultaneously supported by experiences. This will lead to internalization rather than superficial acquisition of the desired goals of education.

Other pedagogical principles that need to be given importance include catering to individual differences, providing scientific basis for learning, etc.

Basic Curricular Areas

The issue of 'what' needs to be taught to enhance spiritual consciousness. It is a very subtle one, as awakening spiritual consciousness is an ultimately personal experience and said to lie in the domain of religion rather than that of education. However, 'complete' education should concern itself with the development of all aspects of the human personality – body, mind and spirit. It also needs to incorporate and integrate all spheres of human activity – secular and religious, which impact the individual. The leading educationist, system scientist and religious leader Revered Prof. P. S. Satsangi considers 'Spiritual Education' as 'the highest form of education'. According to him it is "characterized by three S's: *Satsang*-cum-*Surat Shabda Yoga*; *Seva* in all its forms; and *Sahyog-Sangathan* in all secular, temporal and *Parmarthi* activities" (Discourses on Education in Dayalbagh: A Vision of Complete Education, 2005 p. 244).

Based on this concept of the **Three S's of Spiritual Education** the various components of the content can be classified under the following three heads:

1) Meditation and allied activities (Surat Shabda Yoga)
2) Service to Humanity for all round personal and social upliftment (Seva)
3) Corporate Living (Sahyog – Sangathan)

The above curricular areas are each planned under three stages:

a) Main Content
b) Preparatory Stage- including (i) Fundamental Knowledge (ii) Skills, Attitudes and Values.
c) Syntax

Curricular Area I: Meditation (Surat Shabda Yoga) and Allied Activities

a) **Main content:** Meditation has been defined as "an exercise aiming to prevent thoughts in a natural way by deeply relaxing the physical body and then "concentrating on the source of 'inner sound' leading to the 'inner light'" to reach the highest level of spiritual consciousness (Chalko, 1997).

In the Religion of Saints meditation is said to consist of the three essential progressive stages:

(i) *Sumiran* or 'Contemplation of the Holy Name' ('Om' as practiced by the Hindus; 'Haque' of Sufi saints; and 'Radhasoami' of the followers of Radhasoami Faith) at the seat of the spirit (Agna *chakra*) in the human body.

(ii) *Dhyan* or 'Contemplation of the Holy Form'. This may alongside entail the vision of lights and forms of various spiritual regions.

(iii) *Bhajan* which involves simultaneous concentration on the Holy Name and the Holy Form leading to a state of total peace and bliss.

b) **Preparatory Stage**:

i) **Fundamental Knowledge**: The students should be exposed to fundamental viewpoints regarding all the areas of spiritual education especially Spirituality – its nature, its need and importance, realms of spirituality (for e.g. Pind, Brahmanda and Nirmal Chetan Desh as expounded by the Radhasoami faith) (Satsangi, 2007) and means of attaining it. The knowledge provided should also include familiarity with various religious leaders and religions of the world and fundamental knowledge of metaphysics (as suggested by the Radhakrishnan Commission or the University Education Commission, 1948-49).

Another vital area of knowledge for university graduates is the study of Theology. In his much acclaimed convocation address to the graduates of the Agra University His Holiness Sir Anand Sarup emphatically stated that, "The scientific study of higher consciousness through subjects like parapsychology and consciousness studies may also be included (Sarup, 1935).

The study of Fine Arts is yet another potent area of awakening the higher propensities of man. These include all types of fine arts: Literary texts of Indian mystics like Tagore, Kabir, Meera, etc. and Western transcendentalists like Emerson, T.S. Eliot, Wordsworth, etc.; Paintings and architecture of transcendental thinkers; Music – the highest among fine arts – should include both instrumental and vocal.

ii) Skills, Attitudes and Values required:

Right attitudes and values are the directing forces for right behavior. Inculcation of secular and spiritual values lies at the core of all the three areas of content.

To foster spiritual upliftment we need to nurture in the learners some deep rooted skills like the ability to withdraw oneself from the surroundings at will, contemplative thinking about ones mental processes (mind- watch), focusing attention on a single activity or object, purity of thoughts, faith in an omnipresent Divine Force, scientific attitude to guard against blind faith and superstition, etc.

c) **Syntax: Teaching** –Learning Activities to promote 'Surat-Shabda Yoga'

i. Morning prayers

ii. Guided meditation practice on a daily basis

iii. Attending prayer meetings and collective meditation as a congregation under the guidance of a spiritual educator.

iv. Self-study of texts (e.g. on religions, spiritual consciousness, etc.)

v. Student Presentations and Discussions

vi. Exposition and Demonstration by teachers / invited experts

vii. Research Projects

viii. Screening of films with follow-up discussion

ix. Visit to 'Centers of Consciousness Studies' and meeting with experts

x. Integration of meditative practice while doing routine activities.

Curricular Area II: Service (Seva)

a) **Main Content: Seva:** The ideal of '*seva*' in the 'Religion of Saints' entails service of ones Spiritual Master or Guru as well as that of the community with the (i) body (*Tan*), (ii) mind (*Mana*) (iii) wealth (*Dhana*) and (iv) Spirit (*Surat*). Service with the spirit implies contemplation of the Holy Name and Form all the time even while being engaged in performing worldly duties.

b) **Preparatory Stage:**

i) **Fundamental Knowledge Seva**: its importance to the individual and the society; its various forms; essential principles underlying Seva. E.g. rendering service without the desire of its reward ('nishkama' seva); integrating 'doing' (Seva) with feeling and thinking; not being rigid or selective in performing seva activities according to ones likings, etc.

ii) **Skills, Attitudes and Values required**: To foster the spirit of service (Seva) the learners need to acquire values of empathy, kindness, humility, initiative, endurance, adaptability, respect for physical work, dignity of labour, feelings of equality, fraternity, etc.

c) **Syntax: Teaching** –Learning Activities to promote 'Seva'

i. Service on the campus

ii. Community service – medical and health camps, literary and social awareness campaigns.

iii. Working with hands (in the fields, etc.) with humility and devotion

iv. Helping the intellectually weaker peer group in studies, personal problems, etc.

v. While doing any work keeping the Lord's pleasure in the fore front with internal repetition of the Holy Name (*Surat ki Seva*).

Curricular Area III: Corporate Life(*Sahyog- Sangathan*)

a) Main Content: Corporate Living ('Sahyog – Sangthan') implies mutual co-operation and collective planning, organization and action which leads to success of both the individual and the community. This has to be incorporated in all activities on the campus – in the classroom and outside it.

b) **Preparatory Stage:**

i) Fundamental Knowledge: The concept of **Corporate** Living – its importance (*Sahyog* and *Sangthan* lead to *saphalta* i.e. success).

Various avenues for corporate life on the campus and outside it.

ii) Skills, Attitudes and Values required

To nurture the goal of corporate life among the learners we need to encourage the attitudes of tolerance, patience, team work, fellow-feeling, making individual gains subservient to the interests of a larger group and so on.

c) **Syntax: Teaching**–Learning Activities to promote 'Sahyog – Sangathan'

i. Conducting class activities in groups and pairs (so as to promote the 'co-operative instinct' rather than the 'competitive instinct')

ii. Promoting co-curricular activities which require working in groups.

iii. Carrying out routine chores in the hostel, campus and other places with the spirit of team work and in a well organized manner.

iv. Teachers to be involved in group work as facilitators and co-workers to initiate the students in techniques of collective planning and action.

Component IV: The Social System

This aspect essentially revolves around the roles of the teacher and students.

(a) **Role of the teacher**: It is important that for the proposed model to be effective the teachers must serve as the role model of spiritually enlightened persons themselves. As far as classroom teaching is concerned the teacher must act as facilitators and wise helpers of students in the process of learning rather than domineering providers of information. In this model a good teacher is not merely one with good command over the subject and dexterity in pedagogical strategies. He is one who "will work to create classrooms where people can think, question, speak, write, read critically, critique freely, work cooperatively, consider the common good and link consciousness to conduct" (Ayers 1995, cited in Irwin-De Vitis et al. 1998; 2007).

(b) **Role of Learners**: In this model students are not merely passive listeners and obedient task-doers as in the conventional approach. They play the role of active protagonists in the collective and individual exploration of metaphysical issues related to spiritual consciousness. It has further been pointed out that "students will need not only to take a more active role in constructing their learning, but also to take responsibility of their own thinking outcomes (We, 2006).

Component V: The Support System

The support system includes all possible resources including ideas, activities (based on group work, pair work, individual work etc.) and the material (worksheets, role cards, audio-visual aids, internet resources, etc.).

Component VI: Evaluation and Feedback

Continued evaluation, feedback and renewal are necessary to keep the educational model flexible, updated and to avoid degradation and entropy. Towards this end two types of evaluation processes are required.

a) **Summative**: This is a kind of terminal evaluation done at the end of the implementation cycle. The purpose is to judge the effectiveness of the system.

b) **Formative**: This is a form of continuous evaluation which takes place formally and informally both throughout the implementation cycle. The purpose is to remove the deficiencies and improve the working of the system.

The scope of evaluation must encompass students, teachers, curriculum and the entire educational set up. The agents of evaluation should not be the administrators alone, as in the conventional system. Teachers, students, parents and other concerned groups must be equal partners of the evaluation process.

Conclusion

The educational model for enhancing spiritual consciousness proposed in this paper is intended to bring about an integration of the secular domain with the spiritual domain, thereby, enabling the learners to reach out to their highest faculty, consequently, enhancing their performance at all levels of existence. The goal of the system is, therefore, not to promote unworldliness, but 'better worldliness' by incorporating '*para vidya*' with '*apara vidya*'. It is hoped that by incorporating the three S's of Spiritual Education into the curriculum of higher education we may be able to realize the vision of the leading Spiritualist-cum-educationist Sir Sahabji Maharaj that 'Education, more Education, Education made perfect is the only panacea for all the ills and evils of this world' (Sarup, 1935).

References

Chalko,T.J. (1997). *Meditation* retrieved on 9-8-2006 from http://www.thiaoouba.com/medit.htm

Damasio, A. (2003). *Looking for Spinoza: Joy, Sorrow, and the Feeling Brain*. Orlando, Florida, USA: Harcourt.

Forris, D. (2005). The Effect of Meditation. *Journal of Undergraduate Research Vol. III.*

Glaserfeld, E.Van. (1989). *Constructivism in Education*. Oxford, UK: Pergamum Press.

Irwin-DeVitis, L., & Deitis, J.L. (1998). What Is This Work Called Teaching? Education Theory, 48(2), 267-278.

Joyce, B., & Weil, M. (1996 5th edition). *Models of Teaching.*, New Delhi, India: Prentice Hall Inc.

Le Doux, J. E. (1996). *The Emotional Brain*. New York, USA: Simon & Schuster.

Morris, B. (2008). *Consciousness Based Education Introduced by Maharishi Mahesh Yogi*. Available online.

National Curriculum Framework for School Education (2000). New Delhi, India: NCERT.

Neilson, T. W. (2005). Value Education through Thinking, Feeling and Doing. *The Social Educator*, Vol.23 No. 2.

Novak, J. (1993). Human Constructivism: A Unification of Psychology and Epistemological Phenomena in Meaning Making. *International Journal of Personal Constructivism Psychology.*

Osborne, R.J. et al. (1985). *Learning How to Learn*. New York, USA: Cambridge University Press.

Report of the Education Commission, Government of India (1964-66), Ministry of Education, New Delhi, India.

Report of the University Education Commission (1948-49), New Delhi, India.

Rogers, C. (1994). *Humanistic Education* retrieved on April, 2009 from http://pdfcast.org/pdf/carl-rogers-andhumanistic-education.

Roy, S. (2007). Measurement of Spiritual Intelligence. *DEI Journal of Science and Engineering Research*, Vol. 14, No. 1 and 2.

Sahabji Maharaj [Sir Anand Sarup Kt.] (1935). Convocation Address, Agra University, Agra, India.

Satsangee, N. et al. (2010). Designing a Teaching Model Based on Wisdom Approach for Developing Environmental Values through Teaching of English. *International Conference of Environmental Education.* , Agra, India: Dayalbagh Educational Institute (Deemed University).

Satsangi, P.S. [Revered Prof. Prem Saran Satsangi] (2005). *Discourses on Education in Dayalbagh: A Vision of Complete Education* (2005). Agra, India: Radhasoami Satsang Sabha, Dayalbagh.

Satsangi, P.S. [Revered Prof. Prem Saran Satsangi] (2007). Systems Approach to Understanding Man as a Microcosm, *DEI Journal of Science and Engineering Research*, Vol. 14, No. 1 & 2.

Tan, C. (2004). Indoctrination, Imagination and Moral Education. *The 2nd International Conference on Imagination in Education.* Vancouver, BC, Canada. 14 – 17 July. Available: http://www.ierg.net/pub_conf2004.php

Thayer, P. (2008). *Post Graduate Certificate in Transpersonal and Consciousness Studies*, Akamai University. Available online.

Townsend, K. (2004). *Why Johny Can't Tell Right from Wrong: The Most Important Lesson Our Schools Don't Teach – Values*, Available: http://www.findarticles.com/p/articles/mi_m1316/is_n12_v24/ai_13252028

Valpey, K. (2009). *Love in Indian Culture: Course Outline.* Oxford Centre for Hindu Studies, Oxford University. Oxford, UK.

We, X. (2006). Wisdom Approach to English Language Teaching. *ABAC Journal*, 26(1), pp 19-30.

Chapter 57

Modernity in Radhasoami Faith

SANTOSH KUMARI SRIVASTAVA
Women's Polytechnic
Dayalbagh Educational Institute (Deemed University), Agra, India

SUDHIR SAHNI
Dayalbagh Educational Institute (Deemed University), Agra, India

Abstract

Radhasoami faith has a firm scientific basis and a very modern outlook. It adopts a flexible approach suitable to the times, and eschews rigidity and rituals. Nearly a century ago Huzur Maharaj Sahab gave a scientific exposition of Radhasoami faith in His authoritative book 'Discourses on Radhasoami Faith', and statements made therein are not refuted by any scientific discovery but are actually substantiated by them. This paper discusses the modern outlook of Radhasoami faith since its inception, and briefly describes the cutting-edge or even futuristic scientific studies that are being conducted in Dayalbagh.

Introduction

Radhasoami Faith is a relatively recent faith in the timeline of religions. It was founded in 1861 AD, as compared to Vedic religion and Judaism which were founded around 2000 B.C. It has a firm scientific basis and a very modern outlook. In its literal sense the word 'modern' means 'of or relating to or having characteristics of the present'. In a wider sense it would mean 'involving recent techniques, methods or ideas of approaching things'. Over and above it would mean something which is different from the past, and may be even ahead of the times.

Radhasoami faith displays all the above characteristics. Our revered Sant Satgurus in the past as well as the present have adopted an approach suitable to the times to establish the authenticity of Radhasoami Faith. This idea is reflected in the sayings of our Revered Leaders.

In one of His discourses on April 3, 1935 Huzur Sahabji Maharaj, while advising about the desired point of view of an earnest Satsangi, emphasised the importance of accommodating ourselves to changing circumstances. Without having adaptability, He said, we cannot succeed. Four days after this, on 7th April 1935, commenting on the custom of *Tika* or Tilak, He said "Hindu orthodoxy has had its use. By keeping up old ways and customs, the Hindu resisted the onslaughts of foreign invaders. But when one is developed to the extent that one is ready to sacrifice everything to one's spiritual interest, the outer form of religions do not count. A generation or two ago, religion was traditional. Nobody knew what the *Vedas* were. But people today want reason for their faith. With the advance of education, traditional religion is bound to disappear. But the rational religions will remain". He then concluded by saying

"We have got to remember that it takes a long time to change one's outlook. If religion cannot give such a demonstration and if it cannot be rationalised, it cannot stand the onslaughts of the west" [i].

In His discourse delivered on 8th October 2006 Huzur Satsangi Sahab made it clear that in Radhasoami faith we adopt an approach or methods which are suitable for the period. He explained that "There was a time when it was necessary to hold debates with Pandits. In those times, the Pandits were knowledgeable, experienced and well-versed in *Vedas* and *Vedanta* and had experienced the Truths described in them. In such a time Param Guru Sahabji Maharaj debated with the Pandits and convincingly proved the superiority of the Radhasoami Faith. Now there is no need for debate with the Pandits as the superiority of the Radhasoami Faith has been proven in all respects. You know that the practices adopted in the Radhasoami Faith are according to the needs of times. In the present times, the Pandits are ignorant and are Pandits only for namesake and, so, why should one debate with them? Nowadays debate is carried on with the scientists." [ii]

The first step in this direction was taken by Huzur Maharaj Sahab who presented the spiritual science of consciousness in scientific terms in His authoritative book 'Discourses on Radhasoami Faith'. This book, much ahead of the times, is a clear example of the modernness of Radhasoami Faith. Statements made in this book are being substantiated by subsequent scientific discoveries. Huzur Satsangi Sahab clearly illustrates this with the following example:

Prior to Hubble's work scientists were of the view that the spiral nebulae were mere clouds of gas and that they, along with everything else in the universe, were contained in our own galaxy. In the 1920s, pictures from the Hooker Telescope on Mt. Wilson fundamentally changed our understanding of the cosmos. Astronomer Edwin Hubble, using photographs he took with this telescope, demonstrated that the objects his contemporaries called "spiral nebulae" were actually huge systems of stars - spiral galaxies, similar to our own Milky Way galaxy but incredibly distant. He further observed that these galaxies were not static but in a state of continuous motion. 'Discourses on Radhasoami Faith', written much before these theories were proposed, explains that the entire *Triloki* is revolving around the *Nirmal Chetan Desh*, and that *Pind*, the lowest region of creation, is revolving around *Brahmanda*, and so on.

Most scientists believe the universe was created in the Big Bang around 13.7 billion years ago. Huzur Satsangi Sahab has explained that the big bang known to scientists is only the third big bang and there were two big bangs before this [iii]. Recently Prof. Penrose and Prof. Gurzadyan have uncovered evidence unearthed by Nasa's Wilkinson Microwave Anisotophy Probe that the universe existed before the Big Bang[iv]. Concentric circles discovered in cosmic microwave background radiation (CMB) — the after-effects of the Big Bang — display evidence of events that took place before most scientists believe the universe came into being. They say they have discovered 12 examples of concentric circles, some of which have five rings, meaning the same object has had five massive events in its history.

Systemic experimental studies reinforce the view that there is no disparity between (physical) science and religion (spiritual science), and when spiritual waves come in contact with a physical medium, these take on the form of one of the fundamental physical forces and associated waves. Huzur Satsangi Sahab has designed and guided simple experiments [v] [vi] to determine the effect a meditationist leaves on the environment. These experiments were non-intrusive as well as non-invasive, in so far that they did not intrude upon the privacy of the person who was meditating. The experiments showed that the meditationists, in fact, do generate this kind of effect on the environment in generating or radiating waves of range up to 120 Hz or even beyond [vii].

Further experiments were conducted using random number generators to see how spirituality affects randomness and cohesiveness. Random numbers were generated using a software say MATLAB on a computer, say with a frequency of 120 numbers per second. Besides the experimental measurements, control measurements were taken in a graded fashion. One set of control measurements were taken in a laboratory in the Faculty of Engineering which had not much to do with spirituality. Another set was taken in the Satsang Hall during the time when no prayer session was going on, much before the prayer session, i.e. in the practically vacant Satsang Hall, except for the people required to do the experimentation. But though the Satsang Hall is vacant, it is still charged with spirituality – and this comes out loud and clear from the experimentation. And then, of course, the experiment proper when the meditation-cum-prayer session is going on. It was expected that the process of meditation would produce greater coherence in the numbers which are supposed to be random, purely random. The measure used for determining the order of randomness was to measure the standard deviation. It was found that the standard deviation was highest in the control set taken in the Engineering Laboratory. It was considerably less in the control set taken in the vacant Satsang Hall. It became further less during the meditation-cum-prayer sessions in the Satsang Hall. They also measured it when once there was a Discourse of this sort going on and it turned out to be the lowest at that time. These are some of the preliminary qualitative conclusions which are obtained form the random number generator experiment. They give us some qualitative appreciation that as the spirituality increased the randomness reduced. There was greater cohesiveness, i.e. lesser randomness in the numbers.

The experiment thus brings out the fundamental axiom that the process of *Surat-Shabda-Yoga Abhyas* produces a spiritual wave. There is no chance whatever of measuring the spiritual wave directly. It can only be experienced in the process of *Surat-Shabda-Yoga Abhyas*. The difference here between the scientist and the yogi is that whereas the scientist can only make physical measurements, the yogi experiences the effects of meditation, which are beyond the scientists – physical or life scientists, because they do not approach the whole exploration with an open mind and necessary humility.

We now end with these words of revered Huzur Sahabji Maharaj [viii]

"Providence has located within the human body a special spiritual faculty, and it is the exclusive function of religion to teach man all about that faculty. When that faculty is developed in us like our physical and mental faculties, we shall be able to perceive Truth and realize Ultimate Reality in the same

manner as we now perceive and realize the sun with our physical eyes. And when this takes place, you will be both astonished and amused to find that Truth - the goal of science, Ultimate Reality - the goal of philosophy, and God - the goal of religion, are but three names of the same Supreme Essence."

References

Gurdazyan, V.G., Penrose R. (2010). Unpublished research posted on Arxiv website, 16 -11

Sahabji Maharaj [Sir Anand Sarup Kt.] (1935). Convocation Address, Agra University, Agra, India.

Satsangi P.S. [Revered Prof. Prem Saran Satsangi] (2008). Inaugural Address at XXXII National Systems Conference (NSC 2008), IIT Roorkee, December 17.

Satsangi, P.S. [Revered Prof. Prem Saran Satsangi], & Sahni V. (2007). National Systems Conference, MIT Manipal.

Satsangi, P.S. [Revered Prof. Prem Saran Satsangi], & Sahni V. (2008). National Systems Conference, IIT Roorkee. December 17.

The Dayalbagh Herald (1935). Agra, India: Radhasoami Satsang Sabha, Dayalbagh.

The Dayalbagh Herald (2007), January 9. Agra, India: Radhasoami Satsang Sabha, Dayalbagh.

The Dayalbagh Herald (2007), October 2. Agra, India: Radhasoami Satsang Sabha, Dayalbagh.

Chapter 58

Essentiality of Emergence of a Universal Religion: The Futuristic Religion of Consciousness

PREM PRAKASH SRIVASTAVA
Power Finance Corporation Limited, New Delhi, India

Abstract
Religion is a way of life, based on some specific convictions, which is supposed to be conducive for binding men together in one thread of brotherhood and unity under the Fatherhood of God. But in reality, it has divided more than bound. Lately, a perceived futuristic remedy for the growing menace of worldwide religious conflicts and strife is gaining currency in the form of a universal religion. The important issue to be addressed is whether a universal religion can be considered to be a practical solution for the problems it is supposed to act as a panacea for. A few simplistic and apparently possible models of a universal religion have been considered and analyzed in terms of their practicability. For logical conclusions, the study and analyses of a carefully selected sample set of major world religions was also undertaken. Further, possibilities of a contemporary, practical and practicable futuristic universal religion of consciousness has also been conceptualized and discussed.

Introduction

"Dharma is nothing but common-sense value structure for harmonious co-existence"

This simplistic yet profound thought of Swami Dayanand Saraswati defines the core of religion or Dharma and serves as a beacon for this research paper. The etymology of the word 'religion' indicates that religion is there to bind men together in one thread of brotherhood, but the actual experience has been different. It has divided more than bound.

In this context, the following lines of Swami Vivekanand are relevant even today:

Nothing has made the brotherhood of man more tangible than religion; nothing has made more bitter an enmity between man and man than religion. Nothing has built more charitable institutions, more hospitals for man, and even for animals, than religion; nothing has deluged the world with more blood than religion[1].

We have found that religions of the world both agree and differ amongst themselves on several points. It is wrong and one-sided, therefore, to overem-

---

[1] *Vivekanand. Jnana Yoga.* Advaitashram, Calcutta. 1961, pp 373.

phasize either the similarities alone or the differences alone. People of positive outlook often overemphasize the similarities with the idea of promoting understanding and goodwill amongst the followers of different religions, while fanatics always highlight the differences.

While nothing has been directly responsible for greater philanthropy than religion, nothing has also deluged the world with more blood than religion. Considering the last many centuries and the battlegrounds that were laid out, history is witness to the fact that most of the age-old conflicts and strife of the world have emanated from differences in ways and means of achieving bliss – ananda - or the Ultimate Reality, or God, as postulated by the proponents, seers, and sages of various religions.

The need for a solution to the problem for these conflicts and strife, impinging upon humanity, has always been felt, and today, in the modern age, the need remains alive, more visible, more potent, and more pronounced than ever before. However, modern age, with its scientific and questioning temper, has provided man with that space in which he can speculate logically, coherently and interrogatively numerous possibilities, which hitherto were considered irrational and even sacrilegious, including even the possibility of a universal religion. This backdrop has led to the conceptualization and development of this paper.

Religion: A Basic Deconstruct

Religion and God

Man is a God-seeking creature and is His microcosm. Religion is the path that leads to God. From time immemorial, man has perpetually searched for God. Religion has evolved from signs, symbols, and nature gods, to organized religions like Hinduism, Buddhism, Jainism, Christianity, Islam, Religion of Saints, etc. One of the fundamental reasons why the belief in God continues to this day is that cutting across societies, religions, cultures, races, generations, and geographical barriers is the fact that people have, at one time or another, developed an awareness or an experience of what they consider to be God, which has affected their lives in significant ways. In other words, the awareness of the existence of God is fundamental to human experience and, as such, acts as the raison d' etre or anchor for all religions of the world, one way or the other.

The question 'What is religion?' may be answered differently and the theoretical discussion on the problem as to what a man has or does or becomes when he accepts a particular religion may centre around various points. But seeing the entire thing on a very general and realistic plane one may very easily find that what a man as a matter of fact has with him in having a particular religion like Hinduism or Christianity or any other of this kind as his own religion is that, he entertains certain specific beliefs with regard to the world and life, as a whole, and performs certain specific practices in the light of those beliefs.

Universal Religion: A Possible Panacea

Taking a pessimistic view of the current scenario, as depicted above, many have preached the end of all religion to be in the interest of man. However, without much of argument, it can be seen that this is an untenable and an extreme remedy, if at all it can be considered to be one. In fact, saner persons have sometimes foreseen another remedy and that is in the form of the establishment of a universal religion. What exactly will be the nature of this proposed universal religion is not very clear, but this much seems to be obvious from the very nomenclature that it will not be one more religion, besides the many that are already existing; rather it will be the only religion prevalent all over the world, which will be acceptable to and followed by all religious men alike. It will be the religion of all religious people, and not of one particular group or society.

Universal religion will thus be the universally accepted religion. It is felt that once there is a universal religion, all bloodshed and enmity in the name of religion will be completely over and religion will then have its real role to play – the role of binding all people together in the thread of universal brotherhood, under the Fatherhood of God. Such a situation appears to be highly beneficial for mankind and may therefore be highly desirable. However, the question is whether such a situation is at all feasible, i.e. whether establishment of a universal religion is a real, practical, and practicable possibility. That such a religion is logically possible is undoubted, because there is no contradiction involved in the concept of a universal religion. However, the real question is of its practical possibility.

Formulation of Universal Religion

Based on the above reflections, let us conceptualize the possible models for a universal religion and then test each of them for practicability. Three simple and seemingly implementable optional models for universal religion have been considered as follows:

(a) **Model-I:** A totally new religion is evolved and people all over the world accept it as their common religion.

(b) **Model-II:** Common and essential points of all prevailing religions are drawn to form a new religion with a common set of beliefs and practices.

(c) **Model-III:** One of the prevailing religions is taken universally by all the people of the world to be their religion, instead of the one which they have so far been following.

Universal Religion

A Basic Study of Religions

Based upon the study and analyses of a set of six selected religions, viz. Hinduism, Buddhism, Jainism, Christianity, Islam, and Sikhism, glimpses of broad similarity in the basic tenets of all major religions have been observed. The results of the analyses were considered for drawing out conclusions within the framework of each of the above optional models of universal religion. The concerned prophets and saints have always taught religion in the context of all religious truths that were revealed before their time. They have always stressed upon the essential points of agreement and have highlighted the distinctive features of their own religion. All religions have invariably tried to corroborate their tenets with an appeal to a correct understanding of the religions of the past. Prophets and saints have all taken into consideration all the faiths and emphasized the importance of their own religion for the time.

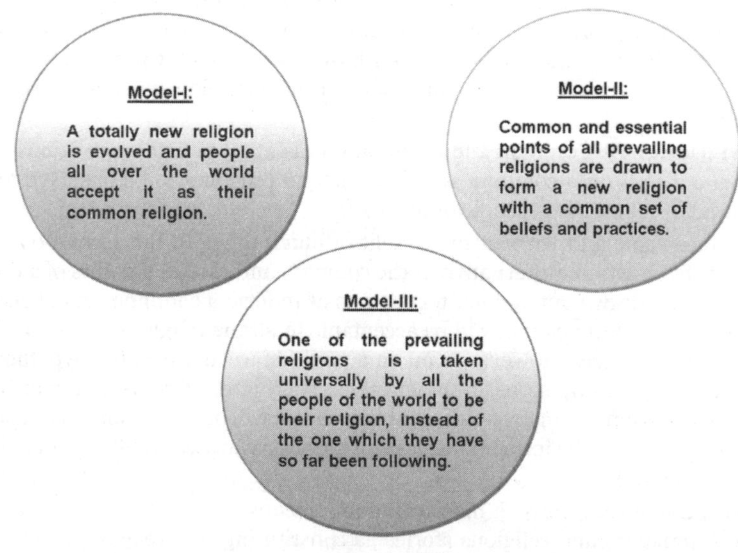

Optional models for universal religion

Appraisal and Analyses

Thus, having studied the basic tenets and features of all of the sample religions, we can formulate the main principles, tenets and features of the proposed universal religion. However, before examining the practical possibility of universal religion in any of the optional forms, as enumerated in this paper, it is necessary to see what actually the acceptance of a religion by a man means. Accepting one specific religion means accepting one set of beliefs and practices and entertaining one set of religious stories and procedures in mind, rather than any other.

Practical possibility of universal religion in any of the above enumerated optional models means its acceptability by all people of the world alike. Hence, let us evaluate in this light the question of the acceptability of the so-called universal religion in any of the three optional models mentioned above by all religious people of the world alike.

(a) Model-I: A totally fresh religion is evolved in a fresh manner and people all over the world accept it as their common religion.

If universal religion comes about as a new religion in any form, whatsoever, it is bound to be nothing more than one more religion, besides the many existing from beforehand. As indicated earlier, no propounder or prophet of a fresh religion has ever wished his religion to be the religion of all the people of the world. But it is an irony of fate that every time when an attempt has been made by a prophet to give man a new religion of universal acceptance, it has resulted merely in giving rise to one more religion besides those existing from beforehand. Hence, it can be inferred that the same will be the fate of the so-called universal religion in its avatar based on the first hypothesis, i.e. if it comes up in the form of a totally new religion. The mere name 'universal' will hardly be able to make it universal. With the above thought-process, the first alternative of the practical possibility of a universal religion appears to be quite dubious.

(b) Model-II: Common and essential points of all prevailing religions are drawn out to form a common set of beliefs and practices to be observed and followed by all religious people of the world.

On face value and without the benefit of much thought, the second option appears to be a viable alternative. If the common and essential points of all the religions are drawn out and put together so as to form a common set of beliefs and practices, perhaps that will be acceptable to all the religious people of the world ungrudgingly. However, even on a preliminary analysis, the hypothesis does not seem to be so easily practicable. There are, of course, similarities amongst religions on many points. But how far we will be able to form a religion in the full sense of the term on the basis of these similarities is still a moot point for consideration.

Accepting a religion by a man commonly means accepting a certain set of beliefs, practices and religious stories as constituting that religion. Now, the point to be considered is, whether there are any similarities between the mythical stories of different religions or not. Whether there are common beliefs pertaining to important religious tenets, such as, perceptions of God, i.e. belief in only one God, or in several gods or no belief in any God at all; whether God is taken as personal or impersonal; whether belief in Karma and rebirth constitutes the central core; whether moksha or nirvana is the ultimate destiny of man or the attainment of heaven is; and so on and so forth.

It is worth considering at this point as to what the common points in all the religions are which can be extracted to form the belief of the universal religion? And most points of belief in different religions are not trivial that they may be left out. As a matter of fact, these constitute the essence of the religions they belong to. Similarly again, although there is considerable commonality amongst various religions regarding the ethical virtues and duties they recognize, there is very little commonality amongst them regarding the various rites, ceremonies and rituals they contain. And however little importance one may be ready to give to these rituals and ceremonies from a higher religious standpoint, they possess indisputably great importance for the common religious man. Thus, it would be difficult to find common religious practices, which may be extracted out of various religions so as to form the rites and rituals of the universal religion.

And most of all, is religion something so external that certain beliefs, practices and religious stories chalked out, formulated and constructed in an artificial manner by taking points from different religions will give real satisfaction to its followers? Religion is primarily a matter of inner conviction, and nothing can be pressed upon a religious man artificially from without. Hence, it is certain that the way in which the proposed set of common beliefs and practices is to be determined for the universal religion will definitely make it external and artificial which will hardly be able to satisfy the core of the religious man. Such a universal religion, therefore, will just not qualify to be called a religion at all.

(c) Model-III: One of the prevailing religions is taken universally by all the people of the world to be their religion, instead of the one, which they have so far been following.

The practical possibility of the universal religion in its third form means the acceptability of the beliefs, practices and religious stories of any one of the prevailing religions by all religious people of the world. For example, if Hinduism becomes universal religion, it will imply that all religious people of the world begin to believe alike in the immortality of the soul, karma and rebirth, bondage and liberations, etc. and all of them adopt the Hindu way of prayer and worship, perform Hindu rituals and observe Hindu moral principles, etc. Not only these, all the people of the world will begin to read, listen and remember with reverence the Hindu sacred stories relating to Rama, Krishna and many other Hindu mythical personalities. But will it ever be possible? Perhaps only when Hindu beliefs, practices and religious stories prove to be the most religiously satisfying, i.e., when they prove to be such which satisfy the religious instinct and hunger of all the people of the world in the most efficient manner. As a matter of fact any religion which claims to be universal or which is taken as being most suitable for this purpose, will have to satisfy this condition, viz. its beliefs, practices and religious stories are most readily acceptable to all the people of the world and are most satisfying in nature. But on what grounds can one prove the supremacy of the set of beliefs and practices of one religion over all others so that it can have the best claim to be the universal religion? Each religion in its own way is most satisfying to its followers, such that its beliefs and practices are most naturally, agreeably and conveniently acceptable to them. What will be the grounds then on which one can claim supremacy for the beliefs and practices of any one religion?

Thus the pervading of one existing religion over all others, such that it is acceptable to all religious people of the world alike as their own religion does not also seem practicable. The basic question is which particular religion is competent for the purpose and why, as all religions appear to have equal claims. However, the most basic question in this regard seems to be, whether it is practically possible that the same set of beliefs, practices and religious stories may be able to satisfy with equal efficiency the religious feelings of persons coming from different traditions and living at different places in different times and different situations. The answer to this question and to this possibility also seems to be negative. And therefore the practical possibility of establishment of a universal religion in the third form also seems to be very much doubtful.

Inference

The obvious and simplistic and, seemingly, practical conceptualization of the universal religion in one of the three conceptualized, simplistic models ultimately turns out to be non-starters when evaluated and assessed with the touchstone of practicality and practicability. Thus, based upon the above analyses, the practical possibility of establishment of a universal religion on any of the three optional models seems to be very bleak. On further reflection on the subject and continuing with the thought-process, we may arrive at the conclusion that as a matter of fact, a universal religion in any of the forms as conceptualized, or even in any other form, may not at all be required. However, with a view to tackle the growing menace of religious fundamentalism, fanaticism and associated conflicts and strife, as highlighted earlier, what is needed is tolerance and sympathy on the part of the followers of every religion towards religions other than their own. In fact, with the above analysis, it may be also inferred that if there is a religion which is universal in any of the above three forms, that will mark the end of true religion.

Religion: ***Quo Vadis***

With an inherent apathy, if not hatred, towards religious ideologies, certain thinkers of this century have developed ideologies of humanism, positivism and secularism as the answer to the crisis of civilization today. These are pseudo-religions or rationalist religions of today that are much talked about. They are mainly moralistic and they appeal to rationalistic thinking. But worldly desires, hoarding, jealousy, hatred and exploitation lie deep in man, that require the aid of religious practices and salutary influences of great men and their example to be rooted out from human mind. The apparently religious teachings of godmen in guise cannot influence and reform man fundamentally. Their influence on national and international levels will never be salutary. So, there is a great need of a true religion and its regenerative work for the salvation of humanity and to extricate civilization out of the present crisis to let it develop in full bloom.

Sahabji Maharaj[2], has said:

...we do not want rationalistic religions but a rationalization of religion.

Relatedly, John Milton Yinger[3] observes:

It seems unlikely that the major existing religions, as embodied in their established institutions, will have a vital part in the reorganization of man's religious life in ways that will deal with the situation that we are in.

Conclusions

Futuristic Religion of Consciousness

The *Kali Yuga* is generally looked upon as an era of spiritual depravation and religious crisis. The Saints, however, have declared that:

...the Kali Yuga is the most suitable Yuga for spiritual regeneration of the highest order, as this is the time of conjunction of the

---

[2] The 5th revered Sant Sat Guru of the Radhasoami Faith

[3] Author of the book, *The Scientific Study of Religion and others.* J. Milton Yinger (1916) is an American sociologist who was president of the American Sociological Association 1976-1977. Yinger is known for his 'functional definition' of religion, reformulating the concept to demonstrate how something is religious in what it does, rather than what it is simply in traditional terms. Thus, various different institutions or movements can be analysed for religious roles.

third grand division of the region of matter and of Brahmanda, the region of mind, with the purely spiritual regions'

-Discourses on Radhasoami Faith, p.144

As a result, a condition more blissful than *Sat Yuga* has been proclaimed for *Kali Yuga*. Similarly, in the words of the philosopher Caleb Rosado[4]:

The third millennium will be dominated by the 'religion/spirituality paradox': the decline of organized religion on one hand coupled with a growing interest in spirituality and wisdom on the other. This demands a reordering of priorities in terms of the spiritual, and an urgent need for a relevant faith. By relevant, I mean a faith that speaks to the current and future concerns of our time.

With the above backdrop, futuristic religion of consciousness could be conceptualized as one that will address and also be equally acceptable to all classes of minds. It will have to be equally philosophic, equally emotional, equally mystical and equally conducive to action. Any religion that does not have all the four elements cannot qualify as a universal religion. It would also have to have a universal appeal to all sections of society and the flexibility to adapt to the intellectual capabilities of different strata of society. *Karma Yoga* and *Bhakti Yoga* philosophies, alongside Raja Yoga philosophy forms that ideal mix of religious doctrines, which when practiced under the guidance of a Self-Realized *(Tattwadarshi) Sadh Purusha* will form a dynamic universal religion to appeal to all sections of society. It is perceived to be dynamic because under the guidance of a Self-Realized *Sadh Purusha*, religious doctrines can be interpreted 'correctly' with a perspective to its basic principles, to suit social conditions of the time.

Futuristic religion of consciousness is, therefore, perceived as a religion of direct experience and not a religion merely of faith. By and large, people are not really content with the idea that the results of a spiritual life may come after death. They are not patient to wait that long; they would like to get direct experience here and now. They may not know how to gain that experience or what is required to gain it, but they long for that experience.

In future, religion would be akin to an educational institution offering a variety of courses and having many different branches of learning where students of different temperaments and talents can find a place. Variety is not to be sacrificed; it is the antagonism to variety because of *Agyana* that is to be condemned. Each one of us shall choose his own way, looking upon all the other ways as equally valid and recognizing that all these different paths lead to the same goal, and satisfy the hunger of an infinite number of individuals.

---

[4] Dr. Caleb Rosado, Department of Sociology, Southern Connecticut State University. A consultant running his consultancy firm, Rosado Consulting for Change in Human Systems having a Mission of Creating Caring Communities.

Salient Tenets of Futuristic Religion of Consciousness

(a) The Living Guru

(b) A New World Order

(c) Better Worldliness

(d) Fatherhood of God and Brotherhood of Man

(a) The Living Guru

Amongst the most important features of the futuristic religion would be paramount emphasis on the existence of the living *Guru*, already available in the *Sant Mat* (Religion of Saints). This is based on a highly religious principle that if the *Guru* is alive the seeker can test him as much as he likes. When he is convinced, he can attend *Satsang* of the true and perfect *Guru* and derive full benefits of his association. Also he can communicate with him and get necessary advice and help in connection with the difficulties he meets with, in the course of his devotional practices. He can discuss with him and get doubts cleared and clarification sought.

It is also said in the *Bhagavad Gita*:

O Arjuna! the Yajna of knowledge is superior to the Yajnas of all kinds because the result of all the acts performed is knowledge. Thou shouldst receive this knowledge from the Guru by falling at his feet i.e. by becoming his humble disciple and by putting questions to him i.e. by being a seeker and by serving him. The Guru who has realised the Truth i.e. he who realised Atman the spirit, would teach you the knowledge.

(b) A New World Order

Aristocratic Democracy (ARIS-DEMO) would be the model for governance under the futuristic religion, as put forth by. Sahabji Maharaj. By Aristocrats He meant *'Spiritual Aristocrats'* who would be practitioners of *Surat Shabda Yoga* and would have an elevated level of consciousness. For it would only be such persons who would have true love for the Lord and compassion for His entire creation, that would treat all on an equal footing. And it will only be such noble men who would be true practitioners of universal brotherhood, *Vaisudhaiva Kutumbakam.*

(c) Better Worldliness

Better Worldliness will be another important hallmark of the futuristic religion. It can be understood as a disposition towards life, by following which, man can achieve the four *Purusharthas* of *Dharma, Artha, Kama* and *Moksha* to attain the status of a *Jivanmukta* during his lifetime itself. A *Jivanmukta* is a realized soul who visualizes the entire creation as the children of God and his love for God translates into brotherhood of man.

Better Worldliness can be explained as a philosophy or a way of life where spiritual pursuits to attain superior consciousness and puritan work ethics make a fine blend. Living in the world comfortably, one should pursue the ideal of achieving the highest spiritual goal. Better worldliness is thus the golden mean between worldliness and unworldliness. To put it another way, Better Worldliness can be seen as a combination of *Karma Yoga, Gyana Yoga* and *Bhakti Yoga.*

Better Worldliness therefore means a disposition towards life that is based on a *Dharmic* way of conduct; a conduct with compassion and forbearance for fellow man, no matter what the nationality, or the color of the skin, religion or caste. Practicing Better Worldliness would usher in *'Brotherhood of Man'* and lead us to an integrated global community.

Better Worldliness would further evolve in response to the four-action framework of 'Blue Ocean Strategy', viz.

(i) Eliminate rituals, orthodoxy, superstition etc.

(ii) Reduce unnecessary costs, wastage etc.

(iii) Raise standard and quality of Satsang, Seva and Abhyasa etc.

(iv) Create New Satsang Polity, New Devotional Method, New Surat Shabda Abhayas etc for Spiritual Value Innovation

Further, striving for achieving snow-white peaks and pinnacles of highest spiritual attainment by all adherents in line with White Mountain Strategy is another facet in the development of the concept of Better Worldliness applicable to the futuristic religion of consciousness.

(d) Fatherhood of God and Brotherhood of Man

Brotherhood, being universal, it is the surest foundation for morality and order, because it dissolves the conflicting interests of man on the material plane and would be another important feature of the futuristic religion of consciousness. It is based on the principle that service of the human brotherhood far from being a hindrance in establishing communion with the Supreme Father, is indeed a positive step in that direction.

In a thoughtful and instructive address at the Kayastha Pathshala Intermediate College, Allahabad, Sahabji Maharaj, expounded the concept of 'Fatherhood of God and Brotherhood of Man, which would be an important feature of the futuristic religion of consciousness:

From time immemorial, religion has been teaching the great truth of the Fatherhood of God and brotherhood of man, but selfish humanity has all along turned a deaf ear to the great teaching. The Divine Plan, however, cannot be set at naught. The great teaching of religion has been ignored, perhaps, because it was imparted in a language, soft and sweet. Naturally therefore, it is now being impressed on us in the somewhat harsh, and altogether unpleasant, language of economic strife. If we do not assimilate the teaching even now, but continue to disregard it as hitherto, you take it from me, the day is not distant when we shall have to learn it, in the extremely harsh language of the machine-gun and the bomb. As said a little while ago the Divine Plan cannot be set

at naught. Believe it or not, Universal Brotherhood must prevail among the nations of the world and humanity must get prepared to recognize the Fatherhood of God.

Ladies and gentlemen, herein lies the solution of India's National Problem and herein lies the solution of England's economic problem. Yes herein and herein alone lies the solution of all the problems of all the countries of the world. It is for the people to accept it at once or keep it pending till they are forced by circumstances to do so.

At this juncture, giving a glimpse of the futuristic religion of consciousness, it would be appropriate to quote Prof. Mark Juergensmeyer of University of California, Berkeley, USA, who says in his much-acclaimed book *Radhasoami Reality: The Logic of a Modern Faith*:

Many in traditional and highly developed area now seek what the adherents of Radhasoami communities have found; a pattern of religious expression and experience that allows them to identify with their cultural past without accepting what they see as its superstitious and greedy excesses, and to embrace modern ways of living without becoming captive to what they perceive as alienating forms of society and sterile forms of thought[5].

Points to Ponder

The above depicted futuristic vision of religion of consciousness is worth pondering over along with four most significant and important historical events, one at the end of the 19th century, from September 11 thru' 27, 1893 at Chicago, USA; the second at the onset of the 21st century, on October 15, 2003 at Surat, India; the third on June 13, 2010 at Murar, India; and the fourth on November 14, 2010 at Dayalbagh, Agra, India.

(a) The Parliament of Religion

In the Parliament of Religions held from September 11 through 27, 1893 at Chicago, USA, Swami Vivekananda expounded in clear and simple terms the Vedanta system of philosophy, where he visualized a futuristic universal religion as follows:

...if there is ever to be universal religion, it must be one which will be infinite, like the God it will preach, and whose sun will shine upon the followers of Krishna and of Christ, on saints and sinners alike; which will not be Brahmanic or Buddhistic, Christian or Mohammedan, but the sum total of all these, and still have infinite space for development; which in its catholicity will embrace in its

[5] In this book, Mark Juergensmeyer seeks to explain why the religious logic of Radhasoami, which is based on the teachings of medieval Hindu saints, is so compelling to hundreds of thousands of businessmen, intellectuals, office managers, and other urban professionals in North India. Juergensmeyer addresses the perplexing relationship between modernity and religious faith and examines it from historical, sociological, and phenomenological points of view.

infinite arms, and find a place for every human being, from the lowest grovelling savage, not far removed from the brute, to the highest man, towering by virtues of his head and heart almost above humanity, making society stand in awe of him and doubt his human nature. It will be a religion which will have no place for persecution or intolerance in its polity, which will recognize divinity in every man and woman, and whose whole scope, whose whole force, will be centered in aiding humanity to realize its own true, divine nature.

(b) The Surat Conclave: Vision India – 2020

A conclave of 15 eminent religious leaders across the leading religions of India was convened on October 15, 2003 at Surat, India, which concluded with the signing of the Surat Declaration. This conclave was also attended by the ex-President of India, Dr APJ Abdul Kalam and gave a peep into the strategic vision in quarters that matter. The Vision Document has as its center-piece Science and Spirituality and the need for them to interact. Rationality and logic are intrinsic to both, Science and Spirituality, but while Spirituality is driven by compassion and love and a spiritual experience is the goal of a deeply religious person, a major discovery or an invention is the goal of the scientific mind. If both aspects are unified we can transcend to that level of thinking, in which unity is a cohesive aspect.

(c) Murar Declaration

The initiative was taken by Radhasoami Satsang Sabha, Dayalbagh by adopting Murar Declaration on June 13, 2010 at Murar, India, for forging Unity among different Radhasoami communities.

(d) SPIRCON 2010: Conclave of Religious Leaders of various Radhasoami Communities

A Conclave of Religious Leaders of various Radhasoami Communities was organized on the occasion of SPIRCON 2010 on November 14, 2010 at Dayalbagh, Agra, India, to promote fraternity, amity and heart-felt love and affection for each other among Satsangis (followers of Radhasoami Faith) across various Radhasoami communities.

Thus, all the major religions have to pass through a process of thorough self-searching and self-criticism. The true, natural and essential teachings of religions should be identified and their fundamental unity should be understood. It should be realized that as all the sciences are one, all religion is one and the natural path of religion has no denominational differences. When the ancient lesson of religion of Fatherhood of God and brotherhood of man is recognized and followed, the way for world peace is naturally laid and in no time will it be achieved.

References

Hopfe, Lewis M. (1983). *Religions of the World*. New York, USA: Macmillan.

Kim, W. Chan and Mauborgne, Renee. (2005). *Blue Ocean Strategy*. Boston, USA: Harvard Business School Press.

Maharaj Sahab [Pandit Brahm Sankar Misra Sahab] (2004). *Discourses on Radhasoami Faith (with Supplement)*, Agra, India: Radhasoami Satsang Sabha, Dayalbagh.

Mark Juergensmeyer. (1991). *Radhasoami Reality: The Logic of a Modern Faith*. Princeton, USA: Princeton University Press.

Matthews, Warren. (1991). *World Religions*. New York, USA: West Publishing Company.

Mohapatra, A.R. (1985). *Philosophy of Religion: An Approach to World Religions*. New Delhi, India: Sterling Publishers.

Post-graduate Diploma in Theology Courseware (2008). THM 201, THM 203, Agra, India: Dayalbagh Educational Institute (Deemed University).

Saxena, Prem K and Chaturvedi, Devendra K. (eds.). (2005). *Theology, Science and Technology: Ethics and Moral Values*. New Delhi, India: Vikas Publishing House.

Singh, Taran (2001). *Religious Situation in the Present Day World*. Patiala, India: Publications Bureau, Punjabi University.

Talib, Gurbachan Singh. (1997). *The Origin and Development of Religion*. Patiala, India: Publications Bureau, Punjabi University.

Talib, Gurbachan Singh. (2001). *Advanced Book of Religious Studies*. Patiala, India: Publications Bureau, Punjabi University.

Tiwari, Kedarnath. (1983). *Comparative Religion*. Varanasi, India: Motilal Banarsidass Indological Publishers & Booksellers.